CAMPING in Australia

CATHY SAVAGE AND CRAIG LEWIS

EXPLORE AUSTRALIA

CONTENTS

MAP AND CAMPING SYMBOLS

Roads and related features

━━━━━━	Freeway
━━━━━━	Highway, sealed
▪▪▪▪▪▪	Highway, unsealed
────────	Main road, sealed
‑‑‑‑‑‑‑‑	Main road, unsealed
────────	Other road, sealed
‑ ‑ ‑ ‑ ‑	Other road, unsealed
············	Vehicle track
┼┼┼┼┼┼	Railway
▪▪ ACT ▪▪	State border
▪▪ ▪▪ ▪▪	Fruit fly exclusion zone boundary
─ ─ ─ ─ ─	Ferry
··········	Dog fence
············	Walking track
M31 31	National highway route marker
A1 1	National route marker
S	Metroad route marker
C141 26	State route marker

Cities, towns, localities and point features

SYDNEY ○	State capital
GEELONG ○	Town, over 50 000
Bundaberg ○	Town, 10 000–50 000
Katherine ○	Town, 5 000–10 000
Narrogin ○	Town, 1 000–5 000
Robe ○	Town, 200–1 000
Bilpin ○	Town, under 200
Gemini Downs	Locality
MANLY ○	Suburb
Wadeye ◌	Major Aboriginal community
Ngunarra ◌	Aboriginal community
Archer River Roadhouse ▣	Roadhouse
Moralana ▢	Homestead
Two Mile Hole ●	Place of interest/landmark feature
Mt Frome +	Hill
❶	Camping location symbol
Horse Swamp ◮	Camping location symbol

Land and water features

River ～～ Lock	Major river, lock, minor river
Lake	Permanent and intermittent lakes
Reef ★ Island Ferry	Sea, reef, lighthouse, island, ferry
▬▬▬	National park
▬▬▬	Other reserve
	Aboriginal / Torres Strait Islander land
╱╱╱╱╱	Prohibited area

$	Camping fees apply
▲	Non-vehicle based camping
⛺	Vehicle-based camping
🚗	4WD access
🚐	Caravan access
	Ranger/staff patrolled
i	Information centre/board
🚻	Toilets
♿	Disabled access (usually to toilets)
🚰	Drinking water
🚿	Showers
	Wood fireplace/barbecue
	Fires prohibited
	Gas/electric barbecue
⛩	Picnic tables
	Picnic shelter/hut
	No rubbish disposal
☎	Public telephone
	Fishing
	Canoeing
	Sailing/sailboarding
	Waterskiing
🏊	Swimming
	No swimming
	Crocodile warning
	Boat launch
🚶	Walking trails
	Hiking trails
	Nature walks
	Lookout/scenic area
🚴	Cycling/mountain-bike riding
🏇	Horseriding
	Scenic drives
🐕	Dogs allowed on lead
🚫🐕	No dogs/pets allowed

MAKING THE MOST OF YOUR TRIP

CAMPING IS ONE OF THE BEST WAYS OF GETTING OUT THERE AND SEEING AUSTRALIA, WHETHER ON A TRIP TO THE COAST, THE RAINFOREST OR THE DESERT, AND WHETHER SETTING OUT FOR A YEAR AT A TIME OR JUST FOR A WEEKEND. IT IS ALL ABOUT GETTING BACK TO BASICS, AND EXPERIENCED CAMPERS HAVE GOT SIMPLICITY DOWN TO A FINE ART. THERE ARE JUST A FEW THINGS THAT CAMPERS NEED TO CONSIDER AND PLAN AHEAD.

Tread lightly when camping

Australia's parks, forests and reserves are some of the country's most precious, and at the same time most sensitive, recreational resources. When enjoying these areas it is important to tread lightly on the environment.

Minimal impact camping is the way to go. When setting up camp there are a few simple guidelines which, if followed, will ensure that parks, forests and reserves are preserved for all to enjoy, now and in the future.

■ **Be prepared**   Plan your trip carefully and make sure your gear is in good order. If you intend to do a lot of camping it pays to invest in good quality equipment.

■ **Protect plants and animals**   Avoid trampling plants or disturbing animals when setting up camp. Do not pick or cut down any vegetation and do not feed native animals.

■ **Leave no rubbish**   Always take home what you brought with you, even if rubbish bins or pits are provided. Don't burn or bury rubbish; animals will dig it up.

■ **Campfire safety**   Use fireplaces where provided or existing campfire sites. Remove combustible material to a distance of three–four metres from the fire. Be sure the fire is out before leaving, and use water not sand or soil to put it out. Better still, use a gas or fuel stove. Follow current fire regulations in the area. No fires or naked flames, including that from gas or fuel stoves, are permitted on days of total fire ban.

- **Waterway care**   Do not pollute waterways. Don't use soap or detergents in or close to waterways and wash at least 100 metres away from them.

- **Toilet time**   Use toilets if provided. If there is no toilet then bury wastes at least 100 metres from campsites and watercourses, in a hole at least 15 centimetres deep. Toilet paper and sanitary items should not be buried, but burned or taken away.

- **Clean camp**   Always leave campsites cleaner and tidier than you found them.

- **Neighbours**   Be considerate of others when camping nearby. Only use generators in areas where they are permitted and follow any time restrictions.

Camping fees and national park entry fees

Camping fees are payable at many of the campsites in this book and are generally quite minimal. They may be collected by a caretaker or ranger or paid at the park entrance, or there may be a system set up for self-payment.

In some states and areas camping fees come under the guise of 'camping permits'. Camping permits generally involve filling out your details (such as number of nights' stay and vehicle registration number) at a self-registration station, paying the required fee, and displaying your permit on your car or tent. At some sites camping permits can be booked and prepaid (this is essential in certain areas at busy times of the year).

For some remote walk-in sites or sites only accessible by canoe, camping permits can be a way for the land managers to monitor who is meant to be camping in a certain area and when, so that if a campers' whereabouts deviate from what was stated on the permit, the land managers can ring the alarm bell.

Some national parks have entrance fees, which in some cases cover camping fees but do not always. If you intend to visit a number of parks within a state, a national parks pass can offer a substantial saving on multiple entry fees. Most states have their own parks pass system.

Please note that all fees in this book are current at the time of research, but fees may increase from time to time or may be applied to an area without warning. When visiting areas with self-payment systems ensure that you have enough small change to cover the camping fee, as change is generally not given. Camping areas that do not have fees may be managed by local volunteers, and if there is a facility to do so, consider leaving a donation.

New South Wales

Some national parks in New South Wales require payment of a park use fee/vehicle entry fee, which may apply to the first day only or may be payable on a per-vehicle per-day basis.

Annual park passes are available for New South Wales national parks, offering substantial savings on entry fees if you plan to visit New South Wales's parks on more than a couple of occasions each year. Different passes are available, including a pass for one nominated national park or a pass covering all parks in New South Wales that have an entry fee. Annual park passes do not generally cover national park camping fees.

National Parks and Wildlife Service (NPWS)
The National Parks Centre
102 George St, The Rocks, Sydney NSW 2000
Tel.: 1300 361 967 or (02) 9253 4600
Website: www.nationalparks.nsw.gov.au

Environment ACT
12 Wattle Street, Lyneham, ACT 2602
Tel.: (02) 6207 9777
Website: www.environment.act.gov.au

Victoria
Most national parks in Victoria do not have entry fees, so there are no park passes in this state. Some of the more popular national park camping areas have a ballot system for peak periods.

Parks Victoria
Tel.: 131 963
Website: www.parkweb.vic.gov.au

South Australia

Camping permits are required when camping in parks managed by National Parks and Wildlife South Australia (NPWSA). Where self-registration stations are not in place all camping fees are payable to and permits arranged from NPWSA offices. Many parks also have entry fees. NPWSA offers a range of park passes, including the Four Week Holiday Parks Pass, the Statewide Parks Pass and the Desert Parks Pass. Some passes include camping fees.

National Parks and Wildlife South Australia (NPWSA)
Tel.: 1300 655 276
Website: www.parks.sa.gov.au

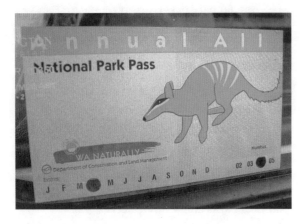

Western Australia

Entry fees apply to many parks in Western Australia. The Department of Conservation and Land Management (CALM) has a range of passes, including Day Passes, Holiday Passes and Annual Passes. These passes do not cover camping fees.

Department of Conservation and Land Management (CALM)
17 Dick Perry Avenue, Kensington WA 6151
Tel.: (08) 9334 0333
Website: www.naturebase.net

Northern Territory

Most parks in the Northern Territory do not have entry fees, except for Kakadu and Uluṟu–Kata Tjuṯa national parks, which are jointly managed by the traditional owners and Environment Australia. The entry fees are levied per person and are valid for up to 14 days in Kakadu and for three consecutive days in Uluṟu–Kata Tjuṯa. An Annual Individual Park Use Ticket is also available, valid for one year for entry into both Kakadu and Uluṟu–Kata Tjuṯa; ID is required to buy this pass, which is not transferable. If you have a Northern Territory drivers licence and registered vehicle you can buy an Annual Territorian Pass. For more information contact the Kakadu National Park Information Centre on tel. (08) 8938 1120 or the Uluṟu–Kata Tjuṯa National Park Information Centre on tel. (08) 8956 3138, or visit the Environment Australia website, www.ea.gov.au/parks

Other national parks in the territory are managed by the Parks and Wildlife Commission of the Northern Territory.

Parks and Wildlife Commission of the Northern Territory
Tel.: (08) 8999 5511
Website: www.nt.gov.au/ipe/pwcnt/

Queensland

Camping permits are required for all campsites in national parks, state forests and some water reserves in Queensland. Some parks and forests have self-registration stations where fees can be paid and permits obtained before setting up camp. Many of Queensland's parks and forests are moving to automated camping permits and fees. These can be pre-booked and paid through Smart Service Queensland, tel. 13 13 04, or via their website, www.qld.gov.au

A Permit to Traverse is required if you wish to travel on restricted-access roads in Queensland's state forests. These permits are free and must be obtained before heading into the bush – failure to do so may result in a fine. Contact the appropriate Queensland Parks and Wildlife Service office for further details.

Queensland Parks and Wildlife Service (QPWS)
Naturally Queensland Information Centre
160 Ann St, Brisbane Qld 4000
Tel.: (07) 3227 7111
Website: www.epa.qld.gov.au

Tasmania

Visitors to Tasmanian national parks require a national parks pass. A range of passes is available, and the right one for you depends on your mode of transport and how long you will be visiting. The Tasmanian parks pass does not cover camping fees and/or overnight walking track fees. Passes are available from Parks and Wildlife offices, at self-registration stations at major parks, and at various other outlets.

Parks and Wildlife Service
Tel.: 1300 135 513
Website: www.parks.tas.gov.au

Restrictions and warnings

Fire

From time to time fire restrictions and bans occur all over Australia. Fire restrictions, fire danger periods and fire ban dates vary from state to state, region to region and year to year. Always confirm fire ban dates and restrictions with local authorities – land managers, councils, police, information centres or fire fighting authorities – before lighting a fire. Remember that on days of total fire ban, no naked flame is allowed in the open, which includes that from a gas or fuel stove.

Some parks, forests and reserves may be closed during periods of extended dry, hot weather (and after heavy rain). Please obey any restrictions advised by authorities as these are for your safety.

New South Wales Rural Fire Service
Tel.: (02) 9684 4411
Website: www.bushfire.nsw.gov.au

Victorian Country Fire Authority
Tel.: (03) 9262 8444
Website: www.cfa.vic.gov.au

South Australian Country Fire Service
Tel.: (08) 8463 4200
Website: www.cfs.org.au

Camping on the Pentecost River, near Wyndham, Western Australia

Fire and Emergency Services Authority
of Western Australia
Tel.: (08) 9323 9300
Website: www.fesa.wa.gov.au

Bushfires Council of the Northern Territory
Tel.: (08) 8922 0844
Website: www.nt.gov.au/ipe/bfc

Queensland Fire and Rescue Service
Tel.: (07) 3247 8100
Website: www.fire.qld.gov.au

Tasmania Fire Service
Tel.: 1800 000 699 (Tasmania only) or
(03) 6230 8600
Website: www.fire.tas.gov.au

Animal dangers

Saltwater crocodiles inhabit many estuarine and inland waterways in the far north of Australia. They are dangerous and caution is required when camping, boating, canoeing or fishing in areas that are known crocodile habitats. Take note of any warning signs in the areas you are travelling through. The absence of a warning sign does not necessarily mean that an area is safe for water-based activities. When travelling through likely crocodile areas please contact the local authorities for up-to-date information on crocodiles.

Box jellyfish and marine stingers can be found in northern Australian waters throughout the year. Swimming is not recommended where these deadly marine creatures are present. Before diving in, check with local authorities for up-to-date information.

Water

Restrictions can apply to local water supplies. Never rely on water supplies at campsites. Ensure that enough water is carried for both cooking and drinking requirements.

General

If visiting state forests where timber harvesting is under way, be aware that there may be heavy traffic and logging vehicles along the access roads. Always observe any restrictions and signs that may be in place.

For safety purposes, restrictions can be placed on specific activities. For example, swimming may be restricted at times of algal growths in waterways and walking tracks may be closed for maintenance or revegetation. Always take heed of all signs and restrictions, and if in doubt make enquiries with the land managers.

Dogs

Travelling and camping with your dog can be very rewarding, however there are some issues that need to be considered before setting out. In some areas, such as national parks, pets – no matter what size or type – are not allowed, while in other areas dogs may be permitted but must be kept on a lead at all times.

When camping near others, ensure that your dog is kept on its lead and does not cause any inconvenience or disturbance to your neighbours.

Extensive fox baiting with the poison 1080 is carried out in forested areas and close to private property. Baited areas are usually signed. Baits are tempting to even the best trained dog so if travelling or camping with a dog in baited areas the dog should be muzzled to prevent it taking the bait. Contact the land managers where you intend to travel for up-to-date information on baiting programs.

In areas inhabited by crocodiles and in the outback where territorial dingoes are common, ensure your dog is kept on a lead and with you at all times. Never leave your dog alone in these regions.

Before leaving home it is a good idea to check with your vet regarding any possible health

A bush track in the Bungle Bungles, Western Australia

problems for the dog that could be encountered, including heartworm, paralysis ticks and grass seeds. A simple injection or some tablets may be necessary to keep your dog healthy.

Don't forget when camping with a pet to pack all its necessary items, including a lead, a long chain/rope to tie it up at night, its bedding, eating and drinking bowls, food, water and favourite toy, along with a muzzle and any necessary medication.

Travelling in the outback

For safety when travelling in remote and desert regions of Australia, you should leave detailed travel plans with a family member or friends. Regular check-ins should be made with them.

When travelling in outback regions always stay on the main public roads. Never venture off on unmarked or unsigned tracks – these are usually on private property and you could be trespassing. Permission must be gained from land owners prior to any travel on private property.

Remember, just because there is no fence it does not mean it is not private property.

It is a good idea to check road conditions, especially after rain and flooding. The states/territories of Australia with significant outback regions have road conditions hotlines and websites:

Transport SA
Tel.: 1300 361 033
Website: www.transport.sa.gov.au

Main Roads Western Australia
Tel.: 1800 013 314
Website: www.mainroads.wa.gov.au

Department of Infrastructure, Planning and Environment (Northern Territory)
Tel.: 1800 246 199
Website: www.nt.gov.au/dtw/roadconditions

Department of Main Roads (Queensland)
Tel.: (07) 3834 2011
Website: www.mainroads.qld.gov.au

There are many things to keep in mind while travelling in remote regions:

- Stay on public main and access roads at all times
- Do not travel on closed roads – heavy penalties apply
- Always leave gates as found
- Never camp beside a water point or creek – it discourages stock accessing the water
- Watch out for livestock on roads and never approach livestock
- Do not use livestock water troughs as baths or wash tubs
- Never camp or stop in a dry creek bed – flash flooding can occur
- Be aware of native animals, kangaroos, emus and camels. Keep travel at dusk to a minimum
- Bury human waste and burn toilet paper. Do not bury garbage – take it away with you
- Always check local fire ban conditions

- Radio contact is recommended – use UHF repeaters

- Do not cut down or take any vegetation, dead or alive, in the outback. Carry your own firewood

- If travelling with a dog keep it with you at all times and always on a lead. Never leave it unattended – territorial dingoes may attack and kill the dog

- Always carry plenty of water. Although some places may have drinking water available, outback areas rely on rain, bores and springs for their water needs

- Always carry enough supplies in case of emergencies and unexpected hold-ups due to wet weather, breakdown, etc.

When to travel

Whether you intend to get away just for the weekend or take a week's leave or an extended holiday, many factors such as weather, school and public holidays, and local events in the area you wish to visit, may influence your decision on when and where to go camping.

New South Wales

Camping in New South Wales can be undertaken year-round, but some regions can be seasonally uncomfortable. The coastal areas are ideal to visit all year, and in spring and summer they are extremely popular and well visited. During summer New South Wales's outback is not generally a comfortable place to camp due to high temperatures, but in autumn and winter temperatures are cooler and conditions more pleasant. In winter camping in the alpine regions of Kosciuszko National Park involves remote snow camping, and should be attempted only by experienced and well-prepared cross-country skiers.

Victoria

The coasts of Victoria are well visited throughout the year, particularly in the warmer summer

Enjoying your camping trip can depend on what time of year you choose to visit

months. In winter much of the high country is closed for safety and track maintenance, but some parks and reserves in the lower sections of the alps are still open. The western and outback regions of Victoria are best visited during the cooler months, from late spring through to autumn, when temperatures are lower and weather conditions are generally more stable.

South Australia

Camping is possible year-round throughout most of South Australia, with the coasts and mountain ranges being well visited. Travel and camping in the outback desert regions is best attempted during the cooler mid-year months, as in summer temperatures can soar.

Western Australia

Campers usually visit the northern parts of the state in late autumn, winter and early spring, in the dry season. From the southern regions of the Pilbara to the south of the state the weather is a little more stable, with camping possible here for most of the year. Camping in the state's central and eastern deserts is best undertaken during the cooler months of winter and early spring.

Northern Territory

Camping and travelling in the Northern Territory is generally best during the dry season, which corresponds with southern Australia's winter. If camping in summer (the wet season) be prepared for extreme temperatures and, especially at the Top End, high humidity.

Queensland

Queensland weather ranges from tropical in the far north to very hot in the outback and cooler in the southern mountains and coastal forests. The south of Queensland can be visited all year round, but the mountains are cool at night and have high rainfall. The outback is only comfortable during the cooler months of the year.

Visits to the far north are best planned during the dry season, when there are warm, sunny days and slightly cooler nights. In the wet season temperatures and humidity rise, and some areas become inaccessible.

Tasmania

The coasts of Tasmania are popular camping destinations; spring through to autumn is the best time to visit. Late summer and autumn provide excellent conditions for camping and hiking through the mountain ranges, although Tasmanian weather can change rapidly – always be prepared and carry a range of clothing. If camping during winter ensure you are prepared for cold temperatures and wet weather.

Fossicking

Fossicking for gems and gold is a popular activity in many areas of Australia. Generally a fossicking permit is required. Whether you intend to fossick by hand or with a detector it is your responsibility to check local rules and conditions before you proceed.

Fossicking is a major attraction in many of Australia's outback regions, such as outback Queensland

New South Wales

No licence required, but regulations apply. Contact the Department of Mineral Resources on tel. (02) 9901 8269 or visit www.minerals.nsw.gov.au

Victoria

Miner's Right required. Contact the Department of Primary Industries – Minerals and Petroleum on tel. 136 186 or visit www.dpi.vic.gov.au

For many, fishing is one of the great joys of camping

South Australia

No licence required, but regulations apply. Contact the Department of Primary Industry and Resources – Minerals on tel. (08) 8463 4154 or visit www.pir.sa.gov.au

Western Australia

Miner's Right required. Contact the Department of Industry and Resources – Minerals on tel. (08) 9222 3628 or visit www.mpr.wa.gov.au

Northern Territory

Fossicker's Permit required. Contact the Department of Business, Industry and Resource Development – Minerals/Mining on tel. (08) 8999 5322 or visit www.dme.nt.gov.au

Queensland

Fossicking Licence required. Contact the Department of Natural Resources and Mines on tel. 1800 803 788 (outside Brisbane) or (07) 3896 3111 or visit www.nrm.qld.gov.au

Tasmania

Prospecting Licence required. Contact the Department of Infrastructure, Energy and Resources – Mineral Resources Tasmania on tel. (03) 6233 8377 or visit www.dier.tas.gov.au

Fishing

If you plan on dropping a line in the ocean or in a river, mountain stream or dam, a recreational fishing licence may be required. Each state has its own regulations, fishing limits and bag sizes. Generally, fishing licences are readily available from retail outlets throughout each state.

New South Wales
New South Wales Fisheries
Tel.: 1300 550 474 or (02) 9527 8411
Website: www.fisheries.nsw.gov.au

Victoria
Department of Primary Industries – Fishing and Aquaculture
Tel.: 131 186 (DPI Information Centre)
Website: www.dpi.vic.gov.au

South Australia
Department of Primary Industries and Resources – Fisheries
Tel.: (08) 8226 2311
Website: www.pir.sa.gov.au

Western Australia
Department of Fisheries
Tel.: (08) 9482 7291
Website: www.fish.wa.gov.au

Northern Territory
Department of Business, Industry and Resource Development – Fisheries
Tel.: (08) 8999 2372
Website: www.nt.gov.au/dbird/dpif/fisheries

Queensland
Department of Primary Industries – Queensland Fisheries Service
Tel.: (07) 3225 1843
Website: www.dpi.qld.gov.au/fishweb

Tasmania
Inland Fisheries Service
Tel.: (03) 6233 4140
Website: www.ifc.tas.gov.au

Department of Primary Industry Water and Environment – Sea Fishing and Aquaculture
Tel.: (03) 6233 7042
Website: www.dpiwe.tas.gov.au

Aboriginal lands

When travelling through Aboriginal lands in Western Australia, the Northern Territory, South Australia and Queensland a travel permit may be required. Generally permits must be arranged up to four weeks prior to travel, but in some cases in Queensland a permit can be obtained on arrival at the community. Contact details are listed in this book where permits may be needed.

Vehicle maintenance and breakdowns

Before embarking on your camping adventure ensure that your vehicle is in good mechanical order and has a reliable spare tyre, adequate water for the cooling system and, if travelling to remote areas, extra fuel supplies.

In the event of a breakdown stay with your vehicle, for two reasons. One, another vehicle is likely to come along, and the people in it should be able to offer assistance. Two, locating a vehicle is easier than locating an individual roaming around the countryside or desert.

Tools

A basic tool kit should be carried in the vehicle at all times. This should include tyre-changing equipment, screwdrivers (Phillips and flat-head), open-ended ring spanners (to suit your vehicle), pliers, hammer, allen keys and a socket set. Your vehicle manual is another handy item to pack.

Planning ahead

When planning your camping trip use this guide to chose a park, forest, town or other area in the region that you wish to visit. Then pick a campsite that has the facilities and activities that you are looking for. Once you have decided on your destination, it may be worthwhile contacting the land mangers to check on current road conditions and access information. Ensure that you allow plenty of time to get to your destination, allowing for varying traffic and road conditions.

Plan your equipment and supplies well before it is time to pack. That way nothing gets forgotten and there are no last-minute trips to the shops.

Food

Where you will be going makes a difference to what food you will carry. Menu planning before departure ensures that you pack all the essentials and also helps when restocking supplies. Many of your favourite meals at home can be cooked while camping but for some great camp cooking and menu planning ideas check out our book, *Australian Bush Cooking* (Boiling Billy Publications, 2002). When travelling through fruit-fly quarantine areas aim to be carrying little or no fresh fruit and vegetables as you will be asked to throw them out.

Cooking equipment

Basic cooking equipment should include a heavy-based frying pan, a saucepan with a lid and a kettle or billy for boiling water. Some campsites have barbecue plates and grills over fireplaces but it is a good idea to carry your own. A gas stove and gas bottle, or fuel stove with fuel, should always be carried for days when solid-fuel fires are banned and for sites where fires are not permitted. A pair of sturdy leather gloves makes handling cooking equipment much safer and a long-handled shovel for moving coals around the bush kitchen is also a good idea.

The camper's kitchen

Camping equipment

A stroll through any camping or outdoor store will reveal a huge range of camping equipment. Before you buy anything, decide what type of camping you wish to do and how often you will be camping. Your budget, along with any specific requirements about the quality of gear, will then dictate what equipment you purchase. You may be taking a camper-trailer or caravan with all sorts of accessories, which will cut down on the equipment you need.

There is a huge variety of tents, from basic two-person tents to family-size dome tents, heavy duty canvas touring tents and roof-top tents. For sleeping, you will have to decide between swags (they come as both single and double), blow-up mattresses (some are self-inflating) and portable fold-up beds. Sleeping bags also vary in thicknesses and temperature ratings.

Optional furniture for campers includes basic camp stools, fold-up table and chairs, but you can also find more luxurious fold-up chairs that are almost lounge like, metal tables with tops that roll up, fold-up cupboards and even portable kitchens. For cooking there are many types of

barbecue plates and grills, gas and fuel stoves, pots, pans, camp ovens and eating utensils.

Clothing

Clothing very much depends on where, when and how you will be camping. Use common sense. A raincoat and sun hat should always be packed, no matter where you will be camping. Bushwalkers wishing to keep their pack size down will need to limit their clothing to good quality lightweight items that are suitable for their destination.

When heading to coastal and northern regions during summer, cool, lightweight clothing will be required, but warm clothes will still be needed for the cooler evenings and occasional inclement days. If heading to the southern states you will need to pack clothes for both cool and warm weather. Travelling in the deserts usually requires warm weather clothing during the day, but at night temperatures can drop dramatically so warm woollen or fleece clothes are needed, along with a beanie and gloves.

Health and safety

A well-stocked first aid kit and first aid book are essential items when camping. It is a good idea that at least one person knows how to use the kit and what all the creams, lotions and tablets are for. Basic kits can be bought at chemists, to which specific items can be added. Do a quick check before each camping holiday, to throw away out-of-date items and replenish stocks. A good quality, high-rating sunscreen should always be packed.

If you take prescribed medications ensure these are safely packed, and if you plan on travelling for an extended period visit your doctor before leaving to obtain prescriptions that will last your trip. If you wear prescription glasses, it is a good idea to pack a second pair, in case of loss or breakage.

In known mosquito areas, such as along waterways and tropical coasts, it is wise to take precautions against these annoying creatures by wearing long-sleeved shirts, long pants and a good quality insect repellent. In the outback bush flies can be a nuisance and wearing a fly veil can provide respite from them.

Camping equipment

Tent, plus poles, pegs and guy ropes
Tarpaulin
Sleeping mats/mattresses
Pillows
Bedding (linen or sleeping bags)
Folding chairs
Folding table
Esky or portable 12 volt/gas fridge
Torch and/or head torch

Cooking equipment

Matches
Firelighters
Gas/fuel stove and gas bottle/fuel
Barbecue plate and grill
Frying pan
Saucepan with lid
Camp oven and lifters
Kettle/billy
Tripod hanger
Shovel
Thick leather gloves
Pie dish and loaf tin to fit in camp oven
Trivet to fit camp oven

Cooking utensils

Tongs
Barbecue scraper
Egg flip
Basting brush
Serving spoon
Slotted serving spoon
Vegetable peeler
Flat grater
Can opener with bottle opener
Swiss army knife – with corkscrew
Flat strainer
Sharp knife
Bread knife
Cutting board
Mesh toaster
General-purpose scissors
Measuring spoon or tablespoon
Extra plate and bowl for serving
Teaspoons

Eating equipment

Plates
Bowls
Mugs
Forks
Spoons
Knives
Steak knives

Miscellaneous

Aluminium foil
Cling wrap
Paper towels
Plastic bottles for milk, cordial, extra water, etc.

Cleaning equipment

Plastic bags
Wash-up bucket
Detergent
Scourer
Cloth
Tea towels

Basic supplies

Water
Tea
Coffee
Sugar
Oil
Selection of sauces
Selection of herbs and spices
Canned foods
Dried packet foods
Flour
Pasta
Rice
Cereals
Biscuits
Salt and pepper

Other equipment – depending on your activity

Camera
Binoculars
Fishing equipment
Bicycles
Canoe
Li-los

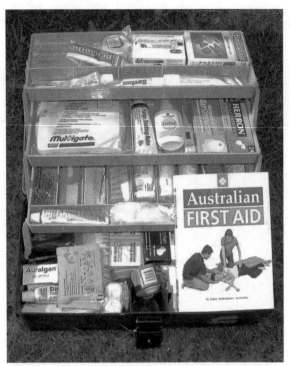

A comprehensive first aid kit will help you prepare for the unexpected

Sources of information

Identification books of birds, animals, plants, trees and flowers are ideal references to have on hand when camping, as are books on the area you are visiting to give you an insight into the local history and geography of the region. National park and state forest brochures usually give detailed information on a park or forest's interesting sites, flora and fauna along with details of walking trails (for popular national parks and state forests, detailed information can often be found on the websites of the relevant state authority, see pages vii–viii). The local visitor centre is always another good place to pick up information.

Maps

A good map or road directory is important on any camping trip, especially when the campsite you have chosen is off the beaten track. Aside from the maps in this book, all campsites listed are referenced to a secondary source. The abbreviations used for these map sources, and their publisher and publication date, are as follows:

NSWRD: The New South Wales Road Directory, Explore Australia Publishing, 1998

VR: VicRoads Country Street Directory of Victoria, Royal Automobile Club of Victoria, 2002

STAWA: Streetsmart Travellers Atlas of Western Australia, Department of Land Administration and Hema Maps, 2002

ANTTM: Australia's Northern Territory Touring Map, Department of Infrastructure, Planning and Environment, 2000

STM Qld: Sunmap Tourist Map Queensland, Department of Natural Resources and Mines, 2000

TVM: Tasmania Visitors Map, Department of Primary Industries, Water and Environment, 2000

In South Australia we have used the series of region maps published by the RAA:

Adelaide and Suburbs, 2002

Mid North, 2001

Barossa Valley and Adelaide Hills, 2002

Yorke Peninsula, 2003

Lower Eyre Peninsula, 2002

Upper Eyre Peninsula and Far West Coast, 2002

Flinders Ranges, 2001

Outback, 2002

Riverland and Central Murray, 2002

Upper South East, 2003

Lower South East, 2001

Fleurieu Peninsula and Southern Adelaide Hills, 2002

Kangaroo Island, 2001

Useful contacts

Contact details for state national park authorities, fire authorities, road authorities (for road conditions reports) and fishing and fossicking authorities are found throughout the preceeding pages. Here are some further contacts that you may find useful during your travels.

Bureau of Meterology
Website: www.bom.gov.au

New South Wales

State Forests of New South Wales
Information Centre
Cumberland State Forest
95 Castle Hill Road, West Pennant Hills,
NSW 2125
Tel.: 1300 655 687 or (02) 9871 3377
Website: www.forest.nsw.gov.au

Department of Land and Water Conservation (DLWC)
23–33 Bridge Street, Sydney, NSW 2000
Tel.: (02) 9228 6111
and
10 Valentine Avenue, Parramatta, NSW 2150
Tel.: (02) 9895 6211
Website: www.dlwc.nsw.gov.au

Tourism New South Wales
Tel.: 132 077
Website: www.visitnsw.com.au

Victoria

Department of Sustainability and Environment (DSE)
Information Centre
8 Nicholson Street, East Melbourne, VIC 3002
Tel.: 136 186
Website: www.dse.vic.gov.au

Tourism Victoria
Tel.: 132 842
Website: www.visitvictoria.com

South Australia

South Australia Tourism Commission
Tel.: 1300 655 276
Website: www.southaustralia.com

Western Australia

Western Australian Tourism Commission
Tel.: 1300 361 351 or (08) 9483 1111
Website: www.westernaustralia.net

Northern Territory

Northern Territory Tourist Commission
Tel.: 136 110 or (08) 8951 8492
Website: www.ntholidays.com

Queensland

Great Barrier Reef Marine Park Authority
Tel.: (07) 4750 0700
Website: www.gbrmpa.gov.au

Tourism Queensland
Tel.: 13 88 33
Website: www.queenslandholidays.com.au

Tasmania

Forestry Tasmania
Tel.: (03) 6233 8203
Website: www.forestrytas.com.au

Tourism Tasmania
Tel.: 1800 808 776
Website: www.tourism.tas.gov.au

Spirit of Tasmania
Melbourne–Devonport ferry
Tel.: 1800 634 906
Website: www.spiritoftasmania.com.au

NEW SOUTH WALES

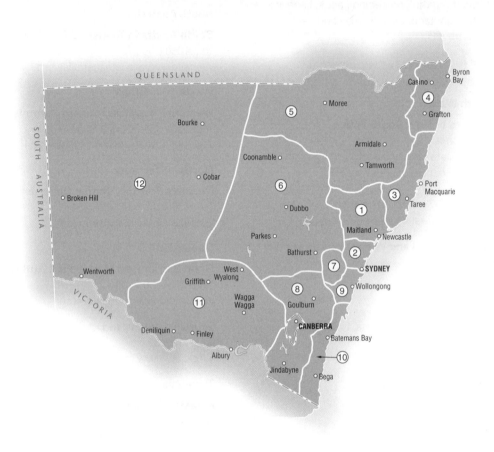

TOP 10 CAMPSITES

Polblue camping area
Barrington Tops National Park, page 5

Mungo Brush camping area
Myall Lakes National Park, page 17

Greenpatch Campground
Booderee National Park, page 62

Geehi camping area
Kosciuszko National Park, page 50

Henry Angel Trackhead
Hume and Hovell Walking Track, page 69

The Barracks camping area
Coolah Tops National Park, page 36

Village Campground
Hill End, page 37

Wollomombi Gorge camping area
Oxley Wild Rivers National Park, page 29

Darling River camping areas
Kinchega National Park, page 75

Homestead Creek camping area
Mutawintji National Park, page 76

New South Wales offers an incredible range of landscapes for the camper, and so much of this has to do with the climate. From east to west, the state stretches from the South Pacific Ocean into the desert, and from south to north it stretches from a rugged southern clime up into the tropics.

Along the 2000-kilometre coastline, small fishing villages and summer holiday destinations merge into cosmopolitan towns like Byron Bay. In between these built up areas is a swathe of magnificent national parks, where the tangle of wilderness often climbs right into the sea. In Ben Boyd National Park, close to the Victorian border, campers can visit Boyds Tower on the edge of Twofold Bay, a failed lighthouse that came to be used as a lookout for whales back in the heady days of a now outlawed industry.

Behind Sydney is one of the state's favourite places – the Blue Mountains. These mountains are all jagged rock escarpments and steep valleys, with some terrific tourism developments set up to make the most of them. To the north, Wollemi National Park is proof for Sydneysiders that you don't have to travel far to get to somewhere remote. Tree-clad mountains sweep down into the gorges of the Colo River, and the mountain-tops give vistas of a wilderness that seems to stretch on forever. This is a great place for bushwalking, as so many areas of the park can only be reached on foot.

In the south-east is the state's largest national park, Kosciuszko. The size of this park makes it a great place for an adventure – a skiing trip in winter, or a horseriding, mountain-bike riding or bushwalking trek in the warmer months.

To the west of Kosciuszko, across the Riverina, you'll find a sparse landscape intercepted with some astonishing places, like Mungo National Park. The remains of an Aboriginal man around 40 000 years old has been discovered here, his bones preserved in the once teeming Willandra Lakes system. Drive across the now dry lakebed, and explore the sandy ridges and miniature peaks of this lunar-like landscape. All through these parts are reminders of our pastoral past, with many old woolsheds and shearing quarters now offering accommodation. This is great if you want an occasional alternative to your tent!

The Walls of China, Mungo National Park

HUNTER VALLEY AND COAST

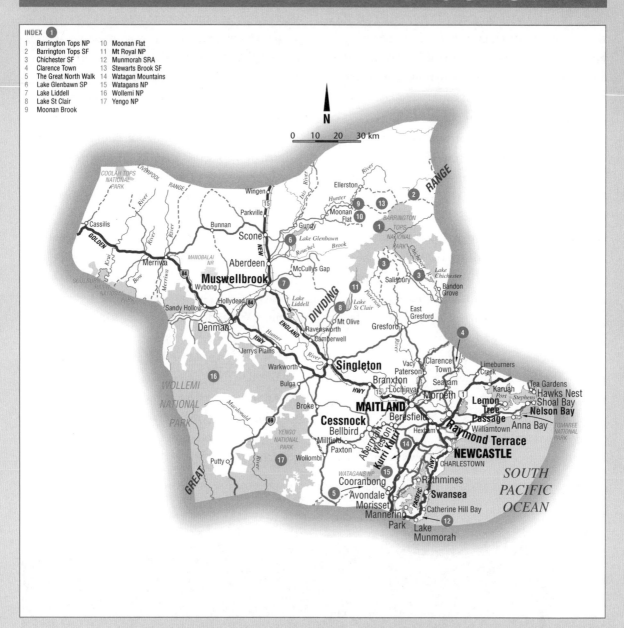

THE HUNTER VALLEY WINE REGION AND THE CITY OF NEWCASTLE ARE THE BEST KNOWN FEATURES OF THIS PART OF THE STATE, BUT IT ALSO HAS SOME SUPERB OPPORTUNITIES FOR CAMPING. FOR SCENERY VISITORS HAVE A CHOICE OF THE MAGNIFICENT HIGH COUNTRY OF BARRINGTON TOPS, THE TOWERING NATIVE FORESTS, CHICHESTER STATE FOREST, THE RUGGED SANDSTONE COUNTRY OF YENGO NATIONAL PARK, AND THE LARGE EXPANSES OF LAKE GLENBAWN AND LAKE LIDDELL.

Barrington Tops, in the north of the region, has camping in a range of surroundings, from expanses of snow gums to rainforest and eucalypt forest. While visiting Barrington Tops throw a line in a mountain stream and try your luck for a trout, enjoy one of the many walking trails – from a short stroll to an overnight hike – take in the magnificent vistas from the numerous lookouts or do some touring by four-wheel drive or mountain bike.

On the southern border of Barrington Tops National Park is Chichester State Forest, home to abundant wildlife. Campers can choose sites beside refreshing waterholes or in secluded forest camping areas. There are scenic drives that will take you to some of the best sites in the forest.

Further to the south, Yengo National Park has some excellent examples of Aboriginal rock carvings and features the historic Old Great North Road. As Yengo is close to the big smoke it makes an ideal weekend getaway. Walk along original sections of the convict-built road or take a tour to Devils Rock and view the rock carvings.

To the east of Yengo National Park are the Watagan Mountains, which include Watagans National Park. Campers will find a number of sites nestled amongst groves of pine trees or casuarinas. In amongst the forests are walking trails and lookouts that can be accessed via the forest drive. Wildflowers bloom in these forests most of the year.

BEST CAMPSITES

Polblue camping area
Barrington Tops National Park

Manning River camping area
Barrington Tops State Forest

The Pines camping area
Watagan Mountains

Frying Pan Creek camping area
Chichester State Forest

Mogo camping area
Yengo National Park

BEST TIME TO VISIT

The region can be visited all year round, with spring and autumn the most comfortable times. Be prepared for all types of weather in Barrington Tops – snow has fallen on the Tops in summer!

1. BARRINGTON TOPS NATIONAL PARK
see page 4

2. BARRINGTON TOPS STATE FOREST

This forest is 40 km west of Gloucester, reached via Barrington Tops Forest Rd. Conventional vehicles can access main areas – other areas require 4WD. There are many recreational opportunities: 4WD touring, camping, walking, mountain-bike riding, fishing, horseriding. This is a remote area and, due to its high altitude, weather conditions can change quickly, even in summer – be prepared.

Banksia camping area

On Dilgry River, reached from Dilgry Circle Rd off Barrington Tops Forest Rd. Water from river. Additional map ref.: NSWRD 117 L8.

Dilgry River camping area

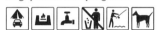

Signposted from Pheasant Creek Rd off Barrington Tops Forest Rd. Bush camping area beside Dilgry River. Water from river. Additional map ref.: NSWRD 117 L8.

Manning River camping area

Beside Manning River – a trout-fishing stream. Access via Pheasant Creek Rd off Dilgry Circle Rd. Water from river – boil before use. Additional map ref.: NSWRD 116 K8.

Further information & bookings: State Forests, Hunter Region **Tel.:** (02) 4927 0977 **General information and brochures:** Cumberland State Forest **Tel.:** 1300 655 687 **Email:** cumberland@sf.nsw.gov.au

3. CHICHESTER STATE FOREST

Chichester State Forest borders the southern section of Barrington Tops National Park. The forest is in two sections – Allyn River and Telegherry River. The Allyn River Section is 55 km north-west of Dungog via Salisbury Rd, while the Telegherry River Section is 20 km north of Dungog and reached via Chichester Dam Rd. It is a popular area for family camping, 4WD touring and trail-bike riding.

ALLYN RIVER SECTION

Dobbie Rim camping area

Access via Allyn River Forest Rd. Water from creek. Additional map ref.: NSWRD 126 K4.

Gunyah Hut

On Mt Allyn Rd. Former forest workers hut. Sleeps up to six people. No power. Water from tank. Dogs allowed on lead outside hut. Bookings well in advance are essential. Additional map ref.: NSWRD 126 K4.

Old camping area

Access via Mt Allyn Rd. Water from creek. Additional map ref.: NSWRD 126 K4.

BARRINGTON TOPS NATIONAL PARK

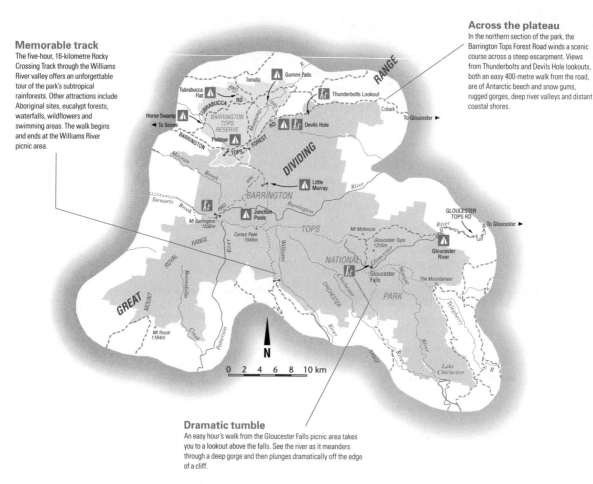

Memorable track
The five-hour, 16-kilometre Rocky Crossing Track through the Williams River valley offers an unforgettable tour of the park's subtropical rainforests. Other attractions include Aboriginal sites, eucalypt forests, waterfalls, wildflowers and swimming areas. The walk begins and ends at the Williams River picnic area.

Across the plateau
In the northern section of the park, the Barrington Tops Forest Road winds a scenic course across a steep escarpment. Views from Thunderbolts and Devils Hole lookouts, both an easy 400-metre walk from the road, are of Antarctic beech and snow gums, rugged gorges, deep river valleys and distant coastal shores.

Dramatic tumble
An easy hour's walk from the Gloucester Falls picnic area takes you to a lookout above the falls. See the river as it meanders through a deep gorge and then plunges dramatically off the edge of a cliff.

The park contains a spectacular subalpine area atop the Great Dividing Range as well as World Heritage-listed rainforests. It is 45 km west of Gloucester. Access to the eastern section is via Gloucester Tops Rd, and to the central and northern section via Barrington Tops Forest Rd. There is access for conventional vehicles to the main areas but other parts require 4WD. There is a wealth of recreational opportunities – car and 4WD touring (there are stunning vistas from the lookouts), camping, walking, mountain-bike riding, fishing and horseriding. This is a remote area. Weather conditions can also change quickly – be prepared.

EASTERN SECTION

Gloucester River camping area

This is 38 km south-west of Gloucester via Gloucester Tops Rd. Access via Cobark Rd off Bucketts Way. Drive to Gloucester Falls. Water from creek – boil before use. Bring firewood. Additional map ref.: NSWRD 127 P2.

NORTHERN SECTION

Devils Hole camping area

Signposted access on Barrington Tops Forest Rd. Bush camping – no facilities. Bring firewood or gas/fuel stove. Additional map ref.: NSWRD 116 K9.

Junction Pools camping area

Beside Barrington River. Access via Barrington Trail off Barrington Tops Forest Rd. 4WD access in dry weather (track closed June–Sept.) or walk-in access. Water from creek. Bring firewood or gas/fuel stove. Additional map ref.: NSWRD 126 J1.

Little Murray camping area

Beside Beean Beean Creek. Access via Barrington Trail off Barrington Tops Forest Rd. 4WD access in dry weather (track closed June–Sept.) or walk-in access. Water from creek. Bring firewood or gas/fuel stove. Additional map ref.: NSWRD 116 K10.

POLBLUE CROWN RESERVE

Gummi Falls camping area

Bush camping – no facilities – beside small cascade. Access via Tuglow Trail. 4WD access in dry weather (track closed June–Sept.) or walk-in access. Water from creek. Bring firewood or gas/fuel stove. Additional map ref.: NSWRD 116 K9.

Horse Swamp camping area

Bush camping – no facilities – on Tubrabucca Rd. Access via Barrington Tops Forest Rd. Bring firewood or gas/fuel stove. Additional map ref.: NSWRD 116 H9.

Polblue camping area

Situated 54 km west of Gloucester via Barrington Tops Rd. Water from creek – boil before use. Bring firewood or gas/fuel stove. Additional map ref.: NSWRD 116 J10.

Tubrabucca Flat camping area

Bush camping – no facilities. Access via Barrington Trail (north). 4WD dry-weather access only (track closed June–Sept.). Bring water and firewood or gas/fuel stove. Additional map ref.: NSWRD 116 J8.

Walk-in camping areas

A number of established walk-in bush campsites exist within the park. Be self-sufficient – no facilities. Gas/fuel stove preferred. Obtain large-scale maps and contact ranger for details.

Further information & bookings:

NPWS, Gloucester **Tel.:** (02) 6558 1478 *or*
NPWS, Muswellbrook **Tel.:** (02) 6543 3533
Camping fees: *Gloucester River:* $5.00 per adult/night, $3.00 per child (age 5–15) per night; fees payable at self-registration station

Manning River, Barrington Tops National Park

Pademelon Park camping area

Access via Mt Allyn Rd. Water from creek. Additional map ref.: NSWRD 126 K4.

White Rock camping area

Access via Allyn River Forest Rd. Beside Allyn River. Water from river. Additional map ref.: NSWRD 126 K3.

TELEGHERRY RIVER SECTION

Coachwood camping area

Reached via Frying Pan Rd (2WD access in dry weather only). Across river from Frying Pan camping area. Good swimming hole. Water from river – boil before use. Additional map ref.: NSWRD 127 R5.

Currawong camping area

Reached via Middle Ridge Rd. On opposite side of Telegherry River to Telegherry Forest Park camping area. 4WD only access – river crossing. Water from river – boil before use. Additional map ref.: NSWRD 127 Q5.

Frying Pan Creek camping area

Access via Frying Pan Rd (2WD access in dry weather only). Beside Telegherry River. Water from river – boil before use. Additional map ref.: NSWRD 127 R5.

Gumleaf Hut

On Skimmings Gap Rd. Former forest workers hut. Sleeps up to six people. No power. Water from tank. Dogs allowed on lead outside hut. Bookings well in advance are essential. Additional map ref.: NSWRD 127 R6.

Telegherry Forest Park camping area

Access via Middle Ridge Rd (2WD access in dry weather only). Beside Telegherry River. Water from river – boil before use. Additional map ref.: NSWRD 127 Q5.

The Knob picnic and camping area

Access via Skimmings Gap Rd. Commanding views over forest. Additional map ref.: NSWRD 127 R6.

Further information & bookings: State Forests, Hunter Region **Tel.:** (02) 4927 0977 **General information and brochures:** Cumberland State Forest **Tel.:** 1300 655 687 **Email:** cumberland@sf.nsw.gov.au **Camping fees:** *Gunyah and Gumleaf huts:* $20.00 per hut/night weekdays; $40.00 per hut/night on Fri./Sat. nights, public holidays and school holidays

4. CLARENCE TOWN

The village of Clarence Town is beside the Willams River, 26 km north of Raymond Terrace. At one time it was a ship-building town but with the coming of the railway it gradually declined in importance. Access is via Clarence Town Rd off the Pacific Hwy. The area is popular for waterskiing and family camping. Bookings are recommended for both camping areas, especially at peak times.

Wharf Reserve camping area

On banks of Willams River. Access via Rifle St in Clarence Town. Additional map ref.: NSWRD 264 E12.

Bridge Reserve camping area

On banks of Willams River. Access via Durham St in Clarence Town. Additional map ref.: NSWRD 264 F10.

Further information & bookings: Caretaker **Tel.:** (02) 4996 4231 **Camping fees:** From $10.00 per site/night

5. THE GREAT NORTH WALK see page 10

5. THE GREAT NORTH WALK see page 10

6. LAKE GLENBAWN STATE PARK

This park consists of the foreshore and land around Glenbawn Dam, a large water storage on the Hunter River 20 km east of Scone. It is reached via Rouchel Rd from Aberdeen or Gundy Rd from Scone. The lake is a very popular summer watersports destination, with good fishing (yellowbelly, bass, murray cod, trout and catfish) and boating.

Eastern Foreshore camping area

Many camping areas on the eastern foreshore of Lake Glenbawn. Access via Eastern Shore Rd from main entrance; campsites also have boat access. Firewood supplied. Additional map ref.: NSWRD 126 A3.

Riverside Caravan Park

Inside main entrace to park. Gas/fuel stove only. Additional map ref.: NSWRD 125 V3.

Further information & bookings: DLWC, Lake Glenbawn **Tel.:** (02) 6543 7193 **Email:** glenbawn@hunterlink.net.au **Camping fees:** From $13.20 for 2 people/night; $16.50 per powered site for 2 people/night (caravan park only)

7. LAKE LIDDELL

Lake Liddell is a water storage supplying the nearby Bayswater Power Station, 15 km south-east of Muswellbrook. It is signposted on Hebden Rd from New England Hwy. The lake is a watersports venue.

Lake Liddell Recreation Area camping area

Firewood supplied. Additional map ref.: NSWRD 125 V8.

Further information & bookings: Manager, Lake Liddell Recreation Area **Tel.:** (02) 6541 2010 **Camping fees:** From $7.00 per site/night; $3.00 additional per site/night for power

8. LAKE ST CLAIR

This lake, formed by the Glennies Creek Dam, is 25 km north of Singleton. It is signposted via Bridgeman Rd from the New England Hwy at Singleton. Activities include swimming, power boating and waterskiing. The lake is stocked with bass and catfish.

Lake St Clair camping area

Large area near lake. Additional map ref.: NSWRD 126 F8.

Further information & bookings: Caretaker
Tel.: (02) 6577 3070 **Camping fees:** Unpowered sites from $12.00 per site/night, powered sites from $18.00 per site/night

9. MOONAN BROOK

Moonan Brook is the site of the old Denison gold diggings; it lies 55 km north-east of Scone and 3 km south-east of Moonan Flat. Access is via Moonan Brook Rd from Moonan Flat in the west or Barrington Tops Forest Rd from Gloucester in the east.

Moonan Brook Forestry Cottage

Reached via Moonan Brook Rd. A former historic school-house (built late 1800s) that sleeps up to 25 people. Camping possible beside cottage. Near Moonan Brook. Dogs allowed on lead outside cottage. Additional map ref.: NSWRD 116 F9.

Further information & bookings: Moonan Forestry Cottage Manager **Tel.:** (02) 6546 3173 **Cottage fees:** *Fri.–Sun., school holidays and public holidays:* $80.00 per night for 4 adults *Mon.–Thurs.:* $65.00 per night for 4 adults. Additional adults $10.00 per night, children under 14 $5.00 per night

10. MOONAN FLAT

This historic village is on the banks of the Hunter River, 50 km north-east of Scone. It is reached via Gundy Rd from Scone. Enjoy the old Victoria Hotel here.

Belmadar camping area

Opposite side of the river to the Victoria Hotel. Bring drinking water and firewood. Additional map ref.: NSWRD 116 E9.

Further information & bookings: Caretaker
Tel.: (02) 6546 3155 **Camping fees:** $4.50 per person/night; powered sites $5.60 per person/night; caretaker collects fees

11. MOUNT ROYAL NATIONAL PARK

This park adjoins the south-west edge of Barrington Tops National Park and is home to the rare Hastings River mouse and rufous scrub bird. It is 50 km north of Singleton and north of Lake St Clair. Access is via Bridgeman Rd from New England Hwy at Singleton then via Mount Royal Rd. Check road conditions after rain.

Youngville camping area

Access via Mt Royal Rd. Bring drinking water and firewood. Additional map ref.: NSWRD 126 F5.

Further information & bookings: NPWS, Bulga
Tel.: (02) 6574 5555

12. MUNMORAH STATE RECREATION AREA

This coastal reserve is 40 km north of Gosford, between Budgewoi and Catherine Hill Bay. It is reached via Blue Wren Drive off Pacific Hwy, or Birdie Beach Drive off Elizabeth Bay Drive. It is a popular destination with anglers and surfers and has stunning ocean views. There are wildflower displays in season.

Frazer camping area

Small area (six sites) in a protected location near Frazer Beach. Access via Frazer Beach Rd from Campbell Drive. Bring drinking water. Gas/fuel stove only. Additional map ref.: NSWRD 35 R3.

Freemans camping area

Large area (50 sites but five caravan sites only) close to Birdie Beach. Access from Birdie Beach Drive. Limited drinking water. Gas/fuel stove only. Bookings are essential for holiday periods and a ballot system applies at peak times. Additional map ref.: NSWRD 35 Q4.

Further information & bookings: Munmorah State Recreation Area **Tel.:** (02) 4358 0400 **Email:** central.coast@ npws.nsw.gov.au **Park use fee:** $6.00 per vehicle/day **Camping fees:** *Frazer:* $9.00 per adult/night and $4.50 per child/night in peak period (Sept.–April); $7.50 per adult/night and $4.00 per child/night in off-peak period (May–Aug.) *Freemans:* $7.50 per adult/night and $4.00 per child/night (peak); $5.00 per adult/night and $3.00 per child/night (off-peak)

13. STEWARTS BROOK STATE FOREST

The forest, which adjoins Barrington Tops National Park, is 15 km east of Moonan Flat. It is reached via Barrington Tops Forest Rd from Moonan Flat in the west and from Gloucester in the east. Activities here include bushwalking and 4WD touring.

Gologolies camping area

A short distance down Boundary Rd, near Dingo Gate on Barrington Tops Forest Rd. 4WD access only. Bring drinking water. Additional map ref.: NSWRD 116 G9.

Further information & bookings: State Forests, Hunter Region **Tel.:** (02) 4927 0977 **Email:** cumberland@sf.nsw. gov.au

14. WATAGAN MOUNTAINS

See also Watagans National Park, *next entry*

The Watagan Mountains cover a large forested area running from behind the Central Coast north to the outskirts of Newcastle – it includes a number of state forests and national parks. Main access roads are the Watagan Forest Rd off Hue Hue Rd from Sydney–Newcastle Freeway in the south; Watagan Forest Rd from Cessnock in the north; Martinsville Rd from Cooranbong and Mount Faulk Rd from Freemans Waterhole from the east; and Watagan Rd from Laguna from the west. The Watagan Mountains offer a wealth of recreational opportunities, ranging from sightseeing and car touring, picnicking, day and overnight walks, camping, 4WD touring, horseriding, mountain-bike riding, photography and nature study.

ONLEY STATE FOREST

Casuarina camping area

Secluded campsites on Watagan Forest Rd. Water from creek. Firewood supplied. Additional map ref.: NSWRD 146 G2.

The Basin camping area

On Basin Forest Rd. Water from creek. Firewood supplied. Additional map ref.: NSWRD 146 E3.

The Pines camping area

On Watagan Forest Rd. Pleasant camping in the vicinity of an old pine plantation. Water from tank. Firewood supplied. Additional map ref.: NSWRD 146 G2.

Turpentine camping area

On Watagan Forest Rd. Secluded campsites. Water from creek. Firewood supplied. Additional map ref.: NSWRD 146 G2.

Wattle Tree camping area

On Watagan Forest Rd. Firewood supplied. Additional map ref.: NSWRD 146 G2.

HEATON STATE FOREST

Watagan Headquarters camping area

On Watagan Forest Rd. Firewood supplied. Additional map ref.: NSWRD 136 J10.

Bush camping
Dispersed bush camping is allowed within the state forests of the Watagan Mountains. Obtain large-scale maps and contact State Forests, Hunter Region, for details.

Further information & bookings: State Forests, Hunter Region **Tel.:** (02) 4927 0977 **General information and brochures:** Cumberland State Forest **Tel.:** 1300 655 687 **Email:** cumberland@sf.nsw.gov.au

15. WATAGANS NATIONAL PARK

Part of the Watagan Mountains, this national park protects many of the area's impressive natural features. It is 30 km south-west of Newcastle, near Cooranbong, and the main access roads are as per the Watagan Mountains (see previous entry). Visit Boarding House Dam, Monkey Face Lookout and Gap Creek Falls.

Bangalow Road camping area

On Bangalow Rd off Mount Faulk Rd. Close to Gap Creek Falls. Bring firewood or gas/fuel stove. Additional map ref.: NSWRD 146 J1.

Gap Creek camping area

On Bangalow Rd off Mount Faulk Rd. Close to Gap Creek Falls. Bring firewood or gas/fuel stove. Additional map ref.: NSWRD 146 J1.

Further information & bookings: NPWS, Munmorah **Tel.:** (02) 4358 0400 **Email:** central.coast@npws.nsw.gov.au

16. WOLLEMI NATIONAL PARK see pages 11 and 41

17. YENGO NATIONAL PARK

This park is to the north of Wisemans Ferry and features rugged sandstone country, spectacular scenery and important Aboriginal sites. There is limited 2WD access. Main access is via Old Great North Rd from Wisemans Ferry and George Downes Drive from Laguna.

Big Yango Homestead
On former grazing property. Accommodation in restored homestead as well as remote camping areas. Advance bookings essential – key access only.

Finchley camping area

On Yango Track. Access via Boree Track from Laguna. Great views from nearby Finchley Trig. Bring water plus firewood or gas/fuel stove. Additional map ref.: NSWRD 146 B1.

Mogo camping area

At northern end of Mogo Creek Rd. Good base to explore top section of Old Great North Rd. Firewood supplied. Additional map ref.: NSWRD 146 B3.

Further information & bookings: NPWS, Gosford **Tel.:** (02) 4324 4911 **Email:** central.coast@npws.nsw.gov.au **Camping fees:** *Mogo:* $5.00 per adult/night, $3.00 per child (age 5–15) per night *Finchley:* $3.00 per adult/night, $2.00 per child (age 5–15) per night. Fees payable at self-registration station at each site

CENTRAL COAST AND HAWKESBURY

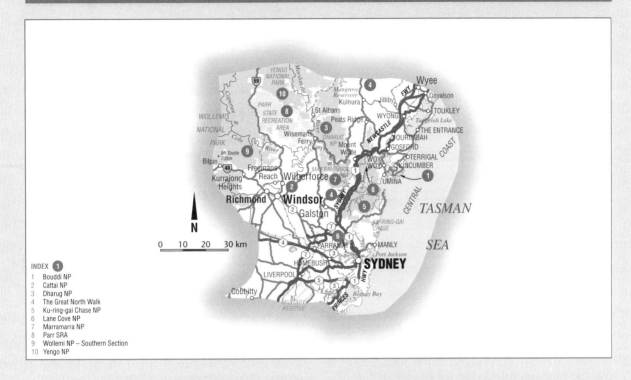

INDEX ①
1 Bouddi NP
2 Cattai NP
3 Dharug NP
4 The Great North Walk
5 Ku-ring-gai Chase NP
6 Lane Cove NP
7 Marramarra NP
8 Parr SRA
9 Wollemi NP – Southern Section
10 Yengo NP

The Central Coast and Hawkesbury region, only a short drive from Sydney, is a perfect place to take time out and set up camp. Those on foot, or with a canoe, can explore the more wild and remote parts of the region.

Bouddi National Park, on the coast just south-east of Gosford, offers stunning vistas of the South Pacific Ocean. Here you can camp at one of the park's three beaches, and there is vehicle access to the main beach, Putty Beach.

The Colo River in the southern section of Wollemi National Park is an extremely popular location for getting out the canoe or li-lo. Vehicle-based camping can be found at the large, grassed Newnes camping area, where campers can explore the nearby mining ruins. Just a short drive, walk or mountain-bike ride away is the fascinating glow worm tunnel. Don't forget to take your torch!

Dharug National Park is on the northern banks of the Hawkesbury River, just east of Wisemans Ferry. The Mill Creek camping area is a perfect place to set up base camp while exploring the park's surrounds by foot or mountain bike.

Wombats and wallaroos are regulars at the camping area, with sugar gliders appearing at night.

More energetic and self-sufficient walkers may wish to attempt a part of or perhaps all of the Great North Walk, which stretches from Sydney through Berowra Waters to Somersby and the Watagan Mountains, finishing at Newcastle.

There are 26 campgrounds set up along this epic track, many of which you can only reach by putting on your boots and walking to them.

BEST CAMPSITES

Mill Creek camping area
Dharug National Park

Putty Beach camping area
Bouddi National Park

Newnes camping area
Wollemi National Park – Southern section

The Basin camping area
Ku-ring-gai Chase National Park

Gentlemans Halt camping area
Marramarra National Park

BEST TIME TO VISIT

All year round, however some access roads to these areas are unsealed and can be closed after periods of wet weather. If you plan on tackling one of the longer walking trails within the region, these are best undertaken during the cooler months and when the fire danger is not high.

1. BOUDDI NATIONAL PARK

This popular coastal park is 20 km south-east of Gosford, near Killcare. There are stunning coastal vistas from lookout points and many walking tracks. Visit the wreck of the SS *Maitland*. The park contains both vehicle-based camping areas and walk-in sites. Prior bookings and payment are essential for all sites in the park and may be made up to three months in advance.

Little Beach camping area

Walk-in access (500 m) from Graham Drive, which is off The Scenic Rd from MacMasters Beach. Six sites close to beach. Bring drinking water. Gas/fuel stove only. Additional map ref.: NSWRD 33 G9.

Putty Beach camping area

Access via Putty Beach Drive from Hardys Bay. Close to beach. 19 sites. Gas/fuel stove only. Additional map ref.: NSWRD 33 E10.

Tallow Beach camping area

Access via Hawke Head Drive from Hardys Bay. Walk-in access only – 1.5 km from carpark. Close to beach. Bring drinking water. Gas/fuel stove only. Additional map ref.: NSWRD 33 D10.

Further information & bookings: NPWS, Gosford **Tel.:** (02) 4320 4200 **Email:** central.coast@npws.nsw.gov.au **Park use fee:** *Putty Beach only:* $6.00 per vehicle/day **Camping fees:** *Putty Beach and Little Beach* $7.50 per adult/night and $4.00 per child (age 5–15) per night in peak period (Sept.–April); $5.00 per adult/night and $3.00 per child (age 5–15) per night in off-peak period (May–Aug.) *Tallow Beach:* $3.00 per adult/night, $2.00 per child (age 5–15) per night

2. CATTAI NATIONAL PARK

The park is on the Hawkesbury River 15 km north-east of Windsor, near Pitt Town. Access is via Cattai Rd from Pitt Town and Wisemans Ferry Rd from Wisemans Ferry.

Cattai camping area

Signposted from Wisemans Ferry Rd. Bring drinking water. Firewood supplied. Sites must be booked before arrival. Additional map ref.: NSWRD 7 U2.

Further information & bookings: NPWS, Scheyville **Tel.:** (02) 4572 3100 **Email:** cumberland.north@npws.nsw.gov.au **Park use fee:** $6.00 per vehicle/day **Camping fees:** $5.00 per adult/night, $3.00 per child (age 5–15) per night

3. DHARUG NATIONAL PARK

The park is north of the Hawkesbury River near Wisemans Ferry, 55 km north of Sydney. It is reached by the Old Northern Rd from Sydney to Wisemans Ferry, or by Wisemans Ferry Rd from Central Mangrove and Spencer. You can inspect convict-built roadworks on the Old Great North Rd. The park is also popular for bushwalking and mountain-bike riding.

Mill Creek camping area

Signposted from Wisemans Ferry Rd. Near Mill Creek. Bring own water. Bookings preferred in peak season. Additional map ref.: NSWRD 146 A9.

Ten Mile Hollow camping area

Walk-in only access via Simpsons Track or historic Old Great North Rd. Be self-sufficient. Bring water and gas/fuel stove. Additional map ref.: NSWRD 146 B7.

Further information & bookings: NPWS, Gosford **Tel.:** (02) 4320 4200 **Email:** central.coast@npws.nsw.gov.au **Camping fees:** *Mill Creek:* $5.00 per adult/night, $3.00 per child (age 5–15) per night; fees payable at self-registration station during off-peak times

4. THE GREAT NORTH WALK

This is a 250-km-long walking track between Macquarie Place Obelisk in Sydney and Queens Wharf in Newcastle. It can be tackled in stages as day and weekend walks and there are numerous access points. It takes up to 14 days to walk the entire track and the full walk is best undertaken by experienced walkers. Facilities vary at the camping areas along the walk. Be self-sufficient and carry water, as water from some of the rivers and creeks may not be suitable for drinking. Gas/fuel stove preferred. Purchase a Great North Walk map/guide kit for details.

Benowie Walking Track
Thornleigh to Berowra, 25 km. Eight camping areas.

Hawkesbury Track
Berowra Waters to Somersby, 78 km. Seven camping areas.

Cedar Brush Walk
Somersby to Flat Rock Lookout, 61 km. Eight camping areas.

Watagan Track
Flat Rock Lookout to Teralba, 61 km. Three camping areas.

Further information & bookings: DLWC, Sydney **Tel.:** (02) 9228 6111

5. KU-RING-GAI CHASE NATIONAL PARK

This is the second oldest national park in New South Wales, and it protects some important Aboriginal sites. It lies 24 km north of Sydney city centre and is signposted from Mona Vale Rd. Vehicle access is confined to the main areas only.

The Basin camping area

Near Soldiers Point on the western shore of Pittwater. Walk in from West Head Rd or access by boat/ferry. Bring water and gas/fuel stove. Bookings essential and fees payable in advance. Additional map ref.: NSWRD 9 S4.

Further information & bookings: NPWS (The Basin booking line) **Tel.:** (02) 9974 1011 **Email:** bobbin.head@npws.nsw.gov.au **Park use fee:** $10.00 per vehicle/day. A landing fee of $2.20 per adult and $1.10 per child applies if arriving by ferry/boat (excludes annual passholders) **Camping fees:** *Peak (Sept.–April):* $9.00 per adult/night, $4.50 per child/night *Off-peak (May–Aug.):* $7.50 per adult/night, $4.00 per child/night

6. LANE COVE NATIONAL PARK

Lane Cove National Park is 10 km north of Sydney's city centre, beside Lane Cove River. Access is via Plassey Rd, off Delhi Rd in North Ryde. Activities here include bushwalking, cycling and boating.

Lane Cove River Caravan Park

Beside Lane Cove River. Signposted from Plassey Rd. Gas/fuel stove only. Camp kitchen and kiosk. Bookings advisable, especially at peak times. Additional map ref.: NSWRD 13 L2.

Further information & bookings: Lane Cove River Caravan Park **Tel.:** (02) 9888 9133 **Email:** lccp@npws.nsw.gov.au
Camping fees: Campsites from $21.00 to $24.00 per site/night

7. MARRAMARRA NATIONAL PARK

The park is 50 km north of Sydney, near Wisemans Ferry and at the junction of Berowra Creek and the Hawkesbury River. It contains many Aboriginal sites and protects a number of rare plant species. There is limited vehicle access via Canoelands Rd off Old Northern Rd and also Bloodwood Rd, but there is no vehicle access to camping areas – walk-in or canoe/boat access only. Bushwalking in the park is best suited to self-sufficient and experienced walkers. The park is closed to all walkers and campers on days of total fire ban. Large groups are asked to register with the information centre, and during the fire danger season all walkers are advised to register and deregister with the information centre for safety purposes.

Berowra Creek camping area

On Berowra Creek near Bar Island. Canoe or boat access only. Not signposted. Gas/fuel stove preferred. Restrictions apply at times – contact NPWS. Additional map ref.: NSWRD 154 C1.

Gentlemans Halt camping area

Beside Hawkesbury River opposite Spencer. Walk-in access from Canoelands Ridge Trail or Singleton Rd, or access by canoe/boat. Not signposted. Gas/fuel stove preferred. Additional map ref.: NSWRD 146 D10.

Marramarra Creek camping area

Beside Marramarra Creek. Walk-in access from Bloodwood Rd or by canoe. Not signposted. Gas/fuel stove preferred. Additional map ref.: NSWRD 154 B1.

Further information & bookings: NPWS, Bobbin Head Information Centre **Tel.:** (02) 9472 8949 **Email:** bobbin.head@npws.nsw.gov.au

8. PARR STATE RECREATION AREA

This area is north-west of Wisemans Ferry, adjoining Yengo National Park. There is limited vehicle access via St Albans Rd from Wisemans Ferry in the east and via Putty Rd from Colo in the west.

Heartbreak Hill camping area

On the Womerah Range Track. Walk-in access only. Closest vehicle access point is from Webbs Creek. Please advise NPWS Gosford of intended stay. Additional map ref.: NSWRD 145 U6.

Further information & bookings: NPWS, Gosford **Tel.:** (02) 4320 4200 **Email:** central.coast@npws.nsw.gov.au

9. WOLLEMI NATIONAL PARK – SOUTHERN SECTION

See also Wollemi National Park – western section, *page 41*

This is a large wilderness park 25 km north-west of Windsor. Vehicle access is limited to the edge of the park; access is via Putty Rd in the east, Blaxlands Ridge Rd and Bells Line of Rd in the south, and Wolgan Rd in the west. Visit the old shale-oil mining town of Newnes and explore the Colo River.

Colo Meroo camping area

Walk-in only access via Bob Turners Track or walk upstream from Upper Colo Rd. Canoe/li-lo access along Colo River. Bring drinking water. Gas/fuel stove preferred. Contact ranger for access details. Additional map ref.: NSWRD 145 P9.

Newnes camping area

This is 47 km north of Lithgow, reached via Wolgan Rd off Mudgee Rd. Explore old mining ruins and walk/cycle to glow worm tunnel. Bring drinking water and firewood or gas/fuel stove. General store open on weekends. Additional map ref.: NSWRD 144 F4.

Wheeney Creek camping area

Access via Comleroy Rd from Bells Line of Rd, 14 km north of Kurrajong. Bring water and firewood. Additional map ref.: NSWRD 145 Q10.

Further information & bookings:
Newnes: NPWS, Blackheath **Tel.:** (02) 4787 8877 **Email:** blue.mountains@ npws.nsw.gov.au
Wheeney Creek and Colo Meroo: NPWS, Richmond **Tel.:** (02) 4588 5247 **Email:** richmond@ npws.nsw.gov.au

10. YENGO NATIONAL PARK see page 8

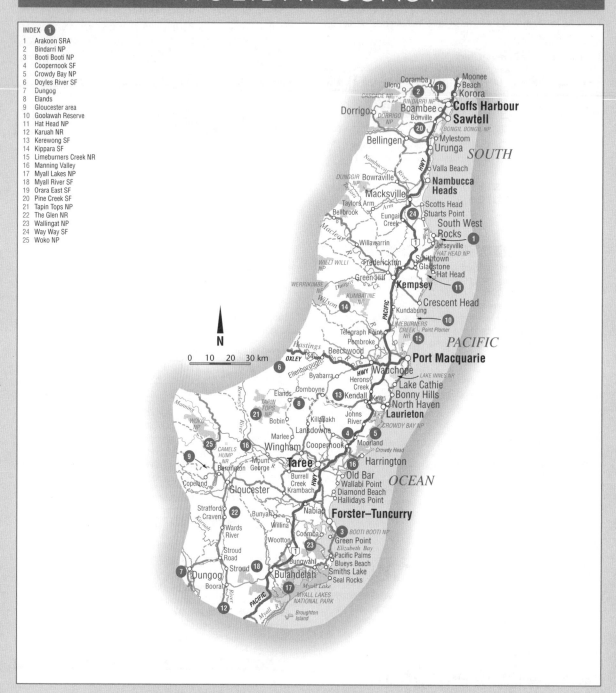

THE STRETCH OF COASTLINE FROM MYALL LAKES IN THE SOUTH THROUGH TO COFFS HARBOUR IN THE NORTH IS A VERY POPULAR HOLIDAY DESTINATION. THE LARGE NUMBER OF NATIONAL PARKS ON THE COAST OFFER EXCELLENT CAMPING OPPORTUNITIES, SPECTACULAR COASTAL VISTAS AND BEACH ACTIVITIES, WHILE FURTHER INLAND THE STATE FORESTS OF THIS REGION ARE GREAT FOR CAR TOURING AND BUSHWALKING THROUGH BEAUTIFUL FORESTS AND RAINFORESTS.

Myall Lakes National Park protects a large, brackish lake system surrounded by paperbarks. It is ideal for boating and canoeing, with some campsites accessible by boat only. Other activities on the lake include fishing, sailboarding and waterskiing. In the north of the park and on the beach, Yagon camping area is popular with swimmers and surfers. The park also has remote beaches that can be reached by four-wheel drive vehicles (permits are required for beach driving).

Further north in the Forster–Tuncurry region, Booti Booti and Wallingat national parks have excellent recreational opportunities. Booti Booti National Park is fronted by the South Pacific Ocean, and its main beach, Seven Mile Beach, is extremely popular with fisherfolk and surfers. To the west of the park is the large Wallis Lake, where sailboard-ing, boating and fishing are popular. Wallingat National Park is on the other side of Wallis Lake. Visitors here can enjoy fishing and boating along Wallingat River or enjoy one of the walks through the forests of mixed gum, oak and mahogany trees.

The rainforests and eucalypt forests surrounding Swans Crossing camping area in Kerewong State Forest, west of Kendall, are home to possums, wallabies and goannas. From the camping area are a couple of walks along Upsalls Creek, where some great swimming spots can be found.

The stunning Limeburners Creek Nature Reserve is home to a number of bird species, including the endangered ground parrot. Campers can enjoy birdwatching, go canoeing on the creek or visit some of the historic Aboriginal sites.

Just to the east of South West Rocks is Arakoon State Recreation Area. Campers here can enjoy the fabulous beaches, spectacular walking trails and magnificent coastal scenery, and visit the historic Trial Bay Gaol, which was used as an internment camp during World War I.

BEST CAMPSITES

Mungo Brush camping area
Myall Lakes National Park

Swans Crossing camping area
Kerewong State Forest

Diamond Head camping area
Crowdy Bay National Park

Arakoon State Recreation Area camping area
Arakoon State Recreation Area

Dingo Tops camping area
Tapin Tops National Park

BEST TIME TO VISIT

This is a popular region in summer, but is a great spot to visit all year round.

1. ARAKOON STATE RECREATION AREA

This excellent beachside destination is 3 km east of South West Rocks. Access from the town is via Phillip Drive. Visit historic Trial Bay Gaol, which was built in 1886. There are also many water-based activities on offer here.

Arakoon State Recreation Area camping area

Reached via Cardwell St in South West Rocks. On sheltered surf beach. Advance bookings essential for peak periods. Additional map ref.: NSWRD 98 B8.

Further information & bookings: NPWS, Arakoon State Recreation Area **Tel.:** (02) 6566 6168 **Email:** trialbay.gaol@npws.nsw.gov.au **Camping fees:** *Peak (Sept.–April):* $9.00 per adult/night, $4.50 per child/night *Off-peak (May–Aug.):* $7.50 per adult/night, $4.00 per child/night

2. BINDARRI NATIONAL PARK

Bindarri contains many spectacular waterfalls and rainforest. It is in a remote area 20 km west of Coffs Harbour on the Dorrigo Escarpment. It is reached via Upper Orara on Dairyville Rd from the east or from Ulong from the west. Roads within the park are accessible by 4WD in dry weather only.

Bush camping

Walk-in bush camping areas with no facilities throughout the park, suitable for experienced and well-equipped walkers. Contact NPWS for best sites. Gas/fuel stove only. Additional map ref.: NSWRD 93 U6 &U7.

Further information & bookings: NPWS, Coffs Harbour **Tel.:** (02) 6652 0900

3. BOOTI BOOTI NATIONAL PARK

At Booti Booti National Park, thick forests spread right to the ocean, fringed by a strip of sandy beach. It is 16 km south of Forster–Tuncurry and stretches from Cape Hawke in the north to Pacific Palms in the south. Wallis Lake, on the west side of the park, is a popular summer destination for surfing, swimming, sailing and powerboating.

The Ruins camping area

At southern end of Seven Mile Beach. Signposted from The Lakes Way. Gas/fuel stove only. Additional map ref.: NSWRD 129 L7.

Further information & bookings: NPWS, Booti Booti **Tel.:** (02) 6591 0300 **Park use fee:** $6.00 per vehicle/day **Camping fees:** $7.50 per adult/night, $4.00 per child (age 5–15) per night

4. COOPERNOOK STATE FOREST

This forest is 20 km north-east of Taree, near Coopernook. It adjoins Coorabach National Park and there are views from Newbys and Flat Rock lookouts. Activities include the scenic Coopernook Forest Drive, swimming at Waitui Falls and climbing Big Nellie.

Coopernook Forest Park

Located 5 km north of Coopernook. Signposted access via Coopernook Forest Way off the Pacific Hwy. Large open grassy area. Additional map ref.: NSWRD 119 N6.

Further information & bookings: State Forests, Wauchope **Tel.:** (02) 6585 3744 **Email:** cumberland@sf.nsw.gov.au

5. CROWDY BAY NATIONAL PARK

This is an idyllic coastal park 5 km south of Laurieton. Access is via Diamond Head Rd from Laurieton or Coral Ville Rd from Moorland on the Pacific Hwy. Diamond Head was named by Captain Cook, and Kylies Hut takes its name from the author Kylie Tennant, who often spent time there. Activities include swimming, surfing, exploring the many walking tracks and 4WD beach driving (permit required).

Diamond Head camping area

Beach frontage with good swimming and surfing 10 km south of Laurieton, on north side of headland. Access via Diamond Head Rd. Bring water and firewood. Additional map ref.: NSWRD 119 R5.

Indian Head camping area

Sheltered site 11 km south of Laurieton at base of headland. Access via Diamond Head Rd. Bring water and firewood. Additional map ref.: NSWRD 119 R5.

Kylies camping area

Sheltered site near beach 12 km south of Laurieton on south side of headland. Access via Diamond Head Rd. 4WD beach access. Bring water and firewood. Additional map ref.: NSWRD 119 R5.

Kylies walk-in camping area

Small sheltered walk-in site near Kylies Hut. Access from Indian Head camping area (200 m). Bring water and firewood. Additional map ref.: NSWRD 119 R5.

Further information & bookings: NPWS, Port Macquarie **Tel.:** (02) 6586 8300 **Park use fee:** $6.00 per vehicle/day **Camping fees:** $5.00 per adult/night, $3.00 per child (age 5–15) per night; ranger collects fees

6. DOYLES RIVER STATE FOREST

This forest, 70 km west of Wauchope, has large stands of towering mountain trees. It is reached via Oxley Hwy from Wauchope; check road conditions after rain. Activities include a scenic drive along Knodingbul Rd, exploring the old goldmining area of The Cells (4WD access only) and taking in the view from Blue Knob.

Maxwells Flat camping area

Grassy area beside small creek reached via Causeway Rd off Knodingbul Rd. Water from creek. Additional map ref.: NSWRD 108 D8.

Diamond Head with North Brother Mountain in the background, Crowdy Bay National Park

The Cells camping area

4WD access, dry weather only, via Eaglehawk and Cells trails. Bush camping – no facilities. Beside Cells River at site of old gold workings. Water from creek. Additional map ref.: NSWRD 108 C9.

Further information & bookings: State Forests, Wauchope **Tel.:** (02) 6585 3744 **Email:** cumberland@sf.nsw.gov.au

7. DUNGOG

The small town of Dungog is on the way to the Barrington Tops National Park. It is 60 km north of Raymond Terrace and is reached via Clarence Town Rd from the Pacific Hwy.

Dungog Showground camping area

Access via Myles St in Dungog. Gas/fuel stove preferred. Camping not available during shows, rodeos etc. Maximum stay 28 days. Additional map ref.: NSWRD 264 D4.

Further information & bookings: Caretaker **Tel.:** (02) 4992 1033 **Camping fees:** Unpowered sites $6.00 per night, powered sites $8.00 per night

8. ELANDS

Elands is a small village 35 km north of Wingham, reached by Elands Rd from Wingham or by forest roads from the Oxley Hwy. In the area is Ellenborough Falls – the highest single-drop falls in the Southern Hemisphere.

Little Plains Sportsground

In Elands township. Pay by donation; overnight stays only. Firewood supplied. Additional map ref.: NSWRD 118 F3.

Further information & bookings: Elands General Store **Tel.:** (02) 6550 4538.

9. GLOUCESTER AREA

Gloucester lies in the foothills of the Great Dividing Range and is the gateway to Barrington Tops. It is a popular camping, canoeing, bushwalking and 4WD area with many natural attractions.

Barrington Reserve camping area

Situated in sportsground 8 km west of Gloucester, beside Barrington River. Access via Gloucester–Scone Rd. Bring drinking water and firewood. Additional map ref.: NSWRD 117 U10.

Bretti Reserve camping area

This is 34 km north of Gloucester, near a river. Access via Gloucester–Nowendoc Rd. Bring drinking water and firewood. Additional map ref.: NSWRD 117 U6.

Copeland Common camping area

A large open area near creek, 12 km west of Gloucester, accessed via Gloucester–Scone Rd. Bring drinking water and firewood. Additional map ref.: NSWRD 117 U10.

Gloryvale Reserve camping area

Near river, 27 km north of Gloucester, reached by Gloucester–Nowendoc Rd. 2WD access in dry weather only. Bring drinking water and firewood. Additional map ref.: NSWRD 117 T8.

Further information & bookings: Gloucester Visitor Information Centre **Tel.:** (02) 6558 1408 **Email:** glosinfo@tpg.com.au **Website:** www.gloucester.org.au

10. GOOLAWAH RESERVE

This reserve is 10 km south of Crescent Head and is signposted from the town via Point Plomer Rd. Explore the swathe of unspoiled beaches and rocky headlands here. Activities include swimming, fishing and surfing. Site allocation is on a first-come basis and it is advisable to phone ahead at peak times.

Delicate Nobby camping area

Signposted from Point Plomer Rd. Road can be rough at times – not recommended for caravans. Firewood supplied. Additional map ref.: NSWRD 109 V6.

Racecourse Headland camping area

Signposted from Point Plomer Rd. Road can be rough at times – not recommended for caravans. Firewood supplied. Additional map ref.: NSWRD 109 V6.

Further information & bookings: Manager **Tel.:** (02) 6566 0515 **Camping fees:** From $14.00 per site/night for 2 people; each extra person $3.00 per night

11. HAT HEAD NATIONAL PARK

A coastal park 20 km east of Kempsey, near Hat Head village. It is reached via South West Rocks Rd from South West Rocks in the north, by Hat Head Rd to get to the centre of the park, and from Crescent Head in the south. Activities include swimming, fishing, surfing, bushwalking and 4WD beach driving (permit required).

Hungry Rest Area

This is 3 km south of Hat Head village. Access via Hungry Rd. Bring drinking water and firewood. Additional map ref.: NSWRD 98 L2 (inset map).

Smoky Rest Area

Set in rainforest near Smoky Cape Lighthouse, 9 km south-east of South West Rocks. Access via Lighthouse Rd from Arakoon Rd. Bring drinking water and firewood. Additional map ref.: NSWRD 98 B9.

Further information & bookings: NPWS, Arakoon State Recreation Area **Tel.:** (02) 6566 6621 **Email:** trialbay.gaol@npws.nsw.gov.au **Park use fee:** $6.00 per vehicle/day

Camping fees: $3.00 per adult/night, $2.00 per child/night; fees payable at self-registration stations

12. KARUAH NATURE RESERVE

The reserve is on the lower reach of the Karuah River, 20 km north of Karuah near Limeburners Creek. Access is via Hobart Rd from Bucketts Way at Limeburners Creek. Activities here include swimming, fishing and canoeing.

Little Mountain camping area

4WD access only via Little Mountain Rd from Hobart Rd. Also boat access; area is beside tidal reach of Karuah River. Bush camping – no facilities. Bring water and firewood. Use of portable toilets preferred. Additional map ref.: NSWRD 137 U3.

Further information & bookings: NPWS, Nelson Bay **Tel.:** (02) 4984 8200 **Email:** hunter@npws.nsw.gov.au

13. KEREWONG STATE FOREST

The forest is part of the Broken Bago Range, about 50 km south-west of Port Macquarie and 15 km west of Kendall. Activities include bushwalking, swimming and cycling.

Swans Crossing camping area

Located 17 km west of Kendall. Signposted from Upsalls Creek Rd off Lorne–Kendall Rd. Bring drinking water. Additional map ref.: NSWRD 119 M3.

Further information & bookings: State Forests, Wauchope **Tel.:** (02) 6585 3744 **Email:** cumberland@sf.nsw.gov.au

14. KIPPARA STATE FOREST

This is 40 km north-west of Wauchope. Activities include bushwalking, swimming, mountain-bike riding, horseriding and car and 4WD touring.

Slippery Rocks camping area

Near creek, 43 km north-west of Wauchope. Signposted via Bobs Ridge Rd from Glen Esk Rd at Rollands Plains. Bring drinking water. Additional map ref.: NSWRD 109 M5.

Further information & bookings: State Forests, Wauchope **Tel.:** (02) 6585 3744 **Email:** cumberland@sf.nsw.gov.au

15. LIMEBURNERS CREEK NATURE RESERVE

The reserve is between Port Macquarie and Crescent Head; the main access is via Crescent Head Rd from Kempsey and Point Plomer Rd from Crescent Head. Activities include surfing, swimming, bushwalking, fishing and canoeing.

Barries Bay camping area

On north side of Point Plomer, near beach, 19 km south of Crescent Head via Point Plomer Rd. Bookings advisable during peak times. Bring firewood. Additional map ref.: NSWRD 109 V7.

Melaleuca camping area

This is 16 km south of Crescent Head via Point Plomer Rd. Bring drinking water and firewood. Additional map ref.: NSWRD 109 V6.

Further information & bookings: NPWS, Arakoon State Recreation Area **Tel.:** (02) 6566 6621 **Email:** trialbay.gaol@ npws.nsw.gov.au **Park use fee:** $6.00 per vehicle/day **Camping fees:** $5.00 per adult/night, $3.00 per child/night

16. MANNING VALLEY

The Manning Valley follows the Manning River to the sea. Taree sits in the valley about 20 km inland, and there are many national parks and unspoiled beaches here.

Farquhar Park Reserve camping area

Secluded estuary location 8 km south of Manning Point, near mouth of Manning River. 4WD access only (at low tide via Smiths Beach from Manning Point) or boat access. Bring drinking water and firewood. Additional map ref.: NSWRD 119 N9.

Rocks Crossing Reserve camping area

This is 21 km north-west of Mount George village, beside Nowendoc River. Signposted from Nowendoc Rd. Bring firewood. Popular over the summer holiday period – sites are on a first-come basis. Additional map ref.: NSWRD 118 B6.

Further information & bookings: Manning Valley Visitor Information Centre **Tel.:** (02) 6552 1900 **Email:** manningvic@ gtcc.nsw.gov.au **Website:** www.retreat-to-nature.com **Camping fees:** *Farquhar Park Reserve*: $6.00 for 2 people/night; each extra person $2.00 per night

17. MYALL LAKES NATIONAL PARK see page 17

18. MYALL RIVER STATE FOREST

This forest is 10 km west of Bulahdelah and is reached via Cabbage Tree Rd from Markwell Rd or Crawford Rd off Booral Rd. Activities include bushwalking and 4WD touring.

Strike-a-light camping area

The area is 22 km north-west of Bulahdelah, beside a creek. Access via Johnsons Creek Rd. Bring drinking water. Additional map ref.: NSWRD 128 B6.

Further information & bookings: State Forests, Hunter Region **Tel.:** (02) 4927 0977 **Email:** cumberland@sf.nsw. gov.au

MYALL LAKES NATIONAL PARK

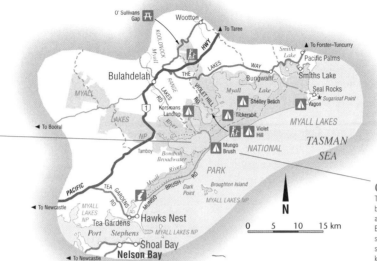

By canoe
Hire a canoe and spend some time cruising the calm lakes, with their large waterbird populations and magnificent foreshore vegetation of paperbarks and gums. Here you'll find one of the tallest trees in the state – a 76-metre flooded gum.

Coastal tramping
This park offers great opportunities for beach and dune tramping, with the best access from Seal Rocks and the Mungo Brush camping area. There are other short walks through the park's forests, scrub and swamps, while the five-kilometre Yacaaba Headland Walk, beginning at Hawks Nest, offers stunning views across the entire coast.

This large coastal park is between Hawks Nest and Seal Rocks. The main routes to it are via Mungo Brush Rd from Hawks Nest in the south and Lakes Rd from Bulahdelah; access to Violet Hill and Seal Rocks is from The Lakes Way. Myall Lake is the largest fresh–brackish lake system on the New South Wales coast and the park has many opportunities for boating, fishing, canoeing, swimming, surfing and bushwalking. 4WD beach driving is allowed but a permit is required. Collection of firewood in the park is prohibited.

Korsmans Landing camping area

Located 4 km north of Bombah Point on Two Mile Lake. Access from Lakes Rd near Bombah Point. Bush camping – be self-sufficient. Bring drinking water and firewood. Gas/fuel stove preferred. Additional map ref.: NSWRD 128 F10.

Mungo Brush camping area

This is 22 km north of Hawks Nest. Access via Mungo Brush Rd. Bring drinking water. Gas/fuel stove only. Additional map ref.: NSWRD 138 G1.

Shelley Beach camping area

Situated 10 km north-east of Bombah Point on Myall Lake. Walk-in access from Bombah Point on The Old Gibber Track or boat access. Bush camping – be self-sufficient. Bring drinking water and firewood. Gas/fuel stove preferred. Additional map ref.: NSWRD 128 H10.

Tickerabit camping area

On Myall Lake, 7 km north-east of Bombah Point. Walk-in access from Bombah Point on The Old Gibber Track or boat access. Bush camping – be self-sufficient. Bring drinking water and firewood. Gas/fuel stove preferred. Additional map ref.: NSWRD 128 H10.

Violet Hill camping area

Located 18 km east of Bulahdelah on Myall Lake. Access via Violet Hill Rd from The Lakes Way near Boolambayte. Bring firewood. Gas/fuel stove preferred. Additional map ref.: NSWRD 128 G10.

Yagon camping area

This popular surfing and fishing spot is 3 km south-west of Seal Rocks. Bring drinking water and firewood. Gas/fuel stove preferred. Additional map ref.: NSWRD 128 K10.

Bush camping
Bush camping is permitted within Myall Lakes National Park; contact NPWS for further details.

Further information & bookings: NPWS, Great Lakes **Tel.:** (02) 6591 0300 **Park use fee:** $6.00 per vehicle/day (annual Park Pass also available) **Camping fees:** $5.00 per adult/night, $3.00 per child (age 5–15) per night

19. ORARA EAST STATE FOREST

The forest is a convenient 9 km west of Coffs Harbour. Main access is via Bruxner Park Rd from the Pacific Hwy. Activities include walking and mountain bike riding.

Bush camping

Numerous bush camping areas located throughout the forest. Obtain large-scale maps and contact ranger for details. Additional map ref.: NSWRD 94 B5.

Further information & bookings: State Forests, Coffs Harbour **Tel.:** (02) 6652 0111 **Email:** cumberland@sf.nsw.gov.au

20. PINE CREEK STATE FOREST

This lies 10 km north of Urunga and a number of roads run to it from the Pacific Hwy. Activities include horseriding and mountain-bike riding.

Bush camping

Many bush camping areas located throughout the forest. Obtain large-scale maps and contact ranger for details. Additional map ref.: NSWRD 94 A9.

Further information & bookings: State Forests, Coffs Harbour **Tel.:** (02) 6652 0111 **Email:** cumberland@sf.nsw.gov.au

21. TAPIN TOPS NATIONAL PARK

This park, 30 km north-west of Wingham, preserves areas of old-growth forest as well as habitats of the parma wallaby and tiger quoll. Access is via Knodingbul Rd from Mount George in the south or via the Oxley Hwy in the north. Features include walking trails and scenic views from Rowleys Rock and Browns Lookout.

Dingo Tops camping area

On Knodingbul Rd, at the site of the former state forest picnic area. Bring water and firewood. Additional map ref.: NSWRD 118 C4.

Further information & bookings: NPWS, Manning Area **Tel.:** (02) 6552 4097

22. THE GLEN NATURE RESERVE

This reserve has impressive stands of blue gum and habitat for endangered animals. It is 25 km south-east of Gloucester near Craven, being reached via Glen Rd from Bucketts Way just south of Craven. Activities include forest drives and bushwalking (the Tops-to-Myalls Heritage Trail passes through the reserve).

Wards Glen camping area

2WD dry-weather-only access via Glen Rd. Bush camping in cleared area 1.5 km in from park boundary – no facilities (facilities are in planning). Bring drinking water and firewood. Additional map ref.: NSWRD 128 A4.

Further information & bookings: NPWS, Gloucester **Tel.:** (02) 6558 1478

23. WALLINGAT NATIONAL PARK

This park, south of Forster–Tuncurry on the west side of Wallis Lake, includes the stunning vistas from Whoota Lookout – about 100 km of coastline. It is reached off The Lakes Way, from Sugar Creek Rd at Bungwahl (the park is 9.7 km from The Lakes Way). Activities here include watersports on the Wallingat River.

Wallingat River Park camping area

On River Rd from Sugar Creek Rd. Beside Wallingat River. Bring drinking water and firewood. Additional map ref.: NSWRD 128 J7.

Further information & bookings: NPWS, Great Lakes **Tel.:** (02) 6591 0300 **Camping fees:** $3.00 per adult/night, $2.00 per child (age 5–15) per night

24. WAY WAY STATE FOREST

This mixed forest – rainforest and blackbutt – is 10 km south of Macksville, near Grassy Head. It is reached via Rosewood Rd off the Pacific Hwy at Warrell Creek, or Grassy Head Rd from Grassy Head. Marvel at the views from Mt Yarrahapinni Lookout. Activities include bushwalking, horseriding and vehicle touring.

Bush camping

Numerous bush camping areas throughout the forest. Obtain large-scale maps and contact ranger for details. Bring water. Additional map ref.: NSWRD 97 U6 (Rosewood Rd).

Further information & bookings: State Forests, Coffs Harbour **Tel.:** (02) 6652 0111 **Email:** cumberland@sf.nsw.gov.au

25. WOKO NATIONAL PARK

This park features rainforest and eucalypts, rocky crags and the Manning River. It is 30 km north-west of Gloucester and is reached via Curricabark Rd off Thunderbolts Way (Gloucester–Nowendoc Rd) near Rookhurst – check road conditions after rain. It is a good bushwalking and bird-watching area.

Woko camping area

Access via Flood Detour from Curricabark Rd. Near Manning River. Water from river – boil before use. Bring firewood. Gas/fuel stove preferred. Additional map ref.: NSWRD 117 R7.

Further information & bookings: NPWS, Gloucester **Tel.:** (02) 6558 1478 **Camping fees:** $5.00 per adult/night, $3.00 per child (age 5–15) per night; fees payable at self-registration station

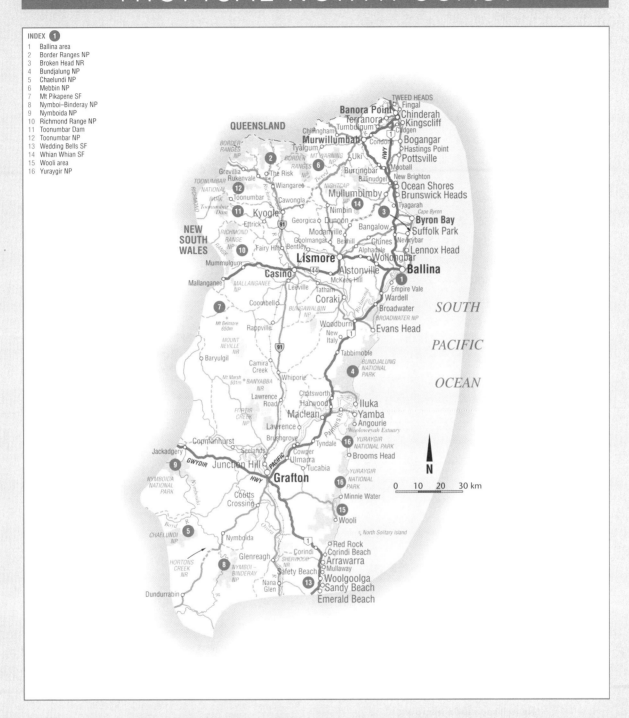

THE FAR NORTH-EAST OF THE STATE BOASTS SPECTACULAR BEACHES, MAGNIFICENT FORESTS AND AREAS OF ABORIGINAL CULTURAL SIGNIFICANCE.

Yuraygir National Park, on the coast, offers camping in its three sections, and campers have a large choice of sites and facilities. While staying in the park, visitors can view beautiful wildflowers during spring and early summer, do some birdwatching and bushwalking, or go swimming, fishing or canoeing on Lake Arragan and Station Creek.

Bundjalung National Park, north of Iluka, is also on this coast. It has bushwalking, canoeing, swimming and fishing. Numerous Aboriginal cultural sites, such as middens and camps, are found throughout the park. Campers have the option of the well-appointed Woody Head camping area, bush camping at Black Rocks camping area behind Ten Mile Beach, or the walk-in bush campsites along Jerusalem Creek Walking Track.

North of Mallanganee is Richmond Range National Park. The grassed Peacock Creek Rest Area is a great place to base yourself while exploring this park and the adjoining Toonumbar National Park. Visitors can enjoy scenic drives through the rainforests, take in spectacular views from Cambridge Plateau, and visit 'Old Spotty', a spotted gum tree up to 300 years old. The park's roads are ideal for mountain-bike riding and the nearby Toonumbar Dam also has camping, excellent fishing, swimming and canoeing opportunities.

On the Queensland border is the beautiful Border Ranges National Park. Within it are stands of ancient trees, untouched forests, spectacular mountain views, abundant wildlife, pure freshwater creeks and waterfalls. The 60-kilometre Tweed Range Scenic Drive takes in some of the park's best features. Campers have a choice of vehicle-based camping amongst eucalypts at Sheepstation Creek – a network of walking trails leave from here – or at the smaller Forest Tops camping area.

BEST CAMPSITES

Peacock Creek Rest Area
Richmond Range National Park

Sheepstation Creek camping area
Border Ranges National Park

Woody Head camping area
Bundjalung National Park

Iron Pot Creek camping area
Toonumbar National Park

Mount Pikapene Campground
Mount Pikapene State Forest

BEST TIME TO VISIT

All year round, but the cooler months of spring and autumn are the ideal time. The roads in some of the higher areas such as Richmond Range National Park can be closed during and after periods of wet weather.

1. BALLINA AREA

Ballina is a fishing town at the mouth of the Richmond River, and a popular holiday destination. Main access is via the Pacific Hwy. Once here, enjoy the region's beaches and rivers; there are many water-based activities to try.

Flat Rock camping ground

Near surf beach, 4 km north-east of Ballina at East Ballina. Access via Coast Rd (Lennox Head Rd). Firewood supplied. Advance bookings essential for peak periods. Additional map ref.: NSWRD 83 N7.

Further information & bookings: Manager
Tel.: (02) 6686 4848 **Camping fees:** From $13.20 per site/night (unpowered) for 2 people

2. BORDER RANGES NATIONAL PARK

A large World Heritage-listed rainforest park 25 km north of Kyogle, adjoining the Queensland border and part of the Scenic Rim. It is reached via Murwillumbah Rd at Lillian Rock from the east or the Summerland Way at Wiangaree from the south. You will find magic rainforests and stunning birdlife including Albert's lyrebird, and you should explore the Tweed Range Scenic Drive. There are also some good bushwalking trails.

Forest Tops camping area

Walk-in site (10–50 m) set in small forest clearing 30 km north of Kyogle. Access via Tweed Range Scenic Drive. Take gas/fuel stove – firewood supplied but is often damp. Additional map ref.: NSWRD 48 F8.

Sheepstation Creek camping area

This is 31 km north of Kyogle. Access via Tweed Range Scenic Drive. Caravan access from Wiangaree. Near creek. Firewood supplied. Additional map ref.: NSWRD 48 F8.

Further information & bookings: NPWS, Kyogle
Tel.: (02) 6632 0000 **Camping fees:** $3.00 per adult/night, $2.00 per child (age 5–15) per night; fees payable at self-registration stations

3. BROKEN HEAD NATURE RESERVE

The reserve is 7 km south of Byron Bay and is reached via Byron Bay–Lennox Head Rd. Here steep rainforest-clad slopes meet magnificent sweeping beaches. You can watch for whales in winter and other activities include surfing, swimming and bushwalking.

Broken Head Caravan Park

On Beach Rd, off Broken Head Rd. Beach frontage. Advance bookings essential for peak periods. Additional map ref.: NSWRD 83 N5.

Further information & bookings: Manager
Tel.: (02) 6685 3245 **Camping fees:** From $18.00 per site/night (unpowered) for 1–2 people

4. BUNDJALUNG NATIONAL PARK

This coastal park between Iluka and Evans Head has 38 km of sweeping beaches. Access is via Iluka Rd in the south and Gap Rd in the north (from the Pacific Hwy near Woodburn). You can explore the Esk River by canoe or enjoy surfing, swimming, beach fishing and 4WD beach driving.

Black Rocks camping area

Beach frontage. 4WD beach-access point 25 km south-east of Woodburn (contact ranger for details). Conventional vehicle access via Gap Rd, 3km south of Woodburn. Bring water. Fires in fireplaces only – bring firewood. Gas/fuel stove preferred. Additional map ref.: NSWRD 86 H5.

Jerusalem Creek camping area

Small walk-in site beside creek 3 km north of Black Rocks camping area, reached via Gap Rd 3 km south of Woodburn. Bring water. Gas/fuel stove only. Additional map ref.: NSWRD 86 H5.

Further information & bookings: NPWS, Alstonville **Tel.:** (02) 6627 0200 **Email:** northernrivers.region@npws. nsw.gov.au **Park use fee:** $6.00 per vehicle/day **Camping fees:** $3.00 per adult/night, $2.00 per child (age 5–15) per night; fees payable at self-registration stations

Woody Head camping area

Located 6 km north of Iluka; access via Iluka Rd. Beach frontage. Kiosk. Fires in fireplaces only, firewood supplied. Advance bookings essential for peak periods. Additional map ref.: NSWRD 86 H8.

Further information & bookings: Manager **Tel.:** (02) 6646 6134 **Camping fees:** From $11.00 per site/night (all sites unpowered) for 2 people

5. CHAELUNDI NATIONAL PARK

The park contains old-growth forest. It is 10 km west of Nymboida village and there is 4WD access only via Boundary Creek Rd from Armidale–Grafton Rd. Activities include bushwalking, birdwatching and 4WD touring.

Chandlers Creek camping area

Bush camping – no facilities – 29 km west of Nymboida. 4WD access off Stockyard Fire Trail off Link Rd, off Boundary Creek Rd. Water from creek. Bring firewood. Additional map ref.: NSWRD 89 L10.

Further information & bookings: NPWS, Dorrigo **Tel.:** (02) 6657 2309 **Email:** dorrigo@npws.nsw.gov.au

6. MEBBIN NATIONAL PARK

This park is 32 km south-west of Murwillumbah, near Tyalgum, and is reached via Byrrill Creek Rd. The park includes large tracts of rainforest and is on the rim of the Mt Warning volcano.

Mebbin Recreation Area

This is 7 km south of Tyalgum; access via Byrrill Creek Rd. Caravan access in dry weather only. Water from creek – boil before use. Bring firewood. Additional map ref.: NSWRD 80 D9.

Further information & bookings: NPWS, Murwillumbah **Tel.:** (02) 6672 6360 **Email:** tweed.area@npws.nsw.gov.au

7. MOUNT PIKAPENE STATE FOREST

This forest is 20 km south of Mallanganee and is reached via Deep Creek Rd from Mallanganee, then Old Lawrence Rd and Busbys Flat Rd. Caravan access via Old Lawrence–Tenterfield Rd from the Summerland Way just north of Whiporie. Activities here include car and 4WD touring.

Mount Pikapene Campground

Large grassed area on site of former forest workers camp, near a pine plantation, 22 km south of Mallanganee. Access via Busbys Flat Rd. Water from creek – boil before use. Additional map ref.: NSWRD 85 Q1.

Further information & bookings: State Forests, Casino **Tel.:** (02) 6662 4499 **Email:** cumberland@sf.nsw.gov.au

8. NYMBOI–BINDERAY NATIONAL PARK

The park includes the popular whitewater rafting and canoeing sections of the Nymboida River, as well as its spectacular gorges. It is 35 km north-west of Dorrigo, near Bostobrick, and is reached via Moonpar Rd from Bostobrick in the south, or Nymboida–Kangaroo River Rd from Nymboida in the north (turn-off south of township).

Platypus Flat camping area

Grassy area beside Nymboida River and a start point for rafters and canoeists, 45 km north-west of Dorrigo. Access via Moonpar Rd from Bostobrick. Water from river – boil before use. Firewood supplied. Additional map ref.: NSWRD 93 P4.

The Junction camping area

On The Junction Rd, 28 km south of Nymboida township at the junction of the Nymboida and Little Nymboida rivers. 4WD-only access via Black Mountain Rd off Nymboida–Kangaroo River Rd. Also canoe access. Water from creek – boil before use. Bring firewood. Additional map ref.: NSWRD 93 R2.

Further information & bookings:
NPWS, Dorrigo **Tel.:** (02) 6657 2309 *or*
NPWS, Grafton **Tel.:** (02) 6641 1500 **Email:** dorrigo@npws.nsw.gov.au

9. NYMBOIDA NATIONAL PARK

The Nymboida and Mann rivers meet in this national park, a challenging whitewater-canoeing area 55 km west of Grafton. There is 4WD-only access via Doboy Rd then Ramornie Rd from Glens Crossing, and also walk-in access from Jackadgery or canoe access. Activities include bushwalking (be self-sufficient).

Ramornie Forest Camp

On T Ridge Rd 57 km west of South Grafton. 4WD access via Doboy Rd then Ramornie Rd from the Old Grafton–Glen Innes Rd at Glens Crossing. Near Nymboida River. Water from river – boil before use. Gas/fuel stove preferred. Additional map ref.: NSWRD 89 M5.

Further information & bookings: NPWS, Grafton **Tel.:** (02) 6641 1500

10. RICHMOND RANGE NATIONAL PARK

This park includes World Heritage-listed rainforest. It is 40 km west of Kyogle near Mallanganee and access is via Cambridge Plateau Forest Drive from Mallanganee or Ettrick Rd then Iron Pot Rd from Kyogle; access from Casino is via Sextonville Rd. 2WD vehicles can reach the park in dry weather only – the clay-based roads are slippery after rain. Activities include self-sufficient bushwalking and birdwatching.

Peacock Creek Rest Area

On Peacock Creek Rd 36 km north of Mallanganee. Access via Cambridge Plateau Forest Drive from Mallanganee or Peacock Creek Rd from Bonalbo. Grassy area on site of old forest workers camp. Limited tank water. Firewood supplied. Additional map ref.: NSWRD 48 D9.

Further information & bookings: NPWS, Kyogle **Tel.:** (02) 6632 0000 **Camping fees:** $3.00 per adult/night, $2.00 per child/night; fees payable at self-registration station

11. TOONUMBAR DAM

This dam is 31 km north-west of Kyogle, via Afterlee Rd. It is a popular fishing area and other activities include boating (8 knot limit), canoeing and swimming.

Bells Bay camping area

On the shore of Toonumbar Dam. Good fishing. Firewood supplied. Additional map ref.: NSWRD 48 D8.

Further information & bookings: DLWC, Toonumbar Dam **Tel.:** (02) 6633 9135 **Camping fees:** From $5.00 per site per night; fees payable at self-registration station

12. TOONUMBAR NATIONAL PARK

The extensive rainforests in this park, 35 km north-west of Kyogle, are World Heritage-listed. Access is via Toonumbar Forest Drive at Afterlee; 2WD vehicles can reach the park in dry weather only as roads may be closed after rain. There is a lookout over the Murray Scrub rainforest and you can go bushwalking and vehicle touring.

Iron Pot Creek camping area

On Murray Scrub Rd 35 km north-west of Kyogle. Water from creek – boil before use. Bring firewood. Additional map ref.: NSWRD 48 D8.

Further information & bookings: NPWS, Kyogle **Tel.:** (02) 6632 0000 **Camping fees:** $3.00 per adult/night, $2.00 per child/night; fees payable at self-registration station

13. WEDDING BELLS STATE FOREST

This is 6 km west of Woolgoolga, reached via Pullen St then Woolgoolga Creek Rd at roundabout on the Pacific Hwy, Woolgoolga. Here you can explore Woolgoolga Creek Reserve; there are walking tracks and opportunities for vehicle touring.

Bush camping

Numerous bush camping areas throughout the forest. Obtain large-scale maps and contact ranger for details. Bring water. Additional map ref.: NSWRD 94 C3.

Further information & bookings: State Forests, Coffs Harbour **Tel.:** (02) 6652 0111 **Email:** cumberland@sf.nsw. gov.au

14. WHIAN WHIAN STATE FOREST

The forest adjoins Nightcap National Park. It is 30 km north of Lismore and access is via Minyon Drive north-east of Dunoon. There are numerous walking tracks and you can explore the Whian Whian Forest Drive by car or bike.

Old Cottage Park camping area

At intersection of Minyon Drive and Telephone Rd 32 km north of Lismore. Small grassy area. Water from creek – boil before use. Additional map ref.: NSWRD 82 H3.

Rummery Park camping area

On Peates Mountain Rd 30 km north of Lismore. Site of former forest workers camp. Limited water from tank. Bring firewood. Additional map ref.: NSWRD 82 H2.

Rummery Park Hut

On Peates Mountain Rd. Former forest workers hut, sleeps up to six people. Water from tank. Bring firewood. Dogs allowed on lead outside hut. Advance bookings essential. Additional map ref.: NSWRD 82 H2.

Further information & bookings: State Forests, Casino **Tel.:** (02) 6662 4499 **Email:** cumberland@sf.nsw.gov.au **Hut fees:** $20.00 per night

15. WOOLI AREA

This coastal area is 45 km south-east of Grafton. It is reached from the Pacific Hwy south of Grafton or from Ulmarra via Wooli Rd. It is a popular area for watersports enthusiasts and beach-goers over summer. The camping area is open only during New South Wales and Queensland school holidays.

Diggers Camp camping area

Beachfront area 12 km north of Wooli on Diggers Camp Rd. Bring water and firewood. Additional map ref.: NSWRD 90 F7.

Further information & bookings: Pristine Waters Council, South Grafton **Tel.:** (02) 6641 7200 **Email:** council@ pristinewaters.nsw.gov.au **Website:** www.pristinewaters. nsw.gov.au **Camping fees:** $10.00 per site per night

16. YURAYGIR NATIONAL PARK

This coastal park is divided into three separate sections. Access to the northern section is via Angourie Rd from Yamba or Brooms Head Rd from Maclean. The central section is reached from Ulmarra or via Wooli Rd from the Pacific Hwy south of Grafton. Access to the southern section is via Barcoongere Way from the Pacific Hwy 46 km north of Coffs Harbour. The park contains large areas of undeveloped coast and you can explore pristine beaches, surf at Angourie Beach and enjoy beach fishing, walking, swimming and canoeing.

NORTHERN SECTION

Lake Arragan Rest Area

Near beach, 5 km north of Brooms Head. Access from Brooms Head Rd. Limited water. Bring firewood. Additional map ref.: NSWRD 90 G2.

Plumbago Head camping area

Walk-in-only site 3 km north of Lake Arragan Rest Area. Access via Shelley Beach Walking Track. Bring water. Gas/fuel stove preferred. Additional map ref.: NSWRD 90 G2.

Red Cliff Rest Area

This is near the beach, 5 km north of Brooms Head. Access from Brooms Head Rd. Bring water and firewood. Additional map ref.: NSWRD 90 G2.

Shelley Head camping area

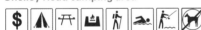

Walk-in-only site 8 km north of Lake Arragan Rest Area. Access via Shelley Beach Walking Track. Bring water. Gas/fuel stove preferred. Additional map ref.: NSWRD 90 H1.

CENTRAL SECTION

Boorkoom Picnic and Camping Area

Near beach 12 km north of Wooli, close to Diggers Camp. Access via Diggers Camp Rd from Wooli Rd. Bring water and firewood. Additional map ref.: NSWRD 90 F7.

Illaroo Rest Area

Near beach 14 km north of Wooli, near Minnie Water. Access via Minnie Water Rd from Wooli Rd, or 4WD beach access (contact ranger for details). Popular in peak periods. Limited drinking water. Firewood supplied. Additional map ref.: NSWRD 90 F6.

Sandon River Rest Area

Near beach and estuary, 10 km south of Brooms Head on Sandon River Rd. Popular in peak periods. Limited drinking water. Bring firewood. Additional map ref.: NSWRD 90 G4.

SOUTHERN SECTION

Freshwater Beach camping area

Bush camping – no facilities – 3 km north of Station Creek Rest Area. Walk-in-only access. Bring water. Gas/fuel stove preferred. Additional map ref.: NSWRD 90 F9.

Pebbly Beach camping area

This is 1 km north of Station Creek Rest Area. 4WD or walk-in access only. Bring water. Firewood supplied. Additional map ref.: NSWRD 90 F9.

Station Creek Rest Area

Area is 30 km north of Woolgoolga. 2WD dry-weather-only access via Barcoongere Way from Pacific Hwy, then Station Creek Rd. Popular in peak periods. Near beach and creek. Bring water. Firewood supplied. Additional map ref.: NSWRD 90 F10.

Further information: NPWS, Grafton **Tel.:** (02) 6641 1500 **Park use fee:** $6.00 per vehicle/day **Camping fees:** $5.00 per adult/night, $3.00 per child (age 5–15) per night; fees payable at self-registration stations or ranger will collect. Site allocation is on a first-come basis

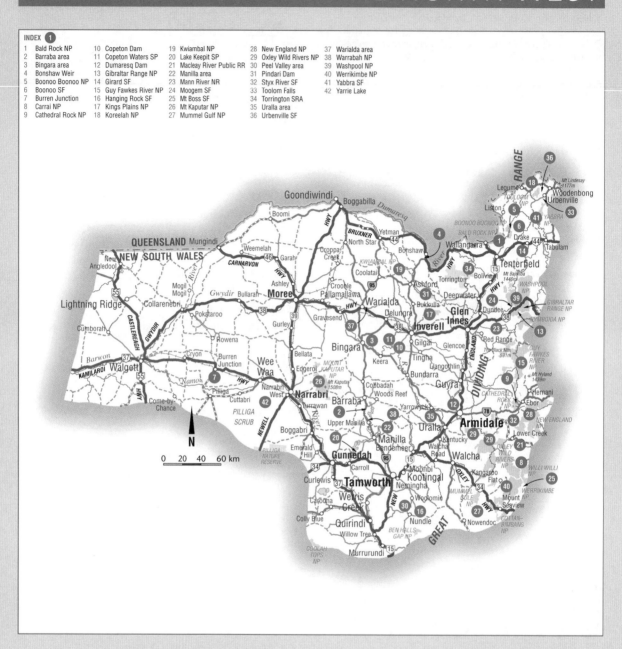

NEW ENGLAND AND THE NORTH-WEST LIE TO THE WEST OF THE GREAT DIVIDING RANGE. THIS REGION IS AN EXCELLENT CAMPING ALTERNATIVE TO THE NORTH COAST OF NEW SOUTH WALES, AND IT BOASTS NUMEROUS WORLD HERITAGE-LISTED PARKS. INDULGE IN THE AREA'S GREAT BUSHWALKING, SPECTACULAR SCENERY, WILD RIVERS AND CASCADING WATERFALLS.

To the east of Armidale is Styx River State Forest. The forest has excellent camping facilities for those who may be travelling with a dog, with the main camping area, Styx River Rest Area, also accessible to caravans. Visitors to the forest can enjoy bushwalking, fishing, swimming, four-wheel drive touring and mountain-bike riding.

Adjacent to the forest is the World Heritage-listed New England National Park – some good bushwalking trails can be found around the camping area here. Within New England National Park is Point Lookout, which has stunning vistas.

In the south of the region, near Nundle, are Hanging Rock State Forest and the Peel Valley.

Camping at Hanging Rock State Forest is at Ponderosa Forest Park, a well-shaded site beside a large dam, in a pine plantation. The Peel Valley campsites offer a number of different possibilities, with Sheba Dams Reserve being one of the most popular. Camping here is beside the dam, which is a good spot for fishing and swimming.

Oxley Wild Rivers National Park, another World Heritage-listed park, has large expanses of wilderness along with spectacular waterfalls, dramatic gorges and scenic rivers. The park is home to rare plants and animals including the Hastings River mouse. There are many campsites throughout the park, in particular near Youdales Hut, which is in one of the most picturesque locations of the park. Access is by four-wheel drive and a permit is required.

In the west of New England camping can be found at reserves near the towns of Barraba, Bingara, Warialda and Burren Junction; campers can relax in the bore baths at Burren Junction, swim and fish in the Gwydir River east of Bingara, or do some gem fossicking at Cranky Rock Recreation Reserve near Warialda.

BEST CAMPSITES

Wattle Flat camping area
Styx River State Forest

Sheba Dams Reserve
Peel Valley area

Wollomombi Gorge camping area
Oxley Wild Rivers National Park

Ponderosa Forest Park
Hanging Rock State Forest

Bellbird camping area
Washpool National Park

BEST TIME TO VISIT

This region experiences all four distinct seasons. The best time to visit is during spring and autumn when there are not too many extremes in temperature.

1. BALD ROCK NATIONAL PARK

This park is 29 km north of Tenterfield, signposted from Mt Lindesay Rd. Bald Rock, a water-streaked dome, is the largest granite rock in Australia. Walk to the summit – it has 360-degree views.

Bald Rock camping area

Area is 30 km north of Tenterfield. Signposted via Bald Rock Rd from Woodenbong Rd. Boil water before use. Bring firewood. Additional map ref.: NSWRD 48 A10.

Further information & bookings: NPWS, Glen Innes **Tel.:** (02) 6732 5133 **Park use fee:** $6.00 per vehicle/day **Camping fees:** $5.00 per adult/night, $3.00 per child (age 5–15) per night; fees payable at self-registration stations

2. BARRABA AREA

Barraba is 90 km north-west of Tamworth. Activities in the area include water-based activities at Split Rock Dam, car touring, sightseeing and bushwalking.

Glen Riddle Reserve camping area

Area is near upper reach of Split Rock Dam, 17 km south of Barraba. Signposted from Crow Mountain Rd at Black Springs turn-off on Fossickers Way. Bring drinking water and firewood. Additional map ref.: NSWRD 55 P8.

Horton Falls camping area

This is 39 km west of Barraba. There is signposted access (2WD in dry weather only) via Mt Lindsay Rd off Trevallyn Rd – the road can be rough at times. Bring drinking water and firewood. Additional map ref.: NSWRD 55 M7.

Little Creek Recreation Reserve

Small area 20 km north-west of Barraba. Access via Trevallyn Rd. Bring drinking water and firewood. Additional map ref.: NSWRD 55 N7.

Further information & bookings: Barraba Visitors Centre **Tel.:** (02) 6782 1255

3. BINGARA AREA

Gems and minerals surround the small town of Bingara, north-east of Narrabri: you should check with Bingara Tourist Information Centre for details of the best sites. It is also a popular fishing area.

Gwydir River camping areas

Numerous camping areas – no facilities – about 18 km east of Bingara on the Gwydir River. Access via Keera Rd east from Bingara. Tracks lead to sites near river after first cattle grid. Check best areas with locals before setting up. Bring drinking water and firewood. Additional map ref.: NSWRD 55 P5.

Rocky Creek camping areas

Dispersed camping areas near Rocky Creek 38 km south-west of Bingara. Access from Bingara–Narrabri Rd. Check best areas with locals before setting up. Bring drinking water and firewood. Additional map ref.: NSWRD 55 M6.

Further information & bookings: Bingara Tourist Information Centre **Tel.:** (02) 6724 0066 **Email:** bingara@northwest.com.au

4. BONSHAW WEIR

This is on the Queensland border 45 km north-east of Ashford, near Bonshaw. It is signposted from Bonshaw Rd off Bruxner Hwy.

Bonshaw Weir camping area

Bring drinking water and firewood. Additional map ref.: NSWRD 55 S1.

Further information & bookings: Inverell Visitor Information Centre **Tel.:** (02) 6728 8161 **Email:** tourism@inverell.nsw.gov.au **Website:** www.inverell-online.com.au

5. BOONOO BOONOO NATIONAL PARK

This park is 36 km north of Tenterfield and signposted via Boonoo Boonoo Falls Rd off Mt Lindesay Rd. The Boonoo Boonoo Falls is worth a visit – it has a drop of 210 m – while spring sees a host of flowering plants. You can also swim in the river.

Cypress Pine camping area

Near river, 35 km north of Tenterfield. Signposted from Boonoo Boonoo Falls Rd. Bring firewood. Additional map ref.: NSWRD 48 A10.

Further information & bookings: NPWS, Glen Innes **Tel.:** (02) 6732 5133 **Park use fee:** $6.00 per vehicle/day **Camping fees:** $5.00 per adult/night, $3.00 per child (age 5–15) per night; fees payable at self-registration stations

6. BOONOO STATE FOREST

This forest is 20 km north of Tenterfield. There is 2WD access in dry weather only via Basket Swamp Rd, off Lindrook Rd from Woodenbong Rd.

Basket Swamp picnic and camping area

Area is 23 km north of Tenterfield. Bring drinking water. Additional map ref.: NSWRD 48 A10.

Further information & bookings: State Forests, Casino **Tel.:** (02) 6662 0900 **Email:** cumberland@sf.nsw.gov.au

7. BURREN JUNCTION

Burren Junction, a cotton-farming town, is 95 km west of Narrabri on the Kamilaroi Hwy. You can relax in warm artesian bore baths here.

Artesian Bore Baths Reserve

This is 3 km east of Burren Junction township. Signposted from Burren Junction–Wee Waa Rd. Bring firewood (no fires during fire danger period). Additional map ref.: NSWRD 54 E6.

Further information & bookings: Walgett Shire Council **Tel.:** (02) 6828 1399 **Email:** admin@walgettshire.com **Website:** www.walgettshire.com

8. CARRAI NATIONAL PARK

This park is high on a plateau 80 km west of Kempsey. Access is via Carrai Rd off Kempsey Rd near Willawarrin – check road conditions after rain before attempting to drive in. Activities here include relaxing, bushwalking and 4WD touring – maybe you will catch a glimpse of the Kookaburra Yowie!

Kookaburra Hut

This old forestry hut is 80 km west of Kempsey, at the old sawmilling settlement of Kookaburra. Access via Carrai Rd. Sleeps up to six people. Bring firewood. Advance bookings essential. Additional map ref.: NSWRD 108 G1.

Further information & bookings: NPWS, Arakoon State Recreation Area **Tel.:** (02) 6566 6168 **Email:** trialbay.gaol@npws.nsw.gov.au **Camping fees:** 1–3 nights $38.50 inclusive; 4–7 nights $77.00 inclusive

9. CATHEDRAL ROCK NATIONAL PARK

This national park contains many striking granite boulder formations. It is 70 km east of Armidale near Ebor and is signposted from Waterfall Way (Armidale–Grafton Rd). Explore the park's walking tracks; wildlife you may see here includes wedge-tailed eagles and kangaroos.

Barokee Rest Area

Situated 14 km south-west of Ebor and 8 km west of Waterfall Way. Bring drinking water. Firewood supplied. Additional map ref.: NSWRD 92 F9.

Native Dog Creek Rest Area

This is 12 km west of Ebor. Signposted from Ebor–Guyra Rd. Bring drinking water. Firewood supplied. Additional map ref.: NSWRD 92 F8.

Further information & bookings: NPWS, Dorrigo **Tel.:** (02) 6657 2309 **Email:** dorrigo@npws.nsw.gov.au **Camping fees:** $3.00 per adult/night, $2.00 per child (age 5–15) per night; fees payable at self-registration stations

10. COPETON DAM

This is a large water storage dam on the Gwydir River, 17 km south-west of Inverell. Part of it is flanked by Copeton Waters State Park (see following entry). The dam is reached by Auburn Vale Rd from Inverell. All types of watersports are popular here and there is good fishing.

Northern Foreshore Reserve camping area

This is on northern foreshore of the dam. Bring firewood. Bookings advised for peak times. Additional map ref.: NSWRD 55 R5.

Further information & bookings: Foreshore reserve ranger **Tel.:** (02) 6723 0250 **Park use fee:** $6.00 per vehicle/day **Camping fees:** Unpowered sites from $5.00 per family (2 adults + 2 school-age children) per night; powered sites from $8.00 per family/night; extra people $2.00 per night

11. COPETON WATERS STATE PARK

This park is on the western edge of Copeton Dam, a large water storage dam on the Gwydir River. It is 40 km south-west of Inverell and reached via Copeton Dam Rd from Inverell. It is a popular watersports destination.

Copeton Waters State Park camping area

On western foreshore of dam. Kiosk and laundry facilities. Also bunkhouse accommodation. Firewood supplied. Bookings preferred for peak times. Additional map ref.: NSWRD 55 Q5.

Further information & bookings: Copeton Waters State Park **Tel.:** (02) 6723 6269 **Email:** copeton@northnet.com.au **Camping fees:** From $10.00 per site/night, powered sites also available; ring for bunkhouse rates

12. DUMARESQ DAM

This was Armidale's original water supply. It is 12 km north-west of Armidale and signposted via Dumaresq Dam Rd and Boorolong Rd from Armidale. Powerboating is not permitted on the dam.

Dumaresq Dam camping area

Foreshore location. Bring firewood. Additional map ref.: NSWRD 55 T8.

Further information & bookings: Armidale Visitors Centre **Tel.:** 1800 627 736 **Email:** armvisit@northnet.com.au **Website:** www.new-england.org/armidale/

13. GIBRALTAR RANGE NATIONAL PARK

This park is 70 km east of Glen Innes and 95 km west of Grafton, adjoining Washpool National Park in the north and Nymboida National Park in the south. It is signposted off the Gwydir Hwy. Its wilderness areas are World Heritage-listed. Take a walk – they range from a one-hour amble to a five-day trek.

Mulligans camping area

Signposted via Mulligans Drive off Gwydir Hwy near NPWS visitor centre. Near creek and hut. Bring firewood. Additional map ref.: NSWRD 88 H1.

Further information & bookings: NPWS, Glen Innes **Tel.:** (02) 6732 5133 **Park use fee:** $6.00 per vehicle/day **Camping fees:** $5.00 per adult/night, $3.00 per child (age 5–15) per night; fees payable at self-registration stations

14. GIRARD STATE FOREST

This former mining area, signposted from the Bruxner Hwy, is 30 km north-east of Tenterfield. Activities include bushwalking and 4WD touring.

Crooked Creek Rest Area

Situated 38 km north-east of Tenterfield and 6 km west of Drake. Reached via Richmond Rd from Bruxner Hwy. Water from tank. Additional map ref.: NSWRD 48 B10.

Further information & bookings: State Forests, Casino **Tel.:** (02) 6662 0900 **Email:** cumberland@sf.nsw.gov.au

15. GUY FAWKES RIVER NATIONAL PARK

This is a rugged and remote park 70 km north-west of Dorrigo. It is signposted from Sheep Station Creek Rd off Armidale– Grafton Rd at Dundurrabin in the east or Chaelundi Rd from the Old Grafton–Glen Innes Rd at Dalmorton to the north. It is a good bushwalking area and there are spectacular views from the lookouts. Check out the Ebor Falls.

Chaelundi Rest Area

Shaded grassy area near a creek. Signposted from Misty Creek Rd off Chaelundi Rd and from Sheep Station Creek Rd. Water from creek – boil before use. Bring firewood. Additional map ref.: NSWRD 92 G2.

Further information & bookings: NPWS, Dorrigo **Tel.:** (02) 6657 2309 **Email:** dorrigo@npws.nsw.gov.au **Camping fees:** $3.00 per adult/night, $2.00 per child (age 5–15) per night; fees payable at self-registration stations

16. HANGING ROCK STATE FOREST

This forest is predominately pine plantation. It is 10 km east of Nundle.

Ponderosa Forest Park

Set in pine plantation 15 km east of Nundle. Signposted via Nundle Forest Way. Bring water. Additional map ref.: NSWRD 106 F10.

Further information & bookings: State Forests, Walcha **Tel.:** (02) 6777 2511 **Email:** cumberland@sf.nsw.gov.au

17. KINGS PLAINS NATIONAL PARK

This is 50 km north-west of Glen Innes via Wellingrove and 48 km north-east of Inverell. There is signposted access via Jindalee Rd from Kings Plains Rd. The park features ironbark and cypress pine woodlands and there are wildflower displays in spring. You can rock-hop along Kings Creek.

Kings Plains Creek camping area

Walk-in site (50 m) from carpark, signposted from Jindalee Rd. Bring water and firewood. Additional map ref.: NSWRD 55 S3.

Further information & bookings: NPWS, Glen Innes **Tel.:** (02) 6732 5133

18. KOREELAH NATIONAL PARK

This park is 30 km north-west of Woodenbong, on the Queensland border. There is access in dry weather only via White Swamp Rd from Summerland Way at Old Koreelah. The park features the state's westernmost rainforest and is home to a number of rare animals and birds.

Koreelah Creek camping area

Located 33 km north-west of Woodenbong. Bring water and firewood. Additional map ref.: NSWRD 48 C7.

Further information & bookings: NPWS, Kyogle **Tel.:** (02) 6632 0000 **Camping fees:** $3.00 per adult/night, $2.00 per child (age 5–15) per night; fees payable at self-registration stations

19. KWIAMBAL NATIONAL PARK

This park is 30 km north-west of Ashford and is signposted from Wallangra Rd. The Severn and MacIntyre rivers flow through the park; view MacIntyre Falls and swim in the rivers. There is prolific wildlife.

Lemon Tree Flat camping area

Beside the Severn River and reached via MacIntyre Falls Rd from Wallangra Rd. Water from river – boil before use. Bring firewood. Additional map ref.: NSWRD 55 Q1.

Further information & bookings: NPWS, Glen Innes
Tel.: (02) 6732 5133

20. LAKE KEEPIT STATE PARK

Lake Keepit, a large water storage dam on the Namoi River, lies between Gunnedah and Tamworth. It is signposted via Keepit Dam Rd from Oxley Hwy. It is a very popular area for watersports and there is good fishing. Advance bookings are required for peak periods.

Eastern Foreshore camping area

On eastern foreshore of lake. Bring drinking water and firewood. Additional map ref.: NSWRD 55 N10.

Lake Keepit State Park camping area

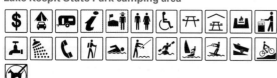

On lake foreshore. Kiosk and laundry facilities. Bring firewood. Additional map ref.: NSWRD 55 N10.

Further information & bookings: Lake Keepit State Park
Tel.: (02) 6769 7605 **Email:** keepit@bigpond.com
Camping fees: *Eastern Foreshore:* From $9.00 per site/night unpowered in off-peak period *Lake Keepit State Park:* From $11.50 per site/night unpowered and $14.50 per site/night powered in off-peak period

21. MACLEAY RIVER PUBLIC RECREATION RESERVE

This reserve is 71 km north-west of Kempsey, on the upper reaches of the Macleay River. Access is via Kempsey–Armidale Rd. Activities include fishing (for bass) and canoeing.

Blackbird Flat Reserve camping area

Beside Macleay River 71 km north-west of Kempsey. Water from river – boil before drinking. Bring firewood. Additional map ref.: NSWRD 96 G6.

Further information & bookings: Kempsey Shire Council
Tel.: (02) 6562 6077 **Email:** ksc@kempsey.nsw.gov.au
Website: www.kempsey.nsw.gov.au

22. MANILLA AREA

Manilla is a pictureque town known for its meadery. It is 44 km north-west of Tamworth and reached via the Fossickers Way.

Split Rock Dam camping area

Beside dam 20 km north of Manilla. Signposted from Oakhampton turn-off on Fossickers Way at Upper Manilla. Good fishing. Bring drinking water and firewood. Additional map ref.: NSWRD 55 P8.

Further information & bookings: Manilla Tourist Information Centre **Tel.:** (02) 6785 1113 **Email:** bigfishmanilla@hotmail.com **Website:** www.manilla-info.net
Camping fees: $2.00 per vehicle/night; fees payable at honesty box

23. MANN RIVER NATURE RESERVE

This is 44 km east of Glen Innes and signposted from the Old Grafton–Glen Innes Rd via Gwydir Hwy or from South Grafton via Newton Boyd. Take in the views from nearby Tommys Rock (4WD access only) and travel through history along the Old Grafton–Glen Innes Rd (2WD in dry weather only).

Picnic and Camping area

Beside the Mann River. Signposted on Old Grafton–Glen Innes Rd. Water from river – boil before use. Bring firewood. Additional map ref.: NSWRD 88 B4.

Further information & bookings: NPWS, Glen Innes
Tel.: (02) 6732 5133

24. MOOGEM STATE FOREST

This forest adjoins Gibraltar Range National Park, north-east of Glen Innes, and is signposted from Slomans Rd off the Gwydir Hwy. Boundary Creek Falls is worth viewing, and other activities here include bushwalking.

Boundary Creek Falls camping area

Former sawmill site 60 km north-east of Glen Innes. Signposted access via Slomans Rd. Bring water. Additional map ref.: NSWRD 88 E1.

Further information & bookings: State Forests, Casino
Tel.: (02) 6662 0900 **Email:** cumberland@sf.nsw.gov.au

25. MOUNT BOSS STATE FOREST

This forest is popular for 4WD touring and lies to the north-west of Wauchope. The forest adjoins Werrikimbe National Park and is reached via Hastings Forest Way from Bellangry. Activities here include bushwalking (be self-sufficient).

Wild Bull camping area

Near Wilson River 45 km from Wauchope. Access via Cobrabald Rd from Hastings Forest Way. Water from river – boil before use. Additional map ref.: NSWRD 109 L5.

Further information & bookings: State Forests, Wauchope
Tel.: (02) 6585 3744 **Email:** cumberland@sf.nsw.gov.au

26. MOUNT KAPUTAR NATIONAL PARK

Mt Kaputar is an extinct volcano 53 km east of Narrabri. It rises to over 1000 m and is signposted on the Kaputar Rd from Narrabri. As a highland and largely wilderness area, visitors should come prepared. There are many bushwalking tracks, from day strolls to multi-day walks.

Bark Hut camping area

This is 60 km east of Narrabri. Signposted from Kaputar Rd. Gas/fuel stove preferred, otherwise bring firewood. Additional map ref.: NSWRD 55 L7.

Dawsons Spring camping area

This is 60 km east of Narrabri. Signposted from Kaputar Rd. Cabin accommodation also available. Gas/fuel stove preferred, otherwise bring firewood. Advance bookings are essential for cabins. Additional map ref.: NSWRD 55 L7.

Further information & bookings: NPWS, Narrabri **Tel.:** (02) 6799 1740 **Camping fees:** $3.00 per adult/night, $2.00 per child (age 5–15) per night; fees payable at self-registration stations *Dawsons Spring cabins*: $55.00 per cabin/night (sleeps up to 6 people); minimum 2-night stay

27. MUMMEL GULF NATIONAL PARK

This park protects old-growth forest and some threatened species. It is 50 km south-east of Walcha and is reached via Enfield Rd from the Oxley Hwy. Activities include remote-area bushwalking and 4WD touring.

New Country Swamp camping area

Access via Enfield Rd. Bring water and firewood. Additional map ref.: NSWRD 107 T7.

Further information & bookings: NPWS, Walcha **Tel.:** (02) 6777 1400

28. NEW ENGLAND NATIONAL PARK

This is a World Heritage-listed park located 75 km west of Dorrigo and 85 km east of Armidale, near Ebor. It is signposted via Point Lookout Rd from Waterfall Way (Armidale–Grafton Rd). Experience the stunning vistas from Point Lookout and try one of the many walking tracks. Cabin accommodation is available.

Thungutti Rest Area

Located 22 km south-east of Ebor. Signposted from Point Lookout Rd. Bring firewood. Additional map ref.: NSWRD 96 H1.

Further information & bookings: NPWS, Dorrigo **Tel.:** (02) 6657 2309 **Camping fees:** $3.00 per adult/night, $2.00 per child (age 5–15) per night; fees payable at self-registration stations

29. OXLEY WILD RIVERS NATIONAL PARK

This is a World Heritage-listed park broken into several sections. Its features include dramatic gorges and waterfalls, scenic rivers and large expanses of wilderness. It lies to the south-east of Armidale and the main access from Armidale is via Waterfall Way (Armidale–Grafton Rd) or the Oxley Hwy from Walcha. Activities include sightseeing, bushwalking and fishing.

ARMIDALE REGION

Dangars Gorge camping area

Located 22 km south of Armidale. Signposted from Dangarsleigh Rd from Armidale. Great views down gorge. Water from tank. Firewood supplied. Additional map ref.: NSWRD 55 U9.

East Kunderang Homestead

A restored 1890s colonial homestead 112 km east of Armidale. 2WD access is possible (4WD is recommended) via Raspberry Rd from Armidale–Kempsey Rd. Sleeps up to ten people (advance bookings essential – key access). Near Kunderang Brook and on Bicentennial National Trail. Firewood supplied. Additional map ref.: NSWRD 96 C7.

Long Point camping area

This is 49 km east of Armidale. Signposted from Hillgrove via Waterfall Way. Splendid views over the ravines of the northern section of the park. Walking tracks nearby. Firewood supplied. Additional map ref.: NSWRD 55 V9.

Wollomombi Gorge camping area

This is 40 km east of Armidale. Signposted access via Waterfall Way. Spectacular flow over falls after rain. Walking tracks. Additional map ref.: NSWRD 96 A1.

Further information & bookings: NPWS, Armidale **Tel.:** (02) 6776 0000 **Email:** armidale@npws.nsw.gov.au **Camping fees:** $3.00 per adult/night, $2.00 per child (age 5–15) per night; fees payable at self-registration stations *East Kunderang Homestead:* Contact NPWS for current rate; permit and key required; advance bookings essential

WALCHA REGION

Apsley Gorge camping area

Located 20 km east of Walcha. Signposted from Oxley Hwy. Views over Apsley Falls. Walking tracks. Water from tank. Firewood supplied. Additional map ref.: NSWRD 63 U1.

Budds Mare Rest Area

Site is 44 km east of Walcha. Signposted via Moona Plains Rd from Winterbourne Rd from Walcha. Walking tracks to Riverside on Apsley River. Water from tank. Firewood supplied. Additional map ref.: NSWRD 55 V10.

Riverside Rest Area

Beside Apsley River 50 km east of Walcha. 4WD-only access via Moona Plains Rd from Winterbourne Rd (access permit required – locked gate). Water from tank. Firewood supplied. Additional map ref.: NSWRD 96 A10.

Tia Falls camping area

Near Tia Falls 43 km south-east of Walcha. Signposted from Oxley Hwy. Walking tracks nearby. Bring drinking water. Firewood supplied. Additional map ref.: NSWRD 63 V1.

Youdales Hut camping area

This hut is in a picturesque location in a valley beside Kundarang Brook. 4WD-only access (permit required) via Youdales Trail off Racecourse Trail. Camping in vicinity of hut (camping in hut not permitted). On the path of the Bicentennial National Trail. Water from creek – boil before use. Bring firewood. Additional map ref.: NSWRD 108 F2.

Further information & bookings: NPWS, Walcha **Tel.:** (02) 6777 1400 **Camping fees:** $3.00 per adult/night, $2.00 per child (age 5–15) per night; fees payable at self-registration stations *Riverside Rest Area and Youdales Hut:* Contact NPWS for current rates; permit and key required; advance bookings essential

30. PEEL VALLEY AREA

The Peel Valley is a fertile farming area; Tamworth is the main centre here.

Bowling Alley Point Recreation Reserve

On foreshore of Chaffey Dam (a water storage on the Peel River), 12 km north-west of Nundle. Signposted from Fossickers Way (Nundle–Tamworth Rd). Firewood supplied. Additional map ref.: NSWRD 106 C8.

Cockburn River campsite

This is 31 km north-east of Tamworth beside the Cockburn River. Access via Kootingal–Limbri Rd. Bring water and firewood. Additional map ref.: NSWRD 106 C2.

Sheba Dams Reserve

Tranquil setting beside dam 11 km east of Nundle, near Hanging Rock. Access via Nundle–Barry Rd. Sheba Dams originally constructed for goldmining. Bring drinking water and firewood. Additional map ref.: NSWRD 106 D10.

Swamp Creek campsite

Located 4 km north of Nundle at junction of Swamp Creek and Peel River. Access via Fossickers Way (Nundle–Tamworth Rd). Popular gold- and gem-fossicking area. Bring drinking water and firewood. Additional map ref.: NSWRD 106 C9.

Teamsters Rest campsite

Located 21 km south of Nundle beside Wombramurra Creek, at the foot of Crawney Pass. 2WD access in dry weather only via Crawney Pass Rd. Water from creek – boil before use or bring own. Bring firewood. Additional map ref.: NSWRD 116 B2.

Woolomin Reserve

At Woolomin village (Munro St) beside the Peel River. Access via Fossickers Way (Nundle–Tamworth Rd). Bring drinking water and firewood. Power available ($5.00 per night; see Goldrush General Store at Woolomin). Additional map ref.: NSWRD 106 C7.

Further information & bookings: Nundle Tourist Information Centre **Tel.:** (02) 6769 3158 **Other contacts:** *Chaffey Dam:* DLWC, Chaffey Dam, tel. (02) 6764 2204 *Cockburn River, Sheba Dams, Swamp Creek and Teamsters Rest:* DLWC, Tamworth, tel. (02) 6764 5100 *Woolomin Reserve:* Goldrush General Store, tel. (02) 6764 2243 **Camping fees:** *Chaffey Dam:* $2.00 per person/night

31. PINDARI DAM

This popular watersports area on the Severn River is 25 km south-east of Ashford and is signposted from Pindari Dam Rd. Activities include boating, swimming, fishing and walking.

Pindari Dam camping area

Access via Pindari Dam Rd. Bring firewood. Additional map ref.: NSWRD 55 S2.

Further information & bookings: DLWC, Pindari Dam **Tel.:** (02) 6725 4007 *or* Inverell Shire Council **Tel.:** (02) 6728 8288 **Camping fees:** Gold coin donation payable at honesty box

32. STYX RIVER STATE FOREST

This forest is 65 km east of Armidale. It is signposted from Styx River Forest Way from the Armidale–Kempsey Rd in the south, and from Point Lookout Rd from Waterfall Way (Armidale–Grafton Rd) in the north. There is good camping beside the Styx River and it is a popular area for trout fishing. Other activities include swimming and 4WD touring. There are some good mountain-bike daytrips.

Hyatts Flat camping area

Beside Styx River 25 km south of Ebor. 2WD access in dry weather only via Hardwood Rd from Styx River Forest Way. Water from river – boil before use. Additional map ref.: NSWRD 56 B8.

Styx River Rest Area

Located 20 km south of Ebor, opposite entrance to New England National Park. Access via Point Lookout Rd. Water from creek – boil before use. Bring firewood. Additional map ref.: NSWRD 56 B8.

Wattle Flat camping area

Beside Styx River 70 km east of Armidale. Signposted via Loop Rd from Styx River Forest Way. Water from river – boil before use. Additional map ref.: NSWRD 56 B8.

Further information & bookings: State Forests, Walcha **Tel.:** (02) 6777 2511 **Email:** cumberland@sf.nsw.gov.au

33. TOOLOM FALLS

This is a small reserve with a strong Aboriginal mythology concerning the creation of the Clarence River. It is 6 km south of Urbenville, near the Queensland border, and is reached via Urbenville–Koorelah Rd.

Toolom Falls camping area

Signposted from Toolom Falls Rd off Urbenville–Koorelah Rd. Near falls. Bring drinking water and firewood. Additional map ref.: NSWRD 48 C8.

Further information & bookings: NPWS, Kyogle **Tel.:** (02) 6632 0000

34. TORRINGTON STATE RECREATION AREA

This is 20 km north of Emmaville, next to Torrington village. It is signposted from Deepwater on the New England Hwy. There are many curious rock formations and great 360-degree views from Thunderbolts Lookout.

Blatherarm Creek camping area

Located 10 km north of Torrington. Access via Blatherarm Rd. Bring drinking water. Gas/fuel stove preferred, otherwise bring firewood. Additional map ref.: NSWRD 55 U2.

Bush camping

Many bush camping areas are located throughout recreation area. Obtain large-scale maps and contact ranger for details. Bring drinking water. Gas/fuel stove preferred.

Further information & bookings: NPWS, Glen Innes **Tel.:** (02) 6732 5133

35. URALLA AREA

Uralla, 22 km south-west of Armidale, was once a rich goldmining town; today it is an attractive historic township.

Fossicking Area camping ground

Fossicking area for gold and gems 6 km west of Uralla on Rocky River Creek. Signposted access via Kingston Rd then Devoncourt Rd. Bring firewood. Additional map ref.: NSWRD 55 T9.

Gwydir River camping areas

These campsites begin around 39 km north-west of Uralla. Turn-off the Thunderbolt Way (Uralla–Bundarra Rd) at Yarrowyck. Tracks to bush campsites start after road crosses river and heads north to Bundarra (now the Gwydir River Road). Check access before towing in a caravan. Water from river – boil before use. Bring firewood. Additional map ref.: NSWRD 55 S8.

Further information & bookings: Uralla Visitor Centre, **Tel.:** (02) 6778 4496 **Email:** uralla@northnet.com.au **Website:** www.new-england.org/uralla/

36. URBENVILLE STATE FOREST

This forest is at Urbenville, which is close to the Queensland border, about 80 km north-west of Casino. Access is via Urbenville–Woodenbong Rd.

Urbenville Forest Park

In Urbenville village. Hot showers and power are available; contact State Forests at Casino to arrange shower key. Bring firewood. Additional map ref.: NSWRD 48 C8.

Further information & bookings: State Forests, Casino **Tel.:** (02) 6662 0900 **Email:** cumberland@sf.nsw.gov.au

37. WARIALDA AREA

Warialda is 55 km north-west of Inverell and is reached via the Gwydir Hwy. It marks the northern end of Fossickers Way and the area is popular with gem fossickers.

Cranky Rock Recreation Reserve

This is 8 km east of Warialda, signposted from the Gwydir Hwy. The reserve takes its name from a Chinese miner who, supposedly in a cranky state, jumped to his death from the rocks. Bring firewood. Additional map ref.: NSWRD 55 P3.

Further information & bookings: Caretaker **Tel.:** (02) 6729 1402 **Camping fees:** From $5.50 per site/night; some powered sites available

38. WARRABAH NATIONAL PARK

This park is north of Tamworth and is reached from Manilla by Namoi River Rd. The Namoi River runs through the park; activities include fishing, swimming, canoeing and rock climbing.

Warrabah camping area

Near Namoi River 35 km north-east of Manilla. Signposted from Namoi River Rd. Bring drinking water and firewood. Additional map ref.: NSWRD 55 Q8.

Further information & bookings: NPWS, Armidale
Tel.: (02) 6776 0000 **Email:** armidale@npws.nsw.gov.au
Park use fee: $6.00 per vehicle/day **Camping fees:** $5.00 per adult/night, $3.00 per child (age 5–15) per night; fees payable at self-registration stations

39. WASHPOOL NATIONAL PARK

This is a World Heritage-listed park protecting areas of rainforest wilderness; it is 75 km north-east of Glen Innes and 90 km west of Grafton, signposted from the Gwydir Hwy. It adjoins Gibraltar Range National Park and there are many walking tracks to enjoy.

Bellbird camping area

Signposted from Coachwood Rd. Bring firewood. Additional map ref.: NSWRD 84 G10.

Coombadjha camping area

Signposted from Coachwood Rd. Firewood supplied. Additional map ref.: NSWRD 84 G10.

Grassy Creek bush campsite

Situated 85 km north-east of Glen Innes. Walk-in-only access via Moogem Fire Trail. Gas/fuel stove preferred. Water from creek – boil before use. Additional map ref.: NSWRD 84 F10.

Further information & bookings: NPWS, Glen Innes
Tel.: (02) 6732 5133 **Park use fee:** $6.00 per vehicle/day
Camping fees: $5.00 per adult/night, $3.00 per child (age 5–15) per night; fees payable at self-registration stations

40. WERRIKIMBE NATIONAL PARK

This World Heritage-listed park is 60 km north-west of Wauchope and 80 km south-east of Walcha. Access to the eastern section is via Hastings Forest Way from Bellangry or via Forbes River Rd from the Oxley Hwy north of Ellenborough; to the western section via Kangaroo Flat Rd then Mooraback Rd from the Oxley Hwy east of Upper Yarrowitch; and to the northern section by 4WD only via Coachwood Rd from Kookaburra. The park has spectacular rainforests and snow gum woodlands and it protects endangered wildlife such as the Hastings River mouse and the rufous scrub bird. Activities include self-sufficient bushwalking and nature study. It is also a popular 4WD touring destination.

EASTERN SECTION

Brushy Mountain Rest Area

This is 62 km north-west of Wauchope. Access via Hastings Forest Way. Caravan access in dry weather only. Water from creek – boil before use. Bring firewood. Additional map ref.: NSWRD 108 H3.

Plateau Beech Rest Area

On Plateau Rd. Signposted off Cockerwombeeba Trail from Hastings Forest Way or from Forbes River Rd. 2WD access in dry weather only. Bring drinking water and firewood. Additional map ref.: NSWRD 108 G4 .

WESTERN SECTION

Mooraback Rest Area

Located 85 km south-east of Walcha. Access via Kangaroo Flat Rd and Mooraback Rd from the Oxley Hwy. Caravan access in dry weather only. Water from creek – boil before use. Firewood supplied. Additional map ref.: NSWRD 108 E3.

Further information & bookings:
Eastern Section: NPWS, Port Macquarie **Tel.:** (02) 6586 8300
or Western Section: NPWS, Walcha **Tel.:** (02) 6777 1400
Email: walcha.area@ npws.nsw.gov.au

41. YABBRA STATE FOREST

This forest is south of Urbenville and is reached via Old Bonalbo Rd.

Yabbra Rest Area

Located 6 km south of Urbenville. Water from tank. Suitable for overnight stays. Additional map ref.: NSWRD 48 C8.

Further information & bookings: State Forests, Casino
Tel.: (02) 6662 0900 **Email:** cumberland@sf.nsw.gov.au

42. YARRIE LAKE

This is a natural lake that is popular for watersports. It is 25 km west of Narrabri and 18 km east of Wee Waa. It is signposted from Yarrie Lake Rd off Narrabri–Wee Waa Back Rd.

Yarrie Lake Reserve camping area

Dispersed camping areas around lake edge. Signposted from Yarrie Lake Rd. Bring drinking water and firewood. Additional map ref.: NSWRD 54 H7.

Further information & bookings: Narrabri Visitors Centre
Tel.: (02) 6799 6760 **Email:** narrtour@turboweb.net.au
Camping fees: From $10.50 per family/night unpowered, $15.00 per night powered; fees payable at Narrabri Visitors Centre or to caretaker on site during summer

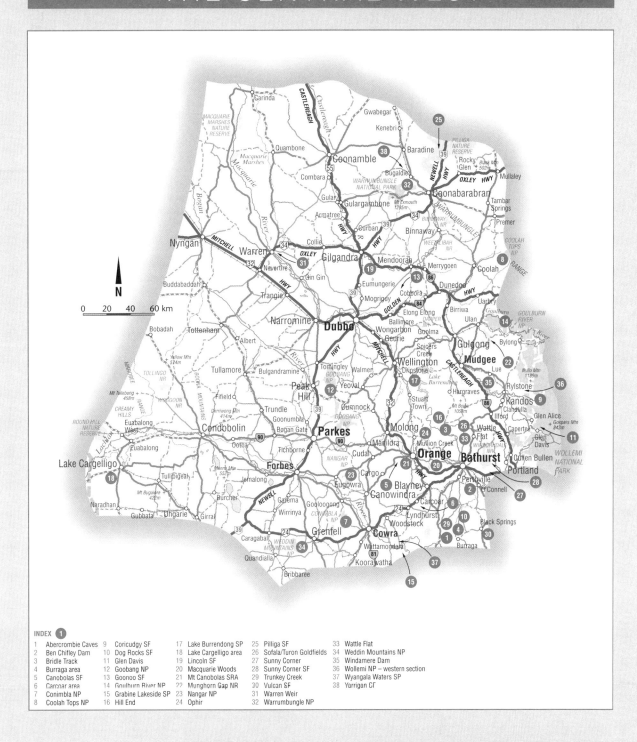

THE CENTRAL WEST REGION OF NEW SOUTH WALES HAS A SUPERB NATURAL ENVIRONMENT AND AN INTERESTING HISTORY. IT IS DOTTED WITH OLD MINING SITES AND TOWNS FROM THE GOLD-RUSH DAYS, AS WELL AS IMPRESSIVE ROCK FORMATIONS FORMED BY VIOLENT VOLCANIC ERUPTIONS MILLIONS OF YEARS AGO.

Along the historic Bridle Track, a horse trail from Bathurst to Hill End, campers have a choice of sites beside the Macquarie River. Some sections of the original Bridle Track can still be viewed today, and the river has some great swimming holes and fishing spots.

In Hill End the Village Campground has excellent camping facilities and visitors should take time to explore the town and the surrounding mining areas. Other historic mining towns with camping nearby include the old gold town of Sofala (camping is along the nearby Turon River) and the former township of Ophir, in Australia's first goldfield.

The mountains of Weddin Mountains National Park, south-west of Grenfell, were once the hideout of bushrangers such as Ben Hall. A walking trail from the park's camping areas leads to Ben Hall's cave. Also in the park, close to Seatons camping area, is the historic Seatons Farm – step back in time and see how the Seaton family lived in the days of the Depression.

The popular Warrumbungle National Park was formed by volcanic activity 13 million years ago and through time has eroded into an impressive mountain range. One of the best-known formations is the 90-metre-high rock wall called the Breadknife. Beautiful wildflowers can be seen during spring and bushwalkers, sightseers and rock climbers all visit the park. Campsites range from powered van sites with hot showers to walk-in bush campsites.

BEST CAMPSITES

Village Campground
Hill End

Turon Crossing Reserve
Bridle Track

The Barracks camping area
Coolah Tops National Park

The Junction picnic and camping area
Ophir

Heritage Grove camping area
Macquarie Woods

BEST TIME TO VISIT

Spring and autumn.

1. ABERCROMBIE CAVES

Abercrombie Caves contain the largest limestone arch in the Southern Hemisphere. They are 70 km south of Bathurst, near Trunkey Creek village, and are reached via Bathurst–Crookwell Rd. Take a guided tour of the caves and walk to Grove Creek Falls. The reserve is a wildlife sanctuary and activities include bushwalking, swimming and fishing.

Abercrombie Caves Reserve

Access via Bathurst–Crookwell Rd. Gas/fuel stove preferred. Bring firewood. Additional map ref.: NSWRD 150 H9.

Further information & bookings: Jenolan Caves Reserve Trust **Tel.:** (02) 6368 8603 **Email:** abercrombie@ jenolancaves. org.au **Website:** www.jenolancaves.org.au **Camping fees:** $6.50 per person/night or $16.00 per family (2 adults + 2–3 school-age children) per night; fees payable at office or kiosk

2. BEN CHIFLEY DAM

This water storage dam was named after former prime minister Ben Chifley, a local. It is 20 km south-east of Bathurst and is signposted off The Lagoon Rd. The area is popular with fisherfolk and other activities include canoeing and waterskiing.

Ben Chifley Dam camping area

Signposted via The Vale Rd from Bathurst then The Lagoon Rd. Bring firewood. Additional map ref.: NSWRD 151 N2.

Further information & bookings: Bathurst City Council **Tel.:** (02) 6333 6100 **Camping fees:** Ring for rates

3. BRIDLE TRACK

This is the original bridle (horse) route between Bathurst and Hill End, now a popular route for 4WD touring. There is 2WD access (but 4WD is recommended) from Kelso on the Great Western Hwy (just east of Bathurst) in the south, or from Hill End in the north. (The low-level concrete causeway over the Turon River, 8 km south of Hill End, may be impassable after rain.) Numerous delightful camping areas exist along the track beside the Macquarie and Turon rivers and you can explore old gold workings (take care around shafts and tunnels), swim, fish and go canoeing. Some sites have disabled toilet access. Bring drinking water. Gas/fuel stove preferred, otherwise bring firewood.

Bruinbun Reserve
43 km north of Bathurst. Additional map ref.: NSWRD 142 K3.

Amy Anderson Reserve
45 km north of Bathurst. Additional map ref.: NSWRD 142 J3.

Tattersalls Hole Reserve
46 km north of Bathurst. Additional map ref.: NSWRD 142 J3.

Black Gate Reserve
47 km north of Bathurst. Additional map ref.: NSWRD 142 J3.

Native Dog Reserve
49 km north of Bathurst. Additional map ref.: NSWRD 142 J3.

Johnsons Hole Reserve
52 km north of Bathurst. Additional map ref.: NSWRD 142 H3.

Randwick Hole Reserve
54 km north of Bathurst. Additional map ref.: NSWRD 142 H3.

Grimleys Hotel Reserve
55 km north of Bathurst. Additional map ref.: NSWRD 142 H2.

Mary Flynn Reserve
10 km south of Hill End. Additional map ref.: NSWRD 142 J2.

Cave Hole Reserve
9 km south of Hill End. Additional map ref.: NSWRD 142 J2.

Turon Crossing Reserve
8 km south of Hill End. Additional map ref.: NSWRD 142 J2.

Further information & bookings:
DLWC, Orange **Tel.:** (02) 6393 4384 or
Bathurst Visitor Centre **Tel.:** (02) 6332 1444
Road conditions: Evans Shire Council **Tel.:** (02) 6331 4200
Camping fees: $5.00 per tent/family/5 persons per night;
ranger collects fees

4. BURRAGA AREA

Burraga is a one-time coppermining town that once boasted 6000 residents. It is located 70 km south of Bathurst and access is via Rockley Rd. The main activity now is agriculture. It is a popular area with fossickers looking for gold, diamonds and sapphires.

Burraga Dam camping area

Located 2 km north-east of Burraga. Access via Arkstone Rd from Burraga (call in at village store for directions). Caravan access in dry weather only. Bring drinking water and firewood. Additional map ref.: NSWRD 151 L9.

Further information & bookings:
DLWC, Carcoar **Tel.:** (02) 6367 3103 or
Burraga Village Store **Tel.:** (02) 6337 0255

5. CANOBOLAS STATE FOREST

This forest is 15 km south-west of Orange and is reached via Cadia Rd off Forest Rd from Orange. There is trout fishing here.

Four Mile Creek camping area

Near creek, 23 km south-west of Orange. Access via Four Mile Creek Rd from Cadia Rd. Bring drinking water. Additional map ref.: NSWRD 141 U9.

Further information & bookings: State Forests, Bathurst **Tel.:** (02) 6331 2044 **Email:** cumberland@sf.nsw.gov.au

6. CARCOAR AREA

This is a historic area – Carcoar is the third oldest settlement west of the Blue Mountains. It is 12 km south-west of Blayney, on the Mid Western Hwy. Around Carcoar there are many old goldmines and the area is popular with fossickers.

Bakers Shaft Reserve

Old goldmining area near Belubula River, west of Carcoar. Access via Mandurama–Orange Rd, from Mandurama. Turn-off 10 km north of Mandurama at Bakers Rd, before Burnt Yards. 2WD access in dry weather only. Bring drinking water. Gas/fuel stove only. Additional map ref.: NSWRD 149 V3.

Carcoar Dam camping area

This camping area is by a water storage dam on the Belubula River, 8 km east of Carcoar. Signposted off the Mid Western Hwy 7 km north of Carcoar. Bring firewood. Additional map ref.: NSWRD 150 D3.

Golden Gully Recreation Reserve

Bush camping – no facilities – near Belubula River 1 km south of Carcoar. Signposted off the Mid Western Hwy. Causeway crossing on Belubula River may be impassable after rain. Bring drinking water and firewood. Additional map ref.: NSWRD 150 B3.

Further information & bookings:
Bakers Shaft and Golden Gully: DLWC, Orange **Tel.:** (02) 6393 4384
Carcoar Dam: Caretaker **Tel.:** (02) 6367 3103

7. CONIMBLA NATIONAL PARK

This park is one of the few 'bushland islands' in the region; it is surrounded by farmland. It is 20 km north-west of Cowra and is signposted via Barryrennie Rd from the Mid Western Hwy (Cowra–Grenfell Rd). There are wildflower displays in season and activities include nature study and bushwalking.

Wallaby picnic and camping area

Small campsite 27 km west of Cowra. Signposted from Barryrennie Rd. Bring water and firewood. Additional map ref.: NSWRD 148 J6.

Further information & bookings: NPWS, Forbes **Tel.:** (02) 6851 4429

8. COOLAH TOPS NATIONAL PARK

This park is on a plateau with tall open forests of snow gums and giant grass trees, 30 km east of Coolah. There is 2WD all-weather access to the main areas signposted via The Forest Rd from Coolah Creek Rd. Some other roads are dry-weather only. The park has plenty of wildlife and waterfalls – visit Norfolk Falls, and take in the vistas from the many lookouts. You can visit explorer Allan Cunningham's Pandora's Pass (off access road to park); the area was also explored by Ludwig Leichhardt. Activities include nature study, bushwalking, mountain-bike riding, fishing and 4WD touring.

Bald Hills camping area

Near Bald Hills Creek Falls, 41 km east of Coolah. 2WD access in dry weather only, via Bald Hills Rd off Hildegard Rd from The Forest Rd. Also walk-in access via track from Norfolk Falls. Water from creek – boil before use. Gas/fuel stove preferred, otherwise bring firewood. Additional map ref.: NSWRD 114 A6.

Brackens Hut

The hut, 40 km east of Coolah, was originally built in 1937 and has recently been restored by NPWS. Access via Hildegard Rd from The Forest Rd. Water from tank. Gas/fuel stove preferred. Firewood supplied. Advance bookings required; contact NPWS Mudgee. Additional map ref.: NSWRD 114 A6.

Cox Creek camping area

Situated 36 km east of Coolah. Signposted from Pinnacle Rd off The Forest Rd. Water from creek – boil before use. Gas/fuel stove preferred, otherwise bring firewood. Additional map ref.: NSWRD 114 A5.

The Barracks camping area

This is 36 km east of Coolah. Signposted from Pinnacle Rd off The Forest Rd. Water from tank. Gas/fuel stove preferred, otherwise bring firewood. Additional map ref.: NSWRD 114 A5.

The Pines camping area

Large area ideal for groups, 39 km east of Coolah. Signposted from Hildegard Rd from The Forest Rd. Bring water. Gas/fuel stove preferred, otherwise bring firewood. Additional map ref.: NSWRD 114 A5.

Further information & bookings:
NPWS, Mudgee **Tel.:** (02) 6372 7199 *or*
NPWS, Blackheath **Tel.:** (02) 4787 8877
Hut use fees: *Brackens Hut:* $22.00 per night

9. CORICUDGY STATE FOREST

This forest is 39 km east of Rylstone, near Wollemi National Park. It is reached via Narango Rd from Rylstone. Check status of roads after wet weather – 2WD vehicles can only reach the forest in dry weather. Activities here include horseriding, bushwalking and 4WD touring.

Kelgoola picnic and camping area

Access via Narango Rd. Bush camping – no facilities. Bring water. Additional map ref.: NSWRD 134 G8.

Further information & bookings: State Forests, Dubbo **Tel.:** (02) 6884 5288 **Email:** cumberland@sf.nsw.gov.au

10. DOG ROCKS STATE FOREST

This forest is 15 km south-east of Rockley and is reached via Swallows Nest Rd from Dog Rocks Rd. The Campbells River, which flows through the forest, is a popular trout-fishing spot.

Campbells River camping area

Large grassed area beside Campbells River. Access via Swallows Nest Rd. Good trout fishing. Bring drinking water and firewood. Additional map ref.: NSWRD 151 N6.

Further information & bookings: State Forests, Bathurst **Tel.:** (02) 6331 2044 **Email:** cumberland@sf.nsw.gov.au

11. GLEN DAVIS

Glen Davis is a historic shale-oil mining town 32 km east of Capertee, on the edge of Wollemi National Park. It is signposted via Glen Davis Rd off the Castlereagh Hwy (Mudgee Rd) 40 km north of Lithgow.

Glen Davis camping area

In Glen Davis village. Additional map ref.: NSWRD 144 F3.

Further information & bookings: Lithgow Visitors Information Centre **Tel.:** (02) 6353 1859 **Email:** lithinfo@lith.com.au **Website:** www.tourism.lithgow.com

12. GOOBANG NATIONAL PARK

Goobang National Park preserves a large tract of western-plains bushland. It is 30 km north-east of Parkes and east of Peak Hill, and is signposted from the Newell Hwy 8 km south of Peak Hill. There are good views from Caloma Trig Lookout. This is a great place for bushwalking.

Greenbah camping area

On Sawpit Gully Track, 6.5 km off the Trewilga–Yeoval Rd from the Newell Hwy south of Peak Hill. 4WD access recommended. Facilities being upgraded. Bring drinking water and firewood. Additional map ref.: NSWRD 130 H3.

Wanda Wandong camping area

Signposted off the Tomingley Rd from the Newell Hwy, 20 km north of Peak Hill. Facilities being upgraded. Bring drinking water and firewood. Additional map ref.: NSWRD 130 G5.

Further information & bookings: NPWS, Forbes **Tel.:** (02) 6851 4429

13. GOONOO STATE FOREST

This forest is a popular birdwatching spot. It is 25 km north-east of Dubbo and reached via Mendooran Rd, also from Mogriguy. Other activities here include horseriding.

No. 2 Bore Dam camping area

Bush camping – no facilities – 38 km north-east of Dubbo. Access via Mendooran Rd. Good birdwatching. Bring drinking water. Additional map ref.: NSWRD 111 V10.

Paddys Dam camping area

Bush camping – no facilities – 36 km north-east of Dubbo, at junction of Samuels Fire Rd and Frost Fire Rd. Access via Samuels Fire Rd from Mendooran Rd. Good birdwatching. Bring drinking water. Additional map ref.: NSWRD 121 T1.

Rileys Dam camping area

Bush camping – no facilities – 31 km north-east of Dubbo. Access via Mogriguy Forest Rd. Bring drinking water. Additional map ref.: NSWRD 121 Q2.

Further information & bookings: State Forests, Dubbo **Tel.:** (02) 6884 5288 **Email:** cumberland@sf.nsw.gov.au

14. GOULBURN RIVER NATIONAL PARK

The Goulburn River runs between spectacular sandstone cliffs in this park, 40 km south of Merriwa near Sandy Hollow. It is signposted off Ringwood Rd from Dubbo Rd in the north, from Denman–Rylstone Rd in the east and from Wollar in the south. It is a rugged and remote area with many Aboriginal sites. There is plenty of wildlife and good views from Lees Pinch. Activities here include bushwalking, swimming and relaxing on li-los (the river is mostly shallow except after rain).

Big River camping area

Beside Goulburn River. Access via Mogo Rd from Wollar. 4WD recommended. Water from river – boil before use. Bring firewood. Additional map ref.: NSWRD 124 B5.

Spring Gully camping area

Beside Goulburn River. Access via Mogo Rd from Wollar; 2WD access in dry weather only. Water from river – boil before use. Bring firewood. Additional map ref.: NSWRD 124 A5.

White Box camping area

Bush camping – no facilities – 40 km south-west of Merriwa. Reached via Ringwood Rd. 2WD access in dry weather only. Bring water and firewood. Additional map ref.: NSWRD 124 B6.

Further information & bookings: NPWS, Mudgee **Tel.:** (02) 6372 7199 **Email:** mudgee@npws.nsw.gov.au

15. GRABINE LAKESIDE STATE PARK

This park is 75 km north-west of Crookwell, on the north-eastern foreshore of Lake Wyangala. Access is via Crookwell–Bathurst Rd, then Bigga Rd. It is a popular watersports area during summer.

Grabine Lakeside State Park camping area

Access via Grabine Rd from Bigga Rd. Foreshore location. Laundry facilities. Other accommodation also available. Bring firewood. Advance bookings essential for peak times. Additional map ref.: NSWRD 150 A10.

Further information & bookings: Grabine Lakeside State Park **Tel.:** (02) 4835 2345 **Park use fee:** $6.00 per vehicle for first night stay **Camping fees:** From $13.50 per site/night

16. HILL END

Hill End is 85 km north of Bathurst via Sofala and 72 km south of Mudgee; 2WD access is also possible (in dry weather only) along the Bridle Track from Bathurst. The village is a living museum from the gold-rush days. Wander the streets and soak up the atmosphere of times long past, and try your luck at prospecting for 'colour'. Other activities include vehicle touring, sightseeing and picnicking.

Glendora camping area

Ideal group-camping area – used by school groups – 1 km north of Hill End's centre. Access via Lees Lane off Beyers Ave. Bring firewood. Additional map ref.: NSWRD 142 J1.

Village Campground

Pleasant grassed area in Hill End. Access via Warry Rd from Clarke St. Bring firewood. Additional map ref.: NSWRD 142 J1.

Further information & bookings: NPWS, Hill End Visitor Centre **Tel.:** (02) 6337 8206 **Camping fees:** *Glendora:* $5.00 per adult/night, $3.00 per child (age 5–15) per night *Village Campground:* Unpowered sites $5.00 per adult/night, $3.00 per child (age 5–15) per night, powered sites $7.50 per adult/night, $4.00 per child (age 5–15) per night. Ranger collects fees

17. LAKE BURRENDONG STATE PARK

Lake Burrendong is a large water storage on the Macquarie River 30 km south-east of Wellington. Access is from the Orange–Dubbo Rd. It is popular for water-based activities and there is good fishing.

Lake Burrendong State Park camping area

Foreshore location. Access via Burrendong Dam Rd off Orange–Dubbo Rd just north of Mumbil. Kiosk and laundry facilities. Bring drinking water and firewood. Additional map ref.: NSWRD 132 C4.

Mookerawa Waters Park camping area

Foreshore location 10 km east of Stuart Town. Access via Mookerawa Rd off Orange–Dubbo Rd at Stuart Town. Kiosk and laundry facilities. Bring drinking water and firewood. Additional map ref.: NSWRD 132 D6.

Further information & bookings: Lake Burrendong State Park **Tel.:** (02) 6846 7435 **Email:** burrdong@australis.com.au **Camping fees:** From $10.00 per site/night unpowered, $14.50 per site/night powered (only unpowered sites at Mookerawa)

18. LAKE CARGELLIGO AREA

This lake is a large irrigation water storage on the edge of the town of Lake Cargelligo, 95 km south-west of Condobolin. Access is via Lachlan Valley Way from Condobolin or via Lake Cargelligo Rd from West Wyalong. There are weirs on the Lachlan River and it is popular for water-based activities.

Lake Brewster Weir camping area

On Lachlan River 42 km west of Lake Cargelligo township. 2WD access in dry weather only via Ballyrogan Channel from Hillston Rd. Bring drinking water and firewood. Additional map ref.: NSWRD 68 K3.

Lake Cargelligo Weir camping area

On Lachlan River 25 km north-east of Lake Cargelligo township. 2WD access in dry weather only. Signposted from Lachlan Valley Way (Condobolin Rd). Bring drinking water and firewood. Additional map ref.: NSWRD 69 N2.

Further information & bookings:
DLWC, Lake Cargelligo **Tel.:** (02) 6898 1009 *or*
Lake Cargelligo Tourist Association **Tel.:** (02) 6898 1501

19. LINCOLN STATE FOREST

This forest is 25 km south-east of Gilgandra and reached via Maila Rd from the Newell Hwy at Balladoran.

Old Lincoln Forest Headquarters camping area

Site of former forestry camp 27 km south-east of Gilgandra. 2WD access in dry weather only, via Flans Rd off Denmire Rd. Bring water. Additional map ref.: NSWRD 111 Q8.

Further information & bookings: State Forests, Dubbo **Tel.:** (02) 6884 5288 **Email:** cumberland@sf.nsw.gov.au

20. MACQUARIE WOODS

Macquarie Woods is located inside Vittoria State Forest and is a demonstration forest 'to showcase the uses and beauty of plantation and native trees'. It is located 29 km west of Bathurst, signposted via Cashens Lane off the Mitchell Hwy.

Heritage Grove camping area

Limited drinking water – best to bring your own. Firewood supplied. Additional map ref.: NSWRD 142 G9.

Further information & bookings: State Forests, Bathurst **Tel.:** (02) 6331 2044 **Email:** cumberland@sf.nsw.gov.au

21. MOUNT CANOBOLAS STATE RECREATION AREA

There are unusual rock formations and varied flora in this recreation area 10 km south-west of Orange. Access is via Pinnacle Rd or Canobolas Rd from Orange. The centrepiece of the park is the 1395-m-high Mt Canobolas. You should take in the views from one of the park's many lookouts; there are also numerous walking tracks to explore.

Federal Falls camping area

Near falls, 15 km south-west of Orange. Signposted via Towac Way from Pinnacle Rd. Bring firewood. Additional map ref.: NSWRD 141 V7.

The Teahouse picnic and camping area

Near park entrance, 13 km south-west of Orange. Signposted via Canobolas Rd from Pinnacle Rd. Bring firewood. Additional map ref.: NSWRD 141 V7.

Further information & bookings: NPWS, Bathurst **Tel.:** (02) 6332 9488 **Email:** central.west@npws.nsw.gov.au

22. MUNGHORN GAP NATURE RESERVE

This reserve is a renowned birdwatching spot, home to lyrebirds, bowerbirds and the rare regent honeyeater. It is 35 km north of Mudgee, near Cooyal, and is reached via Wollar–Mudgee Rd. Explore the walking track to Castle Rocks.

Honeyeater Flat camping area

Large open area suitable for groups. Bring drinking water and firewood or gas/fuel stove. Additional map ref.: NSWRD 123 S9.

Further information & bookings: NPWS, Mudgee **Tel.:** (02) 6372 7199 **Email:** mudgee@npws.nsw.gov.au

23. NANGAR NATIONAL PARK

This park is 10 km east of Eugowra and is signposted off The Escort Way (Eugowra–Orange Rd) east of the township. Roads in the park are dry-weather only. There are good views from Nangar Ridge and good bushwalking.

Bush camping area

Bush camping areas throughout the park – no facilities. Caravan access possible to Dripping Rock Homestead. Bring drinking water and firewood. Additional map ref.: NSWRD 140 K8 (access road).

Further information & bookings: NPWS, Forbes **Tel.:** (02) 6851 4429

24. OPHIR

Ophir is 30 km north-east of Orange and was the site of the first goldfield in Australia, from 1851. It is reached via Ophir Rd or Lewis Ponds Rd from Orange (check conditions if towing a caravan). You can explore the old mine workings (take care near shafts) or try your hand at fossicking, go bushwalking or fish for trout.

The Junction picnic and camping area

At the site of former Ophir township. Access via Ophir Rd from Orange. Caravan access only possible if using a 4WD tow vehicle – steep grades. Camping is possible anywhere in the reserve. Wildlife refuge. Limited drinking water – best to bring own. Bring firewood. Additional map ref.: NSWRD 142 E4.

Further information & bookings: Cabonne Shire Council **Tel.:** (02) 6364 2000 **Website:** www.cabonnecountry.com.au

25. PILLIGA STATE FOREST

This is a large forested area between Baradine, Narrabri and Pilliga. There are many roads into the forest, but the main access is via Pilliga Forest Way Rd from Baradine or from the Newell Hwy south of Narrabri. All roads are dry weather only; many are impassable after rain. It is a remote area with many tracks – navigation can be difficult and you should take maps. Check out the koala colony near The Aloes camping area. The legendary bunyip is also said to live in these forests – keep your camera handy!

Rocky Creek Mill camping area

Large grassed area on site of old sawmill 29 km north of Baradine. Access in dry weather only via Pilliga Forest Way Rd from Baradine. Bring drinking water. Additional map ref.: NSWRD 54 F9.

Salt Caves camping area

Located 37 km north-east of Baradine at junction of Wellyard Rd and County Line Rd. Access in dry weather only via Wellyard Rd from Sixteen Foot Rd off Cumbil Rd from Baradine. Unusual rock formations. Water from tank. Additional map ref.: NSWRD 54 G9.

Schwagers Bore camping area

A small secluded site near bore 51 km north-east of Baradine. Access in dry weather only via Pilliga Forest Way Rd. Bring drinking water. Additional map ref.: NSWRD 54 G9.

The Aloes camping area

Near Etoo Creek 23 km north of Baradine. Access in dry weather only via Pilliga Forest Way Rd. Good koala-spotting area. Bring drinking water. Additional map ref.: NSWRD 54 F9.

Further information & bookings: State Forests, Baradine **Tel.:** (02) 6843 1607

26. SOFALA/TURON GOLDFIELDS

Sofala, 45 km north of Bathurst, is Australia's oldest surviving gold town, founded in 1851. The town is located on the Turon River and is signposted via Peel Rd from Kelso or Illford. Activities include exploring, fossicking, picnicking and fishing for trout. Camping areas are located along the Turon River, with caravan access possible to some sites. These are bush camping areas with no facilities – bring drinking water and firewood.

Coles Bridge
13 km west of Sofala on Turondale Rd. Additional map ref.: NSWRD 143 N2.

Crossley Bridge
500 m west of Sofala over bridge. Additional map ref.: NSWRD 143 P2.

Ration Point
3 km east of Sofala on Upper Turon Rd. Additional map ref.: NSWRD 143 Q2.

Wallaby Rocks
5 km west of Sofala on Hill End Rd. Additional map ref.: NSWRD 143 P2.

Further information & bookings: Sofala General Store **Tel.:** (02) 6337 7025

27. SUNNY CORNER

Sunny Corner is another of this region's gold towns, founded in the 1880s. It is 36 km east of Bathurst and signposted from the Great Western Hwy. Activities here include 4WD touring in the surrounding forests.

Sunny Corner Recreation Reserve

In Sunny Corner village. Access via Sunny Corner Rd. At time of going to press this site was being upgraded – some facilities may change and fees may be introduced. Bring firewood. Additional map ref.: NSWRD 143 T8.

Further information & bookings: DLWC, Orange **Tel.:** (02) 6393 4384

28. SUNNY CORNER STATE FOREST

This forest is a mixture of pine and native trees and is 28 km east of Bathurst, reached from the Great Western Hwy. Activities include 4WD touring in the surrounding forests.

Marys Park camping area

Bush camping – no facilities – 2 km south-west of Sunny Corner village. Signposted off Sunny Corner–Kirkconnell Rd. Bring water. Additional map ref.: NSWRD 143 T8.

Further information & bookings: State Forests, Bathurst **Tel.:** (02) 6331 2044 **Email:** cumberland@sf.nsw.gov.au

29. TRUNKEY CREEK

This village is 56 km south of Bathurst and is reached via the Bathurst–Crookwell Rd. It is the northern gateway to Abercrombie Caves. Wander around the village – there are many old buildings from the gold-rush days.

Trunkey Creek Showground

In Trunkey Creek village. Access via Arthur St. Bring firewood. Additional map ref.: NSWRD 150 G7.

Further information & bookings: Black Stump Hotel **Tel.:** (02) 6368 8604 **Camping fees:** $5.00 per vehicle/night; ranger collects fees or pay at hotel

30. VULCAN STATE FOREST

This forest 24 km south-west of Oberon, near Black Springs, comprises mostly of pine plantation. Access is via Oberon–Black Springs Rd. There are sapphire-fossicking areas close by.

Black Springs camping area

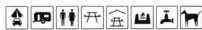

In Black Springs village opposite general store. Bring firewood. Additional map ref.: NSWRD 151 Q7.

Further information & bookings: State Forests, Bathurst **Tel.:** (02) 6331 2044 **Email:** cumberland@sf.nsw.gov.au

31. WARREN WEIR

This weir is on the Macquarie River 5 km south of Warren. Access is from Warren via Ellengerah Rd from the end of Dubbo St. Water activities are not permitted here.

Warren Weir camping area

Bring drinking water and firewood. Additional map ref.: NSWRD 61 V4.

Further information & bookings: DLWC, Warren **Tel.:** (02) 6847 4186

32. WARRUMBUNGLE NATIONAL PARK

This park is an extremely popular one, especially with bushwalkers and rock climbers, located 35 km west of Coonabarabran. It is signposted off John Renshaw Parkway from Coonabarabran and there is also access via Tooraweenah and from Coonamble. The Warrumbungle Range is of volcanic origin. There are plenty of activities – walk to the Breadknife and look at the abundant wildlife.

The Breadknife, Warrumbungle National Park

Balor Hut

Walk-in-only access via Grand High Tops walking track. Hut must be booked and a deposit paid. Permit required. Gas/fuel stove preferred. Additional map ref.: NSWRD 62 E2.

Burbie Camp camping area

Walk-in-only access via Burbie Track from John Renshaw Parkway. Permit required. Gas/fuel stove preferred. Additional map ref.: NSWRD 62 E2.

Camp Blackman camping area

Main camping area in park, signposted from John Renshaw Parkway. Some powered sites available. Bring firewood. Additional map ref.: NSWRD 62 E2.

Camp Elongery camping area

A camping area for booked groups. Signposted from John Renshaw Parkway. Additional map ref.: NSWRD 62 E2.

Camp Pincham camping area

A walk-in site 200 m from the carpark. Signposted from John Renshaw Parkway. Gas/fuel stove preferred. Additional map ref.: NSWRD 62 E2.

Camp Wambelong camping area

A camping area for booked groups. Signposted from John Renshaw Parkway. Bring firewood. Additional map ref.: NSWRD 62 E2.

Gunneemooroo camping area

Located 60 km north-east of Gilgandra. Signposted 4WD-only access via Gummin Rd off Tooraweenah Rd. Permit required – contact visitor centre. Bring water. Gas/fuel stove preferred. Additional map ref.: NSWRD 62 E2.

The Woolshed camping area

Signposted from John Renshaw Parkway. Group camping area only – bookings required. Bring firewood. Additional map ref.: NSWRD 62 E2.

Bush campsites

Bush campsites include Danu Camp on the Burbie Track, Ogma and Dows camps on the Western High Tops Track, and Hurleys Camp via the Grand High Tops Track. Walk-in-only access. Permit required. Gas/fuel stove preferred. Additional map ref.: NSWRD 62 E2.

Further information & bookings: Warrumbungle National Park Visitors Centre **Tel.:** (02) 6825 4364 **Park use fee:** $6.00 per vehicle/day **Camping fees:** *Balor Hut:* $3.00 per adult/night, $2.00 per child/night *Camp Blackman:* $7.50 per adult and $4.00 per child (age 5–15) per night powered, $5.00 per adult and $3.00 per child per night unpowered *Camp Elongery, Camp Wambelong, Gunneemooroo and The Woolshed:* $5.00 per adult/night, $3.00 per child (age 5–15) per night *Camp Pincham:* $3.00 per adult/night, $2.00 per child/night. Call in at visitor centre (open 9 am–4 pm daily) before setting up camp; self-registration applies outside these hours and advance bookings are essential for group camping areas

33. WATTLE FLAT

Wattle Flat was originally settled as a goldmining village in the 1850s. It is 40 km north of Bathurst and signposted off the Bathurst–Sofala Rd from Kelso.

Wattle Heritage Grounds

This is 1 km west of Wattle Flat. Signposted from Thompson St. Contains small stand of rare native argyle apple trees. Bring water and firewood. Additional map ref.: NSWRD 143 P3.

Further information & bookings: Wattle Flat General Store **Tel.:** (02) 6337 7133

34. WEDDIN MOUNTAINS NATIONAL PARK

This park is reputed to have been the hideout of bushranger Ben Hall and his gang. It is 20 km south-west of Grenfell and signposted via Holy Camp Rd or Back Piney Range Rd off the Mid Western Hwy. Explore Seatons Farm – a Depression farm in original condition from the 1930s through to 1960s. Other activities include bushwalking and birdwatching.

Holy Camp camping area

Shaded camping area 15 km west of Grenfell. Signposted from Holy Camp Rd. Bring water and firewood. Additional map ref.: NSWRD 148 A9.

Seatons camping area

Located 29 km west of Grenfell. Signposted via Bimbi Rd from Back Piney Range Rd. Those towing a caravan should check road conditions before travelling. Short walk to Seatons Farm and walk to Ben Halls Cave. Bring water and firewood. Additional map ref.: NSWRD 69 V5.

Further information & bookings: NPWS, Forbes **Tel.:** (02) 6851 4429

35. WINDAMERE DAM

This is a water storage on the Cudgegong River 35 km south-east of Mudgee. It is reached from the Castlereagh Hwy (Ilford–Mudgee Rd).

Cudgegong Waters Park

Access via Castlereagh Hwy. Bring firewood (it is also available for purchase). Bookings necessary for powered sites in peak periods. Additional map ref.: NSWRD 133 S6.

Further information & bookings: Cudgegong Waters Park **Tel.:** (02) 6358 8462 **Park use fee:** $2.00 per vehicle at boom gate **Camping fees:** From $5.00 per adult/night, power additional

36. WOLLEMI NATIONAL PARK – WESTERN SECTION

See also Wollemi National Park – southern section, *page 11*

This World Heritage-listed park is the largest wilderness area in New South Wales. The western section is 25 km east of Rylstone and is reached via Narrango Rd. At Dunns Swamp activities include camping, swimming, fishing and canoeing. Self-sufficient bushwalkers can undertake more extensive trips into the wilderness sections of the park.

Dunns Swamp camping area

Beside Kandos Weir on Cudgegong River. Boil water from dam before use. Limited firewood supplied – best to bring your own. Additional map ref.: NSWRD 134 E7.

Further information & bookings: NPWS, Mudgee **Tel.:** (02) 6372 7199 **Email:** mudgee@npws.nsw.gov.au **Camping fees:** May be collected at peak times

37. WYANGALA WATERS STATE PARK

This is a water storage on the Lachlan River 37 km east of Cowra. It is signposted on Darbys Falls Rd from Cowra. It is another popular watersports area.

Wyangala Waters camping area

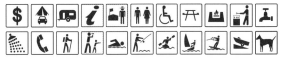

Access via Darbys Falls Rd or Woodstock–Wyangala Rd. Gas/fuel stove preferred. Bookings necessary for powered sites in peak periods. Additional map ref.: NSWRD 149 V10.

Further information & bookings: Wyangala Waters State Park **Tel.:** (02) 6345 0877 **Email:** wyangala@ix.net.au **Camping fees:** From $13.20 per site/night, power additional

38. YARRIGAN STATE FOREST

This forest is 15 km south of Baradine near Bugaldie. It is reached via Bugaldie Rd from Bugaldie or from the Coonabarabran–Baradine Rd.

Yarrigan picnic and camping area

Access in dry weather only via Ridge Rd off Tipperary Rd from Coonabarabran–Baradine Rd south of Barradine. Bring drinking water and firewood. Additional map ref.: NSWRD 62 F1.

Further information & bookings: State Forests, Baradine **Tel.:** (02) 6843 1607 **Email:** cumberland@sf.nsw.gov.au

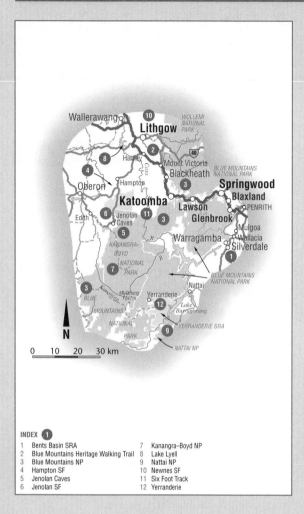

INDEX ①

1 Bents Basin SRA	7 Kanangra–Boyd NP
2 Blue Mountains Heritage Walking Trail	8 Lake Lyell
3 Blue Mountains NP	9 Nattai NP
4 Hampton SF	10 Newnes SF
5 Jenolan Caves	11 Six Foot Track
6 Jenolan SF	12 Yerranderie

THE SPECTACULAR BLUE MOUNTAINS TO THE WEST OF SYDNEY FEATURE MAGNIFICENT MOUNTAIN SCENERY, UNDERGROUND CAVES, DEEP VALLEYS, WILD FORESTS AND GREAT BUSHWALKING TRAILS. FAMOUS LANDMARKS INCLUDE THE THREE SISTERS ROCK FORMATION, THE JENOLAN CAVES AND THE RED HANDS CAVE, WHERE ABORIGINAL STENCILS OF RED-OCHRE HANDS COVER THE WALLS. THE AREA ALSO HAS SOME GREAT CAMPING OPPORTUNITIES.

Within the northern region of the Blue Mountains National Park are a number of vehicle-based campsites along with some remote walk-in bush sites for self-sufficient walkers. In the south of the park camping can be found along the Old Oberon–Colong Stock Route. Camping here is vehicle-based – one area is suitable for caravans and another site is accessible by four-wheel drive only.

Adjoining the northern boundary of Blue Mountains National Park and north-east of Lithgow is Newnes State Forest. The large Bungleboori camping area here is only a short distance from the Zig-Zag Railway, the fascinating glow worm tunnel and the interesting rock formations of the Lost City. Campers can explore the surrounding forests by four-wheel drive vehicle or mountain bike.

Many more interesting rock formations can be found in Kanangra–Boyd National Park. Amazing views can be had at Kanangra Walls lookout, a short distance from Boyd Crossing camping ground. From the lookout are numerous walking trails leading down into the park's valleys.

Along the Jenolan Caves Rd camping can be found at Hampton State Forest and Jenolan State Forest. These sites are ideal for caravanners wishing to visit Jenolan Caves but who cannot take their vans along the narrow, winding access road. Closer to Jenolan Caves vehicle-based camping can be found beside the river at the Jenolan River camping area.

BEST CAMPSITES

Euroka Clearing camping area
Blue Mountains National Park

Mount Werong Campground
Blue Mountains National Park

Jenolan River camping area
Jenolan Caves

Boyd Crossing camping ground
Kanangra–Boyd National Park

Lake Lyell camping ground
Lake Lyell

BEST TIME TO VISIT

Spring and autumn. During summer temperatures can reach the high 30s and during winter snow can fall.

1. BENTS BASIN STATE RECREATION AREA

This is a popular recreation area beside the Nepean River 25 km south of Penrith, near Wallacia. It is signposted from Bringelly and Wallacia. The park is open 9 am–4.30 pm daily and a kiosk is open at weekends and in holidays.

Bents Basin camping area

Bring own firewood – gas/fuel stove preferred. Advance bookings essential. Additional map ref.: NSWRD 10 H10.

Further information & bookings: NPWS, Bents Basin **Tel.:** (02) 4774 8662 **Email:** bentsbsn@ozemail.com.au **Park entry fee:** $6.00 per vehicle/day **Camping fees:** $5.00 per adult/night, $3.00 per child (age 5–15) per night

2. BLUE MOUNTAINS HERITAGE WALKING TRAIL

This trail was part of the original route across the Blue Mountains to Lithgow. It runs to the north-west of Mount Victoria and you can access the walking trail via Mt York Rd from Mount Victoria and from Hartley Vale.

Lockyers Trackhead camping area

Walk-in only access via Lawson Long Alley between Hartley Vale and Collits Inn. Obtain trail brochure from DLWC. Additional map ref.: NSWRD 152 E1.

Further information & bookings: DLWC, Orange **Tel.:** (02) 6393 4300

3. BLUE MOUNTAINS NATIONAL PARK
see page 44

4. HAMPTON STATE FOREST

This forest contains large pine plantations. It is 27 km east of Oberon near Hampton. Access is via Jenolan Caves Rd from the Great Western Hwy or Duckmaloi Rd from Oberon.

Millionth Acre picnic area

At the intersection of Jenolan Caves Rd and Duckmaloi Rd, 4 km south of Hampton. Suitable for overnight stay only.

A platform stop on the Scenic Railway in the Blue Mountains

Bicentennial National Trail passes through forest. Additional map ref.: NSWRD 152 A4.

Further information & bookings: Cumberland State Forest **Tel.:** 1300 655 687 **Email:** cumberland@sf.nsw.gov.au

5. JENOLAN CAVES

These famous and spectacular limestone caves are 50 km south of Lithgow. They are reached via Jenolan Caves Rd from the Great Western Hwy. The final section of the road is steep and windy.

Jenolan River camping area

Beside Jenolan River near caves. Obtain directions after paying fees at ticket office. Bring own firewood. Additional map ref.: NSWRD 152 A7.

Further information & bookings: Jenolan Caves Ticket Office **Tel.:** (02) 6359 3311 **Email:** reception@jenolancaves. org.au **Website:** www.jenolancaves.org.au **Camping fees:** $11.00 per site/night; pay fees at the ticket office at Jenolan Caves

6. JENOLAN STATE FOREST

This forest is 30 km east of Oberon near Hampton. Access is via Jenolan Caves Rd from the Great Western Hwy.

Jenolan camping ground

Beside Jenolan Caves Rd 10 km south of Hampton. Additional map ref.: NSWRD 152 A6.

Further information & bookings: Cumberland State Forest **Tel.:** 1300 655 687 **Email:** cumberland@sf.nsw.gov.au

7. KANANGRA–BOYD NATIONAL PARK

This large, mostly wilderness park is about 50 km south-east of Oberon. There are a number of access routes to the park for 2WD vehicles, including Jenolan Caves Rd and Edith Rd, Shooters Hill Rd and Mt Werong Rd from Oberon. Other routes will require a 4WD vehicle. Once here, take a look at the stunning Kanangra Walls. The park is popular with bushwalkers, mountain-bike riders and trout anglers.

Boyd Crossing camping ground

Main camping area in park. Access via Kanangra Walls Rd. Close to Kanangra Walls and a good base for exploring park. Water from creek – boil before use. Bring firewood or gas/fuel stove. Additional map ref.: NSWRD 152 B10.

Dingo Dell camping area

Large grassed area beside small creek. Access by 4WD only from Kowmung River Trail, off Kanangra Walls Rd. Water from creek – boil before use. Bring firewood or gas/fuel stove. Additional map ref.: NSWRD 151 V10.

BLUE MOUNTAINS NATIONAL PARK

The largest national park in the Sydney region, Blue Mountains National Park is 100 km west of Sydney and covers an area to both the north and south of the Great Western Hwy. There is 2WD vehicle access to the major points of interest: Echo Point and the Three Sisters. The park is popular with daytrippers, bushwalkers and adventure seekers and there are numerous camping areas.

NORTHERN SECTION

Acacia Flat camping area

Walk-in camping for self-sufficient walkers. Contact NPWS, Blackheath, for access details. Drinking water from creek – boil before use. Gas/fuel stove preferred. Additional map ref.: NSWRD 152 G3.

Burra Korain Flat camping area

This is 8 km from Mount Victoria. Walk-in camping for self-sufficient walkers. Area is a three-hour walk from Victoria Falls. Drinking water from creek – boil before use. Gas/fuel stove preferred. Additional map ref.: NSWRD 152 G2.

Burralow picnic and camping area

An open grassy area beside Burralow Creek. Signposted from Patterson Range Fire Trail off Bells Line of Rd 1 km east of Bilpin. 4WD recommended in wet weather. Boil creek water before drinking. Bring own firewood. Additional map ref.: NSWRD 153 M2.

Euroka Clearing camping area

Signposted from Bruce Rd in Glenbrook. Gates closed 6 pm–8.30 am (7 pm–8.30 am during daylight saving). Permit required to camp and bookings required. Bring drinking water. Bring firewood or gas/fuel stove. Advance bookings essential for holiday periods and should be made at least two weeks before intended visit. Additional map ref.: NSWRD 10 G2.

Ingar picnic and camping area

Located 13 km south-east of Wentworth Falls. Access via Queen Elizabeth Drive off Tableland Rd. Access road is slippery after rain (can be closed). Bring drinking water. Gas/fuel stove preferred. Additional map ref.: NSWRD 152 K6.

Murphys Glen camping area

Situated 6 km from Woodford. Access via Bedford Rd. Access road is steep in sections and slippery after rain (can be closed). Bring drinking water. Gas/fuel stove preferred. Additional map ref.: NSWRD 23 K7.

Perrys Lookdown camping area

The area is 9 km from Blackheath. Access (walk-in only) from Hat Hill Rd. Five sites; one-night stay only. Bring drinking water. Gas/fuel stove preferred. Additional map ref.: NSWRD 22 H1.

Further information & bookings:
NPWS, Blackheath **Tel.:** (02) 4787 8877 **Email:** blue.mountains@ npws.nsw.gov.au *or*
NPWS, Richmond **Tel.:** (02) 4588 5247 **Email:** richmond@ npws.nsw.gov.au
Park use fee: *Euroka Clearing only:* $6.00 per vehicle/day
Camping fees: *Euroka Clearing:* $5.00 per adult/night, $3.00 per child (age 5–15) per night

SOUTHERN SECTION

Batsh Camp camping area

A base for wilderness walks. Signposted from Old Oberon–Colong Stock Route (Yerranderie Rd). 2WD access in dry weather only. Bring drinking water and gas/fuel stove. Additional map ref.: NSWRD 160 B3.

Limeburners Flat camping area

Large grassed clearing beside a small creek. Dispersed bush camping – no facilities. Only access is 4WD in dry weather via Limeburners Trail from Wombeyan Caves Rd or Old Oberon–Colong Stock Route. Additional map ref.: NSWRD 159 V3.

Mount Werong Campground

Signposted from Old Oberon–Colong Stock Route (Yerranderie Rd). 2WD access in dry weather. Bring firewood. Additional map ref.: NSWRD 159 V2.

Further information & bookings: NPWS, Oberon **Tel.:** (02) 6336 1972

Across the valley

Govetts Leap, via Blackheath, offers superb views across the misty folds and fissures of the Grose Valley. To explore the valley at ground level, take the Blue Gum Forest Walk, a five-hour walk through forests of blue-trunked gums, or the Grand Canyon Track, a 3.5-hour tour deep into a mountain canyon.

Mountain rides

There are two rides into the Jamison Valley that are as famous as the surrounding scenery. One, the Scenic Skyway, is a cable car that glides 300 metres above the valley. The other, the Scenic Railway, dates back to the 1880s and runs at an angle of 52 degrees down the face of the escarpment. Access to these attractions is from Katoomba.

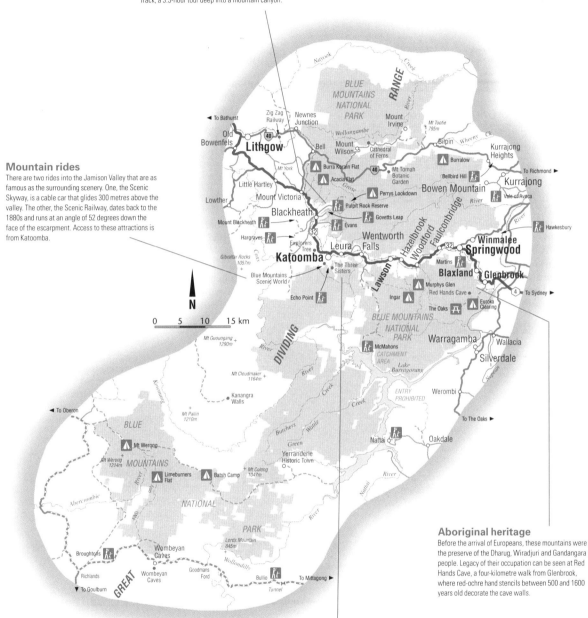

Aboriginal heritage

Before the arrival of Europeans, these mountains were the preserve of the Dharug, Wiradjuri and Gandangara people. Legacy of their occupation can be seen at Red Hands Cave, a four-kilometre walk from Glenbrook, where red-ochre hand stencils between 500 and 1600 years old decorate the cave walls.

Scenic sisters

The Three Sisters rock formation is the scenic icon of the Blue Mountains. The feature, comprising three vertically inclined rock outcrops, is the result of millions of years of erosion. See it from the lookout at Echo Point or take a walk to its base nestled within the forests of the Jamison Valley.

Kowmung Wild River walk-in camping area

Walk-in access from Kowmung River Trail (4WD only). Located 500 m downstream of Kowmung River crossing. Bush camping – no facilities. Water from creek – boil before use. Additional map ref.: NSWRD 151 V10.

Further information & bookings: NPWS, Oberon **Tel.:** (02) 6336 1972 **Email:** oberon@npws.nsw.gov.au **Park use fee:** $6.00 per vehicle/day; fee payable at Boyd Crossing camping area and Kanangra Walls carpark **Camping fees:** May have been implemented since publication

8. LAKE LYELL

Lake Lyell is a large water storage and watersports venue 11 km south-west of Lithgow, on Magpie Hollow Rd. It is reached via Rydal Rd from the Great Western Hwy.

Lake Lyell camping ground

On shores of Lake Lyell. Signposted from Rydal Rd. Bring own firewood. Kiosk. Bookings essential during summer. Additional map ref.: NSWRD 152 B1.

Further information & bookings: Lake Lyell camping ground **Tel.:** (02) 6355 6347 **Email:** lakelyel@lisp.com.au **Camping fees:** From $10.00 per site/night up to 5 people, $2.00 each additional person

9. NATTAI NATIONAL PARK

A wilderness park 30 km south-west of Camden, near Thirlmere and bordering Lake Burragorang. The park protects Sydney's catchments and water supply and is used for low-impact bushwalking and bush camping. There are few vehicle access points.

Starlights Trail camping area

Walk-in access via 5-km track from carpark at end of Wattle Ridge Rd from Hilltop. Campsite is beside Nattai River. Suitable for experienced and self-sufficient walkers only. Contact NPWS Nattai to register. Gas/fuel stoves only. Additional map ref.: NSWRD 160 H5.

Further information & bookings: NPWS, Nattai **Tel.:** (02) 4677 0859

10. NEWNES STATE FOREST

This forest is 10 km north-east of Lithgow, next to Blue Mountains National Park. There is 2WD access in dry weather via State Mine Hill Rd from Lithgow. Once here, visit the majestic glow worm tunnel.

Bungleboori camping area

At the junction of Glow Worm Tunnel Rd and Blackfellow Hand Rd. 2WD access in dry weather only. Road can be rough and corrugated at times. Good base to explore glow worm tunnel, the Lost City and Deep Pass. Gas/fuel stove only during fire danger period (Oct.–March). Additional map ref.: NSWRD 144 D9.

Further information & bookings: Cumberland State Forest **Tel.:** 1300 655 687 **Email:** cumberland@sf.nsw.gov.au

11. SIX FOOT TRACK

This is a long-distance walking track which follows the original bridle (horse) track from Katoomba to Jenolan Caves. It takes three–four days to walk the entire track and a moderate fitness level is required, but it can be walked in stages. The trackhead is at the Explorers Tree 2.5 km west of Katoomba. Campsites along the track have basic facilities. Be self-sufficient. Bring drinking water – water from Coxs River not suitable for drinking. Gas/fuel stove preferred. Purchase the Six Foot Track map/guide published by the DLWC for further details.

Old Ford Reserve camping area

8 km from trackhead. Additional map ref.: NSWRD 21 B5 (Katoomba trackhead).

Coxs River camping area

14 km from trackhead.

Alum Creek camping area

19.5 km from trackhead.

Black Range camping area

31.5 km from trackhead.

Further information & bookings: DLWC, Parramatta **Tel.:** (02) 9895 6225

12. YERRANDERIE

This old silvermining ghost town is on the edge of Blue Mountains National Park. It is signposted off the Old Oberon–Colong Stock Route from Oberon–Goulburn Rd at Porters Retreat. 2WD vehicles can reach Yerranderie in dry weather only – 4WD is recommended. These days Yerranderie is divided into two parts – Government Town and Private Town. Government Town is owned and run by the government, though to make matters confusing, there are also some private residences there. Private Town, about 1 km apart from Government Town, is being gradually restored by a private owner, and there is a small fee to enter it if you are not also camping there. Visit the museum or walk to the old mines. This is a popular 4WD destination.

Government Town camping area

Access via Old Oberon–Colong Stock Route. Limited water supply. Bring firewood or gas/fuel stove. Additional map ref.: NSWRD 160 E3.

Further information & bookings: Sydney Catchment Authority **Tel.:** (02) 4720 0300

Private Town camping area

Access via Old Oberon–Colong Stock Route. Communal kitchen. Firewood supplied. Accommodation also available. Additional map ref.: NSWRD 160 E3.

Further information & bookings: Caretaker **Tel.:** (02) 4659 6165 **Email:** admin@yerranderie.com **Website:** www.yerranderie.com **Camping fees:** $10.00 per adult/night, $5.00 per child under 12 per night

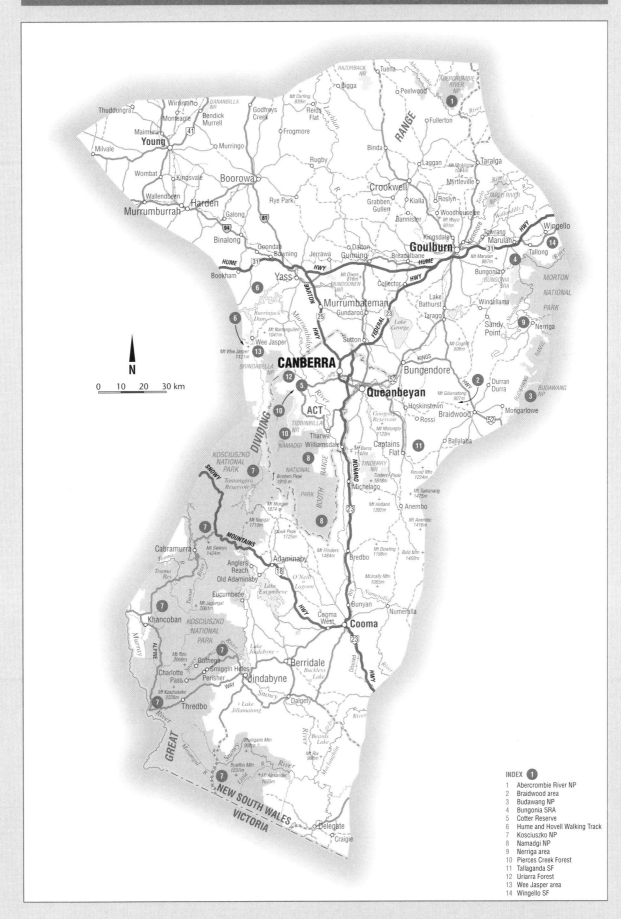

Stretching from the towns of Young and Goulburn down to the Australian Capital Territory, Kosciuszko National Park and the Victorian border, this region is an eclectic mix of city, farming lands, forests, caves and, of course, the famous Snowy Mountains.

Namadgi National Park lies within the boundaries of the ACT. The camping areas here are suitable for vehicle-based camping and small campervans. The park offers some challenging overnight bushwalks along with established day walks from each of the camping areas, and it is also a destination for cycling and horseriding.

Following south from Namadgi is Kosciuszko National Park, home to Australia's highest peak and the famous Snowy River. The park protects some spectacular high country – dotted with old homesteads, huts and mine sites, and crisscrossed with mountain streams, high-altitude touring routes and a vast network of walking, horseriding and mountain bike trails.

In winter the mountains are covered with snow, with the streaked colours of snow gums providing a picturesque break from the dazzling white covering the ground. Parka-clad skiers flock to the slopes from June through to October. In spring and summer the snow-covered fields are transformed into a blaze of colour with alpine wildflowers. Other natural features include the caves at Yarrangobilly and Blue Waterholes, and the Yarrangobilly thermal pool.

Kosciuszko National Park offers a large range of camping options, from remote walk-in sites and sites accessible by four-wheel drive only to sites suitable for caravans.

Campsites along the Alpine Way, in the south of the park, have a range of facilities. All the sites have access to a number of the region's walking trails, and those situated close to the Thredbo, Swampy Plain and Upper Murray rivers offer opportunities to swim, fish and canoe. Along the Barry Way, from Jindabyne to the Victorian border, campsites are located beside the Snowy River, where swimming, fishing and canoeing are also possible.

In the north of the park, travelling along the Snowy Mountains Highway from Tumut to Adaminaby, there are numerous campsites beside the eastern shores of the Blowering Reservoir. Some of these have boat-launching facilities.

BEST CAMPSITES

Cotter Campground
Cotter Reserve

Mount Clear Campground
Namadgi National Park

Geehi camping area
Kosciuszko National Park

Three Mile Dam camping area
Kosciuszko National Park

Cooinbil Hut camping area
Kosciuszko National Park

BEST TIME TO VISIT

Camping in the area north of Canberra is good all year round, though in winter the nights can become quite cool. In alpine areas the best time to camp is in spring, summer and autumn. Camping during the winter months is only recommended for experienced ski tourers.

Snow gum near Adaminaby

1. ABERCROMBIE RIVER NATIONAL PARK

This is a remote park with many rivers and creeks. It is 40 km south of Oberon and 60 km north of Goulburn. There is 2WD access from Arkstone Rd off Goulburn–Oberon Rd and 4WD-only access via Felled Timber Rd off Oberon–Goulburn Rd then Brass Walls Trail. In the park itself there is limited 2WD access – most tracks are suitable for 4WD vehicles only. The park has good trout fishing but Macquarie perch, silver perch, river blackfish and Murray crays are protected – release if caught. Other activities include bushwalking, mountain-bike riding and 4WD touring.

Bumaroo Ford camping area

Located 29 km north of Taralga and 75 km north of Goulburn at Abercrombie River crossing. Signposted from Oberon–Goulburn Rd. Water from river – boil before use. Bring firewood. Additional map ref.: NSWRD 159 Q4.

Silent Creek camping area

This is a large area ideal for groups, 45 km south of Black Springs. 4WD access in dry weather only via Abercrombie Fire Trail from Emden Vale (locality). Bring water – Silent Creek runs underground. Bring firewood. Additional map ref.: NSWRD 159 P4.

The Beach camping area

Beside Abercrombie River 43 km south of Black Springs. 4WD access in dry weather only. Signposted off Abercrombie Fire Trail from Emden Vale (locality). Water from river – boil before use. Bring firewood. Additional map ref.: NSWRD 159 N3.

The Sink camping area

Beside Retreat River, 2.3 km from Abercrombie Fire Trail junction and 41 km south of Black Springs. 4WD access is recommended via Retreat Fire Trail from Emden Vale (locality). Water from river – boil before use. Bring firewood. Additional map ref.: NSWRD 159 P2.

Further information & bookings: NPWS, Oberon **Tel.:** (02) 6336 1972 **Email:** oberon@npws.nsw.gov.au

2. BRAIDWOOD AREA

Braidwood lies 86 km south of Goulburn. It was founded in 1839 and has been declared a historic town by the National Trust. It was a pastoral centre before the discovery of gold in the area in 1851, when it became the principal town of the southern goldfields.

Warri Camping Reserve

Beside the Kings Hwy and the Shoalhaven River, 13 km north-west of Braidwood. Water from river – boil before use. Bring firewood. Additional map ref.: NSWRD 175 Q7.

Further information & bookings: Tallaganda Shire Council **Tel.:** (02) 4842 2225 **Email:** shire@tallaganda.nsw.gov.au **Website:** www.tallaganda.nsw.gov.au

3. BUDAWANG NATIONAL PARK

This remote wilderness park is 18 km east of Braidwood. Access to its western section is via Budawang Rd from Mongarlowe, and to the eastern section via Yadboro Rd and Western Distributor Rd (follow the signs to Pigeon House Mountain from the Princes Hwy at Milton or south of Ulladulla). It is a self-sufficient bushwalking area.

Long Gully camping area

Beside Yadboro River, 36 km west of Milton. Access via Yadboro Rd and Long Gully Rd. One night stay only. Additional map ref.: NSWRD 176 D7.

Further information & bookings: NPWS, Nowra **Tel.:** (02) 4423 2170

4. BUNGONIA STATE RECREATION AREA

This area is 35 km east of Goulburn near Bungonia, and is signposted from the Hume Hwy south of Marulan. It contains the deepest limestone gorge in Australia. You can explore the caves here (for experienced cavers only), take in the views from the lookouts or go bushwalking. The area is also popular with abseilers, rock climbers and canyoners.

Bungonia State Recreation Area camping area

This is 15 km north-east of Bungonia. Signposted from Lookdown Rd. Boil water before use. Bring firewood. Gas/fuel stove preferred. Advance bookings essential. Additional map ref.: NSWRD 168 A7.

Further information & bookings: Bungonia State Recreation Area **Tel.:** (02) 4844 4277 **Email:** bungonia@npws.nsw.gov.au **Park use fee:** $6.00 per vehicle/day **Camping fees:** $5.00 per adult/night, $3.00 per child (age 5–15) per night

5. COTTER RESERVE

This reserve is beside the Murrumbidgee River 22 km west of Canberra. It is reached via Cotter Rd from Canberra. Activities here include swimming, fishing and canoeing.

Cotter Campground

Attractive camping area beside river. Firewood supplied. Site allocation is on a first-come basis. Additional map ref.: NSWRD 173 U7.

Further information: ACT Parks and Conservation Service, Murrumbidgee Corridor Office **Tel.:** (02) 6207 2425 **Website:** www.environment.act.gov.au **Camping fees:** From $11.00 per site/night for up to 2 people, each extra person $2.20; ranger collects fees

6. HUME AND HOVELL WALKING TRACK
see page 68

7. KOSCIUSZKO NATIONAL PARK see page 50

8. NAMADGI NATIONAL PARK

Namadgi National Park is the most northerly of Australia's alpine parks. It is 35 km south of Canberra, reached via Tharwa Rd from Canberra then Naas Rd. Call into Namadgi Visitors Centre on Naas Rd south of Tharwa prior to visiting the park. Activities here include bushwalking, cycling, horseriding and picnicking. Bookings are required to camp in the park and fees are payable in advance. A three-night limit applies to all Namadgi campgrounds.

KOSCIUSZKO NATIONAL PARK

Kosciuszko, one of Australia's most diverse national parks, stretches from Tumut in the north to the Victorian border in the south. There are many access roads, but the main access is via Jindabyne, Adaminaby, Tumut and Khancoban. The park contains Australia's highest mountain – Mt Kosciuszko. During winter the higher areas are snow covered and allow for winter sports such as skiing. Summer is ideal for bushwalking – walk to the top of Mt Kosciuszko – and mountain-bike riding. Late summer has displays of alpine wildflowers. There are many activities: take a tour of Yarrangobilly Caves, explore the limestone area at Blue Waterholes or visit historic cattlemen's huts. Contact one of the NPWS visitor centres for details.

SOUTHERN SECTION

The southern section of the park is the area south of Khancoban to the Victorian border. It is reached via Alpine Way between Jindabyne and Khancoban, and Kosciuszko Rd and Barry Way between Jindabyne and the state border.

ALPINE WAY – JINDABYNE TO KHANCOBAN

Geehi camping area

Large grassy area, popular in summer, at site of former Snowy Mountains Hydro camp beside Swampy Plain River, 31 km south of Khancoban. Signposted from Alpine Way. Caravan access is only possible from Khancoban. You can visit old huts and there is good trout fishing and a wheelchair-accessible walking trail. Water from river – boil before use. Bring firewood. Additional map ref.: NSWRD 188 D8.

Keebles Hut camping area

Located opposite Geehi Rest Area on Bears Flat. 4WD (river crossing) or walk-in access via Geehi Walls Trail from Geehi Rest Area. Near hut. Bring drinking water and firewood. Additional map ref.: NSWRD 188 D8.

Leatherbarrel Creek Rest Area

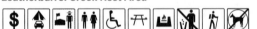

Small area near creek 16 km west of Thredbo. Signposted from Alpine Way. Bring water (do not drink river water) and firewood. Additional map ref.: NSWRD 194 D1.

Ngarigo Rest Area

Near Thredbo River, 24 km south-west of Jindabyne and 8 km north-east of Thredbo. Signposted from Alpine Way. Bring water (do not drink river water) and firewood. Additional map ref.: NSWRD 188 H10.

Old Geehi Hut camping area

Beside Swampy Plains River. 4WD (river crossings) or walk-in access via Geehi Walls Trail from Geehi Rest Area. Near hut. Bring drinking water and firewood. Additional map ref.: NSWRD 188 D8.

Thredbo Diggings camping area

Near Thredbo River 20 km south-west of Jindabyne. Signposted from Alpine Way. Bring water (do not drink river water) and firewood. Additional map ref.: NSWRD 188 J10.

Tom Groggin camping area

Large grassy area, popular in summer, beside Upper Murray River, 24 km west of Thredbo. Signposted from Alpine Way. Caravan access is only possible from Khancoban. Good trout fishing. 4WD access to Alpine National Park (Victoria). Water from river – boil before use. Bring firewood. Additional map ref.: NSWRD 194 C1.

Further information & bookings:
Khancoban Information Centre **Tel.:** (02) 6076 9373 *or* Snowy Region Visitors Centre **Tel.:** (02) 6450 5600
Park use fees: $15.00 per vehicle/day, which includes camping fee; fees payable at entrance station on Alpine Way or at any NPWS visitor centre

KOSCIUSZKO ROAD – JINDABYNE TO CHARLOTTE PASS

Island Bend camping area

Site of former Snowy Mountains Hydro camp near Snowy River, 23 km north-west of Jindabyne. Access via Guthega Rd from Kosciuszko Rd. Bring water (do not drink river water) and firewood. Additional map ref.: NSWRD 188 K7.

Further information & bookings: Snowy Region Visitors Centre **Tel.:** (02) 6450 5600 **Park use fee:** $15.00 per vehicle/day, which includes camping fee; fee payable at entrance station on Kosciuszko Rd or at any NPWS visitor centre

Kosciuszko Mountain Retreat

Located 14 km north-west of Jindabyne at Sawpit Creek. Access via Kosciuszko Rd. Kiosk and laundry facilities. Bring firewood; it is also available for purchase. Advance bookings required for peak times. Additional map ref.: NSWRD 189 L7.

Further information and bookings: Kosciuszko Mountain Retreat **Tel.:** (02) 6456 2224 **Email:** sawpitcreek@ bigpond.com **Website:** www.kositreat.com.au **Park use fee:** $15.00 per vehicle/day; fee payable at entrance station on Kosciuszko Rd or at any NPWS visitors centre **Camping fees:** From $15.00 per 2 people/night plus park use fee

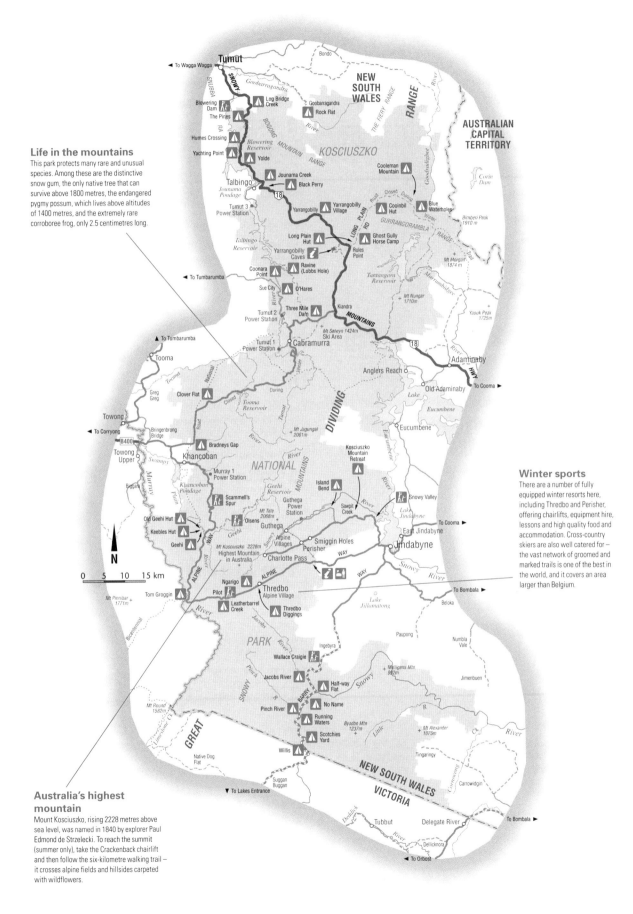

Life in the mountains

This park protects many rare and unusual species. Among these are the distinctive snow gum, the only native tree that can survive above 1800 metres, the endangered pygmy possum, which lives above altitudes of 1400 metres, and the extremely rare corroboree frog, only 2.5 centimetres long.

Winter sports

There are a number of fully equipped winter resorts here, including Thredbo and Perisher, offering chairlifts, equipment hire, lessons and high quality food and accommodation. Cross-country skiers are also well catered for – the vast network of groomed and marked trails is one of the best in the world, and it covers an area larger than Belgium.

Australia's highest mountain

Mount Kosciuszko, rising 2228 metres above sea level, was named in 1840 by explorer Paul Edmond de Strzelecki. To reach the summit (summer only), take the Crackenback chairlift and then follow the six-kilometre walking trail – it crosses alpine fields and hillsides carpeted with wildflowers.

BARRY WAY – JINDABYNE TO THE VICTORIAN BORDER

Half-way Flat camping area

This is 54 km south of Jindabyne near the Snowy River. Access via Barry Way. Bring drinking water and firewood. Additional map ref.: NSWRD 194 J6.

Jacobs River camping area

Located 53 km south of Jindabyne, near junction of Jacob and Snowy rivers. Signposted from Barry Way. Water from creek – boil before use. Bring firewood. Additional map ref.: NSWRD 194 J5.

No Name picnic and camping area

Small area near the Snowy River 57 km south of Jindabyne. Reached from Barry Way. Bring drinking water and firewood. Additional map ref.: NSWRD 194 J6.

Pinch River camping area

Large area on both sides of creek, 59 km south of Jindabyne near junction of Pinch and Snowy rivers. Signposted from Barry Way. Water from creek – boil before use. Bring firewood. Additional map ref.: NSWRD 194 J6.

Running Waters camping area

Located 62 km south of Jindabyne near the Snowy River. Access via Barry Way. Bring drinking water and firewood. Additional map ref.: NSWRD 194 H7.

Scotchies Yard camping area

Situated 70 km south of Jindabyne near the Snowy River. Access via Barry Way. Bring drinking water and firewood. Additional map ref.: NSWRD 194 J8.

Willis camping area

Former site of border customs outpost near the Snowy River, 74 km south of Jindabyne at the Victorian border. Access via Barry Way. Bring drinking water and firewood. Additional map ref.: NSWRD 194 J8.

Further information & bookings: Snowy Region Visitors Centre **Tel.:** (02) 6450 5600 **Camping & park use fees:** Camping and park use fees are not payable along the Barry Way section of Kosciuszko National Park

NORTHERN SECTION

The northern section of the park is the area north of Khancoban to Tumut. Access is via the Snowy Mountains Hwy between Tumut and Cooma, and by Long Plain Rd and the Kiandra–Khancoban Rd.

SNOWY MOUNTAINS HIGHWAY – TUMUT TO ADAMINABY

Black Perry Rest Area

Located 48 km south of Tumut, via Snowy Mountains Hwy. Bring water and firewood. Additional map ref.: NSWRD 180 H2.

Humes Crossing camping area

This is 25 km south of Tumut near Blowering Reservoir. Signposted from Snowy Mountains Hwy. Bring drinking water and firewood. Additional map ref.: NSWRD 172 F10.

Jounama Creek camping area

A sheltered site beside Jounama Creek, 40 km south of Tumut opposite Talbingo turn-off. Signposted from Snowy Mountains Hwy. Water from creek – boil before use. Bring firewood. Additional map ref.: NSWRD 180 G2.

Log Bridge Creek camping area

Located 18 km south of Tumut near Blowering Reservoir. Signposted from Snowy Mountains Hwy. Bring drinking water and firewood. Additional map ref.: NSWRD 172 F9.

The Pines camping area

This is 22 km south of Tumut near Blowering Reservoir. Signposted from Snowy Mountains Hwy. Bring drinking water and firewood. Additional map ref.: NSWRD 172 F9.

Yachting Point camping area

Located 28 km south of Tumut near Blowering Reservoir. Signposted from Snowy Mountains Hwy. Bring drinking water and firewood. Additional map ref.: NSWRD 180 F1.

Yarrangobilly Village Rest Area

Beside Yarrangobilly River, 62 km south of Tumut and 68 km north-west of Adaminaby. Signposted from Snowy Mountains Hwy. This was the site of a gold-, silver- and tin-mining village around the 1860s – only Cotterills Cottage remains. Trout fishing. Water from river – boil before use. Bring firewood. Additional map ref.: NSWRD 180 K3.

Yolde camping area

Located 34 km south of Tumut near Blowering Reservoir. Signposted from Snowy Mountains Hwy. Bring drinking water and firewood. Additional map ref.: NSWRD 180 F1.

Further information & bookings: NPWS, Tumut Visitors Centre **Tel.:** (02) 6947 7025 **Camping & park use fees:** Camping and park use fees are not payable along the Snowy Mountains Hwy section of Kosciuszko National Park

CABRAMURRA AREA – KIANDRA TO KHANCOBAN

Bradneys Gap camping area

Located 10 km north-east of Khancoban. Signposted from Cabramurra–Khancoban Rd. Bring water and firewood. Additional map ref.: NSWRD 188 E2.

Clover Flat camping area

This is 26 km north of Khancoban. Signposted from Cabramurra–Khancoban Rd. Bring water and firewood. Additional map ref.: NSWRD 188 E2.

O'Hares Rest Area

Near site of Sue City (former Snowy Mountains Hydro camp) 20 km north of Cabramurra, near upper reach of Talbingo Reservoir. Signposted from Elliot Way (Cabramurra–Tumbarumba Rd). Popular fishing and boating spot. Bring drinking water and firewood. Additional map ref.: NSWRD 180 H7.

Ravine (Lobbs Hole) camping area

Site of former coppermine during early 1900s, 25 km north of Cabramurra beside Yarrangobilly River. Signposted from Ravine Rd (2WD vehicles check road conditions first), which is off Kiandra–Cabramurra Rd (Link Rd) or Lobbs Hole Rd (4WD only) from the Snowy Mountains Hwy north of Yarrangobilly. Trout fishing. Bring drinking water and firewood. Additional map ref.: NSWRD 180 H6.

Three Mile Dam camping area

Located 14 km north-east of Cabramurra beside Three Mile Dam, near Mt Selwyn ski fields. Signposted from Kiandra–Cabramurra (Link) Rd. No vehicle access during winter – area becomes snow covered. Dam was constructed in 1883; today it is a popular trout-fishing spot. Cross-country skiing in winter. Water from dam – boil before use. Bring firewood. Additional map ref.: NSWRD 180 J8.

Further information & bookings: NPWS, Tumut Visitors Centre **Tel.:** (02) 6947 7025 **Camping & park use fees:** $15.00 per vehicle/day is payable at the entrance station along the Kiandra–Cabramurra Rd (Link Rd) in ski season only. During other times camping and park use fees are not payable in this section of Kosciuszko National Park

LONG PLAIN ROAD – RULES POINT TO BLUE WATERHOLES

Blue Waterholes camping area

Located 26 km north-east of Rules Point. Signposted access via Blue Waterholes Trail off Long Plain Rd. No vehicle access during winter (June–Oct.) – road closed. 2WD access in dry weather only. Explore caves. Bring water and firewood. Additional map ref.: NSWRD 181 P3.

Cooinbil Hut camping area

This is 14 km north-east of Rules Point, off Long Plain Rd. No vehicle access during winter (June–Oct.) – road closed. Access track to hut requires crossing of Murrumbidgee River – may be impassable to 2WD vehicles during wet weather. Camping in vicinity of hut. Water from creek – boil before use. Bring firewood. Additional map ref.: NSWRD 181 M3.

Cooleman Mountain Rest Area

Located 20 km north-east of Rules Point. Signposted via Blue Waterholes Trail off Long Plain Rd. No vehicle access during winter (June–Oct.) – road closed. Bring water and firewood. Additional map ref.: NSWRD 181 N3.

Ghost Gully Horse Camp

Situated 9 km south-east of Rules Point. Access via Port Phillip Fire Trail off Long Plain Rd. No vehicle access during winter (June–Oct.) – road closed. Bring water and firewood. Additional map ref.: NSWRD 181 M4.

Long Plain Hut camping area

This is 4 km north-east of Rules Point (Snowy Mountains Hwy). Signposted off Long Plain Rd. No vehicle access during winter (June–Oct.) – road closed. Camping in vicinity of hut. Bring water and firewood. Additional map ref.: NSWRD 181 L5.

TALBINGO RESERVOIR

Coonara Point camping area

Boat or canoe access only. Site is south of Lobbs Hole near Yorkers Creek Inlet on Talbingo Reservoir. Access boat ramps at Talbingo or O'Hares Rest Area on Elliot Way. Bring drinking water and firewood. Additional map ref.: NSWRD 180 H6.

GOOBARRAGANDRA

Rock Flat camping area

Located 28 km south-east of Tumut. Access via Goobarragandra Rd (Lacmalac Rd). Near Goobarragandra Wilderness and beside Goobarragandra River. Water from river – boil before use. Bring firewood. Additional map ref.: NSWRD 172 J9.

Further information & bookings: NPWS, Tumut Visitors Centre **Tel.:** (02) 6947 7025 **Camping & park use fees:** Camping and park use fees are not payable in Long Plain Rd, Talbingo Reservoir and Goobarragandra sections of Kosciuszko National Park

BUSHFIRES

Bushfires swept through a large portion of Kosciuszko National Park and surrounding areas in early 2003. Due to this, some of the facilities at campsites listed may not be available, and some sites may be temporarily closed. Please check with NPWS before setting out.

Honeysuckle Campground

Site of former space tracking station, 16 km south-west of visitor centre. Signposted via Honeysuckle Rd from Naas Rd. Firewood supplied. Additional map ref.: NSWRD 181 V2.

Mount Clear Campground

Near a creek, 42 km south of visitor centre. Signposted via Boboyan Rd (check on road conditions – can be closed due to rain or snow). Walk or cycle to Horse Gully Hut. Water from creek – boil before use. Firewood supplied. Additional map ref.: NSWRD 181 V4.

Orroral Campground

Near creek 18 km south of visitor centre. Signposted off Orroral Rd from Boboyan Rd. Water from creek – boil before use. Firewood supplied. Additional map ref.: NSWRD 181 V4.

Bush camping

Walk-in bush camping areas – no facilities – are located in the park. Contact visitor centre for details.

Further information & bookings: Namadgi Visitors Centre **Tel.:** (02) 6207 2900 **Email:** namadginationalpark@act.gov.au **Website:** www.environment.act.gov.au **Camping fees:** *Orroral and Honeysuckle:* From $6.70 per 2 people per night *Mount Clear:* From $5.60 per 2 people per night

9. NERRIGA AREA

Nerriga is 50 km north-east of Braidwood and 55 km south-west of Nowra, close to Morton National Park. It is reached from the Braidwood–Nowra Rd (Turpentine Rd). Enjoy refreshments at the rustic Bark Tree Hotel here.

Corang River camping area

Bush camping – no facilities – 8 km south-west of Nerriga on Turpentine Rd at Corang River crossing. Bring firewood. Additional map ref.: NSWRD 176 A5.

Endrick River camping area

Bush camping – no facilities – 4 km north-east of Nerriga on Turpentine Rd at Endrick River crossing. Bring firewood. Additional map ref.: NSWRD 176 C2.

Oallen Ford camping area

Bush camping – no facilities – 18 km west of Nerriga on the Nerriga–Tarago Rd at Shoalhaven River crossing. Bring firewood. Additional map ref.: NSWRD 175 V4.

Stuart Crossing camping area

Bush camping – no facilities – 35 km north of Braidwood on the Mayfield Rd at Lower Boro. Bring firewood. Additional map ref.: NSWRD 175 R4.

Further information & bookings: Bark Tree Hotel, Nerriga **Tel.:** (02) 4845 9120

10. PIERCES CREEK FOREST

This forest – a mixture of pine and native trees – is 30 km west of Canberra. Access is via Cotter Rd from Canberra then Paddys River Rd. Activities include walking, picnicking and camping. Advance bookings are required to camp in the park and fees are payable in advance; contact ACT Forests for application form. Campsite has locked gate – key supplied after payment.

Woods Reserve camping area

This is 45 km south-west of Canberra. Access via Corin Rd from Paddys River Rd. Water from creek – boil before use. Firewood supplied. Additional map ref.: NSWRD 173 U10.

Further information & bookings: ACT Forests **Tel.:** (02) 6207 2486 **Email:** david.whitfield@act.gov.au **Camping fees:** From $15.00 for 2 people/night; $20.00 key deposit for toilet/shower block

11. TALLAGANDA STATE FOREST

This state forest is a mix of old-growth trees and logging areas. It is 10 km east of Captains Flat, straddling the Great Dividing Range, and is reached from Captains Flat, Bungendore, Hoskinstown and Braidwood.

Lowden Forest Park

Site of a 1930s logging camp, 25 km north-east of Captains Flat. Access via Coxs Creek Rd and Lowden Forest Rd from Captains Flat. The old waterwheel at the park was originally used to generate electricity. Bring water. Additional map ref.: NSWRD 183 N1.

Further information & bookings: State Forests Batemans Bay **Tel.:** (02) 4472 6211 **Email:** cumberland@sf.nsw.gov.au

12. URIARRA FOREST

This is the former site of a World War II internment camp. It is 30 km west of Canberra, via Brindabella Rd. Activities include walking, picnicking and camping. Advance bookings are required to camp in the park and fees are payable in advance; contact ACT Forests for application form. Campsite has locked gate – key supplied after payment.

Blue Range Camp camping area

Large grassy area. Signposted off Blue Range Rd from Brindabella Rd. Bring water. Firewood supplied. Hut accommodation also available. Additional map ref.: NSWRD 173 T6.

Further information & bookings: ACT Forests **Tel.:** (02) 6207 2486 **Email:** david.whitfield@act.gov.au **Camping fees:** *Blue Range:* From $12.00 for 2 people/night *Blue Range Hut:* From $25.00 for 2 people/night

13. WEE JASPER AREA

The Goodradigbee River flows through the valley of Wee Jasper, which is 54 km south-west of Yass on the upper reaches of Lake Burrinjuck. Access is via Yass–Wee Jasper Rd. You can explore Careys Cave, go canoeing on Lake Burrinjuck, fish in the Goodradigbee River or take a walk along a section of the Hume and Hovell Walking Track. Site allocation at all reserves is on a first-come basis.

Billy Grace Reserve

Beside Goodradigbee River 6 km south of Wee Jasper. Reached from Wee Jasper–Nottingham Rd. Firewood supplied. Additional map ref.: NSWRD 173 P3.

Careys Reserve

Beside Burrinjuck Dam, 3 km north of Wee Jasper. Access via Caves Valley Rd. Bring water and firewood. Additional map ref.: NSWRD 173 P2.

Micalong Creek Reserve

Beside Micalong Creek, 14 km south of Wee Jasper. Signposted from Nottingham Rd. Water from tank. Bring firewood. Additional map ref.: NSWRD 173 P4.

Swinging Bridge Reserve

A long, narrow area beside Goodradigbee River, 10 km south of Wee Jasper. Signposted from Nottingham Rd. Water from river – boil before use. Bring firewood. Additional map ref.: NSWRD 173 P4.

Further information: DLWC, Wee Jasper **Tel.:** (02) 6227 9626
Camping fees: $6.00 per adult/night; ranger collects fees

14. WINGELLO STATE FOREST

Wingello State Forest is often host to sled dog trials. It is 9 km south of Bundanoon near Wingello and is reached by Forest Rd (Caoura Rd) from Wingello township, which is 45 km east of Goulburn.

Forest Headquarters camping area

Camping area is in pine plantation, 4 km south-east of Wingello. Access via Forest Rd. Take care with fires. Bring water. Additional map ref.: NSWRD 168 D5.

Further information & bookings: State Forests, Bombala **Tel.:** (02) 6458 3177 **Email:** cumberland@sf.nsw.gov.au

View of the Tidbinbilla Valley from Mount Eliza, Tidbinbilla Nature Reserve, close to Namadgi National Park

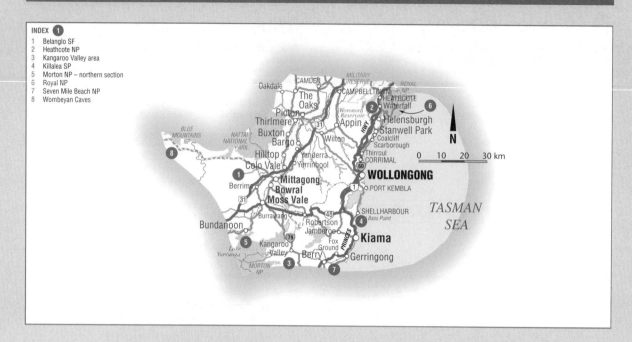

INDEX 1
1 Belanglo SF
2 Heathcote NP
3 Kangaroo Valley area
4 Killalea SP
5 Morton NP – northern section
6 Royal NP
7 Seven Mile Beach NP
8 Wombeyan Caves

The Southern Highlands takes in the breathtaking mountains and cliff faces, rainforests and waterfalls of the Great Dividing Range before dropping down to the flatter regions of the Illawarra coast.

In the very north of the region, just south of Sydney, is Royal National Park. It is a delight for bushwalkers and mountain-bike riders, who can experience the natural beauty of the park at its best. Camping within the park is mainly at walk-in bush sites, however there is an established camping area at Bonnie Vale, near Bundeena, in the north of the park.

Wombeyan Caves is in the west of the region. The Wombeyan Caves Camp Ground is a large grassy area close to the visitor centre, with excellent facilities. Visitors can enjoy a caving experience on a guided or self-guide tour.

The large Morton National Park encompasses all the best that the region offers. It has spectacular waterfalls, cool tree-fern gullies, magnificent escarpments and scenic clifftop lookouts. To the south of the park are the monoliths of The Castle and Pigeon House Mountain. Energetic walkers can climb to the top

of Pigeon House Mountain for one of the coast's most majestic views. Vehicle- and van-based campers can set up at the extremely popular Gambells Rest camping area just south of Bundanoon, while those who prefer a quieter site can hike to some of the more private bush campsites throughout the park.

Campers who prefer the smell of salt water can camp at Seven Mile Beach National Park, south of Gerringong. Surfers, swimmers, windsurfers and fisherfolk all visit this popular summertime destination.

BEST CAMPSITES

Wombeyan Caves Camp Ground
Wombeyan Caves

Gambells Rest camping area
Morton National Park – northern section

Bush camping
Royal National Park

Bendeela camping area
Kangaroo Valley area

Killalea camping area
Killalea State Park

BEST TIME TO VISIT

All year round. Walkers in Morton National Park may wish to avoid the extreme temperatures of winter and summer.

1. BELANGLO STATE FOREST

This forest is 10 km north-west of Moss Vale. It is signposted via Bunnigalore Rd, from the Hume Hwy, and contains areas of pine plantation.

Dalys Clearing camping area

On Dalys Rd. Access via Bunnigalore Rd. Dispersed bush camping is also permitted throughout this forest except in pine plantation area. Bring water. Take extreme care with fires. Additional map ref.: NSWRD 168 E1.

Further information & bookings: State Forests, Bombala **Tel.:** (02) 6458 3177 **Email:** cumberland@sf.nsw.gov.au

2. HEATHCOTE NATIONAL PARK

This national park protects rugged sandstone country 40 km south of Sydney. It is near Heathcote on the western side of the Princes Hwy from Royal National Park. It is reached via Warabin St in Waterfall and Oliver St in Heathcote. Vehicles are restricted, but it is accessible by public transport.

Bush camping

Numerous bush campsites throughout the park. No facilities – be self-sufficient. Bring water. Gas/fuel stove only. Obtain permit from Audley Visitors Centre in Royal National Park. A permit is required to camp and must be carried at all times. Additional map ref.: NSWRD 18 E6 (Heathcote Access).

Further information & bookings: NPWS, Audley Visitors Centre, Royal National Park **Tel.:** (02) 9542 0648 **Camping fees:** $3.00 per adult/night, $2.00 per child (age 5–15) per night

3. KANGAROO VALLEY AREA

Kangaroo Valley, a popular weekend destination, is 20 km north of Nowra and reached via Cambewarra Rd and Kangaroo Valley Rd from Nowra, or from Moss Vale in the west.

Bendeela camping area

Located 8 km west of Kangaroo Valley township. Access via Bendeela Rd. Gas/fuel stoves only. Additional map ref.: NSWRD 169 L5.

Tallowa Dam camping area

The dam is 22 km west of Kangaroo Valley township, surrounded by Morton National Park. Access via Tallowa Dam Rd. Firewood supplied. Boil drinking water. Additional map ref.: NSWRD 168 G6.

Further information & bookings: Sydney Catchment Authority **Tel.:** (02) 4886 4377

4. KILLALEA STATE PARK

This park is about 90 km south of Sydney, between Kiama and Shellharbour. It offers superb surfing beaches and fishing.

Killalea camping area

Campsite is in a gully, a short walk from two beaches. Firewood supplied. Bore water. Additional map ref.: NSWRD 169 T3.

Further information & bookings: Killalea State Park **Tel.:** (02) 4237 8589 **Camping fees:** $16 per 2 adults/night, additional adults $6.00/night, children (over 6) $3.00/night

5. MORTON NATIONAL PARK – NORTHERN SECTION

See also Morton National Park – central and southern sections, *page 63*

This large park runs from Ulladulla to Bundanoon. Access to the northern section is from Bundanoon and Fitzroy Falls. A number of fire trails suitable for walkers and 4WD vehicles provide access to the remote areas of the park. The park contains the Budawang and Ettrema wilderness areas and there is spectacular sandstone scenery. Visit Fitzroy and Belmore Falls; other activities include remote-area bushwalking, sightseeing and 4WD touring.

Gambells Rest camping area

Located 1.5 km south of Bundanoon township. Access via Gullies Rd. Bring water and firewood. Bookings are essential, up to three months in advance, through Fitzroy Falls Visitors Centre. Additional map ref.: NSWRD 392 D5.

Bush camping

Numerous bush camping areas exist throughout the park. Obtain large-scale maps and contact rangers for details. Gas/fuel stove preferred.

Further information & bookings: NPWS, Fitzroy Falls Visitors Centre **Tel.:** (02) 4887 7270 **Park use fee:** $6.00 per vehicle/day **Camping fees:** *Gambells Rest:* $5.00 per adult/night, $3.00 per child (age 5–15) per night

6. ROYAL NATIONAL PARK

Royal National Park was the world's first national park. It is a very popular park with many recreational opportunities. It lies 30 km south of Sydney, near Sutherland, and is signposted via the Princes Hwy and Farnell Ave. Advance bookings for camping are essential and a ballot system applies to the Bonnie Vale camping area during school holidays.

Bonnie Vale camping area

On Port Hacking near Bundeena. Access via Bundeena Rd. Open fires in dedicated areas only. Gas/fuel stove preferred. Additional map ref.: NSWRD 19 L6.

Bush camping

Contact the Audley Visitors Centre for current locations, bookings and permits. Gas/fuel stove only. No pets.

Further information & bookings: NPWS, Audley Visitors Centre **Tel.:** (02) 9542 0648 **Park use fee:** $10.00 per vehicle/day **Camping fees:** *Bonnie Vale:* $7.50 per adult/night, $4.00 per child (age 5–15) per night *Bush camping:* $3.00 per adult/night, $2.00 per child (age 5–15) per night

7. SEVEN MILE BEACH NATIONAL PARK

This park consists of seven miles of unspoiled beach, 6 km south of Gerringong. It is reached via the Gerroa–Shoalhaven Heads Rd from Gerroa or Shoalhaven Heads and via the Princes Hwy from Berry. Activities include fishing, surfing, swimming and windsurfing – the park is popular in summer.

Seven Mile Beach camping area

Located 6 km south of Gerringong. Signposted from Gerroa–Shoalhaven Heads Rd. Surf beach not patrolled. Gas/fuel stove preferred. Additional map ref.: NSWRD 169 R6.

Further information & bookings: NPWS, Nowra **Tel.:** (02) 4423 2170 **Camping fees:** $3.00 per adult/night, $2.00 per child (age 5–15) per night

8. WOMBEYAN CAVES

These caves are 60 km west of Mittagong and 30 km east of Taralga. Access is via Wombeyan Caves Rd from Mittagong or Wombeyan Caves Rd from Goulburn–Oberon Rd 10 km north of Taralga (caravan access from Taralga). Take a guided or self-guide cave tour.

Wombeyan Caves Camp Ground

Large grassy area near visitor centre. Bring firewood. Additional map ref.: NSWRD 159 V7.

Further information & bookings: Wombeyan Caves Visitors Centre **Tel.:** (02) 4843 5976 **Email:** wombeyan@goulburn.net.au **Website:** www.jenolancaves.org.au **Camping fees:** From $6.50 per person/night or $16.00 per family (2 adults + 2 children) per night

The stunning coastal scenery of Royal National Park

FROM NOWRA SOUTH TO THE VICTORIAN BORDER, THE SOUTH COAST OF NEW SOUTH WALES IS A REGION FULL OF UNTOUCHED NATURAL BEAUTY. ITS BEAUTIFUL WHITE SANDY BEACHES AND MAGNIFICENT RIVERS ARE BORDERED TO THE WEST BY THE RAINFORESTS AND ESCARPMENTS OF THE GREAT DIVIDING RANGE. THERE IS A WIDE CHOICE OF CAMPING IN THE REGION: COASTAL AND INLAND NATIONAL PARKS, EASILY ACCESSIBLE STATE FORESTS AND, FOR THE ENERGETIC, WALK-IN SITES ALONG THE SPECTACULAR NADGEE–CAPE HOWE WILDERNESS WALK.

Booderee National Park, on the coast at Jervis Bay, has campsites in natural bush settings. The park is an extremely popular summer holiday destination with swimmers, bushwalkers, divers and snorkellers. Birdwatchers are also drawn to the park – a number of endangered species have been spotted here.

Another popular coastal park is Murramarang National Park. It is well known for the kangaroos at Pebbly Beach camping area. Campsites within this park are all on the beach, encouraging swimming, fishing and diving.

Just south of Narooma is the beautiful Mystery Bay, with wonderful views to Montague Island and its lighthouse. Camping here is set amongst the natural coastal vegetation. The bay has crystal-clear water and is ideal for swimming and snorkelling.

Inland national parks of this region include Deua National Park and Wadbilliga National Park. Deua National Park protects a large area of wild country and numerous caves. Camping with conventional-vehicle access can be found on its western and eastern borders, and at its centre is the remote Bendethera camping area, accessible by four-wheel drive. The Wadbilliga and Tuross rivers flow through Wadbilliga National Park. Camping is possible beside the Wadbilliga River and on the park's western boundary beside the Tuross River. From here it's a short walk to the viewing platform over the falls.

In the south of the area are the wonderful Mimosa Rocks and Ben Boyd national parks. These two offer excellent coastal campsites. Mimosa Rocks National Park is popular for diving, surfing and swimming, while Ben Boyd National Park provides an insight into the area's old whaling industry.

BEST CAMPSITES

Greenpatch Campground
Booderee National Park

Pebbly Beach camping area
Murramarang National Park

Congo camping area
Eurobodalla National Park

Mystery Bay camping area
Mystery Bay

Cascades camping area
Wadbilliga National Park

BEST TIME TO VISIT

All year round.

The Pinnacles, Ben Boyd National Park

1. ARALUEN

The small village of Araluen sits in a picturesque valley between Braidwood and Moruya; it is now famous for its stone fruit but was a gold-prospecting area. Try your luck panning for gold.

Araluen Creek camping area

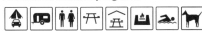

North of Araluen at the junction of the Araluen–Braidwood Rd and Majors Creek Rd beside Araluen Creek. Caravan access from Braidwood. Bring drinking water and firewood. Additional map ref.: NSWRD 183 R3.

Further information & bookings:
Tallaganda Shire Council **Tel.:** (02) 4842 2225 **Email:** shire@ tallaganda.nsw.gov.au **Website:** www.tallaganda.nsw.gov.au or Araluen Hotel **Tel.:** (02) 4846 4023

2. BENANDARAH STATE FOREST

This forest is north of Batemans Bay and is signposted from the Princes Hwy.

Benandarah Rest Area

Beside the Princes Hwy 8 km north of Batemans Bay. Suitable for overnight stays only. Bring water and firewood. Additional map ref.: NSWRD 184 E3.

Further information & bookings: State Forests, South Coast Region **Tel.:** (02) 4472 6211 **Email:** cumberland@sf. nsw.gov.au

3. BEN BOYD NATIONAL PARK

This coastal park with stunning scenery is divided into two sections, one to the north of Eden and the other to the south. The southern section, 30 km south of Eden, permits camping. The park is reached via Edrom Rd from the Princes Hwy. Visit Boyds Tower, originally built as a lighthouse but never commissioned, and look over the Davidson Whaling Station Historic Site. Activities here include swimming, fishing and bushwalking. Advance bookings are essential for peak times and a ballot system operates for Christmas and Easter holiday periods. Bookings are taken from three months in advance of these times, and cottages at Green Cape Lighthouse are also available for rent; contact NPWS Merimbula for details.

Bittangabee camping area

Located 41 km south of Eden. Access via Greencape Rd from Edrom Rd. Bring water and firewood. Additional map ref.: NSWRD 199 L5.

Hegartys Bay camping area

This is 3 km south of Saltwater Creek camping area. Walk-in only access via Light to Light Walking Track from Saltwater to Bittangabee. Bring water. Gas/fuel stove preferred. Additional map ref.: NSWRD 199 L5.

Mowarry Point camping area

Located 3 km north of Saltwater Creek camping area. Walk-in only access via Light to Light Walking Track. Bring water. Gas/fuel stove preferred. Additional map ref.: NSWRD 199 L3.

Saltwater Creek camping area

Near creek, 40 km south of Eden. Access via Duckhole Rd from Greencape Rd off Edrom Rd. Popular family camping area. Bring water and firewood. Additional map ref.: NSWRD 199 K4.

Further information & bookings: NPWS, Merimbula **Tel.:** (02) 6495 5000 **Park use fee:** $6.00 per vehicle/day **Camping fees:** *Saltwater Creek and Bittangabee:* From $5.00 per adult/night, $3.00 per child (age 5–15) per night

4. BODALLA STATE FOREST

This forest is 5 km south of Bodalla and stretches south behind Narooma. It is reached via Eurobodalla Rd from Bodalla and from the Princes Hwy both north and south of Narooma. Activities here include fishing, 4WD touring and horseriding.

Bodalla Forest Park

This is 9 km north of Narooma and is signposted from the Princes Hwy. Overnight stays only. Limited drinking water. Additional map ref.: NSWRD 192 B4.

Red Creek camping area

A small camping area near creek 40 km south-west of Bodalla. Access via Red Creek Rd off Tuross River Rd. Bring drinking water. Additional map ref.: NSWRD 191 T5.

Wagonga picnic area

This small camping area on Wagonga Inlet is 12 km south-west of Narooma and reached via Wagonga Scenic Drive from the Princes Hwy. Bring drinking water. Additional map ref.: NSWRD 192 B5.

Further information & bookings: State Forests, Batemans Bay **Tel.:** (02) 4472 6211 **Email:** cumberland@sf.nsw.gov.au

5. BONDI STATE FOREST

This forest, which contains large areas of pine plantation, is 30 km south of Bombala. Access is via Bondi Forest Way from the Monaro Hwy. Activities here include trout fishing, mountain-bike riding, bushwalking and horseriding.

Bondi Forest Lodge

Self-catering lodge accommodation (no camping) at former forestry camp 32 km south of Bombala. Access via Buldah Rd. Trout-stocked lake nearby. Advance bookings required. Additional map ref.: NSWRD 78 F1.

Further information & bookings: Managers, Bondi Forest Lodge **Tel.:** (02) 6458 7262 **Accommodation fees:** $17.00 per person/night

6. BOODEREE NATIONAL PARK

Booderee National Park has spectacular coastal scenery. It is 35 km south-east of Nowra at Jervis Bay and is reached via Jervis Bay Rd from the Princes Hwy 12 km south of Nowra. It is popular in summer and visitors can enjoy swimming, walking and diving here. A ballot system for site allocations applies for the Christmas holidays; contact the visitor centre for details.

Bristol Point Campground

Off Jervis Bay Rd. Suitable for large groups. Firewood supplied. Additional map ref.: NSWRD 177 Q3.

Cave Beach Campground

Open grassy area on Caves Beach Rd. Walk in to sites (300 m) from carpark. Firewood supplied. Additional map ref.: NSWRD 177 P4.

Greenpatch Campground

On Iluka Rd off Jervis Bay Rd. Secluded campsites. Firewood supplied. Additional map ref.: NSWRD 177 Q3.

Further information & bookings: Booderee National Park Visitors Centre **Tel.:** (02) 4443 0977 **Website:** www.booderee. np.gov.au **Park use fee:** $10.00 per vehicle/day **Camping fees:** *Bristol Point:* Contact visitor centre for current group rates *Cave Beach:* From $8.65 per tent (up to 5 people) per night *Greenpatch:* From $14.00 per tent (up to 5 people) per night

This is a coastal park 10 km north of Merimbula, reached by Bournda Rd from Sapphire Coast Drive. There are many beaches here, as well as the shore of Wallagoot Lake, and it is a very popular summer destination.

Hobart Beach camping area

Near Wallagoot Lake 18 km north of Merimbula. Access via Bournda Rd. Popular with families. Additional map ref.: NSWRD 197 U6.

Further information & bookings: NPWS Discovery Centre, Merimbula **Tel.:** (02) 6495 5000 **Park use fee:** $6.00 per vehicle/day **Camping fees:** From $7.50 per adult/night, $4.00 per child (age 5–15) per night

8. BUNDUNDAH RESERVE

This reserve is in an attractive spotted gum forest set in steep rocky gullies 22 km west of Nowra. Access is via Yalwal Rd from Nowra then Burrier Rd. Activities include bushwalking.

Grassy Gully camping area

Bush camping – no facilities – beside creek, 25 km west of Nowra. Access via Grassy Gully Rd from Burrier Rd. Gas/fuel stove preferred. Additional map ref.: NSWRD 168 J8.

Further information & bookings: NPWS, Nowra **Tel.:** (02) 4423 2170

9. CURROWAN STATE FOREST

This forest is 15 km north-west of Batemans Bay, near Nelligen. It is reached via Lyons Rd from the Kings Hwy (Braidwood–Batemans Bay Rd) west of Nelligen. Activities include 4WD touring.

Currowan Creek camping area

Bush camping – no facilities – 14 km north-west of Nelligen, near Currowan Creek bridge. Access via Lyons Rd. Additional map ref.: NSWRD 184 B2.

Further information & bookings: State Forests, Batemans Bay **Tel.:** (02) 4472 6211

10. DANJERA DAM

Danjera Dam is a water storage and the site of an old gold-rush town (now underwater), 27 km west of Nowra. It is reached via Yalwal Rd off Burrier Rd from Nowra. You can visit the historic cemetery and old mine sites and the area is popular for 4WD touring. Camping is only allowed by prior arrangement; contact council for details.

Danjera Dam camping area

Located 27 km west of Nowra. Access via Yalwal Rd. Camping only permitted in designated areas. Bring drinking water and firewood. Motorised water craft not permitted on dam. Additional map ref.: NSWRD 168 H9.

Further information & bookings: Shoalhaven City Council – Ranger Services **Tel.:** (02) 4429 3111

11. DEUA NATIONAL PARK

This national park is 15 km west of Moruya, and stretches from Araluen in the north to east of Numeralla in the south. There is 2WD access via Araluen Rd or Krawarree Rd and 4WD-only access via Dampier Mountain Trail from Snowball Rd in the west or Little Sugarloaf Rd in the east. Marvel at the Big Hole, a 100-m-deep collapsed cave; bushwalk along the Deua River; explore Bendethera Cave; or enjoy 4WD touring on the park's trails.

Bakers Flat camping area

Near Deua River 31 km north-west of Moruya. Walk-in access from Araluen Rd. Water from river – boil before use. Bring firewood. Additional map ref.: NSWRD 183 U5.

Bendethera camping area

Many campsites beside Deua River 46 km west of Moruya. 4WD-only access, and in dry weather only, via Bendethera Fire Trail from Little Sugarloaf Rd from Moruya, or Dampier Mountain Trail from Snowball Rd in the west. Explore Bendethera Caves. Water from river – boil before use. Bring firewood. Additional map ref.: NSWRD 183 Q9.

Berlang camping area

Near Shoalhaven River 41 km south-west of Braidwood. Signposted from Krawarree Rd. Walk to the Big Hole and Marble Arch. Water from river – boil before use. Bring firewood. Additional map ref.: NSWRD 183 N5.

Deua River camping area

Near Deua River 33 km north-west of Moruya. Access via Araluen Rd. Water from river – boil before use. Bring firewood. Additional map ref.: NSWRD 183 U5.

Dry Creek camping area

Near Deua River 30 km north-west of Moruya. 4WD access via Dry Creek Trail from Araluen Rd. Water from river – boil before use. Bring firewood. Additional map ref.: NSWRD 183 U6.

Further information & bookings: NPWS, Narooma **Tel.:** (02) 4476 2888 **Camping fees:** $3.00 per adult/night, $2.00 per child (age 5–15) per night; fees payable at self-registration stations or to pay collectors

12. EAST BOYD STATE FOREST

This is 20 km south of Eden, reached from the Princes Hwy. The forest adjoins Mt Imlay National Park and offers opportunities for 4WD touring, bushwalking and horseriding.

Scrubby Creek picnic area

A popular overnight stop near the Princes Hwy, signposted. Additional map ref.: NSWRD 199 G5.

Further information & bookings: State Forests, Eden **Tel.:** (02) 6496 1500 **Email:** cumberland@sf.nsw.gov.au

13. EUROBODALLA NATIONAL PARK

Eurobodalla is a coastal park comprising a number of sections; in all it stretches from Moruya in the north to Mystery Bay in the south. There are many roads to it from the Princes Hwy. Activities include swimming, fishing, surfing, bushwalking, canoeing and boating in the lakes.

Congo camping area

Located 10 km east of Moruya. Access via Congo Rd from South Head Rd. Tank water. Firewood supplied. Site allocation is on a first-come basis (area is popular at Christmas and Easter). Additional map ref.: NSWRD 184 D10 .

Further information: NPWS, Narooma **Tel.:** (02) 4476 2888 **Camping fees:** $5.00 per adult/night, $3.00 per child (age 5–15) per night; ranger collects fees

14. MEROO NATIONAL PARK

Meroo National Park is near the beach, 15 km south of Ulladulla. Access is via Meroo Rd off the Princes Hwy north of Termeil. It is a popular destination during summer.

Meroo Head camping area

Bush camping – no facilities – 8 km north-east of Termeil village. Access via Meroo Rd. Bring water. Additional map ref.: NSWRD 176 H10.

Further information & bookings: NPWS, Ulludulla **Tel.:** (02) 4455 3826

15. MIMOSA ROCKS NATIONAL PARK

This coastal park has rugged rocks sculpted by the elements. It is 10 km north of Tathra and reached via Bermagui–Tathra Rd. Explore its secluded headlands, beaches, lagoons and inlets. Activities here include swimming, fishing, surfing, diving, bushwalking, canoeing and boating in the lakes. Site allocation is on a first-come basis and camping is popular at Christmas and Easter.

Aragunnu camping area

Near beach, 24 km south of Bermagui. Signposted on Aragunnu Rd from Bermagui–Tathra Rd. Bring water. Firewood supplied. Additional map ref.: NSWRD 77 L8.

Gillards Beach camping area

Near beach, 14 km north of Tathra. Access via Gillards Rd from Bermagui–Tathra Rd. Bring water. Firewood supplied. Additional map ref.: NSWRD 197 V4.

Middle Beach camping area

A walk-in site (80 m from carpark) near both beach and lagoon. It is 16 km north of Tathra and reached via Middle Beach Rd from Haighs Rd, off Bermagui–Tathra Rd. Bring water and firewood. Additional map ref.: NSWRD 197 W3.

Picnic Point camping area

Near beach, 26 km south of Bermagui. Access via Wapengo Lake Rd from Bermagui–Tathra Rd. Bring water. Firewood supplied. Additional map ref.: NSWRD 197 W3.

Further information: NPWS, Narooma **Tel.:** (02) 4476 2888 **Camping fees:** $5.00 per adult/night, $3.00 per child (age 5–15) per night; fees collected

16. MORTON NATIONAL PARK – CENTRAL AND SOUTHERN SECTIONS

See also Morton National Park – northern section, *page 57*

This large park runs from near Bundanoon to near Milton. The central section is traversed by Turpentine Rd (Braidwood–Nowra Rd) and the southern section is reached by Pointer Gap Rd from the Princes Hwy north of Milton or Yadboro Rd for Pigeon House Mountain. A number of fire trails suitable for walkers and 4WD vehicles provide access to remote areas of the park. The park contains the Budawang and Ettrema wilderness areas and there is spectacular sandstone scenery. Pigeon House Mountain is one of the highlights.

CENTRAL SECTION

Sassafras camping area

This is 15 km east of Nerriga village. Access via Endrick Fire Trail off Turpentine Rd. 2WD access in dry weather only. Walk-in (500 m) from end of road to campsite. Start point for numerous overnight walks in park. Gas/fuel stove preferred. Additional map ref.: NSWRD 392 D5, 176 F3.

Wog Wog camping area

Situated 15 km south of Nerriga village. Access via Charleys Forest Rd off Nerriga–Braidwood Rd. Start point for numerous overnight walks in park. Water from creek – boil before use. Bring firewood. Additional map ref.: NSWRD 176 A6.

SOUTHERN SECTION

Bluegum Flat camping area

Walk-in sites (30 m) beside Clyde River, 33 km south-west of Milton. Access via Blue Gum Flat Rd off Yadboro Rd. Additional map ref.: NSWRD 176 D8.

Bush camping

Numerous bush camping areas exist throughout park. Obtain large-scale maps and contact ranger for details. Gas/fuel stove preferred.

Further information & bookings: NPWS, Nowra
Tel.: (02) 4423 2170 **Park use fee:** $6.00 per vehicle/day

17. MORUYA AREA

Moruya is about 10 km inland from the coast, on the Princes Highway. It is a dairying and oyster-farming centre.

The North Head Campground

Located 7 km east of Moruya, on northern side of Moruya River. Signposted from North Head Drive. Bring firewood. Additional map ref.: NSWRD 371 H8.

Further information & bookings: Caretaker
Tel.: (02) 4474 3072 **Camping fees:** *Peak:* From $16.80 per site/night for 2 people, extra adults $5.00 *Off-peak:* From $8.90 per site/night for 2 people, extra adults $2.20. Fees collected morning and evening

18. MURRAMARANG NATIONAL PARK

This coastal park is 10 km north of Batemans Bay. Numerous access roads are signposted from the Princes Hwy, with the main ones being Durras Rd for the southern area of the park and Mt Agony Rd and Murramarang Rd from Bawley Point for the central and northern areas. It is a popular summer destination and advance bookings are essential for camping, especially for peak times. Pebbly Beach has a large kangaroo population and activities include bushwalking and beach watersports.

Depot Beach camping area

Near beach, 20 km north of Batemans Bay. Access via Mt Agony Rd from the Princes Hwy at East Lynne then North Durras Rd. Firewood supplied. Additional map ref.: NSWRD 184 G3.

North Head Beach camping area

Situated 17 km north of Batemans Bay. Access via North Head Rd. Bring drinking water and firewood. Additional map ref.: NSWRD 184 F5.

Pebbly Beach camping area

Near beach, 26 km north of Batemans Bay, reached via Mt Agony Rd from the Princes Hwy at East Lynne. Firewood supplied. Additional map ref.: NSWRD 184 G3.

Pretty Beach camping area

Near beach, 10 km south of Bawley Point. Access via Murramarang Rd from Bawley Point. Cabins also available. Firewood supplied. Additional map ref.: NSWRD 184 H2.

Bush camping

Numerous bush camping areas exist throughout the park. Campsites must be at least 100 m from any road, walking track or parking area. Camping is not permitted on sand dunes and headlands. Obtain large-scale maps and contact ranger for details. Gas/fuel stove preferred.

Further information & bookings: NPWS, Nowra
Tel.: (02) 4423 2170 **Other contacts:** *Depot Beach*, tel. (02) 4478 6582; *Pebbly Beach*, tel. (02) 4478 6006; *Pretty Beach*, tel. (02) 4457 2019 **Park use fee:** $6.00 per vehicle/day **Camping fees:** *Depot Beach, Pebbly Beach and Pretty Beach:* Unpowered sites $5.00 per adult/night, $3.00 per child (age 5–15) per night, powered sites $7.50 per adult/night, $4.00 per child (age 5–15) per night

19. MYSTERY BAY

This is a beautiful beach 10 km south of Narooma. It is signposted from Mystery Bay Rd off the Princes Hwy. Activities here include swimming, fishing, surfing and boating. Bookings and permits are required.

Mystery Bay camping area

Large camping area set amongst trees on headland. Bring firewood. Additional map ref.: NSWRD 192 C7.

Further information & bookings: Narooma Visitors Centre
Tel.: (02) 4476 2881 **Email:** info@naturecoast-tourism.com. au **Website:** www.naturecoast-tourism.com.au **Camping fees:** *Peak:* From $17.20 per site/night *Off-peak:* From $9.20 per site/night. Fees payable at visitor centre.

20. NADGEE NATURE RESERVE

This coastal reserve – the only coastal wilderness area in New South Wales – is 25 km south of Eden near Wonboyn village and next to the Victorian border. It is reached via Newtons Rd from Wonboyn Rd off the Princes Hwy. It includes the Nadgee–Cape Howe Wilderness Walk, and there is a trackhead facility and ranger station at Merrica River Crossing. There is limited vehicle access to the reserve and it is best explored by self-sufficient bushwalking and sea-kayaking. A permit is required for access and must be obtained prior to departure; contact NPWS at Merimbula for details. Groups are limited to eight persons and only 30 people are permitted in the wilderness area at one time.

Nadgee–Cape Howe Wilderness Walk camping areas

Walk-in access camping areas located along the walking track. Gas/fuel stove preferred. (The camping areas are listed below in the order they are reached from north to south.)

Newtons Beach camping area
7.5 km from ranger station. Additional map ref.: NSWRD 199 J8.

Black Head camping area
15 km from ranger station. Additional map ref.: NSWRD 199 K9.

Harry's Hut camping area
18 km from ranger station. Additional map ref.: NSWRD 199 J9.

Nadgee Lake camping area
17 km from ranger station. Additional map ref.: NSWRD 199 K10.

Cape Howe camping area
20.5 km from ranger station. Additional map ref.: NSWRD 199 K10.

Further information & bookings: NPWS, Discovery Centre Merimbula **Tel.:** (02) 6495 5000 **Camping fees & permits:** $5.00 per person per night

21. SOUTH EAST FOREST NATIONAL PARK

This large park is made up of several sections dotted between Bega and Bombala. There are numerous access roads – it is best to obtain a NPWS brochure and map. The park contains old-growth forest, upland swamps and fern-filled gullies. The Tantawangalo Section is the only section where camping is permitted. This section is 15 km west of Candelo and is reached via Tantawangalo Mountain Rd. Activities include nature study, bushwalking, sightseeing and swimming in the creeks. 4WD touring is also possible.

Postmans Track camping area

Beside Tantawangalo Creek 32 km south of Candelo. 4WD access in dry weather only via Postmans Track off Tantawangalo Rd. Water from creek – boil before use. Bring firewood. Additional map ref.: NSWRD 197 L6.

Six Mile Creek Rest Area

This area is set amongst towering trees beside a creek, 23 km south-west of Candelo via Tantawangalo Rd. Short walk to cascades (wheelchair accessible). Water from creek – boil before use. Bring firewood. Additional map ref.: NSWRD 197 L6.

Further information & bookings: NPWS, Bombala **Tel.:** (02) 6458 4080

22. TIMBILLICA STATE FOREST

This forest is south-west of Eden. It is reached via Imlay Rd from the Princes Hwy. Activities include picnicking, camping and 4WD touring.

Newtons Crossing camping area

A small area beside Wallagaraugh River 43 km south-west of Eden. Access via Allan Brook Rd from Imlay Rd. Water from river – boil before use. Additional map ref.: NSWRD 199 D6.

Further information & bookings: State Forests, Eden **Tel.:** (02) 6496 1500 **Email:** cumberland@sf.nsw.gov.au

23. WADBILLIGA NATIONAL PARK

This park is a mountainous wilderness that protects water catchments. It is 25 km west of Cobargo. Access to the eastern area of the park is via Bourkes Rd off Yowrie Rd at Cobargo; access to the western area, including the Cascades, is via Numeralla. 4WD access in dry weather only is possible via Wadbilliga Trail. Activities here include self-sufficient bushwalking and 4WD touring.

Cascades camping area

Beside Tuross River 43 km east of Cooma. Signposted via Tuross Falls Rd from Badja Forest Rd at Countegany (access road can be rough at times). Walk to viewing platform overlooking falls. Bring water and firewood. Additional map ref.: NSWRD 191 L5.

Lake Creek camping area

Beside Wadbilliga River 34 km west of Cobargo and reached via Bourkes Rd. Water from river – boil before use. Bring firewood. Additional map ref.: NSWRD 191 P6.

Wadbilliga Crossing picnic area

Beside Wadbilliga River 40 km west of Cobargo. Access via Bourkes Rd. Causeway may be impassable after heavy rain. Water from river – boil before use. Bring firewood. Additional map ref.: NSWRD 191 N6.

Further information & bookings: NPWS, Narooma **Tel.:** (02) 4476 2888

24. YADBORO STATE FOREST

This forest south-west of Milton adjoins Morton and Budawang national parks. It is reached via Brooman–Milton Rd from Milton, then Clyde Ridge and Yadboro rds. This forest offers the easiest access to the Pigeon House Mountain walking track. There is good bass fishing in the Clyde River and other activities include bushwalking, swimming and 4WD touring.

Yadboro Flat camping area

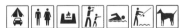

A large grassy area beside the Clyde River, 34 km south-west of Milton. Access via Yadboro Rd from Clyde Ridge Rd. Additional map ref.: NSWRD 176 E7.

Further information & bookings: State Forests, Batemans Bay **Tel.:** (02) 4472 6211 **Email:** cumberland@sf.nsw.gov.au

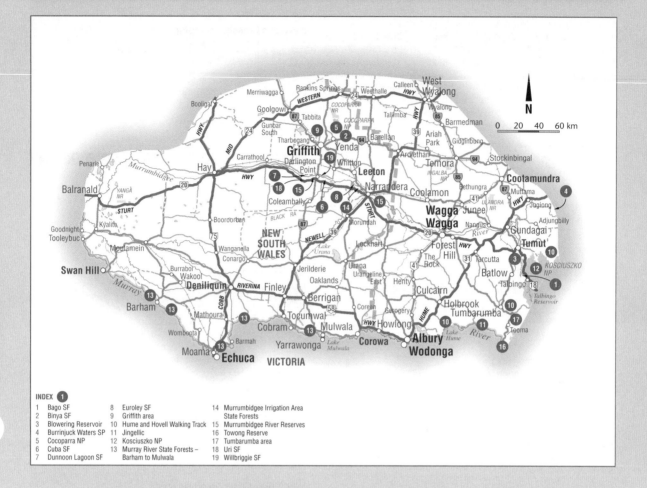

WATERED BY TWO OF THE
COUNTRY'S MIGHTIEST RIVERS –
THE MURRUMBIDGEE AND THE
MURRAY – THIS SOUTHERN
REGION OF NEW SOUTH WALES
IS A MAJOR AGRICULTURAL CENTRE. EVERYTHING
FROM RICE TO STONE FRUIT IS GROWN HERE, MADE
POSSIBLE BY A VAST IRRIGATION AREA, BUT THE
BANKS OF THESE TWO RIVERS ALSO OFFER SOME
SUPERB CAMPING SPOTS.

Camping along the Murrumbidgee is
possible in a host of state forests that begin near
Narrandera and stretch to just east of Hay. The
forests offer vehicle touring along with swimming,
fishing, boating and canoeing. Waterskiing is
possible along some sections of the river.

Along the Murray are a string of state forests
between Mulwala and Barmah, home to some
beautiful river red gums. (Although these majestic
trees look like they provide good shelter, it is wise

not to camp under them as they are prone to
dropping large limbs without warning.)

Due to their excellent location on the
riverbanks, the campsites along both rivers are
very busy during the warmer months. The forests
are also popular with people who travel and camp
with dogs.

There are many other opportunities for
camping in this region. Running through
Cocoparra National Park, north of Griffith, is the
Whitton Stock Route. This route was used in the
nineteenth century by Cobb & Co. coaches
travelling between Queensland and Victoria. The
park is a place of contrast, with valleys of cypress
pine, deep scenic gullies and the cliffs of the
Cocoparra Range, and in spring large blooms of
acacia. The park has numerous picnic areas and
walking trails. Camping is at the large Woolshed
Flat camping area, which is only accessible during
dry weather.

The town of Tumbarumba has a number of excellent campsites in its surrounds, including the Henry Angel Trackhead seven kilometres to the south-east. This is one of the trackheads for the Hume and Hovell Walking Track and is easily reached by vehicle and caravan. Eighteen kilometres from Tumbarumba in the same direction is the large, grassed Paddys River camping area, while to the north-east of the town, in Bago State Forest, is Paddys River Dam campsite, also part of the Hume and Hovell Walking Track. Trout fishing in the dam is a popular pastime. You may even see some brumbies in this area.

BEST CAMPSITES

Woolshed Flat camping area
Cocoparra National Park

Whitton Beach camping area
Murrumbidgee Irrigation Area state forests

Paddys River camping area
Tumbarumba area

Henry Angel Trackhead
Hume and Hovell Walking Track

Millewa State Forest camping area
Murray River state forests – Barham to Mulwala

BEST TIME TO VISIT

Visits to Cocoparra National Park are best saved for the cooler months of the year – spring and autumn. Access to the other areas is possible all year round, however roads into the state forests can be closed during periods of wet weather.

1. BAGO STATE FOREST

See also Paddys River Dam campsite, Hume and Hovell Walking Track, *page 69*

This forest is 10 km south-east of Batlow and it fringes the western shores of Blowering Reservoir and Jounama Pondage. There are numerous access roads from Batlow and Tumbarumba and recreation areas are dotted around the foreshore. Activities include watersports (Blowering Reservoir only) and camping.

Blowering Forest Holiday Camp

A former forestry camp 27 km east of Batlow, on the western shore of Blowering Reservoir. Access via Blowering Camp Rd. Also has bunkhouse (sleeps 58) and cabin accommodation. Ideal for groups. Advance bookings essential. Additional map ref.: NSWRD 172 E10.

Further information & bookings: Blowering Forest Holiday Camp **Tel.:** (02) 6947 5271 **Camping fees:** From $7.70 per person/night for tent camping

Dormans Point, Island Forest Park, Junction Park, Long Point, Platypus Bay, Platypus Park, Willow Bay and Windy Point camping areas

Along the western shore of Blowering Reservoir, 20 km east of Batlow. Access via Blowering Foreshore Rd. Caravan access from Batlow – check road conditions first. Facilities vary between sites. Bring water. Additional map ref.: NSWRD 180 E1.

Jounama Forest Park

Located 9 km north of Talbingo, on the southern shore of Blowering Reservoir. Signposted from Blowering Foreshore Rd. Bring water. Additional map ref.: NSWRD 180 F1.

Further information & bookings: State Forests, Tumut **Tel.:** (02) 6947 3911 **Email:** cumberland@sf.nsw.gov.au

2. BINYA STATE FOREST

This is a cypress-pine forest adjoining Cocoparra National Park, 30 km east of Griffith near Yenda. Access is possible in dry weather only via Whitton Stock Route from Yenda–Ardlethan Rd. There are wildflower displays in late spring and the forest is a popular spot with birdwatchers and bushwalkers.

Binya camping area

Located 10 km west of Yenda. Access via Binya Forest Drive from Whitton Stock Route. Bring water. Solid-fuel ban Dec.–Easter. Gas/fuel stove preferred. Additional map ref.: NSWRD 69 M7.

Further information & bookings: State Forests, Narrandera **Tel.:** (02) 6959 1233

3. BLOWERING RESERVOIR

See Bago State Forest, *above*, Hume and Hovell Walking Track, *page 68*, and Kosciuszko National Park, *page 50*

4. BURRINJUCK WATERS STATE PARK

This park fringes Lake Burrinjuck, 50 km south-west of Yass, and is signposted via Burrinjuck Rd from the Hume Hwy near Bookham. The lake is a watersports venue. Advance bookings are essential for peak periods.

Burrinjuck Waters camping area

On foreshore of Lake Burrinjuck and signposted from Burrinjuck Rd. Kiosk and laundry facilities. Limited firewood supplied. Additional map ref.: NSWRD 165 N10.

Further information & bookings: Burrinjuck Waters State Park **Tel.:** (02) 6227 8114 **Email:** burrinjuckwaters@ bigpond.com **Website:** www.stateparks.nsw.gov.au **Camping fees:** From $13.00 per unpowered site/night, $16.00 per powered site/night

5. COCOPARRA NATIONAL PARK

There is plenty of wildlife in this national park, where cypress pines stand against red rocks, and orchids, wattle and ironbarks also grow. It is 25 km north-east of Griffith, near Yenda, and is signposted via Yenda from Rankins Springs Rd. 2WD access is possible in dry weather only; check on caravan access before attempting. The Whitton Stock Route within the park is part of a historic Cobb & Co. route. There are good views from Mt Bingar.

Woolshed Flat camping area

Located 20 km north of Yenda. Signposted via Whitton Stock Route from Rankins Springs Rd. Bring water and firewood. Additional map ref.: NSWRD 69 M6.

Further information & bookings: NPWS, Griffith **Tel.:** (02) 6966 8100

6. CUBA STATE FOREST

This is a river red gum forest on the north bank of Murrumbidgee River, 40 km south of Griffith near Darlington Point. It is signposted via Cuba Forest Drive from Whitton Rd. Dry-weather access only; check on road conditions for caravan access. There is a solid-fuel ban Dec.–Easter throughout forest – gas/fuel stove only.

Cuba Beach camping area

Beside Murrumbidgee River 19 km east of Darlington Point. Access via Cuba Forest Drive. Bring drinking water. Additional map ref.: NSWRD 69 L9.

Tims Beach camping area

Beside Murrumbidgee River 20 km east of Darlington Point. Access via Cuba Forest Drive. Bring drinking water. Additional map ref.: NSWRD 69 L9.

Further information & bookings: State Forests, Narrandera **Tel.:** (02) 6959 1233 **Email:** cumberland@sf.nsw.gov.au

7. DUNNOON LAGOON STATE FOREST

This forest is on the north bank of the Murrumbidgee River, about 40 km south of Griffith near Darlington Point. It is signposted from Murrumbidgee Rd. Access is possible in dry weather only; check on road conditions for caravan access. Activities here include watersports on the Murrumbidgee River. There is a solid-fuel ban Dec.–Easter throughout forest – gas/fuel stove only.

Nobles Beach camping area

This is 15 km west of Darlington Point. Access off Murrumbidgee River Rd. Bring drinking water. Additional map ref.: NSWRD 68 J8.

Further information & bookings: State Forests, Narrandera **Tel.:** (02) 6959 1233 **Email:** cumberland@sf.nsw.gov.au

8. EUROLEY STATE FOREST

This forest is on the south bank of the Murrumbidgee River, 8 km south-west of Yanco. Access is from Euroley Rd on the southern side of Euroley Bridge (turn-off to forest is 6 km from Yanco). Access is possible in dry weather only; check on road conditions for caravan access. Activities here include watersports on the Murrumbidgee River. There is a solid-fuel ban Dec.–Easter throughout forest – gas/fuel stove only.

Euroley Beach camping area

Located 9 km south-west of Yanco. Access via Euroley Rd. Bring drinking water. Additional map ref.: NSWRD 69 M9.

Further information & bookings: State Forests, Narrandera **Tel.:** (02) 6959 1233 **Email:** cumberland@sf.nsw.gov.au

9. GRIFFITH AREA

Griffith is a thriving city that has developed as a result of the introduction of irrigation. Around it lies fruit and vegetable farms. It is 38 km north of the Sturt Hwy.

Lake Wyangan camping area

Located 10 km north of Griffith. Access via Wyangan Ave. Kiosk operates on weekends during summer. Bring drinking water and firewood. Maximum stay is three nights. Additional map ref.: NSWRD 69 L7.

Further information & bookings: Griffith Visitor Information Centre **Tel.:** 1800 681 141 or (02) 6962 4145 **Email:** griffithvc@griffith.nsw.gov.au

10. HUME AND HOVELL WALKING TRACK

This is a long-distance walking track between Yass and Albury that closely traces the route of the explorers Hume and Hovell's 1824 expedition to Port Phillip. The track, which is fully signposted, covers 440 km and takes about 21 days to walk. The walk can also be done in stages ranging from half-day through to two- and three-day walks. Many of the campsites have vehicle access. Obtain the *Hume and Hovell Walking Track: Map Kit* or *Hume and Hovell Walking Track Guidebook* for details. The campsites are listed below in the order that you would reach them walking north to south.

SECTION ONE – YASS TO THOMAS BOYD TRACKHEAD (130 KM)

The Captain campsite

Walk-in site 28 km west of Yass, reached via Black Range Rd from Yass. Water from creek. Additional map ref.: NSWRD 165 Q8.

Fitzpatrick Trackhead

Vehicle-accessible site 4 km south of Wee Jasper, reached via Tumut–Nottingham Rd. Water from tank. Additional map ref.: NSWRD 173 P3.

Log Bridge Creek campsite

Walk-in site near creek 12.5 km south-west of Fitzpatrick Trackhead. Water from creek. Additional map ref.: NSWRD 173 M4.

Micalong Creek campsite

Walk-in site near creek 26 km south-west of Fitzpatrick Trackhead. Water from creek. Additional map ref.: NSWRD 173 M5.

Bossawa campsite

Walk-in site 49 km east of Tumut, reached from Brindabella Rd. Water from creek. Bring firewood. Additional map ref.: NSWRD 173 L6.

Thomas Boyd Trackhead

Vehicle-accessible site 23 km east of Tumut. Access via Goobarragandra (Lacmalac) Rd. Near river. Additional map ref.: NSWRD 172 J8.

Further information & bookings: DLWC, Wagga Wagga **Tel.:** (02) 6921 2503 **Other contacts:** *Fitzpatrick Trackhead–Wee Jasper,* tel. (02) 6227 9626 **Camping fees:** *Fitzpatrick Trackhead:* From $6.00 per adult/night *Thomas Boyd Trackhead:* From $7.00 per 2 adults/night. Ranger collects fees

SECTION TWO – THOMAS BOYD TRACKHEAD TO HENRY ANGEL TRACKHEAD (130 KM)

Blowering campsite

This site is 15 km south-east of Tumut near the Blowering Dam wall. Walk in (250 m) from carpark. Access from Snowy Mountains Hwy. Additional map ref.: NSWRD 172 E9.

Browns Creek campsite

Walk-in site (or canoe access) 9.5 km south of Blowering campsite, on Blowering Reservoir foreshore. Water from dam. Additional map ref.: NSWRD 172 E10.

Ben Smith campsite

Walk-in site 47 km south of Blowering campsite on Jounama Pondage foreshore, opposite Talbingo village. Water from dam. Additional map ref.: NSWRD 180 F2.

Buddong Hut campsite

Walk in to hut (it is also accessible by 4WD). It is 3.5 km south of Buddong Falls. There is 2WD access in dry weather only to falls carpark via Batlow, Tumbarumba or Kosciuszko National Park Boundary Rd from Jounama Dam. A former Water Commission hut, sleeps 8. Water from creek. Additional map ref.: NSWRD 180 E4.

Paddys River Dam campsite

Vehicle-accessible site 20 km north-east of Tumbarumba in Bago State Forest. 2WD access in dry weather only via Bullongra Rd from JDX Rd and Perkins Rd off Tumbarumba–Batlow Rd. Water from dam. Good fishing. Additional map ref.: NSWRD 180 D5.

Junction campsite

Walk-in site located 6.5 km north of Henry Angel Trackhead. Trout fishing. Water from creek. Additional map ref.: NSWRD 180 B6.

Henry Angel Trackhead

Vehicle-accessible site 7 km south-east of Tumbarumba beside Burra Creek. Access via Tooma Rd. Trout fishing. Water from creek. Additional map ref.: NSWRD 180 B7.

Further information & bookings:
DLWC, Wagga Wagga **Tel.:** (02) 6921 2503 *or* NPWS, Tumut Visitor Information Centre **Tel.:** (02) 6947 7025 **Road conditions:** State Forests, Tumbarumba **Tel.:** (02) 6948 2400

SECTION THREE – HENRY ANGEL TRACKHEAD TO SAMUEL BOLLARD TRACKHEAD (117 KM)

Mannus campsite

Vehicle-accessible site 8 km west of Tumbarumba beside Mannus Creek. Reach from Linden Roth Dr. Water from creek. Additional map ref.: NSWRD 179 U6.

Munderoo campsite

Walk-in site 12.5 km west of Mannus campsite. Water from creek (can cease flowing in extended dry periods). Additional map ref.: NSWRD 179 S7.

Lankeys Creek campsite

Walk-in (40 m) site 16 km north of Jingellic. Access via Holbrook–Jingellic Rd. Water from creek. Additional map ref.: NSWRD 179 N7.

Tin Mines campsite

4WD access in dry weather only to this site, 40 km west of Jingellic. Reach via Tin Mines Rd from Tunnel Rd. Water from

creek (can cease flowing in dry times). Bring firewood. Additional map ref.: NSWRD 178 K8.

Samuel Bollard campsite

Walk-in site 12 km south-east of Woomargama and 28 km west of Tin Mines campsite. Bring drinking water. Additional map ref.: NSWRD 178 G8.

Further information & bookings:
DLWC, Wagga Wagga **Tel.:** (02) 6921 2503 *or*
NPWS, Tumut Visitor Information Centre **Tel.:** (02) 6947 7025

11. JINGELLIC

Jingellic is on the banks of the Murray River. Access is via Jingellic–Khancoban Rd. Activities include fishing, swimming and canoeing.

Jingellic Reserve camping area

On bank of Murray River beside Bridge Hotel in Jingellic. Shower facilities available at hotel. Popular over Christmas holidays. Bring firewood. Additional map ref.: NSWRD 179 Q9.

Further information & bookings: Bridge Hotel
Tel.: (02) 6037 1290

12. KOSCIUSZKO NATIONAL PARK see page 50

13. MURRAY RIVER STATE FORESTS – BARHAM TO MULWALA

See also Murray River State Forests – South Australian border to Euston, *page 76*

Numerous river red gum forests are scattered along the banks of the Murray River from Barham to Mulwala. Access is possible in dry weather only – check on road conditions for caravan access. Flooding may occur after heavy rains. There are numerous bush camping areas (some with limited facilities) throughout these forests; contact State Forests Deniliquin for details. Activities include swimming, fishing, boating, waterskiing and canoeing on the river. There is a solid-fuel fire ban Nov.–Easter throughout these forests – gas/fuel stove only.

Bama State Forest camping areas

Located 13 km north-east of Moama. Access via Barmah Forest Rd from Old Moama–Barmah Rd. Bring drinking water. Additional map ref.: NSWRD 74 E6.

Barooga State Forest camping areas

Adjacent to Barooga township. Reached from Cobram–Barooga Rd. Bring drinking water. Additional map ref.: NSWRD 345 B10.

Boomanoomana State Forest camping areas

These are 16 km west of Mulwala, via Mulwala–Barooga Rd. Bring drinking water. Additional map ref.: NSWRD 74 K5.

Campbells Island State Forest camping areas

Located 5 km west of Barham, via Little Murray Rd off North Barham Rd. Bring drinking water. Additional map ref.: NSWRD 74 A3.

Cottadidda State Forest camping areas

Situated 15 km east of Tocumwal and 2 km west of Barooga. Access is via Tocumwal–Barooga Rd. Bring drinking water. Additional map ref.: NSWRD 74 J5.

Gulpa Island State Forest camping areas

Beside Edward River 9 km north-east of Mathoura. Reached via Millewa Rd (Tocumwal Rd) off Picnic Point Rd. Bring drinking water. Additional map ref.: NSWRD 74 E4.

Koondrook State Forest camping areas

These are 10 km east of Barham. Access via Barham Rd from Barham. Bring drinking water. Additional map ref.: NSWRD 74 B4.

Millewa State Forest camping areas

Located 10 km east of Mathoura, via Tocumwal Rd from Mathoura or from Lower River Rd onto Tocumwal Rd south-east of Deniliquin. Bring drinking water. Additional map ref.: NSWRD 74 F5.

Moira State Forest camping areas

Located 4 km south-east of Mathoura, via Moira Forest Drive off Cobb Hwy south of Mathoura. Bring drinking water. Additional map ref.: NSWRD 74 E5.

Mulwala State Forest camping areas

These are 8 km west of Mulwala. Access is via Mulwala–Barooga Road. Bring drinking water. Additional map ref.: NSWRD 74 K5.

Perricoota State Forest camping areas

These are 35 km north-west of Moama and reached via Nineteen Mile Rd, Yarraman Access Rd or Belbins Rd from Perricoota Forest Rd off Moama–Barham Road. Bring drinking water. Additional map ref.: NSWRD 74 C5.

Further information & bookings: State Forests, Deniliquin
Tel.: (03) 5881 2266 **Email:** cumberland@sf.nsw.gov.au

14. MURRUMBIDGEE IRRIGATION AREA STATE FORESTS

These forests lie beside the Murrumbidgee River, to the west of Narrandera. Dry weather access only; check road conditions for caravan access. There are also numerous bush camping areas – no facilities – throughout the forests; contact State Forests Narrandera for details. Activities include swimming, fishing, boating, canoeing and waterskiing. There is a solid-fuel ban Dec.–Easter throughout the forests – gas/fuel stove only.

MURRUMBIDGEE IRRIGATION AREA 1 STATE FOREST

This forest is on the north bank of the Murrumbidgee River, 10 km west of Narrandera. There is signposted access via M.I.A. Forest Drive (12 km from Narrandera) from Trunk Rd.

Long Beach camping area

Located 8 km east of Yanco. Access off M.I.A. Forest Drive (turn-off to M.I.A. Forest Drive is 3.5 km east of Yanco from Trunk Rd). Bring drinking water. Additional map ref.: NSWRD 69 N9.

Markeys Beach camping area

Located 19 km west of Narrandera. Access off M.I.A. Forest Drive. Bring drinking water. Additional map ref.: NSWRD 69 N9.

Sandy Beach camping area

Located 17 km west of Narrandera. Access via Red Gum Rd off M.I.A. Forest Drive. Bring drinking water. Additional map ref.: NSWRD 69 N9.

MURRUMBIDGEE IRRIGATION AREA 2
STATE FOREST

This forest is on the north bank of the Murrumbidgee River, 5 km south-west of Yanco. Access is signposted via Murrumbidgee Forest Drive (5 km from Yanco) from Euroley Rd.

Middle Beach camping area

Located 6 km south-west of Yanco. Access via Murrumbidgee Forest Drive. Bring drinking water. Additional map ref.: NSWRD 69 M9.

MURRUMBIDGEE IRRIGATION AREA 3
STATE FOREST

This is 20 km south-west of Yanco on the north bank of the Murrumbidgee. It is signposted via Forest Drive (19 km from Yanco) from River Rd.

Whitton Beach camping area

Situated 22 km south-west of Yanco. Access via Forest Drive. Bring drinking water. Additional map ref.: NSWRD 69 M9.

Further information & bookings: State Forests, Narrandera **Tel.:** (02) 6959 1233 **Email:** cumberland@sf.nsw.gov.au

15. MURRUMBIDGEE RIVER RESERVES

Four reserves that allow camping lie along the banks of the Murrumbidgee River to the east of Narrandera and near Darling Point. There is swimming, fishing, boating, waterskiing and canoeing on the Murrumbidgee river.

Buckinbong Reserve camping area

Very small reserve beside river, 16 km east of Narrandera. Access via Buckinbong Rd off Sturt Hwy (near Inland Fisheries Station). Bring drinking water and firewood. Additional map ref.: NSWRD 69 P10.

Bunyip Hole Reserve camping area

Adjacent to Darlington Point township. Access in dry weather only via King St from Darlington Point. Catch a bunyip! Bring drinking water. Additional map ref.: NSWRD 334 B1.

The Murray River, near Tocumwal

Common Beach camping area

Next to Darlington Point township. Access in dry weather only via King St from Darlington Point. Bring water. Additional map ref.: NSWRD 334 B1.

Five Mile Reserve camping area

Located 8 km east of Narrandera beside Bundidgerry Creek. Access via Old Wagga Rd from Narrandera. Bring water and firewood. Additional map ref.: NSWRD 69 P9.

Further information & bookings:
DLWC, Griffith **Tel.:** (02) 6962 7522 *or*
DLWC, Narrandera **Tel.:** (02) 6959 1690 *or*
Narrandera Visitors Centre **Tel.:** 1800 672 392

16. TOWONG RESERVE

This reserve is 2 km north-east of Towong (Victoria), near a bridge across the Murray River. It is reached via Towong–Khancoban Rd. Activities here include fishing, swimming and canoeing.

Towong Reserve camping area

Large grassy area beside Murray River, 2 km north-east of Towong. Access via Towong–Khancoban Rd. Bring drinking water and firewood. Additional map ref.: NSWRD 75 V6.

Further information & bookings: Tumbarumba Shire Council **Tel.:** (02) 6948 9100 **Email:** mail@tumbashire.nsw. gov.au **Website:** www.tumbashire.nsw.gov.au

17. TUMBARUMBA AREA

Tumbarumba lies in the western foothills of the Snowy Mountains. Access is via Batlow, Kiandra, Khancoban, Corryong (Victoria) and the Hume Hwy. Activities include fishing, swimming, horseriding, mountain-bike riding and bushwalking (Hume and Hovell Track).

Paddys River camping area

Large grassy area beside Paddys River, 18 km south-east of Tumbarumba. Access via Tumbarumba–Tooma Rd. Water from creek. Bring firewood. Additional map ref.: NSWRD 180 C8.

Paddys River Falls camping area

Near falls, 15 km south-east of Tumbarumba. Signposted from Tumbarumba–Tooma Rd. Water from creek. Bring firewood. Additional map ref.: NSWRD 180 C8.

Further information & bookings: Tumbarumba Shire Council **Tel.:** (02) 6948 9100 **Email:** mail@tumbashire.nsw. gov.au **Website:** www.tumbashire.nsw.gov.au

18. URI STATE FOREST

This forest is on the south bank of Murrumbidgee River, 9 km south-west of Darlington Point. It is reached via Britts Rd from Hay Rd. Dry weather access only; check road conditions for caravans. There is a solid-fuel ban Dec.–Easter throughout forest – gas/fuel stove only.

Beaumont Beach camping area

Located 9 km south-west of Darlington Point. Access via Britts Rd. Bring drinking water. Additional map ref.: NSWRD 68 K8.

Further information & bookings: State Forests, Narrandera **Tel.:** (02) 6959 1233 **Email:** cumberland@sf.nsw.gov.au

19. WILLBRIGGIE STATE FOREST

This forest is adjacent to Darlington Point township, on the north bank of Murrumbidgee River. Access is via Willbriggie Forest Drive from Whitton Rd and Black Box Rd from Whitton Rd. Dry weather access only; check road conditions for caravans. Bush camping areas – no facilities – are scattered throughout this forest. Contact State Forests Narrandera for details. Swim, fish and boat in the river. There is a solid-fuel ban Dec.–Easter throughout forest (gas/fuel stove only).

Boomerang Beach camping area

Located 7 km east of Darlington Point. Access via Black Box Rd. Bring drinking water. Additional map ref.: NSWRD 68 K8.

Horries Beach camping area

This is 4 km west of Darlington Point and is signposted from Willbriggie Forest Drive. Bring drinking water. Additional map ref.: NSWRD 334 E2 (access road).

Swaggys Beach camping area

Located 7 km west of Darlington Point. Signposted from Willbriggie Forest Drive. Bring drinking water. Additional map ref.: NSWRD 334 E2 (access road).

Further information & bookings: State Forests, Narrandera **Tel.:** (02) 6959 1233 **Email:** cumberland@sf.nsw.gov.au

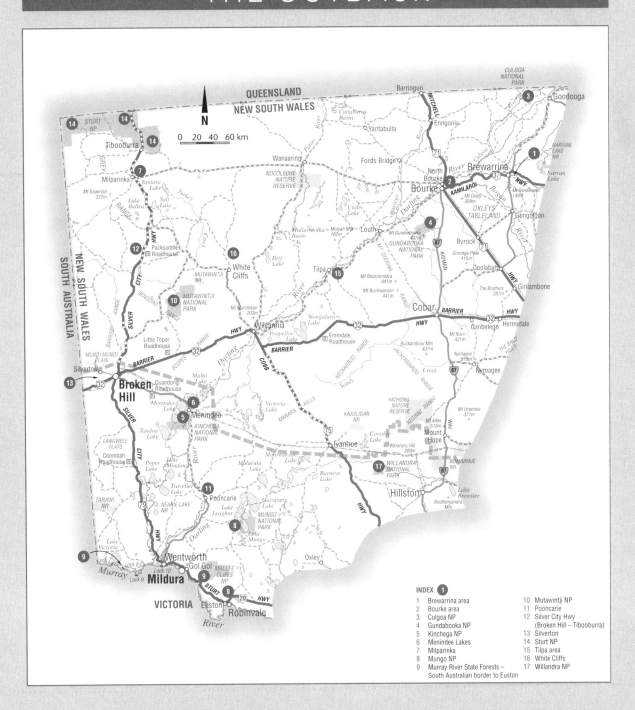

OUTBACK NEW SOUTH WALES HAS MANY DELIGHTS FOR THE VISITOR: THE VAST EXPANSE OF THE MENINDEE LAKES, THE PICTURESQUE JUMP-UP COUNTRY OF STURT NATIONAL PARK, THE SPECTACULAR WALLS OF CHINA IN MUNGO NATIONAL PARK, THE ABORIGINAL ROCK ART IN MUTAWINTJI NATIONAL PARK AND THE POCK-MARKED SURFACES OF WHITE CLIFFS.

Many of the outback's Aboriginal cultural sites and the large sheep and cattle stations of the region are now preserved within national parks, which helps to keep these important sites alive.

In the far north-west corner, Sturt National Park has a mix of landscapes. The central jump-up country consists of flat-topped hills that jut out from the surrounding plains. The park also features the deep-red sand dunes of the Strzelecki desert, seasonal wetlands, and expanses of gibber and grass plains in the east. Dead Horse Gully Campground, near the town of Tibooburra, is beside the Golden Gully Mining Site – well worth a visit. Further into the park are Olive Downs and Fort Grey campgrounds, which are the starting points for some walking tracks.

Mutawintji National Park has deep gorges, rugged ridges and numerous rock-art sites. All these features can be reached on the walking trails in the park. Camping is available at the Homestead Creek camping area.

Around Menindee are a number of campsites to choose from. Some are beside the Menindee Lakes, to the north of the town, while there are various sites located within nearby Kinchega National Park. A visit to Kinchega is a must, with the historic woolshed one of the highlights.

Mungo National Park is home to significant Aboriginal cultural sites and spectacular 70-kilometre vistas. Visitors can enjoy the drive around the lake floor, which takes in many of the attractions. Camping areas are located at the entrance of the park and halfway along the drive tour.

As a pleasant deviation from the outback plains, visitors to this region could take a detour down to the Murray River and camp in one of a handful of state forests that stretch along the river from the South Australian border to Euston. Soak up the magnificent river red gum scenery (but be mindful not to camp under these trees as they can drop limbs without warning).

BEST CAMPSITES

Olive Downs Campground
Sturt National Park

Opal Pioneer Reserve
White Cliffs

Darling River camping areas
Kinchega National Park

Homestead Creek camping area
Mutawintji National Park

Main Camp camping area
Mungo National Park

BEST TIME TO VISIT

Late autumn through to early spring. Summer can bring some extremely high temperatures.

1. BREWARRINA AREA

Brewarrina is 100 km east of Bourke and is reached via Bourke–Brewarrina Rd. It is a historic river town set on the Barwon River with a strong Aboriginal heritage as well – take a look at the Aboriginal fish traps. There is good fishing for yellowbelly and cod.

Four Mile camping area

Beside Barwon River 6 km east of Brewarrina, signposted from Carinda Rd. Fish for yellowbelly and cod. Bring drinking water and firewood. Additional map ref.: NSWRD 53 Q5.

Further information & bookings: Brewarrina Shire Council **Tel.:** (02) 6839 2106 **Email:** breshire@tpg.com.au

2. BOURKE AREA

Bourke is a historic town on the Darling River, dubbed the 'gateway to the outback'. It is reached via the Mitchell Hwy (Kidman Way) from Nyngan in the south or Cunnamulla in the north. Swim, fish and boat on the Darling River.

Mays Bend camping area

Situated 11 km north of North Bourke beside the Darling River. Follow signs to Bullamunta Caravan Park off the Mitchell Hwy (Cunnamulla Rd) from North Bourke. The camping area is on the northern side of the caravan park. Bring drinking water. Additional map ref.: NSWRD 52 K6.

Further information & bookings: Bourke Tourist Information Centre **Tel.:** (02) 6872 1222

3. CULGOA NATIONAL PARK

This isolated park is 100 km north of Brewarrina, near Weilmoringle. Visitors should contact NPWS Bourke for access details. Activities include wildlife watching and exploring the park's walking trails.

Culgoa River Campground

On Tatala Track, 25 km north-west of Weilmoringle near Culgoa River. No wood collection in park – gas/fuel stove preferred. Bring drinking water. Additional map ref.: NSWRD 53 Q1.

Further information & bookings: NPWS, Bourke **Tel.:** (02) 6872 2744 **Camping fees:** Fees may have been implemented since publication

4. GUNDABOOKA NATIONAL PARK

This park's main feature is the Gunderbooka Range, with Mt Gunderbooka rising to 500 m. It is 50 km south of Bourke. Access is via East Toorale Rd from the Mitchell Hwy (Kidman Way) and is possible in dry weather only. You can view Aboriginal artwork (contact NPWS Bourke for details) and walk to Little Mountain. Intending visitors to the park are required to contact NPWS Bourke to obtain detailed directions and information.

Dry Tank Visitor Area

Small camping area (four sites) 60 km south of Bourke (10 km in from the Mitchell Hwy). Access via East Toorale Rd. Bring drinking water. Gas/fuel stove preferred – firewood collection prohibited in park. Shearers quarters accommodation also available. Additional map ref.: NSWRD 52 J8.

Further information & bookings: NPWS, Bourke
Tel.: (02) 6872 2744 **Camping fees:** Fees may have been implemented since publication

This park is a former sheep property with many relics of that era. It is located 5 km south of Menindee and 110 km south-east of Broken Hill, and lies on the Darling River and Menindee Lakes. Access is possible in dry weather only, via Old Pooncarie Rd from Menindee. Visit the historic woolshed. There are also many reminders of Aboriginal occupation here.

Cawndilla camping area

This is 24 km south-west of Menindee with a foreshore location. Signposted from Lake Drive off Old Pooncarie Rd. Bring drinking water and firewood. Additional map ref.: NSWRD 59 M8.

Darling River camping areas

Many campsites along the Darling River within park, commencing 10 km south of Menindee. Signposted via River Drive. Bring drinking water and firewood. Additional map ref.: NSWRD 59 M8.

Emu Lake camping area

Located 24 km south of Menindee, near visitor centre. Signposted from Emu Lake Drive off Old Pooncarie Rd. Bring drinking water and firewood. Additional map ref.: NSWRD 59 M8.

Shearers Quarters

Bunkhouse accommodation in former shearers quarters, 24 km south of Menindee, beside visitor centre. Signposted from Emu Lake Drive. Communal kitchen. Advance bookings essential. Additional map ref.: NSWRD 59 M8.

Further information & bookings: NPWS, Broken Hill
Tel.: (08) 8088 5933 **Park use fee:** $6.00 per vehicle/day
Camping fees: $3.00 per adult/night, $2.00 per child (age 5–15) per night; camping fees payable at self-registration stations *Shearers Quarters:* $16.50 per adult/night, $8.25 per child (age 12–15) per night, $3.30 per child (age 5–12) per night

These are large water storage lakes drawing water from the Darling River. They are about 100 km south-east of Broken Hill and 5 km north-east of Menindee. Access is via Menindee–Broken Hill Rd. Burke and Wills camped in this area on their ill-fated expedition to the Gulf of Carpentaria. There are water-based activities on the lakes as well as on the Darling River.

Burke and Wills Campsite

Camping beside Darling River, 19 km north-east of Menindee near Main Weir. Access via Main Weir Rd (turn-off 8 km from Menindee) from Menindee–Broken Hill Rd. Bring drinking water and firewood. Additional map ref.: NSWRD 59 N7.

Main Weir camping area

Located 20 km north-east of Menindee near Main Weir. Signposted via Main Weir Rd from Menindee–Broken Hill Rd. Bring drinking water and firewood. Additional map ref.: NSWRD 59 N7.

Pamamaroo Lake camping area

This is 16 km north of Menindee. Access via Main Weir Rd from Menindee–Broken Hill Rd. Bring drinking water and firewood. Additional map ref.: NSWRD 59 N7.

Further information & bookings: Menindee Visitor Information Centre **Tel.:** (08) 8091 4274

Milparinka is a former gold-rush town, now almost a ghost town, 42 km south of Tibooburra just off the Silver City Hwy. Access is via Silver City Hwy (Broken Hill–Tibooburra Rd). There is a hospitable bush pub here and the area is popular with outback travellers and fossickers.

Evelyn Creek camping areas

Bush camping areas – no facilities – 1 km east of Milparinka. Access via Milparinka Rd (turn-off 40 km south of Tibooburra) from Silver City Hwy. On east bank of creek. Bring drinking water and firewood. Additional map ref.: NSWRD 50 K4.

Further information & bookings: Albert Hotel
Tel.: (08) 8091 3863

The remote Mungo National Park is part of the Willandra Lakes World Heritage Area and there is much evidence of prior Aboriginal occupation here. The park is 110 km north-east of Mildura and is signposted via Mildura–Arumpo–Ivanhoe Rd. All roads within the park are dry weather only – check on conditions after rain. Once here, marvel at the spectacular Walls of China and take the 70-km Drive Tour.

Belah Camp camping area

This is 35 km east of park visitor centre. Signposted from Drive Tour. Remote area. Bring drinking water. Gas/fuel stove only. Additional map ref.: NSWRD 67 R4.

Main Camp camping area

Situated at park entrance. Signposted from Arumpo Rd. Bring drinking water. Bring firewood; also available for purchase. Additional map ref.: NSWRD 67 Q4.

Shearers Quarters

Near visitor centre. Bunkhouse accommodation in former shearers quarters. Fully equipped kitchen. Bring drinking water. Bring firewood; also available for purchase. Advance bookings essential. Additional map ref.: NSWRD 67 R4.

Further information & bookings: NPWS, Buronga
Tel.: (03) 5021 8900 **Park use fee:** $6.00 per vehicle/day
Camping fees: $3.00 per adult/night, $2.00 per child (age

5–15) per night; camping fees payable at self-registration stations *Shearers Quarters:* $16.50 per adult/night, $5.50 per child (age 12–15) per night

9. MURRAY RIVER STATE FORESTS – SOUTH AUSTRALIAN BORDER TO EUSTON

See also Murray River State Forests – Barham to Mulwala, *page 70*

Numerous river red gum forests are scattered along the banks of the Murray River from the South Australian border to Euston. Access is possible in dry weather only – check road conditions for caravan access. Flooding may occur after heavy rains. There are numerous bush camping areas (some with limited facilities) throughout these forests; contact State Forests Mildura for details. Activities include swimming, fishing, boating, waterskiing and canoeing on the river. There is a solid-fuel fire ban Nov.–Easter throughout these forests – gas/fuel stove only.

Euston State Forest camping areas

Adjacent to Euston. Access via Tapalin Mail Rd from the Sturt Hwy. Gas/fuel stove preferred. Bring drinking water. Additional map ref.: NSWRD 67 P8.

Gol Gol State Forest camping areas

On Murray River 24 km east of Mildura near Monak. Access is from the Sturt Hwy. Gas/fuel stove preferred. Bring drinking water. Additional map ref.: NSWRD 67 M7.

Lake Victoria State Forest camping areas

On Murray River near Lake Victoria, 55 km west of Wentworth. Access via Rufus River Rd. Gas/fuel stove preferred. Bring drinking water. Additional map ref.: NSWRD 66 G6.

Mallee Cliffs State Forest camping areas

Situated 40 km west of Euston. Access via Tapalin Mail Rd from Sturt Hwy. Gas/fuel stove preferred. Bring drinking water. Additional map ref.: NSWRD 67 M8.

Further information & bookings: State Forests, Mildura **Tel.:** (03) 5023 1400 **Email:** cumberland@sf.nsw.gov.au

10. MUTAWINTJI NATIONAL PARK

This is 130 km north-east of Broken Hill and there is signposted access from Broken Hill–White Cliffs Rd, off the Silver City Hwy. All roads to and within the park are dry weather only – check access conditions after rain. The park is jointly managed by the traditional Aboriginal owners and NPWS. Take a guided tour of Mutawintji Historic Site – New South Wales's best Aboriginal art site. The park also contains majestic outback scenery and there are walking tracks to gorges and lookouts.

Homestead Creek camping area

This is 130 km north-east of Broken Hill. Signposted dry-weather-only access via Broken Hill–White Cliffs Rd. Bring drinking water (bore water supplied) and firewood. Additional map ref.: NSWRD 59 M2.

Further information & bookings: NPWS, Broken Hill **Tel.:** (08) 8088 5933 **Camping fees:** $5.00 per adult/night, $3.00 per child (age 5–15) per night; camping fees payable at self-registration stations **Guided tours:** Tours of Mutawintji Historic Site on Wed. and Sat. (April–Nov.) at 11 am. Cost is $20.00 per adult or $40.00 for families (2 adults + 2 children)

11. POONCARIE

Pooncarie is an old river port town on the Darling River 120 km north-east of Wentworth. It is signposted from Pooncarie Rd between Wentworth and Menindee.

P.A.D.D.A. Park

In Tarcoola St beside Darling River. Bring drinking water. Firewood supplied. Additional map ref.: NSWRD 67 N2.

Further information & bookings: Telegraph Hotel **Tel.:** (03) 5029 5205 **Camping fees:** $5.00 per vehicle/night; fees payable at hotel

12. SILVER CITY HIGHWAY (BROKEN HILL–TIBOOBURRA)

The Silver City Hwy runs from Broken Hill to Tibooburra and passes through dramatic outback landscapes.

Fowlers Gap Rest Area

Located 108 km north of Broken Hill. Suitable for overnight stays. Bring drinking water and firewood. Additional map ref.: NSWRD 58 J1.

Packsaddle Rest Area

This is 177 km north of Broken Hill, just north of Packsaddle Roadhouse. Suitable for overnight stays. Bring drinking water and firewood. Additional map ref.: NSWRD 50 K9.

Further information & bookings: RTA, Broken Hill **Tel.:** (08) 8082 6699

13. SILVERTON

A former goldmining town 25 km north-west of Broken Hill. It is signposted from Broken Hill–Silverton Rd. Today there is a vibrant artists' community here.

Penrose Park

Signposted from Silverton. Bunkhouse accommodation also available. Bring drinking water and firewood. Additional map ref.: NSWRD 58 G5.

Further information & bookings: Penrose Park Trust **Tel.:** (08) 8088 5307 **Camping fees:** From $4.00 per adult/night *Bunkhouse:* From $25.00/night

14. STURT NATIONAL PARK

Sturt National Park is a large, remote park 330 km north of Broken Hill near Tibooburra. It is signposted from the Silver City Hwy. There is much to see and do here, and the outback scenery is stunning. Visit in autumn, winter or spring.

Dead Horse Gully Campground

Located 1 km north of Tibooburra. View relics of goldmining days. Bring drinking water. Gas/fuel stove only. Additional map ref.: NSWRD 51 L2.

Fort Grey Campground

This is 109 km north-west of Tibooburra. Signposted dry-weather-only access via Tibooburra–Cameron Corner Rd. Bring drinking water. Gas/fuel stove only. Additional map ref.: NSWRD 50 G1

Mount Wood Campground

Situated 27 km east of Tibooburra. Signposted dry-weather-only access via Gorge Loop Rd from Wanaaring Rd or Silver City Hwy. Bring drinking water. Gas/fuel stove only. Additional map ref.: NSWRD 51 M3.

Olive Downs Campground

Located 55 km north of Tibooburra. Signposted dry-weather-only access via Jump Up Loop Rd from Silver City Hwy. Bring drinking water. Gas/fuel stove only. Additional map ref.: NSWRD 50 K1.

Further information & bookings: NPWS, Tibooburra **Tel.:** (08) 8091 3308 **Park use fee:** $6.00 per vehicle/day **Camping fees:** $3.00 per adult/night, $2.00 per child (age 5–15) per night; camping fees payable at self-registration stations

15. TILPA AREA

Small village on the Darling River 140 km north-east of Wilcannia. Signposted from Wilcannia.

Tilpa Weir camping area

Located 6 km north-east of Tilpa, on eastern side of Darling River at Tilpa Weir. Access from Tilpa–Louth Rd. Popular spot for fishing. Bring drinking water and firewood. Additional map ref.: NSWRD 52 C10.

Further information & bookings: Tilpa Hotel **Tel.:** (02) 6837 3928

16. WHITE CLIFFS

White Cliffs is an opal-mining town 95 km north of Wilcannia. It is signposted from Wilcannia. Noodle for opal and visit a dugout home.

Opal Pioneer Reserve

In White Cliffs. Laundry facilities. Bring firewood. Additional map ref.: NSWRD 51 R10.

Further information & bookings: Opal Pioneer Reserve **Tel.:** (08) 8091 6688 **Camping fees:** $3.30 per adult/night; power $4.40 extra per night

17. WILLANDRA NATIONAL PARK

This large park is a former sheep property. It is 65 km north-west of Hillston, signposted from the Hillston–Mossgiel Rd. All roads are only accessible in dry weather. Willandra Creek, which runs beside the park's homestead, is a haven for wildlife. Explore the old homestead and shearing sheds, and drive the Merton Motor Trail.

Willandra Homestead camping area

Near Willandra Creek. Signposted from Hillston–Mossgiel Rd. Bring drinking water. Firewood supplied. Additional map ref.: NSWRD 68 F1.

Further information & bookings: NPSW, Griffith **Tel.:** (02) 6962 7755 **Park use fee:** $6.00 per vehicle/day **Camping fees:** $3.00 per adult/night, $2.00 per child (age 5–15) per night; camping fees payable at self-registration stations

Mens Quarters

At Willandra Homestead complex. Signposted from Hillston–Mossgiel Rd. Bunkroom accommodation. Bring linen, all food and drinking water. Firewood supplied. Bookings essential. Additional map ref.: NSWRD 68 F1.

Willandra Homestead and Cottage

Willandra Homestead (sleeps up to 15 people) and cottage (sleeps up to 8 people) are for hire. Facilities include beds, eating and cooking utensils, stoves, fridges and hot showers. Contact NPSW Willandra for details and bookings. Bookings essential. Additional map ref.: NSWRD 68 F1.

Further information & bookings: NPSW, Willandra **Tel.:** (02) 6967 8159 **Park use fee:** $6.00 per vehicle/day **Accommodation fees:** Contact NPWS for current rates

VICTORIA

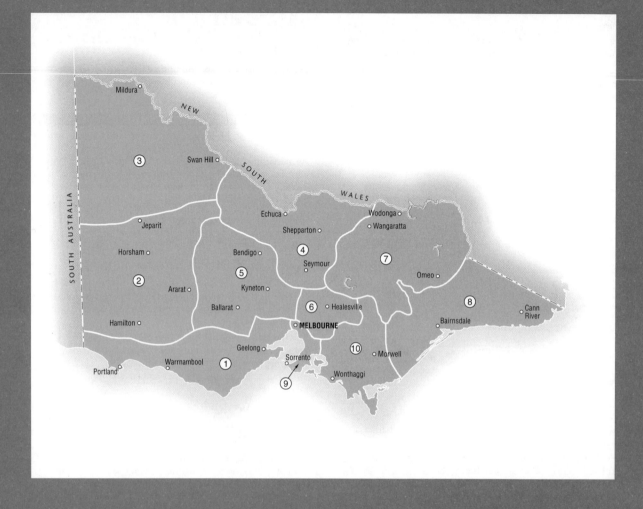

FOR A SMALL STATE IN THE SOUTH-EAST POCKET OF AUSTRALIA, VICTORIA OFFERS A MAGNIFICENT RANGE OF LANDSCAPES – BEACHES, MOUNTAINS, FOREST, RIVERS, EVEN SOME POCKETS OF NEAR DESERT.

In the south the major drawcard is the coast. It weaves a ragged line of cliffs, bays, inlets, islands and lakes, with some classic destinations found amongst them. West of Melbourne are the wind- and sea-swept sandstone formations found along the Great Ocean Road, and to the east is the granite-strewn shoreline of Wilsons Promontory, both great destinations for camping.

In the north is another border of water, this time the long and winding path of the Murray. This famous river rises in the Great Dividing Range. Camp along its banks and take the time to explore the river towns of Echuca and Mildura, which date back to the glorious days of river ports and paddle steamers.

Beneath the Murray, Victoria's north-west is a semi-arid landscape that works another kind of magic on the visitor. This area is characterised by stretches of fragile mallee woodlands, seasonal lake systems, and plains that bloom with wildflowers in spring. Little Desert National Park is one of the gems here – one fifth of the state's indigenous flora is found in the park, including some delicate species of orchid.

Perhaps Victoria's favourite national park, Grampians National Park, is found in the central-west. The lofty ranges of the Grampians are punctuated by weathered rock formations, lakes and waterfalls, and with the rocky terrain comes a strong legacy of Aboriginal rock art – intriguing hand stencils, figures and Dreamtime spirits.

Lower Glenelg National Park, in Victoria's south-west, is another highlight of the state, featuring the peaceful waters of the Glenelg River. Reedy banks meet the deep, green river, tall gums cast reflections on the water, and the sounds of herons and native ducks echo off the limestone walls of Glenelg River Gorge. Campsites here are equipped with their own jetties, great for tying up your canoe or casting in a line.

Great camping spots are spread right across Victoria. You could camp out for a year in this seemingly small state and still not have seen it all!

The Balconies, otherwise known as the Jaws of Death, in Grampians National Park

THE SCENIC SOUTH-WEST COAST IS ONE OF AUSTRALIA'S GREAT DESTINATIONS. IT INCLUDES THE FAMOUS GREAT OCEAN ROAD, WHICH BEGINS SOUTH OF GEELONG AND IS CLASSED AS ONE OF THE WORLD'S MOST SPECTACULAR COASTAL ROUTES. THE SCENERY RANGES FROM MAJESTIC ROCK FORMATIONS TO PICTURESQUE WATERFALLS, TOWERING EUCALYPT FORESTS, ROLLING GREEN HILLS AND JAW-DROPPING CLIFF LINES. THE MAGNIFICENT TWELVE APOSTLES ARE ONE OF THE HIGHLIGHTS, DRAWING THOUSANDS OF VISITORS EACH YEAR.

Many national parks, state forests, coastal parks and foreshore reserves dot this coastline and its hinterland. There are plenty of spots for camping and caravanning, and a huge range of recreational activities on offer.

Otway National Park takes in the Cape Otway Lighthouse and the remains of some tragic shipwrecks. There are a number of campsites throughout the park, with varying facilities and access. Activities include bushwalking, mountain bike riding, swimming and fishing.

The Otway State Forests feature a mix of forest types, while hidden away in their north is the picturesque Lake Elizabeth – this was formed

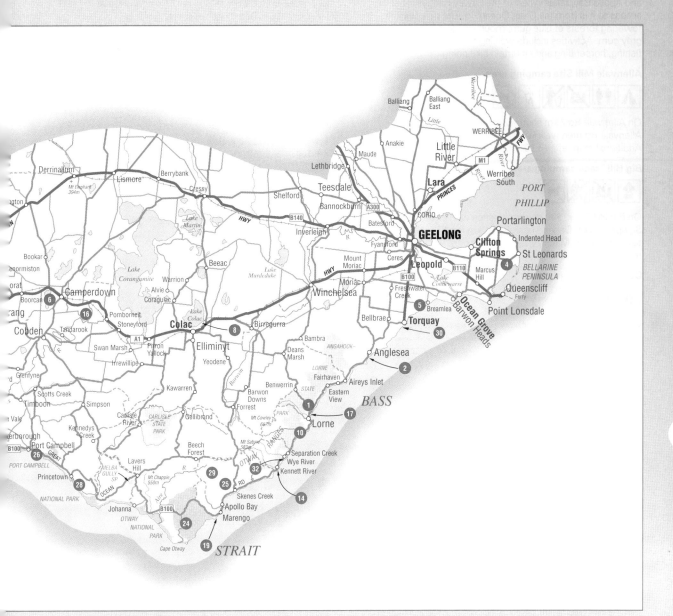

in 1952 as the result of a landslip. Campsites are dotted throughout these forests.

Just to the east of the South Australian border is the large Lower Glenelg National Park. The park is centred around the tranquil waters of the Glenelg River, which has carved a spectacular gorge on its way to the Southern Ocean. Canoeing the Glenelg River is a perfect way to view the cliffs of the gorge. In the west of the park are the magnificent Princess Margaret Rose Caves, and in spring the park comes alive with wildflowers. Campsites are scattered along the northern and southern banks of the river, with some sites only accessible by canoe.

BEST CAMPSITES

Lake Elizabeth camping area
Otway State Forests and Reserves

Fitzroy River Coastal Reserve camping area
Fitzroy River Coastal Reserve

Pritchards camping area
Lower Glenelg National Park

Lake Surprise camping area
Mount Eccles National Park

Aire River West camping area
Otway National Park

BEST TIME TO VISIT

All year round – however, winter can be quite wet.

1. ANGAHOOK–LORNE STATE PARK

This long park, which follows the coast between Anglesea and Apollo Bay, takes in part of the Otway Ranges. The main access to it is from the Great Ocean Rd. The park features towering forests of blue gum, mountain ash and mountain grey gum. Activities include walking trails, 4WD trails, rock fishing, horseriding and mountain bike riding.

Allenvale Mill Site camping area

On Allenvale Rd 2 km south-west of Lorne. Access via Allenvale Rd then walk in 100 m to site. Gas/fuel stove only. Additional map ref.: VR 101 H2.

Big Hill Track camping area

On Big Hill Track, 200 m from junction with Deans Marsh Rd. Signposted off Deans Marsh Rd 11 km from Lorne heading towards Deans Marsh. Gas/fuel stove only. Additional map ref.: VR 92 H9.

Cora Lynn camping area

On Cora Lynn Walking Track. Walk-in only access from Blanket Leaf picnic area on the Erskine Falls Rd. Gas/fuel stove only. Contact ranger for details. Additional map ref.: VR 101 G2.

Hammonds Road camping area

On Hammonds Rd, 10 km from Aireys Inlet in the northern area of the park. Access via Bambra Rd from Aireys Inlet. Gas/fuel stove only. Bring drinking water. Additional map ref.: VR 93 B8.

Jamieson Track camping area

Small site reached via Jamieson Track (seasonally closed), 10 km south of Lorne off the Great Ocean Rd. 4WD only access. Gas/fuel stove only. Additional map ref.: VR 101 G3.

Sharps Track camping area

On Sharps Track, signposted off Allenvale Rd. Conventional vehicle access in dry weather only (4WD recommended). Gas/fuel stove only. Additional map ref.: VR 101 G2.

Wye River Road camping area

Off Wye River Rd, which begins 14 km south of Lorne off the Great Ocean Rd. Gas/fuel stove only. Additional map ref.: VR 101 G3.

Further information & bookings: Parks Victoria information line **Tel.:** 131 963

2. ANGLESEA

This camping spot is close to the shopping centre and signposted from Cameron Rd, which is off the Great Ocean Rd. It has both beach and river frontage.

Anglesea Family Caravan Park

Gas/fuel stove only. Open all year round. Bookings recommended at peak times. Additional map ref.: VR 296 F3.

Further information & bookings: Anglesea Family Caravan Park **Tel.:** (03) 5263 1583 **Email:** info@angleseafcp.com.au **Website:** www.angleseafcp.com.au **Camping fees:** Tent sites from $21.00 per site/night. Cabin accommodation also available

3. ANNYA STATE FOREST

This forest is north of Heywood, near Drumborg.

Annya Camp camping area

Access via Portland–Casterton Rd, off the Princes Hwy. Bring drinking water. Additional map ref.: VR 88 B2.

Further information & bookings: DSE, Heywood **Tel.:** (03) 5527 1302

4. BELLARINE PENINSULA

The Bellarine Peninsula is a popular seaside holiday destination and watersports venue east of Geelong. It forms the western entrance to Port Phillip Bay. There are good fishing grounds for anglers and many camping areas are on foreshore reserves.

Barwon Heads Park caravan and camping area

Access from Ewing Blyth Drive, Barwon Heads. On Barwon Heads Foreshore, close to surf beach. Gas/fuel stove only. Also cabins and backpacker accommodation. Bookings essential during peak times. Additional map ref.: VR 297 S11.

Further information & bookings: Barwon Heads Park **Tel.:** (03) 5254 1115 **Email:** bookings@barwoncoast.com.au **Website:** www.barwoncoast.com.au **Camping fees:** Unpowered sites from $17.00 per site/night

Indented Head foreshore – Anderson Reserve, Batman Park and Taylors Reserve camping areas

Access via The Esplanade. Foreshore frontage to Port Phillip Bay. Gas/fuel stove only. All three reserves are open Melbourne Cup weekend–25 April. Bookings essential during peak times. Additional map ref.: VR 300 J1.

Further information & bookings: Indented Head Foreshore **Tel.:** (03) 5259 2764 **Email:** info@portalingtonresort.com.au **Camping fees:** From $22.00 per site/night

Portarlington Seaside Resort

Access via Sproat St. Foreshore frontage to Port Phillip Bay in Portarlington village. Gas/fuel stove only. Open all year round. Bookings essential for peak periods. Additional map ref.: VR 298 E2.

Further information & bookings: Portarlington Seaside Resort **Tel.:** (03) 5259 2764 or 1800 222 778 **Email:** info@portalingtonresort.com.au **Camping fees:** From $22.00 per site/night

Queenscliff Recreation Reserve caravan and camping area

Foreshore location at Hesse St, Queenscliff. Good access to Port Phillip Bay. Gas/fuel stove only. Open all year round. Bookings essential for peak periods. Additional map ref.: VR 299 R3.

Further information & bookings: Queenscliff Recreation Reserve **Tel.:** (03) 5258 1765 **Email:** queenscliifftourist@ telstra.com **Camping fees:** Unpowered sites from $16.00 per 2 people/ night.

Riverview Family Caravan Park, Ocean Grove

On the Barwon River close to Ocean Grove Beach, reached from Barwon Heads Rd. Natural sites. Gas/fuel stove only. Open all year round. Weekly bookings only during summer and bookings essential during Christmas period. Additional map ref.: VR 298 B12.

Further information & bookings: Riverview Family Caravan Park **Tel.:** (03) 5256 1600 **Email:** bookings@ barwoncoast.com.au **Website:** www.barwoncoast.com.au **Camping fees:** Unpowered sites from $17.00 per site/night

Royal Park caravan and camping area, Point Lonsdale

Access via Point Lonsdale Rd. Close to The Heads, Point Lonsdale. Foreshore location. Gas/fuel stove only. Open 1 Dec.–30 April. Bookings essential for peak periods. Additional map ref.: VR 300 D9.

Further information & bookings: Royal Park **Tel.:** (03) 5258 1765 **Email:** queenscliiftourist@telstra.com **Camping fees:** Unpowered sites from $16.00 per 2 people/ night

St Leonards Foreshore caravan and camping area

Foreshore frontage near The Bluff at St Leonards; signposted from The Esplanade. Gas/fuel stove only. Two camping areas. Open Melbourne Cup weekend–25 April. Bookings essential during peak periods. Additional map ref.: VR 300 J4.

Further information & bookings: St Leonards Foreshore **Tel.:** (03) 5259 2764 **Email:** info@portalingtonresort.com.au **Camping fees:** From $22.00 per site/night

Victoria Park caravan and camping area, Queenscliff

Access via King St, office located in Hesse St. Gas/fuel stove only. Open 1 Dec.–30 April. Bookings essential during peak periods. Additional map ref.: VR 299 Q2.

Further information & bookings: Victoria Park Foreshore **Tel.:** (03) 5258 1765 **Camping fees:** Unpowered sites from $16.00 per 2 people/night

5. BREAMLEA

Breamlea is 18 km south of Geelong, between Barwon Heads and Torquay. It is close to a patrolled ocean beach and tidal estuary.

Breamlea Caravan Park

Access via Horwood Drive. Gas/fuel stove only. Open all year round. Bookings recommended at peak times. Additional map ref.: VR 93 H6.

Further information & bookings: Breamlea Caravan Park **Tel.:** (03) 5264 1352 **Camping fees:** *Off-peak:* Unpowered sites from $12.00 per site/night *Peak:* Unpowered sites from $18.00 per site/night

6. CAMPERDOWN

The caravan park is beside Lake Bullen Merri, 3 km south-west of Camperdown. The lake is part of an extinct volcanic crater and is a popular watersports venue. The route to the park is signposted from Camperdown.

Camperdown Caravan Park

On Park Rd. Fires are permitted; bring fire drum and firewood. Open all year round. Bookings recommended at peak times for powered sites and other accommodation. Additional map ref.: VR 91 C5.

Further information & bookings: Camperdown Caravan Park **Tel.:** (03) 5593 1253 **Camping fees:** Tent sites from $11.50 per site/night

7. COBBOBOONEE STATE FOREST

This state forest is west of Heywood and is reached via the Princes Hwy. The Great South West Walk cuts through the forest.

Jackass Fern Gully camping area

Located 9 km south along T&W Rd from the signposted turn-off on the Princes Hwy, 24 km west of Heywood and 17 km east of Dartmoor. Bring drinking water. Additional map ref.: VR 87 H3.

Surrey Ridge picnic and camping area

Access via Coffeys Lane off the Princes Hwy south of Heywood, then south onto Jackys Swamp Rd and west for 2 km on Cut Out Dam Rd. Bring drinking water. Additional map ref.: VR 88 A4.

Further information & bookings: DSE, Heywood
Tel.: (03) 5527 1302

8. COLAC

Colac is on the shores of Lake Colac, 75 km west of Geelong via the Princes Hwy. The lake is a popular watersports venue.

Central Caravan Park

In Bruce St, Colac. Open all year round. Bookings preferred. Additional map ref.: VR 263 S3.

Further information & bookings: Central Caravan Park **Tel.:** (03) 5231 3586 **Camping fees:** Unpowered tent sites from $10.00 per site/night; powered caravan sites from $15.00 per site/night

Lake Colac Caravan Park

Access via Fyans St in Colac. Open all year round. Bookings recommended at peak times. Additional map ref.: VR 263 Q2.

Further information & bookings: Lake Colac Caravan Park **Tel.:** (03) 5231 5971 **Camping fees:** Tent sites from $10.00 per site/night; coin-operated showers

Meredith Park camping area

On Meredith Park Rd, signposted from the Colac–Ballarat Rd. Additional map ref.: VR 92 B6.

Further information & bookings: Colac Tourist Information Centre **Tel.:** (03) 5231 3730 **Camping fees:** Fees collected by ranger **Fire restrictions:** Fire danger period Nov.–May, check with locals before lighting a fire; fires only in regulation-built fireplaces

9. CRAWFORD RIVER REGIONAL PARK

The park has a diverse flora of heathland and forest, and you may see red-necked wallabies and grey kangaroos. Access is via The Boulevard off the Lyons–Hotspur Rd, which is either off the Princes Hwy 22 km north-west of Heywood (17 km south-east of Dartmoor) or from Hotspur along the Portland–Casterton Rd.

Hiscocks camping area

Dispersed camping along the Crawford River between Hotspur and Dartmoor. Bring drinking water and firewood. Additional map ref.: VR 71 J8.

Further information & bookings: DSE Customer Service Centre **Tel.:** 136 186

10. CUMBERLAND RIVER RESERVE

The Cumberland River reaches the sea 7 km south-west of Lorne. The reserve is signposted from the Great Ocean Rd. There are many walking trails in the area.

Cumberland River Holiday Park

River frontage surrounded by cliffs. Close to beach. Open all year round. Bookings recommended at peak times. Additional map ref.: VR 101 H3.

Further information & bookings: Cumberland River Holiday Park **Tel.:** (03) 5289 1790 **Email:** cumberland@ netconnect. com.au **Camping fees:** Tent sites from $14.00 per site/night. Cabins also available

11. DISCOVERY BAY COASTAL PARK

This coastal park stretches between Portland and Nelson. Attractions in the area include lakes, seal colonies, blowholes, petrified forests and sweeping beaches.

Lake Monibeong camping area

This is 16 km south-east of Nelson. Reached via Lake Monibeong Rd, off the Portland–Nelson Road. Bring drinking water and firewood. Additional map ref.: VR 87 D3.

Swan Lake camping area

This is 30 km north-west of Portland. Reached via Swan Lake Rd, off the Nelson–Portland Rd. Bring drinking water and firewood. Bookings required. Additional map ref.: VR 87 F5.

Further information & bookings: Parks Victoria information line **Tel.:** 131 963 **Camping fees:** *Peak:* From $12.30 per site/night *Off-peak:* From $9.00 per site/night

12. FITZROY RIVER COASTAL RESERVE

The reserve is at the mouth of the Fitzroy River and is reached via a signposted turn-off along the Princes Hwy. The reserve gives access to some beautiful sandy beaches along the Discovery Coast.

Fitzroy River Coastal Reserve camping area

On the eastern side of the Fitzroy River mouth, along Thomsons Rd. Turn-off from the Princes Hwy about half-way between Portland and Yambuk. Bring drinking water and firewood. Additional map ref.: VR 88 F6.

Further information & bookings: Portland Visitor Information Centre **Tel.:** (03) 5523 2671 **Email:** portlandvic@ glenelg.vic.gov.au **Website:** www.maritimediscovery.com **Camping fees:** Free for the first week

13. THE GREAT SOUTH WEST WALK

Stretching for 250 km, the Great South West Walk begins and ends in Portland. From Portland it heads north through native forests before reaching the Glenelg River, then heads for the coast near the South Australia border. From there the walk follows the coast back to Portland. Campsites are located all along the track, and facilities vary from site to site. Water from creeks or rivers may not always be reliable – always carry extra. Obtain a copy of the walk brochure and maps before heading out.

Cubbys Camp
20 km from Portland Visitor Information Centre. Additional map ref.: VR 88 B5.
Cut-out Camp
15 km from Cubbys. Additional map ref.: VR 88 A5.
Cobboboonee Camp
9.4 km from Cut-out. Additional map ref.: VR 87 J4.
Fitzroy Camp
12.5 km from Cobboboonee. Additional map ref.: VR 87 H3.
Moleside Camp
22 km from Fitzroy. Additional map ref.: VR 87 F3.
Post and Rail Camp
12 km from Moleside. Additional map ref.: VR 87 E2.
Murrells Camp
9.5 km from Post and Rail. Additional map ref.: VR 87 D2.
Pattersons Camp
8.5 km from Murrells. Additional map ref.: VR 87 B2.
Simsons Camp
17 km from Pattersons. Additional map ref.: VR 87 A2.
White Sands Camp
13 km from Simsons. Additional map ref.: VR 87 B3.
Lake Monibeong
13 km from White Sands (see Discovery Bay Coastal Park, previous page). Additional map ref.: VR 87 D4.
Swan Lake
16.5 km from Lake Monibeong (see Discovery Bay Coastal Park, previous page). Additional map ref.: VR 87 F5.
The Springs Camp
21 km from Swan Lake. Additional map ref.: VR 87 G7.
Trewalla Camp
15 km from The Springs. Additional map ref.: VR 88 A8.
Mallee Camp
17 km from Trewalla and 16.5 km from Portland Visitor Information Centre. Additional map ref.: VR 88 A8.

Further information & bookings: Parks Victoria information line **Tel.:** 131 963.

14. KENNETT RIVER

Located at Kennett River between Lorne and Apollo Bay. Signposted access via the Great Ocean Rd. Popular surfing area.

Kennett River Caravan Park

Open year round. Bookings required at peak times. Additional map ref.: VR 101 F4.

Further information and bookings: Kennett River Caravan Park **Tel.:** (03) 5289 0272 **Email:** kennettriver@bigpond.com **Camping fees:** Check with office for current fees

15. KILLARNEY

Killarney lies between Port Fairy and Warrnambool, on the Princes Hwy. Set amongst coastal vegetation, the Killarney foreshore is well-sheltered, and the caravan park has grassy sites. Killarney beach offers safe swimming, fishing and walking.

Killarney Caravan Park

Signposted from Princes Hwy, 11 km east of Port Fairy. Bookings recommended during Christmas holidays. Additional map ref.: VR 89 F7.

Further information & bookings: Killarney Hotel **Tel.:** (03) 5568 7290 **Camping fees:** Unpowered sites from $11.00 per site/night, powered from $13.50 per site/night; fees payable at hotel

16. LAKE PURRUMBETE

Lake Purrumbete is 10 km east of Camperdown and is reached via the Princes Hwy and then Purrumbete Estate Road. It is a popular fishing venue.

Lake Purrumbete Caravan Park

Close to lake. Open all year round. Bookings recommended at peak times. Additional map ref.: VR 91 E6.

Further information & bookings: Lake Purrumbete Caravan Park **Tel.:** (03) 5594 5377 **Camping fees:** Tent sites from $6.00 per person/night

17. LORNE

Lorne has been a favourite holiday destination of Victorians for many decades, and is picturesquely situated on the Great Ocean Rd. Its beach is a focus for watersports.

Erskine River camping area

On the northern bank of the Erskine River. Bookings required at peak times. Additional map ref.: VR 265 N4.

Kia-Ora camping area

On the southern bank of the Erskine River. Bookings required at peak times. Additional map ref.: VR 265 N4.

Further information & bookings: Lorne Foreshore Reserve **Tel.:** (03) 5289 1382 **Email:** LFCMD@bigpond.com.au **Website:** www.lorneforeshore.asn.au **Camping fees:** Tent sites from $16.00 per 2 people/night

18. LOWER GLENELG NATIONAL PARK
see page 86

19. MARENGO

Just south of Apollo Bay, Marengo has superb beach frontage. As well as the excellent views the area has great fishing and surfing.

Marengo Holiday Park

On Marengo Crescent in Marengo. Signposted from the Great Ocean Rd. Bookings required in peak periods. Additional map ref.: VR 264 J10.

Further information & bookings: Marengo Holiday Park **Tel.:** (03) 5237 6162 **Email:** marengo@vicnet.net.au **Website:** www.vicnet.net.au/~marengo **Camping fees:** Unpowered sites from $15.50 for 2 people/night

LOWER GLENELG NATIONAL PARK

Impressive gorge
From its humble beginnings in Grampians National Park, the Glenelg River reaches a dramatic conclusion before it spills into Discovery Bay. Craggy limestone cliffs rise as tall as 50 metres, like sentinels peering into the depths of the still, green river.

East meets west
The array of plant life here is a confluence of east and west. Around Moleside Creek are Australia's most westerly tree-fern gullies, and in spring the park brightens up with wildflowers that include some Western Australian species in their furthest reach.

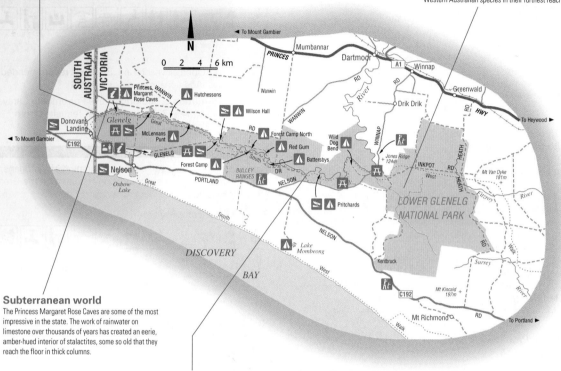

Subterranean world
The Princess Margaret Rose Caves are some of the most impressive in the state. The work of rainwater on limestone over thousands of years has created an eerie, amber-hued interior of stalactites, some so old that they reach the floor in thick columns.

Paddle-perfect
The Glenelg River is a perfect setting for beginner canoeists, or for those who simply prefer a relaxing meander to intense whitewater. Paddle by day and set up at a canoe-only campsite by night – a trip down the Glenelg can feel as though you have virtually left civilisation.

This park is east of Nelson, near Victoria's border with South Australia. Attractions include the tranquil Glenelg River and its estuary. There is excellent canoeing and fishing. You can also explore the Princess Margaret Rose Caves. Bookings and permits are required for all sites in Lower Glenelg National Park.

SOUTHERN RIVERBANK

Battersbys camping area

Located 15 km east of Nelson. Access via Glenelg Drive. Bring drinking water and firewood. Additional map ref.: VR 87 D2.

Forest Camp camping area

Situated 12 km east of Nelson. Access via Glenelg Drive. Bring drinking water and firewood. Additional map ref.: VR 87 D2.

Pritchards camping area

This lies 19 km east of Nelson. Access via Winnap–Nelson Rd. Bring drinking water and firewood. Additional map ref.: VR 87 E3.

Wild Dog Bend camping area

Located 25 km east of Nelson. Access via Winnap–Nelson Rd. Bring drinking water and firewood. Additional map ref.: VR 87 F3.

NORTHERN RIVERBANK

Forest Camp North camping area

Situated 44 km south of Dartmoor, along River Fireline and off the Wanwin Rd. Bring drinking water and firewood. Additional map ref.: VR 87 D2.

Hutchessons camping area

This is 55 km south of Dartmoor, along River Fireline and off Wanwin Rd. Bring drinking water and firewood. Additional map ref.: VR 87 C2.

McLennans Punt camping area

Located 52 km south of Dartmoor, along River Fireline and off Wanwin Rd. Bring drinking water and firewood. Additional map ref.: VR 87 D2.

Princess Margaret Rose Caves camping area

Located 32 km east of Mount Gambier. Access via Princess Margaret Rose Caves Rd. Additional map ref.: VR 87 A1.

Further information & bookings: Princess Margaret Rose Caves office **Tel.:** (08) 8738 4171 **Camping fees:** From $11.00 per site/night

Red Gum camping area

This is 42 km south of Dartmoor, along River Fireline and off the Wanwin Rd. Bring drinking water and firewood. Additional map ref.: VR 87 D2.

Wilson Hall camping area

This lies 48 km south of Dartmoor. Access via Wanwin Rd. Bring drinking water and firewood. Additional map ref.: VR 87 D2.

CANOE ACCESS CAMPING AREAS

Bowds, Deutchers, Georges Rest, Lasletts, Moleside, Pattersons, Pines Landing and Skipworth Springs

These are sites along the Glenelg River that are only accessible by canoe. Permit required. Obtain a copy of the Glenelg River Canoeing Guide from Parks Victoria for details. Additional map ref.: VR 87 C2/D2/E2.

Further information & bookings: For all areas except Princess Margaret Rose Caves, Parks Victoria information line **Tel.:** 131 963 **Camping fees:** *Southern and northern bank sites:* From $12.30 per site/night in peak periods; from $9.00 per site/night in off-peak periods *Canoe access sites:* From $2.20 per person/night

Fishing off the jetty at Forest Camp

20. MOUNT CLAY STATE FOREST

This state forest is a few kilometres east of Narrawong. There is a short walk to Whalers Lookout, an excellent whale-watching spot.

Sawpit picnic and camping area

Access via Boyers Road off the Princes Hwy near Narrawong. Old sawmill site. Bring drinking water and firewood. Additional map ref.: VR 88 D5.

Further information & bookings: DSE, Heywood **Tel.:** (03) 5527 1302

21. MOUNT ECCLES NATIONAL PARK

This national park is 10 km west of Macarthur. Mt Eccles was formed by volcanic activity 20 000 years ago and there are lava caves and tunnels to view. You can swim in the springwater-filled crater of Lake Surprise or go walking on one of the trails.

Lake Surprise camping area

Access via Mt Eccles Rd from Macarthur. There is a specially designed campsite for people with disabilities. Bring firewood (firewood stall 3 km outside park). Bookings required for peak periods: 3rd Fri. of Dec.–1st Sun. of Feb., Labour Day, Easter, Melbourne Cup weekend. Additional map ref.: VR 88 G2.

Further information & bookings: Parks Victoria information line **Tel.:** 131 963 **Camping fees:** *Peak*: From $12.20 per site/night *Off-peak*: From $9.00 per site/night. Fees payable to ranger

22. NARRAWONG

Narrawong is 13 km east of Portland on the Princes Hwy. The Surry River reaches the sea here and there is a beach nearby for swimming and fishing.

Narrawong Holiday Park

Access off the Princes Hwy via Caravan Park Rd. Open all year round. Bookings recommended during peak periods. Additional map ref.: VR 88 D6.

Further information & bookings: Narrawong Holiday Park **Tel.:** (03) 5529 5282 **Email:** nhpark@ansonic.com.au **Camping fees:** Unpowered sites from $15.00 for 2 people/night; powered sites from $17.00 for 2 people/night

23. NELSON

Nelson is close to Lower Glenelg River National Park and the South Australian border. It is also near the Great South West Walk walking trail and the Historic Shipwreck Trail. This camping spot is on North Nelson Rd and is signposted from the Princes Hwy.

Kywong Caravan Park

Only 500 m from the Nelson River. Open all year round. Bookings recommended for peak periods. Additional map ref.: VR 233 T9.

Further information & bookings: Kywong Caravan Park **Tel.:** (08) 8738 4174 **Camping fees:** Unpowered sites from $13.00 for 2 people/night, powered sites from $15.50 for 2 people/night

24. OTWAY NATIONAL PARK

The Great Ocean Rd runs through the middle of this national park, which is 10 km west of Apollo Bay. Attractions include the Cape Otway Lighthouse, Maits Rainforest Walk and the remains of shipwrecks at Wreck Beach. There are many walking trails and other activities include swimming at Blanket Bay and Aire River, fishing, mountain bike riding and horseriding (permit required).

Aire River East camping area

On east bank of Aire River, near mouth. Reached via Hordern Vale Rd from Great Ocean Rd. Bring drinking water and firewood. Additional map ref.: VR 100 J6.

Aire River West camping area

On west bank of Aire River, near mouth. Access via Sand Rd from Glenaire on Great Ocean Rd. Gas/fuel stove only. Bring drinking water. Additional map ref.: VR 100 J6.

Blanket Bay camping area

Access via Lighthouse Rd and Blanket Bay Rd. Bring drinking water and firewood. Bookings required at Easter and Christmas. Additional map ref.: VR 101 B7.

Johanna Beach camping area

Reached via Red Johanna Rd from Great Ocean Rd. Gas/fuel stove only. Campsites behind sand dunes. Popular surfing beach. Additional map ref.: VR 100 H6.

Point Franklin camping area

Access off Blanket Bay Rd from Lighthouse Rd. Access through gate, please close. Gas/fuel stove only. Bring drinking water. Additional map ref.: VR 101 A7.

Parker Hill walk-in camping area

Reached off Blanket Bay Rd from Lighthouse Rd. Access through gate, please close. Walk in to sites. Gas/fuel stove only. Bring drinking water. Additional map ref.: VR 101 A7.

Further information & bookings: Parks Victoria information line **Tel.:** 131 963 **Park use fee:** $4.40 per vehicle/night **Camping fees:** *Aire River East, Aire River West, Blanket Bay and Johanna Beach*: From $10.20 per site/night *Point Franklin and Parker Hill*: $4.40 per site/night

25. OTWAY STATE FORESTS AND RESERVES

The Otway Ranges stretch from the west of Anglesea down to Lavers Hill. As well as Otway National Park, which surrounds Cape Otway, and Angahook–Lorne State Park, which surrounds Lorne, the ranges are protected by state forests and reserves. These areas also boast some great camping spots. The main access roads are Colac–Lavers Hill Rd, Forrest–Apollo Bay Rd and the Great Ocean Rd.

Aire Crossing camping area

Sites beside Aire River. Access via Wait-A-While Rd from Colac–Lavers Hill Rd or Great Ocean Rd then Aire Crossing Track. Additional map ref.: VR 100 J5.

Beauchamp Falls Reserve camping area

On Beauchamp Falls Rd, 33 km north-west of Skenes Creek. From Skenes Creek head north on Skenes Creek Rd then onto Beech Forest Rd for 17 km. Turn into Aire Valley Rd, then Flannagan Rd and finally Beauchamp Falls Rd. Bring drinking water and firewood. Additional map ref.: VR 101 B4.

Dandos camping area

Reached via Lardner Track near Gellibrand River. Water from river – boil before use. Bring firewood. Additional map ref.: VR 101 B2.

Lake Elizabeth camping area

Access via Kaanglang Road from Forrest. Small vans towed by 4WD vehicles can reach this site. Short walk to very picturesque lake which was formed by a natural landslip in 1952. Additional map ref.: VR 101 D2.

Stevenson Falls Reserve camping area

This is 4 km west of Barramunga, and signposted from Gellibrand Road. Bring firewood. Good swimming in the fall's rock pools. Additional map ref.: VR 101 C3.

Further information & bookings: DSE Customer Service Centre **Tel.**: 136 186

26. PORT CAMPBELL

Port Campbell is a small crayfishing village at the eastern end of the Great Ocean Rd. Close by are the world-famous Twelve Apostles, remarkable eroded limestone monoliths that stand off the cliffs. Port Campbell National Park is adjacent to the township. Local activities include swimming, canoeing and fishing.

Port Campbell Cabin and Camping Park

Access via Morris St, Port Campbell. Park is at the head of Campbells Creek, only a short walk to the beach. Open all year round. Gas/fuel stove only. Cabins also available. Bookings required at peak times. Additional map ref.: VR 264 G3.

Further information & bookings: Port Campbell Cabin and Camping Park **Tel.:** (03) 5598 6492 **Email:** campinport@datafast.net.au **Camping fees:** *Off-peak*: Unpowered sites from $15.00 per 2 people/night

The Twelve Apostles, near Port Campbell

27. PORT FAIRY

Port Fairy is home to a large fishing fleet and has an attractive port. The town contains many historic buildings classified by the National Trust. Activities for the visitor include swimming, canoeing and fishing.

Port Fairy Gardens Caravan Park

Access via Griffith St, Port Fairy. River frontage to Moyne River. Close to East Beach. Gas/fuel stove only. Open all year round. Bookings required at peak times. Cabins also available. Additional map ref.: VR 243 Q3.

Further information & bookings: Port Fairy Gardens Caravan Park **Tel.:** (03) 5568 1060 **Email:** portfairygardens@telstra.com **Camping fees:** *Off-peak:* Unpowered sites from $15.00 per 2 people/night

28. PRINCETOWN

Princetown is a small settlement about 20 km east of Port Campbell, beside the Gellibrand River. Local activities include swimming, canoeing and fishing.

Princetown Recreation Reserve

This is 1 km south of Princetown on Old Coach Rd. Additional map ref.: VR 100 D5.

Further information & bookings:
Talk of the Town Restaurant **Tel.:** (03) 5598 8288 *or*
Reserve caretaker **Tel.:** (03) 5237 5221
Camping fees: From $13.00 per site/night. Key access to facilities with a $10.00 refundable deposit; key available from Talk of the Town Restaurant or caretaker

29. SKENES CREEK

Skenes Creek is a small settlement, mainly of holiday homes, 6 km north of Apollo Bay.

Skenes Creek Beachfront Park

Signposted from the Great Ocean Rd. Ocean frontage. Open all year round. Bookings required at peak times. Additional map ref.: VR 265 S4.

Further information & bookings: Skenes Creek Beachfront Park **Tel.:** (03) 5237 6132 **Camping fees:** Unpowered sites from $17.00 per site/night

30. TORQUAY

Torquay is a popular holiday resort; nearby beaches such as Bells Beach are world-famous surfing spots.

Torquay Foreshore Caravan Park

In Bell St, Torquay. Signposted from Surf Coast Hwy. Close to beach and Spring Creek. Gas/fuel stove only. Open all year round. Bookings required at peak times. Additional map ref.: VR 297 M6.

Further information & bookings: Torquay Foreshore Caravan Park **Tel.:** (03) 5261 2496 **Email:** tpri@ozemail.com.au **Website:** www.torquayforeshore.com **Camping fees:** *Off-peak:* Unpowered sites from $19.00 per 2 people/night

31. WARRNAMBOOL

Warrnambool is a lovely seaside city with many parks and gardens. There is an interesting reconstructed 19th-century maritime village and museum where the stories of the many shipwrecks along the local coastline are told.

Surfside Holiday Park

On Pertobe Rd in Warrnambool. Foreshore frontage to Lady Bay and close to Merri River. Open all year round. Gas/fuel stove only. Dogs allowed on lead during off-season; confirm with park prior to arrival. Bookings required at peak times. Additional map ref.: VR 240 K11.

Further information & bookings: Surfside Holiday Park **Tel.:** (03) 5561 2611 **Camping fees:** *Off-peak:* Unpowered sites from $19.00 per 2 people/night

32. WYE RIVER

Wye River is a small holiday destination along the Great Ocean Rd. It is nestled into a bend of the road about 15 km south-west of Lorne.

Wye River Foreshore Reserve

Signposted from Great Ocean Rd, in township. Beach frontage to Bass Strait and beside Wye River. Open 1st week Dec.–end April. Gas/fuel stove only. Bring drinking water. Bookings required at peak times. Additional map ref.: VR 265 S7.

Further information & bookings: Wye River Foreshore Reserve **Tel.:** (03) 5289 0412 **Camping fees:** Unpowered sites from $20.00 per site/night

33. YAMBUK LAKE

Yambuck is near the mouth of the Eumeralla River, 15 km west of Port Fairy. A few kilometres south of the township, the Eumeralla widens to form Yambuk Lake before flowing into the sea. There are great fishing and beachcombing opportunities in the area.

Yambuk Lake Camping Ground

Access via Carrolls Lane or Yambuk Lake Rd, signposted from the Princes Hwy. Gas/fuel stove only. Bookings essential during Easter and Christmas holidays (bookings through caretaker). Additional map ref.: VR 89 B7.

Further information & bookings:
Caretaker **Tel.:** (03) 5568 4201 *or* Moyne Shire Council **Tel.:** (03) 5568 2600
Camping fees: Unpowered sites from $11.00 per 2 people/night

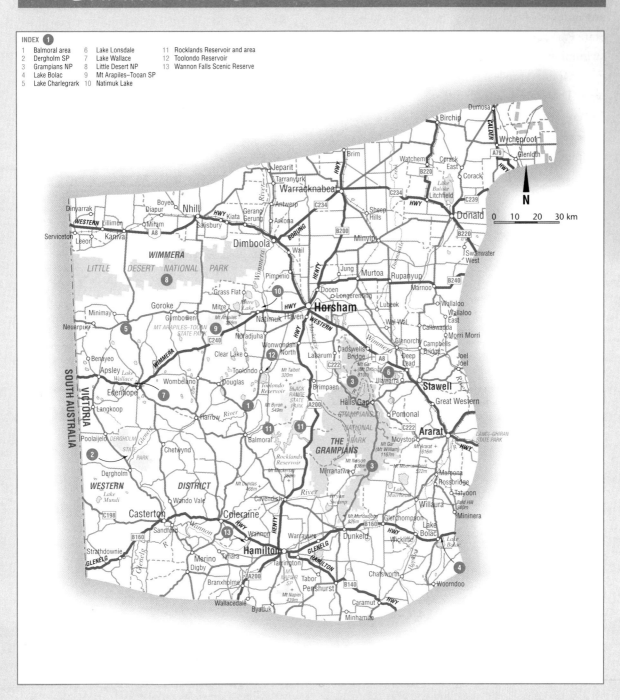

THE MAJOR ATTRACTION OF
VICTORIA'S CENTRAL WEST IS
THE SPECTACULAR GRAMPIANS
NATIONAL PARK. OTHER
NATURAL BEAUTIES IN THE REGION INCLUDE ONE
OF AUSTRALIA'S BEST ROCK-CLIMBING VENUES –
MOUNT ARAPILES–TOOAN STATE PARK – AND THE
REMOTE LITTLE DESERT NATIONAL PARK.

Grampians National Park is ideal for the
outdoor enthusiast. The rugged sandstone and
granite mountains of the Grampians are renowned
for their Aboriginal rock art as well as their
colourful wildflowers, abundant native flora and
fauna, amazing mountain scenery and lookouts.
There are some excellent walking trails – from
short tracks to overnight hikes – as well as cycling
routes and, for the more extreme enthusiast,
abseiling and rock-climbing sites. Campsites are
spread throughout the park, giving visitors easy
access to its varying landscapes and sights.

Just to the west of the Grampians is the Rocklands Reservoir. Here campers can set up at any number of sites, some part of Black Range State Park, and enjoy some fishing, canoeing and swimming.

Mount Arapiles–Tooan State Park is further west. Those not keen on hanging off a rock can still enjoy a thrill by watching the climbers from some of the walking tracks. Centenary Park camping area is near the base of the cliffs on the park's eastern boundary.

On the border with South Australia, Little Desert National Park has a diverse range of plants and a large number of bird species, including the mallee fowl. In spring the park is transformed with colourful wildflower displays. The park is separated into three blocks; camping with facilities can be found in the eastern block, with bush camping allowed in the central and western blocks.

BEST CAMPSITES

Baileys Rocks picnic and camping area
Dergholm State Park

Mountain Dam camping area
Rocklands Reservoir and area

Buandik camping area
Grampians National Park

Horseshoe Bend camping area
Little Desert National Park

Centenary Park camping area
Mount Arapiles–Tooan State Park

BEST TIME TO VISIT

Autumn and spring. Summer temperatures can become uncomfortable.

1. BALMORAL AREA

Red gums surround the small town of Balmoral, which is west of the Grampians, on the banks of the Glenelg River. There is canoeing on the river.

Fulham Streamside Reserve camping area

Signposted off Natimuk–Hamilton Rd, 10 km north of Balmoral near Kanagulk. Sandy track requires 4WD vehicle and seasonal track closures may apply. Bush camping – no facilities. Additional map ref.: VR 54 F4.

Further information & bookings: Parks Victoria, Casterton **Tel.:** (03) 5581 2427

2. DERGHOLM STATE PARK

This park is 40 km north-west of Casterton, near Dergholm. It features large granite tors and unique vegetation. Take a stroll along the Baileys Rocks Loop Walk. Activities include bushwalking, orienteering and 4WD trails.

Baileys Rocks picnic and camping area

Access via Baileys Rocks Rd, off Casterton–Naracoorte Rd. Water from tank – boil before use. Bring firewood. Additional map ref.: VR 53 D6.

Further information & bookings: Parks Victoria information line **Tel.:** 131 963

3. GRAMPIANS NATIONAL PARK see page 94

4. LAKE BOLAC

Lake Bolac is a small township on the Glenelg Hwy, 100 km west of Ballarat. Local activities for holiday-makers include watersports and walking trails.

Lake Bolac Caravan Park

Signposted via Frontage Rd from the Glenelg Hwy. Cabin accommodation also available. Bookings required at peak times. Additional map ref.: VR 229 Q11.

Further information & bookings: Lake Bolac Caravan Park **Tel.:** (03) 5350 2329 **Camping fees:** From $11.00 per site/night

Lake Bolac Foreshore camping area

Located 2 km east of Lake Bolac township, reached from the Glenelg Hwy. Many campsites around lake's edge. Showers in main area and toilets at scattered locations. Bring firewood. Additional map ref.: VR 74 F5.

Further information & bookings: Lake Bolac Foreshore **Tel.:** (03) 5350 2290 **Camping fees:** From $10.00 per site/night

5. LAKE CHARLEGRARK

This lake is 35 km north of Edenhope, near Booroopki. It is signposted from the Kaniva–Edenhope Rd. The lake is a popular watersports venue.

Lake Charlegrark Camping and Cottages

Lakeside location. Cabins also available. Bookings required at peak times. Additional map ref.: VR 38 E6.

Further information & bookings: Lake Charlegrark Camping and Cottages **Tel.:** (03) 5386 6281 **Camping fees:** Unpowered tent sites from $8.00 per site/night, powered tent sites from $10.00 per site/night

6. LAKE LONSDALE

The lake is 12 km west of Stawell. It is reached from Sandbar Rd off the Western Hwy north of Stawell. This is a popular watersports venue when the lake is at full capacity.

Lake Lonsdale camping area

Campsites are on the northern shore of the lake, in designated zones. Additional map ref.: VR 56 C2.

Further information & bookings: Wimmera Mallee Waters **Tel.:** (03) 5382 1244 **Camping fees:** Fees apply and are collected by ranger

7. LAKE WALLACE

The township of Edenhope has been built around the shores of Lake Wallace, which is another watersports centre that is popular in summer.

Lake Wallace Caravan Park

On Lake St, off Wimmera Hwy. Lakeside location. Bookings required at peak times. Additional map ref.: VR 223 O3.

Further information & bookings: Lake Wallace Caravan Park **Tel.:** (03) 5585 1659 **Camping fees:** Unpowered sites from $12.10 per double/night, powered sites from $16.50 per double/night

8. LITTLE DESERT NATIONAL PARK

This park comprises three blocks stretching from the south of the Western Hwy and the east of Dimboola across to the South Australia border. Sealed access roads lead from the Western Hwy and Natimuk Rd. Camping areas are accessible by conventional 2WD vehicles, but most other roads and tracks are sandy and require 4WD. The park is home to the mallee fowl plus a large number of other bird and animal species. Activities include bushwalking (half-day walks through to the four-day, 84-km Desert Discovery Walk) as well as birdwatching, fishing and 4WD touring.

Ackle Bend and Horseshoe Bend camping areas

In the eastern block on the Wimmera River. Signposted from Horseshoe Bend Rd from Dimboola on the Western Hwy. Bring drinking water and firewood. Additional map ref.: VR 25 J10.

Kiata camping area

Signposted via Kiata South Rd from Kiata on the Western Hwy. In the eastern block. Bring drinking water and firewood. Additional map ref.: VR 25 E9.

Bush camping

Vehicle-based bush camping is allowed within the central and western blocks, away from campgrounds and picnic areas. Bring water. Contact ranger for details.

Further information & bookings: Parks Victoria information line **Tel.:** 131 963 **Camping fees:** Fees apply at all camping areas within park and are subject to change; contact Parks Victoria for current fees. Fees are payable at self-registration stations

9. MOUNT ARAPILES–TOOAN STATE PARK

Mt Arapiles is Australia's best-known rock-climbing destination. The first European to climb it was explorer Major Sir Thomas Mitchell in 1836. The park is 9 km west of Natimuk and other activities in the park include walking and cycling.

Centenary Park camping area

Access via Centenary Park Rd off Wimmera Hwy. Collection of firewood not permitted in park – bring own or gas/fuel stove. Additional map ref.: VR 39 F6.

Further information & bookings: Parks Victoria information line **Tel.:** 131 963 **Camping fees:** Fees apply and are subject to change. Current fee structure is at self-registration station in camping area

10. NATIMUK LAKE

The lake is 4 km north of Natimuk township and is reached via Lake Rd. It is another popular summer watersports venue.

Natimuk Lake Caravan Park

Lakeside location. Bookings required at peak times. Additional map ref.: VR 39 H5.

Further information & bookings: Natimuk Lake Caravan Park **Tel.:** (03) 5387 1462 **Camping fees:** Unpowered sites from $4.50 per person/night

11. ROCKLANDS RESERVOIR AND AREA

Rocklands Reservoir is a large water storage to the west of Grampians National Park. It is a popular spot for watersports, and campsites exist virtually all around it. Many of these sites are part of the adjoining Black Range State Park or the Rocklands State Forests, and access to them is either via the Henty Hwy in the east or the Natimuk–Hamilton Rd in the west.

GRAMPIANS NATIONAL PARK

This popular national park is 45 km west of Ararat and to the south of Horsham. Main access is via Grampians Rd in the east, Northern Grampians Rd in the north and Henty Hwy in the west. The area is renowned for spectacular scenery, brilliant wildflower displays in spring and many species of wildlife. There are many Aboriginal rock-art sites. Activities include bushwalking, picnicking, cycling, rock climbing and vehicle touring (both 2WD and 4WD). Bookings are not required for campsites.

NORTHERN GRAMPIANS

Plantation camping area

At the base of Mt Difficult Range, reached by Pines Rd off Mt Zero–Halls Gap Rd. Bring firewood. Additional map ref.: VR 56 A2.

Smith Mill camping area

Signposted via Old Mill Rd off Wartook Rd. Bring drinking water and firewood. Additional map ref.: VR 55 H3.

Stapylton camping area

Access via Olive Plantation Rd off Northern Grampians Rd or Horsham–Halls Gap Rd. Aboriginal art site nearby. Bring firewood. Additional map ref.: VR 40 H8.

Troopers Creek camping area

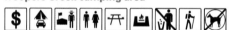

Access via Roses Gap Rd. Bring drinking water and firewood. Additional map ref.: VR 55 H2.

CENTRAL GRAMPIANS

Boreang camping area

Access via Glenelg River Rd. Bring drinking water and firewood. Additional map ref.: VR 55 H4.

Borough Huts camping area

Near Fyans Creek. Access via Grampians Rd. Bring firewood. Additional map ref.: VR 56 A5.

Rosea camping area

At foot of Mt Rosea. Signposted from Silverband Rd. Campsites are over bollards. Bring drinking water and firewood. Additional map ref.: VR 55 J4.

SOUTH-WEST GRAMPIANS

Buandik camping area

Beside Billimina Creek. Access via Billywing Rd, off Henty Hwy. Aboriginal art sites close by. No generators at this site. Bring drinking water. Firewood supplied. Additional map ref.: VR 55 F6.

Strachans camping area

Old sawmill site beside creek. Access via Glenelg River Rd. Campsites reached past bollards. Bring drinking water and firewood. Additional map ref.: VR 55 F8.

SOUTH-EAST GRAMPIANS

Bomjinna camping area

Access via Mitchell Rd. Small secluded site. Bring drinking water and firewood. Additional map ref.: VR 56 B6.

Jimmy Creek camping area

Beside Wannon River, off Grampians Rd. Bring drinking water and firewood. Additional map ref.: VR 56 A7.

Mafeking camping area

Near old goldmining site. Reached by Jimmy Creek Rd from Grampians Rd, or Mafeking Rd from Moyston–Dunkeld Rd. Bring drinking water and firewood. Additional map ref.: VR 56 A8.

Wannon Crossing camping area

Beside Wannon River. Access via Grampians Rd. Bring drinking water and firewood. Additional map ref.: VR 55 J8.

Bush camping

Bush camping is allowed within the park except in the Wonderland Range and the watershed of Lake Wartook. Contact ranger for details.

Further information: Parks Victoria information line **Tel.:** 131 963 **Camping fees:** From $10.40 per site/night; fees are payable at self-registration stations at each site and increase annually

Waterfalls and kangaroos

MacKenzie Falls is perhaps the state's most magnificent waterfall, and after rain the river tumbles over the 40-metre drop with impressive force. A walking track connects the falls with Zumsteins, a picnic area and a meeting spot for kangaroos.

A wonderland

The Wonderland Range is the most popular part of the Grampians. Explore the Elephant Hide or marvel at the bulging walls of rock in the narrow corridor of the Grand Canyon.

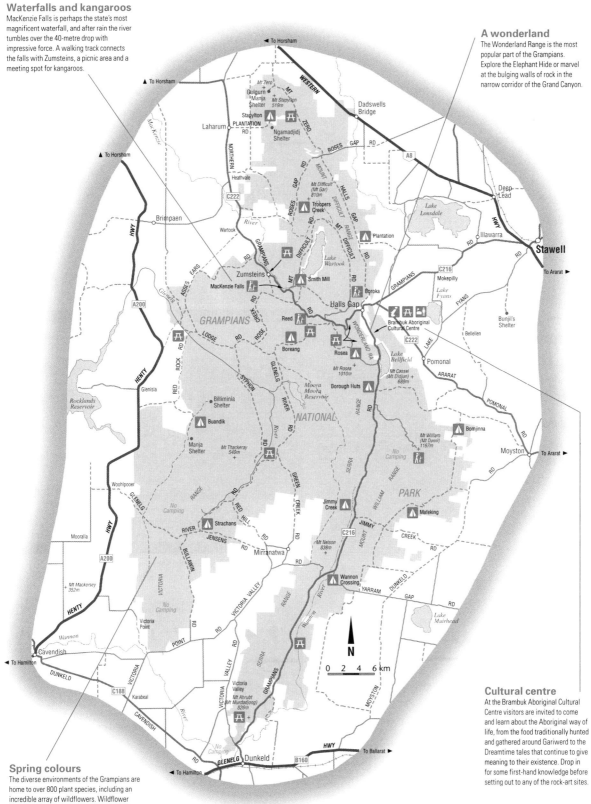

Cultural centre

At the Brambuk Aboriginal Cultural Centre visitors are invited to come and learn about the Aboriginal way of life, from the food traditionally hunted and gathered around Gariwerd to the Dreamtime tales that continue to give meaning to their existence. Drop in for some first-hand knowledge before setting out to any of the rock-art sites.

Spring colours

The diverse environments of the Grampians are home to over 800 plant species, including an incredible array of wildflowers. Wildflower enthusiasts flock here in spring to seek out the delicate Grampians boronia, the flashy flame grevillia and many species in between.

PARKS VICTORIA CAMPING GROUNDS

Brodies camping area

On the north-east shore of the reservoir's western tail, just south of Rocklands Caravan Park. Access via Rocklands–Cherrypool Rd. Bring drinking water. Additional map ref.: VR 54 H5.

Brookes Road camping area

On the northern point of the eastern foreshore of Rocklands Reservoir. Access via Brookes Rd, off Henty Hwy (this is an unofficial campground and is not signposted from the highway). Bring drinking water. Additional map ref.: VR 55 D4.

Cherrypool Highway Park

Beside the Glenelg River and to the north of Rocklands Reservoir. At the junction of Rocklands–Cherrypool Rd and the Henty Hwy, 50 km south of Horsham. The park is suitable for overnight stops. Bring drinking water and firewood. Additional map ref.: VR 55 D3.

Fergusons camping area

In the south of the reservoir's eastern foreshore, just north of Henrys. Access via Fergusons Rd, which is off Gartons Rd, off Henty Hwy. Bring drinking water. Additional map ref.: VR 55 B7.

Glendinning camping area

In the south-west of the reservoir's western tail. Access via Glendinning Rd from Cavendish or Yarramyljup Rd from Natimuk–Hamilton Rd. Bring drinking water and firewood. Additional map ref.: VR 54 H6.

Henrys camping area

Near the southern extremity of Rocklands Reservoir. Reached via Halls Rd, which is off East–West Rd, off Henty Hwy or Natimuk–Hamilton Rd. Bring drinking water. Additional map ref.: VR 55 B7.

Mountain Dam camping area

On the western foreshore of Rocklands Reservoir, roughly opposite Hynes. Access via Rocklands–Cherrypool Rd. Bring drinking water and firewood. Additional map ref.: VR 55 C5.

Bush camping

Bush camping is allowed within these forests. Contact ranger for details.

Further information & bookings: DSE, Cavendish **Tel.:** (03) 5574 2308

OTHER SITES

Hynes Reserve Camping Ground

On the eastern side of the reservoir, just above its widest part. Signposted from Hynes Rd off Henty Hwy. Bring firewood. Additional map ref.: VR 55 C5.

Further information & bookings: Hynes Reserve Camping Ground **Tel.:** (03) 5380 1534 **Email:** hynesatrocklands@telstra.easymail.com.au **Camping fees:** Unpowered from $6.60 per site/night, powered from $11.00 per site/night

Rocklands Caravan Park

Lakeside location 15 km east of Balmoral. Access via Rocklands Rd from Balmoral. Bookings required at peak times. Additional map ref.: VR 54 H5.

Further information & bookings: Rocklands Caravan Park **Tel.:** (03) 5570 1438 **Camping fees:** From $8.00 per person/night

12. TOOLONDO RESERVOIR

This popular fishing (trout and redfin) and watersports venue is next to Toolondo, 40 km south of Horsham. It is reached via Natimuk–Hamilton Rd.

Toolondo Wash Tomorrow Caravan Park

Lakeside location. Signposted along John McPhees Rd off Telangatuk Rd. Bookings required at peak times for caravan sites. Additional map ref.: VR 54 H2.

Further information & bookings: Toolondo Wash Tomorrow Caravan Park **Tel.:** (03) 5388 2231 **Camping fees:** From $6.60 per person/night

13. WANNON FALLS SCENIC RESERVE

This reserve is beside a scenic waterfall on the Wannon River 18 km west of Hamilton. It is signposted from the Glenelg Hwy.

Wannon Falls picnic and camping area

Overnight stop only. Additional map ref.: VR 72 F4.

Further information & bookings: South Grampians Shire Council **Tel.:** (03) 5573 0444 **Email:** council@sthgrampians.mav.asn.au **Website:** www.sthgrampians.vic.gov.au

MALLEE COUNTRY

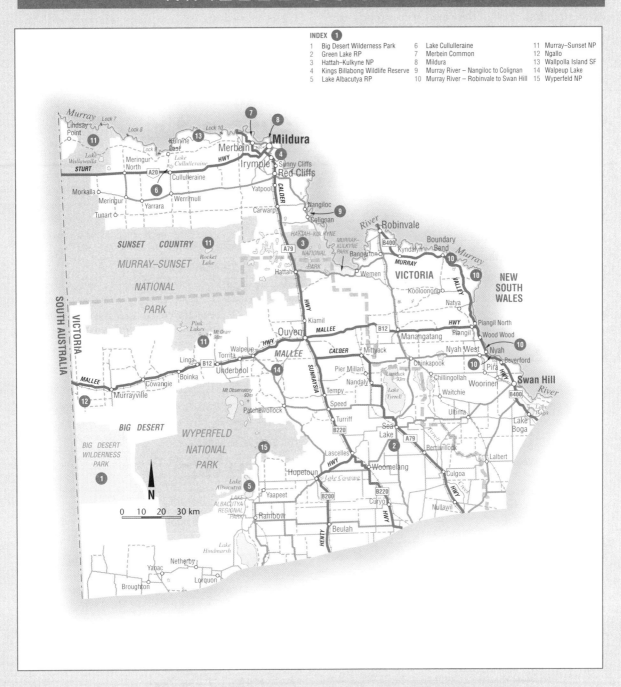

THE MALLEE REGION, NAMED AFTER THE MALLEE SCRUB THAT ONCE COVERED THE AREA, TAKES IN VICTORIA'S NORTH-WEST CORNER. FROM THE SOUTH AUSTRALIAN BORDER IT STRETCHES EAST ALONG THE MURRAY RIVER TO MILDURA AND SWAN HILL, AND EXTENDS SOUTH TO THE MAGNIFICENT MURRAY–SUNSET AND WYPERFELD NATIONAL PARKS.

Campers in this area will find a number of state forests and reserves along the Murray River – to the east and west of Mildura and from Robinvale to Swan Hill. Facilities in these forests and reserves vary from site to site. Here one can swim, fish and canoe in what is arguably Australia's most famous river.

Murray–Sunset National Park and its surrounds are full of contrasts, from the wheat pastures on the park's eastern boundary to the sand dunes and salt flats in the north. To the south is original mallee scrub and the stunning Pink Lakes – salt lakes that take on an unusual pink hue. Camping in the Pink Lakes section of the park is accessible by conventional vehicle and caravan, but the rest of the parks access roads are four-wheel drive only.

North of Dimboola is the cyclic Lake Albacutya. This lake fills and empties in 20-year cycles. There are three designated camping areas around the lake's shores, and when the lake is full fishing and boating are possible.

Wyperfeld National Park, to the north of Lake Albacutya, has wonderful displays of wildflowers during spring. The park has a mix of native plant species that provide homes for a range of native birds and animals. Campers can set up at one of the three camping areas and then enjoy the Eastern Lookout Nature Drive, either by car or mountain bike, or one of the self-guide nature walks.

BEST CAMPSITES

Wonga camping area
Wyperfeld National Park

Lake Hattah camping area
Hattah–Kulkyne National Park

Lake Crosbie camping area
Murray–Sunset National Park

Western Beach camping area
Lake Albacutya Regional Park

Walkool Junction camping area
Murray River – Robinvale to Swan Hill

BEST TIME TO VISIT

Spring and autumn.

1. BIG DESERT WILDERNESS PARK

The Big Desert was Victoria's first wilderness park. Exploration of the park is best undertaken on foot by experienced walkers with map and compass knowledge. Bring water. It is located south of Murrayville and adjoins the South Australian border. Conventional vehicles can access the park in dry weather but 4WD is required after rain and the road may be rough at times. Camping areas are outside the park boundary. Use of fuel/gas stove is preferred.

Big Billy Bore camping area

Access via Murrayville–Nhill Track. Bring drinking water and firewood. Additional map ref.: VR 15 G2.

Broken Bucket camping area

Access via Murrayville–Nhill Track. Bring drinking water and firewood. Additional map ref.: VR 15 H9.

Moonlight Tank camping area

Access via Murrayville–Nhill Track. Bush camping – no facilities. Bring water. Additional map ref.: VR 15 G5.

Red Bluff camping area

Access via Border Track or Red Bluff Track off Murrayville–Nhill Track. Bring drinking water and firewood. Additional map ref.: VR 15 A8.

The Springs camping area

Access via Murrayville–Nhill Track. Bring drinking water and firewood. Additional map ref.: VR 15 G4.

Further information & bookings: Parks Victoria information line **Tel.:** 131 963

2. GREEN LAKE REGIONAL PARK

This park is 10 km south of Sea Lake township. Green Lake is a natural feature filled by irrigation channels and surrounded by mallee woodland. It is a popular camping area, with watersports on the lake.

Green Lake camping area

Access via Birchip–Sea Lake Rd. Additional map ref.: VR 18 F3.

Further information & bookings: Shire of Buloke **Tel.:** (03) 5070 1218 **Camping fees:** Unpowered from $6.00 per site/night; fees payable at self-registration station

3. HATTAH–KULKYNE NATIONAL PARK

This national park, centred around the tranquil Hattah lakes system, is east of Hattah township, between the Calder Hwy and the Murray River. Main access is via Hattah–Robinvale Rd from Hattah. Although conventional vehicles may drive into the park, the roads may be rough at times and caravan access requires care. All park roads are dry weather only and some tracks may be seasonally flooded. Visitors are requested to check conditions before arrival. Use of gas/fuel stove is preferred. Activities include walking, canoeing, swimming, fishing, cycling and vehicle touring. There is a visitor centre near Lake Hattah.

Lake Hattah camping area

On the main park entrance road past the visitor centre. Bring drinking water. Additional map ref.: VR 6 G6.

Lake Mournpall camping area

Access via Mournpall Track. Bring drinking water. Additional map ref.: VR 6 G5.

River Track camping areas

Eight bush camping areas along the Murray River between Wemen and Nangiloc. Access via The River Track. No facilities. Bring drinking water. Additional map ref.: VR 6 J4/J5/J7.

Further information & bookings: Parks Victoria information line **Tel.:** 131 963 **Camping fees:** Fees change annually, contact Parks Victoria for current fees; fees payable at self-registration stations

4. KINGS BILLABONG WILDLIFE RESERVE

The reserve protects a natural floodplain ecosystem and river red gum forest. It is 12 km south-east of Mildura on the banks of the Murray River. Access via Eleventh St, east of Mildura. Conventional vehicles may drive into the park in dry weather only, and some tracks close due to seasonal flooding.

Bush camping

Dispersed bush camping along banks of the Murray River. Additional map ref.: VR 3 E5.

Further information & bookings: Parks Victoria information line **Tel.:** 131 963

5. LAKE ALBACUTYA REGIONAL PARK

Lake Albacutya fills and empties in 20-year cycles. It was last full in 1974 and has been empty since 1984. The lake is 14 km north of Rainbow and is reached on the Hopetoun–Rainbow Rd. Conventional vehicles can access camping areas. Use of gas/fuel stove preferred. Activities include fishing, boating (when lake is full), bushwalking and 4WD touring.

OTIT camping area

On east side of lake. Access via OTIT Track off Wembulin Track. Conventional vehicle access in dry weather only. Bring drinking water. Additional map ref.: VR 17 A5.

Western Beach camping area

On west side of lake. Access via Western Beach Rd off Albacutya Rd. Additional map ref.: VR 16 G6.

Yaapeet Beach camping area

On east side of lake. Access from Yaapeet. Additional map ref.: VR 17 B6.

Further information & bookings: Parks Victoria information line **Tel.:** 131 963

6. LAKE CULLULLERAINE

Lake Cullulleraine is a natural lake filled from Lock 9 on the Murray River. It is 58 km west of Mildura and reached from the Sturt Hwy. All watersports are popular here.

Bushmans Rest Caravan Park

Reached via Bushman Rd, Cullulleraine. Bookings recommended at peak times. Additional map ref.: VR 2 B6.

Further information & bookings: Bushmans Rest Caravan Park **Tel.:** (03) 5028 2252 **Camping fees:** Unpowered from $13.20 per site/night, powered from $15.40 per site/night

Lake Cullulleraine Holiday Park

Signposted off Sturt Hwy in Cullulleraine. Bookings required at peak times. Additional map ref.: VR 2 B6.

Further information & bookings: Lake Cullulleraine Holiday Park **Tel.:** (03) 5028 2226 **Email:** gandrhards@austarnet. com.au **Camping fees:** Unpowered from $12.00 for 2 people/night, powered from $15.00 for 2 people/night

7. MERBEIN COMMON

Merbein Common is on the banks of the Murray River at Horseshoe Bend, near Merbein, 10 km north-west of Mildura. Conventional vehicles have access in dry weather only and some tracks may be closed due to seasonal flooding. Many remnants of Aboriginal occupation, such as middens, are evident here.

Bush camping

Access via Old Wentworth Rd from Merbein. Additional map ref.: VR 3 B4.

Further information & bookings: Parks Victoria information line **Tel.:** 131 963

8. MILDURA

The city of Mildura is the centre of a large irrigation area based on the Murray River; it is particularly important for growing grapes and citrus fruit. Chaffey Bend, the location of Riverbend Tourist Park, is a large, 6.8-ha reserve on the river, 3.5 km north of Mildura. It has a sandbar beach and the river is a venue for all watersports.

Riverbend Tourist Park

On Cureton Ave. Bookings recommended at peak times. Additional map ref.: VR 3 D4.

Further information & bookings: Riverbend Tourist Park
Tel.: (03) 5023 6879 **Email:** riverbendpark@mildura.vic.gov.au
Camping fees: Unpowered from $14.30 for 2 people/night

9. MURRAY RIVER – NANGILOC TO COLIGNAN

This short but scenic stretch of the Murray River between Nangiloc and Colignan is characterised by sharp bends, rock shelves and sandbars. It is 20 km south-east of Mildura.

Bush camping

Access via signposted Kulkyne Way off Calder Hwy south of Red Cliffs (dry weather only; some tracks may be closed due to seasonal flooding). Additional map ref.: VR 6 G1/G2.

Further information & bookings: Parks Victoria information line **Tel.:** 131 963

10. MURRAY RIVER – ROBINVALE TO SWAN HILL

Bush camping is possible on the banks of the Murray River between Robinvale and Swan Hill. There are many roads to the river signposted off the Murray Valley Hwy, but conventional vehicles are advised only to attempt access in dry weather as some tracks may be closed due to seasonal flooding. Check road conditions before setting out. Activities include bushwalking, fishing, swimming and canoeing.

Nyah State Forest bush camping

Next to Nyah township in Nyah State Forest. Signposted off Murray Valley Hwy. Dispersed bush camping along banks of river. Bring drinking water. Additional map ref.: VR 13 H4 (entrance road).

Passage Camp camping area

Located 45 km south-east of Robinvale. Access via Boundary Bend. Signposted off the main road. Dispersed bush camping along banks of river. Bring drinking water. Additional map ref.: VR 8 E5.

Vinifera Murray River Reserve bush camping

This is 20 km north of Swan Hill near Vinifera. Signposted off Murray Valley Hwy. Dispersed bush camping along banks of river. Bring drinking water. Additional map ref.: VR 13 H5 (entrance road).

Walkool Junction camping area

Situated 7 km east of Piambie. Signposted off Murray Valley Hwy. This was the site of Major Mitchell's 'Australia Felix' camp. Dispersed bush camping along banks of river. Bring drinking water. Additional map ref.: VR 8 F7 (entrance road).

Further information & bookings:
Parks Victoria information line **Tel.:** 131 963 or
DSE Customer Service Centre, tel 136 186

11. MURRAY–SUNSET NATIONAL PARK

This is Victoria's second largest national park, once part of a large grazing station with many reminders of station life remaining. It is 40 km south-west of Mildura and the main access is via the Mallee Hwy in the south and Millewa Rd in the north. Conventional vehicles can reach the main camping areas only – others require 4WD. Activities include fishing and boating on the Murray River in the north of the park,

bushwalking near the Pink Lakes and 4WD touring in the remoter sections of the park.

PINK LAKES SECTION

Cattleyards camping area

At intersection of Underbool and Grub Tracks. 4WD vehicles recommended. Bring drinking water. Gas/fuel stove preferred. Additional map ref.: VR 4 J9.

Lake Crosbie camping area

Located 13 km north of the Mallee Hwy, south of Pink Lakes. Access via Linga or Underbool from Mallee Hwy. Bring drinking water. Gas/fuel stove preferred. Additional map ref.: VR 10 D2.

Lake Becking camping area

Located 16 km north of the Mallee Hwy on east side of Lake Becking. Access via Linga or Underbool from Mallee Hwy then Ring Road Nature Drive. from Pink Lakes. Bring drinking water. Gas/fuel stove preferred. Additional map ref.: VR 10 D2.

SOUTHERN SECTION

Large Tank camping area

Access via Mt Crozier Track from Pink Lakes. 4WD vehicles recommended. Bring drinking water. Gas/fuel stove preferred. Additional map ref.: VR 5 D8.

Mopoke Hut camping area

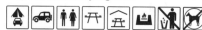

Access via Mt Jess Track from Underbool, then Mopoke Track. 4WD vehicles recommended. Old hut. Bring drinking water. Gas/fuel stove preferred. Additional map ref.: VR 5 E7.

Mount Crozier camping area

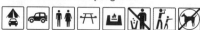

Near Mt Crozier. Reached via Mt Crozier Track from Pink Lakes. 4WD vehicles recommended. Bring drinking water. Gas/fuel stove preferred. Additional map ref.: VR 5 D8.

NORTH-EAST SECTION

Ochre Pit camping area

Access via Henschke Track from Nowingi Line Track or Midnight Tank Track. 4WD vehicles recommended. Bring drinking water. Gas/fuel stove preferred. Additional map ref.: VR 5 H3.

Rocket Lake camping area

Reached via Rocket Lake Track from Pink Lakes or Nowingi Line Track from Nowingi on Calder Hwy. 4WD vehicles recommended. Bring drinking water. Gas/fuel stove preferred. Additional map ref.: VR 5 F4.

Lindsay Island camping areas

Dispersed bush camping on banks of Murray River. Signposted from Sturt Hwy west of Meringur North. Bring drinking water. Gas/fuel stove preferred. Additional map ref.: VR 1 B–F3.

Pheenys Track camping area

On west end of Pheenys Track. 4WD vehicles recommended. Bring drinking water. Gas/fuel stove preferred. Additional map ref.: VR 4 D5.

The Shearers Quarters (hut accommodation)

Historic iron hut built in late 1950s. Sleeps up to 14 people. Access via North–South Settlement Rd from Sturt Hwy. 4WD vehicles recommended. Bring drinking water. Limited firewood supplied – bring own or a gas/fuel stove. Advance bookings essential. Additional map ref.: VR 4 C4.

Accommodation fees: The Shearers Quarters from $55.00 per night; phone Parks Victoria, Weerimull, on (03) 5028 1212

Further information & bookings: Except for Shearers Quarters, Parks Victoria information line **Tel.:** 131 963

12. NGALLO

Ngallo is close to the Big Desert Wilderness Park and is 15 km south-west of Murrayville, near the South Australian border.

Ngallo Park camping

On site of old tennis courts. Signposted off Mallee Hwy and then Ngallo Tennis Court Rd. Bring firewood. Additional map ref.: VR 9 C7.

Further information & bookings: Thurlows Newsagency **Tel.:** (03) 5095 2181

13. WALLPOLLA ISLAND STATE FOREST

Wallpolla Island is a wetlands area with many creeks and billabongs throughout it. It is home to some vulnerable species of birds. The 'island' is 25 km west of Merbein on the south bank of the Murray River. It is reached via Old Mail Rd in dry weather only. Some tracks may be seasonally flooded.

Bush camping

Dispersed bush camping along banks of Murray River. Bring firewood. Campfires are permitted but must be contained as per DSE fire regulations, or risk a fine. Additional map ref.: VR 2 F4 (entrance road).

Further information & bookings: DSE Customer Service Centre **Tel.:** 136 186

14. WALPEUP LAKE

Walpeup is a farming community in the Mallee. The lake is 14 km south-east of Walpeup at Timberoo South.

Walpeup Lake camping area

Lakeside location. Signposted from via Hopetoun–Walpeup Rd. Bring drinking water and firewood. Additional map ref.: VR 11 D5.

Further information & bookings: DSE, Ouyen **Tel.:** (03) 5092 1322

15. WYPERFELD NATIONAL PARK

Wyperfeld is Victoria's third largest national park and protects large areas of undisturbed mallee vegetation. It is usually semi-arid but occasionally a lake system in the park fills with overflow from the Wimmera River. Desert plants then carpet the ground with their flowers. Wyperfeld is west of Hopetoun and is reached either from Yaapeet in the south or Patchewollock in the east. The western section of the park is only suitable for 4WD vehicles. Use of gas/fuel stove preferred. Explore the park by taking the Eastern Lookout Nature Drive or by walking or cycling.

Casuarina camping area

On Meridian Rd. Access via Pine Plains Rd from Baring. Bring drinking water. Additional map ref.: VR 10 H8.

Nine Mile Square Track camping area

Basic overnight camping area, at the intersection of Meridian Rd and Nine Mile Square Track. Reached via Pine Plains Rd from Baring. Bring drinking water. Additional map ref.: VR 10 H9.

Wonga camping area

Located 25 km north of Yaapeet near Lake Brimin; reached via Park Rd from Yaapeet. Additional map ref.: VR 17 B3.

Further information & bookings: Parks Victoria information line **Tel.:** 131 963 **Camping fees:** *Wonga camping area*: from $10.20 per site/night up to 6 people; fees payable at self-registration stations

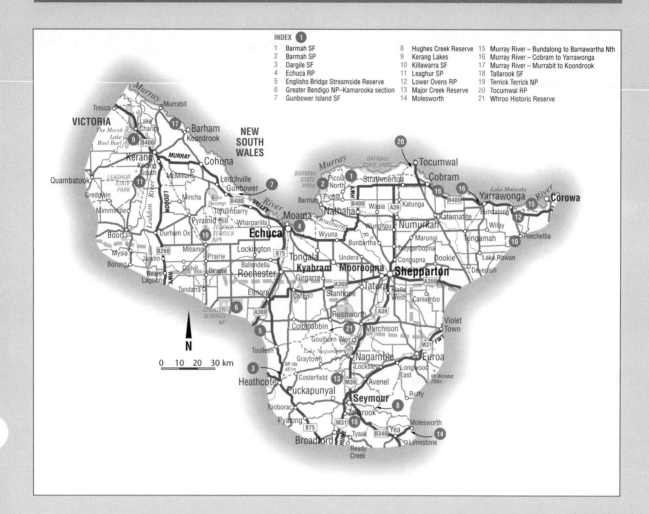

INDEX ①

1 Barmah SF
2 Barmah SP
3 Dargile SF
4 Echuca RP
5 Englishs Bridge Streamside Reserve
6 Greater Bendigo NP–Kamarooka section
7 Gunbower Island SF
8 Hughes Creek Reserve
9 Kerang Lakes
10 Killawarra SF
11 Leaghur SP
12 Lower Ovens RP
13 Major Creek Reserve
14 Molesworth
15 Murray River – Bundalong to Barnawartha Nth
16 Murray River – Cobram to Yarrawonga
17 Murray River – Murrabit to Koondrook
18 Tallarook SF
19 Terrick Terrick NP
20 Tocumwal RP
21 Whroo Historic Reserve

THE GOULBURN AND MURRAY REGION IS A MIX OF RICH AGRICULTURAL LANDS PRODUCING FRUIT AND WINE, HISTORIC RIVER PORTS BOASTING ORIGINAL PADDLE STEAMERS, MAJESTIC RIVER RED GUM FORESTS, WETLANDS AND ABORIGINAL CULTURAL SITES.

Along the banks of the Murray River from Murrabit to Yarrawonga are numerous areas for campers to sit back, relax and soak up the history of the region, while the river itself is a great place for swimming, fishing, boating and canoeing. Bushwalking and birdwatching are other popular activities, as well as taking scenic drives through the forests.

When camping in Barmah State Park don't forget to visit the Dharnya Centre, a cultural centre of the Yorta Yorta people with information and displays on the area's Aboriginal heritage. The state park and the neighbouring Barmah State Forest together make up Victoria's largest river red gum forest.

Stands of white cypress pines, some over 100 years old, can be found in Terrick Terrick National Park, four kilometres north of Mitiamo. The park also has an abundance of native birds, and some vehicle roads that are ideal for mountain bike touring. The camping area is set amongst the white pines at the base of Mount Terrick Terrick.

To the north-west and south of Kerang are the Kerang Lakes, a cluster of some 50 or so lakes. These important wetlands are home to a large number of birds, including ibis. A bird hide is located at Middle Lake, where the ibis rookeries can be seen. Bush camping is allowed around the shores of some of the lakes.

Within Rushworth State Forest, seven kilometres south of Rushworth, is Whroo Historic Reserve. It gives the visitor an excellent insight into the area's mining history. Remnants of those days can be seen while enjoying the walking tracks through the reserve. Other sights not to be missed include the Aboriginal rock well and cemetery.

BEST CAMPSITES

Christies Beach camping area
Echuca Regional Park

Forest Camp camping area
Killawarra State Forest

Terrick Terrick camping area
Terrick Terrick National Park

Greens camping area
Whroo Historic Reserve

Bush camping
Gunbower Island State Forest

BEST TIME TO VISIT

All year round. During periods of wet weather access roads to the Murray River camping areas can be closed.

1. BARMAH STATE FOREST

This large river red gum forest is 10 km north-east of Barmah township on the banks of the Murray River. It is reached via Picola North Rd from Picola and can only be accessed in dry weather. Some tracks may be closed due to seasonal flooding. Activities include fishing and canoeing in the river.

Bush camping

Dispersed bush camping on banks of Murray River. Signposted from Gulf Rd off Murrays Mill Rd. Bring drinking water. Additional map ref.: VR 22 C8 (entrance track).

Further information & bookings: DSE, Nathalia **Tel.:** (03) 5866 2702

2. BARMAH STATE PARK

This park is divided into two sections along the banks of the Murray River. Section 1 (the western area) is north of Barmah, and the Dharnya Centre, a cultural centre run by the local Yorta Yorta people, is in this section. Section 2 (the north-east area) is north of the Murray Valley Hwy. Dry weather access only; some tracks may be closed due to seasonal flooding. There is fishing and canoeing in the Murray River.

Section 1 camping areas

Dispersed bush camping on banks of Murray River north of Barmah. Some areas have facilities. Access via Moira Lakes Rd from Barmah. Bring drinking water. Additional map ref.: VR 22 A9 (entrance track).

Section 2 camping areas

Dispersed bush camping on banks of Murray River from Tongalong Creek to Ulupna Rd. Some areas have facilities. Access via many roads from Murray Valley Hwy. Bring drinking water. Additional map ref.: VR 22 F8/G8/H8.

Further information & bookings: Parks Victoria information line **Tel.:** 131 963

3. DARGILE STATE FOREST

This forest is 40 km east of Bendigo, near Heathcote. Access via Plantation Rd off Heathcote–North Costerfield Rd. Activities include picnicking and cycling. (Dargile State Forest will come under Parks Victoria management in the future; please confirm status of forest before setting out if you plan to bring your dog.)

Dargile Reserve camping area

On Plantation Rd. Bring drinking water. Additional map ref.: VR 45 D7.

Further information & bookings: DSE, Bendigo **Tel.:** (03) 5430 4444

4. ECHUCA REGIONAL PARK

This is a popular river beach 5 km east of Echuca on the banks of the Murray River. Access is signposted via Simmie Rd from Echuca. Dry weather access only; some tracks may be closed due to seasonal flooding. Bring drinking water and firewood.

Christies Beach camping area

Dispersed bush camping on banks of Murray River. Additional map ref.: VR 31 F3.

Further information & bookings: Parks Victoria information line **Tel.:** 131 963

5. ENGLISHS BRIDGE STREAMSIDE RESERVE

The reserve is beside the Campaspe River, approximately 33 km north-east of Bendigo. It is reached via Comer Lane, off the Midland Hwy just north of Goornong.

Englishs Bridge camping area

Situated 47 km east of the Midland Hwy off Comer Lane or Axedelle–Goornong Rd. Comer Lane is 500 m north of Goornong. Bring drinking water and firewood. Additional map ref.: VR 45 A3.

Further information & bookings: Parks Victoria, Bendigo **Tel.:** (03) 5430 4444

6. GREATER BENDIGO NATIONAL PARK – KAMAROOKA SECTION

See also Greater Bendigo National Park – Whipstick section, page 109

This recently proclaimed national park joined together the Kamarooka and Whipstick state parks. The Kamarooka section is 23 km north of Bendigo and it is known for spectacular wildflower displays in spring. Main access is via Camp Rd off Kamarooka West Rd from Burgoyne Rd, signposted from Huntly. Activities include bushwalking, cycling, horseriding and 4WD touring.

Mulga Dam picnic and camping area

Near small dam. Access via Camp Rd off Tennyson Rd. Bring drinking water and firewood. Additional map ref.: VR 44 G2.

Rush Dam picnic and camping area

Located beside small dam. Access via Camp Rd off Millwood Rd. Bring drinking water and firewood. Additional map ref.: VR 44 G.

Further information & bookings: Parks Victoria information line **Tel.:** 131 963

7. GUNBOWER ISLAND STATE FOREST

This large island is a wildlife haven covered with river red gum and box forest. It is sandwiched between the Murray River and Gunbower Creek, stretching for 50 km from Koondrook in the north to Torrumbarry in the south. Access via Koondrook off the Koondrook–Kerang Rd, Spencers Bridge off Koondrook–Cohuna Rd, or Cohuna Island Rd from Cohuna; all are signposted. Dry weather access only; some tracks may be closed due to seasonal flooding. Activities include fishing and watersports on the river.

Bush camping

Numerous dispersed bush campsites (over 100) on the island along the banks of the Murray River and Gunbower Creek. Some sites have facilities. Disabled toilet located near Twin

Bridges via Koondrook access. Caravan access depends on road conditions. Bring drinking water. Additional map ref.: VR 21 D4–E6 (access roads).

Further information & bookings: DSE, Cohuna **Tel.:** (03) 5456 2266

8. HUGHES CREEK RESERVE

This reserve is 20 km east of Seymour via Highlands Rd and Hughes Creek Rd. Access is signposted on Hughes Creek Rd.

Hughes Creek Reserve camping area

Bush camping. There is fishing in the area. Conventional vehicle access. Additional map ref.: VR 61 G2.

Further information & bookings: Parks Victoria information line **Tel.:** 131 963

9. KERANG LAKES

These lakes, to the north-west and south of Kerang township, are one of the country's largest and most important wetland areas, home to a large number of birds. Main access via the Murray Valley Hwy. Activities include picnicking, camping and watersports – each lake permits different activities and you should check those allowed at your destination before visiting. The Kerang Lakes system is subject to potentially toxic blue-green alga blooms from time to time. Please observe any warning signs that may be posted.

Lake Bael Bael camping areas

West of Kerang. Dispersed camping on north-west side of lake. Reached via Fairley Rd off Murray Valley Hwy. Additional map ref.: VR 20 D5.

Lake Boga Caravan Park

On the Murray Valley Hwy in Lake Boga township. Three camping areas around lake; all sites have lake frontage. Bookings essential during Christmas and New Year holiday period. Additional map ref.: VR 14 C8.

Further information & bookings: Lake Boga Caravan Park **Tel.:** (03) 5037 2386 **Email:** lakeboga@telstra.com **Camping fees:** Unpowered from $13.00 for 2 people/night, powered from $16.00 for 2 people/night

Middle Reedy Lake camping areas

North of Kerang. Dispersed camping around lake. Access via Pratt Rd off Murray Valley Hwy. Additional map ref.: VR 20 G4.

The Marshes camping areas

Located west of Lake Charm. Dispersed camping around marsh system. Access via Bael Bael–Boga Rd. 4WD recommended. Additional map ref.: VR 20 D4 (access road).

Further information & bookings: Except for Lake Boga Caravan Park, DSE, Kerang **Tel.:** (03) 5452 1266

10. KILLAWARRA STATE FOREST

This forest is 15 km north-west of Wangaratta, near Peechelba, and is reached via Boweya Rd off the Wangaratta–Yarrawonga Rd. It adjoins Warby Range State Park and is an important habitat for birds including regent honeyeaters, painted honeyeaters, swift and turquoise parrots. (Killawarra State Forest will come under Parks Victoria management in the future; please confirm its current status if you plan to bring your dog.)

Forest Camp camping area

At site of an old wartime internee tent camp, via Camp Rd off Boweya Rd. Bring drinking water. Additional map ref.: VR 34 D5.

Further information & bookings: DSE, Wangaratta **Tel.:** (03) 5721 5022

11. LEAGHUR STATE PARK

The park, which preserves black box woodlands and wetlands, is 25 km south of Kerang. Main access is via Kerang–Boort Rd and is only possible in dry weather. Recreational activities include bushwalking, cycling and horseriding.

Lake Meran picnic and camping area

Located at southern end of lake. Access via Vallance Track off Lake Meran Track. Bring drinking water and firewood. Additional map ref.: VR 20 E8.

Park Entrance picnic and camping area

Near main park entrance. Access off Kerang–Boort Rd. Bring drinking water and firewood. Additional map ref.: VR 20 E8.

Further information & bookings: Parks Victoria information line **Tel.:** 131 963

12. LOWER OVENS REGIONAL PARK

The park is 20 km east of Yarrawonga, at the junction of the Ovens and Murray rivers. Access is possible in dry weather only; some tracks may be seasonally flooded. There is fishing and canoeing in the rivers.

Bush camping

Dispersed bush camping. Access via signposted track off Murray Valley Hwy near Parolas Bridge over Ovens River. Bring drinking water. Additional map ref.: VR 34 E3.

Further information & bookings: Parks Victoria information line **Tel.:** 131 963

13. MAJOR CREEK RESERVE

The reserve is 25 km north of Seymour, near Mitchellstown. There is fishing and canoeing in the river.

Major Creek Reserve camping area

Beside Major Creek and opposite Puckapunyal Military Training Area. Access via Mitchellstown Rd off Goulburn Valley Hwy. Bring drinking water and firewood. Additional map ref.: VR 46 C7.

Further information & bookings: Parks Victoria information line **Tel.:** 131 963

14. MOLESWORTH

Molesworth is 14 km north-east of Yea, signposted from the Goulburn Valley Hwy.

Molesworth Recreational Reserve camping ground

Bring drinking water and firewood. Additional map ref.: VR 62 A4.

Further information & bookings: Molesworth Recreational Reserve **Tel.:** (03) 5797 6278 **Camping fees:** From $10.00 per site/night

15. MURRAY RIVER – BUNDALONG TO BARNAWARTHA NORTH

There are dispersed bush campsites on the banks of the Murray River between Bundalong and Barnawartha North. Some areas have facilities but you should bring drinking water to all. There are many access roads signposted off the Murray Valley Hwy. Dry weather access only to these sites. Activities in the area include fishing, canoeing and swimming.

Doolans Bend camping area
Located 23 km north-west of Wodonga. Access via Barnawartha–Howlong Rd. Additional map ref.: VR 35 C2.

Gooramadda State Forest (Police Paddocks) camping area
Situated 10 km north-east of Rutherglen. Access via Police Paddocks Rd or Up River Rd off Murray Valley Hwy. Additional map ref.: VR 35 A1.

Granthams Bend camping area
This is 5 km north-east of Wahgunyah. Access via Carlyle Rd off All Saints Rd. Additional map ref.: VR 34 H1.

Lumbys Bend camping area
Located 15 km west of Rutherglen. Access via Kellys Rd or Raitts Rd off Murray Valley Hwy. Additional map ref.: VR 34 F2.

Richardsons Bend camping area
About 21 km north-west of Wodonga. Access via Kings Rd off Old Barnawartha Rd. Additional map ref.: VR 35 D2.

Shaws Flat camping area
Situated 7 km north of Rutherglen. Access via Shaws Flat Rd off Up River Rd. Additional map ref.: VR 34 J1.

Stantons camping area
This is 5 km west of Rutherglen. Access via Moodemere Rd off Murray Valley Hwy. Additional map ref.: VR 34 G2.

Taylors Bend camping area
Situated 18 km west of Rutherglen. Reached via Brimin Rd off Murray Valley Hwy. Additional map ref.: VR 34 F2.

Further information & bookings: Parks Victoria information line **Tel.:** 131 963

16. MURRAY RIVER – COBRAM TO YARRAWONGA

There are dispersed bush campsites on the banks of Murray River between Cobram and Yarrawonga. There are many signposted roads off the Murray Valley Hwy but these are dry weather access only; some tracks may be closed due to seasonal flooding. Some areas have facilities but you should bring drinking water to all. Activities include bushwalking, fishing, swimming, canoeing, powerboating and waterskiing.

Bourkes Bend camping areas

Located 20 km south-east of Cobram. Access via Bourkes Bend Track off Murray Valley Hwy. Additional map ref.: VR 23 F9.

Bruces Bend camping areas

Located 8 km west of Yarrawonga. Access via Bruces Rd. Additional map ref.: VR 23 G9.

Chinamans Bend camping area

Located 3 km west of Yarrawonga. Access via Brears Rd off Murray Valley Hwy. Additional map ref.: VR 33 H2.

Cobrawonga Island camping areas

This is 16 km south-east of Cobram. Access via Grinter Rd off Murray Valley Hwy. Additional map ref.: VR 23 E9.

Horseshoe Beach camping area

Situated 5 km south-east of Cobram. Access via Horseshoe Track. Additional map ref.: VR 23 D8.

Nevins Bend camping areas

This is 11 km west of Yarrawonga. Access via Thoms Rd. Additional map ref.: VR 23 F9.

Scotts Beach camping area

Located 3 km south-east of Cobram. Access via River Rd. Additional map ref.: VR 23 C8.

Yarrawonga Bends camping areas

Situated 5 km west of Yarrawonga. Access via Forges Pump Rd. Additional map ref.: VR 23 H9.

Further information & bookings: Parks Victoria information line **Tel.:** 131 963

17. MURRAY RIVER – MURRABIT TO KOONDROOK

There are many bush campsites along the Murray River between Murrabit and Koondrook. Main access (in dry weather only) is via River Track from Murrabit or Koondrook; some tracks may be closed due to seasonal flooding. Activities include fishing and watersports.

Benwell State Forest

Dispersed bush campsites on banks of Murray River. Access via Murray Rd from Murrabit or via Hall Lane or Watsons Lane from Murrabit–Koondrook Rd. Bring drinking water. Additional map ref.: VR 21 B3.

Guttrum State Forest

Dispersed bush campsites on banks of river. Access via River Track off Cassidys Lane from Koondrook. Bring drinking water. Additional map ref.: VR 21 C3.

Further information & bookings: Parks Victoria, Kerang **Tel.:** (03) 5450 3951

18. TALLAROOK STATE FOREST

The Tallarook State Forest is a gazetted military training area. It is about 80 km north of Melbourne, between Broadford and Seymour. It is reached via Ennis Rd, off the Hume Fwy. Activities include 4WD touring, motorbike riding, bushwalking and horseriding.

Falls Creek Reservoir camping area

4WD only access via East Falls Rd. Site beside old water supply dam. Water from dam – boil before use. Additional map ref.: VR 61 E4.

Freemans picnic and camping area

Access via Ennis Rd off Hume Hwy. Conventional vehicle access. Ideal site for groups and families. Bring drinking water. Additional map ref.: VR 61 D4.

Further information & bookings: DSE, Broadford **Tel.:** (03) 5784 0600

19. TERRICK TERRICK NATIONAL PARK

This recently gazetted national park, which is 4 km north of Mitiamo and 60 km north of Bendigo, protects a significant area of white cypress pine woodland and original northern plains grassland. Access (in dry weather only) is off the Echuca–Mitiamo Rd. Activities include bushwalking and cycling.

Terrick Terrick camping area

On Allen Track at the base of Mt Terrick Terrick. Access via Cemetery Track or Allen Track. Bring drinking water. Gas/fuel stove preferred. Additional map ref.: VR 30 E4.

Further information & bookings: Parks Victoria information line **Tel.:** 131 963

20. TOCUMWAL REGIONAL PARK

This is on the Victorian side of the Murray River, near Tocumwal, and is accessed in dry weather only from the Goulburn Valley Hwy.

Apex Beach camping area

This is 2 km south-west of Tocumwal, reached via Pumps Bend Track. Dispersed bush camping on banks of river. Bring drinking water. Additional map ref.: VR 23 A7.

Finley Beach camping area

Located 2 km south of Tocumwal. Access via Finely Track. Dispersed bush camping on banks of river. Bring drinking water. Additional map ref.: VR 23 A7.

Pebbly Beach camping area

Adjacent to Tocumwal. Access via Goulburn Valley Hwy. Dispersed bush camping on banks of river. Bring drinking water. Additional map ref.: VR 23 A7.

Further information & bookings: Parks Victoria information line **Tel.:** 131 963

21. WHROO HISTORIC RESERVE

Once a goldmining settlement, little evidence now remains of Whroo except the cemetery. Whroo Historic Area is 7 km south of Rushworth and is reached via the Rushworth–Nagambie Rd.

Greens camping area

On Greens Rd. Bring drinking water. Additional map ref.: VR 46 B4.

Further information & bookings: Parks Victoria information line **Tel.:** 131 963

THE GOLDFIELDS

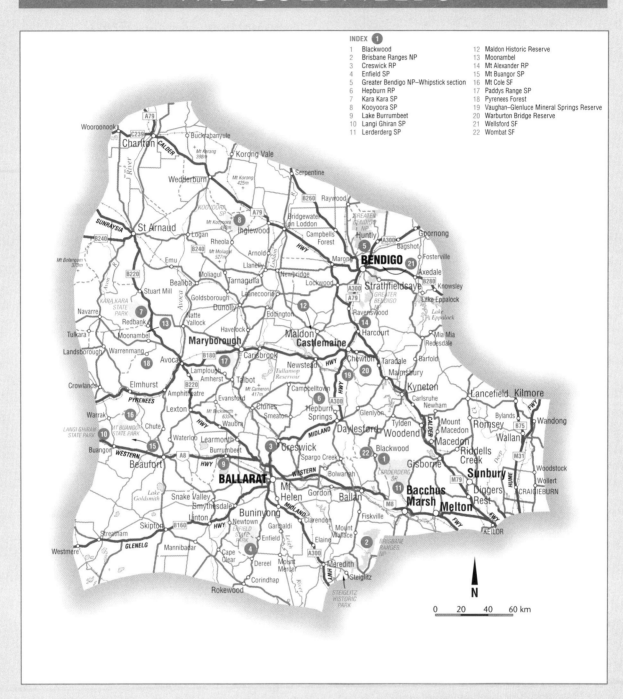

INDEX 1

1 Blackwood
2 Brisbane Ranges NP
3 Creswick RP
4 Enfield SP
5 Greater Bendigo NP–Whipstick section
6 Hepburn RP
7 Kara Kara SP
8 Kooyoora SP
9 Lake Burrumbeet
10 Langi Ghiran SP
11 Lerderderg SP

12 Maldon Historic Reserve
13 Moonambel
14 Mt Alexander RP
15 Mt Buangor SP
16 Mt Cole SF
17 Paddys Range SP
18 Pyrenees Forest
19 Vaughan–Glenluce Mineral Springs Reserve
20 Warburton Bridge Reserve
21 Wellsford SF
22 Wombat SF

THE HISTORIC GOLDFIELDS REGION OF VICTORIA WAS ONCE FILLED WITH THE SOUND OF THOUSANDS OF HOPEFUL GOLDMINERS, AND AT THE END OF 1854, WITH THE ANGER OF THE BALLARAT REFORM LEAGUE CALLING FOR THE ABOLITION OF GOVERNMENT LICENCE FEES. NOW THE REGION'S HISTORY IS A MAJOR DRAWCARD FOR VISITORS FROM AROUND THE WORLD.

Significant relics of the goldmining and eucalyptus oil industries can be found in the recently proclaimed Greater Bendigo National Park – Whipstick section, north of Bendigo. The park is alive with colour from August to November, when the wildflowers bloom. Camping, bushwalking, car touring, birdwatching and recreational fossicking can be done here.

To the west of Beaufort are Langi Ghiran State Park, Mount Buangor State Park and Mount

Cole State Forest, each offering great camping opportunities. Langi Ghiran State Park houses two old water reservoirs, built in 1880 to supply water to Ararat, and has attractive woodlands of red gum and yellow box trees. Mount Buangor State Park contains the area's highest peak as well as a handful of good walking trails. Some continue into Mount Cole State Forest. During the day a large number of birds, kangaroos, swamp wallabies and echidnas can be seen, while night time brings out the owls, bats, gliders and possums.

On either side of Bacchus Marsh are Lerderderg State Park and Brisbane Ranges National Park. Lerderderg's dominant feature is the striking, 300-metre-deep Lerderderg Gorge, carved by the Lerderderg River as it winds its way south. Visitors to the park can enjoy some wonderful four-wheel drive touring and bush-walking. The energetic may wish to attempt the challenging two-to-three day, 20-kilometre gorge hike.

The Brisbane Ranges feature stunning wildflower displays in spring and some diverse wildlife. Mountain-bike riding is popular in the park, though riders must keep off the management trails.

Another feature of the region are the charming spa towns of Daylesford and Hepburn Springs, north-east of Ballarat, where Melburnians have been coming to revitalise themselves for well over a century. The campground within Hepburn Regional Park is located conveniently close by for those wanting to acquaint themselves with the healing mineral waters.

BEST CAMPSITES

Shadbolt picnic and camping area
Greater Bendigo National Park – Whipstick section

Langi Ghiran camping area
Langi Ghiran State Park

Middle Creek picnic and camping area
Mount Buangor State Park

Firth Park picnic and camping area
Wombat State Forest

Waterfalls picnic and camping area
Pyrenees Forest

BEST TIME TO VISIT

All year round.

1. BLACKWOOD

Blackwood is part of Victoria's mineral springs district and was at one time the scene of a gold rush.

Blackwood Mineral Springs Caravan Park

In Blackwood beside the Lerderderg River, with the Wombat State Forest nearby. Gold panning. Bookings recommended during peak periods. Additional map ref.: VR 290 H2.

Further information & bookings: Blackwood Mineral Springs Caravan Park **Tel.:** (03) 5368 6539 **Camping fees:** Unpowered sites from $13.00 for 2 people/night, powered sites from $15.00 for 2 people/night

2. BRISBANE RANGES NATIONAL PARK

The Brisbane Ranges National Park is 80 km west of Melbourne, near Anakie. It has rugged ranges formed millions of years ago by a fault line. There are scenic walks, and native plant species and wildlife abound. Mountain bike riders are not permitted to access trails behind management gates.

Boar Gully camping area

Reached via Reids Rd. Boil water before use. Bring drinking water and firewood. Catch yabbies in the dam. Bookings preferred. Additional map ref.: VR 77 F6.

Bush camping
Permit required, contact ranger for details.

Further information & bookings: Parks Victoria information line **Tel.:** 131 963 **Camping fees:** From $10.20 per site/night; fees payable at self-registration station

3. CRESWICK REGIONAL PARK

The area was once mined heavily for gold, but the vegetation has since regenerated. The park is 18 km north of Ballarat, near Creswick. Access is via Bungaree–Creswick Rd, off Midland Hwy. Activities include bushwalking, mountain biking, picnicking, canoeing and nature study.

Slaty Creek picnic and camping area

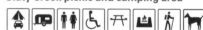

On Slaty Creek Rd. Short-term camping only. Bring drinking water and firewood. Additional map ref.: VR 58 G9.

Further information & bookings: Parks Victoria information line **Tel.:** 131 963

4. ENFIELD STATE PARK

Enfield State Park is home to numerous goldmining sites and 19th-century relics. Try your luck fossicking for gold (Miners Right licence required). During spring there are prolific wildflower displays.

Surface Point camping area

This is 30 km south of Ballarat, reached via Misery Creek Rd, signposted off the Ballarat–Colac Rd. Bring drinking water and firewood. Additional map ref.: VR 76 D6.

Further information & bookings: Parks Victoria information line **Tel.:** 131 963

5. GREATER BENDIGO NATIONAL PARK – WHIPSTICK SECTION

See also Greater Bendigo National Park – Kamarooka section, *page 104*

The park protects Whipstick mallee-type vegetation as well as relics from goldmining and the eucalyptus oil distillation industry. It is 8 km north of Bendigo and reached via Neilborough Rd off Simpsons Rd from Eaglehawk on the Loddon Valley Hwy. Activities include bushwalking and 4WD touring.

Loeser picnic and camping area

Access via Loeser Rd. Bring drinking water and firewood. Additional map ref.: VR 44 F3.

Notley picnic and camping area

Access via Neilborough Rd. Bring drinking water and firewood. Additional map ref.: VR 44 F4.

Shadbolt picnic and camping area

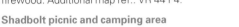

Near Flagstaff Hill. Access via Neilborough Rd. Bring drinking water and firewood. Additional map ref.: VR 44 E4.

Further information & bookings: Parks Victoria information line **Tel.:** 131 963

6. HEPBURN REGIONAL PARK

This park is close to the famous mineral springs towns of Daylesford and Hepburn Springs. It features natural mineral springs and goldmining relics. Activities include bushwalking, mountain biking, picnicking and nature study.

Mount Franklin Reserve camping area

Located 8 km north of Daylesford. Signposted from the Midland Hwy. Short-term camping only. Bring drinking water and firewood. Additional map ref.: VR 59 D6.

Further information & bookings: Parks Victoria information line **Tel.:** 131 963

7. KARA KARA STATE PARK

This park is 23 km south of St Arnaud, near Stuart Mill, and is reached via Teddington Rd, off Sunraysia Hwy. Conventional vehicles can access the park in dry weather only. Activities include fishing, bushwalking, fossicking and 4WD touring.

Teddington camping area

Beside Teddington Reservoir. Signposted from Teddington Rd. Group camping at Teddington Hut (bookings required). Collection of firewood not permitted in park – bring own or use gas/fuel stove. Additional map ref.: VR 42 F7.

Further information & bookings: Parks Victoria information line **Tel.:** 131 963

8. KOOYOORA STATE PARK

This attractive park includes hill ranges and box-ironbark forest. It is 15 km west of Inglewood, near Kingower. It is signposted off Dunolly–Wedderburn Rd. There are panoramic views from the park's granite tors. Activities include bushwalking, fossicking, rock climbing and horseriding.

Melville Caves camping area

A short distance from Melville Caves. Access via Melville Caves Rd. Bring drinking water and firewood or use fuel/gas stove. Additional map ref.: VR 43 C3.

Further information & bookings: Parks Victoria information line **Tel.:** 131 963

9. LAKE BURRUMBEET

Lake Burrumbeet is a popular fishing (trout and redfin) and summer watersports venue 16 km west of Ballarat, near Burrumbeet, which is on the Western Hwy.

Lake Burrumbeet Caravan Park

Cabin accommodation also available. Bookings required at peak times. Additional map ref.: VR 58 C9.

Further information & bookings: Lake Burrumbeet Caravan Park **Tel.:** (03) 5344 0583 **Email:** lbcp@netconnect. com.au **Camping fees:** Unpowered sites $14.30 per site/night for 1–2 people, powered from $16.50 per site/night for 1–2 people.

10. LANGI GHIRAN STATE PARK

The park is 12 km east of Ararat and is reached via Kartuk Rd, off Western Hwy. There are panoramic views from the park's granite peaks and attractive red gum and yellowbox woodlands. Take a walk to two old water reservoirs that once served Ararat. Activities include bushwalking and vehicle touring.

Langi Ghiran camping area

Signposted from Kartuk Rd. Additional map ref.: VR 57 C6.

Bush camping
Bush camping is allowed within the mountainous sections of the park. Bring water. Contact ranger for details.

Further information & bookings: Parks Victoria information line **Tel.:** 131 963

11. LERDERDERG STATE PARK

Lerderderg State Park is north of Bacchus Marsh and to the east of Blackwood. Access is via the Greendale–Trentham Rd or the Bacchus Marsh–Gisborne Rd. The park's main feature is the 300-metre-deep Lerderderg Gorge.

O'Briens Crossing camping area

On the Lerderderg River, 8 km from Blackwood via O'Briens Road, in the north-west section of the park. Access road is steep in places. Bring drinking water and firewood. Additional map ref.: VR 59 G9.

Bush camping
Walk-in bush campsites within park for self-sufficient bushwalkers. Contact ranger for details.

Further information & bookings: Parks Victoria information line **Tel.:** 131 963

12. MALDON HISTORIC RESERVE

The reserve, adjacent to Maldon township, protects many historical features from the gold-rush era. Take one of the walking tracks to explore mining relics such as a 'puddler'. For safety, please stay on marked tracks due to old mine shafts.

The Butts camping area

Access via Franklin St in Maldon. Bring drinking water. Additional map ref.: VR 59 B1.

Further information & bookings: Parks Victoria information line **Tel.:** 131 963

13. MOONAMBEL

Moonambel, in the Pyrenees, is the centre of a winegrowing area. It lies on the Stawell–Avoca Rd, 19 km north-west of Avoca.

Mountain Creek camping area

Located 300 m north of Moonambel. Take Greens Lane in Moonambel to Mountain Creek picnic area. Additional map ref.: VR 42 F9.

Further information & bookings: DSE, Maryborough **Tel.:** (03) 5461 1055

14. MOUNT ALEXANDER REGIONAL PARK

The park is 3 km east of Harcourt and 120 km north-west of Melbourne, near Castlemaine. Access is via Mt Alexander Tourist Rd from Faraday or from Harcourt North Rd. Walk to one of the park's panoramic lookouts.

Bush camping

Dispersed bush camping at rear of day-use area. Bring drinking water. Additional map ref.: VR 59 F2.

Further information & bookings: Parks Victoria information line **Tel.:** 131 963

15. MOUNT BUANGOR STATE PARK

This park is 21 km west of Beaufort. It is reached from the Western Hwy. Mt Buangor is the area's highest peak. Activities include camping, bushwalking and mountain biking.

Ferntree picnic and camping area

Five sites only. Signposted from Ferntree Waterfall Rd. Bring firewood. Additional map ref.: VR 57 E7.

Middle Creek picnic and camping area

Large area suitable for groups. Signposted off Jimmy Smith Rd, from Ferntree Gully Rd. Bring drinking water and firewood. Additional map ref.: VR 57 E7.

Further information & bookings: Parks Victoria information line **Tel.:** 131 963

16. MOUNT COLE STATE FOREST

Mt Cole State Forest is 25 km north-west of Beaufort. Access roads may be rough at times. Activities include bushwalking, mountain biking and 4WD touring.

Chinamans camping area

Beside Chinaman Creek, 4–5km from Warrak. Access via Mt Cole Rd from Warrak. Additional map ref.: VR 57 D6.

Ditchfields camping area

Near a small creek. Signposted via Camp Rd from Mt Cole Rd. Old forest hut. Additional map ref.: VR 57 F7.

Mugwamp camping area

Near Mugwamp Creek. Access via Dawson Rock Rd from Mt Cole Rd. Old hut. Additional map ref.: VR 57 E6.

Richards camping area

Short walk from carpark to these sites beside Fiery Creek. Access via The Glut Rd. Additional map ref.: VR 57 F6.

Smiths Bridge camping area

Located 19 km north-west of Beaufort and 13 km from Elmhurst, on the Beaufort–Elmhurst Rd. Additional map ref.: VR 57 F6.

Bush camping
Bush camping is allowed within the forest. Contact ranger for details.

Further information & bookings: DSE Customer Information Centre **Tel.:** 136 186

17. PADDYS RANGE STATE PARK

This park is 4 km south-west of Maryborough, reached by Old Avoca Rd off the Pyrenees Hwy. There is limited space for caravans. There are many old goldmining sites and relics and stunning wildflowers in spring. Activities include bushwalking, exploring old mine workings, birdwatching, horseriding and fossicking.

Karri Track camping area

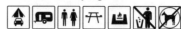

Access via signposted Karri Track off Old Avoca Rd. Notify ranger before camping. No bush camping. Bring drinking water and firewood. Additional map ref.: VR 58 D3.

Further information & bookings: Parks Victoria information line **Tel.:** 131 963

18. PYRENEES FOREST

The forest is in the Pyrenees Range west of Avoca. Access is via Vinoca Rd from Avoca.

Camerons Track Shelter camping area

On Camerons Track, 20 km west of Avoca via Vinoca Rd. Bring firewood. Additional map ref.: VR 57 G3.

Waterfalls picnic and camping area

Signposted from Vinoca Rd, about 11 km west of Avoca. Bring drinking water and firewood. Additional map ref.: VR 57 G3.

Further information & bookings: DSE, Maryborough **Tel.:** (03) 5461 1055

19. VAUGHAN–GLENLUCE MINERAL SPRINGS RESERVE

The local area has many historic mining sites and mineral springs. The reserve is 10 km south of Castlemaine at Vaughan, on the Loddon River. Access is via Vaughan Springs Rd from Guildford on the Midland Hwy. Activities include bushwalking, cycling, fishing and picnicking.

Vaughan Springs picnic area

Reached via Grenville St at Vaughan. Additional map ref.: VR 59 E4.

Further information & bookings: Parks Victoria information line **Tel.:** 131 963 **Camping fees:** Fees may apply at times

20. WARBURTON BRIDGE RESERVE

This is 4 km south of Fryerstown, beside the Loddon River. It is reached via Vaughan Springs Rd from the Midland Hwy at Yapeen, then Vaughan–Drummond Rd. Swimming and fishing are popular here.

Bush camping

Dispersed bush camping on banks of Loddon River. Bring drinking water and firewood. Additional map ref.: VR 59 E4.

Further information & bookings:
Parks Victoria information line **Tel.:** 131 963 *or*
Parks Victoria, Castlemaine, **Tel.:** (03) 5472 5272

21. WELLSFORD STATE FOREST

This popular area for picnicking and horseriding is 5 km east of Bendigo. It is reached via Plant Rd from Bendigo. (Wellsford State Forest will come under Parks Victoria management in the future; please confirm the park's status if you plan to bring your dog.)

Bush camping

Dispersed bush camping away from day-use areas. Bring drinking water. Additional map ref.: VR 44 G5.

Further information & bookings: DSE, Bendigo **Tel.:** (03) 5430 4444

22. WOMBAT STATE FOREST

Located north-west of Melbourne between Macedon and Daylesford. The forest is popular for drives. Activities include 4WD touring, horseriding and walking.

Firth Park picnic and camping area

Access via Firth Rd off the Bacchus Marsh–Gisborne Rd or from Trentham. Bring drinking water and firewood. Old sawmill site. Additional map ref.: VR 59 H9.

Nolans Creek picnic and camping area

Located 11 km west of Blackwood on Lerderderg Rd. Bring drinking water and firewood. Additional map ref.: VR 59 E9.

Bush camping
Permitted within the forest. Contact ranger for details.

Further information & bookings: DSE Customer Service Centre **Tel.:** 136 186

Sovereign Hill, Ballarat, where all the splendour of the gold-rush days is relived

VICTORIA

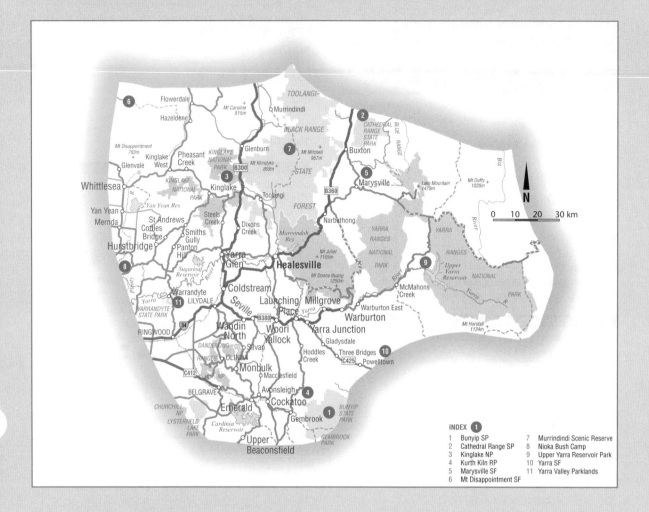

INDEX

1 Bunyip SP
2 Cathedral Range SP
3 Kinglake NP
4 Kurth Kiln RP
5 Marysville SF
6 Mt Disappointment SF
7 Murrindindi Scenic Reserve
8 Nioka Bush Camp
9 Upper Yarra Reservoir Park
10 Yarra SF
11 Yarra Valley Parklands

THE YARRA VALLEY AND THE DANDENONG RANGES ARE AREAS OF GREAT NATURAL BEAUTY.

Yarra State Forest is 80 kilometres east of Melbourne. Here magnificent stands of mountain ash cover the hills, one of the most tremendous examples being the Ada Tree. This giant mountain ash, believed to be one of Victoria's largest trees, towers over the surrounding rainforest.

Criss-crossing the forest are three drives which also take in some interesting man-made features, including the remains of the sawmilling days. And for those who prefer to see the sights on foot, the walk from Powelltown to East Warburton traverses the forest following a disused tramway, visiting a number of old sawmill sites and passing through both campsites in the forest – Starlings Gap and Latrobe River.

Kinglake National Park is a large park on the slopes of the Great Dividing Range, 65 kilometres north of Melbourne. The park offers some excellent walking tracks of varying lengths and grades. Scenic views can be had from Mount Sugarloaf and Lady Stonehavens Lookout. Natural features here include the mixed eucalypt forest, beautiful wildflowers during autumn and spring, Wombelano Falls and a large variety of birds and wildlife. The Gums camping area is beside Island Creek, ten kilometres north of Kinglake, where trout, blackfish and yabbies are caught.

The beautiful Murrindindi Scenic Reserve provides excellent riverside camping. The reserve has much to offer the visitor: walking trails, lookouts, beautiful waterfalls, picnic areas, mountain-bike riding and vehicle touring. There are nearly 100 campsites within the reserve, all along the Murrindindi River. Although the river is not deep enough for swimming, it is suitable for a paddle and is safe for the littlies.

The Upper Yarra Reservoir Park camping area is surrounded by tall eucalypt forest and has spectacular scenery. Close by is the short self-guide Fern Gully walking trail and a walk to the restored McVeighs Water Wheel. There is abundant wildlife in the park, including common wombats, king parrots and lyrebirds.

BEST CAMPSITES

Starlings Gap camping area
Yarra State Forest

The Gums camping area
Kinglake National Park

Upper Yarra Reservoir Park camping area
Upper Yarra Reservoir Park

Cooks Mill camping area
Cathedral Range State Park

Murrindindi Scenic Reserve camping areas
Murrindindi Scenic Reserve

BEST TIME TO VISIT

All year round.

1. BUNYIP STATE PARK

Bunyip State Park boasts magnificent mountain ash forests and the area has a strong timber-getting background. It is in the foothills of the Great Dividing Range, 65 km east of Melbourne, near Gembrook. There are possibilities for hiking, mountain biking and horseriding and while you are there, go bunyip spotting!

Dyers picnic and camping area

Access via Black Snake Creek Rd. Bring drinking water and firewood. Additional map ref.: VR 80 D9.

Mile Pit camping ground

Access via Tonimbuk Rd. Bring drinking water and firewood. Additional map ref.: VR 80 B9.

Nash Creek camping ground

Access via Black Snake Creek Rd. Bring drinking water and firewood. Additional map ref.: VR 80 D9.

Old Tynong Camp camping ground

Access via Camp Rd. Bring drinking water and firewood. Additional map ref.: VR 80 C9.

Rysons Creek camping ground

Access via Forest Rd. Bring drinking water and firewood. Additional map ref.: VR 80 E9.

Further information & bookings: Parks Victoria information line **Tel.:** 131 963

2. CATHEDRAL RANGE STATE PARK

This park is 100 km north-east of Melbourne and is reached from the Maroondah Hwy near Taggerty and Buxton. Entry is from Cathedral Lane or Mt Margaret Rd. The park contains a number of clear mountain streams and a variety of walking and hiking trails. Things to do include rock climbing, horseriding and fishing. Wood collection in the park is prohibited.

Cooks Mill camping area

Access via Little River Rd. Site of old sawmill beside Little River. Bring drinking water and firewood. Additional map ref.: VR 62 E8.

Neds Gully camping area

Access via Little River Rd. Walk-in site beside Little River. Bring drinking water and firewood. Additional map ref.: VR 62 E7.

The Farmyard camping area

Walk-in site. No facilities: self-sufficient camping. Access from Jawbone carpark on Cerberus Road. Bring drinking water. Gas/fuel stove preferred. Additional map ref.: VR 62 D8.

Further information & bookings: Parks Victoria information line **Tel.:** 131 963 **Camping fees:** $10.20 per site/night; fees payable at self-registration stations at Cooks Mill and Neds Gully

3. KINGLAKE NATIONAL PARK

This is the largest national park close to Melbourne and is near Kinglake township. It is reached via the Maroondah Hwy. Kinglake is an eucalypt forest on the Great Dividing Range and there are many walking trails in the park. It is a popular destination for bird watching and nature study.

The Gums camping area

Located 10 km north of Kinglake via Eucalyptus Rd. Ten sites (three with caravan access). Bring drinking water. Firewood supplied. Book well in advance for peak periods. Additional map ref.: VR 61 H9.

Further information & bookings: Parks Victoria information line **Tel.:** 131 963 **Camping fees:** From $10.20 per site/night

4. KURTH KILN REGIONAL PARK

Kurth Kiln is 65 km east of Melbourne, near Gembrook. Access is via Launching Place Rd or Beenak. The historic kilns here were used to produce charcoal for gas-producer units fitted to cars during World War II. Activities include walking and horseriding.

Kurth Kiln picnic and camping area

This is located 9 km along Soldiers Rd, off Gembrook Rd, or reached via Beenak Rd off the Gembrook–Launching Place Rd. Bring drinking water and firewood. Additional map ref.: VR 80 B8.

Further information & bookings: Parks Victoria information line **Tel.:** 131 963

5. MARYSVILLE STATE FOREST

This lies to the north-east of Marysville and is reached via Lady Talbot Drive. There are spectacular waterfalls and rainforests along the way in Yarra Ranges National Park.

Keppel Hut camping area

Seasonal access by 4WD only from Keppel Hut Track off Lady Talbot Drive. Bring drinking water and firewood. Small walk-in camping area near hut. Part of the Bicentennial National Trail. Additional map ref.: VR 62 F9.

Further information & bookings: DSE, Marysville **Tel.:** (03) 5963 3555

6. MOUNT DISAPPOINTMENT STATE FOREST

Mt Disappointment State Forest is 60 km north of Melbourne near Broadford. Access is via Heathcote Junction and North Mountain Rd. Mt Disappointment was named by Hume and Hovell in 1824. Activities in the area include car and motorbike touring, bushwalking and horseriding.

No. 1 Camp camping area

Access via Flowerdale Rd. Large area suited to groups. Bring drinking water and firewood. Additional map ref.: VR 61 D7.

Regular Camp camping area

Vehicle access to campsites restricted by bollards. Access via Main Mountain Rd or Spur Rd. Bring drinking water and firewood. Additional map ref.: VR 61 D7.

Further information & bookings: DSE, Broadford **Tel.:** (03) 5784 0600

7. MURRINDINDI SCENIC RESERVE

This reserve is situated in the northern section of Toolangi–Black Range State Forest. Located north-east of Yarra Glen, near Toolangi, it is reached from Myers Creek Rd or the Melba Hwy. There is excellent riverside camping here and activities include walking trails – walk to Wilhelmina Falls – motorbike riding, 4WD touring, mountain bike riding and fishing. You should visit the Toolangi Forest Discovery Centre and, if you have a car, wind your way along the Toolangi–Black Range Forest Drive.

Bull Creek camping area

Access via Murrindindi Rd. Bring drinking water and firewood. Additional map ref.: VR 62 B8.

SEC camping and picnic area

Walk-in site, access via Murrindindi Rd. Bring drinking water. Additional map ref.: VR 62 A8.

Suspension Bridge camping ground

Access via Murrindindi Rd. Small caravans can reach campsite, not large ones. Bring drinking water and firewood. Additional map ref.: VR 62 A8.

The Ferns, Water Gauge, Pine Tree and Blackwood camping areas

There are signposts to each site off Murrindindi Rd. Bring drinking water and firewood. Additional map ref.: VR 62.

Further information & bookings: DSE Customer Service Centre **Tel.:** 136 186 **Camping fees:** From $5.00 per vehicle/night; fees payable at self-registration stations

8. NIOKA BUSH CAMP

This is a nature-based recreational area only 20 km north-east of Melbourne, near Morang South in the Plenty Gorge Parklands. Access is signposted via Plenty Rd. There is a wide range of activities here.

Nioka Bush Camp camping area

Bookings essential – locked access. Firewood supplied. Additional map ref.: VR 79 C4.

Forests of mountain ash and tree ferns are found throughout this part of Victoria

Further information & bookings: Parks Victoria information line **Tel.:** 131 963 **Camping fees:** Contact Parks Victoria for latest fee schedule

9. UPPER YARRA RESERVOIR PARK

The park is the uppermost point of the Yarra River accessible to the public, and the reservoir is the third largest of Melbourne's water supplies. It is 24 km north-east of Warburton, and reached by Woods Point–Warburton Rd. Features include walking trails, lookout points and the restored McVeighs Water Wheel. The park is open 8.30 am–6 pm during summer daylight saving time, and 8.30 am–5 pm for the rest of the year.

Upper Yarra Reservoir Park camping area

Signposted from Woods Point Rd. Ideal area for groups and families. Bring firewood. Bookings essential. Locked gate access only – entry code supplied at time of booking. Additional map ref.: VR 80 G4.

Further information & bookings: Parks Victoria information line **Tel.:** 131 963 **Camping fees:** From $5.50 per adult/night and $3.30 per child/night; families from $18.00 per night

10. YARRA STATE FOREST

The forest is about 80 km east of Melbourne, near Powelltown, and is reached via Warburton, Powelltown, Yarra Junction and Noojee. The forest contains the upper reaches of the Yarra, Latrobe and Bunyip river systems and is a popular area for forest drives. There are over 100 km of walking trails in the forest, including 'Walk into History' – a two-day hike from Powelltown to East Warburton. Visit the Ada Tree – a giant mountain ash which is one of the largest trees in Victoria. Activities include 4WD touring, horseriding and mountain biking.

Ada No. 2 Mill, Big Pats Creek and Federal Mill camping areas

Walk-in sites located along the Walk into History trail. No facilities – toilet at Big Pats Creek only. Trail brochure available from DSE.

Latrobe River camping area

The camping area is beside the Latrobe River, on Ada River Rd. Access via Noojee Rd from Powelltown. Additional map ref.: VR 80 G8.

Starlings Gap camping area

On Big Creek Rd. Best access is Black Sands Rd off the Yarra Junction–Noojee Rd; turn-off is just south-east of small village of Gladysdale. Additional map ref.: VR 80 E7.

Bush camping
Permitted within forest. Contact ranger for details.

Further information & bookings: DSE Customer Service Centre **Tel.:** 136 186

11. YARRA VALLEY PARKLANDS

These parklands in a bushland setting are along the Yarra River near Warrandyte, just to the north-east of Melbourne. Access is via Warrandyte Rd. Activities include walking, canoeing and swimming.

Longridge camping area

Ideal area for group camping. Maximum two-night stay. Bookings essential. Locked gate – entry code supplied at time of booking. Additional map ref.: VR 79 E5.

Further information & bookings: Parks Victoria information line **Tel.:** 131 963 **Camping fees:** From $5.00 per adult/night and $3.30 per child/night; families from $16.50 per night

THE HIGH COUNTRY

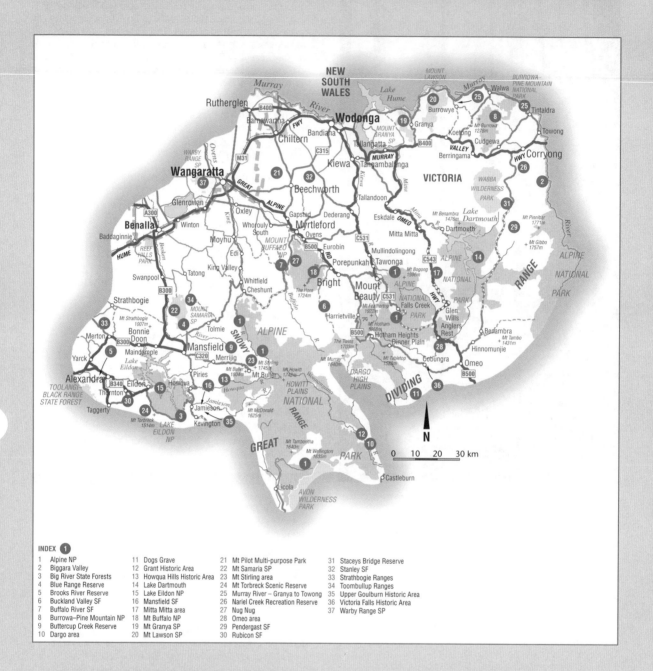

THE MAGNIFICENT VICTORIAN ALPS CONTAIN SOME OF THE STATE'S MOST DIVERSE AND SPECTACULAR COUNTRYSIDE, AND THE UNSPOILED NATURAL BEAUTY OF THIS AREA CAN BE ENJOYED THROUGHOUT THE YEAR.

In winter downhill and cross-country skiers visit the Alps. For the rest of the year these mountains are a major destination for bushwalking, vehicle touring, camping, mountain bike riding, fishing, canoeing, sightseeing and horseriding.

The region is also home to a number of historic areas protecting our early pioneering and mining heritage. Visitors will find some interesting reminders of the early settlements, including abandoned mine equipment and mine shafts, ruins of old goldmining towns and cemeteries. Areas that are extremely interesting to visit and also provide camping opportunities include the historic areas of Grant, Howqua Hills, Upper Goulburn and Victoria Falls.

Other places where camping is allowed include Buckland Valley State Forest, where the Buckland Riots took place in 1857, and Dogs Grave, where a monument to man's best friend is erected.

Victoria's largest national park, Alpine National Park, is largely undeveloped and has wonderful opportunities for camping and recreation. A number of established camping areas are located throughout the park, with remote bush camping also possible. There are hundreds of kilometres of walking trails here, with the major walking trails of the Australian Alps Walking Track, the Bicentennial National Trail and McMillans Walking Track passing through the park. The alpine vegetation is spectacular, with alpine ash and snow gums on the higher ground and eucalypt forests lower down. Come spring and summer and the beautiful alpine wildflowers are in bloom.

BEST CAMPSITES

Buttercup Creek camping areas
Buttercup Creek Reserve

Sheepyard Flat camping area
Howqua Hills Historic Area

Italian Flat camping area
Dargo area

Doctors Creek camping reserve
Upper Goulburn Historic Area

Nariel Creek Recreation Reserve camping area
Nariel Creek Recreation Reserve

BEST TIME TO VISIT

All year round, depending on your choice of activity. Remember that this is alpine country, and weather and conditions can change dramatically and without warning.

1. ALPINE NATIONAL PARK see page 120

2. BIGGARA VALLEY

Biggara is a small township beside the Murray River southeast of Corryong. Access is via Upper Murray Rd off the Corryong–Khancoban Rd. This is a popular fishing area.

Bunroy Junction camping area

On edge of Alpine National Park, beside Murray River on Bunroy Creek Track off Bunroy Rd, which is off Upper Murray Rd. Bring drinking water and firewood. Additional map ref.: VR 37 J7.

Hairpin Bend camping area

On edge of Alpine National Park, beside Murray River on Indi River Track off Bunroy Rd, which is off Upper Murray Rd. South of Bunroy Junction. Bring drinking water and firewood. Additional map ref.: VR 37 J7.

Indi Bridge Reserve camping area

On Upper Murray Rd 4 km south of Towong Upper. Bring drinking water and firewood. Additional map ref.: VR 37 J5.

Further information & bookings: Corryong Tourist Information Centre **Tel.:** (02) 6076 2277 **Email:** faithd@towong.vic.gov.au

3. BIG RIVER STATE FORESTS

LOWER BIG RIVER STATE FOREST
This forest is 240 km north-east of Melbourne, to the southeast of Eildon. Access is via the Eildon–Jamieson Rd in the north and via Marysville and the Cumberland Rd in the south. It is a popular area for gold fossicking, bushwalking, fishing and 4WD touring.

Big River camping area

Access via Eildon–Jamieson Rd. Bring drinking water and firewood. Additional map ref.: VR 63 B7.

Burnt Bridge camping ground

Access via Eildon–Jamieson Rd. Bring drinking water and firewood. Additional map ref.: VR 63 B7.

Bulldog Flat camping area

Access via Eildon–Jamieson Rd. Bring drinking water and firewood. Additional map ref.: VR 63 B7.

Chaffe Creek camping area

Access via Lower Big River Rd. Bring drinking water and firewood. Additional map ref.: VR 63 C8.

Jimmy Bullocks camping area

Access via Eildon–Jamieson Rd. Bring drinking water and firewood. Additional map ref.: VR 63 B7.

Old Coach Road camping area

Access via Lower Big River Rd. Bring drinking water and firewood. Additional map ref.: VR 63 C8.

Railway Creek camping area

Access via Lower Big River Rd. 4WD access only. Bring drinking water and firewood. Additional map ref.: VR 63 C8.

The Pines camping ground

Access via Eildon–Jamieson Rd. Bring drinking water and firewood. Additional map ref.: VR 63 B7.

Further information & bookings: DSE Customer Service Centre **Tel.:** 136 186

UPPER BIG RIVER STATE FOREST

This forest is 130 km north-east of Melbourne and to the east of Marysville. Access is via the Cumberland Rd from Marysville or the Reefton Spur Rd from Warburton. This is a popular area for gold fossicking, bushwalking, fishing and 4WD touring.

Big River Camp camping area

Access via Big River Rd. Bring drinking water and firewood. Additional map ref.: VR 81 A1.

Frenchmans Creek camping area

Access via Big River Rd. Bring drinking water and firewood. Additional map ref.: VR 81 B2.

Snowy Road camping area

Access via Snowy Rd. 4WD access only. Bring drinking water and firewood. Additional map ref.: VR 81 B2.

Stockmans Reward camping area

Access via Big River Rd. Bring drinking water and firewood. Additional map ref.: VR 81 B2.

Big Bend Creek, Bobuck Ridge, Catford, Dairy Flat, Fishbone Flat, Gang Gang Gully, McClelland, Married Mens, Miners Flat, Peppermint Ridge, Petroffs, Reids, Specimen Creek, Twenty-five Mile Creek and Vennells camping areas

Access via Big River Rd. Some sites require 4WD vehicle. Bring drinking water and firewood.

Further information & bookings: DSE, Marysville **Tel.:** (03) 5963 3555

4. BLUE RANGE RESERVE

This is 15 km north of Mansfield and is reached via Blue Range Creek Rd off the Mansfield–Whitfield Rd. Activities include 4WD touring, mountain biking and horseriding.

Blue Range camping reserve

Small site beside Blue Range Creek. Water from creek – boil before use. Additional map ref.: VR 48 C9.

Further information & bookings: DSE Customer Service Centre **Tel.:** 136 186

5. BROOKS RIVER RESERVE

The reserve is near Alexandra, on the Goulburn River towards Yarck.

Brooks River Reserve camping area

Access from Swanns Lane on the north side of Alexandra. Bring drinking water and firewood. Additional map ref.: VR 62 C5.

Further information & bookings: Parks Victoria information line **Tel.:** 131 963

6. BUCKLAND VALLEY STATE FOREST

The forest is 22 km south-west of Bright and is reached via Buckland Valley Rd off Great Alpine Rd at Porepunkah. It is an old mining area.

Buckland River Valley camping areas

Camping allowed between road and west side of Buckland River except on private land. Tracks lead off from Buckland River Rd to sites beside river. First track from Great Alpine Way is at 14.5 km and last track is a further 19 km on. Bring drinking water. Additional map ref.: VR 49 F7.

Maguire Point camping area

Main camping area is a large grassed area beside Buckland River, 18 km from Great Alpine Way. Signposted access along Buckland River Rd: road can be rough and potholed. Bring drinking water. Additional map ref.: VR 49 F6.

Further information & bookings:
DSE Customer Service Centre **Tel.:** 136 186 or
DSE, Ovens **Tel.:** (03) 5731 1222

7. BUFFALO RIVER STATE FOREST

This is 35 km south of Myrtleford, via Abbeyards Rd off Buffalo River Rd.

Blades, Manna Gum and Tea-Tree picnic and camping areas

Signposted from Abbeyards Rd. Bring drinking water and firewood. Additional map ref.: VR 49 C6.

Further information & bookings:
DSE Customer Service Centre **Tel.:** 136 186 or
DSE, Ovens **Tel.:** (03) 5731 1222

8. BURROWA–PINE MOUNTAIN NATIONAL PARK

The park consists of two blocks connected by a vegetated corridor and is 120 km east of Wodonga near Cudgewa. Views of the Snowy Mountains can be had from a number of lookouts. Activities include bushwalking and nature study.

Blue Gum Camp camping area

On Falls Rd. Access via Cudgewa North–Walwa Rd. Additional map ref.: VR 37 E4.

Bluff Creek picnic and camping area

On Bluff Falls Rd. Access via Cudgewa North–Walwa Rd. Additional map ref.: VR 37 E3.

Hinces Creek Camp camping area

On Upper Dogman Track. Access via Cudgewa North–Walwa Rd. Additional map ref.: VR 37 E3.

Further information & bookings: Parks Victoria information line **Tel.:** 131 963

9. BUTTERCUP CREEK RESERVE

Buttercup Creek Reserve is 23 km from Mansfield. Conventional vehicle and caravan access are possible via Carters Rd, off the Mansfield–Mt Buller Rd 13 km east of Merrijig. 4WD access is via signposted Buttercup Rd 13 km from Mansfield. There are five sites beside Buttercup Creek and it is a good base to explore the surrounding areas. Activities include bushwalking, fishing, mountain bike riding, horseriding (permits may apply) and 4WD touring.

Buttercup Creek camping areas

These sites are signposted along Buttercup Creek Rd. Facilities vary at sites. Bring drinking water and firewood. Additional map ref.: VR 63 F3/G3.

Further information & bookings: DSE Customer Service Centre **Tel.:** 136 186

10. DARGO AREA

The village of Dargo is 50 km north-west of Bairnsdale. It is reached via the bitumen Lindenow–Dargo Rd from Bairnsdale, or from the north via the gravel Dargo High Plains Rd from the Great Alpine Rd at Mt St Bernard.

Black Snake Creek camping area

This is 24 km north-west of Dargo at junction of Wonnangatta River and Black Snake Creek. Signposted via Wonnangatta Rd off Crooked River Rd. Additional map ref.: VR 65 D9.

DARGO HIGH PLAINS

Twenty-five Mile Creek camping area

Small site beside creek, 10 km along Ritchie Rd from its junction with Dargo High Plains Rd, which is 45 km north of Dargo. Bring drinking water and firewood. Additional map ref.: VR 65 D4.

Thirty Mile Creek camping area

Small site beside creek, 22 km along Ritchie Rd from its junction with Dargo High Plains Rd, which is 45 km north of Dargo. Bring drinking water and firewood. Additional map ref.: VR 65 D4.

UPPER DARGO

Black Flat camping area

The area is 17 km north of Dargo along Upper Dargo Rd, turn-off 6 km north of Dargo. Signposted conventional vehicle access. Additional map ref.: VR 65 F7.

Collins Flat camping area

Located 21 km north of Dargo. 4WD vehicle only access via Upper Dargo Rd, turn-off 6 km north of Dargo. Additional map ref.: VR 65 F7.

Italian Flat camping area

Located 9 km north of Dargo near Two Mile Creek along Upper Dargo Rd, turn-off 6 km north of Dargo. Signposted conventional vehicle access. Additional map ref.: VR 65 F8.

Jimmy Iversons camping area

This is 10 km north of Dargo along Upper Dargo Rd, turn-off 6 km north of Dargo. Signposted conventional vehicle access. Additional map ref.: VR 65 F8.

Ollies Jump-Up camping area

Situated 13 km north of Dargo along Upper Dargo Rd, turn-off 6 km north of Dargo. Signposted conventional vehicle access. Additional map ref.: VR 65 F8.

Two Mile Creek camping area

This is 8 km north of Dargo, near Two Mile Creek along Upper Dargo Rd, turn-off 6 km north of Dargo. Signposted conventional vehicle access. Additional map ref.: VR 65 F8.

Further information & bookings: DSE, Dargo **Tel.:** (03) 5140 1243

11. DOGS GRAVE

Dogs Grave is 35 km west of Swifts Creek. It is an isolated spot that is home to a monument mourning a working dog that died of strychnine poisoning. Access is via Birregun Rd from Upper Livingstone Rd, off Cassilis Rd from Swifts Creek.

Dogs Grave camping area

Signposted conventional vehicle access via Birregun Rd from Omeo or Dargo. Caravan access from Omeo only. Bring drinking water and firewood. Additional map ref.: VR 65 H5.

Further information & bookings: DSE, Swifts Creek **Tel.:** (03) 5159 5100

Bush camping

Numerous 4WD and walk-in campsites throughout the area, notably beside Crooked River. Bush camping – no facilities. Follow Parks Victoria bush camping regulations. Obtain large-scale maps and contact park ranger for further details.

Further information & bookings: Parks Victoria information line **Tel.:** 131 963

ALPINE NATIONAL PARK

See also Lake Dartmouth, *page 126, and* Suggan Buggan, *page 138*

Huts and history

Many white settlers dreamed of a life in the high country. They negotiated the mountainous terrain on horseback, some tilling the soil, others panning for gold. Many finally found the isolation overwhelming, a story told by the string of empty bush huts now found in the area. Wallaces Hut has walls of solid snow-gum slabs and dates back to 1889.

Well-trodden track

While Mount Bogong is Victoria's highest peak, the hike to the summit of Mount Feathertop (1922 metres) along the exposed Razorback Ridge is one of the most popular walks here. This 22-kilometre-return walk has magnificent views all the way up.

Secret lake

It is claimed that even the local Aboriginal people were unaware of Lake Tali Karng until two members of the Welwenduk clan happened upon it in the 1800s. The sapphire lake lies high up in the mountains, 850 metres above sea level, and is only accessible by foot.

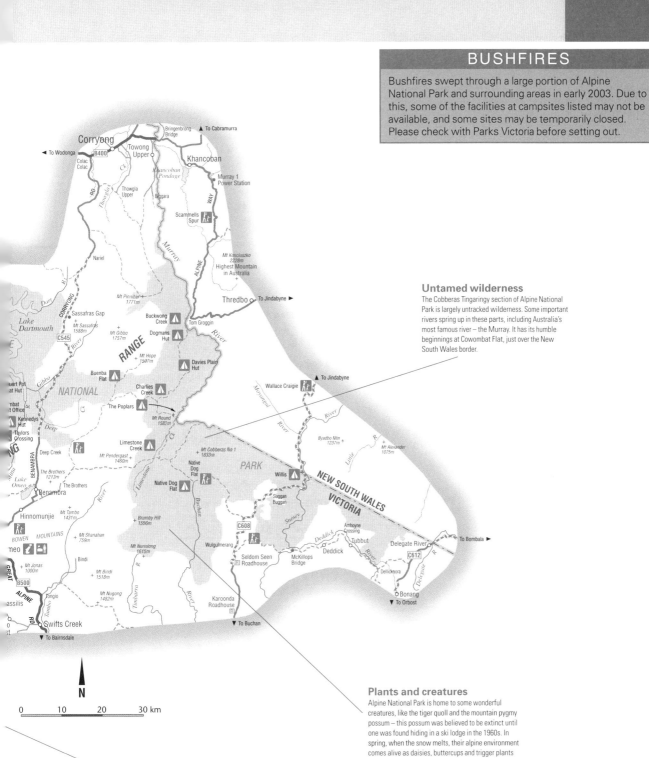

BUSHFIRES

Bushfires swept through a large portion of Alpine National Park and surrounding areas in early 2003. Due to this, some of the facilities at campsites listed may not be available, and some sites may be temporarily closed. Please check with Parks Victoria before setting out.

Untamed wilderness

The Cobberas Tingaringy section of Alpine National Park is largely untracked wilderness. Some important rivers spring up in these parts, including Australia's most famous river – the Murray. It has its humble beginnings at Cowombat Flat, just over the New South Wales border.

Plants and creatures

Alpine National Park is home to some wonderful creatures, like the tiger quoll and the mountain pygmy possum – this possum was believed to be extinct until one was found hiding in a ski lodge in the 1960s. In spring, when the snow melts, their alpine environment comes alive as daisies, buttercups and trigger plants all burst into bloom.

Unsolved mystery

In the early 1900s the remote Wonnangatta Valley was home to John Barclay, a cattleman, and his cook. On Christmas Eve 1917 the pair rode into Talbotville and never returned. Their bodies were later found severed and dumped, and to this day their deaths remain the unsolved murder mystery of the Victorian high country.

For campsite listings, see following pages

This huge park – Victoria's largest – stretches across Victoria's north-east. From the New South Wales border it sweeps down across the Bogong High Plains to as far south as Licola, and stops just short of Mansfield in the west. The park protects a vast area of the southern Great Dividing Range, and there are myriad opportunities for camping.

Many roads pass through the park and there is conventional vehicle access to all the main areas. Many other areas of the park are only accessible by 4WD vehicles and some roads are closed to all vehicles during winter. Be prepared for sudden changes in weather.

The park features the state's highest mountains and stunning alpine scenery. There are wildflower displays during summer and you can discover historic cattlemen's huts. It is a popular destination for bushwalking, skiing, 4WD touring, horseriding, fishing and mountain biking. The huts within Alpine National Park are refuge huts and should not be relied upon except in an emergency. Horseriding season is Dec.–April; permits are required.

BOGONG AREA
The Bogong area takes in the central section of Alpine National Park, including two of the park's highest mountains – Moung Bogong and Mount Feathertop. Located 365 km north-east of Melbourne and 90 km south-east of Wodonga, it is reached from the south via Great Alpine Rd, or from Bogong High Plains Rd from Omeo Hwy if aiming for Falls Creek. From the north-west take Kiewa Valley Hwy or Great Alpine Rd. Use of gas/fuel stove preferred.

Faithfuls Hut camping area

Located 18 km south of Falls Creek. Access via Bogong High Plains Rd. Camping in hut vicinity. Bring drinking water. Additional map ref.: VR 50 G9.

J. B. Plain camping area

This is 11 km south-east of Mt Hotham. Access via Great Alpine Rd. Walk-in site near hut. Bring drinking water. Additional map ref.: VR 65 E2.

Langford West camping area

Located 13–14 km south of Falls Creek. Access via Bogong High Plains Rd. Horseyards can be booked. Additional map ref.: VR 50 F8.

Mountain Creek camping area

This is 16 km east of Tawonga. Access via Mountain Creek Rd off Kiewa Valley Hwy. Water from creek – boil before use or bring your own. Additional map ref.: VR 50 E5.

Raspberry Hill camping area

Located 16–17 km south of Falls Creek. Access via Bogong High Plains Rd. Bring drinking water. Additional map ref.: VR 50 G9.

4WD and bush camping areas

There are numerous 4WD and walk-in campsites throughout the area, many near huts. Bush camping – no facilities. Follow Parks Victoria bush camping regulations. Obtain large-scale maps and contact park ranger for further details.

Further information & bookings: Parks Victoria information line **Tel.:** 131 963

COBBERAS–TINGARINGY AREA
The Cobberas–Tingaringy area is 450 km north-east of Melbourne and 60 km north-east of Omeo. Access from south is via Gelantipy Rd from Buchan, from the east via MacKillops Rd from Bonang, from the north via Barry Way (New South Wales) or from the west via Benambra–Black Mountain Rd. It is a remote area – be prepared. Use of gas/fuel stove preferred.

Native Dog Flat camping area

Located 45 km east of Benambra beside Buchan River. Access via Black Mountain Rd. Water from river – boil before use or bring own water. Additional map ref.: VR 52 C8.

Willis camping area

Near Snowy River 90 km north of Buchan at the New South Wales border. Access via Snowy River Rd/Barry Way. Bring drinking water. Additional map ref.: VR 52 H8.

4WD and bush camping areas

Numerous 4WD and walk-in campsites throughout the park, many in the vicinity of huts. Bush camping – no facilities. Follow Parks Victoria bush camping regulations. Obtain large-scale maps and contact park ranger for further details.

Further information & bookings: Parks Victoria information line **Tel.:** 131 963

DAVIES HIGH PLAIN AREA
The Davies High Plain area covers the far north-eastern part of the park, bound by the Murray River to the east. This area is 55 km north-east of Omeo, near the New South Wales border. It is reached from Benambra–Black Mountain Rd or Beloka Rd from Benambra or from Tom Groggin (New South Wales). Mainly 4WD vehicle, walking and horse access. Remote area – be prepared. Many tracks have seasonal closures. Check with Parks Victoria for details.

Buckwong Creek camping area

Located 5 km south of New South Wales border crossing at Tom Groggin. 4WD only access via Davies Plain Track. Bush camping near creek. Additional map ref.: VR 52 C3.

Buenba Flat camping area

Dispersed bush camping near Beunba Creek, 44 km north-east of Benambra. Conventional vehicle access via Beloka Rd. Additional map ref.: VR 51 G5.

Charlies Creek Plain camping area

Bush camping beside Charlies Creek. 4WD only access via Davies Plain Rd, 13 km south of Davies Hut. Bring drinking water and firewood. Additional map ref.: VR 52 C5.

Davies Plain Hut camping area

On Davies High Plain. 4WD only access via Davies Plain Track. Bring drinking water. Camping in hut vicinity. Horseyards. Additional map ref.: VR 52 C4.

Dogmans Hut camping area

Signposted off Tom Groggin Track, near Murray River crossing, 4 km from Alpine Way (New South Wales). 4WD only access. Bring drinking water and firewood. Additional map ref.: VR 52 D2.

Limestone Creek camping area

Beside Limestone Creek. 4WD only access via Limestone Creek Track. Bring drinking water. Additional map ref.: VR 52 B7.

The Poplars camping area

Beside Murray River. 4WD only access via McCarthys Track off Limestone Creek Track (1.1 km in from junction). Bring drinking water and firewood. Additional map ref.: VR 52 C6.

4WD and bush camping areas

Numerous 4WD and walk-in campsites throughout the area, many near huts. Bush camping – no facilities. Follow Parks Victoria bush camping regulations. Obtain large-scale maps and contact park ranger for further details.

Further information & bookings: Parks Victoria information line **Tel.:** 131 963

LAKE DARTMOUTH AREA

See also Lake Dartmouth, *page 126*

This area is approximately 50 km north of Omeo, near Mitta Mitta and surrounding Lake Dartmouth. Access from Omeo Hwy in the west or Benambra–Corryong Rd from the east. Mainly 4WD vehicle and boat access. Remote area – be prepared. Many tracks have seasonal closures. Check with Parks Victoria for details.

Kennedys Hut camping area

Located 40 km north of Omeo beside Mitta Mitta River. Access via Four Mile Creek Track off Wombat Track. 4WD only access. Camping in hut vicinity. Bring drinking water and firewood. Additional map ref.: VR 51.

Quart Pot Flat Hut camping area

Located 45 km south-east of Mitta Mitta near Mt Cooper. 4WD only access via Limestone Gap Track. Bring drinking water and firewood. Additional map ref.: VR 51 B5.

Taylors Crossing camping area

On the Mitta Mitta River. The Australian Alps Walking Track crosses here. 2WD vehicle access from east via Uplands or 4WD vehicle access from west via Four Mile Creek Track. Bring drinking water and firewood. Gas/fuel stove preferred. Additional map ref.: VR 51 C7.

Wombat Post Office camping area

This is 30 km north of Benambra beside Wombat Creek. 4WD only access via Wombat Creek Track. Camping near hut. Bring drinking water and firewood. Additional map ref.: VR 51 B6.

4WD and walk-in bush camping areas

Numerous 4WD and walk-in access campsites throughout the area, many in the vicinity of huts. Bush camping – no facilities. Follow Parks Victoria bush camping regulations. Obtain large-scale maps and contact park ranger for further details.

Further information & bookings: Parks Victoria information line **Tel.:** 131 963

WONNANGATTA–MOROKA AREA

This huge part of the park is around 200 km east of Melbourne. It stretches from Licola in the south to Cheshunt in the north, and from Howqua Hills Historic Area in the west to Grant Historic Area in the east. Access from the south is via Tamboritha Rd from Licola, from the west via Circuit Rd from Mansfield, and from the north via Myrtleford–Buffalo River Rd from Myrtleford or Buckland Valley Rd from Bright. From the east take Crooked River Rd from Dargo. It is a remote area – be prepared. Use of gas/fuel stove preferred.

NORTH-WESTERN REGION

Bennies camping area

Located 29 km south of Whitfield beside Rose River. Access via Cobbler Lake Rd off Whitfield–Myrtleford Rd. Bring drinking water. Additional map ref.: VR 49 A9.

Evans Creek Hut camping area

Located 8 km south of Lake William Hovell. 4WD only access via Evans Creek Track from Top Crossing Track. Additional map ref.: VR 48 H9.

King Hut camping area

Situated 35 km east of Mt Stirling on King Basin Rd near King River. 4WD only access via Speculation Rd off Circuit Rd from Mt Stirling. Water from river – boil before use. Horseyards. Additional map ref.: VR 64 B3.

Lake Cobbler camping area

This is 47 km south of Whitfield beside Lake Cobbler. Access via Cobbler Lake Rd off Whitfield–Myrtleford Rd. 4WD recommended or high clearance 2WD. Water from lake – boil before use. Near hut. Additional map ref.: VR 64 C2.

Pineapple Flat camping area

Located 10 km north of Mt Stirling near King River. 4WD only access via Burnt Top Track off Circuit Rd from Mt Stirling. Water from river – boil before use. Additional map ref.: VR 63 J3.

Sandy Flat camping area

Dispersed camping beside King River 9 km south-east of Lake William Hovell picnic area. 4WD only access via Sandy Flat Track from Lake William Hovell or Basin Track off Lake Cobbler Rd. Additional map ref.: VR 48 H8.

Top Crossing Hut camping area

Beside King River 13 km south of Lake William Hovell picnic area. 4WD only access via Top Crossing Track from Lake William Hovell. Additional map ref.: VR 48 H9.

Further information & bookings: Parks Victoria information line **Tel.:** 131 963

NORTH-EASTERN REGION

Beveridges Station camping area

Beside Buckland River, 40 km south of Great Alpine Rd, turn-off at Porepunkah. Signposted access via Buckland River Rd. Bring drinking water and firewood. Additional map ref.: VR 49 H9.

Further information & bookings: Parks Victoria information line **Tel.:** 131 963

CENTRAL REGION

Barkly River camping area

Bush camping at bridge over Barkly River. On Licola–Glencairn Rd 15 km north-west of Licola. Road is narrow and steep. Additional map ref.: VR 82 B3.

Bullock Flat camping area

Located 46 km north-west of Dargo beside Wonnangatta River. Access via Wonnangatta Rd. Additional map ref.: VR 65 B8.

Eaglevale camping area

Located 54 km north-west of Dargo beside Wonnangatta River. Access via Wonnangatta Rd. Additional map ref.: VR 64 H7.

Gantner Hut camping area

Located 37 km north of Arbuckle Junction near Mt Howitt. Walk-in only access via Howitt Rd. Near hut. Bring drinking water. Gas/fuel stove preferred. Additional map ref.: VR 64 D4.

Guys Hut camping area

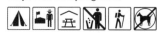

This is 20 km north of Arbuckle Junction near Bryces Gorge. Walk-in access via Howitt Rd from Bryces Gorge carpark. Bring drinking water. Gas/fuel stove preferred. Additional map ref.: VR 64 D6.

Holmes Plains camping area

Situated 5 km north of Arbuckle Junction. Access via Howitt Rd from Arbuckle Junction then Kellys Lane. Bring drinking water. Additional map ref.: VR 64 E8.

Horseyard Flat camping area

Located 65 km north-east of Licola. Signposted via Moroka Rd from Arbuckle Junction – it is 31 km east of Arbuckle Junction. Camping near hut. Water from river – boil before use. Additional map ref.: VR 64 H9.

Howitt Plains camping area

This is 30 km north of Arbuckle Junction beside Caledonia River. Access via Howitt Rd from Arbuckle Junction. Near Howitt Hut. Bring drinking water. Horse paddocks. Additional map ref.: VR 64 D5.

Kellys Lane camping areas

Dispersed bush camping 8 km south-west of Arbuckle Junction beside Shaws Creek. Access via Kellys Lane off Tamboritha Rd. Additional map ref.: VR 64 D9.

Lake Tali Karng camping area

This is 15 km south of Arbuckle Junction near the Sentinels, a 12-km walk from McFarlane Saddle on Moroka Rd. Bring drinking water. Gas/fuel stove preferred. Additional map ref.: VR 82 E2.

McFarlane Saddle camping area

This is 12 km south-east of Arbuckle Junction. Access via Moroka Rd from Arbuckle Junction. Bring drinking water. Bush camping – no facilities. Additional map ref.: VR 64 H9.

Millers Hut camping area

Situated 5 km south-west of Mt Wellington summit. 4WD access via Mt Wellington Track off Moroka Rd. Track junction is 17 km south-east of Arbuckle Junction. Bring drinking water. Near hut. Additional map ref.: VR 82 F2.

Moroka Bridge camping area

This is 26 km south-east of Arbuckle Junction. Access via Moroka Rd from Arbuckle Junction. Bring drinking water. Bush camping – no facilities. Additional map ref.: VR 64 H9.

Moroka Junction camping area

Located 62 km north-west of Dargo, 1 km before the junction of Moroka and Wonnangatta rivers. 4WD only access via Wonnangatta Rd off Crooked River Rd. Additional map ref.: VR 64 G7.

Wellington River camping areas

Many sites beside the Wellington River. Sites start 10 km north of Licola via Tamboritha Rd. Water from river – boil before use. Facilities vary at sites. Horseyards. Additional map ref.: VR 82 B2.

Wonnangatta Station camping area

This is 65 km north of Arbuckle Junction on Wonnangatta Track, beside the Wonnangatta River. 4WD only access via Zeka Spur Track off Howitt Rd from Licola, Humffray River Track off Abbeyards Rd from Myrtleford, or Wombat Spur Track from Crooked River Rd near Dargo. Additional map ref.: VR 64 E5.

Further information & bookings: Parks Victoria information line **Tel.:** 131 963

WESTERN REGION

Bindaree Hut camping area

4WD access only via Bindaree Rd off Circuit Rd. This area is 6 km past Bindaree Falls beside the Howqua River. Camping on flats in hut vicinity. Bring drinking water and firewood. Additional map ref.: VR 64 A4.

Bluff Hut camping area

4WD access only. Located 67 km south-east of Mansfield on Bluff Track off Brocks Rd. Bring drinking water. Horseyards. Bush campsites are 300 m north of hut. Additional map ref.: VR 63 J5.

Eight Mile camping area

Beside Howqua River. Signposted along Brocks Rd. Seasonal access. Small creek crossing to reach campsite. This area is 47 km south-east of Mansfield. Additional map ref.: VR 63 H5.

Lovick Hut camping area

4WD access only. Area is 74 km south-east of Mansfield via Bluff Track off Brocks Rd. Hut is 300 m from junction of Bluff Track and Cairn Creek Track. Horseyards. Camping in hut vicinity. Additional map ref.: VR 64 A5.

Mitchells Flat camping area

4WD access only. Area is 52 km east of Jamieson and is reached via Mitchells Track off the Jamieson–Licola Rd, and 56 km south-east of Mansfield, reached via Sheepyard Flat and Tobacco Flat. Dispersed bush camping. Site of old homestead. Bring drinking water and firewood. Additional map ref.: VR 63 G6.

Pikes Flat camping area

4WD access only via Bindaree Rd off Circuit Rd. Area is past Bindaree Hut beside the Howqua River. Dispersed bush camping on flats beside river. Bring drinking water and firewood. Additional map ref.: VR 64 A4.

Seven Mile camping area

Small campsite beside Howqua River 45 km south-east of Mansfield. Signposted along Brocks Rd. Additional map ref.: VR 63 H5.

Upper Howqua camping area

4WD access only via Bindaree Rd off Circuit Rd. Located 10 km along Bindaree Rd. Bring drinking water and firewood. Additional map ref.: VR 64 A4.

4WD and bush camping areas

Numerous 4WD and walk-in only campsites throughout the park, many near huts. Bush camping – no facilities. Follow Parks Victoria bush camping regulations. Obtain large-scale maps and contact park ranger for further details.

Further information & bookings: Parks Victoria information line **Tel.:** 131 963

12. GRANT HISTORIC AREA

This historic goldmining area is 16 km north-west of Dargo. It is reached via McMillan Rd off the Dargo High Plains Rd and is a popular area for 4WD touring.

Grant camping area

Near Mt Grant. Bring drinking water and firewood. Additional map ref.: VR 65 D7.

Talbotville camping areas

Dispersed camping at Talbotville beside Crooked River. Access via McMillan Track. Water from river – boil before use. Bring firewood. Additional map ref.: VR 65 C7.

4WD and bush camping areas

Numerous 4WD and walk-in campsites throughout the park, notably beside the Crooked River. Follow Parks Victoria bush camping regulations. Obtain large-scale maps and contact Parks Victoria for further details.

Further information & bookings: Parks Victoria information line **Tel.:** 131 963

13. HOWQUA HILLS HISTORIC AREA

The campsites here are beside the Howqua River, 35 km south-east of Mansfield. They are reached on the Howqua Track off Mansfield–Mt Buller Rd. The road can be rough and narrow in places, not recommended for caravans. It is a historic goldmining area and a popular area for camping and 4WD touring.

Blackbird Flat camping area

Signposted from Howqua Track. Bring drinking water and firewood. Additional map ref.: VR 63 G5.

Davons Flat camping area

Signposted from Howqua Track. Bring drinking water and firewood. Horseyards. Additional map ref.: VR 63 G5.

Frys Flat camping area

Reached through Sheepyard Flat off Howqua Track. Seasonally closed. Bring drinking water and firewood. Additional map ref.: VR 63 G5.

Noonans Flat camping area

Signposted from Howqua Track. Seasonally closed. Bring drinking water and firewood. Additional map ref.: VR 63 G5.

Pickerings Flat camping area

Signposted from Howqua Track. Bring drinking water and firewood. Additional map ref.: VR 63 G5.

Sheepyard Flat camping area

Signposted from Howqua Track. Bring drinking water and firewood. Additional map ref.: VR 63 G5.

Tobacco Flat camping area

Signposted 4WD only access through Sheepyard Flat on Howqua Track. Bring drinking water and firewood. Additional map ref.: VR 63 G5.

Tunnel Bend Flat camping area

Signposted from Howqua Track. Bring drinking water and firewood. Additional map ref.: VR 63 G5.

Further information & bookings: Parks Victoria information line **Tel.:** 131 963

14. LAKE DARTMOUTH

These campsites on the shores of Lake Dartmouth are managed by Goulburn–Murray Water; their management area is surrounded by Alpine National Park (see page 120). The lake is 20 km west of Mitta Mitta. It is a popular fishing venue.

Dart Arm camping area

At Dart Arm on eastern side of Lake Dartmouth. Boat access only. Additional map ref.: VR 51 D2.

Eight Mile Creek camping area

At Eight Mile Creek on southern side of Lake Dartmouth. Additional map ref.: VR 51 A4.

Eustace Creek camping area

Beside lake, near Eustace Gap Creek and 55 km north of Benambra. 4WD vehicle recommended for access via Eustace Gap Track off Benambra–Corryong Rd; boat access also possible. Additional map ref.: VR 51 C4.

Further information & bookings:
Goulburn–Murray Water **Tel.:** (02) 6072 4411 *or*
Parks Victoria information line **Tel.:** 131 963

15. LAKE EILDON NATIONAL PARK

This is a large national park 145 km north-east of Melbourne. Access is via Alexandra, Mansfield and Jamieson. There are many camping areas here and it is a popular venue for fishing, sailing and canoeing. Large populations of kangaroos roam the park and there are many bird species.

CAR-ACCESS CAMPING

Candlebark, Devils Cove and Lakeside camping areas

These camping areas are around the shore of Lake Eildon's Coller Bay, 12 km north-east of Alexandra. Access is via U. T. Creek Rd. There are 200 campsites in total and they are open year round. Bring firewood. Bookings essential for peak times. In addition to the facilities listed above, Candlebark and Devils Cove have disabled-access toilets, Devils Cove has undercover tables, and Devils Cove and Lakeside have boat jetties nearby. Additional map ref.: VR 62 F4.

Further information & bookings: Lake Eildon Camping and Cabins **Tel.:** (03) 5772 1293 **Camping fees:** From $14.00 per site/night. Cabin accommodation also available

Delatite Arm Reserve camping areas

Delatite Arm Reserve has 24 camping zones on the southern shore of the Delatite Arm of Lake Eildon. Access from Mansfield or Jamieson via Goughs Bay along Walshes Rd. Open fires prohibited Nov.–April inclusive. Gas/fuel stove preferred. Bookings required for Christmas and Easter. Additional map ref.: VR 62 G4/62 H4.

Further information & bookings: DSE/Parks Victoria, Mansfield **Tel.:** (03) 5733 0120 **Camping fees:** From $10.00 per site/night; ranger collects fees

Jerusalem Creek camping area

On Jerusalem Inlet at the southern end of Lake Eildon, 10 km from Eildon township. Access via Jerusalem Creek Rd. Eight camping areas. Bring drinking water and firewood. Bookings essential for peak times. Additional map ref.: VR 62 H5.

Further information & bookings: Lake Eildon Camping and Cabins **Tel.:** (03) 5772 1293 **Camping fees:** From $8.30 per site/night

BOAT-BASED CAMPING

Coopers Point camping area

Boat-based campsite on eastern foreshore of Lake Eildon, opposite Coller Bay. Bring drinking water. Contact ranger for details. Additional map ref.: VR 62 J6.

Mountaineer Inlet camping area

Boat-based or walk-in campsite at Stone Bay. Bring drinking water and firewood. Contact ranger for details. Additional map ref.: VR 62 F4.

Taylors Creek camping area

Boat-based or walk-in campsite at Big River Arm. Bring drinking water and firewood. Contact ranger for details. Additional map ref.: VR 62 J6.

Further information & bookings: Parks Victoria information line **Tel.:** 131 963

16. MANSFIELD STATE FOREST

This state forest is located to the east of Jamieson.

Running Creek camping reserve

Located 12 km north-east of Jamieson. Signposted access via Howqua River Rd. Water from river – boil first. Additional map ref.: VR 63 E5.

Grannys Flat camping reserve

Located 8 km east of Jamieson. Access via Jamieson–Licola Rd. Bring drinking water and firewood. Additional map ref.: VR 63 D6.

Wrens Flat camping reserve

Located 44 km east of Jamieson. Access via Mt Sunday Rd off Jamieson–Licola Rd. Bring drinking water and firewood. Additional map ref.: VR 63 E6.

Further information and bookings: DSE Customer Service Centre **Tel.:** 136 186

17. MITTA MITTA AREA

The Mitta Mitta River valley is one of the most beautiful in Victoria. It lies on the Omeo Hwy.

Lightning Creek camping area

Situated 20 km south of Mitta Mitta beside Lightning Creek on Omeo Hwy. Additional map ref.: VR 50 J4.

Snowy Creek camping area

This is 12 km south of Mitta Mitta near Snowy Creek. Access via Holloways Log Rd off Omeo Hwy. Caravan acccess in dry weather only. Additional map ref.: VR 50 H3.

The Walnuts camping area

Located 14 km south of Mitta Mitta near Snowy Creek off Omeo Hwy. Additional map ref.: VR 50 H3.

Further information & bookings: DSE, Mitta Mitta **Tel.:** (02) 6072 3410

18. MOUNT BUFFALO NATIONAL PARK

The park is 35 km south of Myrtleford and is reached via Mt Buffalo Rd off the Great Alpine Rd at Porepunkah. It boasts superb alpine scenery and is popular for snow sports in winter and bushwalking, fishing and adventure activities in summer.

Lake Catani campground

Fifty campsites beside Lake Catani. Access via Mt Buffalo Tourist Rd. Camping area open 1 Nov.–30 April. Fires only in communal fireplaces; bring firewood. Gas/fuel stove preferred. Bookings recommended for peak periods. Additional map ref.: VR 49 E5.

Further information & bookings: Parks Victoria information line **Tel.:** 131 963 **Camping fees:** From $12.50 per site/night for up to 6 people

19. MOUNT GRANYA STATE PARK

This is 60 km east of Wodonga near Lake Hume; access is via Murray River Rd off Murray Valley Hwy. There are good views from Mt Granya and you can walk to Granya Falls. Bushwalking, 4WD touring and mountain biking are popular here.

Cottontree picnic and camping area

Access via Webb Lane from Granya township. Bring drinking water. Additional map ref.: VR 36 F3.

Further information & bookings: Parks Victoria information line **Tel.:** 131 963

20. MOUNT LAWSON STATE PARK

This park is adjacent to the Murray River, 70 km east of Wodonga and near Lake Hume. It is reached via Murray Valley Hwy in the south or Murray River Rd in the north – dry weather access only. There are good views from summit of Mt Lawson and wildflowers in spring. Bushwalking, mountain biking and 4WD touring are popular activities.

Koetong Creek camping area

Near Koetong Creek. Access via Firebrace Track and Koetong Link off Murray Valley Hwy (4WD recommended). Additional map ref.: VR 36 H3.

Kurrajongs camping area

Near Lake Hume. Access via Murray River Rd. Additional map ref.: VR 36 J1.

Further information & bookings: Parks Victoria information line **Tel.:** 131 963

21. MOUNT PILOT MULTI-PURPOSE PARK

This is 20 km east of Wangaratta. Conventional vehicles should access with care – there are some creek crossings to negotiate. Activities include fishing and fossicking (Miners Right required).

Reedy Creek camping area

Dispersed bush camping west of the Woolshed Falls day-use area to Eldorado. Access via Woolshed Rd from Beechworth–Chiltern Rd or Eldorado Rd from Eldorado. No facilities. Additional map ref.: VR 35 A7/B7.

Further information & bookings: Parks Victoria information line **Tel.:** 131 963

22. MOUNT SAMARIA STATE PARK

Mt Samaria State Park is 14 km north of Mansfield. It is reached via Tolmie Rd in the south or Samaria Rd from Swanpool in the north. Seasonal road closures apply during winter and a total fire ban exists throughout the park during summer; bring a gas/fuel stove. Visit Mt Samaria's summit and Wild Dog Creek Falls. There are numerous walking trails.

Camphora camping area

Walk-in (500 m) camping area set amongst large gum trees. Signposted from Mt Samaria Rd. Bring drinking water. Additional map ref.: VR 48 C8.

Samaria Well camping area

In the north of the park. Access via Mt Samaria Rd. Bring drinking water. Additional map ref.: VR 48 B7.

The Kilns camping area

Access via Mt Samaria Rd. Bring drinking water. Additional map ref.: VR 48 C7.

Wild Dog Creek Falls camping area

Walk-in (800 m) camping area set amongst blue gums. Access via Mt Samaria Rd. Bring drinking water. Additional map ref.: VR 48 C7.

Further information & bookings: Parks Victoria information line **Tel.:** 131 963

23. MOUNT STIRLING AREA

Mt Stirling is about 40 km east of Mansfield and is reached via Mt Buller Rd. There is conventional vehicle access to some areas; others require a 4WD vehicle. The Circuit Rd (seasonal access) provides access to many points of interest in the area. Mt Stirling is a very popular area for skiing, bushwalking, horseriding and 4WD touring.

Carters Road camping area

Located 500 m along Carters Rd off Mt Buller Rd, 13 km east of Merrijig. Additional map ref.: VR 63 G3.

Craigs Hut camping area

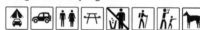

This is 20 km east of Telephone Box Junction. 4WD only access via Clear Hills Track off Circuit Rd. Walk-in access from Circuit Rd picnic area. The hut was built for *The Man from Snowy River* film. Bring water. Additional map ref.: VR 64 A3.

Razorback Hut camping area

This area is 5 km north of Telephone Box Junction. Access via track prior to No. 3 Rd intersection on Circuit Rd. 2WD access in dry weather only – 4WD recommended. Large hut. Horseyards. Additional map ref.: VR 63 J3.

Further information & bookings: DSE Customer Service Centre **Tel.:** 136 186

24. MOUNT TORBRECK SCENIC RESERVE

Mt Torbreck is a venue for cross-country skiing in winter. It is 14 km south of Eildon. In summer take the 2-km walk (2 hour return) to the summit of Mt Torbreck. Access roads and tracks are subject to seasonal closures during winter.

Barnewall Plains camping area

4WD access only. Area is 6 km along Barnewall Plains Rd from the Eildon–Jamieson Rd junction. Additional map ref.: VR 62 G7.

Further information & bookings: DSE Customer Service Centre **Tel.:** 136 186

25. MURRAY RIVER – GRANYA TO TOWONG

These camping areas are between Granya and Towong beside the Murray River and are signposted off Murray River Rd. Activities include camping, fishing, canoeing and swimming.

Burrowye Reserve camping area

This is 24 km west of Walwa. Additional map ref.: VR 37 A1.

Clarke Lagoon Reserve camping area

Located 6 km north of Tintaldra. Additional map ref.: VR 37 G2.

Jingellic Reserve camping area

Situated 6 km north-west of Walwa. Additional map ref.: VR 37 D1.

Neils Reserve camping area

Located 7 km east of Walwa near Eighty Acre Rd junction. Additional map ref.: VR 37 E1.

Further information & bookings: Parks Victoria information line **Tel.:** 131 963

26. NARIEL CREEK RECREATION RESERVE

This reserve, a large area beside Nariel Creek, is 9 km south of Corryong.

Nariel Creek Recreation Reserve camping area

Signposted via Corryong–Benambra Rd from Colac Colac on the Murray Valley Hwy. Additional map ref.: VR 37 F5.

Further information & bookings: Corryong Tourist Information Centre **Tel.:** (02) 6076 2277 **Email:** faith@towong.vic.gov.au **Camping fees:** From $15.00 per car/night

27. NUG NUG

Nug Nug is 15 km south of Myrtleford, beside the Buffalo River.

Nug Nug Reserve camping area

Signposted access via Buffalo River Rd from Myrtleford. Open Dec.–April. Additional map ref.: VR 49 D4.

Further information & bookings: Nug Nug management committee **Tel.:** (03) 9439 3962 **Camping fees:** Fees apply

28. OMEO AREA

Omeo is an old goldmining town set in the mountains on the Omeo Hwy.

Anglers Rest camping area

Located 29 km north of Omeo near Cobungra River on Omeo Hwy. Additional map ref.: VR 50 J9.

Big River Bridge camping area

This is 42 km north of Omeo near Big River Bridge on Omeo Hwy. Additional map ref.: VR 50 J8.

Gibbo River camping areas

Situated 30 km north-east of Omeo, south of Exhibition Creek Bridge on Corryong–Benambra Rd. No facilities. Fishing and canoeing area. Additional map ref.: VR 51 D5.

Grassy Flat camping area

Located 16 km north of Omeo near Mitta Mitta River on Omeo Valley Rd. Bush camping – no facilities. Popular canoeing spot. Additional map ref.: VR 66 C2.

Craigs Hut, in the Mount Stirling area, was built for the film The Man from Snowy River

The Joker camping area

This is 38 km north of Omeo near Mitta Mitta River on Omeo Hwy. Additional map ref.: VR 50 J9.

Victoria River Track camping area

Located 23 km west of Omeo on Victoria River Track off Great Alpine Rd. No facilities. Additional map ref.: VR 65 G3.

Further information & bookings:
Parks Victoria, Omeo **Tel.:** (03) 5159 1660 *or*
Parks Victoria information line **Tel.:** 131 963

29. PENDERGAST STATE FOREST

The forest is 65 km south of Corryong and is reached via Wheeler Creek Logging Rd off Benambra–Corryong Rd. There is conventional vehicle access to main areas; other roads may require 4WD. It is a popular 4WD touring area.

O'Hagens camping area

Along Wheeler Creek Logging Rd. Additional map ref.: VR 51 F2.

Wheelers Creek Hut camping area

Along Wheeler Creek Logging Rd. Near hut. Additional map ref.: VR 51 F2.

Bush camping

Numerous bush campsites along Dunstans Logging Rd, some near old logging huts. Conventional vehicle access to some sites, others require 4WD. No facilities. Dogs allowed on lead. Contact ranger for details.

Further information & bookings: DSE, Corryong **Tel.:** (02) 6076 3100

30. RUBICON STATE FOREST

This forest is 150 km north-east of Melbourne and reached via the Maroondah Hwy at Taggerty or the Goulburn Valley Hwy at Thornton. Activities include 4WD touring, bushwalking, fishing and horseriding.

Kendalls A and Kendalls B camping areas

Access via Rubicon Rd. Basic camping beside the Rubicon River. Bring drinking water. Additional map ref.: VR 62 F7.

Further information & bookings: DSE Customer Service Centre **Tel.:** 136 186

31. STACEYS BRIDGE RESERVE

The reserve is 46 km south of Corryong at Nariel. Access is via Corryong–Benambra Rd from Corryong.

Staceys Bridge camping area

Signposted access via Corryong–Benambra Rd. Water from river – boil before use. Additional map ref.: VR 37 F9.

Further information & bookings: Corryong Tourist Information Centre **Tel.:** (02) 6076 2277 **Email:** faithd@towong.vic.gov.au

32. STANLEY STATE FOREST

This forest is 32 km south of Wodonga and 4 km south of Yackandandah. Access is via Bells Flat Rd from Yackandandah. Visit the old township site of Yackandandah Junction and travel along the Yackandandah Forest Drive.

Stanley Forest camping areas

Numerous dispersed camping areas beside Yackandandah Creek, on the Yackandandah Forest Drive (Yack Gate Rd and Number One Rd). Additional map ref.: VR 35 E7.

Further information & bookings:
DSE, Beechworth **Tel.:** (02) 5720 8190 *or*
DSE Customer Service Centre **Tel.:** 136 186

33. STRATHBOGIE RANGES

This large area is 25 km north-west of Mansfield and bounded by Benalla, Euroa and Bonnie Doon. Main access is via Midland Hwy, Merton and Violet Town. The area was once used by the Kelly Gang as a hide out. Activities include cycling, bushwalking and 4WD touring.

James Camping Reserve

Small reserve beside Moonee Moonee Creek on Lima East Rd near Swanpool. Signposted from Gandinis Lane off Midland Hwy. Water from creek – boil before use. Additional map ref.: VR 47 H7.

Further information & bookings: DSE, Mansfield **Tel.:** (03) 5733 0120

34. TOOMBULLUP RANGES

These ranges are in state forest 18 km south-east of Tatong. Access is via Tatong–Tolmie Rd from Benalla. Fishing, 4WD touring, trail bike riding and horseriding are popular here.

Jones camping reserve

This is 18 km south of Tatong near Hollands Creek. Access via Jones Rd off Tatong–Tolmie Rd. Water from creek. Additional map ref.: VR 48 D7.

Stringybark Creek camping reserve

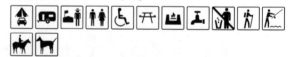

Situated 28 km south of Tatong near Stringybark Creek, via Tatong–Tolmie Rd. Water from creek. Additional map ref.: VR 48 E7.

Toombullup East School Site camping area

Located 30 km south of Tatong, via Tatong–Tolmie Rd. Additional map ref.: VR 48 E8.

Further information & bookings: DSE, Mansfield **Tel.:** (03) 5733 0120

35. UPPER GOULBURN HISTORIC AREA

This area lies along the Upper Goulburn River between Jamieson and Woods Point. There is conventional vehicle access on the Mansfield–Woods Point Rd. Numerous reserves beside the river offer camping. It was the site of Victoria's second gold rush and the area is still mined for gold. It is popular for fossicking, bushwalking, fishing, swimming and 4WD touring.

Blue Hole camping reserve

Located 21 km south of Jamieson and 32 km north of Woods Point. Access via Mansfield–Woods Point Rd. Water from river. Additional map ref.: VR 63 E8.

Comet Flat camping reserve

Located 4 km south-east of Woods Point beside river. Access via Johnson Hill Track from Woods Point (4WD vehicle recommended). Additional map ref.: VR 81 F3.

Doctors Creek camping reserve

This is 4 km south of Jamieson. Access via Mansfield–Woods Point Rd. Water from creek. Additional map ref.: VR 63 D7.

Gaffneys Creek camping reserve

Situated 37 km south of Jamieson and 17 km north of Woods Point. Access via Mansfield–Woods Point Rd. Water from river. Additional map ref.: VR 63 E9.

J. H. Scott camping reserve

The reserve is 2 km north-west of Woods Point. Access via Mansfield–Woods Point Rd. Additional map ref.: VR 81 E2.

Knockwood camping reserve

Located 29 km south of Jamieson and 25 km north of Woods Point. Access via Mansfield–Woods Point Rd. Water from river. Additional map ref.: VR 63 E8.

L. R. Skipworth camping reserve

The reserve is 7 km south of Jamieson. Access via Mansfield–Woods Point Rd. Water from tank. Additional map ref.: VR 63 D7.

Picnic Point camping reserve

Situated 23 km south of Jamieson and 30 km north of Woods Point. Access via Mansfield–Woods Point Rd. Water from river. Additional map ref.: VR 63 E8.

Snakes camping reserve

Located 26 km south of Jamieson and 28 km north of Woods Point. Access via Mansfield–Woods Point Rd. Water from river. Additional map ref.: VR 63 E8.

Tunnel Bend camping reserve

This is 19 km south of Jamieson. Access via Mansfield–Woods Point Rd. Water from creek. Additional map ref.: VR 63 D7.

Twelve Mile camping reserve

Located 20 km south of Jamieson. Access via Mansfield–Woods Point Rd. Water from creek. Additional map ref.: VR 63 E8.

Further information & bookings:
Parks Victoria information line **Tel.:** 131 963 *or* Woods Point General Store **Tel.:** (03) 5777 8220
Camping fees: *Doctors Creek and L. R. Skipworth:* From $5.00 per tent/night or $20.00 per week; fees collected by volunteer *J. H. Scott and Comet Flat:* $2.00 donation per site/night; donation payable at Woods Point General Store

36. VICTORIA FALLS HISTORIC AREA

The area is 22 km west of Omeo. It is signposted from the Great Alpine Rd.

Victoria Falls Historic Area camping area

Near Cobungra Station. Bring drinking water. Additional map ref.: VR 65 H3.

Further information & bookings: Parks Victoria information line **Tel.:** 131 963

37. WARBY RANGE STATE PARK

The Warby Range was used by Ned Kelly and his gang as a refuge during the late 1800s. It is 15 km west of Wangaratta. Access is via Wangandary Rd from Wangaratta. There are many walking tracks to explore.

Wenhams Camp camping area

Large open area on site of old farm on Booth Rd. Access via Gerrets Rd. Bring drinking water. Groups contact ranger first. Additional map ref.: VR 34 E7.

Bush camping
Bush camping is available in the park. Contact ranger for details.

Further information & bookings: Parks Victoria information line **Tel.:** 131 963

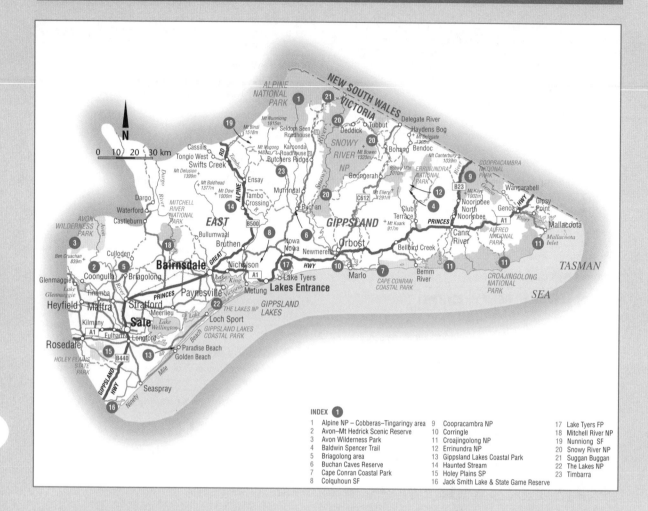

INDEX ①

1 Alpine NP – Cobberas–Tingaringy area	9 Coopracambra NP	17 Lake Tyers FP
2 Avon–Mt Hedrick Scenic Reserve	10 Corringle	18 Mitchell River NP
3 Avon Wilderness Park	11 Croajingolong NP	19 Nunniong SF
4 Baldwin Spencer Trail	12 Errinundra NP	20 Snowy River NP
5 Briagolong area	13 Gippsland Lakes Coastal Park	21 Suggan Buggan
6 Buchan Caves Reserve	14 Haunted Stream	22 The Lakes NP
7 Cape Conran Coastal Park	15 Holey Plains SP	23 Timbarra
8 Colquhoun SF	16 Jack Smith Lake & State Game Reserve	

SOUTH OF THE HIGH COUNTRY, THE MAGNIFICENT EAST GIPPSLAND REGION STRETCHES ACROSS TO THE COASTLINE DOWN TO SALE. ITS BEAUTIFUL INLAND WATERWAYS ATTRACT BOATERS, CANOEISTS AND FISHERFOLK, WHILE THE COASTAL BEACHES ARE POPULAR WITH SURFERS.

The circular Baldwin Spencer Trail is a drive of 262 kilometres following Baldwin Spencer's route during his 1889 expedition to the region. Along the trail are two campsites, beside the Ada and Delegate rivers. The trail also passes through beautiful forests along the Errinundra Plateau.

On the coast from Mallacoota to Sale, visitors have a choice of wonderful parks and foreshore reserves to camp in, including the spectacular Croajingolong National Park, Cape Conran Coastal Park, Lake Tyers Forest Park,

The Lakes National Park and Gippsland Lakes Coastal Park. All of these parks have beautiful coastal scenery. They offer water activities – swimming, fishing and canoeing – as well as bushwalking.

Next to the township of Buchan are the Buchan Caves, an underground world of surprising beauty and colour. The caves were first explored by Europeans in the early 1900s and are now a major tourist destination. There are guided tours throughout the year, and self-guide bushwalking trails in the above-ground parts of the reserve. The Buchan Caves Campground is a large shaded area with excellent facilities.

Mitchell River National Park is a remote mountain wilderness popular for canoeing and rafting. The Den of Nargun, within the park, is a limestone cave featuring impressive stalactites – access is via a moderate-to-hard walking track.

There are a couple of vehicle-based campsites in the park with basic facilities.

The spectacular Snowy River National Park is dominated by deep gorges carved by the Snowy River on its way to the Tasman Sea. The river is the park's main attraction and is popular with canoeists. Near the impressive McKillops Bridge in the north of the park are a number of camping areas with great views of the river and gorge only a short walk away.

BEST CAMPSITES

Wingan Inlet camping area
Croajingolong National Park

Ada River camping area
Baldwin Spencer Trail

Corringle Slips camping area
Corringle

Snowy River camping area
Snowy River National Park

The Honeysuckles camping area
Gippsland Lakes Coastal Park

BEST TIME TO VISIT

All year round, however the inland areas can get a bit cool during the winter months.

1. ALPINE NATIONAL PARK – COBBERAS–TINGARINGY AREA see page 120

2. AVON–MOUNT HEDRICK SCENIC RESERVE

This reserve is 20 km north-west of Maffra on the Avon River. A number of access roads run to it off the Newry–Glenmaggie Rd. There is conventional vehicle access to some areas; others require a 4WD vehicle. You can walk to the summit of Mt Hedrick or go fishing, swimming, walking and 4WD touring.

Dermody Camp camping area

Beside Avon River. Access via Dermody Rd off Warrigal–Toms Creek Rd. Conventional vehicle access in dry weather only. Additional map ref.: VR 82 F7.

Huggetts Crossing camping area

Beside Avon River. 4WD vehicle only access via Huggett–Mt Angus Track from Green Hill. Bush camping – no facilities. Additional map ref.: VR 82 F6.

Wombat Crossing camping area

Beside Avon River. 4WD access (river crossing) from south via O'Keefe Track off Back Wombat Rd or from the east 2WD access via Valencia Creek. Additional map ref.: VR 82 G6.

Further information & bookings: DSE, Heyfield
Tel.: (03) 5139 7777

3. AVON WILDERNESS PARK

This park is 40 km north of Heyfield near Licola, abutting Alpine National Park. Vehicle access is restricted to the edge of park only. It is reached via Mt Margaret Track from Licola Rd and Mt Wellington Track from Moroka Rd via Arbuckle Junction. Walkers must register with ranger.

Bush camping

Dispersed bush camping for self-sufficient walkers. Gas/fuel stove preferred. Contact ranger for details. Additional map ref.: VR 82 F2 (Mt Wellington).

Further information & bookings: Parks Victoria information line **Tel.:** 131 963

4. BALDWIN SPENCER TRAIL

This is a 262-km driving trail following the route of Baldwin Spencer's 1889 expedition to East Gippsland. The circular route from Orbost takes in the Cann Valley Hwy and Errinundra Plateau. Activities include vehicle touring, walking trails and camping.

Ada River camping area

Beside the Ada River. Access via Errinundra Valley Rd off Club Terrace–Combienbar Rd. Water from river – boil before use. Additional map ref.: VR 68 G8.

Delegate River camping area

Beside Delegate River 8.4 km from Bendoc. Access via Gap Rd from Bendoc. Water from river – boil before use. Additional map ref.: VR 68 F5.

Further information & bookings: DSE, Bendoc
Tel.: (02) 6458 1456

5. BRIAGOLONG AREA

Briagolong is 15 km north of Stratford. There are many secluded campsites beside the Freestone and Valencia creeks, which are popular swimming spots.

Blue Pools camping area

The area is 10 km north of Briagolong. Signposted from Freestone Creek Rd. Additional map ref.: VR 83 C6.

Johnstones Flat camping area

Located 20 km north of Briagolong along Freestone Creek Rd. Additional map ref.: VR 83 D5.

Lee Creek camping area

Located 28 km north of Briagolong along Freestone Creek Rd. Additional map ref.: VR 83 D5.

McKinnon Point camping area

Located 14 km north of Briagolong along Freestone Creek Rd. Additional map ref.: VR 83 D5.

Shadys Place camping area

Located 19 km north of Briagolong along Freestone Creek Rd. Additional map ref.: VR 83 D5.

The Quarries camping area

Located 3 km north of Briagolong. Signposted along Freestone Creek Rd. Additional map ref.: VR 83 C7.

Valencia Creek camping area

This is 8 km north of Valencia Creek on the banks of Valencia Creek. Access via Valencia Creek–Morgan Rd. Additional map ref.: VR 83 B6.

Winki Creek camping area

Located 20 km north of Briagolong along Freestone Creek Rd. Additional map ref.: VR 83 D5.

Further information & bookings: DSE, Briagolong
Tel.: (03) 5145 5215 **Camping fees:** *The Quarries*: From

$5.00 per site/night; fees payable at local stores or to caretaker

6. BUCHAN CAVES RESERVE

The caves, which contain some of the most spectacular limestone formations found in Australia, are adjacent to Buchan township. Access is via Buchan Rd. Activities include cave tours, walking trails and camping. There is abundant wildlife in the reserve.

Buchan Caves Campground

At Buchan Caves, signposted from Caves Rd. Other accommodation also available. Bookings essential at peak times. Additional map ref.: VR 67 D9.

Further information & bookings:
Parks Victoria information line **Tel.:** 131 963 *or* Parks Victoria, Buchan **Tel.:** (03) 5155 9264
Camping fees: *Off-peak*: Unpowered from $11.30 per site/night, powered from $15.90 per site/night *Peak*: Unpowered from $14.90 per site/night, powered from $19.50 per site/night. (These fees apply for up to 3 people)

7. CAPE CONRAN COASTAL PARK

This park is 19 km east of Marlo and has outstanding coastal scenery. Access is via Princes Hwy or from Marlo.

Banksia Bluff camping area

Access from Marlo Rd. Bring drinking water and firewood. Bookings essential at peak times – there is a ballot system Dec.–Jan. and Easter. Additional map ref.: VR 86 D6.

Further information & bookings: Cape Conran Coastal Park **Tel.:** (03) 5154 8438 **Camping fees:** *Off-peak*: From $13.50 per tent site/night *Peak*: From $18.40 per tent site/night

8. COLQUHOUN STATE FOREST

The forest is worth visiting for its wildflowers and bird-watching. It is 12 km north-west of Lakes Entrance.

Bush camping

Dispersed bush camping away from day-use areas. Access via Log Crossing Rd off Princes Hwy. Additional map ref.: VR 84 G7.

Further information & bookings: DSE, Nowa Nowa **Tel.:** (03) 5155 7203

9. COOPRACAMBRA NATIONAL PARK

The park is one of the most remote and least disturbed in Victoria. It lies 30 km north of Cann River and the main access is via Monaro Hwy. There is conventional vehicle access to Beehive Falls but all other roads are only suitable for 4WD vehicles or walkers. Activities include 4WD touring and bushwalking.

Bush camping

Dispersed bush camping – no facilities. For self-sufficient campers; 4WD or walk-in access only. Additional map ref.: VR 69 E3 (Beehive Falls).

Further information & bookings: Parks Victoria information line **Tel.:** 131 963

10. CORRINGLE

This campsite is in the Corringle Foreshore Reserve, which is in a natural bush setting close to the beach, 18 km south of Newmerella near the mouth of the Snowy River estuary. Activities include swimming, boating, canoeing, fishing and walking.

Corringle Slips camping area

Access via Corringle Rd from Newmerella. Bring drinking water. Bookings essential at peak times; a ballot system operates Dec.–Jan. and Easter. Additional map ref.: VR 86 A6.

Further information & bookings: Parks Victoria, Orbost **Tel.:** (03) 5161 1222 **Camping fees:** *Off-peak:* From $9.20 per site/night *Peak:* From $11.50 per site/night. Fees apply for up to 5 people and are payable at self-registration station

11. CROAJINGOLONG NATIONAL PARK
see page 137

12. ERRINUNDRA NATIONAL PARK

The park protects large areas of cool temperate rainforest and old-growth eucalypt forest. It lies 70 km north-east of Orbost near Goongerah. Access is via Bonang Hwy from Orbost or Combienbar Rd from Club Terrace. Conventional vehicles can access the park but in dry weather only. Use of gas/fuel stove preferred. Activities include vehicle touring (the Baldwin Spencer Trail) and bushwalking.

Frosty Hollow camping area

Signposted from Coast Range Rd. Access via Back Creek Rd and Hensleigh Rd from Bendoc. Additional map ref.: VR 68 H6.

Further information & bookings: Parks Victoria information line **Tel.:** 131 963

13. GIPPSLAND LAKES COASTAL PARK

The park lies along a coastal strip between Lakes Entrance and Seaspray. Main road access is via the Longford–Lochsport Rd from Longford. Some areas of the park are only accessible by boat. Many water-based activities are popular on the lakes and there are also walking trails and horseriding.

Bunga Arm boat-based camping

Boat-based camping at seven designated areas on Bunga Arm of Lake Victoria. Each site has 10–12 sites. Boat access only. Bring drinking water and firewood. Additional map ref.: VR 84 E9.

Eel Farm camping area

Beside McLennans Strait. Access via Eel Farm Track off Lakeside Track. Bush camping – no facilities. Bring drinking water and firewood. Additional map ref.: VR 99 J3.

Paradise Beach camping area

Signposted from Shoreline Drive east of Golden Beach. Bring firewood. Additional map ref.: VR 99 H5.

Red Bluff camping area

Lakeside location at Red Bluff on Lake Victoria. Access via Beacon Swamp Track. Bring drinking water and firewood. Additional map ref.: VR 99 K2.

Seacombe camping area

At Seacombe on McLennans Strait. Access via Seacombe Rd off Longford–Lochsport Rd. Bring drinking water and firewood. Additional map ref.: VR 99 H3.

Spoon Bay camping area

Lakeside location at Spoon Bay on Lake Victoria. Access via Lakeside Track. Bush camping. Bring drinking water and firewood. Additional map ref.: VR 99 J3.

Thalia Point camping areas

Dispersed camping beside Lake Victoria between Spoon Bay Track and Beacon Swamp Track. Access via Lakeside Track. Bush camping – no facilities. Bring drinking water and firewood. Camping here only during hunting season, contact Parks Victoria for further details. Additional map ref.: VR 99 J3.

The Honeysuckles to Golden Beach camping areas

Camping in a number of designated sites in the sand dunes. Access via The Boulevarde and Shoreline Drive from Seaspray or Golden Beach. Bring drinking water and firewood. Additional map ref.: VR 99 H5 (Golden Beach).

Further information & bookings: Parks Victoria information line **Tel.:** 131 963 **Camping fees:** *Bunga Arm:* $4.30 per site/night; permit required from Parks Victoria, Bairnsdale, tel. (03) 5152 0600

14. HAUNTED STREAM

Haunted Stream is an old mining area 25 km south of Swifts Creek. Access is via Brookville Rd and Angora Range Rd from Swifts Creek or Haunted Stream Track off Omeo Hwy near Tambo Crossing. Conventional vehicle access (high clearance) to Stirling town site from south but all other tracks are 4WD vehicle access only.

Haunted Stream camping areas

Dispersed bush camping located along Haunted Stream Track, at Stirling and Dogtown town sites. 4WD vehicle access only (seasonal closure) via Haunted Stream Track off Angora Range Rd or Omeo Hwy. Additional map ref.: VR 66 D9.

Further information & bookings: DSE Customer Service Centre **Tel.:** 136 186

15. HOLEY PLAINS STATE PARK

This park is 30 km south-west of Sale and it is reached via Limestone Quarry Rd off Willung–Rosedale Rd. Activities include bushwalking, picnicking and nature study.

Harriers Swamp camping area

On Long Ridge Track off West Boundary Track, off Limestone Quarry Rd. Additional map ref.: VR 98 F5.

Holey Hill camping area

On Holey Hill, the highest point in the park. Access via Holey Hill Track off Limestone Quarry Rd. Bring drinking water. Additional map ref.: VR 98 G5.

Further information & bookings: Parks Victoria information line **Tel.:** 131 963

16. JACK SMITH LAKE AND STATE GAME RESERVE

The reserve is 25 km north-east of Yarram near Woodside. Access is via Middle Rd off South Gippsland Hwy or Stringy Bark Lane from Woodside. The main feature of the park is Jack Smith Lake.

Bush camping

Dispersed bush camping – no facilities. Bring drinking water. Additional map ref.: VR 99 B9.

Further information & bookings: Parks Victoria information line **Tel.:** 131 963

17. LAKE TYERS FOREST PARK

This park surrounds Lake Tyers and is 20 km north-east of Lakes Entrance. Access roads lead off Princes Hwy. It is possible to enter the park in dry weather only. The use of portable toilets is preferred. Activities include picnicking, camping, fishing, canoeing and boating.

Camerons Arm camping area

On Camerons Arm No. 1 Track, on Nowa Nowa Arm. Access via Lake Tyers House Rd from Princes Hwy. Bring drinking water. Gas/fuel stove preferred. Additional map ref.: VR 85 D6.

The Glasshouse camping area

Near Glasshouse Beach. Access via Lake Tyers House Rd from Princes Hwy. No facilities. Bring drinking water. Gas/fuel stove preferred. Additional map ref.: VR 85 C7.

Bush camping

Bush camping is permitted on the east side of Nowa Nowa Arm away from established picnic areas. Contact ranger for details.

Further information & bookings: Parks Victoria information line **Tel.:** 131 963

18. MITCHELL RIVER NATIONAL PARK

This national park is 45 km north-west of Bairnsdale. Access is via Dargo Rd. The park has excellent canoeing and there are also walking trails, rock climbing and 4WD touring.

Angusvale camping area

Beside Mitchell River. Reached via Mitchell Dam Rd off Dargo Rd. Camping area is 16 km in from Dargo Rd. Additional map ref.: VR 83 G3.

Billy Goat Bend camping area

On Billy Goat Bend Rd. Mitchell River Walking Track passes through. Additional map ref.: VR 83 H4.

Rock Creek Track camping area

Beside Mitchell River. Access via Angusvale Track near Rock Creek Track junction, off Mitchell Rd. 4WD, walk-in or river access. Additional map ref.: VR 83 G3.

Woolshed Creek camping area

Access via Mitchell River Walking Track. Walk-in or river access only. Additional map ref.: VR 83 G5.

Further information & bookings: Parks Victoria information line **Tel.:** 131 963

19. NUNNIONG STATE FOREST

The forest, which is a popular 4WD touring destination, is 35 km north-east of Swifts Creek. Access is via Nunniong Rd off Bindi Rd from the Great Alpine Rd. Pay a visit to 'The Washington' steam winch to get a feel for the old timber-getting days.

Bentlys Plain Reserve camping area

Access via Bentlys Plain Rd off Nunniong Rd. Additional map ref.: VR 66 G5.

Moscow Villa Hut camping area

Access via Bentlys Plain Rd off Nunniong Rd. Camping in vicinity of hut. Additional map ref.: VR 66 G5.

Nunniong Plains camping areas

At the headwaters of the Tambo River. Access via Nunniong Rd. Bush camping – no facilities. Water from creek. Additional map ref.: VR 66 G4.

Further information & bookings: DSE, Swifts Creek **Tel.:** (03) 5159 5100

20. SNOWY RIVER NATIONAL PARK

The Snowy River National Park stretches from north of Orbost near Buchan to the Deddick River/Snowy River junction. Main access into the park is via the Bonang–Gelantipy Rd (McKillops Bridge) off the Buchan Rd or from Bonang. Main areas are accessible by conventional vehicle; other roads and tracks are only suitable for 4WD vehicles. This spectacular park takes in the unspoilt scenery of the mighty Snowy River, inviting sandy river beaches and towering craggy peaks. Activities include bushwalking, canoeing, rafting, 4WD touring, horseriding and fishing.

NORTHERN SECTION (MCKILLOPS BRIDGE CAMPING AREAS)

Little River Junction camping area

At junction of Little and Snowy rivers. Access off Bonang–Gelantipy Rd. 4WD vehicle (seasonal), canoe or walk-in access. Additional map ref.: VR 67 G3.

CROAJINGOLONG NATIONAL PARK

Mountain to sea
A one-hour uphill hike is a small price to pay for the views afforded at the top of Genoa Peak. Atop the final stretch of steel ladders is a vista of tree-clad hills stretching all the way to the glimmering Southern Ocean.

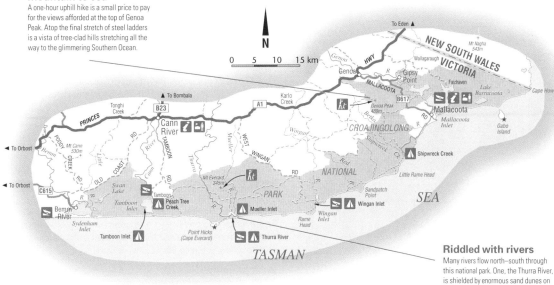

Riddled with rivers
Many rivers flow north–south through this national park. One, the Thurra River, is shielded by enormous sand dunes on one side and a scramble of wilderness on the other. Take the Dunes Walk from the camping area to view this scenic part of the park.

This large national park stretches for over 100 km along Victoria's far eastern coastline. Access is via a sealed road to Mallacoota and by unsealed roads off the Princes Hwy. There is conventional vehicle access, but you should check road conditions after rain. Explore the unspoiled beaches and tranquil waterways and see the abundant birdlife. Activities include swimming, boating, canoeing, fishing and walking. Bookings are recommended at all times and are essential at peak times; a ballot system applies to all sites for Christmas/New Year and Easter, when the minimum stay is one week. Contact Parks Victoria, Cann River, for further information.

Mueller Inlet camping area

On Bald Hills Track on the western shore of Mueller Inlet. Signposted off Point Hicks Rd, which is off Tamboon Rd from Cann River. Eight sites (three are walk-in). Bring drinking water. Gas/fuel stove only. Additional map ref.: VR 69 G10.

Peach Tree Creek camping area

Beside Cann River near Tamboon Inlet. Access via Fishermans Track off Point Hicks Rd. Twelve sites. Caravan access with care. Bring drinking water. Additional map ref.: VR 69 D9.

Shipwreck Creek camping area

Near the mouth of Shipwreck Creek. Access via Betka Track from Mallacoota then Old Coast Track. Five sites. Additional map ref.: VR 70 D8.

Tamboon Inlet boat-based camping areas

Nine areas around shores of Tamboon Inlet. Bush camping – no facilities. Use of portable toilets preferred. Bring drinking water and firewood. Be self-sufficient. Additional map ref.: VR 69 D9.

Thurra River camping area

Forty-six sites near the mouth of Thurra River. Access via Cape Everard Rd off Tamboon Rd from Cann River. Access for cars and small vans only. Water from river – boil before drinking. Bring firewood. Additional map ref.: VR 69 F10.

Wingan Inlet camping area

Twenty-four sites on the western side of Wingan Inlet. Access via West Wingan Rd off Princes Hwy. Firewood supplied. Additional map ref.: VR 69 J9.

Further information & bookings:
Parks Victoria information line **Tel.:** 131 963 or Parks Victoria, Cann River, **Tel.:** (03) 5158 6351
Camping fees: Fees apply and change annually; contact Parks Victoria, Cann River, for current fee schedule

McKillops Bridge, in Snowy River National Park

Bull Flat, Snowy River and White Box camping areas

In the north of the park near McKillops Bridge. Access via Bonang–Gelantipy Rd. Caravan access with care via Bonang – check road conditions first. Additional map ref.: VR 67 H3.

Waratah Flat camping area

Near Rodger River at Waratah Flat. Access via Waratah Flat Rd off Yalmy Rd. Bring drinking water. Additional map ref.: VR 68 B6.

SOUTHERN SECTION

Balley Hooley camping area

Near Snowy River east of Buchan. Signposted off Buchan–Orbost Rd. Bring drinking water and firewood. Additional map ref.: VR 67 F9.

Hicks camping area

Beside Yalmy River. Access via Varneys Track off Yalmy Rd. 4WD vehicle access in dry weather only or walk-in access. Water from river – boil before use or bring your own drinking water. Additional map ref.: VR 67 G8.

Jacksons Crossing camping area

Beside Snowy River. Access via Varneys Track off Yalmy Rd. 4WD access in dry weather only, plus canoe and walk-in access. Bush camping – no facilities. Bring drinking water. Additional map ref.: VR 67 G8.

Raymond Falls camping area

Has 4 sites only, beside Raymond Creek. Access via Moresford Track off Yalmy Rd. Bring drinking water and firewood. Additional map ref.: VR 67 F9.

Further information & bookings: Parks Victoria information line **Tel.:** 131 963 **Camping fees:** *McKillops Bridge camping areas:* $10.20 per site/night; fees payable at self-registration station

21. SUGGAN BUGGAN

This area is 75 km north of Buchan and is reached from Snowy River Rd. It is surrounded by Alpine National Park. There are numerous bush campsites from the old Suggan Buggan township site north to the New South Wales border at Willis. Many tracks lead to the Snowy River.

Bush camping

Dispersed bush camping north of Suggan Buggan. Some areas have facilities. Be fully self-sufficient. Additional map ref.: VR 52 G9.

Further information & bookings: Parks Victoria, Buchan **Tel.:** (03) 5155 9264

22. THE LAKES NATIONAL PARK

The park is 60 km east of Sale, near Loch Sport, and is reached via Longford–Loch Sport Rd from Longford. There is also boat access from Paynesville. Activities include boating, walking, fishing and birdwatching.

Emu Bight camping area

On the shore of Lake Victoria. Access via Lake Victoria Track. Bookings recommended. Additional map ref.: VR 84 C9.

Rotamah Island
Booked group camping only. Contact Parks Victoria, Loch Sport, for details.

Further information & bookings:
Parks Victoria information line **Tel.:** 131 963 *or* Parks Victoria, Loch Sport **Tel.:** (03) 5146 0278
Camping fees: *Off-peak:* From $8.80 per site/night *Peak:* From $12.00 per site/night

23. TIMBARRA

This is 23 km north-west of Buchan on the Timbarra River. It is reached via Timbarra Rd off Nunnett Rd. There is excellent trout fishing here.

Bush camping

Dispersed bush camping downstream from Timbarra community. No facilities. Be fully self-sufficient. Additional map ref.: VR 67 C8.

Further information & bookings: Parks Victoria, Buchan **Tel.:** (03) 5155 9264

MORNINGTON PENINSULA

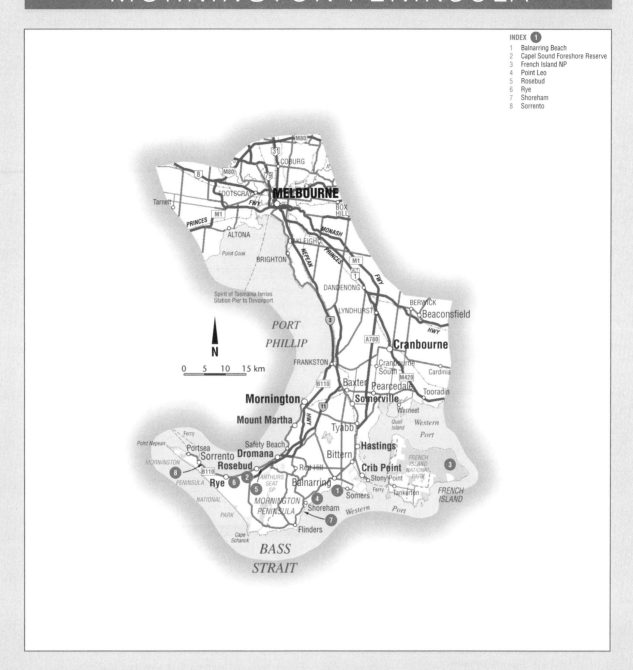

Facing three bodies of water – Port Phillip, Western Port and Bass Strait – Mornington Peninsula has long been a popular summer holiday destination. The sheltered bayside beaches in the north attract many families, and the ocean beaches in the south and east are popular with surfers. The peninsula's inland countryside is also not without charms – it is a picturesque mix of cool-climate vineyards, eucalypt forests and scenic farmlands.

Mornington Peninsula National Park is one of the region's prime attractions – it stretches from Cape Schanck up to Port Phillip Heads. While camping is not permitted in the park, there are plenty of camping spots close by.

On the eastern side of the peninsula camping is possible at the Balnarring Beach camping reserves, Point Leo Foreshore Reserve and Shoreham Foreshore Reserve. All reserves are accessible to caravans and offer a range of facilities plus swimming, fishing, boating, sailing and canoeing. Balnarring Beach A Reserve has gum trees that are home to koalas.

Facing Port Phillip, on the western side of the peninsula, are the Rosebud, Capel Sound, Rye and Sorrento foreshore reserves. These offer camping on the waterfront, and easy access to the bay for sailing, boating, swimming and fishing.

For those after a camping holiday with a difference, catch the ferry from Stony Point to French Island in Western Port. Nearly half of the island is national park. Parks Victoria provides a camping area with basic facilities five kilometres north of the ferry jetty at Tankerton. As no vehicles are allowed on the island, be prepared to walk everywhere or take a pushbike with you. The island's attractions include the large koala colony, prolific wildflower displays in spring, wonderful coastal views and, of course, the great opportunity to go walking and bike riding.

BEST CAMPSITES

Balnarring Beach A Reserve
Balnarring Beach

Fairhaven camping area
French Island National Park

Shoreham Foreshore Reserve caravan and camping area
Shoreham

Rosebud Foreshore Reserve caravan and camping area
Rosebud

Capel Sound Foreshore Reserve camping area
Capel Sound Foreshore Reserve

BEST TIME TO VISIT

All year round, but the area is a popular destination in summer.

1. BALNARRING BEACH

Balnarring, 80 km from Melbourne on the eastern side of Mornington Peninsula, offers the closest ocean beaches to the city. The waters of Western Port provide for all types of aquatic recreation. There are walking and nature trails.

Balnarring Beach camping reserves – A Reserve, B Reserve and C Reserve

Access to A Reserve from Mason Smith Rd, B Reserve from Balnarring Beach Rd, and C Reserve from Feathers Rd. Close to sheltered surf beach. Gas/fuel stove only. Open Sept.–June long weekend. Advance bookings recommended during peak periods. Additional map ref.: VR 95 C8.

Further information & bookings: Balnarring Beach Camping Reserve **Tel.:** (03) 5983 5582 or 0419 596 549
Camping fees: Unpowered sites from $17.00 per family (2 adults and 3 children under 17) per night

2. CAPEL SOUND FORESHORE RESERVE

This reserve is situated on the Port Phillip side of the Mornington Peninsula, near Rosebud. Many sites are scattered from West Rosebud to Tootgarook; access is via Point Nepean Rd, Tootgarook.

Capel Sound Foreshore Reserve camping area

Foreshore location. Open Dec.–Easter. Gas/fuel stove only. Bookings recommended during Christmas period. Additional map ref.: VR 94 F7.

Further information & bookings: Capel Sound Foreshore **Tel.:** (03) 5986 4382 **Email:** capel@cdi.com.au **Camping fees:** *Peak*: Dec.–Jan. from $22.00 per 2 people/site *Off-peak*: From $11.00 per 2 people/site

3. FRENCH ISLAND NATIONAL PARK

This island in Western Port is reached by a passenger ferry from Stony Point or Phillip Island. The island is popular for cycling, and there are walking trails. In season you will see prolific wildflowers. French Island has great coastal scenery and extensive wetlands.

Airs Farm camping ground

Private campground on 3 ha of bushland 10 km east of Tankerton. Access via private bus, cycling or walking. Plentiful wildlife. Firewood supplied. Additional map ref.: VR 95 G7.

Further information & bookings: Airs Farm **Tel.:** (03) 5980 1241 **Camping fees:** From $3.00 per adult/night

Fairhaven camping area

Located 5 km north of Tankerton. Access via cycling or walking. Camping permit required. No fees apply. Basic camping. Bring drinking water. Gas/fuel stove only. Additional map ref.: VR 95 F7.

Further information & bookings:
Parks Victoria information line **Tel.:** 131 963 *or*
Parks Victoria, Rosebud **Tel.:** (03) 5986 8987
French Island Ferry **Tel.:** (03) 9585 5730

The rugged coastline of Diamond Bay, Mornington Peninsula National Park

4. POINT LEO

The reserve is on the Mornington Peninsula at Point Leo, adjacent to Western Port. There are good surfing beaches nearby.

Point Leo Foreshore Reserve caravan and camping area

Generally open all year. Bookings recommended during peak periods. Additional map ref.: VR 95 C8.

Further information & bookings: Point Leo Foreshore Reserve **Tel.:** (03) 5989 8333 **Camping fees:** Unpowered sites from $20.00 per family/night

5. ROSEBUD

Rosebud is on the Mornington Peninsula 5 km south-west of Dromana. The reserve is on the foreshore of Port Phillip, a popular watersports area. There are boat-hire facilities nearby.

Rosebud Foreshore Reserve caravan and camping area

Gas/fuel stove only. Bookings recommended during peak periods. Additional map ref.: VR 94 G7.

Further information & bookings: Parks Victoria/Rosebud Foreshore Reserve **Tel.:** (03) 5986 8286 **Camping fees:** Unpowered sites from $16.50 per site/night

6. RYE

Rye is on the Mornington Peninsula and the foreshore reserve is beside a beach of Port Phillip. Rye is reached via the Nepean Hwy.

Rye Foreshore Reserve caravan and camping area

Gas/fuel stove only. Open Nov.–April. Bookings essential during peak periods. Additional map ref.: VR 94 F7.

Further information & bookings: Rye Foreshore Reserve **Tel.:** (03) 5985 2405 or 0407 304 048 **Camping fees:** From $20.00 plus GST per site/night

7. SHOREHAM

Shoreham is on the south-east side of the Mornington Peninsula. The reserve is reached via Prout–Webb Rd. There is foreshore frontage to the Western Port entrance.

Shoreham Foreshore Reserve caravan and camping area

Gas/fuel stove only. Open Aug.–May. Bookings recommended during peak periods. Additional map ref.: VR 95 C8.

Further information & bookings: Shoreham Foreshore Reserve **Tel.:** (03) 5989 8325 **Camping fees:** Tent sites from $19.80 per 2 people/night

8. SORRENTO

The reserve is 1 km east of Sorrento on the Mornington Peninsula. Access is via the Nepean Hwy. The reserve has foreshore frontage to Port Phillip.

Sorrento Foreshore Reserve caravan and camping area

Gas/fuel stove only. Open Nov.–April. Bookings essential during peak period (15 Dec.–end Jan.). Additional map ref.: VR 94 D7.

Further information & bookings: Sorrento Foreshore Reserve **Tel.:** (03) 5984 2797 **Camping fees:** Tent sites from $20.00 plus GST per site/night

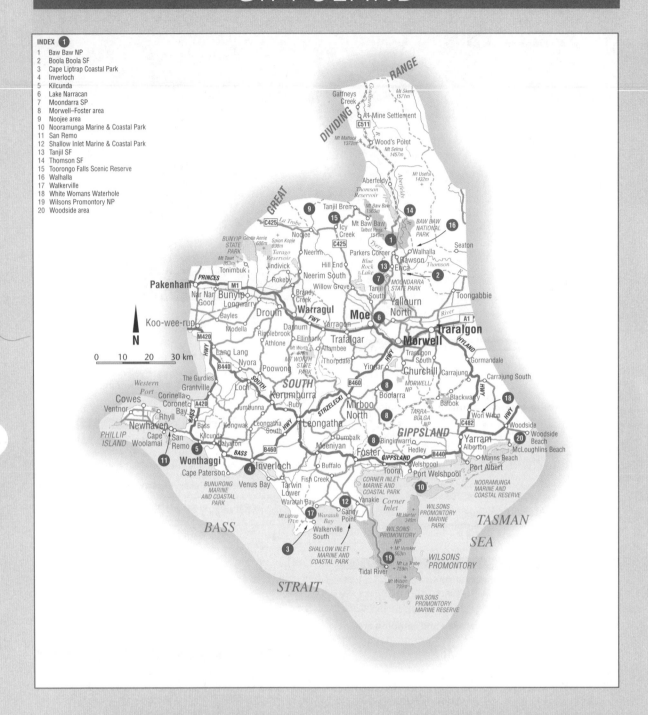

THIS REGION HAS MANY BEAUTIFUL HIGHLIGHTS, INCLUDING THE COASTS OF BASS STRAIT AND THE TASMAN SEA, THE HIGH PEAKS OF MOUNT BAW BAW, THE HISTORIC TOWNSHIP OF WALHALLA, PHILLIP ISLAND'S PENGUIN PARADE AND THE FORESTS OF TARRA–BULGA NATIONAL PARK.

Wilsons Promontory National Park, on the southernmost tip of mainland Australia, is another highlight. The 'Prom' would have to be one of Victoria's most-loved national parks, consisting of superb mountains, granite headlands, forests and beaches. There are over 150 kilometres of walking trails here, while the large camping area at Tidal River has excellent facilities and is very popular, especially during holiday periods. If you are after a more remote break, there are also 11 walk-in campsites throughout the park.

Walhalla is a scenic town with a number of restored buildings and miners cottages along a creek and clinging to the hillsides above it. Campers can set up at the delightful North Gardens camping ground and spend days walking through Walhalla and visiting its historic sites, or alternatively, touring through the surrounding mountains and valleys.

Flowing through tall mountain forests in the picturesque Toorongo Falls Scenic Reserve are the Toorongo and Little Toorongo rivers. Visitors can follow a walking track to the base of the spectacular Toorongo Falls. Camping is permitted on a large grassy flat beside the river, near the reserve's entry.

Moondarra State Park protects a variety of native flora and fauna. Of particular appeal are the wildflower displays that include a number of native orchids, and the sightings of koalas. Camping at Seninis Recreation Area allows for scenic drives, cycling, bushwalking and swimming.

BEST CAMPSITES

Toorongo Falls picnic and camping area
Toorongo Falls Scenic Reserve

Tidal River camping area
Wilsons Promontory National Park

Bear Gully camping area
Cape Liptrap Coastal Park

North Gardens camping ground
Walhalla

Seninis Recreation Area
Moondarra State Park

BEST TIME TO VISIT

All year round.

1. BAW BAW NATIONAL PARK

Baw Baw is a popular bushwalking and cross-country skiing area 40 km north of Moe, near Rawson. It is reached via Thomson Valley Rd from Rawson. The Australian Alps Walking Track passes through the park.

Aberfeldy Bridge camping area

Beside Aberfeldy River, 17 km north-west of Walhalla. Signposted from Walhalla–Aberfeldy Rd. Water from river – boil before use or bring own drinking water. Many 4WD touring tracks nearby. Additional map ref.: VR 81 H7.

Baw Baw Plateau bush camping

On Australian Alps Walking Track. Walk-in access only. Bring drinking water. Gas/fuel stove preferred. Limit of two nights' stay. Contact ranger for further details. Additional map ref.: VR 81 G8.

Eastern Tyers camping area

On Australian Alps Walking Track. Walk-in access only. Bring drinking water. Gas/fuel stove preferred. Additional map ref.: VR 81 H8.

Further information & bookings: Parks Victoria information line **Tel.:** 131 963

2. BOOLA BOOLA STATE FOREST

The area was once heavily mined. It is south-east of Rawson and reached via Tyers–Thomson Valley Rd.

Bruntons Bridge camping area

Beside Thomson River. 4WD access (river crossing) via Brunton Bridge Rd off Cowwarr Rd; conventional vehicle access from Walhalla via Cowwarr–Walhalla Rd. Additional map ref.: VR 97 J2.

Coopers Creek camping area

Conventional vehicle access via Coopers Creek Rd off Walhalla Rd. Additional map ref.: VR 81 H9.

Thomson Bridge camping area

Access via Walhalla Rd. Additional map ref.: VR 81 H9.
Further information & bookings: Parks Victoria, Erica **Tel.:** (03) 5165 2200

3. CAPE LIPTRAP COASTAL PARK

Cape Liptrap Coastal Park stretches from Point Smythe, north-west of Venus Bay, to Waratah Bay, about 30 km west of Wilsons Promontory. Access is from Cape Liptrap Rd off either the Tarwin Lower or Waratah rds. The park has good swimming beaches.

Bear Gully camping area

On Bear Gully Rd 10 km west of Walkerville. Access via Walkerville South Rd. Additional map ref.: VR 102 J8.

Further information & bookings: Parks Victoria information line **Tel.:** 131 963

4. INVERLOCH

Inverloch is 12 km east of Wonthaggi. Access to the reserve is via The Esplanade.

Inverloch Foreshore Reserve caravan and camping area

Foreshore location. Gas/fuel stove only. Open all year round. Bookings required during the Dec.–Feb. peak season. Additional map ref.: VR 358 G4.

Further information & bookings: Inverloch Foreshore Reserve **Tel.:** (03) 5674 1236 **Email:** redmond@nex.net.au **Camping fees:** Unpowered sites from $15.00 per 2 people/night

5. KILCUNDA

Kilcunda is between Wonthaggi and San Remo.

Kilcunda Caravan Park

Access from Bass Hwy, Kilcunda. Beachside location. Gas/fuel stove only. Open all year round. Bookings required in peak season. Dogs allowed on lead at discretion of management. Additional map ref.: VR 102 A2.

Further information & bookings: Kilcunda Caravan Park **Tel.:** (03) 5678 7260 **Camping fees:** Unpowered sites from $11.00 per 2 people/night

6. LAKE NARRACAN

The lake is 5 km north-east of Moe and access is via South Shore Rd. Lake Narracan is a watersports venue.

Lake Narracan Caravan Park

On North Moe Rd. Park open Nov.–March (opening dates may change). Bookings required at peak times. Additional map ref.: VR 97 F4.

Further information & bookings: Lake Narracan Caravan Park **Tel.:** (03) 5127 8724 **Camping fees:** Unpowered sites from $10.00 per site/night, powered sites from $15.00 per site/night

7. MOONDARRA STATE PARK

This park is 13 km north of Moe and is reached via Moe–Erica Rd. Koalas live in the park and there are scenic drives and opportunities for bushwalking, swimming, mountain-bike riding and nature study.

Seninis Recreation Area

Access via Seninis Track off Moe–Erica Rd. Additional map ref.: VR 97 G2.

Further information & bookings: Parks Victoria information line **Tel.:** 131 963

8. MORWELL–FOSTER AREA

Morwell is 150 km south-east of Melbourne, in the heart of the Latrobe Valley. Although Morwell is an industrial city, the bush country around it is attractive.

Middle Creek camping area

This is 10 km south-east of Yinnar beside Middle Creek. Access via Middle Creek Rd. Bush camping – no facilities. Additional map ref.: VR 97 H8.

Morwell River camping areas

This is 5 km south-east of Boolarra. Many camping areas located along Morwell River Rd. Access via Morwell River Rd. Additional map ref.: VR 97 G9.

Turtons Creek camping area

This bush camp is 12 km north of Foster, near Tarwin East, beside Turtons Creek. Access via Turtons Creek Rd off Boolarra–Foster Road. Bush camping – no facilities. Additional map ref.: VR 103 D2.

Further information & bookings: Parks Victoria, Foster **Tel.:** (03) 5682 2133

9. NOOJEE AREA

See also Toorongo Falls Scenic Reserve, *opposite page*

Noojee lies on the way to Mt Baw Baw, 105 km east of Melbourne.

Hawthorn Bridge camping area

Dispersed camping on both sides of bridge beside Latrobe River, 25 km north-east of Neerim South on Latrobe River Rd. Access via Neerim East Rd from Neerim South, then Latrobe River Rd. Conventional vehicle access. Additional map ref.: VR 81 C9.

Loch Valley camping area

Dispersed camping beside the Loch River, 7 km north of Noojee. Access via Henty St off Powelltown Rd, at junction with Bennett St. Conventional vehicles can access the area, but note that logging trucks use this road. Additional map ref.: VR 80 H7.

Further information & bookings: DSE Customer Service Centre **Tel.:** 136 186

10. NOORAMUNGA MARINE AND COASTAL PARK

This park stretches north-east from Port Welshpool to the southern end of Ninety Mile Beach. There is only boat access to the islands; charter boat operators can provide transport to them. Activities include bushwalking, picnicking, swimming, fishing and nature study.

Little Snake Island camping areas

Offshore from Port Welshpool. Boat access only. Dispersed bush camping at The Bluff on south-west side of island. Bring drinking water. Gas/fuel stove preferred. Additional map ref.: VR 104 A5.

Snake Island camping areas

Offshore from Port Welshpool. Boat access only. Dispersed bush camping on island. Toilets and water at The Huts. Bring drinking water. Gas/fuel stove preferred. Additional map ref.: VR 104 A5/B6.

Further information & bookings: Parks Victoria information line **Tel.:** 131 963 **Camping permit**: Permit required, contact Parks Victoria, Forster, tel. (03) 5682 2133

11. SAN REMO

San Remo is immediately to the east of Phillip Island, on the mainland.

San Remo Foreshore Caravan Park

Access via Davis Point Rd. Foreshore frontage to Bass Strait. Gas/fuel stove only. Open year round. Bookings recommended during during peak periods. Additional map ref.: VR 303 S9.

Further information & bookings: San Remo Foreshore Caravan Park **Tel.:** (03) 5678 5251 **Camping fees:** From $16.50 per site/night

12. SHALLOW INLET MARINE AND COASTAL PARK

Shallow Inlet is a watersports venue 28 km south of Fish Creek, near Yanakie.

Shallow Inlet camping ground

Access via Lester Rd, off Wilsons Promontory Rd. Gas/fuel stove only. Bookings essential at peak times. Additional map ref.: VR 103 C7.

Further information & bookings: Shallow Inlet Camping Ground **Tel.:** (03) 5687 1365 **Camping fees:** Tent sites from $8.00 per family/site/night; fees apply Nov.–Easter only

13. TANJIL STATE FOREST

This forest is 10 km west of Rawson and reached via Telbit Rd, off Moe–Rawson Rd south of Erica. Activities here include bushwalking, fishing and 4WD touring.

Caringal camping area

Near Tyers River junction. Additional map ref.: VR 81 G9.

Western Tyers camping area

Beside Western Tyers River. Signposted from Western Tyers Rd off Telbit Rd. Additional map ref.: VR 81 F9.

Further information & bookings: DSE, Erica **Tel.:** (03) 5165 2200

14. THOMSON STATE FOREST

The forest is north of Walhalla. It is reached by Walhalla Rd, and some sections of the road are windy. The area is popular for fishing and 4WD touring and there are many historic sites to explore.

Andersons campground

Small site beside Aberfeldy River. 4WD only access via Donnelly Creek Track from Walhalla Rd. Additional map ref.: VR 81 H5.

Merringtons camping area

South of Cast Iron Pot Lookout. Access via Merringtons Track off Walhalla Rd. Additional map ref.: VR 81 H6.

O'Tooles camping area

Beside Donnelly Creek. 4WD only access via signposted Donnelly Creek Track from Walhalla Rd. Additional map ref.: VR 81 H5.

The Junction campground

Beside Aberfeldy River. 4WD only access via The Junction Track off Merringtons Track (1.3 km from Merringtons turn-off). Short walk to toilet facilities. Additional map ref.: VR 81 H5.

Further information & bookings: DSE, Erica **Tel.:** (03) 5165 2200

15. TOORONGO FALLS SCENIC RESERVE

The reserve, which is notable for the Toorongo Falls and for its tall mountain forests, is 8 km north-east of Noojee. Access is via Toorongo Falls Rd from Mt Baw Baw Tourist Rd.

Toorongo Falls picnic and camping area

Located beside Toorongo River. Access via Toorongo Falls Rd off Mt Baw Baw Tourist Rd from Noojee. Not suitable for large caravans. Walk to falls. Additional map ref.: VR 81 B7.

Further information & bookings: DSE, Customer Service Centre **Tel.:** 136 186

16. WALHALLA

Walhalla is an interesting historic town set in scenic surrounds. It is reached via Walhalla Rd from Rawson. Explore the town – there are many goldmining sites. Activities include sight-seeing, 4WD touring and horseriding. (*Phytophthora* (root rot), which kills plants, is prevalent in this area. Please observe signs and take steps to help combat the spread of this disease to other areas. Further information is available from DSE and Parks Victoria.)

North Gardens camping ground

Beside Stringer Creek in Walhalla township. Additional map ref.: VR 81 J9.

Further information & bookings: Parks Victoria information line **Tel.:** 131 963

17. WALKERVILLE

Walkerville is 30 km south-west of Foster and reached by Walkerville–Fish Creek Rd. The reserve fronts on to Waratah Bay.

Walkerville Foreshore Reserve camping area

Dogs on lead in off-peak periods only. Additional map ref.: VR 102 J7.

Further information & bookings: Walkerville Foreshore Reserve **Tel.:** (03) 5663 2224 **Camping fees:** *Off-peak*: Unpowered from $13.00 per site/night, powered from $16.00 per site/night *Peak*: Unpowered from $15.00 per site/night, powered from $18.00 per site/night

18. WHITE WOMANS WATERHOLE

This is 15 km north of Yarram and access is via Won Wron Road.

White Womans Waterhole picnic and camping area

On the corner of Napier and Lowes rds. Signposted from Won Wron Rd off Hyland Hwy. Additional map ref.: VR 98 E9.

Further information & bookings: DSE, Yarram **Tel.:** (03) 5183 9100

19. WILSONS PROMONTORY NATIONAL PARK
see page 147

20. WOODSIDE AREA

Woodside lies on the South Gippsland Hwy about 70 km south-east of Traralgon. It is an access point for Ninety Mile Beach.

McGaurans Beach camping area

On Ninety Mile Beach, 20 km north-east of Woodside. Reached from McGaurans Beach Rd. Bring drinking water. Additional map ref.: VR 99 C9.

McLoughlins Beach camping area

On Ninety Mile Beach, 11 km south-east of Woodside. Reached from McLoughlins Beach Rd. Also walk-in sites in dune system. Bring drinking water. Additional map ref.: VR 104 H3.

Reeves Beach camping area

On Ninety Mile Beach, 10 km south-east of Woodside. Access via Reeves Beach Rd. Bring drinking water. Additional map ref.: VR 104 J3.

Further information & bookings: Parks Victoria information line **Tel.:** 131 963

Windsor House, in historic Walhalla

WILSONS PROMONTORY NATIONAL PARK

Joined but separate

Wilsons Prom once formed part of a land bridge to Tasmania, and today the granite-strewn beaches are reminiscent of the islands of Bass Strait and some coastal parts of the island state. The prom is only connected to the mainland by a sandbar – the narrow Yanakie isthmus.

Picturesque river

The park's main camping area is also one of its most scenic spots, where the tea-brown Tidal River winds past lichen-covered boulders before flowing into Norman Bay. Take a lazy afternoon stroll along the sandy riverbank and the nearby beach.

Hikers' dream

Like many parts of the Prom, the lighthouse on South East Point is only accessible by foot. Adding to its appeal is the cottage-style accommodation located at its base – the sort of thing that hikers dream of. Walk the 19 kilometres from Tidal River and bed-down in comfort on the mainland's southernmost tip.

This very popular park has stunning coastal scenery. It is 200 km south-east of Melbourne and reached via Wilsons Promontory Rd from Foster. There are excellent facilities here and at Tidal River, the main camping area, the park caters for people with limited mobility. There are many walking tracks and facilities for watersports. Cabin and lighthouse accommodation are available. Booking is essential for Christmas, Easter and long weekends; a ballot system for the Christmas holidays is drawn 1 July each year – contact Parks Victoria, Tidal River, for details.

Tidal River camping area

Access via Wilsons Promontory Rd. There are 480 sites. Additional map ref.: VR 102 C7.

Walk-in camping areas

There are 11 remote walk-in camping areas within the park. Gas/fuel stove only. Camping permit required. Contact Parks Victoria for details.

Further information & bookings:

Parks Victoria information line **Tel.:** 131 963 *or* Parks Victoria, Tidal River **Tel.:** (03) 5680 9555
Camping fees: *Tidal River:* $18.00 per site/night (3 people + 1 car), extra persons $3.90 per person/night and $5.60 per extra vehicle *Walk-in sites:* $5.00 per person/night plus park entry fee of $9.00 per vehicle **Fire restrictions:** *Tidal River:* campfires prohibited Nov.–April

SOUTH AUSTRALIA

TOP 10 CAMPSITES

Stringybark Campground
Deep Creek Conservation Park, page 194

Rocky River camping area
Flinders Chase National Park, page 197

Hacks Peninsula camping area
Bool Lagoon Game Reserve, page 190

Long Point camping area
Coorong National Park, page 187

Border Cliffs Customs House camping area
Chowilla Game Reserve, page 182

Cable Bay camping area
Innes National Park, page 155

Mambray Creek Campground
Mount Remarkable National Park, page 177

Burners Beach camping area
Yorke Peninsula reserves, page 156

Little Yangie Bay camping area
Coffin Bay National Park, page 161

Wilpena Pound Campground
Flinders Ranges National Park, page 175

South Australia, with an area of just under a million square kilometres, is the site of some of the country's most unusual and arresting landscapes. Much of the state is either unsettled or sparsely populated, and many areas are preserved within well-managed national parks and other conservation zones. It is an outdoor adventurer's paradise.

Although much of the state is arid, it claims areas of remarkable abundance that have become, over time, symbols of South Australia's penchant for the good life. Most notable of these are the major Clare and Barossa wine regions, interwoven with a clutch of nineteenth-century towns and villages.

The Murray River incorporates more vineyards as well as acres of orchards and a natural landscape of rugged valleys and river red gums. The river empties into Lake Alexandrina on the coast and feeds the magnificent wetlands preserved within Coorong National Park.

The state's 3700-kilometre coast is as diverse as it is spectacular. The south-east takes in the historic fishing settlement of Robe and the famous red-wine district of the Coonawarra. The Fleurieu Peninsula is a classic summer holiday destination – a place of calm green-water coves, surf beaches and subdued cliff scapes, all within an hour of Adelaide. Offshore lies Kangaroo Island, rugged and windswept, offering some of Australia's best wildlife-watching opportunities.

Wildlife is also a feature of the Yorke and Eyre peninsulas, to the west of Adelaide, as are stunning beaches, quiet holiday towns, great fishing spots and magnificent pockets of national park. In the west lies the Nullarbor – a flat, treeless plain that drops suddenly into the swell of the Southern Ocean from a seemingly endless line of cliffs.

The Flinders Ranges form another spectacular landscape, a long strip of reddened mountains striking north towards the continent's desert heart. The attractions of the ranges include Aboriginal art, rare rock formations and vivid spring wildflowers, and the facilities for walking and camping in the national parks here have gained an international reputation.

Beyond are the arid plains and deserts that constitute two thirds of the state. While seemingly barren on the surface, these places are ecologically rich, and replete with indigenous and European history; they are accessed by a series of rough tracks, which, despite their remoteness, attract thousands of four-wheel-drive adventurers each year.

The Remarkable Rocks, in Flinders Chase National Park, Kangaroo Island

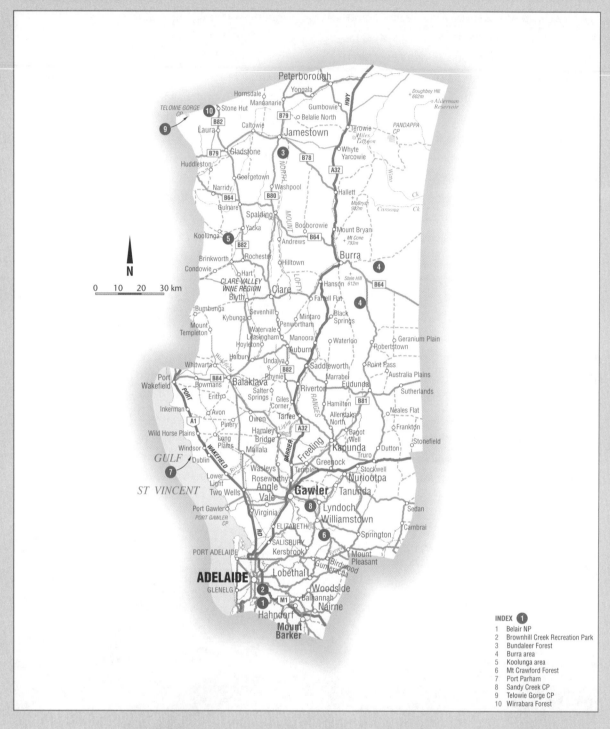

Peterborough
Hornsdale
Yongala
Doughboy Hill
+ 602m
Alderman
Reservoir
Manganarie
Gumbowie
TELOWIE GORGE CP
10 Stone Hut
B79
Belalie North
HWY
PANDAPPA
CP
9
B82
Terowie
Miles
Lagoon
Laura
Caltowie
Jamestown
Whyte
Yarcowie
B79
Gladstone
3
B78
A32
Witto
Ck
Huddleston
Geergetown
Washpool
Hallett
Curoona
Ck
Narridy
B64
Mt Bryan
902m
Gulnare
B80
Boaborowie
Mount Bryan
Spalding
B64
Mt Cone
+ 793m
Koolunga
5
Yacka
Andrews
Burra
B82
Hilltown
Stein Hill
612m
4
Brinkworth
Rochester
B64
Condowie
Hart
Hanson
4
CLARE VALLEY
WINE REGION
Clare
Farrell Flat
Black
Springs
0 10 20 30 km
Blyth
N
Bumbunga
Sevenhill
Mintaro
Geranium Plain
Kybunga
Penwortham
Robertstown
Watervale
Manoora
Waterloo
Mount
Templeton
Leasingham
Point Pass
Hoyleton
Auburn
Australia Plains
Halbury
Undalya
Saddleworth
Whitwarta
B82
Rhynie
Marrabel
Eudunda
Port
Wakefield
B84
Balaklava
Riverton
Sutherlands
Bowmans
Salter
Springs
Giles
Corner
Hamilton
B81
Neales Flat
Erith
Allendale
North
Inkerman
Avon
Owen
Tarlee
Frankton
A1
Purery
A32
Bagot
Well
Stonefield
Wild Horse Plains
Hamley
Bridge
Freeling
Kapunda
Dutton
Windsor
Long
Plains
Mallala
Truro
GULF
Dublin
Wasleys
Greenock
Stockwell
ST VINCENT
7
Lower
Light
Roseworthy
Templers
Nuriootpa
Two Wells
Angle
Vale
Gawler
Tanunda
Sedan
Port Gawler
Virginia
8
Lyndoch
Williamstown
PORT GAWLER
CP
ELIZABETH
Cambrai
SALISBURY
6
Springton
PORT ADELAIDE
Kersbrook
Mount
Pleasant
Birdwood
Lobethal
ADELAIDE
Woodside
GLENELG
2
Balhannah
M1
Nairne
1
Hahndorf
Mount
Barker

THIS REGION OF SOUTH
AUSTRALIA STRETCHES FROM
THE EDGE OF ADELAIDE TO
THE TOP OF THE MOUNT
LOFTY RANGES, TAKING IN THE
BAROSSA VALLEY –
AUSTRALIA'S MOST FAMOUS WINE REGION –
ALONG THE WAY. THIS IS A MAGNIFICENT PLACE

FOR INDULGING IN SOUTH AUSTRALIA'S UNIQUE
HISTORY AND LANDSCAPE.

Two destinations close to the city are
Brownhill Creek Recreation Park and Belair
National Park. Brownhill Creek flows through a
steep-sided valley lined with river red gums, some
more than 300 years old. Belair National Park is
home to a variety of beautiful orchids and

wildflowers, many colourful native birds and the southern brown bandicoot. Both parks offer excellent camping within caravan parks.

A short distance west of Mount Pleasant is the Mount Crawford Forest. Horseriding, mountain-bike riding and bushwalking are popular here, and there are six established camping areas as well as remote bush camping along the Heysen Trail, which traverses the park.

In the Barossa Valley proper, visitors can tour historic Lutheran churches, take hot-air balloon rides, travel the scenic drive from Angaston to Tanunda and visit any number of wineries. Also in the area is Sandy Creek Conservation Park, a short distance west of Lyndoch. This is a good place to see how the Barossa Valley was before vineyards took over. The Wren and Honeyeater walking trails within the park are well marked and pass through tall grasslands, woodlands and heathlands that bloom with wildflowers in spring.

North of the Barossa is the Clare Valley wine region, and north again is Telowie Gorge Conservation Park. The rare yellow-footed rock wallaby can be found amongst the rocky landscapes of this park, as can euros, possums, honeyeaters, the sacred kingfisher and numerous reptiles.

To the east of Burra are two more places to camp – Burra Creek Gorge and Redbanks Reserve. At Redbanks campers can visit the picturesque red alluvial cliffs along Baldina Creek. This town has a strong coppermining heritage – pick up a 'Burra Passport' from the visitor centre to see old mine shafts, dugouts and lock-ups.

BEST CAMPSITES

Sandy Creek camping area
Sandy Creek Conservation Park

Rocky Paddock camping area
Mount Crawford Forest

Telowie Gorge camping area
Telowie Gorge Conservation Park

Ippinitchie Campground
Wirrabara Forest

Redbanks Reserve – Mallee camping area
Burra area

BEST TIME TO VISIT

All year round.

1. BELAIR NATIONAL PARK

Belair National Park is South Australia's oldest national park, declared in 1891. It is 13 km from Adelaide and is easily accessible via conventional vehicle or train. There are numerous scenic walks in the park and other activities include cycling, horseriding or visiting Old Government House. Tennis courts, cricket pitches and football ovals are available for hire here. The park is open from 8 am to sunset each day and a park entrance fee is payable. The park may be closed on days of total fire ban. Within the park is the Belair Park Caravan Park, which has camping and a range of other accommodation.

Belair Park Caravan Park

Signposted from Upper Sturt Rd. Gas/fuel stove only. Bookings recommended during school holidays, Easter and Christmas. Additional map ref.: *RAA Adelaide & Suburbs* K19.

Further information & bookings:
NPWSA, Belair **Tel.:** (08) 8278 5477 *or*
Belair Park Caravan Park **Tel.:** (08) 8278 3540
Camping fees: From $14.00 per unpowered site/night for 2 people

2. BROWNHILL CREEK RECREATION PARK

In the foothills of the Mt Lofty Ranges, 8 km from Adelaide, is Brownhill Creek Recreation Park. The creek's Aboriginal home is Wirraparinga and it was a camping, hunting and gathering place for the Kaurna Aboriginal tribe. Stunning river red gums, some as old as 300 years, guard the banks of Brownhill Creek. Activities include walks and wildlife-spotting. The park may be closed on days of total fire ban.

Brownhill Creek Recreation Caravan Park

Signposted from Brownhill Creek Rd, off Blythewood Rd. Gas/fuel stove only. Bookings recommended during school holidays, Easter and Christmas. Additional map ref.: *RAA Adelaide & Suburbs* K17.

Further information & bookings:
NPWSA, Belair **Tel.:** (08) 8278 5477 *or*
Brownhill Creek Caravan Park **Tel.:** (08) 8271 4824
Camping fees: From $15.00 per unpowered site/night for 2 people

3. BUNDALEER FOREST

Bundaleer Forest, south of Jamestown, was the first forest reserve declared in South Australia – in 1875. The forest offers activities such as walking, picnicking, cycling, horseriding and camping. Permits and fees apply for horseriding; contact office for details.

Curnows Hut camping area

This is 15 km south of Jamestown and is reached from Bundaleer Gardens Rd. Permit required. Bring water. Gas/fuel stove preferred. Bookings required; access to camping area is padlocked. Hut can also be booked. Additional map ref.: *RAA Mid North* G7.

Further information & bookings: Forestry SA, Wirrabara **Tel.:** (08) 8668 4163 **Email:** forestry.recreation@saugov.sa.gov.au **Website:** www.forestry.sa.gov.au **Camping fees:** From $3.00 per adult/night, $1.00 per child/night; fees payable to and permit available from forestry office **Fire restrictions:** Solid-fuel fire ban 1 Nov.–1 May; total fire ban 1 Nov.–30 April; camping prohibited 15 Nov.–31 March

4. BURRA AREA

Close to the township of Burra are the Burra Gorge and nearby Redbanks Reserve, with its red alluvial cliffs, one of Burra's main attractions.

Burra Creek Gorge camping area

This area is 26 km south-east of Burra. Signposted from Robertstown Rd, off Burra–Morgan Road. Bring firewood. Gas/fuel stove preferred. Additional map ref.: *RAA Mid North* K12.

Redbanks Reserve – Mallee camping area

Situated 15 km east of Burra. Signposted from Eastern Rd. Bring firewood. Gas/fuel stove preferred. Additional map ref.: *RAA Mid North* L11.

Further information & bookings: Burra Visitors Centre **Tel.:** (08) 8892 2154 **Email:** bvc@capri.net.au **Camping fees:** *Burra Creek Gorge:* Donations greatly appreciated, use donation box at gorge **Fire restrictions:** Solid-fuel fire ban 15 Nov.–15 April

5. KOOLUNGA AREA

The small farming community of Koolunga is known for its many bunyip sightings. In 1883 attempts were made to capture this mythical creature after it was seen beside a waterhole. If you choose to camp beside the Broughton River or at Bunyip Park you could be the next to I-spy the bunyip!

Broughton River camping area

Conventional vehicle access via Koolunga–Yacka Rd, 5 km east of Koolunga. Bring water and firewood. Gas/fuel stove preferred. Additional map ref.: *RAA Mid North* E10.

Bunyip Park camping area

Access off Koolunga Rd, in township. Bring water and firewood. Gas/fuel stove preferred. Additional map ref.: RAA *Mid North* E10.

Further information & bookings: Port Pirie Regional Tourism **Tel.:** (08) 8633 0439 **Email:** fretwell@a1.com.au **Camping fees:** *Bunyip Park:* Donations greatly appreciated; use donation box **Fire restrictions:** Solid-fuel fire ban 15 Nov.–30 April

6. MOUNT CRAWFORD FOREST

This forest is in the northern Adelaide Hills, one hour's drive from Adelaide CBD, and is easily accessible by conventional vehicle. There are numerous forest roads and tracks that are popular with bushwalkers. Longer walks include the Mawson and Heysen trails, which both pass through the forest. The forest is also popular for cycling and horseriding. Horses are not permitted in the camping areas; contact forestry office for further information and horseriding permits. The forest is closed on days of total fire ban and all camping is prohibited during the total fire ban season (1 Dec.–31 March).

Centennial Road camping area

On Centennial Rd 12 km south-east of Williamstown. Permit required. Additional map ref.: *RAA Barossa Valley & Adelaide Hills* Q8.

Chalks camping area

This is 11 km south-east of Williamstown, on Chalks Rd off Warren Rd. Permit required. Additional map ref.: *RAA Barossa Valley & Adelaide Hills* Q8.

Cromer Shed camping area

On Cricks Mill Rd 7 km west of Mount Pleasant. Large shelter shed. Bookings necessary. Additional map ref.: *RAA Barossa Valley & Adelaide Hills* R9.

Fromms Farm Campground

On Mount Rd 13 km west of Mount Pleasant. Large shelter shed. Bookings necessary. Additional map ref.: *RAA Barossa Valley & Adelaide Hills* Q8.

Rocky Paddock camping area

This is 9 km south-east of Williamstown, signposted from Tower Rd. Permit required. Additional map ref.: *RAA Barossa Valley & Adelaide Hills* Q8.

The Old School House Campground

Situated 9 km east of Williamstown and reached from Springton Rd. School house has eight bunks. Bookings necessary. Additional map ref.: *RAA Barossa Valley & Adelaide Hills* Q7.

Bush camping

There are numerous bush camping areas along the Heysen Trail. Walk-in access only. Permit required. Gas/fuel stove preferred. Contact forestry office for further details.

Further information & bookings: Forestry SA, Mt Crawford Forest **Tel.:** (08) 8524 6004 **Email:** forestry.recreation@saugov.sa.gov.au **Website:** www.forestry.sa.gov.au **Camping fees:** From $3.00 per adult/night, $1.00 per child/night *Cromer Shed, Fromms Farm and The Old School House:* Exclusive hire fee of $20.00 per night plus camping fees; bookings are necessary; fees payable to and permits from Mt Crawford headquarters (Warren Rd) **Horseriding:** Permits required and fees payable for horseriding **Fire restrictions:** Solid-fuel fire ban 1 Nov.–30 April; total fire ban 1 Dec.–31 March, when camping is also prohibited

There are opportunities for wine tasting throughout this region

7. PORT PARHAM

This council reserve, on the shores of Gulf St Vincent, provides excellent camping and is a very popular spot for crabbing.

Port Parham camping area

This is 10 km north-west of Dublin. It is signposted 1 km north of Dublin on Port Wakefield Rd. Boat ramp in Port Parham village. Gas/fuel stove preferred. Additional map ref.: *RAA Barossa Valley & Adelaide Hills* E3.

Further information & bookings: General Inspector, District Council of Mallala **Tel.:** (08) 8527 2006
Fire restrictions: Solid-fuel fire ban 15 Nov.–30 April

8. SANDY CREEK CONSERVATION PARK

This park is an important habitat for over 130 bird species; the spring wildflowers here attract numerous small birds. Take a stroll along the Wren Trail or Honeyeater Trail.

Sandy Creek camping area

The camping area is 4 km west of Lyndoch and is reached via Conservation Park Rd off the Barossa Valley Way. Permit required. Gas/fuel stove only. Additional map ref.: *RAA Barossa Valley & Adelaide Hills* P6.

Further information & bookings: NPWSA, Para Wirra **Tel.:** (08) 8280 7048 **Camping fees:** From $6.00 per vehicle/night; fees payable to and permits from NPWSA office **Fire restrictions:** Solid-fuel fire ban throughout the year; park closed on days of total fire ban

9. TELOWIE GORGE CONSERVATION PARK

The rocky ridges of Telowie Gorge Conservation Park are home to the rare yellow-footed rock wallaby. The park is east of the Princes Hwy, north-east of Port Pirie, and is easily reached by conventional vehicle.

Telowie Gorge camping area

This is 27 km north-east of Port Pirie, signposted from the Princes Hwy. Permit required. Bring water and firewood. Gas/fuel stove preferred. Additional map ref.: *RAA Mid North* C5.

Bush camping

Walk-in bush campsites for experienced and self-sufficient walkers. Permit required. Bring water. Gas/fuel stove only. Additional map ref.: *RAA Mid North* C5.

Further information & bookings: NPWSA, Mt Remarkable National Park **Tel.:** (08) 8634 7068 **Camping fees:** *Telowie Gorge:* From $6.00 per vehicle/night *Bush camping:* From $3.50 per person/night. Fees payable to and permits from NPWSA office **Fire restrictions:** Solid-fuel fire ban 1 Nov.–30 April. Camping prohibited at walk-in sites during this period; day walks only

10. WIRRABARA FOREST

Wirrabara is an Aboriginal word for a place of big trees. The forest, which lies about 25 km north-east of Port Pirie, has numerous walks and lookout points. Experienced walkers who make the steep climb to The Bluff will be rewarded with vistas to Port Pirie and upper Spencer Gulf.

Ippinitchie Campground

On Forest Rd 8 km south-west of Wirrabara. Permit required from self-registration station at forest headquarters, 4 km south of campground. Fees and permits apply for horse-riding. Bring water. Gas/fuel stove preferred. Additional map ref.: *RAA Mid North* D5.

Further information & bookings: Forestry SA, Wirrabara **Tel.:** (08) 8668 4163 **Camping fees:** From $3.00 per adult/night, $1.00 per child/night; fees payable to and permit from forestry office **Fire restrictions:** Solid-fuel fire ban 1 Nov.–30 April; total fire ban 1 Dec.–31 March; camping prohibited 15 Nov.–31 March

YORKE PENINSULA

SOUTH AUSTRALIA · YORKE PENINSULA

154

INDEX

1 Innes NP
2 Redhill area
3 Yorke Peninsula reserves

THE COASTLINES OF THE YORKE PENINSULA, FACING THE GULF ST VINCENT AND SPENCER GULF, ARE POPULAR HOLIDAY DESTINATIONS FOR THOSE WHO ENJOY FISHING, SWIMMING, SURFING AND DIVING. IN THE NORTH OF THE PENINSULA ARE THE COPPERMINING TOWNS OF WALLAROO, MOONTA AND KADINA AND ON THE SOUTHERN TIP OF THE PENINSULA IS THE RUGGED AND BEAUTIFUL INNES NATIONAL PARK.

Over the years, the Southern Ocean and the strong winds have sculptured the rocky coastline of Innes National Park. Its shores and waters are well visited by surfers, divers and fisherfolk, and are home to around 40 shipwrecks. Innes National Park caters well for the camper, with a large number of sites close to the coast and its beaches. All are accessible by conventional vehicles and offer a range of facilities and activities. The park is home to the rare great western whipbird; other birds to be seen here include malleefowl and ospreys. Whales can be sighted during the winter months from Stenhouse Bay and Cape Spencer.

The local council manages other bush campsites scattered around the peninsula – some are in its most picturesque and scenic locations. In particular, good campsites in the northern reserves of Yorke Peninsula are Tiparra Rocks, The Gap and The Bamboos along the north-west coast, while the southern reserves offer Wauraltee Beach, Barker Rocks, Berry Bay, Gravel Bay, Swincer Rocks and Gleesons Landing. Along the southern coastline are Foul Bay, Sturt Bay, Mozzie Flat, Kemp Bay, Troubridge Hill and Sheoak Flat camping areas. At most of these sites campers must be self-sufficient, carry their own water supply and take all rubbish away.

BEST CAMPSITES

Stenhouse Bay camping area
Innes National Park

Cable Bay camping area
Innes National Park

Pondalowie Well camping area
Innes National Park

The Bamboos camping area
Yorke Peninsula reserves

Burners Beach camping area
Yorke Peninsula reserves

BEST TIME TO VISIT

All year, however during winter the coastal areas can get quite windy.

This coastal reserve on the tip of the Yorke Peninsula, three hours' drive from Adelaide, was set aside to conserve the habitat of the rare great western whipbird. Innes National Park has a rich history and much to offer visitors. Activities include fishing, surfing, diving and snorkelling, birdwatching and bushwalking. Whale-watching is also popular during the winter months. As well as camping, heritage accommodation is available in the park; contact the office for details.

Browns Beach camping area

Access via Browns Beach Rd, 26 km north-west of Marion Bay. Permit required from self-registration station. Popular salmon-fishing spot. Bring water and firewood. Gas/fuel stove preferred. Additional map ref.: *RAA Yorke Peninsula* C16.

Cable Bay camping area

Off Pondalowie Bay Rd 10 km south of Marion Bay. Popular area for snorkelling. Boat launch facilities. Permit required from self-registration station. Bring water and firewood. Gas/fuel stove preferred. Additional map ref.: *RAA Yorke Peninsula* C17.

Casuarina camping area

Signposted from Pondalowie Bay Rd, 20 km west of Marion Bay. Permit and key required for access – refundable deposit for key; contact office. Bring water and firewood. Gas/fuel stove preferred. Additional map ref.: *RAA Yorke Peninsula* C17.

Gym Beach camping area

This is 14 km north-west of Marion Bay and 64 km south-west of Warooka, reached off the Corny Point–Marion Bay Rd. Permit required from self-registration station. Bring water and firewood. Gas/fuel stove preferred. Additional map ref.: *RAA Yorke Peninsula* C16.

Jollys Beach camping area

Signposted from park headquarters, 6 km south of Marion Bay. Permit required from self-registration station. Bring water and firewood. Gas/fuel stove preferred. Additional map ref.: *RAA Yorke Peninsula* D17.

Pondalowie Well camping area

Signposted from Pondalowie Bay Rd, 18 km west of Marion Bay. Permit required from self-registration station. Beach launch for boats. Bring water and firewood. Gas/fuel stove preferred. Additional map ref.: *RAA Yorke Peninsula* B17.

Shell Beach camping area

Reached via Browns Beach Rd, 24 km north-west of Marion Bay. Permit required from self-registration station. Bring water and firewood. Gas/fuel stove preferred. Additional map ref.: *RAA Yorke Peninsula* C17.

Stenhouse Bay camping area

Signposted from Stenhouse Bay Rd, 6 km south of Marion Bay. Disabled toilets nearby at park headquarters. Permit required from self-registration station. Bring water and firewood. Gas/fuel stove preferred. Additional map ref.: *RAA Yorke Peninsula* C17.

Surfers camping area

Access from Browns Beach Rd, 20 km west of Marion Bay. Permit required from self-registration station. Popular surfing site. Bring water and firewood. Gas/fuel stove preferred. Additional map ref.: *RAA Yorke Peninsula* C17.

Further information & bookings: NPWSA, Yorke District **Tel.:** (08) 8854 4040 **Camping fees:** *Browns Beach, Cable Bay, Gym Beach, Jollys Beach, Shell Beach, Stenhouse Bay and Surfers*: From $6.00 per vehicle per night *Casuarina*: From $18.00 per vehicle/night *Pondalowie Well*: From $15.00 per vehicle/night. Fees payable to and permits from self-registration station at park headquarters, Stenhouse Bay, or NPWSA office **Fire restrictions:** Solid-fuel fire ban 1 Nov.–30 April

2. REDHILL AREA

A bustling agricultural centre in the late 1860s, Redhill is now a small rural town with a population of around 200. There are historic buildings here; in the Old District Council Building there is a museum containing much local history. Contact the general store for access details.

Redhill Recreation Ground

In Redhill, on the access road off the Princes Hwy. Bring firewood. Additional map ref.: *RAA Mid North* D9.

Further information & bookings: Redhill General Store **Tel.:** (08) 8636 7020

3. YORKE PENINSULA RESERVES

The District Council of Yorke Peninsula has a number of approved bush campsites. They are all accessible by conventional vehicles.

NORTHERN RESERVES

Maitland Overnight Camping Bay

On Robert St at north end of Maitland township, which is in the central-north of the peninsula. This is an overnight bay only – no extended stays allowed. Additional map ref.: *RAA Yorke Peninsula* K9.

Port Arthur Roadside Rest Area

On the north-east coast, signposted from the Coast Rd, 9 km north of Port Clinton. Bring water and firewood. Gas/fuel stove preferred. Additional map ref.: *RAA Yorke Peninsula* N7.

The Bamboos camping area

On the north-west coast of the peninsula 12 km north of Balgowan. Access via Balgowan. Beach launch for boats.

Bring water and firewood. Gas/fuel stove preferred. Additional map ref.: *RAA Yorke Peninsula* H8.

The Gap camping area

On the north-west coast of the peninsula 15 km north of Balgowan. Access via Balgowan. Beach launch for boats. Bring water and firewood. Gas/fuel stove preferred. Additional map ref.: *RAA Yorke Peninsula* H7.

Tiparra Rocks camping area

On the north-west coast of the peninsula, 8 km north of Balgowan. Access via Balgowan. Beach launch for boats. Bring water and firewood. Gas/fuel stove preferred. Additional map ref.: *RAA Yorke Peninsula* H8.

SOUTHERN RESERVES

Barker Rocks camping area

On the west coast of the peninsula, 12 km north-west of Minlaton on Barker Rocks Rd. Bring water and firewood. Additional map ref.: *RAA Yorke Peninsula* H12.

Berry Bay camping area

On the west coast of the foot of the peninsula, on Berry Bay Rd, 15 km west of Corny Point. Permit required. Popular spot for surfing. Bring water and firewood. Additional map ref.: *RAA Yorke Peninsula* D14.

Burners Beach camping area

On the north coast of the foot of the peninsula, on Point Souttar Rd, 22 km north-west of Warooka. Permit required. Natural boat ramp. Bring water and firewood. Additional map ref.: *RAA Yorke Peninsula* F14.

Corny Point Lighthouse camping area

On the north coast of the foot of the peninsula, on Corny Point–Lighthouse Rd, 7 km west of Corny Point. Permit required. Popular spot for surfing and snorkelling. Bring water and firewood. Additional map ref.: *RAA Yorke Peninsula* D14.

Foul Bay camping area

On the south coast of the peninsula 39 km south-west of Warooka. Access via Happy Valley Rd. Permit required. Bring water and firewood. Additional map ref.: *RAA Yorke Peninsula* F17.

Gleesons Landing camping area

On the west coast of the foot of the peninsula, 19 km south-west of Corny Point. Access off Corny Point–Marion Bay Rd. Permit required. 4WD beach boat ramp. Bring water and firewood. Additional map ref.: *RAA Yorke Peninsula* D15.

Gravel Bay camping area

On the west coast of the foot of the peninsula, on Berry Bay Rd, 18 km west of Corny Point. Permit required. Popular spot for surfing. Bring water and firewood. Additional map ref.: *RAA Yorke Peninsula* D14.

Kemp Bay camping area

On the south coast of the peninsula 13 km south of Yorketown, on South Coast Rd. Permit required. Popular fishing spot. Bring water and firewood. Additional map ref.: *RAA Yorke Peninsula* J16.

Mozzie Flat camping area

On the south coast of the peninsula, 23 km south-east of Warooka and 17 km south-west of Yorketown. Access via Sturt Bay Rd. Permit required. Bring water and firewood. Additional map ref.: *RAA Yorke Peninsula* H16.

Port Julia Oval camping area

In Port Julia village, on the east coast of the peninsula. Signposted off the Coast Rd 17 km north of Port Vincent. Area maintained by volunteers – please leave it clean and tidy. Bring water and firewood. Additional map ref.: *RAA Yorke Peninsula* L12.

Sheoak Flat camping area

On the south coast of the peninsula 10 km south of Edithburgh. On Hancock Rd. Permit required. Bring water and firewood. Additional map ref.: *RAA Yorke Peninsula* K16.

Sturt Bay camping area

On the south coast of the peninsula 13 km south of Warooka. Access via Sturt Bay Rd. Permit required. Bring water and firewood. Additional map ref.: *RAA Yorke Peninsula* G16.

Sturt Bay Private camping area

On the south coast of the peninsula 15 km south of Warooka. Access via Sturt Bay Rd. Permit required. Key access only – key from council's general inspector. 4WD beach boat ramp. Bring water and firewood. Additional map ref.: *RAA Yorke Peninsula* G16.

Swincer Rocks camping area

On the west coast of the foot of the peninsula, on Wurlie Rd, 41 km west of Warooka. Permit required. Bring water and firewood. Additional map ref.: *RAA Yorke Peninsula* D14.

Troubridge Hill camping area

On the south coast of the peninsula, 19 km south of Yorketown and 15 km south-west of Edithburgh. On South Coast Rd. Permit required. Popular fishing spot. Bring water and firewood. Additional map ref.: *RAA Yorke Peninsula* J16.

Wauraltee Beach camping area

On the west coast of the peninsula, 17 km south of Port Victoria on Wauraltee Beach Rd. Bring water and firewood. Additional map ref.: *RAA Yorke Peninsula* H11.

Further information & bookings:

Northern Reserves and Port Julia Oval: District Council of Yorke Peninsula, Maitland office **Tel.:** (08) 8832 2701
Southern Reserves: District Council of Yorke Peninsula, Warooka office **Tel.:** (08) 8854 5055
Camping fees: *Berry Bay, Burners Beach, Corny Point Lighthouse, Foul Bay, Gleesons Landing, Gravel Bay, Kemp Bay, Mozzie Flat, Sheoak Flat, Sturt Bay, Sturt Bay Private, Swincer Rocks and Troubridge Hill*: From $5.00 per site/night; fees payable and permits from council offices, council's general inspector or local stores *Sturt Bay Private*: Access key available from council's general inspector
Fire restrictions: Solid-fuel fire ban 15 Nov.–30 April

An old miner's cottage in Moonta

EYRE PENINSULA AND NULLARBOR

THIS VAST REGION OFFERS A RANGE OF LANDSCAPES – FROM UNDULATING FARMING LANDS TO GRANITE OUTCROPS, AND FROM SPECTACULAR COASTLINES TO THE TREELESS PLAINS OF THE NULLARBOR. TO THE NORTH-WEST OF PORT LINCOLN IS A RUGGED COASTLINE THAT OFFERS SOME EXCELLENT SURFING BREAKS. FURTHER ALONG, FRINGING THE NULLARBOR, ARE THE CLIFFS OF THE GREAT AUSTRALIAN BIGHT.

The beautiful coastal landscapes of Coffin Bay National Park include massive sand dunes, limestone cliffs and headlands, wide white beaches, surf beaches and sheltered bays. The beaches provide breeding sites and habitat for many seabirds, including the endangered hooded plover. Conventional vehicle access is possible to Little Yangie Bay camping area, where a number of walking trails begin. All other campsites within the park can only be reached by four-wheel drive. Coffin Bay National Park is on the south-west coast of the Eyre Peninsula and is popular for sightseeing, walking, swimming and fishing.

On the opposite side of the peninsula is Lincoln National Park. This rugged park has spectacular ocean scenery, steep limestone cliffs and beautiful sheltered beaches. It is popular with birdwatchers, as it is a stopover point for birds migrating from Siberia and the Arctic Circle. Camping is at designated sites along the northern coast of the park. In the south of the park is Memory Cove camping area, a beautiful place; bookings are required here and camper numbers are limited.

Around Streaky Bay – named by Matthew Flinders in reference to the streaks of seaweed in the bay – are a number of council-approved bush campsites. Campers can swim, fish and sail here.

To the west of the delightful town of Fowlers Bay is the Fowlers Bay Conservation Park, a popular area for fishing and birdwatching. Campers here will find spectacular coastal scenery and long sandy beaches.

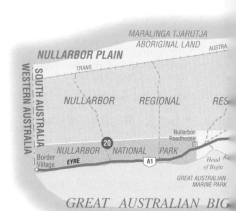

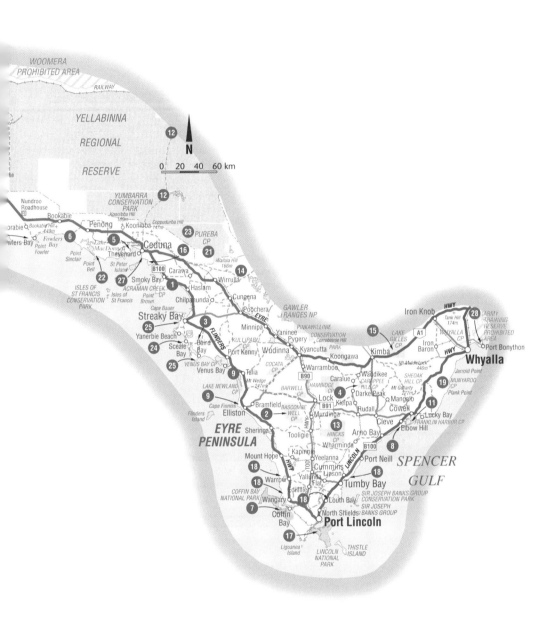

SOUTH AUSTRALIA

BEST CAMPSITES

Little Yangie Bay camping area
Coffin Bay National Park

Point Westall camping area
Streaky Bay area

Memory Cove camping area
Lincoln National Park

Surfleet Cove camping area
Lincoln National Park

Fitzgerald Bay camping area
Whyalla area

BEST TIME TO VISIT

All year round.

1. ACRAMAN CREEK CONSERVATION PARK

This is north of Streaky Bay, which is on the Flinders Hwy. Activities here include canoeing. Caravan and conventional access is possible but call NPWSA for road conditions before setting out.

Acraman Creek camping area

Sites beside Acraman Creek, 53 km north of Streaky Bay and 56 km south of Ceduna. Signposted from Flinders Hwy. Permit required. 4WD beach boat launch. Bring water and firewood. Gas/fuel stove preferred. Additional map ref.: *RAA Upper Eyre Peninsula and Far West Coast* C3.

Further information & bookings: NPWSA, Ceduna **Tel.:** (08) 8625 3144 **Email:** Dawes.Rhiannon@saugov.sa. gov.au **Camping fees:** From $6.00 per vehicle/night; fees payable to and permits from NPWSA office **Fire restrictions:** Solid-fuel fire ban 1 Nov.–30 April

2. BASCOMBE WELL CONSERVATION PARK

This conservation park, 22 km south-west of Lock and 68 km north-west of Cummins, has areas of mallee and woodlands. In spring orchids come into flower. It is a remote park and visitors should check with the NPWSA for conditions and accessibility. It is suitable for self-sufficient campers only.

Bush camping

Access via Murdinga or Warrachie off Tod Hwy. Permit required. Contact office for details of internal tracks. Bring water and firewood. Gas/fuel stove preferred. Additional map ref.: *RAA Lower Eyre Peninsula* F1.

Further information & bookings: NPWSA, Port Lincoln **Tel.:** (08) 8688 3111 **Camping fees:** From $6.00 per vehicle/night; fees payable to and permits from NPWSA office **Fire restrictions:** Solid-fuel fire ban 1 Nov.–30 April

3. CALPATANNA WATERHOLE CONSERVATION PARK

This park is 40 km south-east of Streaky Bay. The Calpatanna Waterhole is on the southern boundary of the park and was used as a watering point by the early Aboriginal inhabitants. Caravan access is possible, however check with a ranger first.

Wedina Well camping area

Access via Calca Rd off the Flinders Hwy. Enter through gate signposted 'Reserve' on the Calca Rd. Permit required. Bring water and firewood. Gas/fuel stove preferred. Additional map ref.: *RAA Upper Eyre Peninsula and Far West Coast* E7.

Further information & bookings: NPWSA, Ceduna **Tel.:** (08) 8625 3144 **Email:** Dawes.Rhiannon@saugov. sa.gov.au **Camping fees:** From $6.00 per vehicle/night; fees payable to and permits from NPWSA office **Fire restrictions:** Solid-fuel fire ban 1 Nov.–30 April

4. CARAPPEE HILL CONSERVATION PARK

This park, which protects beautiful native orchids and wildflowers, is 8 km east of Darke Peak and 42 km south-west of Kimba. It is reached via the Darke Peak Rd off the Eyre Hwy. The highest granite rock mass on the Eyre Peninsula is found within the park.

Bush camping

Permit required. Bring water and firewood. Gas/fuel stove preferred. Additional map ref.: *RAA Upper Eyre Peninsula and Far West Coast* Q9.

Further information & bookings: NPWSA, Port Lincoln **Tel.:** (08) 8688 3111 *or* Cleve Visitor Information Centre **Tel.:** (08) 8628 2183 **Camping fees:** From $6.00 per vehicle/night; fees payable to and permits from NPWSA **Fire restrictions:** Solid-fuel fire ban 1 Nov.–30 April

5. CEDUNA AREA

Ceduna comes from the Aboriginal word 'chedoona' and means 'resting place'. The town is on the western edge of Eyre Peninsula, on the shores of Murat Bay. Access to the camping areas is via the unsealed Denial Bay Rd; check road conditions before attempting. Both areas offer excellent swimming and fishing.

Davenport Creek camping area

Located 41 km west of Ceduna and signposted off Denial Bay Rd. There are three main camping areas here; conventional vehicle access is possible to the Cocklebeds and Ocean Beach camping areas, and 4WD access only to the Davenport Creek camping area. 4WD beach boat launch. Bring water and firewood. Gas/fuel stove preferred. Additional map ref.: *RAA Upper Eyre Peninsula and Far West Coast – Far West Coast Map* N3.

Nadia Landing camping area

This is 25 km west of Ceduna and is signposted off Denial Bay Rd. 4WD beach boat launch. Bring water and firewood. Gas/fuel stove preferred. Additional map ref.: *RAA Upper Eyre Peninsula and Far West Coast – Far West Coast Map* N3.

Further information & bookings: Ceduna Gateway Visitors Information Centre **Tel.:** (08) 8625 2780 or 1800 639 413 **Email:** travelce@tpg.com.au **Fire restrictions:** Solid-fuel fire ban 1 Nov.–30 April

6. CHADINGA CONSERVATION RESERVE

This reserve, south-west of Penong, is known by locals as Tuckamore. Conventional vehicle access is possible to the beach, 4WD is necessary thereafter. To reach the park contact the ranger or ask locals for directions and road conditions.

Tuckamore bush camping

Situated 25 km west of Penong. Access via Edwards Rd off the Eyre Hwy. Permit required. Bring water and firewood. Gas/fuel stove preferred. Additional map ref.: *RAA Upper Eyre Peninsula and Far West Coast – Far West Coast Map* L3.

Further information & bookings: NPWSA, Ceduna **Tel.:** (08) 8625 3144 **Email:** Dawes.Rhiannon@saugov.sa.gov.au *or* Penong General Store **Tel.:** (08) 8625 1027 **Camping fees:** From $6.00 per vehicle/night; fees payable to and permits from NPWSA **Fire restrictions:** Solid-fuel fire ban 1 Nov.–30 April

7. COFFIN BAY NATIONAL PARK

This park is on the Coffin Bay Peninsula 5 km south of Coffin Bay township. There is much for visitors to see and do: walks, fishing, bird- and wildlife-watching. Within the park travel is on foot or by 4WD. Conventional vehicle access is possible to Little Yangie Bay camping area but all other areas are reached by 4WD only. Some camping areas can be accessed by 4WD along Seven Mile Beach; check tide times before attempting and do not drive on vegetated dunes.

Black Springs camping area

Signposted off the Coffin Bay National Park Access Rd, 28 km north-west of the rangers headquarters. 4WD access only. Permit required. Bring water and firewood. Gas/fuel stove preferred. Additional map ref.: *RAA Lower Eyre Peninsula* E9.

Little Yangie Bay camping area

On the Coffin Bay National Park Access Rd 15 km west of the rangers headquarters. Permit required. Bring water and firewood. Gas/fuel stove preferred. Additional map ref.: *RAA Lower Eyre Peninsula* E10.

Morgans Landing camping area

Signposted off the Coffin Bay National Park Access Rd, 45 km north-west of the rangers headquarters. Access also via Seven Mile Beach. Permit required. Bring water and firewood. Gas/fuel stove preferred. Additional map ref.: *RAA Lower Eyre Peninsula* D8.

Sensation Beach camping area

Access via Coffin Bay National Park Access Rd, 50 km north-west of the rangers headquarters. Access also via Seven Mile Beach. Permit required. Bring water and firewood. Gas/fuel stove preferred. Additional map ref.: *RAA Lower Eyre Peninsula* D9.

The Pool camping area

Access via Coffin Bay National Park Access Rd, 55 km north-west of the rangers headquarters. Access also via Seven Mile Beach. Permit required. Bring water and firewood. Gas/fuel stove preferred. Additional map ref.: *RAA Lower Eyre Peninsula* D8.

Further information & bookings: NPWSA, Port Lincoln **Tel.:** (08) 8688 3111 **Email:** dwray@deh.sa.gov.au **Camping fees:** From $6.00 per vehicle/night, non-vehicle campers from $3.50 per person/night; fees payable to and permits from NPWSA or self-registration station at rangers headquarters at park entrance **Fire restrictions:** Solid-fuel fire ban 1 Nov.–30 April

8. COWELL AREA

Cowell is 108 km south-west of Whyalla, on the almost landlocked Franklin Harbor.

The cliffs that fringe the Nullarbor, with the thundering Southern Ocean down below

The Knob camping area

The Knob is 13 km south of Cowell, signposted from Wellington Rd. Its sheltered beach is popular with swimmers and fisherfolk. Bring water and firewood. Gas/fuel stove preferred. Additional map ref.: *RAA Lower Eyre Peninsula* R2.

Further information & bookings: Cowell Visitor Information Centre **Tel.:** (08) 8629 2034
Fire restrictions: Solid-fuel fire ban 15 Nov.–15 April

9. ELLISTON AREA

Elliston is on the west coast of the Eyre Peninsula, 166 km north-west of Port Lincoln. The local council has set aside three beautiful coastal reserves for bush camping. These offer visitors excellent swimming and fishing opportunities.

Sheringa Beach camping area

Situated 51 km south of Elliston. Signposted via Sheringa Beach Rd, which is off the Flinders Hwy 39 km south of Elliston. Permit required from self-registration station. Bring water and firewood. Gas/fuel stove preferred. Additional map ref.: *RAA Lower Eyre Peninsula* C3.

Talia Caves camping area

This is 48 km north of Elliston, signposted off the Flinders Hwy 42 km north of Elliston. Permit required. Bring water and firewood. Gas/fuel stove preferred. Additional map ref.: *RAA Upper Eyre Peninsula and Far West Coast* G9.

Walkers Rocks camping area

The area is 12 km north of Elliston, signposted off the Flinders Hwy 9 km north of Elliston. Permit required from self-registration station. Bring water and firewood. Gas/fuel stove preferred. Additional map ref.: *RAA Upper Eyre Peninsula and Far West Coast* G10.

Further information & bookings: Elliston District Council **Tel.:** (08) 8687 9177 **Email:** dce@elliston.sa.gov.au
Camping fees: From $5.00 per site/night or $30.00 per site/week; fees payable to and permits from self-registration stations at Sheringa Beach and Walkers Rocks or Elliston District Council **Fire restrictions:** Solid-fuel fire ban 15 Nov.–15 April

10. FOWLERS BAY CONSERVATION PARK

This spectacular coastal park has sandy beaches and is popular with fisherfolk and birdwatchers. It is west of the town of Fowlers Bay, which is 172 km west of Ceduna. Conventional vehicle access is possible via an unsealed road from Coorabie.

Bush camping

Access from Coorabie–Fowlers Bay Rd, off Eyre Hwy. Permit required. Locals are happy to provide directions. Camp only in designated areas. Bring water and firewood. Gas/fuel stove preferred. Additional map ref.: *RAA Upper Eyre Peninsula and Far West Coast – Far West Coast Map* K3.

Further information & bookings: NPWSA, Ceduna **Tel.:** (08) 8625 3144 **Email:** Dawes.Rhiannon@saugov.sa.gov.au **Camping fees:** From $6.00 per vehicle/night; fees payable to and permits from NPWSA **Fire restrictions:** Solid-fuel fire ban 1 Nov.–30 April

11. FRANKLIN HARBOR CONSERVATION PARK

This is 16 km south of Cowell, on the Spencer Gulf. Access to the park is by 4WD only and campers need to be fully self-sufficient.

Bush camping

Access via Wellington Rd. Permit required. Bring water and firewood. Gas/fuel stove preferred. Additional map ref.: *RAA Lower Eyre Peninsula* S2.

Further information & bookings: NPWSA, Port Lincoln **Tel.:** (08) 8688 3111 **Camping fees:** From $6.00 per vehicle/night; fees payable to and permits from NPWSA **Fire restrictions:** Solid-fuel fire ban 1 Nov.–30 April

12. GOOGS TRACK

This 154-km-long track traverses both Yumbarra Conservation Park and Yellabinna Regional Reserve, which lie north of Ceduna. Here you should visit Googs Lake, Mt Finke and the monuments to the track's builders: John 'Goog' Denton and his son Martin 'Dinger' Denton. Caution is required when approaching vehicles on sand ridges. This is a remote area and all travellers must be fully self-sufficient.

YELLABINNA REGIONAL RESERVE

Mount Finke camping area

This is 40 km south of Malbooma Railway Siding (which is 161 km west of Glendambo) and 160 km north of Ceduna on Googs Track. Permit required. Bring water and firewood. Gas/fuel stove preferred. Additional map ref.: *RAA Outback* E9.

YUMBARRA CONSERVATION PARK

Googs Lake camping area

Situated 85 km north of Ceduna, on Googs Track. Access is through private property, contact NPWSA for details; alternative access signposted via Y Rd off OTC Rd. Permit required. Bring water and firewood. Gas/fuel stove preferred. Additional map ref.: *RAA Upper Eyre Peninsula and Far West Coast – Far West Coast Map* P2.

Further information & bookings: NPWSA, Ceduna **Tel.:** (08) 8625 3144 **Email:** Dawes.Rhiannon@saugov.sa.gov.au **Camping fees:** From $6.00 per vehicle/night; fees payable to and permits from NPWSA **Fire restrictions:** Solid-fuel fire ban 1 Nov.–30 April

13. HINCKS CONSERVATION PARK

This large, predominantly mallee park is 85 km north of Port Lincoln and 8 km east of Tooligie. Conventional vehicle access to the park is limited. All visitors should check with NPWSA for road conditions and access. It is a popular park with naturalists and experienced bushwalkers.

Nicholls Track camping area

Situated 54 km north-east of Cummins on Nicholls Track, reached via Reserve Rd from Mt Isabella. Permit required. Bring water and firewood. Gas/fuel stove preferred. Additional map ref.: *RAA Lower Eyre Peninsula* J3.

Further information & bookings: NPWSA, Port Lincoln **Tel.:** (08) 8688 3111 **Camping fees:** From $6.00 per vehicle/night; fees payable to and permits from NPWSA **Fire restrictions:** Solid-fuel fire ban 1 Nov.–30 April

14. KOOLGERA CONSERVATION PARK

This park encompassing some 44 700 ha of red sand dunes is north of the Eyre Hwy, 27 km east of Wirrulla. Visitors here need to be fully self-sufficient and experienced outback travellers. Contact office for detailed information on access and camping spots.

Bush camping

Access via Gawler Ranges Rd from Wirrulla – 4WD only. Permit required. Bring water and firewood. Gas/fuel stove preferred. Additional map ref.: *RAA Upper Eyre Peninsula and Far West Coast* G3.

Further information & bookings: NPWSA, Ceduna **Tel.:** (08) 8625 3144 **Email:** Dawes.Rhiannon@saugov. sa.gov.au **Camping fees:** From $6.00 per vehicle/night; fees payable to and permits from NPWSA **Fire restrictions:** Solid-fuel fire ban 1 Nov.–30 April

15. LAKE GILLES CONSERVATION PARK

Lake Gilles is a large salt lake north of the Eyre Hwy, about 120 km west of Port Augusta. The conservation park lies between the highway and the lake; it is popular with birdwatchers and those who enjoy remote travelling. A 4WD vehicle is recommended; if travelling in a conventional vehicle check access with NPWSA first.

Lakes Edge camping area

This is 17 km north of the Eyre Hwy, signposted off it 87 km west of Iron Knob and 35 km east of Kimba. Contact NPWSA ranger for detailed access information. Permit required. Bring water and firewood. Gas/fuel stove preferred. Additional map ref.: *RAA Upper Eyre Peninsula and Far West Coast* S7.

Further information & bookings: NPWSA, Port Lincoln **Tel.:** (08) 8688 3111 **Camping fees:** From $6.00 per vehicle/night; fees payable to and permits from NPWSA **Fire restrictions:** Solid-fuel fire ban 1 Nov.–30 April

16. LAURA BAY CONSERVATION PARK

The exposed coast of this small park, 21 km south-east of Ceduna, has rocky headlands and a sandy beach but Laura Bay itself is well sheltered. Activities include birdwatching, beachcombing, bushwalking, swimming and fishing.

Bush camping

Signposted off Eyre Hwy or via Decres Bay Rd. Camp in designated sites only. Permit required. Bring water and firewood. Gas/fuel stove preferred. Additional map ref.: *RAA Upper Eyre Peninsula and Far West Coast* B2.

Further information & bookings: NPWSA, Ceduna **Tel.:** (08) 825 3144 **Email:** Dawes.Rhiannon@saugov. sa.gov.au **Camping fees:** From $6.00 per vehicle/night; fees payable to and permits from NPWSA **Fire restrictions:** Solid-fuel fire ban 1 Nov.–April

17. LINCOLN NATIONAL PARK see page 164

18. LOWER EYRE PENINSULA RESERVES

On the coasts of the peninsula are a number of reserves with bush camping opportunities. Activities include fishing, swimming, canoeing and surfing.

Coles Point camping area

On the west coast 27 km north of Wangary. Access via Coles Point Rd from Flinders Hwy. Popular surfing spot. Bring water and firewood. Gas/fuel stove preferred. Additional map ref.: *RAA Lower Eyre Peninsula* E7.

Convention Beach camping area

Bush camping behind sand dunes, on the west coast 36 km north of Wangary. Access via Ulina Lane off Flinders Hwy. Popular fishing and surfing spot. Bring water and firewood. Gas/fuel stove preferred. Additional map ref.: *RAA Lower Eyre Peninsula* E6.

Farm Beach camping area

On the west coast 37 km north of Coffin Bay and 10 km west of Wangary. Access via Farm Beach Rd. 4WD beach boat launch. Bring water and firewood. Gas/fuel stove preferred. Additional map ref.: *RAA Lower Eyre Peninsula* E8.

Greenly Beach camping area

On the west coast 29 km north of Wangary. Access via Greenly Beach Rd from Flinders Hwy. Popular salmon-fishing and surfing spot. Bring water and firewood. Gas/fuel stove preferred. Additional map ref.: *RAA Lower Eyre Peninsula* E7.

Lipson Cove camping area

On the east coast 24 km north of Tumby Bay. Access via Lipson Cove Rd, signposted from Lincoln Hwy. Bring water and firewood. Gas/fuel stove preferred. Additional map ref.: *RAA Lower Eyre Peninsula* M6.

Louth Bay camping area

On the east coast 29 km south of Tumby Bay and 21 km north of Port Lincoln. Access via The Haven Drive off Lincoln Hwy. Beach boat launch. Bring water and firewood. Gas/fuel stove preferred. Additional map ref.: *RAA Lower Eyre Peninsula* J9.

Further information & bookings:
Lipson Cove: Tumby Bay District Council **Tel.:** (08) 8688 2101
All other areas: Lower Eyre Peninsula District Council
Tel.: (08) 8676 2106
Fire restrictions: Solid-fuel fire ban 1 Nov.–30 April

19. MUNYAROO CONSERVATION PARK

On the western shores of Spencer Gulf, south of Whyalla. The park offers beach fishing, walking and birdwatching. It is suitable for self-sufficient campers only. Access to the park is through private property – contact NPWSA for access details.

Bush camping

Signposted off Lincoln Hwy, 44 km south of Whyalla. Permit required. Bring water and firewood. Gas/fuel stove preferred. Additional map ref.: *RAA Upper Eyre Peninsula and Far West Coast* W9.

LINCOLN NATIONAL PARK

Seawards to Sleaford
Sleaford Bay, facing the full force of the Southern Ocean, preserves a wild landscape of limestone cliffs, wave-battered beaches and the magnificent wind-sculptured Wanna Dunes. Access is by four-wheel drive. Southern right whales can be spotted off the coast between July and November.

Following Flinders
The Investigator Trail is a long-distance walking track exploring some of South Australia's prettiest and least traversed coastal areas. It is named for the ship of the great explorer/navigator Matthew Flinders, who surveyed the rugged Eyre Peninsula coastline in 1802, losing eight men in the process.

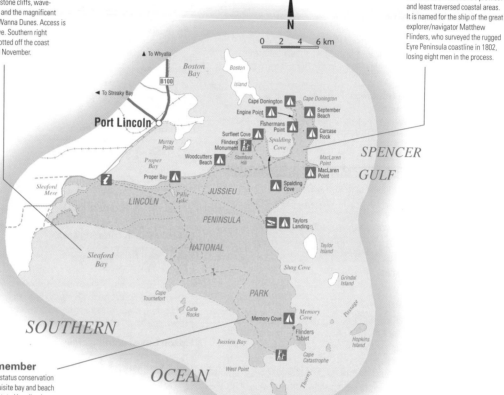

A place to remember
Memory Cove is a high-status conservation zone containing an exquisite bay and beach flanked by densely vegetated headlands. Access is by four-wheel drive and is limited to 15 vehicles and five campers per day; contact Port Lincoln's National Parks & Wildlife office for details.

This rugged peninsula park protects coastal vegetation and is a summer refuge for migrating birds. The spectacular coastline has scenic views, sandy beaches and sheltered camping areas. It is 11 km south of Port Lincoln and offers visitors activities such as bushwalking, fishing, swimming, sightseeing and 4WD touring.

Cape Donington camping area

Access via Lincoln National Park Access Rd, 27 km north-east of park entrance. Permit required. Bring water and firewood. Gas/fuel stove preferred. Additional map ref.: *RAA Lower Eyre Peninsula* K10.

Carcase Rock camping area

Signposted from Lincoln National Park Access Rd, 29 km north-east of park entrance. Permit required. Bring water and firewood. Gas/fuel stove preferred. Additional map ref.: *RAA Lower Eyre Peninsula* K11.

Engine Point camping area

Access via Lincoln National Park Access Rd, 25 km north-east of park entrance. Permit required. Bring water and firewood. Gas/fuel stove preferred. Additional map ref.: *RAA Lower Eyre Peninsula* K10.

Fishermans Point camping area

Access via Lincoln National Park Access Rd, 24 km north-east of park entrance. Small boat access from beach. Permit required. Bring water and firewood. Gas/fuel stove preferred. Additional map ref.: *RAA Lower Eyre Peninsula* K11.

MacLaren Point camping area

Reached via Lincoln National Park Access Rd, 29 km north-east of park entrance. Permit required. Bring water and firewood. Gas/fuel stove preferred. Additional map ref.: *RAA Lower Eyre Peninsula* K11.

Stamford Hill Lookout, in the north of the park

Memory Cove camping area

Signposted from Lincoln National Park Access Rd, 29 km south-east of park entrance. Key access only – refundable deposit on key. Bookings essential and permit required. Bring water. Gas/fuel stove only. Additional map ref.: *RAA Lower Eyre Peninsula* K12.

Proper Bay camping area

Access via Lincoln National Park Access Rd, 10 km east of park entrance. Permit required. Bring water and firewood. Gas/fuel stove preferred. Additional map ref.: *RAA Lower Eyre Peninsula* J11.

September Beach camping area

Reached via Lincoln National Park Access Rd, 28 km north-east of park entrance. Permit required. Bring water and firewood. Gas/fuel stove preferred. Additional map ref.: *RAA Lower Eyre Peninsula* K10.

Spalding Cove camping area

Signposted from Lincoln National Park Access Rd, 20 km north-east of park entrance. Permit required. Bring water and firewood. Gas/fuel stove preferred. Additional map ref.: *RAA Lower Eyre Peninsula* J11.

Surfleet Cove camping area

Signposted from Lincoln National Park Access Rd, 22 km north-east of park entrance. Permit required. Bring water and firewood. Gas/fuel stove preferred. Additional map ref.: *RAA Lower Eyre Peninsula* J11.

Taylors Landing camping area

Access via Lincoln National Park Access Rd, 23 km east of park entrance. Care required when using boat ramp; check tides. Permit required. Bring water and firewood. Gas/fuel stove preferred. Additional map ref.: *RAA Lower Eyre Peninsula* J11.

Woodcutters Beach camping area

Signposted from Lincoln National Park Access Rd, 15 km east of park entrance. Two sites only. Permit required. Bring water and firewood. Gas/fuel stove preferred. Additional map ref.: *RAA Lower Eyre Peninsula* J11.

Further information & bookings:
NPWSA, Port Lincoln **Tel.:** (08) 8688 3111
Email: dwray@deh.sa.gov.au *or*
Port Lincoln Visitor Information Centre **Tel.:** (08) 8683 3544
Email: plvic@camtech.net.au
Camping fees: *Memory Cove*: From $18.00 per vehicle/night *All other areas*: From $6.00 per vehicle/night. Fees payable to and permits from self-registration station at park entrance or NPWSA office **Fire restrictions:** Solid-fuel fire ban 1 Nov.–30 April

Further information & bookings: NPWSA, Port Lincoln **Tel.:** (08) 8688 3111 **Camping fees:** From $6.00 per vehicle/night; fees payable to and permits from NPWSA **Fire restrictions:** Solid-fuel fire ban 1 Nov.–30 April

20. NULLARBOR NATIONAL PARK

Many features such as sinkholes, blowholes and caves are protected within Nullarbor National Park and the neighbouring regional reserve. From May to October the Nullarbor cliffs are an excellent spot for viewing southern right whales.

Koonalda Homestead camping area

Camping in the vicinity of the homestead, which is on a dirt road off the Eyre Hwy, 15 km north of the highway. Road is not signposted; it is 100 km west of Nullarbor Roadhouse and 90 km east of Border Village. Homestead also for rent (bookings are essential; contact NPWSA for details). Permit required. Bring water and firewood. Gas/fuel stove preferred. Additional map ref.: *RAA Upper Eyre Peninsula and Far West Coast – Far West Coast Map* C1.

Bush camping

Many parking bays are positioned in the scrub along the Eyre Hwy between Nullarbor Roadhouse and Border Village; some are signposted. These are overnight bays only, no extended stays. Pets allowed but must be kept on lead at all times. Bring water and firewood. Gas/fuel stove preferred. Additional map ref.: *RAA Upper Eyre Peninsula and Far West Coast – Far West Coast Map* A2/B2/C2/D2/E2/F2.

Further information & bookings: NPWSA, Ceduna **Tel.:** (08) 8625 3144 **Email:** Dawes.Rhiannon@saugov. sa.gov.au **Camping fees:** *Koonalda Homestead*: From $6.00 per vehicle/night; fees payable to and permits from NPWSA **Fire restrictions:** Solid-fuel fire ban 1 Nov.–30 April

21. NUNNYAH CONSERVATION RESERVE

This reserve is located north of the Eyre Hwy 37 km north-west of Wirrulla. Visitors to the park must be fully self-sufficient and experienced outback travellers. Contact NPWSA Ceduna for detailed information on access and camping areas.

Bush camping

Situated 24 km north of Eyre Hwy. 4WD access only via Oak Hill. Permit required. Bring water and firewood. Gas/fuel stove preferred. Additional map ref.: *RAA Upper Eyre Peninsula and Far West Coast* E1.

Further information & bookings: NPWSA, Ceduna **Tel.:** (08) 8625 3144 **Email:** Dawes.Rhiannon@saugov. sa.gov.au **Camping fees:** From $6.00 per vehicle/night; fees payable to and permits from NPWSA **Fire restrictions:** Solid-fuel fire ban 1 Nov.–30 April

22. POINT BELL CONSERVATION RESERVE

This coastal reserve west of Ceduna has excellent beaches for swimming and fishing.

Point Bell camping area

This is 87 km west of Ceduna, reached via Shady Lane off Denial Bay Rd. Camp in designated sites only. Permit required. Bring water and firewood. Gas/fuel stove preferred. Additional map ref.: *RAA Upper Eyre Peninsula and Far West Coast – Far West Coast Map* M3.

Further information & bookings: NPWSA, Ceduna **Tel.:** (08) 8625 3144 *or* Ceduna Gateway Visitor Information Centre **Tel.:** (08) 8625 2780 **Camping fees:** From $6.00 per vehicle/night; fees payable to and permits from NPWSA **Fire restrictions:** Solid-fuel fire ban 1 Nov.–30 April

23. PUREBA CONSERVATION PARK AND RESERVE

This park and reserve adjoin Nunnyah Conservation Reserve and Koolgera Conservation Reserve. Activities include birdwatching and bushwalking. Contact NPWSA Ceduna for detailed information on access and camping areas.

Bush camping

Located 15 km north of Eyre Hwy, just north of Ceduna. 4WD access only, via Mudamuckla. Permit required. Bring water and firewood. Gas/fuel stove preferred. Additional map ref.: *RAA Outback* E10.

Further information & bookings: NPWSA, Ceduna **Tel.:** (08) 8625 3144 **Camping fees:** From $6.00 per vehicle/night; fees payable to and permits from NPWSA **Fire restrictions:** Solid-fuel fire ban 1 Nov.–30 April

24. SCEALE BAY CONSERVATION RESERVE

Recently dedicated, this reserve conserves coastal dunes and Seagull Lake. Activities include birdwatching and fishing.

Bush camping

This is 15 km south of Streaky Bay and is reached from Streaky Bay–Sceale Bay Rd. Permit required. Bring water and firewood. Gas/fuel stove preferred. Additional map ref.: *RAA Upper Eyre Peninsula and Far West Coast* D6.

Further information & bookings: NPWSA, Ceduna **Tel.:** (08) 8625 3144 **Camping fees:** From $6.00 per vehicle/night; fees payable to and permits from NPWSA **Fire restrictions:** Solid-fuel fire ban 1 Nov.–30 April

25. STREAKY BAY AREA

There are a number of excellent bush camping areas around Streaky Bay. Recreational activities here include swimming, fishing, sailing, surfing, car touring and sailboarding.

Baird Bay Campground

This is 50 km south-east of Streaky Bay. Access via Baird Bay Rd off Flinders Hwy. Bring water and firewood. Gas/fuel stove preferred. Additional map ref.: *RAA Upper Eyre Peninsula and Far West Coast* E8.

Haslam Jetty camping area

Situated 40 km north of Streaky Bay and 33 km south-west of Wirrulla. Signposted access from Flinders Hwy. Bring water and firewood. Gas/fuel stove preferred. Additional map ref.: *RAA Upper Eyre Peninsula and Far West Coast* D4.

Perlubie Beach camping area

Located 20 km north of Streaky Bay. Signposted from Flinders Hwy. Beach boat launch. Bring water and firewood. Gas/fuel stove preferred. Additional map ref.: *RAA Upper Eyre Peninsula and Far West Coast* D5.

Point Westall camping area

Situated 9 km south of Streaky Bay along the Westall Way Scenic Drive. Many sites signposted along the drive at High Cliffs, The Granites and Smooth Pool. Bring water and firewood. Gas/fuel stove preferred. Additional map ref.: *RAA Upper Eyre Peninsula and Far West Coast* C6.

Further information & bookings: Streaky Bay District Council **Tel.:** (08) 8626 1001 **Email:** dcstreaky@streakybay. sa.gov.au **Camping fees:** From $2.00 per person/night; fees payable to honesty box at each site **Fire restrictions:** Solid-fuel fire ban 1 Nov.–30 April

26. WAHGUNYA CONSERVATION RESERVE

This reserve, 15 km south of Yalata Roadhouse and the Eyre Hwy, has long windswept beaches, sand dunes and dense coastal mallee vegetation. Detailed information on access is available from NPWSA Ceduna.

Cape Adieu camping area

Situated 40 km south-west of Nundroo Roadhouse, off Eyre Hwy. Contact ranger for access details. Camping areas behind the main sand dunes. Limited conventional-vehicle access; 4WD recommended. Permit required. Bring water and firewood. Gas/fuel stove preferred. Additional map ref.: *RAA Upper Eyre Peninsula and Far West Coast – Far West Coast Map* J3.

Dog Fence Beach camping area

This is 37 km south-west of Nundroo and 28 km south-east of Yalata. Reached off Eyre Hwy. Contact ranger for access details. Permit required. Bring water and firewood. Gas/fuel stove preferred. Additional map ref.: *RAA Upper Eyre Peninsula and Far West Coast – Far West Coast Map* J2.

Further information & bookings: NPWSA, Ceduna **Tel.:** (08) 8625 3144 **Email:** Dawes.Rhiannon@saugov. sa.gov.au **Camping fees:** From $6.00 per vehicle/night; fees payable to and permits from NPWSA **Fire restrictions:** Solid-fuel fire ban 1 Nov.–30 April

27. WITTELBEE CONSERVATION PARK

This small park 10 km south-east of Ceduna has fine sandy beaches. Access is via the unsealed Decres Bay Rd, which is suitable for conventional vehicles and caravans.

Bush camping

Signposted from Decres Bay Rd. Small area. Camp in designated sites only. Permit required. Bring water and firewood. Gas/fuel stove preferred. Additional map ref.: *RAA Upper Eyre Peninsula and Far West Coast* A2.

Further information & bookings: NPWSA, Ceduna **Tel.:** (08) 8625 3144 **Email:** Dawes.Rhiannon@saugov. sa.gov.au **Camping fees:** From $6.00 per vehicle/night; fees payable to and permits from NPWSA **Fire restrictions:** Solid-fuel fire ban 1 Nov.–30 April

28. WHYALLA AREA

Whyalla, the largest provincial city in South Australia, lies on the western shores of upper Spencer Gulf. The region around Whyalla has much to offer visitors in the way of scenery, tours, museums, wildlife sanctuaries, parks and beaches.

Fitzgerald Bay camping area

Situated 32 km north-east of Whyalla and signposted from Point Lowly Rd, 10 km north of Whyalla off Lincoln Hwy. Boat ramp nearby at Point Lowly. Popular area for snorkelling and diving. Bring water and firewood. Gas/fuel stove preferred. Additional map ref.: *RAA Upper Eyre Peninsula and Far West Coast* Y6.

Further information & bookings: Whyalla Visitor Centre **Tel.:** (08) 8645 7900 **Email:** tourist.centre@whyalla.sa.gov.au **Website:** www.whyalla.sa.gov.au **Fire restrictions:** Solid-fuel fire ban 1 Nov.–30 April

29. YALATA

Yalata is 200 km west of Ceduna on the Eyre Hwy. South of the Yalata Roadhouse are a number of excellent fishing and whale-watching spots. Permits for these activities are available from the roadhouse, which is operated by the Yalata Aboriginal community. Please note that Yalata lands are dry areas – no alcohol allowed.

Yalata Roadhouse Caravan Park

Bring firewood (it is also available for purchase here). Gas/fuel stove preferred. Additional map ref.: *RAA Upper Eyre Peninsula and Far West Coast – Far West Coast Map* H1.

Further information & bookings: Yalata Roadhouse **Tel.:** (08) 8625 6986 **Camping fees:** From $5.00 per site/night; fees payable at roadhouse (fees are donated to the RFDS) **Fire restrictions:** Solid-fuel fire ban 1 Nov.–30 April

THIS ENORMOUS AREA OF SOUTH AUSTRALIA STRETCHES FROM THE WESTERN AUSTRALIAN BORDER TO NEW SOUTH WALES, AND FROM THE NORTHERN TERRITORY BORDER SOUTH TO PORT AUGUSTA. INCLUDED IN THESE BOUNDARIES ARE THE SPECTACULAR LAKES EYRE, TORRENS AND FROME, COOPER CREEK, THE SIMPSON, STRZELECKI AND STURT STONY DESERTS, AND THE FLINDERS AND GAMMON RANGES.

The extremely popular touring trails of the Oodnadatta and Birdsville tracks are also in this region. Along both of these are a number of campsites; in the case of the Oodnadatta Track there are some commercial camping areas while the Birdsville Track has bush camping. The bush campsites along the Birdsville Track are on private property.

On the New South Wales border is the large Innamincka Regional Reserve, protecting Cooper Creek and the Coongie Lakes. The creek has a number of permanent waterholes but it flows only after periods of heavy rain in Queensland's central-west. This area is well marked in Australia's history as the ill fated Burke and Wills expedition camped beside Cooper Creek. Today's travellers can still camp alongside Cooper Creek and at Coongie Lakes, and camping is also possible in Innamincka, at the Town Common.

Visitors to Flinders Ranges National Park will find rugged mountain scenery, Aboriginal art sites, spectacular gorges, historical homesteads, abundant wildlife and in early spring, beautiful wildflowers. The park has strong Aboriginal ties, and the names of many sights are taken from the local Aboriginal language. Places to explore include Wilpena Pound, Bunyeroo Valley, Brachina Gorge, Sacred Canyon, Wilkawillana Gorge and Aroona Valley, just to name a few. The park's lookouts, walking trails and scenic drives take in many of these beautiful spots. Caravan and tent camping is possible at Wilpena Pound Campground, which has good facilities,

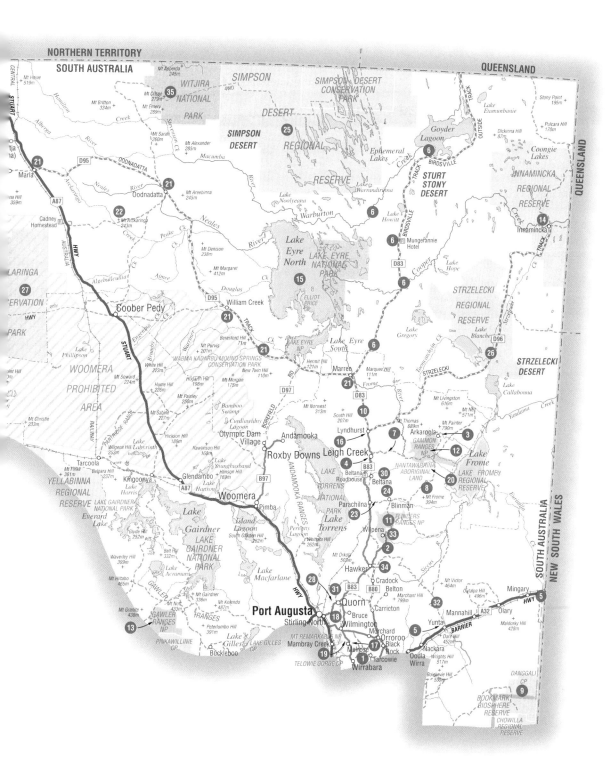

while seven other campsites are located throughout the park.

Gammon Ranges National Park has Aboriginal Dreamtime significance. Its deep gorges and rugged ranges are home to a variety of plant and animal life. The centre of the park is accessible mainly by foot, but there are a couple of four-wheel drive tracks. Camping areas here include Italowie Gorge, which is accessible to caravans.

BEST CAMPSITES

Coward Springs Campground
Oodnadatta Track

Cullyamurra Waterhole camping area
Innamincka Regional Reserve

Mambray Creek Campground
Mount Remarkable National Park

Wilpena Pound Campground
Flinders Ranges National Park

Italowie Gorge camping area
Gammon Ranges National Park

BEST TIME TO VISIT

The cooler months of the year, from April through to October.

NPWSA DESERT PARKS PASS

The pass covers one car, costs $85.00, and is valid for 12 months. It entitles you to unlimited access to the parks listed below. With the pass you will receive a handbook, park maps and wildlife information.

Parks covered by the pass are:
• Strzelecki Regional Reserve
• Innamincka Regional Reserve
• Simpson Desert Conservation Park
• Simpson Desert Regional Reserve
• Witjira National Park
• Lake Eyre National Park

You may not enter these parks without a Desert Parks Pass. The pass can be bought at NPWSA offices. For more information ring the Desert Parks Hotline on 1800 816 078.

1. APPILA SPRINGS

This permanent waterhole is north of the small farming and grazing settlement of Appila, which is about 100 km south-east of Port Augusta. Here you will find pleasant, secluded grassy areas to camp. Please note that there is no camping here during the fire ban season, which runs 1 Nov.–30 April.

Appila Springs picnic and camping area

Situated 8 km north of Appila. Signposted off Appila–Tarcowie Rd. Bring water and firewood. Gas/fuel stove preferred. Additional map ref.: *RAA Mid North* F4.

Further information & bookings: Northern Areas Council **Tel.:** (08) 8664 1139 **Email:** nacouncil@ozemail.com.au

2. ARKAPENA

This bush camping area is on a working sheep property, north-east of Hawker and south of Flinders Ranges National Park. Please note that the camping area is closed Nov.–April, during period of solid-fuel fire ban.

Bush camping

Access via Martins Well Rd, 35 km north of Hawker. Signposted 2.2 km along Martins Well Rd. Self-registration and payment box at campsite. Gas/fuel stove preferred. Additional map ref.: *RAA Flinders Ranges – Flinders Ranges National Park Map* B7.

Further information & bookings: Information brochure available at signposted letterbox at entrance **Camping fees:** From $12.00 per vehicle/night; fees are payable at self-registration box at campsite

3. ARKAROOLA–MOUNT PAINTER WILDLIFE SANCTUARY

Rugged mountains, magnificent gorges and waterholes are some of the features of this 610-sq.-km wilderness sanctuary. Activities include bushwalking and 4WD touring. Drivers of conventional vehicles and caravans should check road conditions prior to travelling.

Arkaroola Campground

This is 30 km north of Balcanoona which is in Gammon Ranges National Park. Access is via the Arkaroola–Balcanoona Rd, subject to road conditions. Bush campsites along Wywhyana Creek. Bring water and firewood. Gas/fuel stove preferred. Additional map ref.: *RAA Flinders Ranges – Gammon Ranges National Park & Arkaroola–Mount Painter Sanctuary Map* F4.

Further information & bookings: Arkaroola Village **Tel.:** 1800 676 042 or (08) 8648 4848 **Email:** res@arkaroola.on.net **Website:** www.arkaroola.on.net **Camping fees:** From $11.00 per unpowered site/night **Fire restrictions:** Solid-fuel fire ban 1 Nov.–30 April

4. AROONA SANCTUARY

Aroona Dam was built in 1955 to supply water to the township of Leigh Creek, and the area surrounding Aroona Dam was declared a sanctuary in 1996. The sanctuary is south-west of Leigh Creek.

Aroona Dam camping area

On Aroona Dam Rd. Signposted off Leigh Creek–Hawker Rd, 9 km south of Leigh Creek. Bring water and firewood. Gas/fuel stove preferred. Additional map ref.: *RAA Flinders Ranges* E5.

Further information & bookings:
Leigh Creek Visitor Information Centre **Tel.:** (08) 8675 2723 *or* Flinders Power **Tel.:** (08) 8675 4272
Camping fees: From $10.00 per vehicle/night; payable to caretaker **Fire restrictions:** Solid-fuel fire ban 1 Nov.–30 April

5. BARRIER HIGHWAY

The Barrier Hwy runs from Adelaide north-east to the New South Wales border and beyond. From Yunta an unsealed road heads north to the northern Flinders Ranges. There is a solid-fuel fire ban in the camping areas 1 Nov.–30 April.

Cockburn Caravan and Camping Area

Signposted off the Barrier Hwy in Cockburn, 50 km west of Broken Hill and 148 km north-east of Yunta. Bring firewood. Additional map ref.: *RAA Outback* N11.

Further information & bookings: Cockburn Progress Association **Tel.:** (08) 8091 1999 **Email:** cockburntelecentre@hotmail.com **Camping fees:** From $5.00 per unpowered site/night for 2 people

Yunta Recreational Ground

Located in Yunta on the Barrier Hwy, 85 km north-east of Peterborough. Bring water. Gas/fuel stove only. Additional map ref.: *RAA Flinders Ranges* J14.

Further information & bookings: Yunta Police **Tel.:** (08) 8650 5004

6. BIRDSVILLE TRACK

From Marree to Birdsville, this 520-km track was once a hazardous stock route used by drovers moving cattle from Queensland to the railhead at Marree. Nowadays the Birdsville Track is one of Australia's most famous roads. The track is maintained and during dry weather it is suitable for conventional vehicles and caravans, however it is always best to check on road conditions before attempting. The designated camping areas along the track are on private property. Please respect the landowners' property and take all rubbish with you. Do not cut down any vegetation, dead or live, and stay on the main road.

Clayton Station camping area

Signposted along the Birdsville Track 44 km north of Marree and 466 km south of Birdsville. Bring water and firewood. Gas/fuel stove preferred. Donation to be left in honesty box. Additional map ref.: *RAA Outback* K6.

Cooper Creek camping area

Signposted along Birdsville Track 137 km north of Marree and 383 km south of Birdsville. Bring water and firewood. Gas/fuel stove preferred. Donation to be left in honesty box. Additional map ref.: *RAA Outback* L5.

Kalamurina Homestead camping area

This is 60 km north-west of Mungerannie and is reached by the Kalamurina Access Rd off the Birdsville Track just north of Mungerannie. Campsites beside the Warburton Creek. Call into homestead first for directions to campsites. Bring water and firewood. Gas/fuel stove preferred. Additional map ref.: *RAA Outback* K4.

Further information & bookings: Kalamurina Homestead **Tel.:** (08) 8675 8310 **Camping fees:** From $25.00 per vehicle/night

Mungerannie Hotel camping area

Signposted on Birdsville Track 205 km north of Marree and 315 km south of Birdsville. Situated beside the Derwent River. Bring water and firewood. Gas/fuel stove preferred. Additional map ref.: *RAA Outback* L4.

Further information & bookings: Mungerannie Hotel **Tel.:** (08) 8675 8317 **Camping fees:** From $5.50 per adult/night

Tippipila Creek camping area

Signposted along Birdsville Track 336 km north of Marree and 178 km south of Birdsville. Camping only on Birdsville side of creek. Bring water and firewood. Gas/fuel stove preferred. Additional map ref.: *RAA Outback* L3.

Road conditions: Transport SA Road Conditions Hotline **Tel.:** 1300 361 033 **Fire restrictions:** Solid-fuel fire ban 1 Nov.–30 April

7. BOOLYEROO GOLDFIELDS

This fossicking area is on private property east of Leigh Creek. Those who wish to camp and visit the goldfields must contact the station owners before visiting.

Boolyeroo Goldfields camping area

For detailed access and information visitors must contact owners via phone or mail, or drop into Patsy Springs Homestead on Copley–Balcanoona Rd, 29 km east of Leigh Creek. Bring water and firewood. Gas/fuel stove preferred. Dogs welcome but must be on lead as poison is laid on the property. Additional map ref.: *RAA Flinders Ranges* F5.

Further information & bookings: John and Jeff Mengersen **Tel.:** (08) 8675 2553 (7 pm–9 pm only) **Post:** 'Patsy Springs', via Copley, SA 5732 **Fire restrictions:** Solid-fuel fire ban 1 Nov.–30 April

8. CHAMBERS GORGE

This gorge is on private property off the Blinman–Arkaroola Rd. Campers need to be fully self-sufficient as there are no facilities. Please respect the landowner's property, stay on public main roads, don't cut down any dead or live vegetation, and take all rubbish with you.

Bush camping

Signposted along Blinman–Arkaroola Rd, 63 km north-east of Blinman and 92 km south of Arkaroola. Camp in designated areas only. Conventional vehicles can access with care. Bring water and firewood. Gas/fuel stove preferred. Additional map ref.: *RAA Flinders Ranges* H7.

Fire restrictions: Solid-fuel fire ban 1 Nov.–30 April

9. DANGGALI CONSERVATION PARK

This vast wilderness park on the New South Wales border 90 km north of Renmark is mainly dominated by mallee scrubland. It covers an area of more than 253 000 ha and is the combination of four old sheep stations: Canopus, Hypurna, Morgan Vale and Postmark. There are many campsites within the park for those who enjoy remote camping and privacy, and the Shearers Hut is also available for hire. The park can be closed after heavy rain or flood; contact NPWSA for details.

Black Oak Country, Little Rock, Mallee Country, Marys and Olympic Dam camping areas

Signposted from Renmark–Wentworth Rd then signposted all the way to park entrance. Permit required. Bring water. Firewood supplied. Gas/fuel stove preferred. Additional map ref.: *RAA South Australia State Road Map – 7th edition* W17.

Further information & bookings: NPWSA, Danggali **Tel.:** (08) 8595 8010 **Camping fees:** From $6.00 per vehicle/night; fees payable to and permits from NPWSA *Shearers Hut:* From $46.00 per night for up to 10 people; extra persons at additional cost **Fire restrictions:** Solid-fuel fire ban 1 Nov.–30 April

10. FARINA

Farina is a ghost town on the Lyndhurst–Marree Rd. Enjoy the easy-grade walking trail from the campground or join a guided tour of Farina and its ruins.

Farina Campground

Signposted off Lyndhurst–Marree Rd, 25 km north of Lyndhurst and 53 km south of Marree. Bring water. Gas/fuel stove preferred. Tours available. Additional map ref.: *RAA Flinders Ranges* D3.

Further information & bookings: Kevin and Anne Dawes **Tel.:** (08) 8675 7790 **Camping fees:** From $3.50 per person/night; fees payable at honesty box at campground **Fire restrictions:** Solid-fuel fire ban 1 Nov.–30 April

11. FLINDERS RANGES NATIONAL PARK
see page 174

12. GAMMON RANGES NATIONAL PARK

The park headquarters at Balcanoona is 99 km east of Leigh Creek along the Copley–Balcanoona Rd. The park has significant Aboriginal Dreamtime association and the rugged ranges and deep gorges within the park are home to a variety of wildlife and flora. Experienced bushwalkers can explore the gorges and valleys via a number of walking trails. Drivers of conventional vehicles and those towing caravans must check road conditions first. Temporary park closures occur throughout the year; contact park headquarters for further information. In addition to camping, Grindells Hut, Nudlamutana Hut and Balcanoona Shearers Quarters are available for hire; contact park headquarters or NPWSA Hawker for details and fees. Wood collection within the park is prohibited.

Arcoona Creek camping area

Signposted 23 km along Mt Serle–Yankaninna Access Rd, which is off Copley–Balcanoona Rd, 45 km east of Leigh Creek. Access through private property – please leave gates as found. Camping permit required from self-registration station. Bring water and firewood. Gas/fuel stove preferred.

Additional map ref.: *RAA Flinders Ranges – Gammon Ranges National Park & Arkaroola–Mount Painter Sanctuary Map – B5.*

Grindells Hut camping area

On Loop Rd, 26 km north-west of park headquarters. Sections of Loop Rd are one-way. Please check road access and conditions with park ranger. Camping permit required from self-registration station on Loop Rd. Bring water and firewood. Gas/fuel stove preferred. Additional map ref.: *RAA Flinders Ranges – Gammon Ranges National Park & Arkaroola–Mount Painter Sanctuary Map* E6.

Italowie Gorge camping area

Signposted along the Copley–Balcanoona Rd, 82 km east of Leigh Creek and 17 km west of park headquarters. Camping permit required from self-registration station. Limited caravan access. Bring water and firewood. Gas/fuel stove preferred. Additional map ref.: *RAA Flinders Ranges – Gammon Ranges National Park & Arkaroola–Mount Painter Sanctuary Map* D7.

Loch Ness Well camping area

This is 31 km north-west of park headquarters, on Loop Rd. Sections of Loop Rd are one-way. Please check road access and conditions with ranger. Camping permit required from self-registration station on Loop Rd. Bring water and firewood. Gas/fuel stove preferred. Additional map ref.: *RAA Flinders Ranges – Gammon Ranges National Park & Arkaroola–Mount Painter Sanctuary Map* D5.

Weetootla Gorge camping area

Signposted along Weetootla Trail, 7 km north-west of park headquarters. Camping permit required from self-registration station. Bring water and firewood. Gas/fuel stove preferred. Additional map ref.: *RAA Flinders Ranges – Gammon Ranges National Park & Arkaroola–Mount Painter Sanctuary Map* E6.

Further information & bookings:
NPWSA, Balcanoona **Tel.:** (08) 8648 4829 *or* NPWSA, Hawker **Tel.:** (08) 8648 4244
Camping fees: Non vehicle-based campers from $3.50 per person/night, vehicle-based campers from $6.00 per vehicle/night; fees payable to and permits from NPWSA Balcanoona or at self-registration stations within park **Fire restrictions:** Solid-fuel fire ban 1 Nov.–30 April

13. GAWLER RANGES NATIONAL PARK

This 120 000-ha park is north of the Eyre Hwy and is accessible from Iron Knob, Kimba, Wudinna and Minnipa. The park is rich in Aboriginal and European history, and there are many historic sites to visit. Travel within the park is not recommended for low-clearance vehicles. All roads in the park are dry-weather access only.

Chillunie camping area

This is 51 km north of Wudinna and 110 km north-west of Kimba. Signposted from LP Track. 4WD access only. Permit required. Bring water and firewood. Gas/fuel stove preferred. Additional map ref.: *RAA Upper Eyre Peninsula and Far West Coast – Gawler Ranges National Park Map* C9.

Mattera camping area

Situated 81 km north-west of Wudinna. Signposted from Mattera Track. 4WD recommended. Permit required. Bring water and firewood. Gas/fuel stove preferred. Additional map ref.: *RAA Upper Eyre Peninsula and Far West Coast – Gawler Ranges National Park Map* B9.

Old Paney camping area

Located 75 km north-west of Wudinna and 45 km north-east of Minnipa. Signposted from Old Paney Scenic Route. Permit required. Bring water and firewood. Gas/fuel stove preferred. Additional map ref.: *RAA Upper Eyre Peninsula and Far West Coast – Gawler Ranges National Park Map* A9.

Waganny camping area

Situated 63 km north-west of Wudinna. Signposted from Old Paney Scenic Route. Permit required. Bring water and firewood. Gas/fuel stove preferred. Additional map ref.: *RAA Upper Eyre Peninsula and Far West Coast – Gawler Ranges National Park Map* B11.

Further information & bookings: NPWSA, Port Augusta **Tel.:** (08) 8648 5300 **Camping fees:** From $6.00 per vehicle per night, plus park entrance fee of $7.00; fees payable to and permits from NPWSA or local businesses in Kimba, Wudinna and Minnipa **Fire restrictions:** Solid-fuel fire ban 1 Nov.–30 April

14. INNAMINCKA REGIONAL RESERVE

Innamincka Regional Reserve was proclaimed in 1988 to protect the area's wetlands. It is a large and remote area on the Queensland border and is reached via the Strzelecki Track from Lyndhurst. The area is rich in history with sites such as the graves of Burke and Wills. Activities include swimming, fishing and canoeing. All roads within the reserve are rated 4WD, however conventional vehicles and caravans can access the reserve depending on road conditions. Collection of firewood is not allowed within the campgrounds – please bring your own firewood. Dogs are allowed in some areas of the reserve but must be on lead and with owner at all times. A Desert Parks Pass is required to enter this park (see page 170).

Burkes Memorial camping area

Signposted off Innamincka–Nappamerrie Rd, 7 km east of Innamincka. Permit required. Bring water and firewood. Gas/fuel stove preferred. Additional map ref.: *RAA Outback – Innamincka Region Map.*

Coongie Lakes camping area

On the Coongie Track 106 km north-west of Innamincka. Permit required. 4WD access only. Bring water. Gas/fuel stove only. Located in the Coongie Conservation Zone; no fires, pets, fishing, generators or powerboats allowed. Additional map ref.: *RAA Outback* N3.

Cullyamurra Waterhole camping area

This is 14 km east of Innamincka and is signposted from Innamincka–Nappamerrie Rd, 7 km east of Innamincka.

Permit required. Bring water and firewood. Gas/fuel stove preferred. Powerboats with motors up to 10 h.p. are permitted, speed to be under 10 knots. Additional map ref.: *RAA Outback – Innamincka Region Map.*

Innamincka Town Common camping area

In the township of Innamincka. Bring water and firewood. Gas/fuel stove preferred. Additional map ref.: *RAA Outback – Innamincka Region Map.*

Kings Marker camping area

Signposted along Fifteen Mile Track, 5 km south-west of Innamincka. Permit required. Bring water and firewood. Gas/fuel stove preferred. Powerboats with motors up to 10 h.p. are permitted, speed to be under 10 knots. Additional map ref.: *RAA Outback – Innamincka Region Map.*

Kudriemitchie camping area

On Coongie Track 85 km north-west of Innamincka. Permit required. 4WD access only. Bring water and firewood. Gas/fuel stove preferred. Additional map ref.: *RAA Outback* N4.

Minkie Waterhole camping area

Signposted along Fifteen Mile Track, 9 km south-west of Innamincka. Permit required. Bring water and firewood. Gas/fuel stove preferred. Additional map ref.: *RAA Outback – Innamincka Region Map.*

Policemans Waterhole camping area

Signposted along Fifteen Mile Track, 2 km south-west of Innamincka. Permit required. Bring water and firewood. Gas/fuel stove preferred. Powerboats with motors up to 10 h.p. are permitted, speed to be under 10 knots. Additional map ref.: *RAA Outback – Innamincka Region Map.*

Scrubby Camp camping area

On Coongie Track 45 km north-west of Innamincka. Permit required. 4WD access only. Bring water and firewood. Gas/fuel stove preferred. Additional map ref.: *RAA Outback* N4.

Ski Beach camping area

Signposted along Fifteen Mile Track, 4 km south-west of Innamincka. Permit required. Bring water and firewood. Gas/fuel stove preferred. Powerboats with motors up to 10 h.p. are permitted, speed to be under 10 knots. Additional map ref.: *RAA Outback – Innamincka Region Map.*

Wills Memorial camping area

Signposted along Fifteen Mile Track, 13 km south-west of Innamincka. Permit required. Bring water and firewood. Gas/fuel stove preferred. Additional map ref.: *RAA Outback – Innamincka Region Map.*

FLINDERS RANGES NATIONAL PARK

Wildflowers of the ranges
If the rainfall is adequate during winter, spring will produce spectacular displays of wildflowers throughout the region, which includes the easily accessed Wilpena Pound area. Favourites include Sturt's nightshade, silver tails, yellow buttons and the vivid Sturt's desert pea.

Desert dish
The dish-shaped crater named Wilpena Pound – 'Wilpena' meaning cupped hand in the language of the Adnyamathanha people – is the scenic centrepiece of the Flinders Ranges. A network of well-marked walking trails leads to various points around its ragged rim, and for those after great views with the least effort, a shuttle bus from Wilpena leads to an easy 30-minute walk to the ridge.

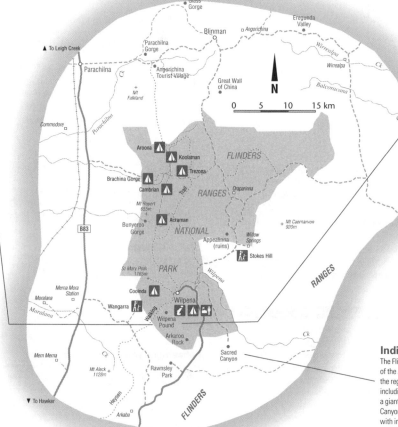

Indigenous heritage
The Flinders Ranges are the traditional home of the Adnyamathanha people. Throughout the region are a number of significant sites, including art sites at Arkaroo Rock, named for a giant Dreamtime serpent, and Sacred Canyon, where the rock walls are engraved with images of animal tracks, human figures and waterholes.

Flinders Ranges National Park, with a rich Aboriginal and European history, offers visitors magnificent scenery, rugged mountains, peaceful gorges and abundant wildlife and flora. The park is popular with artists, bushwalkers, photographers and nature lovers. Enjoy one of the numerous walking trails of varying grades and visit picturesque valleys, peaceful waterholes or Aboriginal rock engravings. Alternatively, view the ranges from above on a scenic flight. Note that wood collection within the park is prohibited.

Acraman Campground

Close to Bunyeroo carpark and walks. Signposted from Bunyeroo Gorge Rd, 32 km north-west of Park Headquarters. Permit from self-registration station. Bring water and firewood. Gas/fuel stove preferred. Additional map ref.: RAA *Flinders Ranges – Flinders Ranges National Park Map* A4.

Aroona Campground

Signposted along Aroona Rd, 48 km north of Park Headquarters. Caravan access via Blinman Rd only. Check with Park Headquarters on road conditions. Permit from self-registration station. Bring firewood. Gas/fuel stove preferred. Additional map ref.: *RAA Flinders Ranges – Flinders Ranges National Park Map* B2.

Brachina Gorge Campground

Signposted along Brachina Rd, 48 km north-west of Park Headquarters. Two sites, East Brachina and West Brachina. Permit from self-registration station. Bring water and firewood. Gas/fuel stove preferred. Additional map ref.: *RAA Flinders Ranges – Flinders Ranges National Park Map* A3/B3.

Cambrian Campground

Signposted along Bunyeroo Gorge Rd, 37 km north-west of Park Headquarters. Permit from self-registration station. Bring water and firewood. Gas/fuel stove preferred. Additional map ref.: *RAA Flinders Ranges – Flinders Ranges National Park Map* B3.

Cooinda camping area

In Wilpena Pound. Walk-in site via Loop Walk, 10–12 km from Park Headquarters. Permit required. Bring water. Gas/fuel stove only. Additional map ref.: *RAA Flinders Ranges – Flinders Ranges National Park Map* B6.

Koolaman Campground

Along Aroona Rd, 46 km north of Park Headquarters. Permit from self-registration station. Bring water and firewood. Gas/fuel stove preferred. Additional map ref.: *RAA Flinders Ranges – Flinders Ranges National Park Map* B2.

Trezona Campground

Signposted along Brachina Rd, 44 km north of Park Headquarters. Caravan access via Blinman Rd only.

Check with Park Headquarters on road conditions. Permit from self-registration station. Bring water and firewood. Gas/fuel stove preferred. Additional map ref.: *RAA Flinders Ranges – Flinders Ranges National Park Map* B3.

Wilpena Pound Campground

Signposted off Wilpena Rd, 52 km north of Hawker. Permit required. Park entrance fee applies. Bring firewood. Gas/fuel stove preferred. Powered sites, bookings recommended April–Oct. Additional map ref.: *RAA Flinders Ranges – Flinders Ranges National Park Map* B5.

Further information & bookings: Wilpena Pound Visitors Centre **Tel.:** (08) 8648 0048 **Email:** wilpena@adelaide.net.au **Web:** www.wilpenapound.on.net **Camping fees:** *Cooinda*: From $3.50 per person/night *Wilpena Pound*: From $16.00 per night for 2 people; park entry fee of $6.00 applies to first night *All other areas*: From $6.00 per vehicle/night; fees payable to and permits from Park Headquarters at Wilpena Pound Visitors Centre or at self-registration stations **Fire restrictions:** Solid-fuel fire ban 1 Nov.–30 April

The famous Cazneaux Tree, with Wilpena Pound in the background

Further information & bookings: NPWSA, Innamincka **Tel.:** (08) 8675 9909 **Camping fees:** *Innamincka Town Common:* From $5.00 per vehicle/night *All other areas:* Covered under NPWSA Desert Parks Pass; fees payable to and permits from NPWSA **Fire restrictions:** Solid-fuel fire ban 1 Nov.–30 April

15. LAKE EYRE NATIONAL PARK

Lake Eyre National Park covers a total area of 1228 million hectares. Lake Eyre is the world's largest salt lake and is Australia's lowest point, at 16 m below sea level. The lake and its foreshore are home to numerous waterbird species and reptiles such as the Lake Eyre dragon. 4WD vehicle access to the park is via the signposted road south of William Creek on the Oodnadatta Track and via the road north out of Marree. Conventional vehicles can use the road from Marree to as far as the camping area at Muloorina Station. A Desert Parks Pass is required to enter this park (see page 170). At both campsites campfires must be kept small and in a hole; leave no trace of fire and ensure it is out before covering with earth. Gas/fuel stove preferred.

Halligan Point camping area

This is 71 km east of William Creek. Signposted 4WD-only access off the Oodnadatta Track just south of William Creek. Permit required. Sites are on western foreshore of Halligan Bay. Bring water and firewood. Gas/fuel stove preferred. Please note that the journey from ABC Bay to Halligan Point requires 10 km of soft-sand driving. Additional map ref.: *RAA Outback J5.*

Muloorina Homestead camping area

On Muloorina Station access road 51 km north of Marree. Signposted from Marree. Bring water and firewood. Gas/fuel stove preferred. Additional map ref.: *RAA Outback K6.*

Further information & bookings: NPWSA, Port Augusta **Tel.:** 1800 816 078 **Camping fees:** *Halligan Point:* Covered under NPWSA Desert Parks Pass *Muloorina Homestead:* Donation to be left in honesty box at site; all donations go to the RFDS
Fire restrictions: Solid-fuel fire ban 1 Nov.–30 April

16. LYNDHURST

Lyndhurst, 33 km north of Leigh Creek, is at the start of the Strzelecki Track. Visit the spectacular ochre cliffs nearby. Camping is available at the Elsewhere Hotel.

Elsewhere Hotel camping area

Camping area beside hotel. Gas/fuel stove preferred. Additional map ref.: *RAA Outback K8.*

Further information & bookings: Elsewhere Hotel **Tel.:** (08) 8675 7781 **Camping fees:** From $10.00 per site/night for powered sites **Fire restrictions:** Solid-fuel fire ban 1 Nov.–30 April

17. MELROSE AREA

Melrose was first settled in 1853 when a nearby coppermine opened; it is the oldest settlement in the Flinders Ranges. is located at the foot of Mt Remarkable, about 80 km south-east of Port Augusta.

The Showgrounds camping area

This area is beside a creek amongst shady gum trees. It is signposted from Wilmington–Melrose Rd 2 km north of Melrose. Key access to shower – for key contact ranger. Power available. Bring own firewood. Additional map ref.: *RAA Mid North D3.*

Further information & bookings: Mt Remarkable–Melrose Show Society Trust **Tel.:** (08) 8666 2158 **Camping fees:** From $2.00 per adult/night, $1.00 per child/night; power additional and fees payable to ranger/caretaker **Fire restrictions:** Solid-fuel fire ban 15 Nov.–30 April

18. MOUNT BROWN CONSERVATION PARK

Mt Brown Conservation Park is 14 km south of Quorn. The challenging self-guide Mt Brown Bush Walk passes through varying landscapes and vegetation to the summit of Mt Brown; the Heysen Trail also traverses the park. Self-sufficient bush camping is available. Camping is prohibited during the fire ban period, 1 Nov.–30 April.

Bush camping

Access via Richman Valley Rd. Walk-in sites only. Permit required. Bring water. Gas/fuel stove only. Additional map ref.: *RAA Flinders Ranges C13.*

Further information & bookings: NPWSA, Mt Remarkable National Park **Tel.:** (08) 8634 7068 **Camping fees:** From $3.50 per person/night; fees payable to and permits from NPWSA

19. MOUNT REMARKABLE NATIONAL PARK

Mt Remarkable National Park is 55 km south-east of Port Augusta. The park's dramatic scenery and diverse flora and fauna are the main attractions for visitors. There are numerous walking trails of varying grades and lengths within the park. In the solid-fuel fire ban season, 1 Nov.–30 April, camping is prohibited at the park's walk-in sites; there are day walks only during this period.

Eaglehawk Dam and Longhill Camp bush campsites

Walk-in sites on Ring Route Trail; Eaglehawk Dam is 4 km west of Alligator Gorge carpark, Longhill Camp is 1 km south-west of carpark. Permit required from self-registration station. Bring water. Gas/fuel stove only. Additional map ref.: *RAA Mid North C2.*

Fricks Dam bush campsite

Walk-in site on Fricks Trail 10 km north of Mambray Creek. Permit required from self-registration station. Bring water. Gas/fuel stove only. Additional map ref.: *RAA Mid North C2.*

Hidden Camp and Kingfisher Flat bush campsites

Walk-in sites on Alligator Gorge–Mambray Creek Trail; Hidden Camp is 8 km north of Mambray Creek, Kingfisher Flat is 4 km south of Alligator Gorge carpark. Toilets at Kingfisher Flat. Permit required from self-registration station. Bring water. Gas/fuel stove only. Additional map ref.: *RAA Mid North C2.*

Mambray Creek Campground

Signposted off Princes Hwy, 45 km north of Port Pirie. Permit required from self-registration station. Bring firewood. Gas/fuel stove preferred. Additional map ref.: *RAA Mid North* C3.

Stony Creek Camp bush campsite

Walk-in site on Stony Creek Track, 8 km north of Alligator Gorge carpark. Permit required from self-registration station. Bring water. Gas/fuel stove only. Additional map ref.: *RAA Mid North* C2.

Sugar Gum Dam bush campsite

Walk-in site on Mambray Creek Track, 11 km east of Mambray Creek. Permit required from self-registration station. Bring water. Gas/fuel stove only. Additional map ref.: *RAA Mid North* C2.

Summit Camp bush campsite

Walk-in site on Mt Remarkable Range Track/Heysen Trail, 6 km north-west of Melrose. Permit required from self-registration station. Bring water. Gas/fuel stove only. Additional map ref.: *RAA Mid North* D3.

Further information & bookings: NPWSA, Mambray Creek **Tel.:** (08) 8634 7068 **Camping fees:** *Mambray Creek:* From $15.00 per vehicle/night *Bush campsites:* From $3.50 per person/night. Fees payable to and permits from self-registration stations at Mambray Creek Campground, Alligator Gorge carpark and NPWSA Mambray Creek office **Fire restrictions:** Solid-fuel fire ban 1 Nov.–30 April

20. NANTAWARRINA ABORIGINAL LAND

On the eastern boundary of the Nantawarrina Aboriginal Land, south of Gammon Ranges National Park, is Moro – or Big Moro – Gorge. Bush camping is allowed within the gorge on a permit basis. Contact the Nepabunna Aboriginal Community Centre on the Copley–Balcanoona Rd 58 km east of Leigh Creek for permits and road conditions.

Bush camping

Access via Balcanoona–Wertaloona Rd, 14 km south of Balcanoona opposite Wertaloona access track. Access depends on road conditions. Permit required. Bring water and firewood. Gas/fuel stove preferred. Additional map ref.: *RAA Flinders Ranges – Gammon Ranges National Park & Arkaroola–Mount Painter Sanctuary Map* E8.

Further information & bookings: Nepabunna Aboriginal Community Centre **Tel.:** (08) 8648 3764 **Camping fees:** Contact the community centre for details of permits and current fee structure **Fire restrictions:** Solid-fuel fire ban 1 Nov.–30 April

21. OODNADATTA TRACK

Following the route of the historic Ghan Railway, the Oodnadatta Track stretches north-west from Marree to Oodnadatta, then turns west to finish at Marla on the Stuart Hwy. Conventional vehicles and caravans can travel this route with care. Check road conditions prior to travelling. Along the track are a number of designated camping areas.

MARREE

Marree Caravan and Campers Park

Just south of Marree. Bring water. Additional map ref.: *RAA Outback* K7.

Further information & bookings: Marree Caravan and Campers Park **Tel.:** (08) 8675 8371 **Camping fees:** From $6.00 per person/night.

Marree Oasis Town Centre Caravan Park

In Marree township. Bring water. Additional map ref.: *RAA Outback* K7.

Further information & bookings: Marree Oasis Town Centre Caravan Park **Tel.:** (08) 8675 8352 **Camping fees:** From $5.50 per adult/night.

COWARD SPRINGS

Coward Springs Campground

Signposted along Oodnadatta Track, 128 km west of Marree. Site of old railway siding. Natural spa. Bring water. Gas/fuel stove preferred. Additional map ref.: *RAA Outback* H6.

Further information & bookings: Coward Springs Campground **Tel.:** (08) 8675 8336 **Camping fees:** From $15.00 per vehicle/night

WILLIAM CREEK

William Creek Campground

In William Creek. Bring water. Additional map ref.: *RAA Outback* H6.

Further information & bookings: William Creek Campground **Tel.:** (08) 8670 7746 **Camping fees:** From $8.00 per vehicle and driver per night, $5.00 per extra person per night

William Creek Hotel camping area

In William Creek. Camping area behind hotel. Bring firewood. Additional map ref.: *RAA Outback* H6.

Further information & bookings: William Creek Hotel **Tel.:** (08) 8670 7880 **Camping fees:** From $3.50 per person/night

OODNADATTA

Oodnadatta Caravan Park

In Oodnadatta. Bring water and firewood. Additional map ref.: *RAA Outback* G4.

Further information & bookings: Oodnadatta Caravan Park **Tel.:** (08) 8670 7822 **Camping fees:** From $9.50 per vehicle and driver per night, $5.00 per extra person per night

MARLA

Marla Travellers Rest

In Marla, which is at the junction of the Oodnadatta Track and the Stuart Hwy. Additional map ref.: *RAA Outback* D3.

Further information & bookings: Marla Travellers Rest **Tel.:** (08) 8670 7001 **Email:** marla@internode.on.net **Camping fees:** From $5.00 per person/night **Fire restrictions:** Solid-fuel fire ban 1 Nov.–30 April (all sites)

22. PAINTED DESERT

The ever-changing colours of the Painted Desert about 80 km south-west of Oodnadatta, are one of nature's wonders. Camping is not permitted in the desert itself, however there is a pleasant bush campsite just to the east. Arckaringa Homestead, 15 km west of Goorikianna Creek, also offers accommodation.

Goorikianna Creek bush camping

Bush camping beside Goorikianna Creek, 80 km south-west of Oodnadatta and 7 km east of the Painted Desert. Signposted along Oodnadatta–Cadney Park Rd. Bring water and firewood. Gas/fuel stove preferred. Additional map ref.: *RAA Outback* F4.

Further information & bookings: Pink Roadhouse, Oodnadatta **Tel.:** (08) 8670 7822 **Fire restrictions:** Solid-fuel fire ban 1 Nov.–30 April

23. PARACHILNA GORGE

Parachilna is 89 km north of Hawker and 67 km south of Leigh Creek. The beautiful Parachilna Gorge, to the east of the village, offers some excellent bush campsites. The access road is the Parachilna–Blinman Rd, which has numerous creek crossings that can rise suddenly after rain. Always check road conditions first. Caravan access is possible with care.

Bush camping

Bush camping along Parachilna–Blinman Rd through Parachilna Gorge. Travel 9 km east of Parachilna for start of camping areas; designated areas are signposted. Bring water and firewood. Gas/fuel stove preferred. Additional map ref.: *RAA Flinders Ranges* E7.

Further information & bookings: Leigh Creek Visitor Information Centre **Tel.:** (08) 8675 2723 **Fire restrictions:** Solid-fuel fire ban 1 Nov.–30 April

24. PUBLIC ACCESS ROUTES (PARs)

Public Access Routes (PAR) are routes that cross private property to an area of value or interest and are available for the public to traverse. Camping is permitted within 50 m of a PAR. Rules and conditions apply to travelling and camping alongside PARs (see box following this entry).

Nuccaleena Mine (PAR 3)

The mine is 42 km north-east of Parachilna via PAR 3 off Glass Gorge Rd. Do not camp close to buildings or ruins. Bring water and firewood. Gas/fuel stove preferred. Additional map ref.: *RAA Flinders Ranges* E7.

Artimore Ruins (PAR 4)

The ruins are 28 km north-east of Blinman via PAR 4. Do not camp close to ruins. Bring water and firewood. Gas/fuel stove preferred. Additional map ref.: *RAA Flinders Ranges* F7.

Patawarta Gap (PAR 6)

Situated 42 km north-east of Blinman via PAR 6. Bring water and firewood. Gas/fuel stove preferred. Additional map ref.: *RAA Flinders Ranges* F7.

Further information & bookings: DEHAA Pastoral Board **Tel.:** (08) 8204 8860 **Website:** www.rangelands.sa.gov.au or *PAR 3, PAR 6*: Moolooloo Station **Tel.:** (08) 8648 4861 *PAR 4*: Oratunga Station **Tel.:** (08) 8648 4881 **Fire restrictions:** Solid-fuel fire ban 1 Nov.–30 April

---

PAR RULES AND CONDITIONS

- Traversing PARs is possible without permission, but if you wish to venture off the track permission is required from station owners.
- PARs may be closed from time to time by the station owners or the Pastoral Board for stock management or because of weather conditions.
- Do not drive along a PAR in wet weather or immediately after rain. Delay travel for at least 24 hours after heavy rain.
- Camping is permitted along a PAR within 50 m of the track so long as it is more than 500 m from any constructed stock watering point and more than 1 km from any house or occupied building.
- Leave all gates as found.
- Do not contaminate stock water or waterways with soap and detergents; never bathe in tanks or troughs.
- Never interfere with stock.

---

25. SIMPSON DESERT REGIONAL RESERVE AND CONSERVATION PARK

The Simpson Desert is the world's largest parallel sand dune desert, covering an area of 3 million ha. It straddles the corners of South Australia, Queensland and the Northern Territory. A large variety of desert flora and fauna is conserved within the reserve. Travelling through the desert is for well-equipped and self-sufficient travellers and campers only and 4WD vehicles are essential. A NPWSA Desert Parks Pass (see page 170) is required to enter this desert.

Bush camping

Bush camping throughout the desert. Recommended positions are 100 m from the main track along the swales between dunes. Permit required. Be aware of other vehicles. Bring water and firewood. Gas/fuel stove preferred. Additional map ref.: *RAA Outback* H2/J2/K2.

Further information & bookings: NPWSA, Port Augusta **Tel.:** 1800 816 078 **Camping fees:** Covered under NPWSA Desert Parks Pass **Fire restrictions:** Solid-fuel fire ban 1 Nov.–30 April.

26. STRZELECKI REGIONAL RESERVE

Situated between Innamincka and Lyndhurst, on the Strzelecki Track. The pale sand dune country of the Strzelecki and Cobbler deserts is included in the reserve. Drivers of conventional vehicles and those towing caravans need to check road conditions prior to travel. A Desert Parks Pass is necessary to enter this reserve (see page 170). The collection of firewood is prohibited in the camping area.

Montecollina Bore camping area

On the Strzelecki Track, 221 km north-east of Lyndhurst and 193 km south-west of Innamincka. Access in dry weather only. Bring water and firewood. Gas/fuel stove preferred. Additional map ref.: *RAA Outback* M7.

Further information & bookings: NPWSA, Innamincka **Tel.:** (08) 8675 9909 **Camping fees:** Fees not applicable at time of research but may apply in future **Fire restrictions:** Solid-fuel fire ban 1 Nov.–30 April

27. TALLARINGA CONSERVATION PARK

Tallaringa Conservation Park, 100 km west of Coober Pedy, is bordered by the Great Victoria Desert. Access is by 4WD vehicle only, via the Anne Beadell Hwy through areas of private property. This is a remote area, for self-sufficient and well-equipped travellers only. A NPWSA Desert Parks Pass is required to enter this park (see page 170).

Bush camping

Bush camping only in cleared areas within 50 m of Anne Beadell Hwy. Permit required. Bring water and firewood. Gas/fuel stove preferred. Additional map ref.: *RAA Outback* D6.

Further information & bookings: NPWSA, Port Augusta **Tel.:** 1800 816 078 **Camping fees:** Covered under NPWSA Desert Parks Pass **Fire restrictions:** Solid-fuel fire ban 1 Nov.–30 April

28. THE DUTCHMANS STERN CONSERVATION PARK

This park is 10 km north-west of Quorn, reached via Arden Vale Rd. There are two excellent self-guide walks here, and those who climb The Dutchmans Stern will be rewarded with magnificent views of the surrounding ranges and Spencer Gulf. Bush camping opportunities are available for self-sufficient campers. The Heysen Trail passes through the park. Camping is prohibited during the period of solid-fuel fire ban, 1 Nov.–30 April.

Bush camping

Walk-in sites on the western side of the Dutchman Range. Permit required. Bring water. Gas/fuel stove only. Additional map ref.: *RAA Flinders Ranges* C12.

Further information & bookings: NPWSA, Mt Remarkable National Park **Tel.:** (08) 8634 7068 **Camping fees:** From $3.50 per person/night; fees payable to and permits from NPWSA

29. UNNAMED CONSERVATION PARK

This park, on the Western Australia border, is only accessible by 4WD. Access is from the east via the Anne Beadell Hwy through private property and Aboriginal land or from the Nullarbor in the south via Cook through Aboriginal land (the eastern boundary is 403 km west of Coober Pedy; the southern boundary is 268 km north of Cook). Three permits are required to travel through this park; contact NPWSA Ceduna for details. Travel to the park is for self-sufficient, well-equipped and experienced outback travellers only.

Bush camping

Bush camping only in natural cleared areas within 50 m of Anne Beadell Hwy. Permits required and trip intention form

must be lodged. Bring water and firewood. Gas/fuel stove preferred. Additional map ref.: *RAA Outback* A5.

Further information & bookings: NPWSA, Ceduna **Tel.:** (08) 8625 3144 **Email:** cedunanp@dove.net.au **Camping fees:** From $6.00 per vehicle/night; fees payable to and permits from NPWSA **Fire restrictions:** Solid-fuel fire ban 1 Nov.–30 April

30. WARRAWEENA CONSERVATION PARK

There is much pastoral and mining heritage to be seen throughout this park, which lies to the east of the Hawker–Leigh Creek Rd at Beltana. It is also a popular bird- and wildlife-watching park. Access by conventional vehicle is possible in dry weather only; check road conditions. Once in the park a 4WD vehicle is required to reach remote areas. Bookings apply for camping. There are shearers quarters and huts available for hire.

Sliding Rock camping area

Situated 30 km east of Beltana Roadhouse and 5 km west of Warraweena Homestead. Signposted from Beltana. Bring water and firewood. Bookings apply. Additional map ref.: *RAA Flinders Ranges* E6.

Further information & bookings: Warraweena Homestead **Tel.:** (08) 8675 2770 **Camping fees:** From $10.00 per adult/night **Fire restrictions:** Solid-fuel fire ban 1 Nov.– 30 April

31. WARREN GORGE

This beautiful council reserve, 22 km north of Quorn, is home to the yellow-footed rock wallaby. Within Warren Gorge are a number of walking trails, and the Heysen Trail also passes through here.

Warren Gorge camping area

Access via Arden Vale Rd. Bring water and firewood. Gas/fuel stove preferred. Additional map ref.: *RAA Flinders Ranges* C12.

Further information & bookings: Flinders Ranges Council **Tel.:** (08) 8648 6031 **Email:** council@flindersrangescouncil. sa.gov.au **Website:** www.flindersrangescouncil.sa.gov.au **Fire restrictions:** Solid-fuel fire ban 1 Nov.–15 April

32. WAUKARINGA RUINS

These ruins are north of Yunta, on the unsealed Yunta–Arakaroola Rd off the Barrier Hwy. Camping is possible on the main road in the vicinity of the ruins. Please do not travel off the main road as this is private property.

Waukaringa Ruins camping area

Signposted on Yunta–Arakaroola Rd, 35 km north of Yunta. Bring water and firewood. Additional map ref.: *RAA Flinders Ranges* H12.

Fire restrictions: Solid-fuel fire ban 1 Nov.–15 April

33. WILLOW SPRINGS

This large sheep station north-east of Wilpena Pound offers secluded bush camping. There is also a 70-km self-guide 4WD track on the property.

Bush camping

Signposted off Wilpena–Blinman Rd, 13 km north-east of the Wilpena Pound Resort turn-off. Bookings essential. Additional map ref.: *RAA Flinders Ranges – Flinders Ranges National Park Map* C4.

Further information & bookings: Mr B. Reynolds, Willow Springs Homestead **Tel.:** (08) 8648 0016 (during working hours) **Camping fees:** From $15.00 per vehicle/night **Fire restrictions:** Solid-fuel fire ban 1 Nov.–30 April

34. WILLOW WATERS RUINS

These ruins are on private property 20 km east of Hawker. Campers need to be fully self-sufficient as there are no facilities. Please respect the landowner's property, stay on public main roads, don't cut down any dead or live vegetation and take all rubbish with you. Drivers of conventional vehicles and those towing caravans should check road conditions first.

Bush camping

Signposted off Orroroo–Hawker Rd. Bring water and firewood. Additional map ref.: *RAA Flinders Ranges* E11.

Further information & bookings:
Mr and Mrs McInnis **Tel.:** (08) 8648 4180 *or*
Hawker Information Centre **Tel.:** (08) 8648 4014
Fire restrictions: Solid-fuel fire ban 1 Nov.–30 April

35. WITJIRA NATIONAL PARK

Covering an area of 7770 sq. km, Witjira National Park is on the western edge of the Simpson Desert, 120 km north of Oodnadatta. The Dalhousie Springs, where artesian water bubbles up from the Great Artesian Basin, are one of the main features of the park. Swimming in the warm waters of Dalhousie Springs is very popular. Access is recommended for 4WD vehicles only. A Desert Parks Pass is necessary to enter this park (see page 170).

Dalhousie Springs camping area

This is 180 km north of Oodnadatta via Pedirka Siding and 71 km south-east of Mount Dare, on Purni Bore Access Rd. Permit required. Bring water and firewood. Gas/fuel stove preferred. Additional map ref.: *RAA Outback – Dalhousie Springs Map*.

Mount Dare Homestead camping area

Situated 250 km north of Oodnadatta and signposted from Oodnadatta–Witjira National Park Rd. Bookings recommended. Gas/fuel stove preferred. Additional map ref.: *RAA Outback* F1.

Purni Bore camping area

At the start of the French Line, 70 km east of Dalhousie Springs and 363 km west of Birdsville. Permit required. Bring water and firewood. Gas/fuel stove preferred. Additional map ref.: *RAA Outback* H2.

Three O'Clock Creek camping area

Situated 10 km west of Dalhousie Springs and 61 km south-east of Mount Dare Homestead. Access via Mount Dare–Dalhousie Springs Rd. Permit required. Bring water and firewood. Gas/fuel stove preferred. Additional map ref.: *RAA Outback – Dalhousie Springs Map*.

Further information & bookings:
NPWSA, Port Augusta **Tel.:** 1800 816 078 *or*
Mount Dare Homestead **Tel.:** (08) 8670 7835
Email: braithwaite10@hotmail.com
Camping fees: *Dalhousie Springs*: From $18.00 per vehicle/night for single night visit *Mount Dare Homestead*: From $6.50 per adult/night, $3.50 per child/night *All other areas*: Covered under NPWSA Desert Parks Pass; fees payable to and permits from NPWSA **Fire restrictions:** Solid-fuel fire ban 1 Nov.–30 April

Dawn at Port Augusta, the gateway to South Australia's outback

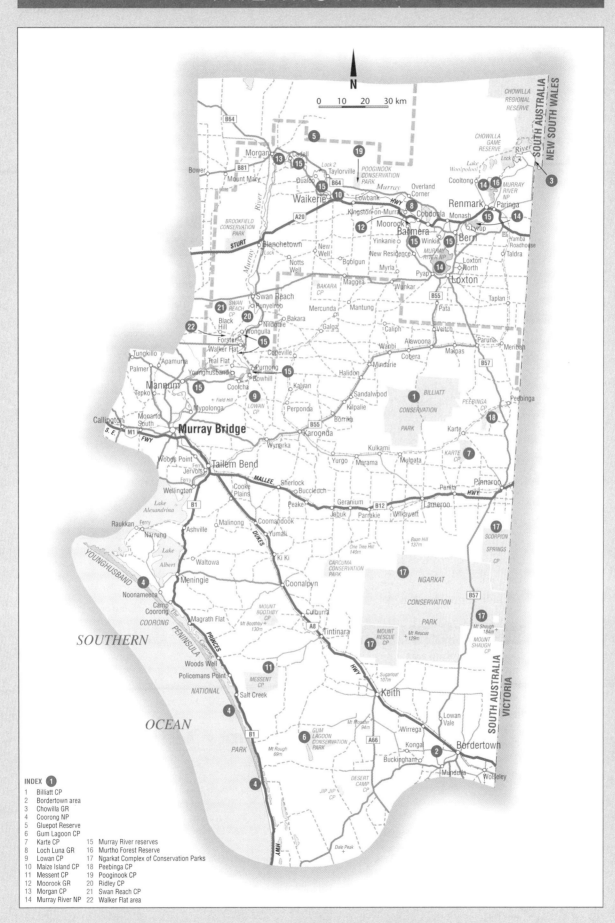

INDEX ①

1   Billiatt CP
2   Bordertown area
3   Chowilla GR
4   Coorong NP
5   Gluepot Reserve
6   Gum Lagoon CP
7   Karte CP   15 Murray River reserves
8   Loch Luna GR   16 Murtho Forest Reserve
9   Lowan CP   17 Ngarkat Complex of Conservation Parks
10 Maize Island CP   18 Peebinga CP
11 Messent CP   19 Pooginook CP
12 Moorook GR   20 Ridley CP
13 Morgan CP   21 Swan Reach CP
14 Murray River NP   22 Walker Flat area

THE GREAT MURRAY RIVER WINDS
ITS WAY THROUGH THE EAST OF
SOUTH AUSTRALIA, PAST
WONDERFUL RIVER TOWNS AND
HIGH YELLOW CLIFFS ON ITS WAY
TO LAKE ALEXANDRINA AND THE
SOUTHERN OCEAN. THE RIVER RED GUM-LINED
BANKS PROVIDE SOME EXCELLENT CAMPING – IN
VARIOUS PARKS AND RESERVES THAT STRETCH
FROM THE NEW SOUTH WALES/VICTORIA BORDER
ALL THE WAY TO MANNUM.

Bulyong Island, Katarapko and Lyrup Flats
are the three sections of Murray River National
Park. They protect floodplain and wetlands areas,
as well as Aboriginal and European heritage sites.
Bulyong Island offers remote camping – it is
upriver from Renmark and is only accessible by
boat or houseboat. Katarapko, opposite the town
of Loxton, has a number of campsites along the
river and Katarapko Creek. Campers here can
explore the Murray and the creek by canoe, enjoy
the self-guided Kai Kai walking trail, and fish or
birdwatch.

Lying adjacent to the mouth of the Murray
River is Coorong National Park. It protects a long
shallow lagoon that stretches for over 100 kilometres, separated from the Southern Ocean by the
Younghusband Peninsula. The Coorong has
abundant birdlife and during the summer months
is visited by migratory birds from as far away as
Siberia. There are some wonderful scenic
campsites on both sides of the lagoon.

BEST CAMPSITES

Long Point camping area
Coorong National Park

Pine Hut Soak camping area
Ngarkat Complex of Conservation Parks

Border Cliffs Customs House camping area
Chowilla Game Reserve

Colligans campground
Murray River National Park

Chambers Creek camping area
Loch Luna Game Reserve

BEST TIME TO VISIT

**All year round, however temperatures in this region
can soar in summer.**

1. BILLIATT CONSERVATION PARK

This large mallee park lies 37 km north of Lameroo. Along
with numerous bird, reptile and mammal species the park is
home to the tiny marsupial mouse, ningaui.

Bush camping

Access via Lameroo–Alawoona Rd. Self-sufficient camping,
no facilities. Permit required. Contact ranger for detailed
information on campsites. Bring water. Gas/fuel stove only.
Additional map ref.: *RAA Riverland & Central Murray* N13.

Further information & bookings: NPWSA, Lameroo
Tel.: (08) 8576 3690 **Email:** lawrence.darrell@saugov.
sa.gov.au **Camping fees:** From $6.00 per vehicle/night; fees
payable to and permits from NPWSA **Fire restrictions:** Solid-
fuel fire ban 1 Nov.–30 April

2. BORDERTOWN AREA

To the west of Bordertown, are the Mundulla and Poocher
swamps, both with camping opportunities. Canoeing and
fishing are allowed here.

Jimmies Waterhole camping area

Access off Rowney Rd via Mundulla Oval in Mundulla, 10 km
west of Bordertown. Bring water and firewood. Additional
map ref.: *RAA Upper South East* H11.

Poocher Swamp camping area

On Cannawigara Rd 9 km west of Bordertown. Bring water
and firewood. Additional map ref.: *RAA Upper South East* H11.

Further information & bookings:
Jimmies Waterhole: Bordertown Visitor Information Centre
Tel.: (08) 8752 0700 **Email:** btowninfo@lm.net.au
Poocher Swamp: NPWSA, Naracoorte **Tel.:** (08) 8762 3412
Fire restrictions: Solid-fuel fire ban 15 Nov.–15 April

3. CHOWILLA GAME RESERVE

This reserve is north-east of Renmark on the Murray River,
adjoining the New South Wales border. It features stands of
majestic river red gums and numerous activities. The reserve
can be closed after heavy rain; contact NPWSA for details.

Border Cliffs Customs House camping area

Signposted from Murtho Rd, 34 km north-east of Renmark.
Permit required. Bring water and firewood. Gas/fuel stove
preferred. Additional map ref.: *RAA Riverland & Central
Murray* S1.

Bush camping

Signposted off Renmark–Wentworth Rd, 32 km north-east of
Renmark. Dispersed camping along Murray River floodplains.
Limited caravan access. Permit required. Bring water and
firewood. Gas/fuel stove preferred. Additional map ref.: *RAA
Riverland & Central Murray* S1/T1.

Further information & bookings: NPWSA, Berri
Tel.: (08) 8595 2111 **Email:** fitzpatrick.leah@saugov.sa.gov.au
Camping fees: From $6.00 per vehicle/night; fees payable to
and permits from NPWSA **Fire restrictions:** Solid-fuel fire
ban 1 Nov.–30 April

4. COORONG NATIONAL PARK see page 186

5. GLUEPOT RESERVE

Gluepot Reserve is a large bird sanctuary in mallee country north of Waikerie. Bike riders should carry puncture repair kits due to the spinifex.

Gluepot Reserve camping area

Situated 64 km north of Waikerie. Signposted via Lunn Rd off Morgan–Renmark Rd. Bring water. Self-sufficient camping only. Key (from Shell Roadhouse, Waikerie, with refundable deposit) and permit required. If towing a caravan check road conditions first. Gas/fuel stove only. Additional map ref.: *RAA South Australia State Road Map – 7th edition* V18.

Further information & bookings:
Birds Australia – Gluepot Reserve Management Committee **Tel.:** (08) 8892 9600 (6 pm–8 pm) **Email:** gluepot@riverland. net.au **Website:** www.riverland.net.au/gluepot *or* Shell Roadhouse, Waikerie **Tel.:** (08) 8541 2621 **Camping fees:** $10.00 per vehicle per night

6. GUM LAGOON CONSERVATION PARK

This park offers good trails for experienced and self-sufficient walkers. Around Gum Lagoon are large areas of low melaleuca heathland and in the north-west, high sandy ridges. The park is 44 km south-west of Keith, off the Dukes Hwy.

Bush camping

Walk-in sites for self-sufficient walkers. Signposted off Keith–Cantara Rd. Conventional-vehicle access to this point; 4WD needed for rest of park. Permit required. Gas/fuel stove preferred. Additional map ref.: *RAA Upper South East* D10.

Further information & bookings: NPWSA, Naracoorte **Tel.:** (08) 8762 3412 **Email:** jpaech@deh.sa.gov.au **Camping fees:** Campers from $3.50 per person/night; fees payable to and permits from NPWSA **Fire restrictions:** Solid-fuel fire ban 1 Nov.–30 April

7. KARTE CONSERVATION PARK

This park is 30 km north-west of Pinnaroo, which lies on the Mallee Hwy. Its name comes from an Aboriginal word meaning thick, low scrub – dense scrub covers the magnificent sand dunes here.

Bush camping

Signposted off Karte Rd, 30 km north-west of Pinnaroo. Self-sufficient camping. Permit required. Bring water and firewood. Gas/fuel stove preferred. Additional map ref.: *RAA Upper South East* H1.

Further information & bookings: NPWSA, Lameroo **Tel.:** (08) 8576 3690 **Email:** lawrence.darrell@saugov. sa.gov.au **Camping fees:** From $6.00 per vehicle/night; fees payable to and permits from NPWSA **Fire restrictions:** Solid-fuel fire ban 1 Nov.–30 April

8. LOCH LUNA GAME RESERVE

This large wetland has a network of small, narrow creeks perfect for fishing and boating. There is conventional vehicle access – in dry weather only – signposted from the Sturt Hwy 14 km north-west of Barmera.

Chambers Creek camping area

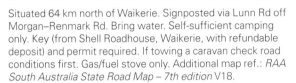

Signposted entrance at Nappers Bridge, 11 km north-west of Barmera on Morgan Rd. Permit required. Bring water and firewood. Gas/fuel stove preferred. Additional map ref.: *RAA Riverland and Central Murray – Central Riverland Map* B2/B3.

Further information & bookings: NPWSA, Berri **Tel.:** (08) 8595 2111 **Email:** fitzpatrick.leah@saugov.sa.gov.au **Camping fees:** From $6.00 per vehicle/night; fees payable to and permits from NPWSA **Fire restrictions:** Solid-fuel fire ban 1 Nov.–30 April

9. LOWAN CONSERVATION PARK

'Lowan' is an old word for the malleefowl, a bird that nests within this park. The park is also home to a variety of other wildlife and lies about 30 km north-east of Murray Bridge.

Bush camping

Conventional vehicle access from the main entrance on the park's northern boundary, via Bowhill–Karoonda Rd 13 km south east of Bowhill. Self-sufficient camping only. Permit required. Bring water and firewood. Gas/fuel stove preferred. Additional map ref.: *RAA Riverland and Central Murray* E13.

Further information & bookings: NPWSA, Lameroo **Tel.:** (08) 8576 3690 **Email:** lawrence.darrell@saugov. sa.gov.au **Camping fees:** From $6.00 per vehicle/night; fees payable to and permits from NPWSA **Fire restrictions:** Solid-fuel fire ban 1 Nov.–30 April

10. MAIZE ISLAND CONSERVATION PARK

This park on the Murray River, east of Waikerie, offers excellent fishing and canoeing opportunities.

Bush camping

Situated 7 km east of Waikerie. Signposted off Sturt Hwy. Self-sufficient camping only. Permit required. Bring water and firewood. Gas/fuel stove preferred. Additional map ref.: *RAA Riverland and Central Murray* J3.

Further information & bookings: NPWSA, Berri **Tel.:** (08) 8595 2111 **Email:** fitzpatrick.leah@saugov.sa.gov.au **Camping fees:** From $6.00 per vehicle/night; fees payable to and permits from NPWSA **Fire restrictions:** Solid-fuel fire ban 1 Nov.–30 April

11. MESSENT CONSERVATION PARK

This park, which lies to the east of Salt Creek, off the Princes Hwy, is home to numerous wildlife species and extensive native flora. Conventional vehicle access is possible only to the park boundary; travel within the park is by foot or 4WD.

Bush camping

Located 6 km east of Salt Creek; reached via Bellara Rd from the north or Salt Creek Rd from the south. 4WD or walk-in access to bush camping areas. Permit required. Additional map ref.: *RAA Upper South East* C9.

Further information & bookings: NPWSA, Coorong **Tel.:** (08) 8575 1200 **Camping fees:** Non-vehicle campers $3.50 per person/night, or from $6.00 per vehicle/night; fees payable to and permits from NPWSA **Fire restrictions:** Solid-fuel fire ban 1 Nov.–30 April

12. MOOROOK GAME RESERVE

On the western banks of the Murray River, Moorook Game Reserve is west of Barmera. There are excellent canoeing and fishing opportunities here and dispersed bush camping along the Murray River.

Moorook camping area

Signposted off Sturt Hwy then off Moorook–Loxton Rd 17 km south-west of Barmera. Bring water and firewood. Permit required. Gas/fuel stove preferred. Additional map ref.: *RAA Riverland and Central Murray – Central Riverland Map* B3/B4.

Further information & bookings: NPWSA, Berri
Tel.: (08) 8595 2111 **Email:** fitzpatrick.leah@saugov.sa.gov.au
Camping fees: From $6.00 per vehicle/night; fees payable to and permits from NPWSA **Fire restrictions:** Solid-fuel fire ban 1 Nov.–30 April

13. MORGAN CONSERVATION PARK

Another of the Murray River parks, Morgan Conservation Park offers swimming, fishing and canoeing. The park is on the east side of the Murray, opposite the town of Morgan.

Bush camping

Signposted via Cadell Rd on the eastern side of the river from Morgan. Permit required. Bring water and firewood. Gas/fuel stove preferred. Additional map ref.: *RAA Riverland and Central Murray* E1.

Further information & bookings: NPWSA, Berri
Tel.: (08) 8595 2111 **Email:** fitzpatrick.leah@saugov.sa.gov.au
Camping fees: From $6.00 per vehicle/night; fees payable to and permits from NPWSA **Fire restrictions:** Solid-fuel fire ban 1 Nov.–30 April

14. MURRAY RIVER NATIONAL PARK

Murray River National Park consists of three sections which are important in conserving floodplain environments. The dispersed camping along the creeks and river provides opportunities for swimming, fishing and canoeing.

BULYONG ISLAND

Bush camping

Bulyong Island is north of Renmark. Boat access only via Murray River. Self-sufficient camping. Permit required. Bring water and firewood. Gas/fuel stove preferred. Additional map ref.: *RAA Riverland and Central Murray – Central Riverland Map* K1.

KATARAPKO

Eckerts Creek Section camping area

Signposted 12 km south-west of Berri via Lower Winkie Rd off Sturt Hwy. Permit required from self-registration station at park entrance. Bring water and firewood. Gas/fuel stove preferred. Additional map ref.: *RAA Riverland and Central Murray – Central Riverland Map* E6.

Katarapko Extension Section camping area

Signposted 5 km south-west of Berri off Draper Rd. Permit required from self-registration station. Bring water and firewood. Gas/fuel stove preferred. Additional map ref.: *RAA Riverland and Central Murray – Central Riverland Map* F6.

Katarapko Section camping area

Signposted 16 km south-west of Berri off Katarapko Rd. Permit required from self-registration station. Bring water and firewood. Gas/fuel stove preferred. Additional map ref.: *RAA Riverland and Central Murray – Central Riverland Map* E6/E7/E8/D8.

LYRUP FLATS

Colligans campground

Signposted off the Sturt Hwy 9 km south-west of Renmark. Permit required. Bring water and firewood. Gas/fuel stove preferred. Additional map ref.: *RAA Riverland and Central Murray – Central Riverland Map* H4.

Tea Tree campground

Signposted off the Sturt Hwy 9 km south-west of Renmark. Permit required. Bring water and firewood. Gas/fuel stove preferred. Additional map ref.: *RAA Riverland and Central Murray – Central Riverland Map* H4.

Bush camping

Signposted off Sturt Hwy 9 km south-west of Renmark. Permit required. Bring water and firewood. Gas/fuel stove preferred. Additional map ref.: *RAA Riverland and Central Murray – Central Riverland Map* H4/J3/J4.

Further information & bookings: NPWSA, Berri
Tel.: (08) 8595 2111 **Email:** fitzpatrick.leah@saugov.sa.gov.au
Camping fees: From $6.00 per vehicle/night; fees payable to and permits from NPWSA **Fire restrictions:** Solid-fuel fire ban 1 Nov.–30 April

15. MURRAY RIVER RESERVES

There are many bush camping areas (some with limited facilities) along the banks of the Murray River between Renmark and Mannum. A range of activities is on offer. Access is possible in dry weather only and drivers towing caravans should check road conditions. There is a solid-fuel fire ban in the reserves 15 Nov.–15 April.

RENMARK TO MORGAN

Hogwash Bend camping area

Signposted off Morgan–Waikerie Rd, 21 km north-west of Waikerie. Bring water and firewood. Gas/fuel stove preferred. Additional map ref.: *RAA Riverland and Central Murray* G2.

Further information & bookings: Waikerie Visitor Information Centre **Tel.:** (08) 8541 2332

Martin Bend camping area

This is 2–3 km east of Berri. Signposted via Martin Rd off Riverview Drive. Bring water and firewood. Gas/fuel stove preferred. Additional map ref.: *RAA Riverland and Central Murray – Central Riverland Map* G5.

Further information & bookings: Berri Tourist and Travel Centre **Tel.:** (08) 8582 5511

Moorook Reserve camping area

Situated off Moorook–Loxton Rd. Bring water and firewood. Gas/fuel stove preferred. Additional map ref.: *RAA Riverland and Central Murray – Central Riverland Map* B4.

Further information & bookings: Loxton Waikerie District Council, Loxton office **Tel.:** (08) 8584 7221 *or* Loxton General Store **Tel.:** (08) 8583 9289
Camping fees: From $4.00 per site/night; fees payable to ranger

Plushs Bend picnic and camping area

On 23rd Street, 6 km south of Renmark. Bring water and firewood. Gas/fuel stove preferred. Additional map ref.: *RAA Riverland and Central Murray – Central Riverland Map* K3.
Further information & bookings: Renmark Paringa Visitor Information Centre **Tel.:** (08) 8586 6704

Ramco Point camping area

Situated 5 km west of Waikerie on Ramco Point Rd. Signposted off Waikerie–Cadell Rd. Bring water and firewood. Gas/fuel stove preferred. Additional map ref.: *RAA Riverland and Central Murray* H3.

Further information & bookings:
Loxton Waikerie District Council, Waikerie office **Tel.:** (08) 8541 2077 *or*
Waikerie Visitor Information Centre **Tel.:** (08) 8541 2332

MORGAN TO MANNUM

Bolto Reserve camping area

On Khartoum Rd, on east side of river from Mannum, south of ferry. Bring water and firewood. Gas/fuel stove preferred. Additional map ref.: *RAA Riverland and Central Murray* A12.

Caurnamont Riverside Reserve camping area

On Caurnamont Rd in Caurnamont, beside ferry. Bring water and firewood. Gas/fuel stove preferred. Additional map ref.: *RAA Riverland and Central Murray* D11.

Haythorpe Reserve camping area

On Bowhill Rd, on east side of river from Mannum and north of ferry. Natural boat ramp. Bring water and firewood.

Gas/fuel stove preferred. Additional map ref.: *RAA Riverland and Central Murray* A12.

Hettner Landing camping area

Located on Walker Flat Rd, on northern side of Walker Flat village. Bring water and firewood. Gas/fuel stove preferred. Additional map ref.: *RAA Riverland and Central Murray* D10.

Purnong Riverside Reserve camping area

On Purnong Rd in Purnong, beside ferry. Bring water and firewood. Gas/fuel stove preferred. Additional map ref.: *RAA Riverland and Central Murray* D11.

Walker Flat Boat Ramp Reserve camping area

On southern side of Walker Flat village, 31 km north-east of Mannum. Bring water and firewood. Gas/fuel stove preferred. Additional map ref.: *RAA Riverland and Central Murray* D10.

Wongulla Boat Ramp Reserve camping area

On Wongulla Rd 8 km north of Walker Flat. Bring water and firewood. Gas/fuel stove preferred. Additional map ref.: *RAA Riverland and Central Murray* D10.

Further information & bookings:
Bolto and Haythorpe reserves: Mid Murray Council **Tel.:** (08) 8569 1600 *or*
Mannum Visitor Information Centre **Tel.:** (08) 8569 1303
Hettner Landing, Walker Flat Boat Ramp Reserve and Wongulla Boat Ramp Reserve: Mid Murray Council **Tel.:** (08) 8569 1600 *or*
Walker Flat General Store **Tel.:** (08) 8570 8050

16. MURTHO FOREST RESERVE

Also known as Headings Cliff, this bush camping area on the southern banks of the Murray River is 20 km north-east of Renmark.

Headings Cliff/Murtho Forest Landing camping area

Self-sufficient camping beside Murray River. Signposted off Paringa–Murtho Rd, 16 km north-east of Renmark. Bring water and firewood. Gas/fuel stove preferred. Additional map ref.: *RAA Riverland and Central Murray* S2.

Further information & bookings: Renmark Paringa Visitor Information Centre **Tel.:** (08) 8586 6704 **Email:** tourist@riverland.net.au **Fire restrictions:** Solid-fuel fire ban 15 Nov.–30 April

17. NGARKAT COMPLEX OF CONSERVATION PARKS

These are on the Victoria border, with the towns Pinnaroo and Lameroo to their north and Keith to their south. The complex of parks covers about 262 700 ha and includes Mt Rescue Conservation Park, Ngarkat Conservation Park and Scorpion Springs Conservation Park. The low heath and mallee vegetation within the parks is home to many birds, mammals and reptiles. The parks have a rich Aboriginal history – the name 'Ngarkat' is also the name of the local Aboriginal people.

COORONG NATIONAL PARK

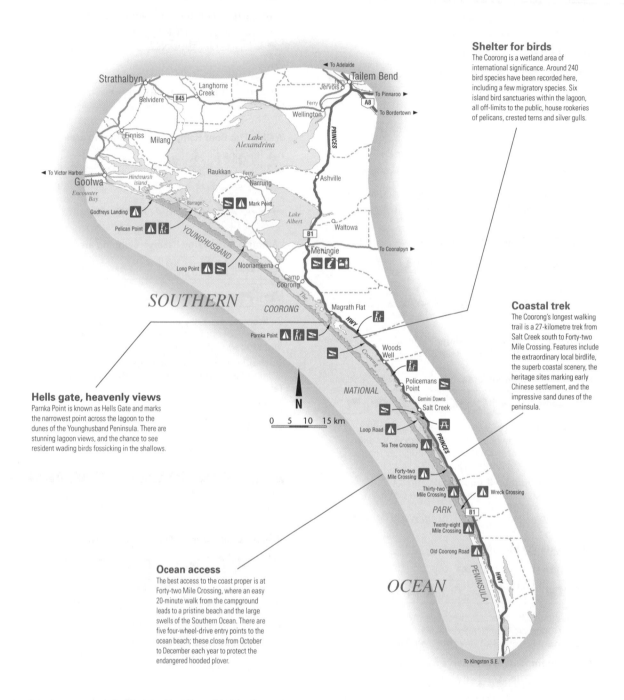

Shelter for birds

The Coorong is a wetland area of international significance. Around 240 bird species have been recorded here, including a few migratory species. Six island bird sanctuaries within the lagoon, all off-limits to the public, house rookeries of pelicans, crested terns and silver gulls.

Coastal trek

The Coorong's longest walking trail is a 27-kilometre trek from Salt Creek south to Forty-two Mile Crossing. Features include the extraordinary local birdlife, the superb coastal scenery, the heritage sites marking early Chinese settlement, and the impressive sand dunes of the peninsula.

Hells gate, heavenly views

Parnka Point is known as Hells Gate and marks the narrowest point across the lagoon to the dunes of the Younghusband Peninsula. There are stunning lagoon views, and the chance to see resident wading birds fossicking in the shallows.

Ocean access

The best access to the coast proper is at Forty-two Mile Crossing, where an easy 20-minute walk from the campground leads to a pristine beach and the large swells of the Southern Ocean. There are five four-wheel-drive entry points to the ocean beach; these close from October to December each year to protect the endangered hooded plover.

Coorong National Park consists of a shallow saltwater lagoon some 100 km long, located at the mouth of the Murray River and separated from the Southern Ocean by the Younghusband Peninsula. As well as a rich history of Aboriginal occupation, the park offers visitors many recreational activities including birdwatching, walking, canoeing, boating and fishing, as well as many scenic viewpoints throughout the park.

Forty-two Mile Crossing camping area

This is 22 km south of Salt Creek and 48 km north of Kingston S.E. Signposted off Princes Hwy. Permit from self-registration station. 4WD access to beach. Bring water and firewood. Gas/fuel stove preferred. Additional map ref.: *RAA Upper South East* B10.

Godfreys Landing camping area

Boat access only via The Coorong or Lake Alexandrina. Permit from self-registration station. Bring water and firewood. Gas/fuel stove preferred. Additional map ref.: *RAA Fleurieu Peninsula & Southern Adelaide Hills* P12.

Long Point camping area

Signposted from Long Point Rd, 26 km west of Meningie. Permit from self-registration station. Bring water and firewood. Gas/fuel stove preferred. Additional map ref.: *RAA Fleurieu Peninsula & Southern Adelaide Hills* T15.

Loop Road camping area

Situated 4 km south of Salt Creek and 60 km south of Meningie on Loop Rd. Signposted off Princes Hwy. Permit from self-registration stations within park. Bring water and firewood. Gas/fuel stove preferred. Additional map ref.: *RAA Upper South East* B9/B10.

Mark Point camping area

Signposted via Mark Point Rd, 35 km north-west of Meningie. Permit from self-registration stations within park. Bring water and firewood. Gas/fuel stove preferred. Additional map ref.: *RAA Fleurieu Peninsula & Southern Adelaide Hills* S14.

Ocean beach camping areas

Bush camping at marked areas along the ocean beach. 4WD beach access via Twenty-eight Mile Crossing, Wreck Crossing, Thirty-two Mile Crossing, Forty-two Mile Crossing and Tea Tree Crossing (only possible here in late summer).

Permits from self-registration stations within the park. Bring water and firewood. Gas/fuel stove preferred. Please note that the ocean beach is closed north of Tea Tree Crossing 24 Oct.–24 Dec. to protect breeding hooded plovers.

Old Coorong Road camping areas

Signposted access to many bush campsites along Old Coorong Rd, around 26 km north of Kingston S.E. Permit from self-registration stations within park. Bring water and firewood. Gas/fuel stove preferred. Additional map ref.: *RAA Upper South East* C11/C12.

Parnka Point camping area

Situated 24 km south of Meningie, signposted off Princes Hwy. Permit from self-registration station. Bring water and firewood. Gas/fuel stove preferred. Additional map ref.: *RAA Upper South East* A7.

Pelican Point camping area

On Pelican Point Rd 41 km north-west of Meningie. Popular birdwatching spot. Permit from self-registration stations within park. Bring water and firewood. Gas/fuel stove preferred. Additional map ref.: *RAA Fleurieu Peninsula & Southern Adelaide Hills* R13.

Tea Tree Crossing camping area

Situated 9 km south of Salt Creek. Signposted off Loop Rd. 4WD access in late summer only when lagoon is low. Permit from self-registration stations within park. Bring water and firewood. Gas/fuel stove preferred. Additional map ref.: *RAA Upper South East* B10.

Thirty-two Mile Crossing camping area

This is 39 km north of Kingston S.E. Signposted off Princes Hwy. Permit from self-registration station. Bring water and firewood. Gas/fuel stove preferred. Additional map ref.: *RAA Upper South East* C11.

Twenty-eight Mile Crossing camping area

Situated 30 km north of Kingston S.E. Signposted off Old Coorong Rd. Permit from self-registration station. Bring water and firewood. Gas/fuel stove preferred. Additional map ref.: *RAA Upper South East* C12.

Further information & bookings: NPWSA, Coorong **Tel.:** (08) 8575 1200 **Email:** jflavel@deh.sa.gov.au **Camping fees:** *Godfreys Landing*: From $3.50 per person/night *All other areas*: From $6.00 per vehicle/night. Fees payable to and permits from self-registration stations or NPWSA **Fire restrictions:** Solid-fuel fire ban 1 Nov.–30 April

MOUNT RESCUE CONSERVATION PARK

Bucks Camp Soak camping area

On Bucks Camp Track, 24 km north of Keith. Permit required. Bring water and firewood. Additional map ref.: *RAA Upper South East* F8.

Rabbit Island Soak camping area

To the right of Bucks Camp Soak 30 km north of Keith. Permit required. Bring water and firewood. Additional map ref.: *RAA Upper South East* F8.

NGARKAT CONSERVATION PARK

Box Flat camping area

Signposted off The Baan Hill Track, 38 km south-west of Lameroo. Permit required. Bring water and firewood. Additional map ref.: *RAA Upper South East* F5.

Comet Bore camping area

On Pinnaroo–Bordertown Rd, 75 km north of Bordertown. Permit required. Bring water and firewood. Additional map ref.: *RAA Upper South East* H6.

Pertendi Hut camping area

Signposted from Pinnaroo–Bordertown Rd, 48 km south of Pinnaroo. Permit required. Bring water and firewood. Additional map ref.: *RAA Upper South East* H6.

SCORPION SPRINGS CONSERVATION PARK

Pine Hut Soak camping area

Access via Rosy Pine Rd, 21 km south of Pinnaroo. Check with ranger after rain for road and access conditions. Permit required. Bring water and firewood. Additional map ref.: *RAA Upper South East* J4.

Further information & bookings: NPWSA, Lameroo **Tel.:** (08) 8576 3690 **Email:** lawrence.darrell@saugov. sa.gov.au **Camping fees:** From $6.00 per vehicle/night; fees payable to and permits from NPWSA **Fire restrictions:** Solid-fuel fire ban 1 Nov.–30 April

Peebinga Conservation Park was declared to protect the habitat of the rare western whipbird. It is a popular spot for birdwatchers and experienced bushwalkers.

Bush camping

Signposted off Pinnaroo–Loxton Rd, 37 km north of Pinnaroo. Self-sufficient camping. Permit required. Contact ranger for detailed information. Gas/fuel stove preferred. Additional map ref.: *RAA Riverland and Central Murray* S13.

Further information & bookings: NPWSA, Lameroo **Tel.:** (08) 8576 3690 **Email:** lawrence.darrell@saugov.sa.gov.au **Camping fees:** From $6.00 per vehicle/night; fees payable to and permits from NPWSA **Fire restrictions:** Solid-fuel fire ban 1 Nov.–30 April

This park covers an area of 2852 ha. It is home to a variety of wildlife and birds.

Bush camping

Located along Morgan–Renmark Rd, 28 km north-east of Waikerie. Permit required. Bring water and firewood. Gas/fuel stove preferred. Additional map ref.: *RAA Riverland and Central Murray* K2.

Further information & bookings: NPWSA, Berri **Tel.:** (08) 8595 2111 **Email:** fitzpatrick.leah@saugov.sa.gov.au **Camping fees:** From $6.00 per vehicle/night; fees payable to and permits from NPWSA **Fire restrictions:** Solid-fuel fire ban 1 Nov.–30 April

This long, narrow conservation park was set aside to protect the habitat of the region's wombats. It is beside the Swan Reach–Mannum Rd south of Swan Reach.

Bush camping

Signposted off Swan Reach–Mannum Rd. Self-sufficient camping. Permit required. Bring water and firewood. Gas/fuel stove preferred. Additional map ref.: *RAA Riverland and Central Murray* D9.

Further information & bookings: NPWSA, Lameroo **Tel.:** (08) 8576 3690 **Email:** lawrence.darrell@saugov.sa.gov.au **Camping fees:** From $6.00 per vehicle/night; fees payable to and permits from NPWSA **Fire restrictions:** Solid-fuel fire ban 1 Nov.–30 April

This mallee park is on the Swan Reach–Sedan Rd 14 km west of Swan Reach. It is popular with birdwatchers.

Bush camping

Signposted off Swan Reach–Sedan Rd. Self-sufficient camping. Permit required. Bring water and firewood. Gas/fuel stove preferred. Additional map ref.: *RAA Riverland and Central Murray* C8.

Further information & bookings: NPWSA, Lameroo **Tel.:** (08) 8576 3690 **Email:** lawrence.darrell@saugov.sa.gov.au **Camping fees:** From $6.00 per vehicle/night; fees payable to and permits from NPWSA **Fire restrictions:** Solid-fuel fire ban 1 Nov.–30 April

Walker Flat is about 50 km north-east of Mannum. Near the town you can visit historic Shell Hill, a natural oyster shell deposit some five million years old.

John S. Christian Reserve camping area

The reserve is 15 km north-west of Walker Flat on Marne Valley Rd, beside Marne River. Bring water and firewood. Additional map ref.: *RAA Riverland and Central Murray* C10.

Further information & bookings: Mid Murray Council **Tel.:** (08) 8569 1600 *or* Walker Flat General Store **Tel.:** (08) 8570 8050 **Fire restrictions:** Solid-fuel fire ban 15 Nov.–15 April

THE SOUTH-EAST POCKET OF SOUTH AUSTRALIA FEATURES A WONDERFUL COASTLINE OF RUGGED CLIFFS, SURFING BEACHES AND FISHING VILLAGES. INLAND IS THE RICH TERRA ROSA SOIL OF THE COONAWARRA WINE REGION AND THE FASCINATING LIMESTONE CAVES AROUND NARACOORTE AND MOUNT GAMBIER. THIS IS A POPULAR HOLIDAY DESTINATION.

South of Naracoorte the large wetland system of Bool Lagoon Game Reserve is home to over 150 bird species, providing a refuge for some rare and migratory birds. Boardwalks have been constructed for walkers to view the different sections of the reserve. Tent and caravan camping is at Hacks Peninsula.

Not far away, beside the World Heritage-listed Naracoorte Caves Conservation Park, is the Naracoorte Caves Caravan Park, which has good facilities. The caves display beautiful and delicate calcite formations and the fossils of extinct animals; they are also home to a colony of bent-wing bats. There are guided tours of the caves and those who don't mind crawling and sliding through tunnels can take an adventure tour through some of the undeveloped caves.

The 40-kilometre coastline of Canunda National Park offers excellent fishing opportunities for salmon and mulloway. Facing the Southern Ocean, the park has long stretches of beaches and sand dunes in the south, while in its north are limestone cliffs, offshore reefs and sea stacks. Campers here can enjoy fishing, crayfishing, surfing, bushwalking and birdwatching.

Little Dip Conservation Park protects part of the foreshore of Lake Eliza along with a large area of coastal dunes and rugged coastline. Early Aboriginal occupation is evident in the middens found here. While camping in the park take one of the many walks along the beaches or around Fresh Water Lake.

Between Little Dip Conservation Park and Canunda National Park is Beachport Conservation Park. This park has more spectacular coastal scenery along with fishing and camping opportunities.

BEST CAMPSITES

Hacks Peninsula camping area
Bool Lagoon Game Reserve

Cape Banks Lighthouse camping area
Canunda National Park

Number Two Rocks camping area
Canunda National Park

Long Gully camping area
Little Dip Conservation Park

Three Mile Bend camping area
Beachport Conservation Park

BEST TIME TO VISIT

All year round.

1. BEACHPORT CONSERVATION PARK

Lying between the Southern Ocean and Lake George, Beachport Conservation Park has spectacular rugged coastal scenery. In the north at Five Mile Drift there are safe, white sandy beaches around the lake. Enjoy the 1.2-km Woolley Lake Walk.

Rooney Point camping area

This is 7 km north of Beachport. Access via Five Mile Rd. Permit required from self-registration on Five Mile Rd. Bring water and firewood. Gas/fuel stove preferred. Additional map ref.: *RAA Lower South East* D10.

Three Mile Bend camping area

Situated 5 km north of Beachport. Access via Five Mile Rd. Permit required from self-registration station. Bring water and firewood. Gas/fuel stove preferred. Additional map ref.: *RAA Lower South East* D10.

Further information & bookings: NPWSA, Southend **Tel.:** (08) 8735 6053 **Camping fees:** From $6.00 per vehicle/night; fees payable to and permits from self-registration station or NPWSA **Fire restrictions:** Solid-fuel fire ban 1 Nov.–30 April

2. BIG HEATH CONSERVATION PARK

Big Heath Conservation Park, 35 km south-west of Naracoorte, protects areas of low-lying wet heathland. These are sheltered by stony rises vegetated with blue gum, pink gum, some banksia and she oak. Camping within the park is for experienced, self-sufficient walkers only.

Bush camping

Park access via Bool Lagoon Rd, 35 km south-west of Naracoorte. Walk-in bush campsites. Permit required. Obtain large-scale maps and contact ranger for further details. Gas/fuel stove preferred. Additional map ref.: *RAA Lower South East* K7.

Further information & bookings: NPWSA, Naracoorte **Tel.:** (08) 8762 3412 **Email:** jpaech@deh.sa.gov.au **Camping fees:** From $3.50 per person/night; fees payable to and permits from NPWSA **Fire restrictions:** Solid-fuel fire ban 1 Nov.–30 April

3. BOOL LAGOON GAME RESERVE

Bool Lagoon, south of Naracoorte, is home to over 150 bird species. The reserve is one of the largest wetland systems in southern Australia and provides drought refuge for many migratory species. Enjoy one of the numerous boardwalks and do a bit of birdwatching, or take one of the drives. Don't forget your bird identification book and binoculars.

Hacks Peninsula camping area

This is 27 km south of Naracoorte. Signposted via Bool Lagoon Rd off Naracoorte–Penola Rd. Permit from self-registration station. Gas/fuel stove only. Additional map ref.: *RAA Lower South East* L7.

Further information & bookings: NPWSA, Naracoorte **Tel.:** (08) 8762 3412 **Email:** kheyne@deh.gov.sa.au **Camping fees:** From $15.00 per vehicle/night; fees payable to and permits from self-registration station or NPWSA

4. CANUNDA NATIONAL PARK

This large park just north of Mount Gambier is dominated by sand dunes and spectacular coastal scenery – there are numerous opportunities for keen fisherfolk along the 40 km coastline. Other recreational activities include birdwatching, nature study, surfing, 4WD touring and bushwalking. In the north of the park three walks follow the coast's clifftops, while in the south two easy walks commence from Coola Outstation.

Bevilaqua Ford camping area

Situated 28 km west of Millicent. Signposted access via South Coast Track off Canunda Frontage Rd. Permit from self-registration stations within park. Bring firewood. Gas/fuel stove preferred. Additional map ref.: *RAA Lower South East* F12.

Cape Banks Lighthouse camping area

Signposted access via Cape Banks Rd from Carpenter Rocks, 4 km north of Carpenter Rocks. Permit from self-registration stations within park. Bring water and firewood. Gas/fuel stove preferred. Additional map ref.: *RAA Lower South East* G16.

Number Two Rocks camping area

This is 15 km north of Carpenter Rocks. Signposted – 4WD access only – via South Coast Track along beach. Permit from self-registration stations within park. Bring water and firewood. Gas/fuel stove preferred. Additional map ref.: *RAA Lower South East* G15.

Oil Rig Square camping area

Situated 14 km west of Millicent. Signposted via Oil Rig Square Track off Canunda Causeway Rd. Permit from self-registration stations within park. Bring firewood. Gas/fuel stove preferred. Additional map ref.: *RAA Lower South East* F13.

Further information & bookings: NPWSA, Southend **Tel.:** (08) 8735 6053 **Camping fees:** From $6.00 per vehicle/night; fees payable to and permits from self-registration stations or NPWSA **Fire restrictions:** Solid-fuel fire ban 1 Nov.–30 April

5. FAIRVIEW CONSERVATION PARK

Fairview Conservation Park centres on Kangoora Lagoon, part of an important wetland area. It is north-west of Naracoorte. Forest, consisting mainly of swamp paperback, red gum and manna gum, surrounds the lagoon's banks.

Bush camping

The park is 45 km north-west of Naracoorte and 25 km north-east of Lucindale. Access is signposted off Woolumbool Rd. Walk-in bush campsites for self-sufficient walkers. Some restricted areas due to weed problems. Contact ranger for further details and camping permit. Gas/fuel stove preferred. Additional map ref.: *RAA Lower South East* H3.

Further information & bookings: NPWSA, Naracoorte **Tel.:** (08) 8762 3412 **Email:** jpaech@deh.sa.gov.au **Camping fees:** From $3.50 per person/night; fees payable to and permits from NPWSA **Fire restrictions:** Solid-fuel fire ban 1 Nov.–30 April

6. LITTLE DIP CONSERVATION PARK

Little Dip Conservation Park protects an area of coastal dunes as well as a rugged coastline of the Southern Ocean and part of the foreshore around Lake Eliza. Other lakes included in the park are Big Dip and Fresh Water. Activities here include beach fishing, a variety of walks and 4WD touring.

A boardwalk in Bool Lagoon Game Reserve, a haven for many bird species

Long Gully camping area

Access via Long Gully Track off Nora Creina Drive, 10 km south of Robe. Permit from self-registration stations in park. Bring firewood. Gas/fuel stove preferred. Additional map ref.: *RAA Lower South East* B8.

Old Man Lake camping area

On Nora Creina Drive 14 km south of Robe. Permit from self-registration stations in park. Bring water. Gas/fuel stove only. Additional map ref.: *RAA Lower South East* C8.

Stony Rise camping area

Access via Stony Rise Track off Robe St, 4 km south of Robe. Popular rock-fishing spot. Permit from self-registration stations in park. Bring water and firewood. Gas/fuel stove preferred. Additional map ref.: *RAA Lower South East* B7.

The Gums camping area

Access via The Gums Track off Eastern Boundary Track, 5 km south of Robe. Permit from self-registration stations in park. Bring water and firewood. Gas/fuel stove preferred. Additional map ref.: *RAA Lower South East* B7.

Further information & bookings: NPWSA, Robe **Tel.:** (08) 8768 2543 **Camping fees:** From $6.00 per vehicle/night; fees payable to and permits from self-registration stations at park entrances or NPWSA **Fire restrictions:** Solid-fuel fire ban 1 Nov.–30 April

7. NARACOORTE CAVES CONSERVATION PARK

Within the caves of this World Heritage-listed park you will see beautiful calcite decorations and fossils of animals long extinct. Join a cave tour – or an adventure cave tour. Visit the Wonambi Fossil Centre where you will be taken back 200 000 years to view the landscapes and animals of that time.

Naracoorte Caves Caravan Park

On Caves Rd 14 km south of Naracoorte. Firewood supplied. Other accommodation available. Additional map ref.: *RAA Lower South East* M6.

Further information & bookings: NPWSA, Naracoorte **Tel.:** (08) 8762 3412 **Email:** sbourne@deh.sa.gov.au **Camping fees:** From $18.00 per vehicle/night **Fire restrictions:** Solid-fuel fire ban 1 Nov.–30 April

8. PADTHAWAY CONSERVATION PARK

Within the West Naracoorte Ranges, Padthaway Conservation Park is made up of low open woodland and tall heathland. Access is by 4WD vehicle or on foot.

Bush camping

Access via Padthaway–Bordertown Rd, 4 km north-east of Padthaway. Limited 4WD and walk-in access. Permit required. Contact ranger for further details. Bring water and firewood. Gas/fuel stove preferred. Additional map ref.: *RAA Upper South East* G13.

Further information & bookings: NPWSA, Naracoorte **Tel.:** (08) 8762 3412 **Email:** jpaech@deh.sa.gov.au **Camping fees:** Non-vehicle campers $3.50 per person/night, or from $6.00 per vehicle/night; fees payable to and permits from NPWSA **Fire restrictions:** Solid-fuel fire ban 1 Nov.–30 April

9. PICCANINNIE PONDS CONSERVATION PARK

This park is 32 km south of Mount Gambier on Discovery Bay, close to the Victorian border. For those who enjoy snorkelling or diving, the crystal-clear waters of Piccaninnie Ponds are a must-see. The ponds have formed over thousands of years with the water filtering through layers of limestone. Permits are necessary for diving and snorkelling and time slots for these activities must be booked through NPWSA.

Piccaninnie Ponds camping area

Access on Piccaninnie Ponds Rd, which is signposted off Glenelg River Rd, 29 km south of Mount Gambier. Permit required from self-registration station. Swimming prohibited in ponds, however swimming and fishing is possible in Discovery Bay. Gas/fuel stove only. Additional map ref.: *RAA Lower South East* M18.

Further information & bookings: NPWSA, Mount Gambier **Tel.:** (08) 8735 1111 **Email:** barnett.trudy@saugov.sa.au **Camping fees:** From $6.00 per vehicle/night; fees payable to and permits from self-registration station or NPWSA

FLEURIEU PENINSULA

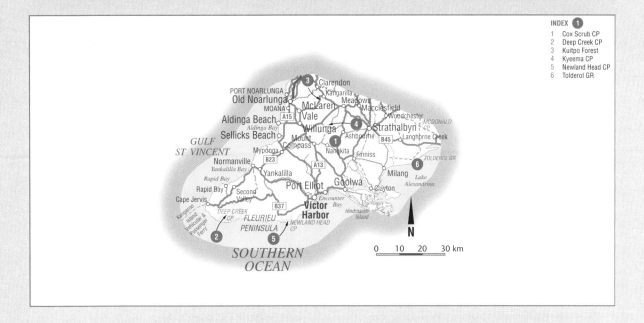

ONLY A SHORT DRIVE SOUTH OF ADELAIDE, THE FLEURIEU PENINSULA IS A POPULAR HOLIDAY DESTINATION. BUSIEST IN SUMMER, IT IS KNOWN FOR ITS BEAUTIFUL COASTLINE, SURF BEACHES, WINERIES AND PICTURESQUE LANDSCAPES.

Deep Creek Conservation Park has spectacular scenery encompassing mountain ridges, steep valleys and gorges, waterfalls, cliffs along the coast dropping into the Southern Ocean and wonderful views across to Kangaroo Island. The park has an extensive network of walking trails, with Stringybark Campground at the start of the easy Spring Wildflower Walk and Forest Circuit. There are four other campgrounds within the park.

Campsites in Newland Head Conservation Park are set amongst the shade of pink gums and wattles behind Waitpinga Beach. The park is south-west of Victor Harbor, and there is excellent beach fishing for salmon here. The park is home to the rare southern pygmy possum, which feeds on the nectar of banksia flowers.

Tolderol Game Reserve is on the northern shores of Lake Alexandrina. The park's swamp and low shrub areas provide feeding grounds for a large number of birds, including swans, ducks, ibis and the white-faced heron, making it a wonderful birdwatching site. Camping is possible in the reserve, however caravan access is only possible in dry weather.

In the southern Mount Lofty Ranges is the large Kuitpo Forest, which has many picnic sites, camping areas and walking trails. The delightful Chookarloo Campground is beside a small creek amongst tall gums. The forest is popular with cyclists, horseriders and bushwalkers.

BEST CAMPSITES

Stringybark Campground
Deep Creek Conservation Park

Trig Campground
Deep Creek Conservation Park

Newland Head camping area
Newland Head Conservation Park

Chookarloo Campground
Kuitpo Forest

Tolderol Game Reserve camping area
Tolderol Game Reserve

BEST TIME TO VISIT

All year round, however temperatures can soar in January and February and rain falls regularly in winter.

1. COX SCRUB CONSERVATION PARK

This park covers an area of 544 ha and is about 22 km north of Goolwa. It has rejuvenated since the 1983 Ash Wednesday fires with many kinds of vegetation uncommon to the area. It is a popular spot for birdwatchers and bushwalkers. There is a total fire ban 1 Nov.–30 April and camping is prohibited during this time.

Coles Crossing camping area

Situated 17 km east of Mount Compass. Access via Cole Crossing Rd off Mt Magnificent Rd. Camping area is 6 km south of the Mt Magnificent Rd. Permit required. Gas/fuel stove only. Additional map ref.: *RAA Fleurieu Peninsula & Southern Adelaide Hills* L8.

Further information & bookings: NPWS, Victor Harbor **Tel.:** (08) 8552 3677 **Camping fees:** From $6.00 per car/night, non-vehicle campers from $3.50 per person/night; fees payable to and permits from NPWSA

2. DEEP CREEK CONSERVATION PARK

Stretching for over 10 km on the southern coast of the Fleurieu Peninsula, this park covers a total area of 4180 ha. With steep cliffs dropping to the Southern Ocean the park offers some spectacular views. There are numerous walks of different grades here and excellent fishing on the coast.

Cobbler Hill Campground

On Blowhole Creek Rd 12 km south of Delamere. Permit from self-registration station. Bring wood. Gas/fuel stove preferred. Additional map ref.: *RAA Fleurieu Peninsula & Southern Adelaide Hills* C13.

Eagle Waterhole Campground

On the Heysen Trail. Walk-in access. Limited water supply. Permit from self-registration station. Gas/fuel stove preferred. Additional map ref.: *RAA Fleurieu Peninsula & Southern Adelaide Hills* C13.

Stringybark Campground

On Tapanappa Rd 9 km south-east of Delamere. Permit from self-registration station. Bring wood. Gas/fuel stove preferred. Additional map ref.: *RAA Fleurieu Peninsula & Southern Adelaide Hills* D13.

Tapanappa Campground

On Tapanappa Rd 16 km south-east of Delamere. Permit from self-registration station. Bring wood. Gas/fuel stove preferred. Additional map ref.: *RAA Fleurieu Peninsula & Southern Adelaide Hills* D13.

Trig Campground

On Tent Rock Rd 12 km south of Delamere. Permit from self-registration station. Bring wood. Gas/fuel stove preferred.

Additional map ref.: *RAA Fleurieu Peninsula & Southern Adelaide Hills* C14.

Further information & bookings: NPWSA, Deep Creek Conservation Park **Tel.:** (08) 8598 0263 **Camping fees:** *Eagle Waterhole*: From $3.50 per person/night *Stringybark*: From $15.00 per vehicle/night *All other areas*: From $6.00 per vehicle/night. Fees payable to and permits from self-registration stations or NPWSA **Fire restrictions:** Solid-fuel fire ban 1 Nov.–30 April

3. KUITPO FOREST

This forest is located 45 minutes from Adelaide in the southern Mt Lofty Ranges. The forest is popular with walkers, horseriders and cyclists. Fees apply and permits are necessary for horseriding. The forest is closed on days of total fire ban, and camping is prohibited during the total fire ban season, 1 Dec.–31 March.

Chookarloo Campground

On Brookman Rd 8 km south-west of Meadows. Permit required. Gas/fuel stove preferred. Additional map ref.: *RAA Fleurieu Peninsula & Southern Adelaide Hills* L6.

Jacks Paddock Campground

On Brookman Rd 11 km south of Meadows. Horseyards. Permit required. Key access only. Gas/fuel stove preferred. Additional map ref.: *RAA Fleurieu Peninsula & Southern Adelaide Hills* L7.

Rocky Creek Campground

On Razor Back Rd 7 km north-west of Meadows. Sites are a short walk from carpark. Permit required. Gas/fuel stove preferred. Can be exclusively hired; booking essential. Additional map ref.: *RAA Fleurieu Peninsula & Southern Adelaide Hills* M5.

Rocky Creek Hut Campground

On Razor Back Rd 7 km north-west of Meadows. Hut sleeps up to ten people. Permit required. Gas/fuel stove preferred. Can be exclusively hired; booking essential. Additional map ref.: *RAA Fleurieu Peninsula & Southern Adelaide Hills* M5.

Further information & bookings: Forestry SA, Kuitpo Forest **Tel.:** (08) 8388 3267 **Camping fees:** From $3.00 per adult/night, $1.00 per child/night *Jacks Paddock and Rocky Creek Hut*: Exclusive hire, $20.00 per night plus camping fees. All fees payable to and permits from forest headquarters on Brookman Rd **Fire restrictions:** Solid-fuel fire ban 1 Nov.–30 April

4. KYEEMA CONSERVATION PARK

Conventional vehicle access to this park is off the Willunga Rd 18 km south of Meadows. Kyeema is home to around 70 bird species as well as the southern brown bandicoot. During the fire ban season, 1 Nov.–30 April, there is no access to this park.

Kyeema camping areas

Access via Woodgate Hill Rd. Permit required. Gas/fuel stove preferred. Additional map ref.: *RAA Fleurieu Peninsula & Southern Adelaide Hills* K7/L7.

Further information & bookings: NPWSA, Victor Harbor **Tel.:** (08) 8552 3677 **Camping fees:** From $6.00 per vehicle/night; fees payable to and permits from NPWSA

5. NEWLAND HEAD CONSERVATION PARK

This park, 16 km south-west of Victor Harbor, encompasses two beautiful beaches where salmon fishing is popular.

Newland Head camping area

This is 16 km south-west of Victor Harbor. Access via Dennis Rd. Permit required. Gas/fuel stove only. Additional map ref.: *RAA Fleurieu Peninsula & Southern Adelaide Hills* H13.

Further information & bookings: NPWSA, Victor Harbor **Tel.:** (08) 8552 3677 **Camping fees:** From $6.00 per vehicle/night; fees payable to and permits from NPWSA

6. TOLDEROL GAME RESERVE

An excellent waterbird-watching spot on the shore of Lake Alexandrina. There is evidence of early Aboriginal occupation in the form of burial sites and freshwater mussel middens. Caravan access is limited to dry weather only.

Tolderol Game Reserve camping area

Situated 13 km south-east of Langhorne Creek. Signposted via Dog Lake Rd off Langhorne Creek–Wellington Rd. Permit required. Gas/fuel stove preferred. Additional map ref.: *RAA Fleurieu Peninsula & Southern Adelaide Hills* T9.

Further information & bookings: NPWSA, Victor Harbor **Tel.:** (08) 8552 3677 **Camping fees:** From $6.00 per vehicle/night; fees payable to and permits from NPWSA **Fire restrictions:** Solid-fuel fire ban 1 Nov.–30 April

The coast near Aldinga Beach

KANGAROO ISLAND

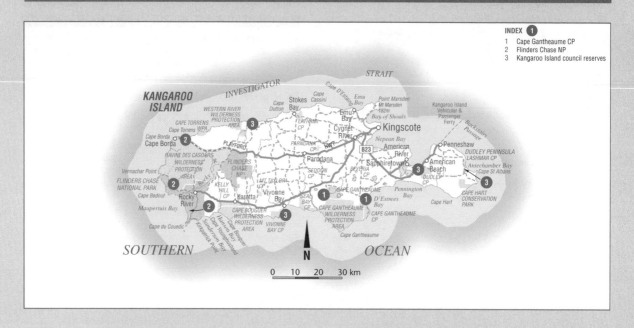

THE BACKSTAIRS PASSAGE SEPARATES AUSTRALIA'S THIRD LARGEST ISLAND, KANGAROO ISLAND, FROM THE MAINLAND. THE ISLAND'S MAJOR ATTRACTIONS INCLUDE ITS MAGNIFICENT COASTLINE, ABUNDANT NATIVE WILDLIFE, CORAL REEFS AND SHIPWRECKS, WILDFLOWERS AND FISHING. DUE TO THE ABSENCE OF INTRODUCED PESTS SUCH AS FOXES AND RABBITS, KANGAROOS, BANDICOOTS AND POSSUMS ARE COMMON AND EASILY SEEN WHILE TRAVELLING.

A large number of activities can be enjoyed on the island. There are safe swimming beaches along the north coast, while surfing beaches exist along the south coast. There is scuba diving in the sheltered waters off the east and north coasts. Fishing from the island's jetties, beaches and rocky coastline results in catches of a large variety of fish, from garfish to salmon, flathead and mullet.

Scattered around the island are a number of council reserves where camping is possible. These reserves have only limited facilities, but they are located in some of the island's most scenic locations, and they offer great opportunities for fishing, boating and canoeing.

Occupying the island's western end is the large Flinders Chase National Park. The park has many beautiful natural sights, such as Admirals Arch – a rock archway formed by the pounding sea – and Remarkable Rocks – a group of sculptured boulders balanced on top of a high granite dome. Other interesting spots include the lighthouses at Cape Borda and Cape du Couedic and the large fur seal colony near Admirals Arch. There are walking trails throughout the park and camping is possible at Rocky River, Snake Lagoon and West Bay in the southern section of the park and at Harveys Return in the north. Campers at Rocky River have the opportunity to do some excellent wildlife-spotting, with kangaroos, koalas, possums and Cape Barren geese regularly making an appearance.

BEST CAMPSITES

American River camping area
Kangaroo Island council reserves

Vivonne Bay camping area
Kangaroo Island council reserves

Rocky River camping area
Flinders Chase National Park

West Bay camping area
Flinders Chase National Park

D'Estrees Bay camping area
Cape Gantheaume Conservation Park

BEST TIME TO VISIT

The months between October and May offer the best temperature ranges and least likelihood of rain.

1. CAPE GANTHEAUME CONSERVATION PARK

Cape Gantheaume Conservation Park and neighbouring Seal Bay Conservation Park provide shelter for sea lions and fur seals. Inland, Murray Lagoon is a feeding ground for numerous waterbirds, ducks and swans. At D'Estrees Bay, which was the site of an early whaling station, you will find quiet beaches to enjoy.

D'Estrees Bay camping area

Situated 68 km south of Kingscote. Signposted off D'Estrees Bay Rd. Permit required. Bring water. Gas/fuel stove only. Additional map ref.: *RAA Kangaroo Island* M6.

Murray Lagoon camping area

Kangaroo Island's largest wetland habitat, 46 km south-west of Kingscote. Signposted from Seagers Rd. Permit required. Gas/fuel stove only. Additional map ref.: *RAA Kangaroo Island* L6.

Further information & bookings: NPWSA, Murray Lagoon **Tel.:** (08) 8553 8233 **Camping fees:** From $6.00 per vehicle/ night; fees payable and camping permits from ranger headquarters or Seal Bay Visitors Centre

2. FLINDERS CHASE NATIONAL PARK

Covering 32 600 ha, Flinders Chase National Park occupies the western end of Kangaroo Island. The park headquarters is 102 km south-west of Kingscote. As well as campsites, historic cottage accommodation is also available; contact park headquarters for further details.

Harveys Return camping area

Located 63 km west of Parndana. Access via Playford Hwy. Historic site. Bring drinking water. Gas/fuel stove only. Permit required. Additional map ref.: *RAA Kangaroo Island* B4.

Rocky River camping area

Situated 105 km south-west of Kingscote near park headquarters on South Coast Rd. Permit required and bookings recommended during summer school holidays. Gas/fuel stove only. Additional map ref.: *RAA Kangaroo Island* C6.

Snake Lagoon camping area

Small camping area 8 km west of park headquarters. Access via West Bay Track. Bring drinking water. Gas/fuel stove only. Bookings and permit required. Additional map ref.: *RAA Kangaroo Island* B6.

West Bay camping area

Small camping area 22 km north-west of park headquarters. Access via West Bay Track. Bring drinking water. Gas/fuel

stove only. Bookings and permit required. Additional map ref.: *RAA Kangaroo Island* A6.

Further information & bookings: NPWSA, Rocky River **Tel.:** (08) 8559 7235 **Email:** kiparksaccom@dehaa.sa.gov.au **Camping fees:** *Rocky River*: From $15.00 per vehicle/night *All other areas*: From $6.00 per vehicle/night. Fees payable to and camping permits from park headquarters

3. KANGAROO ISLAND COUNCIL RESERVES

Kangaroo Island has a handful of council-managed campsites. Please note that Antechamber Bay and Browns Beach are populated by penguins; dogs must be kept on lead at all times. During the fire danger period, 1 Dec.–15 April, gas/fuel stoves are preferred and conditions apply to solid-fuel fires; contact information centre or council for further details.

American River camping area

On Tangara Drive 1 km south of American River. Bring drinking water and firewood. Permit required. Additional map ref.: *RAA Kangaroo Island – American River Map.*

Antechamber Bay camping area

Access via Willoughby Rd, 19 km south-east of Penneshaw. Permit required. Bring firewood. Additional map ref.: *RAA Kangaroo Island* S5.

Browns Beach camping area

On Hog Bay Rd 12 km south-west of Penneshaw. Gas/fuel stove only. Bring drinking water. Permit required. Additional map ref.: *RAA Kangaroo Island* Q5.

Vivonne Bay camping area

Access via South Coast Rd from village of Vivonne Bay. Good whale-watching spot May–Oct. Permit required. Bring firewood. Additional map ref.: *RAA Kangaroo Island* H7.

Western River camping area

On Western River Cove Rd, 44 km north-west of Parndana. Permit required. Bring firewood. Additional map ref.: *RAA Kangaroo Island* F3.

Further information & bookings:
Tourism Kangaroo Island **Tel.:** (08) 8553 1185
Email: tourki@kin.on.net *or*
Kangaroo Island Council **Tel.:** (08) 8553 2015
Camping fees: From $3.50 per site/night; fees payable and permits from Tourism Kangaroo Island (Howard Drive, Penneshaw) or council (Dauncy St, Kingscote) *Vivonne Bay*: Ranger collects fees daily

WESTERN AUSTRALIA

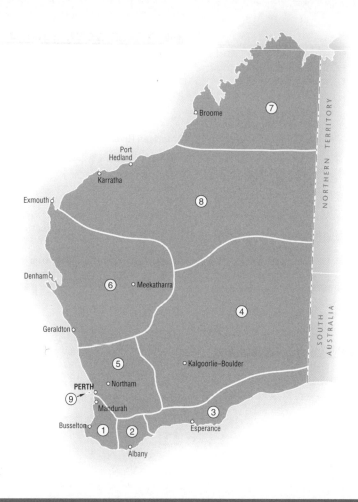

TOP 10 CAMPSITES

Hills Forest Discovery campground
Hills Forest Discovery Centre, page 229

Gooralong picnic and camping area
Serpentine National Park, page 231

Cape Riche camping area
Albany area, page 212

Conto Campground
Leeuwin–Naturaliste National Park, page 205

Thomas River camping area
Cape Arid National Park, page 215

Eagle Bluff camping area
Denham area, page 238

Neds Camp camping area
Cape Range National Park, page 236

Deep Reach Pool camping area
Millstream–Chichester National Park, page 252

Punamii-unpuu (Mitchell Falls) camping area
Ngauwudu (Mitchell Plateau), page 246

Kurrajong camping area
Purnululu National Park, page 247

Western Australia covers approximately one-third of the continent. Its population congregates along the seaboard but peters out in the far north, and the vast deserts of the west are all but unpopulated. The great age of the landscape – greater than any other on Earth – has helped create unique landforms and rich ecologies. From the azure waters and fine sands of the south to the worn magnificence of the Bungle Bungles in the north, Western Australia offers outdoor enthusiasts a world of sublime natural beauty and mystery and, in places, considerable personal challenge.

In the much-visited southern reaches of the state, campers and others are eminently well catered for. Here you'll find the summer-holiday island of Rottnest and the busy south-west touring region, known for its wineries, national park-protected coastline, great surfing and glorious old-growth forests. The Great Southern region incorporates the historic port of Albany and some of the state's most prolific wildflower areas, including Stirling Range National Park.

In the east, distances are greater and the landscapes are sparser. On the coast lies Esperance, surrounded by some of the country's most beautiful beaches. Further east lie the arid reaches of the great Nullarbor Plain. Inland, you can relive the excitement of the gold-rush days in the dusty but elegant townships of the Goldfields.

The Heartlands and Outback Coast reach inland, but the attractions are predominately coastal. The Heartlands is where you'll find the monastic town of New Norcia, built in the mid-1800s to resemble a Spanish mission; the Pinnacles, a bizarre desert landscape of limestone pillars; and the wildflower fields of the Avon Valley. The Outback Coast incorporates the famous dolphins of Monkey Mia, the gorge, river and bush landscapes of Kalbarri and Cape Range national parks, and Ningaloo Reef, an underwater paradise to rival the Great Barrier Reef.

The Kimberley, bigger than Germany but with a population of just 25 000, is Western Australia's signature landscape, a place where the themes of isolation, adventure and ancient beauty come together with spectacular results. Here you'll find the frontier pearling town of Broome, remote Aboriginal communities, rock shelters liberally inscribed with indigenous art, and the surreal spectacle of the striped domes of the Bungle Bungles rising up out of the desert.

Mitchell Falls in Ngauwudu, otherwise known as the Mitchell Plateau, the Kimberley

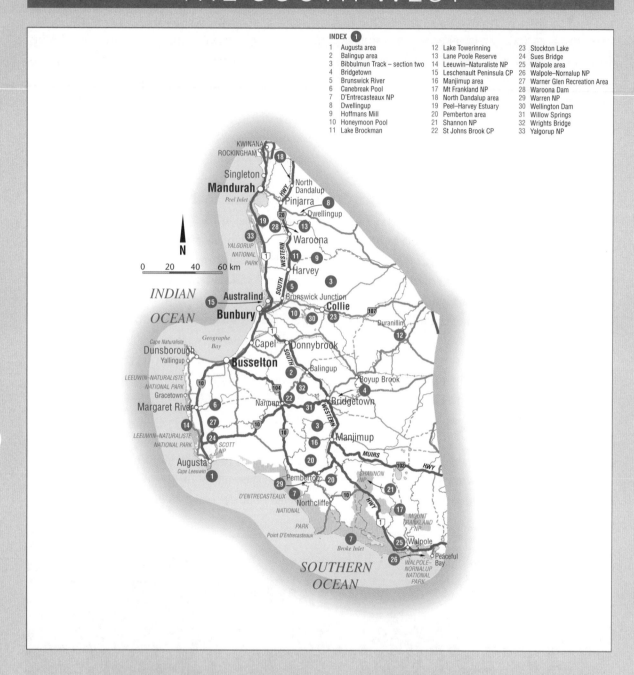

THE SOUTH-WEST CORNER OF
WESTERN AUSTRALIA FEATURES
SPECTACULAR COASTLINES,
TOWERING FORESTS, WINDING
RIVERS, RUGGED MOUNTAIN
RANGES, EXCELLENT WINERIES AND
INTERESTING TOWNS. AND IT HAS A PLETHORA OF
CAMPING OPPORTUNITIES. THE HARDEST DECISION
IN THIS REGION IS CHOOSING WHERE TO GO!

In the north of the region, south of
Mandurah, campers could set up beside the
Peel–Harvey Estuary at Heron Point, where
prawning, fishing and walking can be enjoyed.
Tent-based campers may choose Martins Tank
campsite in Yalgorup National Park, where a
walking trail visits the park's lake system,
including its interesting stromatolites and
thrombolites. Further inland is Lane Poole
Reserve, with a number of campsites along the
Murray River. Waroona Dam and Lake Brockman
both have an established caravan park with full
amenity blocks as well as foreshore bush camping.

The rivers of the region's south provide excellent canoeing, fishing, swimming and camping opportunities. Campsites well worth spending some time at include Honeymoon Pool beside the Collie River, Canebreak Pool on the Margaret River and Alexandra Bridge, Sues Bridge and Wrights Bridge along the Blackwood River.

The large Leeuwin–Naturaliste National Park has magnificent coastal scenery, excellent surf beaches, caves, walking trails and scenic drives through towering karri forests. The large, grassed and shady Conto Campground in the southern half of the park is a popular spot for caravans and tents. Those after a more secluded site might choose Point Road camping area; it is accessed by four-wheel drive only.

Warren National Park near Pemberton features magnificent karri forests. The park surrounds the Warren River, popular for swimming, fishing and canoeing. Campsites here are beside the river, along the scenic Heartbreak Trail.

BEST CAMPSITES

Warren River campsites
Warren National Park

Workers Pool camping area
St Johns Brook Conservation Park

Canebreak Pool camping and picnic area
Canebreak Pool

Conto Campground
Leeuwin–Naturaliste National Park

Shannon Campground
Shannon National Park

BEST TIME TO VISIT

All year round, however during winter the region can receive high rainfalls.

1. AUGUSTA AREA

At the mouth of the Blackwood River, Augusta is 330 km south of Perth. Augusta and its surrounds offer fishing, boating, swimming, surfing and sightseeing for visitors. In June–Dec. Augusta is a perfect whale-watching spot as humpback and southern right whales migrate north along the coast. Cape Leeuwin, 8 km south of Augusta, is where the Indian and Southern oceans meet.

Alexandra Bridge Camping Ground

On east side of bridge, signposted off Brockman Hwy, 10 km east of Karridale and 26 km north-east of Augusta. Firewood supplied. Additional map ref.: STAWA 15 D3.

Further information & bookings: Caretaker **Tel.:** (08) 9758 2244 **Camping fees:** From $3.85 per adult/night, $1.65 per school-aged child/night

Flinders Bay Caravan Park

Signposted off Leeuwin Rd, off Albany Terrace in Augusta. Firewood supplied. Closed from May to the Sept./Oct. school holidays. Bookings recommended. Additional map ref.: STAWA 15 D5.

Further information & bookings: Manager **Tel.:** (08) 9758 1380 **Camping fees:** Unpowered from $13.20 per site/night for 2 adults, powered from $16.50 per site/night for 2 adults

Turner Caravan Park

Signposted from Blackwood Ave in Augusta. On the Blackwood River. Firewood supplied. For peak season (Dec.–April) bookings are required 12 months in advance. Additional map ref.: STAWA 15 D5.

Further information & bookings: Manager **Tel.:** (08) 9758 1593 **Email:** turnercpark@amrsc.wa.gov.au **Camping fees:** *Off-peak (May–Nov.):* Unpowered from $13.20 per site/night for 2 adults, powered from $16.50 per site/night for 2 adults *Peak:* Ring for fee schedule

2. BALINGUP AREA

Surrounded by forests, Balingup is on the South Western Hwy between Donnybrook and Bridgetown. It is well known for its arts and crafts centre, wineries and speciality shops.

Balingup Caravan Transit Park

On Walter St in Balingup. Firewood supplied. Refundable deposit of $10.00 on key for ablution block. Additional map ref.: STAWA 28 C3.

Further information: Balingup General Store **Tel.:** (08) 9764 1051 **Camping fees:** From $11.00 per site/night for 2 people; fees payable at general store

Grimwade Townsite bush camping

Dispersed bush camping at dam and old mill site with no facilities, 11 km north-east of Balingup and 16 km east of

Kirup. Access off Grimwade Rd. Grimwade Rd is signposted 1 km north of Balingup. Travel for 9.6 km to a gravel road turn-off on the left – it leads into the forest to a clearing by a dam – or travel a further 700 m to a large junction and turn left into the old mill site. Bring drinking water and firewood. Additional map ref.: STAWA 28 C3.

Further information: CALM, Kirup **Tel.:** (08) 9731 6232
Fire restrictions: Solid-fuel fire ban 15 Dec.–15 March. Bring gas/fuel stove during this period. Dates may vary; check with local CALM office before lighting a fire

3. BIBBULMUN TRACK – SECTION TWO

See also Bibbulmun Track – section one, *page 226, and* Bibbulmun Track – section three, *page 212*

For an introduction to the Bibbulmun Track, see section one. This section of the track begins at White Horse Hills south of the Albany Hwy and traverses the forested regions between Dwellingup and Pemberton before hitting the coast close to Walpole. All walkers should be well prepared and self-sufficient. Water may not be reliable – always carry extra. Gas/fuel stove preferred. No fires at Yourdamung and Blackwood campsites or throughout the Lane Poole Special Conservation Zone. Fire restrictions occur Oct.–May; please contact local authorities to obtain current details. Purchase of the excellent Bibbulmun Track guides and maps published by CALM is essential.

White Horse Hills campsite
17.6 km from Gringer Creek (see section one). Additional map ref.: STAWA 58 B5.
Mount Wells campsite
14.5 km from White Horse Hills.
Chadoora campsite
14.8 km from Mt Wells.
Swamp Oak campsite
32.4 km from Chadoora.
Murray campsite
18.6 km from Swamp Oak.
Dookanelly campsite
17.8 km from Murray.
Possum Springs campsite
19.3 km from Dookanelly.
Yourdamung campsite
18.7 km from Possum Springs.
Harris Dam campsite
13.5 km from Yourdamung.
Yabberup campsite
41.0 km from Harris Dam.
Noggerup campsite
17.7 km from Yabberup.
Grimwade campsite
21.9 km from Noggerup.
Blackwood campsite
40.1 km from Grimwade.
Gregory Brook campsite
18.0 km from Blackwood.
Donnelly River Village
20.6 km from Gregory Brook.
Tom Road campsite
15.9 km from Donnelly River Village.
Boarding House campsite
22.8 km from Tom Rd.
Beavis campsite
19.1 km from Boarding House.
Beedelup campsite
19.5 km from Beavis.
Warren campsite
45.4 km from Beedelup.
Schafer campsite
21.1 km from Warren.

Gardner campsite
29.1 km from Schafer.
Lake Maringup campsite
15.9 km from Gardner.
Dog Pool campsite
24.5 km from Lake Maringup.
Mount Chance campsite
19.4 km from Dog Pool.
Woolbales campsite
20.4 km from Mt Chance.
Long Point campsite
17.2 km from Woolbales.
Mount Clare campsite
12.2 km from Long Point.
Frankland River campsite
27.5 km from Mt Clare.
Giants campsite
13.7 km from Frankland River.
Rame Head campsite
15.6 km from Giants, 33.2 km from Boat Harbour (see section three). Additional map ref.: STAWA 2 C2.

Further information:
CALM Bibbulmun Track Coordinator, Kensington **Tel.:** (08) 9334 0265 **Email:** bibtrack@calm.wa.gov.au *or* The Friends of the Bibbulmun Track **Tel.:** (08) 9481 0551 **Email:** friends@bibbulmuntrack.org.au **Website:** www.bibbulmuntrack.org.au *or* CALM offices: Dwellingup, tel. (08) 9538 1078; Collie, tel. (08) 9734 1988; Kirup, tel. (08) 9731 6232; Manjimup, tel. (08) 9771 7988; Pemberton, tel. (08) 9776 1207; Walpole, tel. (08) 9840 1027

4. BRIDGETOWN

Bridgetown, on the Blackwood River, is 90 km south-east of Bunbury on the South Western Hwy. Bridgetown is known for its beautiful countryside and surrounding jarrah forests.

Bridgetown Caravan Park

On South Western Hwy at the southern end of town beside Blackwood River. Camp kitchen. Firewood supplied. Pets allowed, but conditions apply; contact office for details. Additional map ref.: STAWA 28 D5.

Further information & bookings: Bridgetown Caravan Park **Tel.:** (08) 9761 1053 **Email:** colit@wn.com.au
Camping fees: Unpowered from $15.00 per site/night for 2 people, powered from $18.00 per site/night for 2 people

5. BRUNSWICK RIVER

The Treasure Bridge camping area is set amongst a grove of pine trees on the banks of the Brunswick River, north-east of Brunswick Junction, which is on the South Western Hwy about 20 km east of Bunbury. Conventional vehicles can only reach it in dry weather and the route is not suitable for caravans; 4WD is recommended as the track into the site is steep. The Brunswick River is suitable for fishing and Moonlight Pool is a good spot for swimming.

Treasure Bridge camping area

Beside the Brunswick River 22 km north-east of Brunswick Junction. Access via Sandlewood Rd, 5 km north of Brunswick Junction, then Big Tree Rd for 3.7 km. No facilities. Self-sufficient camping. Bring drinking water and firewood. Additional map ref.: STAWA 36 C2.

Further information:
CALM, Collie **Tel.:** (08) 9734 1988 *or*
Harvey District Tourist Bureau **Tel.:** (08) 9729 1122

6. CANEBREAK POOL

Canebreak Pool is on the Margaret River 25 km east of Margaret River township and offers swimming, fishing and canoeing. Campsites are beside the river. Drivers towing caravans should check road conditions before attempting access.

Canebreak Pool camping and picnic area

Signposted from Cane Brake Rd, 25 km east of Margaret River. From Bussell Hwy take Osmington Rd, which is 4 km north of Margaret River and 7 km south of Cowaramup. Travel for 15.5 km then take signposted Cane Brake Rd. Signposted access to Canebreak Pool is 5.5 km along Cane Brake Rd. Bring drinking water. Firewood supplied. Camp hosts are on-site during peak periods. Additional map ref.: STAWA 27 A5.

Further information: CALM, Margaret River
Tel.: (08) 9757 2322 **Camping fees:** From $5.00 per person/night; fees payable at self-registration station

7. D'ENTRECASTEAUX NATIONAL PARK

D'Entrecasteaux National Park stretches for 130 km, from Black Point in the north-west to Walpole in the south-east. The park features limestone cliffs, basalt columns, swamps, lakes, pristine sandy beaches, mobile sand dunes and jarrah and karri forests. Visitors can enjoy bushwalking and beachcombing, and excellent fishing, boating and canoeing in the rivers and lakes. Access to the majority of campsites within D'Entrecasteaux National Park is by 4WD, with Windy Harbour and Crystal Springs accessible to conventional vehicles. All visitors travelling in 4WDs should contact CALM for up-to-date access information. Caution is required at all river crossings.

SOUTH-EAST AREA

Banksia campsite

This campsite is in a popular surfing area and is signposted off Mandalay Beach Rd. It is 5 km west of Mandalay Beach, 14 km west of Crystal Springs campground and 28 km west of Walpole. Self-sufficient campers only. Bring drinking water. Gas/fuel stove only. Additional map ref.: STAWA 1 D2.

Canebreak Pool on the Margaret River

Crystal Springs campground

On Mandalay Beach Rd. Signposted off South Western Hwy, 13 km west of Walpole. Firewood supplied. Additional map ref.: STAWA 2 A2.

Further information: CALM, Walpole **Tel.:** (08) 9840 1027
Park entrance fee: $9.00 per vehicle, but not required for Crystal Springs **Camping fees:** *Crystal Springs:* From $5.00 per person/night; fees payable at self-registration station

CENTRAL AREA

Coodamurrup Beach camping area

Dispersed bush camping along beach and behind dunes at Coodamurrup Beach, 3 km south of Moores Hut. Access via Moores Track and Moores Hut. Bring drinking water and fire bin/bucket. Firewood supplied. Additional map ref.: STAWA 9 A5.

Fish Creek camping area

Located 13 km south of Chesapeake Rd. Access via signposted Fish Creek Track off Moores Track off Chesapeake Rd. Bring drinking water. Bring fire bin/bucket and firewood. Additional map ref.: STAWA 1 B1.

Malimup Beach camping area

Located 25 km south-west of Northcliffe. Access via Summertime Track off Windy Harbour Rd. Self-sufficient campers only. Bring drinking water. Bring fire bin and firewood or gas/fuel stove. Additional map ref.: STAWA 8 C4.

Moores Hut

Access via Moores Track off Chesapeake Rd. Located 13 km south of Chesapeake Rd and 40 km south-east of Northcliffe. Bring drinking water. Firewood supplied. Additional map ref.: STAWA 9 B5.

Mouth of Gardner camping area

Dispersed bush camping behind dunes beside the Gardner River. Access from Windy Harbour Rd. Access road is seasonally closed. Bring drinking water. Firewood supplied. Additional map ref.: STAWA 8 D5.

Windy Harbour camping area

Access via Windy Harbour Rd, 27 km south of Northcliffe. Popular surfing area. No powered sites. Bring drinking water. Firewood supplied. Additional map ref.: STAWA 8 D5.

Further information:
CALM, Pemberton **Tel.:** (08) 9776 1207 *or*
CALM, Walpole **Tel.:** (08) 9840 1027
Windy Harbour: Caretaker **Tel.:** (08) 9776 8398
Park entrance fee: $9.00 per vehicle, but not required for

Windy Harbour **Camping fees:** *Windy Harbour.* From $5.50 per person/night, family (2 adults and 2 children) $12.00 per site/night; fees payable to caretaker

NORTH-WEST AREA

Black Point Recreation Site

Located in a popular surfing area 70 km south-west of Nannup. Access via Black Point Rd from May until after Christmas; winter access is via Roberts and Woodarburrup rds from Milyeannup Coast Rd or via Wapet Track from Jasper Beach. Bring drinking water. Firewood supplied. Additional map ref.: STAWA 8 (Pt Map 7 C1).

Donnelly River Mouth camping area

Self-sufficient bush camping at mouth of Donnelly River. Boat access only; boat launch on Donnelly Boat Landing Rd. Bring drinking water, fire bin and firewood or gas/fuel stove. Additional map ref.: STAWA 8 (Pt Map 7 D1).

Jasper Beach camping area

Dispersed bush camping at Jasper Beach. Access via Jasper Beach Rd off Scott Rd. Self-sufficient campers only. Bring drinking water. Bring fire bin and firewood or gas/fuel stove. Additional map ref.: STAWA 8 (Pt Map 7 D1).

Lake Jasper camping area

Access via Lake Jasper Rd off Scott Rd off Vasse Hwy. It is 14 km from Vasse Hwy and 64 km south of Nannup. Signposted off Vasse Hwy. Bring drinking water. Firewood supplied. Additional map ref.: STAWA 16 D5.

Warren Beach camping area

Dispersed bush camping at Warren Beach and along access track. Use existing campsites only. Access via Warren Beach Rd off Lewis Rd. Self-sufficient campers only. Bring drinking water. Bring fire bin and firewood or gas/fuel stove. Additional map ref.: STAWA 8 B3.

Yeagarup Beach camping area

Dispersed bush camping at Yeagarup Beach. Access via Ritter Rd off Old Vasse Rd. Self-sufficient campers only. Bring drinking water. Bring fire bin and firewood or gas/fuel stove. Additional map ref.: STAWA 8 B2.

Further information:
CALM, Nannup **Tel.:** (08) 9756 1101 *or*
CALM, Pemberton **Tel.:** (08) 9776 1207
Park entrance fee: $9.00 per vehicle **Camping fees:** *Black Point and Lake Jasper.* From $5.00 per person/night, $2.00 per child (under 16) per night; fees payable at self-registration stations

8. DWELLINGUP

Dwellingup is 110 km south of Perth and to the east of the South Western Hwy.

Marrinup camping area

This is 2 km west of Dwellingup. Access via Grey Rd. Bring drinking water and firewood. Additional map ref.: STAWA 49 C1.

Further information: CALM, Dwellingup
Tel.: (08) 9538 1078

9. HOFFMANS MILL

Hoffmans Mill was once the centre of a thriving mill town, established in the early 1900s. Remains of the old mill can still be seen today. It is north-east of Harvey and signposted from the South Western Hwy.

Hoffmans Mill camping area

Signposted on Clarke Rd. Mill is 17 km east of South Western Hwy, 22 km east of Yarloop and 28 km north-east of Harvey. Water from river – boil before use. Bring firewood. Gas/fuel stove preferred. Hoffmans Mill is closed for camping from the end of Easter until 1 Nov. annually. Additional map ref.: STAWA 49 D5.

Further information: CALM, Collie **Tel.:** (08) 9734 1988
Camping fees: From $5.00 per person/night; fees collected by ranger **Fire restrictions:** Solid-fuel fire ban applies 15 Dec.–14 March; dates can change, check with local authorities for current dates

10. HONEYMOON POOL

Honeymoon Pool is 28 km west of Collie, on the banks of the Collie River. It is a popular area for bushwalkers, swimmers, canoeists and fisherfolk. There are three sites here: a group camping area, a lightweight/walk-in camping area and an area with individual car-based sites.

Honeymoon Pool camping areas

Signposted off River Rd, which is 5 km along Wellington Dam Rd, off the Coalfields Hwy. Drinking water from river – boil before use. Firewood supplied. Additional map ref.: STAWA 36 C4.

Further information: CALM, Collie **Tel.:** (08) 9734 1988
Camping fees: From $5.00 per person/night; fees collected by ranger or by campsite host on site during peak season
Fire restrictions: Solid-fuel fire ban 15 Dec.–15 March; bring gas/fuel stove during this period. Dates may change; check with local CALM office before lighting a fire

11. LAKE BROCKMAN

Lake Brockman is on Logue Brook Dam Rd, 6 km east of the South Western Hwy and south-east of Yarloop. The lake is a popular swimming and recreation area and offers great fishing, with trout often restocked.

Lake Brockman Tourist Park

Signposted from Logue Brook Dam Rd. Bring firewood or available for sale. Bookings recommended mid-Dec.–end Jan. Additional map ref.: STAWA 49 C5.

Bush camping

Lake foreshore camping. Access via Logue Brook Dam Rd. Bring drinking water. Additional map ref.: STAWA 49 C5.

Further information & bookings: Lake Brockman Tourist Park **Tel.:** (08) 9733 5402 **Camping fees:** *Lake Brockman Tourist Park*: Unpowered tent sites from $8.00 per adult/night, powered sites from $9.00 per adult/night *Bush camping*: $5.00 per adult/night, $2.00 per child/night

12. LAKE TOWERINNING

Lake Towerinning is a large lake surrounded by farmland. It is a haven for waterbirds and is a popular spot for birdwatchers. The lake is also popular for water-based activities. It is reached from Darkan Rd South, 2 km north of the Boyup Brook–Arthur River Rd and 8 km south of Duranillin.

Lakeside camping area

Signposted off Darkan Rd South. Firewood available. Bookings necessary during peak holiday periods. Additional map ref.: STAWA 30 C1.

Further information & bookings: Lakeside camping area **Tel.:** (08) 9863 1040 **Email:** lakesidecamping@westnet.com.au **Camping fees:** From $4.00 per adult/night, $3.00 per child/night; day visitors fee from $5.00 per adult/day, $3.50 per child/day

13. LANE POOLE RESERVE see page 206

14. LEEUWIN–NATURALISTE NATIONAL PARK

Covering 20 000 ha, Leeuwin–Naturaliste National Park stretches from Cape Naturaliste in the north to Cape Leeuwin in the south. The park features magnificent coastal scenery, beautiful surfing beaches, walking trails, caves, scenic drives and towering karri forests. At both capes are lighthouses that are open daily for visitors. Two caves within the park, Calgardup and Giants Cave, have self-guide tours while guided tours are available for Ngilgi, Lake, Mammoth, Jewel and Moodyne caves. The park is also popular with fisherfolk, swimmers and whale-watchers.

Boranup Forest camping area

Signposted from Boranup Drive off Caves Rd, 10 km north-west of Karridale. Access for cars and small vans only. Bring drinking water. Firewood supplied. Additional map ref.: STAWA 15 C2.

Conto Campground

Located 18 km south-west of Margaret River. Signposted on Conto Rd off Caves Rd. Access is 2 km west of Caves Rd. Access for cars and small vans only. Tank water – boil before use. Firewood supplied. Additional map ref.: STAWA 15 B2.

Hamelin Bay Caravan Park

Signposted on Hamelin Bay West Rd off Caves Rd, 8 km west of Karridale. Firewood supplied. Bookings necessary during school and public holidays and long weekends. Additional map ref.: STAWA 15 B3.

Point Road camping area

Close to fishing and surfing beach. 4WD access only, from Point Rd off Boranup Drive. Area is 4 km from Boranup Drive. and 21 km south-west of Margaret River. Bring drinking water. Firewood supplied. Additional map ref.: STAWA 15 B2.

Further information & bookings:
CALM, Busselton **Tel.:** (08) 9752 1677
Conto Campground: **Tel.:** (08) 9757 7025
Hamelin Bay Caravan Park: **Tel.:** (08) 9758 5540
Email: hamelinbay@westnet.com.au
Camping fees: *Hamelin Bay Caravan Park*: Unpowered from $15.00 per site/night for up to 2 people, powered from $20.00 per site/night for up to 2 people *All other areas*: From $6.00 per adult/night for $2.00 per child/night; fees collected by rangers

15. LESCHENAULT PENINSULA CONSERVATION PARK

Leschenault Peninsula separates the Leschenault Estuary from the Indian Ocean, west of Australind. The conservation park has long white beaches perfect for swimming and fishing. The peppermint and tuart woodlands are home to brushtail and ringtail possums. Access to Leschenault Peninsula Conservation Park is by boat or from the north via Buffalo Rd, 10 km north of Australind off the Old Coast Rd. Conventional vehicles can reach the park, but drivers towing caravans should check road conditions before attempting.

Belvedere Camping Ground

Off Buffalo Rd off Old Coast Rd, 16 km north of Australind. Bring drinking water and firewood. Additional map ref.: STAWA 35 D2.

The Cut camping area

Boat access only. Area is at end of peninsula. Bring drinking water and firewood. Additional map ref.: STAWA 35 D2.

Tuart Grove camping area

Boat access only. Area is halfway along peninsula. Bring drinking water and firewood. Additional map ref.: STAWA 35 D2.

Further information: CALM, Collie **Tel.:** (08) 9734 1988 **Camping fees:** From $5.00 per person/night; fees collected by ranger

16. MANJIMUP AREA

West of Manjimup is Greens Island camping area, once the Green family farm dating back to the 1921 settlement scheme. Signposted access to the camping area is off

LANE POOLE RESERVE

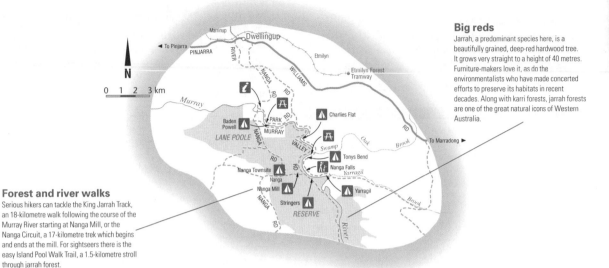

Big reds

Jarrah, a predominant species here, is a beautifully grained, deep-red hardwood tree. It grows very straight to a height of 40 metres. Furniture-makers love it, as do the environmentalists who have made concerted efforts to preserve its habitats in recent decades. Along with karri forests, jarrah forests are one of the great natural icons of Western Australia.

Forest and river walks

Serious hikers can tackle the King Jarrah Track, an 18-kilometre walk following the course of the Murray River starting at Nanga Mill, or the Nanga Circuit, a 17-kilometre trek which begins and ends at the mill. For sightseers there is the easy Island Pool Walk Trail, a 1.5-kilometre stroll through jarrah forest.

Lane Poole Reserve covers nearly 55 000 ha. Running through the reserve is the Murray River, which is ideal for swimming, fishing and canoeing, and visitors will also find forests of jarrah, blackbutt and marri, and wildflowers in spring. Abundant wildlife can be seen, including the chuditch (western quoll) and quokka, along with numerous bird and reptile species. Access is along Nanga Rd from Dwellingup. All roads within Lane Poole Reserve are gravel surfaces and are suitable for conventional vehicles. Collection of firewood within the reserve is not permitted; please bring it from home or purchase from supplier on the Pinjarra–Williams Rd near Nanga Rd junction. Keep dogs on leash at all times as fox baiting is carried out here.

Baden Powell Campground

Signposted from Park Rd off Nanga Rd, 9.5 km south of Dwellingup and 2 km east of reserve entry. Limited drinking water, bring own. Bring firewood. Additional map ref.: STAWA 49 D2.

Charlies Flat Campground

On River Rd off Park Rd, off Nanga Rd, 14 km south of Dwellingup and 7 km south-east of reserve entry. Bring drinking water and firewood. Additional map ref.: STAWA 49 D2.

Nanga Mill Campground

Signposted off Murray Valley Rd then Park Rd, River Rd and Bobs Crossing. It is 18 km south-east of Dwellingup and 11 km south-east of reserve entry. Boil water first. Bring firewood. Additional map ref.: STAWA 49 D2.

Nanga Townsite Campground

Signposted along Nanga Rd, 13.5 km south of Dwellingup and 6 km south of reserve entry. Bring drinking water and firewood. Additional map ref.: STAWA 49 D2.

Stringers Campground

On Murray Valley Rd via Bobs Crossing off River Rd, which is off Park Rd, 19 km south-east of Dwellingup and 11.5 km south-east of reserve entry. Bring drinking water and firewood. Additional map ref.: STAWA 49 D2.

Tonys Bend Campground

On River Rd off Park Rd, off Nanga Rd, 17 km south of Dwellingup and 9.4 km south-east of reserve entry. Bring drinking water and firewood. Additional map ref.: STAWA 49 D2.

Yarragil Campground

On River Rd off Park Rd, off Nanga Rd, 20 km south of Dwellingup and 12 km south-east of reserve entry. Bring drinking water and firewood. Additional map ref.: STAWA 49 D3.

Further information: CALM, Dwellingup
Tel.: (08) 9538 1078 **Email:** dwell.dis@calm.wa.gov.au
Camping fees: From $5.00 per adult/night; $3.00 per child (16 and under) per night; fees payable at park entry station on Park Rd or to ranger **Fire restrictions:** Solid-fuel fire ban 15 Dec.–15 March, bring gas/fuel stove during this period. Dates can change so check first with local CALM office

Donnelly Drive. The Bibbulmun Track passes through this region and One Tree Bridge and the Four Aces are nearby and well worth a visit.

Greens Island camping area

Signposted off Donnelly Drive off Graphite Rd, 26 km west of Manjimup. Bring drinking water. Firewood supplied. Additional map ref.: STAWA 17 C3.

Further information:
CALM, Pemberton **Tel.:** (08) 9776 1207 or
Manjimup Tourist Bureau **Tel.:** (08) 9771 1831

17. MOUNT FRANKLAND NATIONAL PARK

Mt Frankland National Park contains some of the state's largest stands of karri trees. Overlooking the forests is the large granite peak of Mt Frankland – the walk to the summit is hard, involving a climb up a steel ladder then a steep walk, and is best attempted by fit walkers only. Mt Frankland National Park is north of Walpole.

Mount Frankland camping area

A small site at start of walking track to summit. Accessed via Mt Frankland Rd off North Walpole Rd, 27 km north of Walpole. Limited drinking water, best to bring own. Firewood supplied. Additional map ref.: STAWA 10 C5.

Further information: CALM, Walpole **Tel.:** (08) 9840 1027

18. NORTH DANDALUP AREA

Whittakers Mill, an old mill town, is 8 km east of North Dandalup. It is a good place to see birds and wildlife.

Whittakers Mill camping area

Signposted from Scarp Rd off Del Park Rd, off the South Western Hwy just south of North Dandalup. Bring drinking water and firewood. Additional map ref.: STAWA 57 C5.

Further information: CALM, Dwellingup **Tel.:** (08) 9538 1078
Camping fees: None at time of printing, however fees may be introduced at a later date **Fire restrictions:** Solid-fuel fire ban 15 Dec.–15 March. Bring gas/fuel stove during this period. Check with local CALM office before lighting a fire

19. PEEL–HARVEY ESTUARY

Herron Point camping area is on the Peel–Harvey Estuary 23 km south-west of Pinjarra. This is an ideal site for fishing, prawning and walking. Abundant and varied birdlife can be found here.

Herron Point camping area

On Herron Point Rd 7 km west of Old Bunbury Rd. Bring drinking water and firewood. There is a two-night limit for camping. Area is baited, keep dogs on lead at all times. Additional map ref.: STAWA 48 D2.

Further information:
Murray Shire Council **Tel.:** (08) 9531 7777 or
Pinjarra Tourist Centre **Tel.:** (08) 9531 1438
Camping fees: $5.50 per site/night 1 Nov.–31 April only, caretaker on site during this time **Fire restrictions:** Solid-fuel

fire ban 1 Nov.–15 March, bring gas/fuel stove during this period. These dates may change, check with local authorities prior to lighting any fire

20. PEMBERTON AREA

Pemberton is 76 km south of Nannup on the Vasse Hwy. Pemberton and its surrounds have many natural attractions: visitors can climb the Gloucester Tree or the Dave Evans Bicentennial Tree, swim or fish at Big Brook Dam or drive the scenic Rainbow Trail.

Big Brook Arboretum

Signposted from Rainbow Trail, 11 km north-west of Pemberton. Caravan access via Range Rd off Mullineaux Rd, which is off Golf Links Rd from Pemberton. Bring drinking water. Firewood supplied. Maximum of three nights' stay only. Additional map ref.: STAWA 17 C5.

Moons Crossing camping and picnic area

Small site beside Warren River. Access via Moons Crossing Rd off Spring Gully Rd from the Gloucester Tree, 16 km east of Pemberton. Conventional vehicle access in dry weather only. Bring drinking water. Firewood supplied. Additional map ref.: STAWA 9 A1.

Further information:
CALM, Pemberton **Tel.:** (08) 9776 1207 or
Pemberton Tourist Centre **Tel.:** (08) 9776 1133

21. SHANNON NATIONAL PARK

Covering 53 500 ha, Shannon National Park east of Pemberton protects karri, jarrah and marri forests. Visitors can enjoy the park's wildflowers, one of the several walks, or the self-guide Great Forest Trees Drive. The Shannon campground is at the old Shannon townsite, which once boasted a general store, butcher, church and school.

Shannon Campground

Signposted from South Western Hwy, 53 km south of Manjimup and 41 km north-west of Walpole. Camp hosts are on site Dec.–April. Firewood supplied. Additional map ref.: STAWA 9 C2.

Further information: CALM, Pemberton **Tel.:** (08) 9776 1207
Park entrance fee: $9.00 per vehicle **Camping fees:** From $12.50 per site/night for 2 people, use of hut extra $5.00 per night; fees payable at self-registration station

22. ST JOHNS BROOK CONSERVATION PARK

Visitors to St Johns Brook Conservation Park can enjoy a refreshing swim in St Johns Brook or take in the area's logging history along the Old Timberline Walking Trail. You may even spot the Nannup tiger! Conventional vehicle access to the park is the signposted Mowen Rd, 1.5 km north of Nannup off the Vasse Hwy.

Workers Pool camping area

Signposted along Mowen Rd, 9.5 km west of Nannup. Bring drinking water. Some firewood supplied. Additional map ref.: STAWA 27 D5.

Further information:
CALM, Kirup **Tel.:** (08) 9731 6232 *or*
Nannup Tourist Information Centre **Tel.:** (08) 9756 1211
Camping fees: From $5.00 per person/night; fees payable at self-registration station

23. STOCKTON LAKE

The old Stockton open-cut mine is now filled with water, an artificial lake popular for water activities. It is 8 km east of Collie and reached from the Coalfields Hwy.

Stockton Lake camping area

On Piavanini Rd off Coalfields Hwy. Bring drinking water and firewood. Additional map ref.: STAWA 37 A4.

Further information: CALM, Collie **Tel.:** (08) 9734 1988

24. SUES BRIDGE

On the banks of the Blackwood River, Sues Bridge is an ideal canoeing venue. It is 9 km north of the Brockman Hwy on Sues Rd (the Sues Rd turn-off is 29 km east of Karridale). It is proposed that this area will become national park, so dog laws may change; check before leaving if you are intending to bring your dog.

Sues Bridge picnic and camping area

Signposted from Sues Rd. Cars and small vans only. Bring drinking water. Firewood supplied. This area is baited, keep dogs on leash. Additional map ref.: STAWA 16 B2.

Further information: CALM, Margaret River
Tel.: (08) 9757 2322 **Camping fees:** From $5.00 per person/night; fees payable at self-registration station

25. WALPOLE AREA

The town of Walpole is on the South Western Hwy west of Denmark, on the Walpole Inlet which is connected to the Nornalup Inlet. The Frankland, Walpole and Deep rivers feed into the two inlets. To the north-west of Walpole on the Deep River are two campsites. Conventional vehicle access to both is off the South Western Hwy. It is proposed that this area will become national park, so dog laws may change; check before leaving if you are intending to bring your dog.

Centre Road camping area

Located 5 km east of the South Western Hwy on Centre Rd (turn-off is 20 km north-west of Walpole). Shelter hut on site. Limited tent sites. Firewood supplied. There is a limit of three nights' stay here. Additional map ref.: STAWA 2 A1.

Fernhook Falls camping area

Located 6 km east of the South Western Hwy on Beardmore Rd (turn-off is 37 km north-west Walpole). Shelter huts on site. Bring drinking water. Firewood supplied. Additional map ref.: STAWA 10 A5.

Further information: CALM, Walpole **Tel.:** (08) 9840 1027
Camping fees: *Fernhook Falls:* From $10.00 per site/night for the first 2 people, use of hut additional $10.00; fees payable at self-registration station

26. WALPOLE–NORNALUP NATIONAL PARK

Surrounding Walpole and Nornalup inlets, Walpole–Nornalup National Park is home to the giant tingle tree, pristine bushland and limestone cliffs. Visitors can enjoy scenic drives, bushwalking, swimming, canoeing and 4WD touring. The park is well known for the Valley of the Giants Tree Top Walk, along with the Valley of the Giants Ancient Empire Walk and the Hilltop Giant Tingle Tree Trail. Coastal walks include the easy Conspicuous Cliff Walks and the harder 6-km Coalmine Beach Heritage Trail. Two caravan parks are located close to the park – one near Walpole and the other at Peaceful Bay.

Coalmine Beach Caravan Park

On Knoll Drive off the South Coast Hwy, 3 km east of Walpole. Popular surfing and birdwatching spot. Firewood supplied. Bookings essential during Christmas and New Year holidays. Additional map ref.: STAWA 2 B2.

Bookings: Coalmine Beach Caravan Park **Tel.:** 1800 670 026
Email: coalmine@agn.net.au **Camping fees:** Unpowered sites from $18.00 per site/night for 2 people, powered sites from $20.00 per site/night for 2 people

Peaceful Bay Caravan Park

On Peaceful Bay Rd off the South Coast Hwy, 34 km east of Walpole and 45 km west of Denmark. Beach boat launch. Popular surfing spot. Some firewood supplied. Bookings essential during Christmas, New Year and Easter holidays. Additional map ref.: STAWA 2 D2.

Bookings: Peaceful Bay Caravan Park **Tel.:** (08) 9840 8060
Camping fees: Unpowered sites from $14.00 per site/night for 2 people, powered sites from $16.00 per site/night for 2 people

Park information: CALM, Walpole **Tel.:** (08) 9840 1027

27. WARNER GLEN RECREATION AREA

This recreation area is a popular canoeing site. It is at Warners Bridge on the banks of Chapman Brook, near where the brook enters the Blackwood River, and is 25 km south-east of Margaret River via Warner Glen Rd off the Bussell Hwy.

Chapman Pool camping area

Signposted off Warner Glen Rd. Bring drinking water. Some firewood supplied. Additional map ref.: STAWA 15 D2.

Further information: CALM, Margaret River
Tel.: (08) 9757 2322 **Camping fees:** From $5.00 per person/night; fees payable at self-registration station

28. WAROONA DAM

This irrigation dam is 8 km east of Waroona on the South Western Hwy. It was completed in 1968. Waroona Dam is popular with visitors for swimming, fishing, bushwalking, wildflowers, canoeing and waterskiing. Access from Waroona to the camping areas is via Nanga Brook Rd on to Scarp Rd then Invarell Rd. There is a $20.00 refundable dog bond at both camping areas.

Lake Navarino Forest Resort

On Invarell Rd, signposted from Scarp Rd. Bring drinking water and firewood. Additional map ref.: STAWA 49 C3.

Navarino Lakeside Camping

Lake foreshore camping. Access via Lake Navarino Forest Resort. Bring drinking water and firewood. Additional map ref.: STAWA 49 C3.

Further information & bookings: Lake Navarino Forest Resort **Tel.:** (08) 9733 3000 or 1800 650 626 **Email:** info@navarino.com.au **Website:** www.navarino.com.au
Camping fees: *Lake Navarino Forest Resort:* Unpowered tent sites from $7.00 per adult/night, $3.50 per child/night; powered van sites from $17.00 per site/night for 2 people *Navarino Lakeside Camping:* From $5.50 per adult/night, $2.75 per child (age 3–16) per night; fees to be paid at office prior to setting up camp **Fire restrictions:** Solid-fuel fire ban 15 Dec.–15 March; bring gas/fuel stove during this period

29. WARREN NATIONAL PARK

One of the most outstanding features of Warren National Park is its tall karri trees. The park is south-west of Pemberton and surrounds the Warren River, which is popular for fishing, swimming and canoeing. Take a stroll along the Heartbreak Walk Trail and visit the Dave Evans Bicentennial Tree, or even climb it!

Warren River campsites

Three separate campsites signposted along Heartbreak Trail and Maidenbush Trail off Old Vasse Rd, off the Vasse Hwy south-west of Pemberton. Bring drinking water. Firewood supplied. Additional map ref.: STAWA 8 C1.

Further information: CALM, Pemberton
Tel.: (08) 9776 1207 **Park entrance fee:** $9.00 per vehicle
Camping fees: From $10.50 per site/night for 2 people; fees payable at self-registration station near the Dave Evans Bicentennial Tree

30. WELLINGTON DAM

Wellington Dam is 29 km west of Collie and is surrounded by jarrah forests. The waters of Wellington Dam are popular for fishing, catching marrons and canoeing. At the dam wall visitors will find a lookout and walking trails. Conventional vehicle access is via Wellington Weir Rd off the Coalfields Rd.

Potters Gorge camping area

Signposted off Wellington Weir Rd. Water from dam – boil before use. Firewood supplied. Additional map ref.: STAWA 36 C4.

Further information: CALM, Collie **Tel.:** (08) 9734 1988
Camping fees: From $5.00 per person/night; fees collected by ranger or by campsite host on-site during peak season

31. WILLOW SPRINGS

Set amongst jarrah forests between Nannup and Bridgetown along Gold Gully Rd, Willow Springs was a once a forestry site. The Bibbulmun Track passes through here. Conventional vehicle access is off the Brockman Hwy 22 km east of Nannup and 23 km west of Bridgetown.

Willow Springs camping area

Signposted off Gold Gully Rd 5 km south of Brockman Hwy. Self-sufficient campers only. Bring drinking water and firewood. Additional map ref.: STAWA 17 C1.

Further information: CALM, Kirup **Tel.:** (08) 9731 6232

32. WRIGHTS BRIDGE

Beside the Blackwood River, Wrights Bridge offers visitors the opportunity to throw in a line for trout or marron as well as swim and canoe. For walkers there are a number of short trails around the camping area or for those after a longer walk there is one along the river. Wrights Bridge is reached from the scenic Nannup–Balingup Rd.

Wrights Bridge camping area

Signposted from Nannup–Balingup Rd, 29 km north-east of Nannup and 12 km south-west of Balingup. Bring drinking water. Firewood supplied. Additional map ref.: STAWA 28 B4.

Further information: CALM, Kirup **Tel.:** (08) 9731 6232
Camping fees: From $5.00 per adult/night and $2.00 per child (up to 16) per night; fees payable at self-registration station

33. YALGORUP NATIONAL PARK

Just south of Mandurah, Yalgorup National Park preserves some of the coastal vegetation of the Swan Coastal Plain. Within the park is a chain of ten lakes, with Lake Clifton and Lake Preston being the largest. The lakes provide shelter for migrating birds from the Northern Hemisphere as well as many local species. Visitors can view the algae growth structures of stromatolites and thrombolites at the northern end of Lake Clifton, while in the south of the park they can enjoy either the Lake Pollard Trail or Heathlands Walk. Martins Tank campsite is in the south of the park, 8 km north of Preston Beach. Conventional vehicle access is via Preston Beach North Rd off Old Coast Rd.

Martins Tank campsite

This site is signposted 6.8 km along Preston Beach North Rd. Bring drinking water and firewood. Additional map ref.: STAWA 48 D3.

Further information: CALM, Mandurah **Tel.:** (08) 9582 9333
Camping fees: From $5.00 per person/night; fees collected by ranger **Fire restrictions:** Solid-fuel fire ban Oct.–March; bring gas/fuel stove during this period. Dates may change; check with local CALM office before lighting a fire

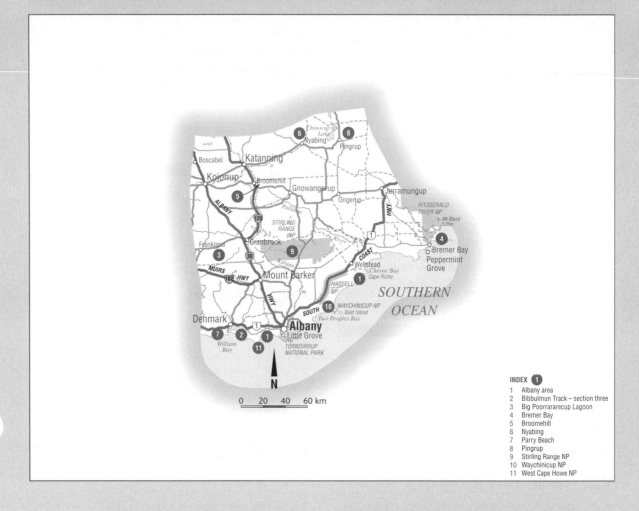

THE GREAT SOUTHERN REGION COVERS THE COASTLINE FROM DENMARK EAST TO BREMER BAY, STRETCHING NORTH TO THE SMALL TOWNS OF KOJONUP AND KATANNING. THE COASTLINE BOASTS SPECTACULAR SCENERY, AND IN THE NORTH ARE THE MAGNIFICENT MOUNTAINS OF STIRLING RANGE AND PORONGURUP NATIONAL PARKS.

Just to the west of Denmark, on William Bay, is Parry Beach. Campers here can set up amongst the coastal vegetation, which offers good protection from coastal winds. This site is beside a swimming beach with a beach boat launch, making it popular with fisherfolk.

The City of Albany has set aside a number of bush campsites along the coast, stretching from Lowlands Beach, 40 kilometres west of Albany, to Boat Harbour, 127 kilometres north-east. Facilities and activities vary from site to site.

Camping at West Cape Howe National Park is at the undeveloped Shelley Beach camping area. Campers here can enjoy the rugged coastline of dolerite rising above the Southern Ocean. Fishing, scuba diving and four-wheel-drive touring are popular in this park.

Waychinicup National Park boasts unspoiled coastal scenery, granite outcrops and the lower reaches of the Waychinicup River. Camping in the park is at Waychinicup Inlet, and the river and its inlet are popular canoeing and fishing areas.

In the north of the region, the Stirling and Porongurup ranges rise up from the surrounding farmlands. There is camping at Moingup Springs along Chester Pass Road in Stirling Range National Park. The Stirling Range stretches for over 65 kilometres and rises 1000 metres above sea level. It features excellent walking trails with magnificent views, and there are brilliant wildflower displays during spring and early summer.

BEST CAMPSITES

Moingup Springs camping area
Stirling Range National Park

Parry Beach recreation area
Parry Beach

Big Poorrarecup Lagoon camping area
Big Poorrarecup Lagoon

Perkins Beach camping area
Albany area

Cape Riche camping area
Albany area

BEST TIME TO VISIT

All year round for the coastal regions, but the mountains are best visited from spring through to autumn.

Two Peoples Bay, east of Albany

1. ALBANY AREA

See also Waychinicup National Park, *page 213*

Albany is located 408 km from Perth via the Albany Hwy. Visitors to Albany and its surrounding region will find historical sites, magnificent coastal scenery, nature reserves, rivers and mountains. Activities include boating, fishing, swimming, bushwalking, sightseeing and much more. The City of Albany has established many camping areas within the shire, along its beautiful coastline.

WEST OF ALBANY

Cosy Corner (east) camping area

Signposted from Cosy Corner Rd, off Lower Denmark Rd, 30 km west of Albany. Self-sufficient campers only. Bring drinking water and firewood (fire restrictions apply to this site; check with local authorities before lighting a fire). Additional map ref.: STAWA 4 B3.

Cosy Corner (west) camping area

On Cosy Corner Rd off Lower Denmark Rd, 30 km west of Albany. 4WD boat launch. Self-sufficient campers only. Bring drinking water and firewood. Please note that this site is closed to camping 1 Dec.–22 April. Additional map ref.: STAWA 4 B3.

Lowlands camping area

On Tennessee South Rd off Lower Denmark Rd, 40 km west of Albany. Self-sufficient campers only. Bring drinking water and firewood. Dogs not recommended at this site as it is beside a national park. Additional map ref.: STAWA 4 A3.

Mutton Bird (east) camping area

On Mutton Bird Rd off Elleker–Grasmere Rd, off Lower Denmark Rd, 17 km west of Albany. Drivers towing caravans should check road conditions before attempting. Self-sufficient campers only. Bring drinking water and firewood. Additional map ref.: STAWA 4 C2.

Perkins Beach camping area

On Perkins Beach Rd off Lower Denmark Rd, 28 km west of Albany. Self-sufficient campers only. Bring drinking water and firewood. Additional map ref.: STAWA 4 B2.

Torbay Inlet (east) camping area

On Torbay Rd off Mutton Bird Rd, which is off Elleker– Grasmere Rd off Lower Denmark Rd, 28 km west of Albany. 4WD boat launch. Self-sufficient campers only. Bring drinking water and firewood. Additional map ref.: STAWA 4 C2.

Torbay Inlet (west) camping area

On Torbay Inlet Rd off Perkins Beach Rd, which is off Lower Denmark Rd, 28 km west of Albany. Self-sufficient campers only. Bring drinking water and firewood. Additional map ref.: STAWA 4 C2.

EAST OF ALBANY

Bettys Beach (Two Peoples Bay) camping area

This is 52 km north-east of Albany on Two Peoples Bay, along Bettys Beach Rd. Take Homestead Rd off the South Coast Hwy then drive 14 km to Bettys Beach Rd. Self-sufficient campers only. Bring drinking water and firewood. Additional map ref.: STAWA 5 D1.

Boat Harbour camping area

Signposted from Boat Harbour Rd off South Coast Hwy, 127 km north-east of Albany and 96 km west of Bremer Bay. Access road is seasonal; check road conditions before attempting. Self-sufficient campers only. Bring drinking water and firewood. Additional map ref.: STAWA 24 B3.

Cape Riche camping area

Signposted from the South Coast Hwy via Sandalwood Rd, 115 km north-east of Albany and 100 km south-west of Bremer Bay. Bring drinking water and firewood. 4WD boat ramp. Additional map ref.: STAWA 24 B4.

Normans Beach camping area

Located 49 km north-east of Albany. Take Homestead Rd off the South Coast Hwy and travel for 9 km to Normans Beach Rd. Site is 2 km along Normans Beach Rd. Self-sufficient campers only. Bring drinking water and firewood. Additional map ref.: STAWA 5 D1.

Further information:
City of Albany **Tel.:** (08) 9841 9333 *or*
Albany Visitor Centre **Tel.:** (08) 9841 1088
Website: www.albanytourist.com.au
Cape Riche: On-site caretaker **Tel.:** (08) 9847 3088
Camping fees: *Cape Riche:* From $5.50 per site/night up to 2 people, each additional person $2.75 per night and children under 16 free **Fire restrictions:** These apply in the region; check with local authorities before lighting any fires

2. BIBBULMUN TRACK – SECTION THREE

See also Bibbulmun Track – section one, *page 226*, and Bibbulmun Track – section two, *page 202*

For an introduction to the Bibbulmun Track, see section one. This section of the track covers the distance between Rame Head (in Walpole–Nornalup National Park) and Albany, taking in some beautiful coastal scenery along the way. All walkers should be well prepared and self-sufficient. Water may not be reliable – always carry extra. Gas/fuel stove preferred. Fire restrictions occur Oct.–May; please contact local authorities to obtain current details. Purchase of the excellent Bibbulmun Track guides and maps published by CALM is essential.

Boat Harbour campsite
33.2 km from Rame Head (see section two). Additional map ref.: STAWA 3 A2.

William Bay campsite
19.9 km from Boat Harbour.
Nullaki campsite
31.5 km from William Bay.
West Cape Howe campsite
16.5 km from Nullaki.
Torbay campsite
16.4 km from West Cape Howe.
Hidden Valley campsite
17.5 km from Torbay.
Albany trackhead
19.3 km from Hidden Valley. Additional map ref.: STAWA 4 D2.

Further information:
CALM Bibbulmun Track Coordinator, Kensington
Tel.: (08) 9334 0265 **Email:** bibtrack@calm.wa.gov.au *or*
The Friends of the Bibbulmun Track **Tel.:** (08) 9481 0551
Email: friends@bibbulmuntrack.org.au **Website:**
www.bibbulmuntrack.org.au *or*
CALM offices: Walpole, tel (08) 9840 1027; Albany, tel. (08) 9842 4500

3. BIG POORRARECUP LAGOON

Big Poorrarecup Lagoon is west of the Albany Hwy, about 50 km west of Cranbrook and 20 km east of Frankland. It is popular for water activities.

Big Poorrarecup Lagoon camping area

On northern edge of lake. Signposted from Poorrarecup Rd off Frankland–Cranbrook Rd; camping area is 10 km south of Frankland–Cranbrook Rd. Natural boat ramp. Flush toilets. Childrens playground. Bring drinking water and firewood. Additional map ref.: STAWA 20 C5.

Further information: Shire of Cranbrook **Tel.:** (08) 9826 1008 **Email:** cbkshire@wn.com.au **Fire restrictions:** Solid-fuel fire ban Nov.–March; bring gas/fuel stove during this period. Dates may change; check with local authorities before lighting a fire

4. BREMER BAY AREA

The town of Bremer Bay is 183 km north-east of Albany and is reached off the South Coast Hwy. The coastal scenery here is one of the highlights of this region and it is a deservedly popular area for boating, fishing and scuba diving.

Gordon Inlet camping area

Located 20 km north-east of Bremer Bay, just south of Fitzgerald River National Park, accessed via Gordon Inlet Rd off Gairdner Rd. 4WD access only. Bring drinking water. Gas/fuel stove only. Additional map ref.: STAWA 24 (Pt Map 25 A2).

House Beach camping area

Signposted – 4WD only – off Gordon Inlet Rd, off Gairdner Rd, 43 km north-east of Bremer Bay. Bring drinking water. Gas/fuel stove only. Additional map ref.: STAWA 24 (Pt Map 25 A2).

Millers Point Reserve

On Beaufort Inlet, reached via Millers Point Rd off Borden–Bremer Bay Rd. It is 6 km south of Borden–Bremer Bay Rd and 55 km west of Bremer Bay. Bring drinking water and firewood. Additional map ref.: STAWA 24 B3.

Further information: Shire of Jerramungup
Tel.: (08) 9835 1022 **Camping fees:** *Millers Point:* From $5.00 per site/night; fees payable to on-site caretaker

5. BROOMEHILL

The village of Broomehill is 160 km north of Albany on the Great Southern Hwy. Visitors can take in the sites and history on the town's Heritage Trail walking track.

Broomehill Village Caravan Park

Corner of Morgan Rd and Journal St in Broomehill. Gas/fuel stove only. Laundry facilities. Additional map ref.: STAWA 32 B4.

Further information & bookings: Shire of Broomehill
Tel.: (08) 9824 1245 **Camping fees:** Unpowered tent sites from $8.00 per site/night for 1–2 people, powered van sites from $16.00 per site/night for 2 people; fees payable at shire office on the Great Southern Hwy or collected by caretaker

6. NYABING

Nyabing and its surrounding regions were first visited in the 1800s by sandalwood cutters. It is 65 km east of Katanning, which lies on the Great Southern Hwy.

Nyabing Recreation Reserve

On Martin St in Nyabing. Firewood supplied. Key for ablution block from shire office. Additional map ref.: STAWA 33 C1.

Further information & bookings: Shire of Kent
Tel.: (08) 9829 1051 **Email:** admin@kent.wa.gov.au
Camping fees: From $11.60 per site/night for up to 2 people; fees payable at shire office (Richmond St)

7. PARRY BEACH

Parry Beach is on William Bay 29 km west of Denmark and offers excellent swimming, fishing and boating. It is signposted off the South Coast Hwy.

Parry Beach recreation area

At the end of Parry Rd. Beach boat launch. Bring firewood. Additional map ref.: STAWA 3 B2.

Further information:
Shire of Denmark **Tel.:** (08) 9848 1106 *or*
Denmark Tourist Bureau **Tel.:** (08) 9848 2055
Camping fees: Tent sites from $5.00 per site/night for up to 2 people, caravan sites from $10.00 per site/night for up to 2 people

8. PINGRUP

Pingrup is a small rural centre with a population of around 80 people. It lies 38 km east of Nyabing.

Pingrup Caravan Park

On Sanderson St in Pingrup. Key for ablution block from general store – $10.00 refundable deposit. Additional map ref.: STAWA 34 C1.

Further information & bookings: Pingrup General Store
Tel.: (08) 9820 1010 **Camping fees:** From $11.60 per site/night for up to 2 people; fees payable at general store (Sanderson St)

9. STIRLING RANGE NATIONAL PARK

The rugged peaks of the Stirling Range stretch for 65 km, rising up from the surrounding farmland. The range is home to a large and diverse array of plants and animals. The main wildflower season is Sept.–Nov. A number of walks leave from the camping area. The park is signposted from the Chester Pass Rd 76 km north-east of Albany.

Moingup Springs camping area

Signposted from Chester Pass Rd 76 km north-east of Albany. Gas/fuel stove only. Additional map ref.: STAWA 22 C5.

Further information: CALM, Stirling Range National Park
Tel.: (08) 9827 9230 or (08) 9827 9278 **Park entrance fee:** $9.00 per vehicle **Camping fees:** From $5.00 per person/night; fees collected by ranger

10. WAYCHINICUP NATIONAL PARK

Waychinicup National Park stretches from Normans Beach in the west across Mt Manypeaks to Cheyne Beach in the east. It protects the picturesque Waychinicup River, which is popular with canoeists and fisherfolk. The park has magnificent coastal scenery and in spring is carpeted with colourful wildflowers. For conventional vehicles access to the camping area is off Cheyne Beach Rd from the South Coast Hwy.

Waychinicup Inlet camping area

Signposted off Cheyne Beach Rd, 60 km east of Albany. Nine tent sites only, some walk-in. Bring drinking water. Gas/fuel stove only. Additional map ref.: STAWA 5 (Pt Map 6 A1).

Further information:
CALM, Albany **Tel.:** (08) 9841 7133 *or*
CALM, Two Peoples Bay Nature Reserve **Tel.:** (08) 9846 4276
Camping fees: From $10.00 per site/night for 1–2 people; fees collected by ranger or by campsite host on-site during peak season

11. WEST CAPE HOWE NATIONAL PARK

West Cape Howe National Park has a stunning coastline of dolerite cliffs framed against the Southern Ocean. The vegetation here ranges from karri forest to low coastal heath and from groups of peppermints to colourful spring wildflowers. Visitors can enjoy scuba diving at Shelley Beach (please be aware of strong rips in this area) or go 4WD touring to some of the remote scenic areas within the park. It is 40 km west of Albany and reached from Shelley Beach Rd off Coombes Rd, off Cosy Corner Rd.

Shelley Beach camping area

Access off Shelley Beach Rd. Bring drinking water. Gas/fuel stove only. Additional map ref.: STAWA 4 B3.

Further information:
CALM, Albany **Tel.:** (08) 9841 7133 *or*
CALM, West Cape Howe National Park **Tel.:** (08) 9844 4090
Camping fees: From $5.00 per person/night; fees collected by ranger or by campsite host on-site during peak season

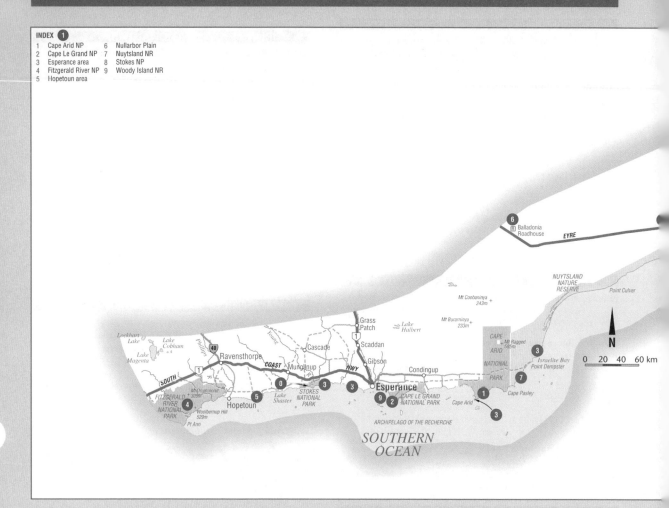

STRETCHING EAST FROM ESPERANCE IS SOME OF AUSTRALIA'S MOST BEAUTIFUL AND REMOTE COASTLINE – WHITE SANDY BEACHES AND AZURE WATERS, SHEER CLIFFS AND DRIFTING DUNES. BEYOND IS THE VAST NULLARBOR PLAIN, WITH ITS NETWORK OF UNDERGROUND LIMESTONE CAVES.

Esperance is well known for spectacular beaches and clear waters, great for fishing, swimming, diving, snorkelling and surfing. On the scenic 36-kilometre Great Ocean Drive travellers can indulge in sheltered swimming at Pink Lake and Twilight Cove and in the wonderful coastal views from Wireless Hill and Observatory Point. Council-run camping areas are located both west and east of Esperance.

To the east of Esperance is the spectacular Cape Le Grand National Park, with magnificent coastal scenery, rocky headlands, stunning beaches and rugged mountains. It has a variety of vegetation, including spring wildflowers, and a range of native animals and birds. In the waters off the park fur seals and southern right whales can be seen. Other activities include bushwalking, fishing, swimming and boating. Both of Cape Le Grand's camping areas are accessible and suitable for caravans.

Further east again, Cape Arid National Park and neighbouring Nutysland Nature Reserve form a continuous arc of nature conservation stretching east almost to the South Australian border. Camping in Cape Arid is at the coastal sites of Thomas River, Seal Creek, Jorndee Creek and Thomas Fishery, and inland at Mount Ragged, only reachable by four-wheel drive. The park is popular with fisherfolk, swimmers, walkers and four-wheel-drive tourers. During spring the park is awash with wildflowers.

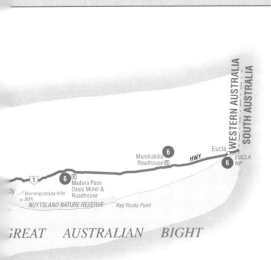

Mundrabilla Roadhouse · 6 · HWY · Eucla
EUCLA NP · 6
WESTERN AUSTRALIA
SOUTH AUSTRALIA
1 · 6 · Madura Pass Oasis Motel & Roadhouse
Warrengoodyea Hills +90m
NUYTSLAND NATURE RESERVE · Red Rocks Point
GREAT AUSTRALIAN BIGHT

BEST CAMPSITES

Thomas River camping area
Cape Arid National Park

Lucky Bay camping area
Cape Le Grand National Park

Stokes Inlet North camping area
Stokes National Park

Munglinup Beach camping area
Esperance area

Israelite Bay camping area
Esperance area

BEST TIME TO VISIT

All year round, however the climate is best spring to autumn.

1. CAPE ARID NATIONAL PARK

The isolated Cape Arid National Park is known for its beautiful sandy beaches and rocky headlands. A stunning display of wildflowers can be seen during spring, summer and autumn. Beach fishing and 4WD touring are popular activities here. There are walks of various lengths. Cape Arid National Park is 120 km east of Esperance; access is via Fisheries or Merivale rds from Esperance or Balladonia Rd from the Eyre Hwy (4WD required). Camping areas in the park are remote and for self-sufficient campers only. Carry sufficient water and a gas/fuel stove.

Jorndee Creek camping area

Signposted off Poison Creek Rd, which is off Merivale and Fisheries rds. It is south of Seal Creek. 4WD access only. Bring drinking water. Gas/fuel stove only. Additional map ref.: STAWA 107 A5.

Mount Ragged camping area

Signposted off Balladonia Rd. 4WD access only. This site can be closed during wet weather. Bring drinking water. Gas/fuel stove only. Additional map ref.: STAWA 107 A5.

Seal Creek camping area

Located on Poison Creek Rd 24 km south-east of Merivale Rd. Drivers towing caravans should check road conditions as Poison Creek Rd can be corrugated. Bring drinking water. Gas/fuel stove only. Additional map ref.: STAWA 107 A5.

Thomas Fishery camping area

Signposted off Poison Creek Rd, which is off Merivale and Fisheries rds. 4WD access only. This site can be closed during wet weather. Bring drinking water. Gas/fuel stove only. Additional map ref.: STAWA 107 A5.

Thomas River camping area

Signposted along Thomas River Rd off Merivale Rd, located 9.5 km south of Merivale Rd. Bring drinking water. Gas/fuel stove only. Additional map ref.: STAWA 107 A5.

Further information:

CALM, Cape Arid National Park **Tel.:** (08) 9075 0055 *or* CALM, Esperance **Tel.:** (08) 9071 3733
Park entrance fee: $9.00 per vehicle **Camping fees:** There are no set camping fees for Cape Arid National Park; please put an appropriate donation in one of the donation boxes at the campsites

2. CAPE LE GRAND NATIONAL PARK

Cape Le Grand National Park boasts the beautiful beaches of Le Grand, Hellfire, Lucky Bay and Rossiter Bay. The park also features rocky headlands and rugged coastal scenery. During spring and early summer wildflowers are abundant. It is a popular swimming, fishing and whale-watching area. Access to Cape Le Grand National Park is via Cape Le Grand Rd off Merivale Rd, turn-off 36 km east of Esperance.

Le Grand Beach camping area

Signposted off Cape Le Grand Rd. It is 58 km east of Esperance and 22 km south of Merivale Rd. Camp kitchen. Solar hot showers. Gas/fuel stove only. Additional map ref.: STAWA 47 A5.

Lucky Bay camping area

Signposted on Lucky Bay Rd off Cape Le Grand Rd. It is 62 km east of Esperance and 26 km south of Merivale Rd. Camp kitchen. Solar hot showers. Beach boat launch, 4WD recommended. Gas/fuel stove only. Additional map ref.: STAWA 47 A5.

Further information:
CALM, Cape Le Grand National Park **Tel.:** (08) 9075 9072 or CALM, Esperance **Tel.:** (08) 9071 3733
Park entrance fee: $9.00 per vehicle **Camping fees:** From $6.50 per adult/night; fees payable to ranger or campsite hosts on-site during peak periods

3. ESPERANCE AREA

The Esperance region is well known for its beautiful beaches – ideal for swimming, surfing, fishing, diving, snorkelling and sailboarding – as well as its magnificent coastal scenery. The crystal-clear waters here are also perfect for spotting whales, seals and dolphins. One of the best ways to view the region's wonderful attractions is via the scenic Great Ocean Drive. The Shire of Esperance runs a number of good campsites within its area, which stretches from Nuytsland Nature Reserve west to Munglinup. Please note that Cape Arid, Cape Le Grand and Stokes national parks as well as the western part of Nuytsland Nature Reserve are all within this shire area, but campsites in these places are listed under the individual park/reserve names.

Alexander Bay camping area

On Alexander Rd off Merivale Rd. Located 11 km south of Merivale Rd and 90 km east of Esperance. Bring drinking water and firewood. Additional map ref.: STAWA 47 D5.

Israelite Bay camping area

At the end of Fisheries Rd, 240 km east of Esperance through Cape Arid National Park (4WD required). This shire-run camping spot is surrounded by Nuytsland Nature Reserve. Self-sufficient campers only. Bring drinking water and firewood. Gas/fuel stove preferred. Additional map ref.: STAWA 107 B5.

Munglinup Beach camping area

On Munglinup Beach Rd, off Springdale Rd off Fuss Rd. Fuss Rd turns off the South Coast Hwy 5 km east of Munglinup. Munglinup is 134 km west of Esperance. Bring firewood. Additional map ref.: STAWA 45 C5.

Quagi Beach camping area

On Farrells Rd off the South Coast Hwy, 70 km west of Esperance. Bring firewood. Additional map ref.: STAWA 46 A4.

Further information:
Shire of Esperance **Tel.:** (08) 9071 0666 **Website:** www.esperance.wa.gov.au or
Esperance Tourist Bureau **Tel.:** (08) 9071 2330
Camping fees: From $2.00 per person/night; fees collected by ranger **Fire restrictions:** Solid-fuel fire ban 1 Nov.–31 March; use a gas/fuel stove during this period. Dates may change; check with local authorities before lighting any fire

4. FITZGERALD RIVER NATIONAL PARK

See also Hopetoun area, Hamersley Inlet – shire camping area, *opposite page*

Covering an area of 329 039 ha, Fitzgerald River National Park features a diverse landscape of rugged coastal cliffs, protected beaches and river valleys. During spring an array of wildflowers are in bloom, and during Aug.–Nov. whales are frequently spotted as they move along the coast. Fishing and bushwalking are other popular activities. It is situated between the towns of Bremer Bay in the west and Hopetoun in the east. Conventional vehicle access to the eastern side of the park is from Hopetoun via Hamersley Drive. In the west conventional vehicle access is via Collets Rd from Bremer Bay.

WESTERN SECTION

Fitzgerald Inlet camping area

Signposted from Fitzgerald River Track off Collets Rd. It is 20 km east of Collets Rd and 80 km north-east of Bremer Bay. Bring drinking water. Gas/fuel stove only. Additional map ref.: STAWA 24 (Pt Map 25 A1).

St Marys Inlet camping ground

Signposted from Point Ann Rd off Collets Rd, 67 km north of Bremer Bay. Bring drinking water. Gas/fuel stove only. Additional map ref.: STAWA 24 (Pt Map 25 A1).

EASTERN SECTION

Four Mile Beach camping area

Signposted from Hamersley Drive 10 km west of Hopetoun. Bring drinking water. Gas/fuel stove only. Additional map ref.: STAWA 44 C5.

Hamersley Inlet camping area

Signposted from Hamersley Inlet Rd off Hamersley Drive, 23 km west of Hopetoun. Bring drinking water. Gas/fuel stove only. Additional map ref.: STAWA 44 C5.

Quoin Head camping area

Signposted on Telegraph Track off Hamersley Drive, 45 km west of Hopetoun. Bring drinking water. Gas/fuel stove only. Additional map ref.: STAWA 44 B5.

Whale Bone Beach camping area

Signposted on Telegraph Track off Hamersley Drive, 45 km west of Hopetoun. Swimming not recommended here due to large rips. Bring drinking water. Gas/fuel stove only. Additional map ref.: STAWA 44 C5.

Further information:
Ranger in charge **Tel.:** (08) 9835 5043 or
Western section ranger **Tel.:** (08) 9837 1022 or
Eastern section ranger **Tel.:** (08) 9838 3060
Park entrance fee: $9.00 per vehicle **Camping fees:** From $5.00 per person/night, $2.00 per child (under 16) per night; fees payable at self-registration stations at park entrances

5. HOPETOUN AREA

The town of Hopetoun is 50 km south of Ravensthorpe, which is on the South Coast Hwy. The area boasts some great spots for swimming and fishing (including Mason Bay and Starvation Boat Harbour, both with camping areas listed below), and the town gives access to the eastern section of Fitzgerald River National Park.

Hamersley Inlet – shire camping area

This camping area is within Fitzgerald River National Park but is run by the Shire of Ravensthorpe. Signposted access on Hamersley Inlet Rd off Hamersley Drive, 35 km west of Hopetoun. Bring drinking water. Gas/fuel stove only. Additional map ref.: STAWA 44 C5.

Mason Bay camping area

Located 34 km east of Hopetoun via Southern Ocean Rd. 4WD beach boat launch. Bring drinking water. Some firewood supplied. Additional map ref.: STAWA 45 A5.

Starvation Boat Harbour camping area

This is 50 km east of Hopetoun. Access via Starvation Boat Harbour Rd or Southern Ocean Rd, both off Springdale Rd off Hopetoun–Ravensthorpe Rd. Walk-in and vehicle-based sites on offer. 4WD beach boat launch. Bring drinking water. Some firewood supplied. Additional map ref.: STAWA 45 B5.

Further information:
Shire of Ravensthorpe **Tel.:** (08) 9838 1001 or
Ravensthorpe Tourist Information **Tel.:** (08) 9838 1277
Camping fees: May be introduced in the future

6. NULLARBOR PLAIN

The Nullarbor Plain, a limestone plateau, was formed more than 50 million years ago. Over time weathering has sculptured underground caves, blowholes and sinkholes, formed by rain trickling through the limestone. There are spectacular coastal views and areas for whale-watching as well as historical memorials and museums. The Eyre Hwy across the Nullarbor Plain is one of Australia's greatest drives. The caravan parks and roadhouses on the highway can advise you of the local attractions and provide directions. They are listed below in the order they are reached west–east.

Balladonia Caravan Park

On Eyre Hwy at Balladonia, 191 km east of Norseman. Open 6 am–10 pm. Camp kitchen. Limited rain water, best to bring drinking water. Firewood supplied. Additional map ref.: STAWA 107 A3.

Further information & bookings: Balladonia Hotel Motel **Tel.:** (08) 9039 3453 **Camping fees:** Unpowered from $6.00 for 1 per night and $12.00 for 2, then $3.00 for each additional person; powered from $12.00 for 1 per night and $18.60 for 2, then $3.00 for each additional person

Caiguna Roadhouse

On Eyre Hwy at Caiguna, 181 km east of Balladonia. Open 24 hours. Bring firewood. Additional map ref.: STAWA 107 D3.

Further information & bookings: Caiguna Roadhouse **Tel.:** (08) 9039 3459 **Camping fees:** Unpowered from $12.00 per site/night for 2 adults, powered from $18.00 per site/night for 2 adults

Cocklebiddy Roadhouse

On Eyre Hwy at Cocklebiddy, 66 km east of Caiguna. Open Mon.–Sat. 6.30 am–10 pm, Sun. until 9 pm. Additional map ref.: STAWA 107 D3.

Further information & bookings: Cocklebiddy Roadhouse **Tel.:** (08) 9039 3462 **Camping fees:** Unpowered from $8.50 per site/night for 2 adults, powered from $18.00 per site/night for 2 adults

Madura Pass Oasis Motel

On Eyre Hwy at Madura, 92 km east of Cocklebiddy. Open 6.30 am–9 pm. Bring firewood. Key access to ablution block, refundable $5.00 deposit. Additional map ref.: STAWA 108 A3.

Further information & bookings: Madura Pass Oasis Motel **Tel.:** (08) 9039 3464 **Camping fees:** Unpowered from $12.00 per site/night for 2 adults, powered from $18.00 per site/night for 2 adults

Mundrabilla Roadhouse

On Eyre Hwy, 116 km east of Madura and 66 km west of Eucla. Open 5.30 am–11 pm. Firewood supplied. Key access to ablution block, refundable $5.00 deposit. Additional map ref.: STAWA 108 C3.

Further information & bookings: Mundrabilla Roadhouse **Tel.:** (08) 9039 3465 **Camping fees:** Unpowered from $10.00 per site/night for 2 people, powered from $15.00 per site/night for 2 people

Eucla Pass Caravan Park

On Eyre Hwy at Eucla, 66 km east of Mundrabilla Roadhouse and 12 km west of the South Australian border. Open 6 am–10 pm. Firewood supplied. Additional map ref.: STAWA 108 D3.

Further information & bookings: Eucla Pass Caravan Park **Tel.:** (08) 9039 3468 **Camping fees:** Unpowered tent sites from $2.00 per person/night, powered from $11.00 per site/night

7. NUYTSLAND NATURE RESERVE

See also Esperance area, Israelite Bay camping area, *page 216*

Incorporating cliffs and ocean beaches of the Great Australian Bight, Nuytsland Nature Reserve encompasses close to 500 km of coastline and stretches from Cape Arid National Park eastwards to Red Rock Point. The Eyre Bird Observatory and sections of the old Overland Telegraph Line, constructed in 1876, are within the reserve. Access to Point Malcolm in the west of the park is by 4WD along Fisheries Rd through Cape Arid National Park. It is a remote area and recommended for self-sufficient campers only.

Point Malcolm camping area

Signposted along Point Malcolm Rd off Fisheries Rd. Located 13 km south of Fisheries Rd and 237 km east of Esperance. Bring drinking water. Gas/fuel stove only. Additional map ref.: STAWA 107 B5.

Further information:
CALM, Cape Arid National Park **Tel.:** (08) 9075 0055 *or*
CALM, Esperance **Tel.:** (08) 9071 3733

8. STOKES NATIONAL PARK

The picturesque Stokes Inlet, popular for fishing, canoeing and birdwatching, is within Stokes National Park, west of Esperance. The coastal areas of Skippy Rock in the west and Fanny Cove and Shoal Cape in the east of the park offer spectacular coastal scenery, and those with a 4WD vehicle can reach the historic Moir family homestead – the Moirs were granted a lease around Stokes Inlet in 1888.

Fanny Cove camping area

Signposted 4 km along Farrells Rd off the South Coast Hwy; Fanny Cove further 16 km from Farrells Rd. 4WD access. Popular surfing and snorkelling spot. Bring drinking water. Gas/fuel stove only. Additional map ref.: STAWA 46 A5.

Skippy Rock camping area

Signposted off Torradup Rd, off the South Coast Hwy; turn-off is 4 km from highway and Skippy Rock is a further 6 km on. 4WD access. Popular surfing and snorkelling spot. Bring drinking water. Gas/fuel stove only. Additional map ref.: STAWA 45 D5.

Stokes Inlet North camping area

Signposted on Stokes Inlet Rd off South Coast Hwy, located 6 km south of the highway. Bring drinking water. Gas/fuel stove only. Additional map ref.: STAWA 45 D4.

Stokes Inlet South camping area

Signposted on Stokes Inlet Rd off South Coast Hwy, located 8 km south of the highway. Bring drinking water. Gas/fuel stove only. Additional map ref.: STAWA 45 D4.

Further information:
CALM, Stokes National Park **Tel.:** (08) 9076 8541 *or*
CALM, Esperance **Tel.:** (08) 9071 3733
Park entrance fee: $9.00 per vehicle **Camping fees:** *Stokes Inlet North and South*: From $5.00 per adult/night, $2.00 per child (age 5–15) per night; fees payable at self-registration station at Stokes Inlet North

9. WOODY ISLAND NATURE RESERVE

Woody Island is one of a number of islands in the Archipelago of the Recherche, south of Esperance. The archipelago has a rich history of whalers, sealers and pirates. Woody Island Nature Reserve is a nature lover's paradise. Here one can indulge in diving, snorkelling, birdwatching, bushwalking, fishing and swimming. Reaching Woody Island Nature Reserve involves a cruise of one hour and forty-five minutes from Esperance. The island is only accessible Sept.–April.

Woody Island Eco-stays

On Woody Island Nature Reserve. Camp kitchen with fridges. Campers can bring a gas/fuel stove or use facilities at the campground. Additional map ref.: STAWA 46 D5.

Further information & bookings: MacKenzies Island Cruises **Tel.:** (08) 9071 5757 **Email:** macruise@emerge.net.au **Website:** www.emerge.net.au/~macruise **Camping fees:** From $10.00 per person/night **Accommodation fees:** Medium-size erected tents from $41.00 per night, safari huts from $75.00 per night **Boat fares:** Return $54.00 per adult, $20.00 per child (age 5–16)

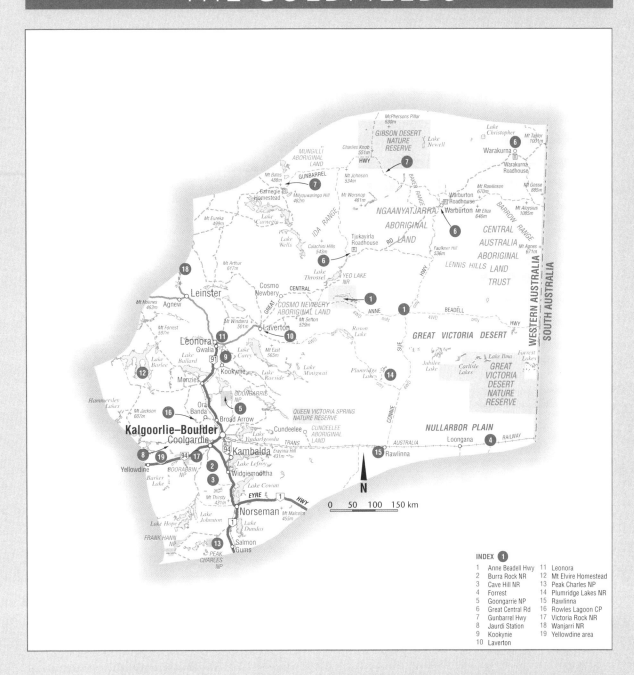

INDEX ①

THE HISTORIC MINING TOWNS OF KALGOORLIE–BOULDER, KAMBALDA AND NORSEMAN ARE INCLUDED IN THE GOLDFIELDS REGION, ALONG WITH A NUMBER OF INTRIGUING GHOST TOWNS. THEY SIT AMONGST A LANDSCAPE OF ALLUVIAL FLATS, ROCKY OUTCROPS, OUTBACK TRACKS AND DESERT.

From the summit of Peak Charles in Peak Charles National Park, south-west of Norseman, there are extensive views of the surrounding salt lakes and mallee woodlands. Camping is possible in the park and those camped here in spring will be rewarded with a beautiful wildflower display.

Burra Rock, Cave Hill and Victoria Rock nature reserves all have camping within landscapes of spectacular granite outcrops. The dams in Burra Rock and Cave Hill nature reserves were once used to supply water to steam trains taking timber to Kalgoorlie–Boulder during the late 1920s and 1930s. It is possible to catch yabbies in these dams, but check local regulations first.

The freshwater Rowles Lagoon and Carnage, Clear and Muddy lakes are all part of Rowles Lagoon Conservation Park, an important wetland home to a large variety of bird species, including the rare freckled duck and visiting migratory waders. Campers beside Rowles Lagoon can indulge in birdwatching, canoeing, yabbying, swimming and waterskiing.

Goongarrie National Park is 90 kilometres north of Kalgoorlie. It was once a large station and camping here is in the vicinity of the old homestead. Visitors can view the salt lakes and Twenty-five Mile Rock.

Niagara Dam, near Kookynie, and Malcolm Dam, east of Leonora, were also constructed to supply water to steam trains. Nowadays they offer recreational activities such as camping, fishing and yabbying.

BEST CAMPSITES

Niagara Dam camping area
Kookynie

Rowles Lagoon camping area
Rowles Lagoon Conservation Park

Burra Rock camping area
Burra Rock Nature Reserve

Victoria Rock camping area
Victoria Rock Nature Reserve

Peak Charles camping area
Peak Charles National Park

BEST TIME TO VISIT

All year round. Winter and spring are the busiest time of the year for this region.

1. ANNE BEADELL HIGHWAY

See also Unnamed Conservation Park *and* Tallaringa Conservation Park, *page 179*

Constructed in stages between 1953 and 1962, the Anne Beadell Hwy covers 1340 km, running east from Laverton through the Great Victoria Desert to Coober Pedy in South Australia. The Anne Beadell Hwy is sometimes called Serpentine Lakes Rd. The 'highway' is rugged and remote, with sections of the road being narrow and twisted as well as badly corrugated. Travellers must be self-sufficient as fuel, water and supplies are not available for its entire length. Permits are needed to travel the Anne Beadell Hwy as sections pass through Aboriginal land.

Yeo Homestead Ruins

In Yeo Lake Nature Reserve on Anne Beadell Hwy, 112 km north-east of Laverton via White Cliffs and Yarmarna rds or 65 km south of Great Central Rd via Point Sunday Rd. Bring drinking water. Gas/fuel stove only. Additional map ref.: STAWA 126 B2.

Neale Junction

At junction of Anne Beadell Hwy and Connie Sue Hwy, 167 km east of Yeo Homestead and 307 km south of Warburton. Located in Neale Junction Nature Reserve. Camping area is 600 m west of the junction. Bring drinking water. Gas/fuel stove only. Additional map ref.: STAWA 126 D3.

Bush camping

Bush camping is allowed along most parts of the highway. Campsites are to be no more than 30 m off the side of the road. Please take note of any signs. Bring drinking water and firewood.

Further information:
CALM, Kalgoorlie **Tel.:** (08) 9021 2677 *or* NPWSA, Ceduna **Tel.:** (08) 8625 3144
Permits: *WA*: Ngaanyatjarraku Council, tel.: (08) 8950 1711; *SA*: Maralinga–Tjarutja Council, tel.: (08) 8625 2946
Road conditions: Shire of Laverton **Tel.:** (08) 9031 1202

2. BURRA ROCK NATURE RESERVE

Burra Rock is a large granite outcrop 60 km south of Coolgardie. At the base of the rock is a dam originally used to supply water to steam trains during the late 1920s. A walk to the summit of Burra Rock offers views over surrounding woodlands. Conventional vehicle access to the reserve is possible, but some sections close to the rock may be sandy. Access from Coolgardie is via Hunt St and the nature reserve is on Burra Rock Rd.

Burra Rock camping area

Signposted along Burra Rock Rd, 60 km south of Coolgardie. Bring drinking water and firewood. Additional map ref.: STAWA 83 A1.

Further information: CALM, Kalgoorlie **Tel.:** (08) 9021 2677

3. CAVE HILL NATURE RESERVE

The granite outcrop of Cave Hill stretches for almost 1.5 km. On its western side is a walking track leading to a large cave. The best way to reach Cave Hill Nature Reserve is to follow the signs from Widgiemooltha on the Coolgardie–Esperance Hwy.

Cave Hill camping area

4WD access only. Signposted from Widgiemooltha, 50 km to the north-east. Alternative access is from the north from Burra Rock Nature Reserve or via Higginsville Pump Station Rd off Coolgardie–Esperance Hwy. Bring drinking water and firewood. Additional map ref.: STAWA 83 A1.

Further information: CALM, Kalgoorlie **Tel.:** (08) 9021 2677

4. FORREST

Forrest is beside the Transcontinental Railway, 639 km east of Kalgoorlie and 126 km north of the Eyre Hwy. Used by aircraft flying across the Nullarbor as a refuelling spot, Forrest has the largest bitumen airstrip outside major airports. Access to Forrest is by 4WD vehicle only. Please note that use of the Transcontinental Railway Access Rd is not permitted; it is a private road from Rawlinna east to Tarcoola in South Australia.

Forrest camping area

On the Transcontinental Railway Access Rd, 126 km north of Eyre Hwy. 4WD access via Forrest–Mundrabilla Rd, turn-off 34 km west of Mundrabilla. Firewood supplied. Additional map ref.: STAWA 108 C1.

Further information: Forrest Airport **Tel.:** (08) 9022 6403
Camping fees: From $7.00 per person/night

5. GOONGARRIE NATIONAL PARK

North of Kalgoorlie, Goongarrie National Park encompasses an old homestead, salt lakes on Planto Rd and Twenty-five Mile Rock. It is 90 km north of Kalgoorlie.

Goongarrie Homestead camping area

Signposted 90 km north of Kalgoorlie along Menzies–Kalgoorlie Rd. It is 14 km west of this turn-off. Camping in homestead vicinity with use of its facilities. Bring drinking water and firewood. Bookings are necessary, contact CALM. Hosts are on-site during busy periods. Additional map ref.: STAWA 125 B5.

Further information & bookings: CALM, Kalgoorlie **Tel.:** (08) 9021 2677 **Camping fees:** From $5.00 per person/night

6. GREAT CENTRAL ROAD

See also Laverton, *page 222, and* Kaltukatjara (Docker River), *page 276*

The Great Central Rd runs east from Laverton through to Yulara in the Northern Territory. (Over the Northern Territory border it is known as Tjukaruru Rd, and another name for the route, both states inclusive, is the Outback Hwy.) Travellers along the road will be treated to typical central Australian desert landscapes of red sand, spinifex and mulga. The Great Central Rd passes through Aboriginal land and permits are required. Although the road is sandy in sections it can be travelled in a conventional vehicle, however a 4WD is recommended.

Tjukayirla Roadhouse

On Great Central Rd, 318 km north-east of Laverton and 244 km south-west of Warburton. Open Mon.–Fri. 7 am– 6 pm, Sat.–Sun. and public holidays 8 am–5 pm. Fuels

available: diesel, avgas, unleaded. Camp kitchen. Dogs allowed but conditions apply. Bring firewood. Additional map ref.: STAWA 126 C1.

Warburton Roadhouse

On Great Central Rd, 244 km north-east of Tjukayirla Roadhouse and 231 km south-east of Warakurna Roadhouse. Open Mon.–Fri. 8 am–5 pm, Sat.–Sun. 9 am–3 pm, public holidays 9 am–noon. Fuels available: diesel, avgas. Camp kitchen. Bring firewood. Additional map ref.: STAWA 135 A5.

Warakurna Roadhouse

On Great Central Rd, 231 km north-east of Warburton Roadhouse and 92 km west of Docker River. Open Mon.– Fri. 8.30 am–6 pm, Sat.–Sun. 9 am–3 pm, public holidays 8.30 am–12.30 pm. Fuels available: diesel, avgas. Bring firewood. Additional map ref.: STAWA 135 D3.

Further information:
Tjukayirla Roadhouse: **Tel.:** (08) 9037 1108
Warburton Roadhouse: **Tel.:** (08) 8956 7656
Warakurna Roadhouse: **Tel.:** (08) 8956 7344
Camping fees: From $8.00 per person/night at all three roadhouses
Permits: Ngaanyatjarraku Council **Tel.:** (08) 8950 1711 *or* Department of Indigenous Affairs **Tel.:** (08) 9235 8000
Website: www.dia.wa.gov.au

7. GUNBARREL HIGHWAY

The Gunbarrel Hwy was the first major road constructed by Len Beadell and the Gunbarrel Construction Party, and is still their best known. The final section to Carnegie Station was completed in 1958. Much of the original Gunbarrel is not accessible to today's traveller, with the present-day route considered as beginning at Yulara in the Northern Territory and following the Great Central Road to Warakurna and Warburton, then continuing on all the way to Wiluna (which also happens to be at the beginning, or end, depending on which way you travel, of the Canning Stock Route). For campsites between Yulara and Warburton, see Kaltukatjara (Docker River), page 276, and Great Central Road, this page. The section of the Gunbarrel Hwy proper that is approved for travel runs north from a turn-off 41 km south-west of Warburton up to Everard Junction and then south-west to Carnegie. A 4WD vehicle is necessary, a permit is required and conditions apply.

Camp Beadell

On Gunbarrel Hwy, 62 km south-east of Everard Junction and 165 km north-west of Warburton. Bring drinking water and firewood. Gas/fuel stove preferred. Additional map ref.: STAWA 134 D4.

Geraldton Bore

On Gunbarrel Hwy, 206 km east of Carnegie Station and 32 km west of Everard Junction. It is just west of the Gibson Desert Nature Reserve. Bring drinking water and firewood. Gas/fuel stove preferred. Additional map ref.: STAWA 134 C3.

Carnegie Station

On Gunbarrel Hwy, 353 km north-east of Wiluna and 462 km north-west of Warburton. Fuels available: diesel, unleaded. Firewood supplied. Additional map ref.: STAWA 134 A4.

Further information: Ngaanyatjarraku Council **Tel.:** (08) 8950 1711 **Website:** www.dia.wa.gov.au **Other contact:** Carnegie Station **Tel.:** (08) 9981 2991 **Permits:** Department of Indigenous Affairs **Tel.:** (08) 9235 8000 **Website:** www.dia.wa.gov.au **Camping fees:** *Carnegie Station:* From $10.00 per site/night **Road conditions**: Shire of Ngaanyatjarraku **Tel.:** (08) 8956 7966

8. JAURDI STATION

Jaurdi Station is 178 km west of Kalgoorlie and 50 km north of the Great Eastern Hwy. Formerly a sheep-grazing property, Jaurdi Station now offers visitors a chance to experience how station life once was. There are rare flora species and a large number of birds, mammals and reptiles, while reminders of the station's history can be found in the way of old graves and mines. Conventional vehicle access is possible, however a 4WD vehicle is recommended.

Jaurdi Station Homestead camping area

On Ryans Find Rd off Great Eastern Hwy. Turn-off is 59 km west of the Bullabulling Hotel and 99 km east of Southern Cross. Homestead accommodation or camping in homestead vicinity using homestead facilities. Limited drinking water, best to bring own. Bring firewood. Advance bookings are necessary. Additional map ref.: STAWA 103 D3.

Further information & bookings: CALM, Kalgoorlie **Tel.:** (08) 9021 2677 **Camping fees:** From $5.00 per person/night; fees to be paid at CALM Kalgoorlie

9. KOOKYNIE

The ghost town of Kookynie is 68 km south of Leonora. Evidence of the town's early goldmining days still exists, including the Grand Hotel, once one of six hotels here. South of Kookynie is Niagara Dam, built as a water supply for steam trains; it is signposted off the Kookynie Rd off the Goldfields Highway.

Niagara Dam camping area

Signposted 13 km along Kookynie Road from highway. Bring drinking water and firewood. Keep dogs on lead as this area is baited. Additional map ref.: STAWA 125 C4.

Further information: Grand Hotel, Kookynie **Tel.:** (08) 9031 3010 *or* Shire of Menzies **Tel.:** (08) 9024 2041

10. LAVERTON

On the edge of the Great Victoria Desert, Laverton is at the start of the Great Central Road. The Windarra Nickel Project mined nickel 20 km west of Laverton for 25 years. Visitors can enjoy walking the Mt Windarra Heritage Trail with its interpretative signs. Laverton is 124 km north-east of Leonora and 361 km north-east of Kalgoorlie.

Laverton Caravan Park

On Weld Drive in Laverton. Camp kitchen. Gas/fuel stove only. Additional map ref.: STAWA 125 D3.

Further information: Laverton Caravan Park **Tel.:** (08) 9031 1072 **Camping fees:** Unpowered from $16.00 per site/night for 2 people, powered from $18.00 per site/night for 2 people

11. LEONORA

The town of Leonora is on the Goldfields Hwy, 234 km north of Kalgoorlie. Leonora and neighbouring Gwalia thrived during the heady goldmining days of the early 1900s and Leonora has a number of buildings still standing from this time. Malcolm Dam is east of Leonora and was built in 1902 to provide water for the railway.

Malcolm Dam camping area

Signposted along Leonora–Laverton Rd, 10 km east of Leonora. Bring drinking water and firewood. Additional map ref.: STAWA 125 C3.

Further information: Leonora Information Centre **Tel.:** (08) 9037 6888 *or* Shire of Leonora **Tel.:** (08) 9037 6044

12. MOUNT ELVIRE STATION

Mt Elvire is west of Menzies and was a working station before being purchased by CALM. Today's visitor here can experience the solitude of station life. Menzies is 132 km north of Kalgoorlie, and access to Mt Elvire is via gravel roads. Access details should be confirmed with CALM Kalgoorlie before attempting.

Mount Elvire Homestead camping area

Take Diemals Rd for 175 km west of Menzies to turn-off, then travel 40 km north. Camping in the vicinity of homestead or shearers quarters. Hot-water donkey shower system. Bring drinking water. Firewood supplied. Advance bookings are necessary. Additional map ref.: STAWA 125 A4.

Further information & bookings: CALM, Kalgoorlie **Tel.:** (08) 9021 2677 **Camping fees:** From $5.00 per person/night; fees to be paid at CALM Kalgoorlie

13. PEAK CHARLES NATIONAL PARK

Peak Charles National Park is south-west of Norseman. Visitors who are fit and agile can tackle the moderately difficult climb to the summit of Peak Charles for extensive views over the surrounding mallee woodlands and salt lakes to the east. During spring the park is ablaze with wildflowers. Access for conventional vehicles is off the Lake King–Norseman Rd. Check road conditions before attempting, especially after wet weather.

Peak Charles camping area

At the end of Peak Charles Rd, off Lake King–Norseman Rd. It is 107 km south-west of Norseman and 202 km east of Lake King. Self-sufficient campers only. Bring drinking water. Gas/fuel stove preferred. Additional map ref.: STAWA 83 A5.

Further information:
CALM, Stokes National Park **Tel.:** (08) 9076 8541 *or*
CALM, Esperance **Tel.:** (08) 9071 3733
Road conditions: Shire of Dundas **Tel.:** (08) 9039 1205

14. PLUMRIDGE LAKES NATURE RESERVE

Plumridge Lakes Nature Reserve is 85 km west of the Connie Sue Hwy and 341 km south-east of Laverton. Access is by 4WD vehicle only. The lakes were named in 1908 by Frank Hann and they are a popular birdwatching site. The road off the Connie Sue Hwy begins 136 km north of Rawlinna and 203 km south of Neale Junction. Access from Laverton is via Rason Lake Rd. This is a remote area and visitors need to be self-sufficient and well prepared. Contact local authorities for detailed access information and conditions. Those travelling the Connie Sue Hwy from Warburton will need a permit.

Bush camping

Self-sufficient, no-trace camping only. Bring drinking water. Gas/fuel stove only. Additional map ref.: STAWA 126 C4.

Further information:
CALM, Kalgoorlie **Tel.:** (08) 9021 2677 *or*
Laverton Visitor Information Centre **Tel.:** (08) 9031 1750
Permits: Ngaanyatjarraku Council **Tel.:** (08) 8950 1711

15. RAWLINNA

Rawlinna is beside the Transcontinental Railway 380 km east of Kalgoorlie. Once a railway siding, Rawlinna is now the base for Loongana Lime Mine. Access by 4WD vehicle is possible on the Transcontinental Railway Access Rd via the Super Pit Lookout in Kalgoorlie. The mine operators allow people to camp in the town, however as a courtesy all visitors should contact them on UHF radio, channel 11, on arrival. Please note that from Rawlinna east to Tarcoola in South Australia the Transcontinental Railway Access Rd is a private road and access is not permitted.

Rawlinna camping area

Self-sufficient campers only. Bring drinking water. Campfires are not encouraged, please use gas/fuel stove. Additional map ref.: STAWA 107 D1.

Further information: Kalgoorlie–Boulder Visitor Centre
Tel.: (08) 9021 1966

16. ROWLES LAGOON CONSERVATION PARK

Rowles Lagoon, along with Carnage, Clear and Muddy lakes, make up the Rowles Lagoon Conservation Park. Of these freshwater lakes, Rowles Lagoon is the deepest and largest. The lakes are visited by a large number of birds and waterfowl, making the area popular with birdwatchers. They are also a good setting for recreational activities such as swimming, picnicking, canoeing and waterskiing. Conventional-vehicle access is possible.

Rowles Lagoon camping area

Signposted 67 km north of Coolgardie along Coolgardie North Rd. Natural beach boat launch. Bring drinking water and firewood. Additional map ref.: STAWA 104 C1.

Further information: CALM, Kalgoorlie **Tel.:** (08) 9021 2677

17. VICTORIA ROCK NATURE RESERVE

Victoria Rock Nature Reserve features one of the most impressive granite outcrops in the Goldfields. There is a walking track to the summit. Surrounding the outcrop are regrowth woodlands of redwood and salmon gum. Access is via Victoria Rock Rd from Coolgardie.

Victoria Rock camping area

On Victoria Rock Rd, 46 km south of Coolgardie. Bring drinking water and firewood. Additional map ref.: STAWA 104 C5.

Further information: CALM, Kalgoorlie **Tel.:** (08) 9021 2677

18. WANJARRI NATURE RESERVE

Wanjarri Nature Reserve is 74 km north of Leinster. Within the reserve is the old Wanjarri shearing shed. Access is off the Goldfields Hwy approximately 58 km north of Leinster; turn-off is just south of the bridge over Jones Creek. Conventional vehicles can access the site.

Wanjarri Shearing Shed camping area

Camping in vicinity of shearing shed, which is 16 km east of highway. Use of shearing shed facilities. Hot-water donkey shower system. Bring drinking water and firewood. Bookings necessary. Additional map ref.: STAWA 125 B1.

Further information & bookings: CALM, Kalgoorlie
Tel.: (08) 9021 2677 **Camping fees:** From $5.00 per person/night

19. YELLOWDINE AREA

Yellowdine is located 400 km east of Perth on the Great Eastern Hwy, the route to Kalgoorlie–Boulder. Karalee Rock and Dam are 18 km east of Yellowdine and 5 km north of the highway. The dam was originally built in 1897 to supply water to steam trains travelling to the goldfields. A walk to the top of the rock affords visitors views across the region.

Karalee Rock and Dam picnic and camping area

Signposted off the Great Eastern Hwy. Bring drinking water and firewood. Maximum of three nights' stay. Additional map ref.: STAWA 103 B5.

Further information: Shire of Yilgarn **Tel.:** (08) 9049 1001

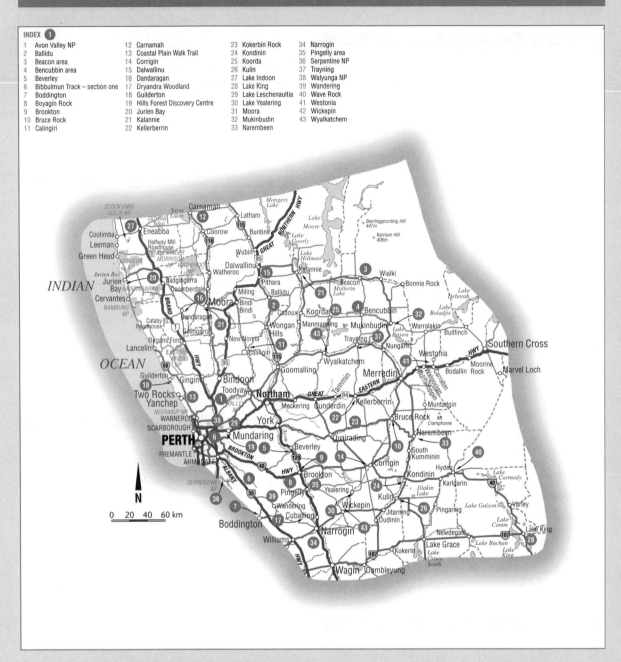

THIS LARGE REGION IS MADE UP OF DIVERSE LANDSCAPES, FROM COASTAL BEACHES AND FISHING VILLAGES TO THE GOLDEN PADDOCKS OF THE WHEAT BELT. EVERY SPRING THE WHOLE AREA HAS WONDERFUL WILDFLOWER DISPLAYS, WHICH CAN BE ENJOYED ALONG A NUMBER OF SCENIC DRIVES. TO THE NORTH ARE THE LIMESTONE PILLARS OF THE PINNACLES (IN NAMBUNG NATIONAL PARK) AND TO THE SOUTH-EAST THE GRANITE OUTCROP OF WAVE ROCK (NEAR HYDEN).

Serpentine National Park is located just south of Perth. At Gooralong, in the park's north, there is a large, shaded camping area which inquisitive local parrots often visit. Bushwalking and mountain-bike riding are possible in this section, and in the east of the park are the stunning Serpentine Falls.

Dryandra Woodland, north of Williams and north-west of Narrogin, is home to a number of native ground-dwelling mammals including the numbat, tammar wallaby and woylie. This is a popular area for walking, picnicking and cycling.

On the paths of the Swan and Avon rivers are Avon Valley and Walyunga national parks. These are great places for exploring the state's impressive forests of jarrah and marri. Avon Valley National Park is home to rufous treecreepers, western yellow robins and honeyeaters, with the sacred kingfisher arriving in spring to breed. Walyunga National Park boasts a variety of walking trails, ranging from the 45-minute Aboriginal Heritage Trail to the five-hour Echidna Trail, with its superb views across the Swan and Avon valleys. Camping is possible in both parks.

Just south of Mundaring is Hills Forestry Discovery Centre, an excellent venue for children – and adults – to learn more about biodiversity and the values of Australia's natural heritage. The camping area here is suitable for tents and caravans, and has facilities including hot showers and a camp kitchen.

With so many campsites close to Perth, visitors to this region also have easy access to that other great attraction here – wining and dining in the Swan Valley.

BEST CAMPSITES

Gooralong picnic and camping area
Serpentine National Park

Congelin Campground
Dryandra Woodland

Homestead campsite
Avon Valley National Park

Boyagin Rock picnic and camping area
Boyagin Rock

Hills Forest Discovery campground
Hills Forest Discovery Centre

BEST TIME TO VISIT

All year round.

1. AVON VALLEY NATIONAL PARK

This park is 45 km north-east of Midland. It features granite outcrops, forests and views over the Avon Valley. The park is a popular spot for birdwatchers, with over 90 species of birds identified here. Entry to the southern side of the park is via Quarry Rd off Morangup Rd off the Toodyay Rd and to the northern side from Plunkett Rd.

Thirty-seven Mile Road campsite

Signposted on Thirty-seven Mile Rd off Plunkett Rd. Located 40 km west of Toodyay. Bring drinking water. Firewood supplied. Additional map ref.: STAWA 75 A4.

Bald Hill campsite

Signposted off Governors Drive off Quarry Rd; it is west of Drummonds campsite. Firewood supplied. Additional map ref.: STAWA 75 A4.

Drummonds campsite

Signposted off Governors Drive off Quarry Rd. To the west of Homestead campsite. This area is suitable for small pop-top vans. Firewood supplied. Additional map ref.: STAWA 75 A4.

Homestead campsite

Signposted from Governors Drive off Quarry Rd. Located 30 km west of Toodyay and 55 km north-east of Midland. This site is suitable for small pop-top vans. Firewood supplied. Additional map ref.: STAWA 75 A4.

Sappers campsite

Signposted on Sappers Rd off Plunkett Rd. Located 25 km west of Toodyay. Bring drinking water. Firewood supplied. Additional map ref.: STAWA 75 A4.

Valley campsite

Signposted off Forty-one Mile Rd off Quarry Rd. Firewood supplied. Additional map ref.: STAWA 75 A4.

Further information: Avon Valley National Park
Tel.: (08) 9571 3066 **Park entrance fee:** $9.00 per vehicle
Camping fees: From $5.00 per person/night, $2.00 per child (under 16) per night; fees payable at park entrance stations on Quarry Rd and Plunkett Rd

2. BALLIDU

The small town of Ballidu, 240 km north-east of Perth, was originally settled in 1909. Ballidu is the service and social centre for the surrounding grain and sheep farms. Many of its original buildings from the 1920s and 30s are still standing. It is a wildflower viewing area.

Ballidu Caravan Park

On Wallis St in Ballidu. Bring firewood. Additional map ref.: STAWA 97 B3.

Further information & bookings:
Ballidu Caravan Park **Tel.:** (08) 9674 1317 *or*
Shire of Wongan–Ballidu **Tel.:** (08) 9671 1011
Camping fees: Tent sites from $7.70 per site/night up to 2 people, powered sites from $14.30 per site/night up to 2 people; fees collected by ranger

3. BEACON AREA

Beacon is 315 km north-east of Perth, in the north-eastern wheat belt. The region is popular with birdwatchers and wildflower lovers.

Beacon Caravan Park

On Lucas St in Beacon. Bring gas/fuel stove. Additional map ref.: STAWA 100 A1.

Further information & bookings:
Beacon Caravan Park **Tel.:** (08) 9686 1002 **Camping fees:** Unpowered from $5.50 per site/night, powered from $8.80 per site/night

Billiburning Rock camping area

This is 34 km north of Beacon. Signposted from White Rd off Beacon North Rd. Unmarked walks to the top of the rock. Bring drinking water and firewood. Enquire at shire office for fire restrictions. Additional map ref.: STAWA 118 A5.

Further information:
Shire of Mount Marshall **Tel.:** (08) 9685 1202
Email: admin@mtmarshall.wa.gov.au

4. BENCUBBIN AREA

Bencubbin, 273 km north-east of Perth, is the centre of the north-eastern wheat belt. The area has a rich farming history of grain, wheat and sheep. During wildflower season (June–Oct.) a large variety of beautiful wildflowers are in bloom.

Bencubbin Caravan Park

On Bencubbin–Trayning Rd at the southern end of Bencubbin. Additional map ref.: STAWA 100 A5.

Marshall Rock camping area

Located 10 km south of Bencubbin. Signposted from Marshall Rock South Rd off Mukinbudin Rd. Bring drinking water and firewood. Gas/fuel stoves preferred. Enquire at shire office for fire restrictions. Additional map ref.: STAWA 91 A1.

Further information & bookings: Shire of Mount Marshall **Tel.:** (08) 9685 1202 **Email:** admin@mtmarshall.wa.gov.au
Camping fees: *Bencubbin Caravan Park*: From $8.80 per site/night; fees payable at council offices on Monger St, Bencubbin (office hours 8.30 am–5 pm weekdays)

5. BEVERLEY

Beverley is 135 km east of Perth. The town, which was established in 1838, is on the banks of the Avon River and is within the central wheat belt.

Beverley Caravan and Camping Ground

Behind the council chambers on Council Rd in Beverley. Bring gas/fuel stove. Additional map ref.: STAWA 68 D5.

Further information & bookings: Shire of Beverley
Tel.: (08) 9646 1200 **Email:** admin@beverley.wa.gov.au
Camping fees: From $11.00 per site/night; fees payable on weekdays at council offices at 136 Vincent St, Beverley (office hours 8 am–4 pm) and at honour box at caravan park on weekends

6. BIBBULMUN TRACK – SECTION ONE

See also Bibbulmun Track – section two, *page 202*, and Bibbulmun Track – section three, *page 212*

The Bibbulmun Track is Western Australia's longest walking track, 963 km in all. The track runs from the Perth suburb of Kalamunda to Albany on the south coast and is marked the full length. It was originally designed to allow urban people to 'go bush'. Walkers will traverse some of the south-west's most beautiful and scenic regions and experience a variety of forest types. The track can be tackled in one go for those with the time and energy or can be walked in sections – there are many vehicle access points. This section of the track takes walkers past Mundaring Weir and Hills Forest before heading south over the Brookton and Albany highways into more forested terrain. All walkers should be well prepared and self-sufficient. Water may not be reliable – always carry extra. Gas/fuel stove preferred. Fire restrictions occur Oct.–May; please contact local authorities to obtain current details. Purchase of the excellent Bibbulmun Track guides and maps published by CALM is essential.

Hewetts Hill campsite
10.3 km from the Kalamunda trackhead. Additional map ref.: STAWA Perth & Environs P2 I8.
Ball Creek campsite
10.6 km from Hewetts Hill.
Helena campsite
8.6 km from Ball Creek.
Waalegh campsite
9.5 km from Helena.
Beraking campsite
8.5 km from Waalegh.
Mount Dale campsite
11.5 km from Beraking.
Brookton campsite
8.3 km from Mt Dale.
Canning campsite
11.1 km from Brookton.
Monadnocks campsite
15.6 km from Canning.
Mount Cooke campsite
12.7 km from Monadnocks.
Nerang campsite
12.6 km from Mt Cooke.
Gringer Creek campsite
16.6 km from Nerang; 17.6 km from White Horse Hills (see Bibbulmun Track – section two). Additional map ref.: STAWA 58 C5.

Further information:
CALM Bibbulmun Track Coordinator, Kensington
Tel.: (08) 9334 0265 **Email:** bibtrack@calm.wa.gov.au *or*
The Friends of the Bibbulmun Track **Tel.:** (08) 9481 0551
Email: friends@bibbulmuntrack.org.au **Website:**
www.bibbulmuntrack.org.au *or*
CALM offices: Mundaring, tel. (08) 9295 1955; Dwellingup, tel. (08) 9538 1078

7. BODDINGTON

Boddington is west of the Albany Hwy, 123 km south-east of Perth. The surrounding region is a mix of agricultural, forestry and mining industries. Situated on the Hotham River, the Boddington Caravan Park has fishing for redfin and perch.

Boddington Caravan Park

On Wuraming Ave in Boddington. Bring gas/fuel stove. Key for ablution block – $10.00 refundable deposit. Bookings recommended during Nov. Additional map ref.: STAWA 50 D2.

Further information & bookings: Boddington Caravan Park **Tel.:** (08) 9883 8018 **Camping fees:** Unpowered tent site from $9.90 per site/night for 2 adults, powered caravan sites from $16.50 per site/night for up to 4 people

8. BOYAGIN ROCK

Boyagin Rock is within the Boyagin Nature Reserve to the west of Pingelly and the Great Southern Hwy. The Boyagin Nature Reserve protects woodlands and heaths, along with numerous marsupials. Within the reserve are two large granite outcrops that offer wonderful views. The best time to visit is during the cooler months of July to September when the wildflowers are in bloom. Please note that camping is not allowed within the nature reserve but there is a picnic and camping area located adjacent to it.

Boyagin Rock picnic and camping area

Access is signposted via Boyagin Rd from Walwalling Rd and Kulyaling West Rd off the Great Southern Hwy. From the east signposted access is off the York Williams Rd from the Brookton Hwy. Bring drinking water and firewood. Additional map ref.: STAWA 59 D4.

Further information:
Camping area: Shire of Pingelly **Tel.:** (08) 9887 1066
Boyagin Nature Reserve: CALM, Narrogin **Tel.:** (08) 9881 1113
Fire restrictions: Solid-fuel fire ban Oct.–March; please check with shire office for current fire restrictions

9. BROOKTON

The town of Brookton is on the Brookton Hwy, 138 km south-east of Perth. It is an ideal base to explore the local attractions, such as Nine Acre Rock and the Yenyenning Lakes.

Brookton Caravan Park

On Brookton Hwy in Brookton. Laundry facilities. Additional map ref.: STAWA 60 A3.

Further information & bookings: Brookton Caravan Park **Tel.:** (08) 9642 1434 **Camping fees:** Unpowered tent sites from $5.50 per person/night, powered caravan sites from $15.00 per site/night up to 2 people

10. BRUCE ROCK

Bruce Rock is 247 km east of Perth.

Bruce Rock Caravan Park

On Dunstall St in Bruce Rock. Laundry facilities. Additional map ref.: STAWA 71 C2.

Further information & bookings: Caretaker, Bruce Rock Caravan Park **Tel.:** (08) 9061 1070 **Camping fees:** Tent sites from $5.00 per person/night, caravan sites from $15.00 per site/night; fees payable at Bruce Rock Post Office or to caretaker

11. CALINGIRI

Calingiri is 141 km north-east of Perth. It is a good base for visiting the attractions of the Shire of Victoria Plains, which include the Benedictine community, the Wyening Mission, historic buildings at Bolgart and the wildflowers in Piawaning and Gillingarra.

Calingiri Caravan Park

On Cavell St in Calingiri. Gravel surface not suitable for tents. Gas/fuel stove only. Additional map ref.: STAWA 87 C3.

Further information & bookings: Shire of Victoria Plains **Tel.:** (08) 9628 7004 **Website:** www.victoriaplains.wa.gov.au **Camping fees:** Unpowered from $5.50 per site/night for 2 people, powered from $11.00 per site/night for 2 people; fees payable at council office, 28 Cavell St

12. CARNAMAH

On the Midlands Rd 290 km north of Perth, the town of Carnamah has a rich history and many historical buildings still standing, including McPherson Homestead, built in 1869. Visitors can take in the expansive views of the Yarra Yarra Lakes from Lakes Lookout.

Carnamah Caravan Park

On King St off McPherson St in Carnamah. Gas/fuel stove only. Additional map ref.: STAWA 110 C2.

Further information & bookings: Shire of Carnamah **Tel.:** (08) 9951 1055 **Email:** shire@carnamah.wa.gov.au **Camping fees:** Unpowered from $7.70 per site/night for 2 people, powered from $11.00 per site/night per 2 people; fees payable at honesty box at park or at shire offices on McPherson St on weekdays, 8.30 am–4 pm

13. COASTAL PLAIN WALK TRAIL

The Coastal Plain Walk Trail traverses the Swan Coastal Plain from Yanchep National Park to Melaleuca Conservation Park. The plain has diverse flora and walkers are treated to coastal heath, jarrah forests, woodlands and wildflowers. Walkers need to be self-sufficient and carry water – water at campsites is for emergency use only. The Coastal Plain Walk Trail map and the Wild About Walking brochure are available from CALM. Trail trackhead is at Ghost House Ruins 5 km north of the McNess Visitors Centre, Yanchep National Park. The campsites are listed in the order they are reached from the trackhead.

Shapcotts campsite

Located 300 m from trackhead. Bring drinking water. Gas/fuel stove preferred. Additional map ref.: STAWA 73 D4.

Ridges campsite

Located 15.6 km from Shapcotts campsite. Bring drinking water. Gas/fuel stove preferred. Additional map ref.: STAWA 73 D4.

Moitch campsite

Located 19.9 km from Ridges campsite. Bring drinking water. Gas/fuel stove preferred. Additional map ref.: STAWA 74 B5.

Prickly Bark campsite

Located 17 km from Moitch campsite and 3.2 km from Cooper Rd trackhead (end of trail) in Melaleuca Conservation Park. Bring drinking water. Gas/fuel stove preferred. Additional map ref.: STAWA 74 C5.

Further information: Yanchep National Park, **Tel.:** (08) 9561 1004 **Park entrance fee:** $9.00 per vehicle (for Yanchep National Park)

14. CORRIGIN

The small town of Corrigin is 235 km south-east of Perth along the Brookton Hwy. The town and surrounding region has many attractions, including the Dog Cemetery and the Pioneer Museum. There are wildflower displays in season.

Corrigin Caravan Park

On the corner of Larke Crescent and Kirkwood St. Close to all town facilities. Additional map ref.: STAWA 62 A2.

Further information & bookings: Corrigin Caravan Park **Tel.:** (08) 9063 2515 **Camping fees:** Unpowered from $5.00 per person/night, powered from $13.50 per site/night for 2 people

15. DALWALLINU

The first town on Western Australia's famous Wildflower Way, Dalwallinu is 254 km north-east of Perth on the Great Northern Hwy. Dalwallinu and its surrounding region offer many cultural and natural attractions for the visitor. Wildflower season is July–Oct.

Dalwallinu Caravan Park

On Dowie St in Dalwallinu. Gas/fuel stoves only. Additional map ref.: STAWA 111 C5.

Further information & bookings: Dalwallinu Caravan Park **Tel.:** (08) 9661 1253 **Camping fees:** Unpowered site from $13.20 per site/night for 2 people, powered from $15.40 per site/night for 2 people

16. DANDARAGAN

Dandaragan is 180 km north of Perth and just east of the Brand Hwy. Dandaragan and its surrounds are a popular wildflower spot in Sept.–Oct.

Pioneer Park

On Dandaragan Rd in Dandaragan. Additional map ref.: STAWA 94 D4.

The Pinnacles, in Nambung National Park, south of Jurien Bay

Further information & bookings: Shire of Dandaragan **Tel.:** (08) 9651 4010 **Email:** council@dandaragan.wa.gov.au **Website:** www.dandaragan.wa.gov.au **Camping fees:** From $8.00 per site/night for 2 people; fees payable to shire office, Dandaragan Rd, or to caretaker

17. DRYANDRA WOODLAND

Dryandra Woodland is 27 km north of Williams on the Albany Hwy via the York Williams Rd and 24 km north-west of Narrogin via the Wandering Narrogin Rd. Dryandra is popular with bushwalkers, wildlife-spotters, picnickers, cyclists, horseriders and campers. Visitors to Dryandra will see a variety of flora – from spring wildflowers to woodlands of white-barked wandoo and powderbark. The 'Return to Dryandra' project is helping the repopulation of threatened native marsupials in the area. There are numerous walking trails of varying lengths and grades, and visitors can learn about the region's history while travelling the Dryandra Drive Trail and tuning the radio into the signposted frequency. A range of activities such as stargazing and traditional bushcraft are run by CALM; contact CALM at Narrogin for further information.

Congelin Campground

Bring drinking water and firewood. Additional map ref.: STAWA 51 D2.

Further information: CALM, Narrogin **Tel.:** (08) 9881 9200 **Camping fees:** From $5.00 per person/night; fees payable via self-payment reply-paid envelopes from the information station

18. GUILDERTON

Guilderton is 94 km north of Perth, at the mouth of the Moore River. This is a great location that offers safe swimming, pleasant beaches, canoeing on the Moore River and ocean and river fishing. Access to Guilderton is via Guilderton Rd off the Wanneroo Rd.

Guilderton Caravan Park

At the mouth of Moore River. Reached from Guilderton Rd in Guilderton. Gas/fuel stove only. Bookings recommended. Additional map ref.: STAWA 73 B1.

Further information & bookings: Guilderton Caravan Park **Tel.:** (08) 9577 1021 **Website:** www.iinet.net.au/~ginginwa **Camping fees:** Unpowered from $16.00 per site/night for 2 people, powered from $19.50 per site/night for 2 people

19. HILLS FOREST DISCOVERY CENTRE

The Hills Forest Discovery Centre, 6 km south of Mundaring, has much to offer visitors. Throughout the year there is a range of organised nature-based activities including bush crafts, Aboriginal culture sessions, animal encounters and an outdoor cinema during the warmer months. Alternatively, enjoy one of the scenic walks, wander along a section of the Bibbulmun Track or enjoy the views over Mundaring Weir. The Discovery Centre is signposted from Mundaring via the Mundaring Weir Rd.

Hills Forest Discovery campground

Signposted on Allens Rd off Mundaring Weir Rd, 6 km south of Mundaring. Firewood supplied. Bookings essential. Additional map ref.: STAWA 67 A3.

Patens Brook campsite

Walk-in site on Patens Brook Trail, 3 km from Hills Forest Discovery Centre. Limited water supply, best to take own. Firewood supplied. Gas/fuel stove preferred. Bookings advisable. Additional map ref.: STAWA 67 A3.

Further information & bookings: Hills Forest Discovery Centre **Tel.:** (08) 9295 2244 **Email:** hillsforest@calm.wa.gov.au **Camping fees:** *Hills Forest Discovery*: From $8.80 per adult/night, $6.60 per child (16 and under) per night *Patens Brook*: From $3.30 per person/night

20. JURIEN BAY

The popular holiday town of Jurien Bay is on the coast 266 km north of Perth, off the Brand Hwy. Jurien Bay is home to a large crayfishing fleet. The region offers safe swimming, fishing, sailboarding and diving, and Jurien Bay is 24 km from the Pinnacles.

Jurien Bay Caravan Park

On Roberts Rd in Jurien Bay. Wood barbecues, firewood supplied. Bookings recommended. Campfires prohibited. Additional map ref.: STAWA 109 C5.

Further information & bookings: Jurien Bay Caravan Park **Tel.:** (08) 9652 1595 **Camping fees:** *Off-peak*: From $17.50 per site/night for 2 people *Peak*: From $18.50 per site/night for 2 people

21. KALANNIE

Within the wildflower region, Kalannie is 45 km east of the Dalwallinu. To the west of Kalannie is Petrudor Rock, a great spot for a day visit and picnic.

Kalannie Caravan Park

On Roche St North in Kalannie. Bring gas/fuel stove. Additional map ref.: STAWA 98 B1.

Further information & bookings: Kalannie Caravan Park **Tel.:** (08) 9666 2120 **Camping fees:** Unpowered tent sites from $6.60 per site/night for 1 person, $2.20 for extra adults; powered sites from $15.40 per site/night for 2 people. Fees collected by caretaker

22. KELLERBERRIN

Kellerberrin is 202 km to the east of Perth along the Great Eastern Hwy. The Kellerberrin Caravan Park is a small park at the Kellerberrin Sports Ground.

Kellerberrin Caravan Park

On Connelly St. Additional map ref.: STAWA 78 C5.

Further information & bookings: Shire of Kellerberrin **Tel.:** (08) 9045 4006 **Camping fees:** Unpowered from $8.00 per site/night, powered from $10.00 per site/night; fees payable to on-site caretaker

23. KOKERBIN ROCK

This large granite outcrop offers panoramic views of the surrounding countryside. Visitors will find caves and rock formations to explore, along with walking trails and wildflowers. It is located 10 km north of Kwolyin, which is on the Bruce Rock–Quairading Rd.

Kokerbin Rock camping area

On Kwolyin West Rd and signposted from Kwolyin. Bring firewood. Additional map ref.: STAWA 70 C2.

Further information:
Shire of Bruce Rock **Tel.:** (08) 9061 1377 *or* Bruce Rock Tourist Information Centre **Tel.:** (08) 9061 1002

24. KONDININ

Kondinin is 280 km east of Perth and 60 km west of Hyden and Wave Rock. There is a council caravan park in town.

Kondinin Caravan Park

On Gordon St, Kondinin. Key access to ablution block – $10.00 refundable deposit. Additional map ref.: STAWA 62 D4.

Further information & bookings: Kondinin Shire **Tel.:** (08) 9889 1006 **Email:** enquiries@kondinin.wa.gov.au **Website:** www.kondinin.wa.gov.au **Camping fees:** Unpowered site from $6.60 per site/night, powered site from $13.20 per site/night; fees payable to shire office on Gordon St or to Kondinin Roadhouse Motel, corner Gordon and Graham sts

25. KOORDA

Koorda is 235 km north-east of Perth. The council caravan park is surrounded by natural bushland and wildflower displays in season.

Koorda Caravan Park

On Scott St in Koorda. Bring firewood. Additional map ref.: STAWA 90 A1.

Further information & bookings: Shire of Koorda **Tel.:** (08) 9684 1219 **Email:** corndoll@agn.net.au **Website:** www.koorda.wa.gov.au **Camping fees:** Tent sites from $3.00 per person/night, powered sites from $9.90 per site/night; fees payable to shire office, Allenby St

26. KULIN

Kulin is 110 km east of Narrogin, which is on the Great Southern Hwy.

Kulin Caravan Park

On Rankin St in Kulin. Firewood supplied. Laundry facilities. Additional map ref.: STAWA 54 C1.

Further information & bookings: Kulin Caravan Park **Tel.:** (08) 9880 1053 **Camping fees:** Tent sites from $3.30 per person/night, powered van sites from $11.00 per site/night for 2 people; fees collected by caretaker

27. LAKE INDOON

Lake Indoon is 12 km west of Eneabba, which is 145 km south of Geraldton on the Brand Hwy. The lake is a watersports destination for swimming, canoeing, sailing and waterskiing. With over 50 bird species recorded, the area is also popular with birdwatchers.

Lake Indoon camping area

Signposted along Eneabba–Coolimba Rd, 12 km west of Eneabba and 18 km east of Indian Ocean Drive. Gas/fuel stove only. Additional map ref.: STAWA 109 D3.

Further information: Shire of Carnamah **Tel.:** (08) 9951 1055 **Camping fees:** From $8.00 per car/night; fees collected by ranger

28. LAKE KING

The town of Lake King is in Lake Grace Shire, commonly known as The Lakes District for its abundance of salt lakes. It is in the far south-east of the Heartlands region, 117 km east of Lake Grace on the Newdegate–Ravensthorpe Rd.

Lake King Caravan Park

On Critchley Ave in Lake King. Additional map ref.: STAWA 82 A5.

Further information & bookings: Lake King Caravan Park **Tel.:** (08) 9874 4119 **Camping fees:** Unpowered from $9.90 per site/night for 2 people, powered from $13.20 per site/night for 2 people; fees collected by caretaker

29. LAKE LESCHENAULTIA

Lake Leschenaultia is 2 km north-west of Chidlow, which is just north of the Great Eastern Hwy about 15 km from Mundaring. The lake was built in 1897 by the Western Australian Government Railway to replenish steam engines travelling to Northam, York and beyond. Today's visitors can enjoy water-based activities such as swimming, fishing and canoeing. It is a popular area for bird- and wildlife-spotting ane there is a beautiful wildflower display in season. Motorised and sailing boats are prohibited on the lake.

Lake Leschenaultia camping area

Signposted from Rosedale Rd. Gates are locked at night but a key is available with a $20.00 refundable deposit. Bookings essential. Additional map ref.: STAWA 67 A2.

Further information & bookings: Lake Leschenaultia rangers office **Tel.:** (08) 9572 4248 **Email:** allanhill@ mundaring.wa.gov.au **Website:** www.mundaring.wa.gov.au **Camping fees:** $5.50 per person/night, plus a one-off booking fee of $5.50 for all sites

30. LAKE YEALERING

Lake Yealering is east of the town of Yealering, which is 63 km east of Pingelly. The lake is popular for waterskiing, canoeing, swimming and other watersports.

Lake Yealering Caravan Park

On Wickepin–Corrigin Rd from Yealering. Key for ablution block. Firewood supplied. Bookings recommended. Additional map ref.: STAWA 61 B5.

Further information & bookings: Yealering General Store **Tel.:** (08) 9888 7013 **Camping fees:** Tent sites from $3.00 per site/night, unpowered van sites from $5.00 per site/night, powered van sites from $10.00 per site/night; fees payable at general store

31. MOORA

Moora is 172 km north of Perth and is a popular stop for those travelling the wildflower trail. It is on the picturesque Moore River.

Shire of Moora Caravan Park

On Dandaragan St in Moora, near all town facilities. Additional map ref.: STAWA 95 C4.

Further information & bookings: Shire of Moora **Tel.:** (08) 9651 1401 **Website:** www.moora.wa.gov.au **Camping fees:** Unpowered tent sites from $9.00 per site/night for 2 people, powered tent sites from $10.00 per site/night for 2 people, powered van sites from $17.00 per site/night for 2 people; fees payable at council office, 34 Padbury St, or collected by ranger

32. MUKINBUDIN

Mukinbudin is to the north-east of Perth, and 82 km north of Merredin.

Mukinbudin Caravan Park

On Cruickshank Rd in Mukinbudin, near all town facilities. Additional map ref.: STAWA 91 D2.

Further information & bookings: Caretaker, Mukinbudin Caravan Park **Tel.:** (08) 9047 1103 **Camping fees:** Unpowered from $6.05 per site/night, powered from $13.75 per site/night

33. NAREMBEEN

This town is 290 km east of Perth. Narembeen's major industries are wheat and sheep. Visit the local Machinery Museum and Roe Lookout for views over the district. The local reserves of Mt Walker Rock, Twine Reserve and Anderson Rock have unusual rock formations and wildflowers.

Narembeen Caravan Park

On Curral St in Narembeen. Bring gas/fuel stove. Additional map ref.: STAWA 72 B4.

Further information & bookings: Shire of Narembeen **Tel.:** (08) 9064 7308 **Website:** www.narembeen.wa.gov.au

Camping fees: From $5.00 per person/night; fees payable at council office, 1 Longhurst St

34. NARROGIN

Narrogin is on the Great Southern Hwy, 210 km south-east of Perth.

Narrogin Caravan Park

On Williams Rd in Narrogin. Firewood supplied. Additional map ref.: STAWA 52 B4.

Further information & bookings: Narrogin Caravan Park **Tel.:** (08) 9881 1260 **Camping fees:** Unpowered from $4.40 per person/night, powered from $14.85 per site/night

35. PINGELLY AREA

Pingelly is 158 km south-east of Perth via the Brookton Hwy. Kulyaling Park is north of Pingelly, along the Great Southern Hwy – this former town site is suitable for an overnight stop only.

Kulyaling Park overnight stop

Located 10 km north of Pingelly, signposted from Great Southern Hwy. Bring drinking water and gas/fuel stove. Additional map ref.: STAWA 60 A4.

Further information: Shire of Pingelly **Tel.:** (08) 9887 1066 *or* Pingelly Tourist Information Centre **Tel.:** (08) 9887 1351

36. SERPENTINE NATIONAL PARK

Serpentine National Park is east of the South Western Hwy, between Serpentine and Jarrahdale. The Serpentine Falls, one of the park's major features, cascade 15 m over granite outcrops into rock pools below. In spring the park is carpeted by wildflowers including spider orchids, grevillas and dryandras. The park is also popular with birdwatchers and wildlife-spotters. There are three recreational areas: the Serpentine Falls area is signposted off the South Western Hwy; the Gooralong picnic and camping area is in the north-east of the park and reached from Jarrahdale; and the Pipehead Dam picnic area is on Day Rd off Kingsbury Drive from Jarrahdale.

Gooralong picnic and camping area

Signposted from Jarrahdale Rd in Jarrahdale, then on to Oak Way and then Atkins St. Travel 1 km from Jarrahdale Rd to an unsealed dirt road on the right, which leads for 500 m to the large, cleared camping area. Only cars and small vans can access this site. Flush toilets. Bring drinking water and firewood. Additional map ref.: STAWA 57 D2.

Further information: CALM, Serpentine National Park **Tel.:** (08) 9525 2128 *or* CALM, Mundaring **Tel.:** (08) 9295 1955

Fire restrictions: Solid-fuel fire ban Nov.–March inclusive; bring gas/fuel stove during this period. Dates may change, check with local CALM office before lighting a fire

37. TRAYNING

Trayning is 235 km north-east of Perth and 76 km north of Kellerberrin, which is on the Great Eastern Hwy. Trayning has a rich history dating back to the time when prospectors travelled through here on their way to the goldfields. Cereal crops and sheep are the region's main industries.

Trayning Caravan Park

On Sutherland St in Trayning. Bring gas/fuel stove. Laundry facilities. Additional map ref.: STAWA 90 D4.

Further information & bookings: Shire of Trayning
Tel.: (08) 9683 1001 **Email:** admin@trayning.wa.gov.au
Website: www.trayning.wa.gov.au **Camping fees:** Tent sites from $4.00 per night for 1 person, $1.00 per night for each extra person; powered van sites from $8.80 per site/night. Fees payable at shire office, Railway St, or after hours in honesty box on site

38. WALYUNGA NATIONAL PARK

Walyunga National Park is well known for its abundant native animals, its beautiful wildflowers during winter and spring and its rugged valley scenery. The Avon River runs through the middle of the park and provides one of the country's best whitewater canoeing courses – it is the setting for the Avon Descent each August. There are many walking trails of varying lengths and grades. The park is also a popular area for birdwatching. Walyunga National Park is 40 km north-east of Perth and is reached via Walyunga Rd off the Great Northern Hwy. The park is closed during the summer, end Nov.–end April. The park is locked each evening at 5 pm and all campers must be in by that time.

Walyunga camping area

Signposted via Walyunga Rd off Great Northern Hwy, 17 km north of Midland. Bring drinking water. Firewood supplied. Bookings essential. Additional map ref.: STAWA 66 D1.

Further information & bookings:
Ranger **Tel.:** (08) 9571 1371 *or*
CALM, Mundaring **Tel.:** (08) 9295 1955
Park entrance fee: $9.00 per vehicle **Camping fees:** From $5.00 per person/night, $2.00 per child (under 16) per night

39. WANDERING

The town of Wandering is east of the Albany Hwy and can be reached from the south via Crossman or from the north via North Bannister. The town has many historical buildings. Take a wildflower walk along Wandering Rd North or visit nearby Boyagin Rock (visitors can also camp at Boyagin Rock, see page 227).

Wandering Caravan Park

On Cheetaning St in Wandering. Some firewood supplied but best to bring own. Additional map ref.: STAWA 51 A1.

Further information & bookings: Shire of Wandering
Tel.: (08) 9884 1056 **Email:** ceo@wandering.wa.gov.au
Camping fees: From $7.00 per site/night for 2 adults, $2.50 for each additional person; fees payable at shire office, 22 Watts St

40. WAVE ROCK

The well-known Wave Rock is a granite cliff 110 m long and 15 m high, formed millions of years ago, by weather and water erosion. Visitors can enjoy walks in the surrounding bushland, visit the cave of the Aboriginal outlaw Mulka, go animal and bird spotting and enjoy the spring wildflowers. Wave Rock is just outside Hyden, 340 km east of Perth via the Brookton Hwy.

Wave Rock Caravan Park

Signposted on Wave Rock Rd, 4 km east of Hyden. Gas/fuel stove only. Additional map ref.: STAWA 64 B2.

Further information & bookings: Wave Rock Caravan Park
Tel.: (08) 9880 5022 **Website:** www.waverock.com.au
Camping fees: Unpowered from $17.00 per site/night for 2 people, powered from $20.00 per site/night for 2 people

41. WESTONIA

The town of Westonia is in Western Australia's wheat belt, 316 km east of Perth and 52 km east of Merredin. The region has a history of sandalwood cutting, goldmining and agriculture. Visitors to the area can view many natural features such as Boodalin Soak, Sandford Rocks, Baladjie Rock, Elachbutting Rock, Chiddarcooping Reserve and the Edna May Goldmine just north of town.

Westonia Caravan Park

On Wolfram St in Westonia. Gas/fuel stove only. Additional map ref.: STAWA 81 A1.

Further information & bookings:
Shire of Westonia **Tel.:** (08) 9046 7063
Website: www.westonia.wa.gov.au *or*
Westonia Community Resource Centre **Tel.:** (08) 9046 7077
Camping fees: From $14.00 per site/night; fees payable at Community Resource Centre, Wolfram St

42. WICKEPIN

Wickepin is south-east of Perth and 38 km north-east of Narrogin.

Wickepin Caravan Park

On Wogolin Rd in Wickepin. Firewood supplied. Additional map ref.: STAWA 53 A2.

Further information & bookings: Wickepin Caravan Park
Tel.: (08) 9888 1089 **Camping fees:** Unpowered sites from $6.00 per site/night, powered sites from $12.00 per site/night

43. WYALKATCHEM

Wyalkatchem is 191 km north-east of Perth via Toodyay and 115 km north-west of Merredin. The town has a number of heritage buildings. Wyalkatchem is a great base for exploring the surrounding nature reserves, lakes and wells.

Wyalkatchem Caravan Park

On Goomalling–Merredin Rd in Wyalkatchem. Additional map ref.: STAWA 89 D4.

Further information & bookings: Shire of Wyalkatchem
Tel.: (08) 9681 1166 **Email:** sowyalk1@comswest.net.au
Camping fees: Tent sites from $6.05 per site/night for 2 people, van sites from $14.30 per site/night; fees payable at shire office, corner of Honour Ave and Flint St, or after hours at Wyalkatchem Roadhouse on Hands Drive.

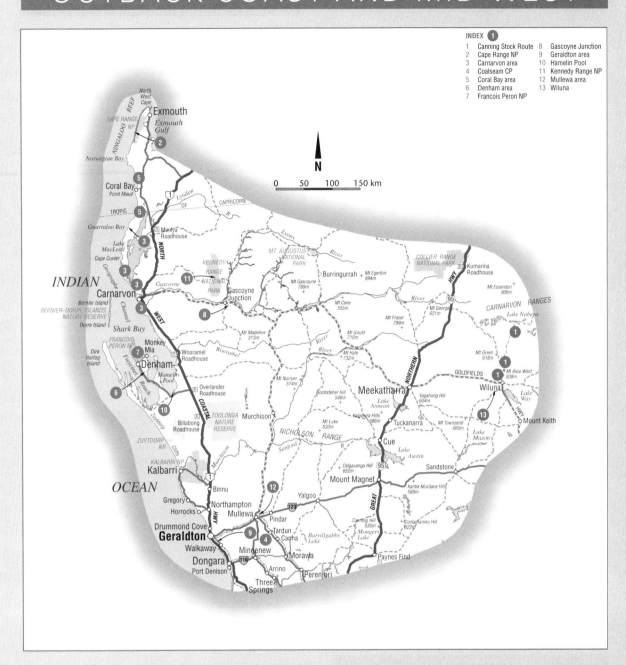

THE STRIKING BLUE WATERS OF
THE INDIAN OCEAN, HOME TO
DUGONG, DOLPHINS AND MANY
OTHER MARINE CREATURES, FRINGE
THE OUTBACK COAST. THE TOWNS
ALONG THIS COASTLINE OFFER
EXCELLENT HOLIDAY FACILITIES, AND INLAND ARE
MANY OTHER ATTRACTIONS FOR THE VISITOR –
RIVERS, GORGES, LARGE GRANITE FORMS,
ABORIGINAL ART SITES, OLD MINE SITES AND
DIVERSE FLORA.

The site of Western Australia's first coalmine
is within Coalseam Conservation Park. Visitors
exploring the park will find old mine shafts, coal
seams and ancient fossils along the riverbank and
around the cliffs. The park is home to many
different animals and from August to October it is
carpeted with everlastings. Campsites here offer
remote and self-sufficient camping.

En route to Denham from the North West
Coastal Highway is the historic Telegraph Station,
established in 1884 to service the Perth-to-

Roebourne line. Once here, walk to the Coquinite Quarry, and see the world-renowned Hamelin Pool stromatolites, rocks made up of layers of fossilised algae. Camping is at the nearby Hamelin Pool Caravan Park.

Closer to Denham are four camping areas facing Henri Freycinet Harbour. These natural bush campsites are managed by the local council and permits are required prior to setting up. Activities here include swimming, boating and fishing – or just relaxing.

At the tip of the Peron Peninsula is Francois Peron National Park. This is where the term 'Outback Coast' seems a true definition, where the park's huge red sand dunes meet the ocean. Visitors here will see a variety of marsupials, birds and reptiles, while the surrounding waters are home to turtles, dugong and dolphins. Project Eden, an interesting conservation project, is underway in the park – feral animals are being eradicated so that native species can be safely reintroduced. Camping is possible at a number of coastal sites here; they each have basic facilities and are accessed by four-wheel drive only.

BEST CAMPSITES

Miners Camp camping area
Coalseam Conservation Park

Neds Camp camping area
Cape Range National Park

Eagle Bluff camping area
Denham area

Gregories camping area
Francois Peron National Park

Ellendale Pool camping area
Geraldton area

BEST TIME TO VISIT

All year round.

1. CANNING STOCK ROUTE see page 249

2. CAPE RANGE NATIONAL PARK see page 236

3. CARNARVON AREA

Carnarvon is 904 km north of Perth via the North West Coastal Hwy, where the Gascoyne River meets the Indian Ocean. Along the river are tropical fruit plantations growing bananas, mangos, paw paws and melons. Fishing, including game-fishing, is a popular pastime. Carnarvon and its surrounds have a number of historic landmarks and natural attractions.

SOUTH OF CARNARVON

New Beach camping area

Signposted turn-off along North West Coastal Hwy 33 km south of Carnarvon. Area is 8 km west of the highway along New Beach Rd. Bring drinking water and firewood. Additional map ref.: STAWA 129 B1.

Bush Bay camping area

Signposted turn-off along North West Coastal Hwy 33 km south of Carnarvon. Area is 10 km west of the highway. Small boats can be launched off the beach. Bring drinking water and firewood. Additional map ref.: STAWA 129 B1.

Gladstone camping area

Signposted turn-off along North West Coastal Hwy 146 km south of Carnarvon. Area is 6 km west of the highway. Small boats can be launched from the beach. Bring drinking water and firewood. Additional map ref.: STAWA 129 C4.

Further information:
Shire of Carnarvon – Ranger Services **Tel.:** (08) 9941 0030 *or* Carnarvon Tourist Bureau **Tel.:** (08) 9941 1146
Camping fees: *Gladstone*: From $1.10 per person/night; fees payable at self-registration station on site

NORTH OF CARNARVON

Miaboolya Beach camping area

On Miaboolya Beach Rd off Bibbawarra Rd, 16 km north of Carnarvon. Camping in carpark area only. Access road may be closed in wet weather. Bring drinking water and firewood. Please note that this site is under review and may be closed for camping at a later date. Additional map ref.: STAWA 136 A5.

Further information:
Shire of Carnarvon – Ranger Services **Tel.:** (08) 9941 0030 *or* Carnarvon Tourist Bureau **Tel.:** (08) 9941 1146

The Blowholes camping area

Signposted along Blowholes Rd off North West Coastal Hwy, 73 km north of Carnarvon. 4WD boat ramp. Popular surfing, snorkelling and scuba-diving spot. Bring drinking water and firewood. Additional map ref.: STAWA 136 A5.

Further information:
Shire of Carnarvon – Ranger Services **Tel.:** (08) 9941 0030 *or* Carnarvon Tourist Bureau **Tel.:** (08) 9941 1146
Camping fees: From $5.50 per site/night; fees payable to ranger or at shire office, Francis St, Carnarvon

Quobba Station Homestead camping area

On Gnaraloo Rd off Blowholes Rd, 80 km north of Carnarvon. Donkey hot water system. Bring drinking water. Firewood supplied. Pets only by prior arrangement. Other accommodation available. Bookings required. Additional map ref.: STAWA 136 A4.

Further information & bookings: Quobba Station **Tel.:** (08) 9941 2036 **Email:** quobba@wn.com.au
Camping fees: Unpowered from $7.00 per person/night, powered from $9.00 per person/night

Red Bluff camping area

Access via Gnaraloo Rd off Blowholes Rd, 141 km north of Carnarvon. Popular surfing spot. Drivers towing caravans should check road conditions before attempting. Bring drinking water and firewood. Additional map ref.: STAWA 136 A3.

Further information & bookings: Caretakers **Tel.:** (08) 9948 5001 **Camping fees:** From $6.60 per adult/night

Three Mile Camp camping area

On Gnaraloo Station, 145 km north of Carnarvon. Access via Blowholes Rd. Caravan access is possible during dry weather only. Popular surfing and windsurfing spot. Bring drinking water, firewood, barbecue plate and grate. Dogs charged at $2.00 per dog/night; there is also a $50.00 refundable dog bond. Bookings preferred during July holidays. No fishing in the lagoon. Additional map ref.: STAWA 136 A3.

Further information & bookings: Gnaraloo Station **Tel.:** (08) 9388 2881 **Email:** gnarloo@wn.com.au
Camping fees: From $12.00 per adult/night, $5.00 per child (age 5–13) per night

EAST OF CARNARVON

Rocky Pool camping area

Signposted turn-off along Carnarvon–Mullewa Rd (Gascoyne Junction Rd) 52 km east of Carnarvon. Area is 4 km north of Carnarvon–Mullewa Rd. Bring drinking water and firewood. Additional map ref.: STAWA 136 C5.

Further information:
Shire of Carnarvon – Ranger Services **Tel.:** (08) 9941 0030 *or* Carnarvon Tourist Bureau **Tel.:** (08) 9941 1146

4. COALSEAM CONSERVATION PARK

Coalseam Conservation Park, the site of the state's first coalmine, is 32 km north of Mingenew and 51 km south of Mullewa. Coal was discovered here in 1846, by the Gregory brothers along the banks of the Irwin River. Today visitors can view old mine shafts, coal seams and fossils along with diverse and colourful vegetation. During Aug.–Oct. the park is carpeted with everlastings. Be cautious around mine shafts and do not enter them. Access to the park is via Coalseam Rd off Mingenew–Mullewa Rd.

Breakaway camping area

Signposted off Coalseam Rd. Bring drinking water. Gas/fuel stove only. Additional map ref.: STAWA 115 A3.

Miners Camp camping area

Signposted off Coalseam Rd, 5 km from the park entrance and south-east of the Irwin River. Bring drinking water. Gas/fuel stove only. Additional map ref.: STAWA 115 A3.

Further information: CALM, Geraldton **Tel.:** (08) 9921 5955

5. CORAL BAY AREA

The sea off the coast of Coral Bay forms the southern part of Ningaloo Marine Park. The town is located 218 km north of Carnarvon, on the Minilya–Exmouth Rd.

Nine Mile Camp camping area

On Cardabia Station north of Coral Bay. 4WD access recommended. Signposted from Coral Bay Rd off Minilya–Exmouth Rd. It is approximately 15 km north of the turn-off from Coral Bay Rd. Beach camping. Bring drinking water and firewood. All campers must contact Cardabia Station, either by phone or in person at homestead, prior to setting up camp. Additional map ref.: STAWA 140 B5.

Further information & bookings: Cardabia Station **Tel.:** (08) 9942 5935 **Camping fees:** None at time of printing, however fees may be introduced at a later time

Warroora Station camping areas

Numerous camping areas on Warroora Station, some with 4WD access only, approximately 60 km south of Coral Bay. Access via Warroona North Rd off Minilya–Exmouth Rd. Surfing and scuba-diving spot. Bring drinking water and firewood. No facilities. Self-sufficient campers only. There is an access fee of $5.00 per adult/day (children under 18 are free). Campers must call into homestead to pay fees and obtain map to camping areas. There are shower and toilet facilities at homestead ($2.50 per person) and other accommodation is available. Additional map ref.: STAWA 136 B2.

Further information & bookings: Warroora Station **Tel.:** (08) 9942 5920

6. DENHAM AREA

See also Francois Peron National Park, *next entry.*

The Shire of Shark Bay, based in Denham, runs a number of natural bush campsites. Denham and its surrounds feature safe swimming beaches, rugged coastal cliffs and scenic drives. Visitors can enjoy the World Heritage-listed Shark Bay Marine Park and the dolphins at Monkey Mia, view 'living fossils' at Hamelin Pool, or try a spot of boating or fishing – or just relax in the beautiful surrounds. Access to all the campsites is possible for conventional vehicles off the Shark Bay Rd. There is a maximum of three nights' stay at each site. Camping permits must be obtained before setting up camp; if camping on the weekend a permit must be obtained on the Friday before. Fines are applied for not holding a permit.

CAPE RANGE NATIONAL PARK

Cape Range National Park, just south of Exmouth, has an abundance of natural delights. As well as its magnificent coastal scenery, delightful beaches and crystal-clear waters, there are spectacular views from Thomas Carter Lookout and Charles Knife Rd. In addition there are walks to Shothole Canyon, Mandu Mandu Gorge and to the bird and fauna hides from Mangrove Bay carpark. The waters off Cape Range National Park offer excellent fishing and boating opportunities and give scuba divers and snorkellers the chance to explore coral reefs. The park entrance is in the north, 36 km from Exmouth. The main road through the park, Yardie Creek Rd, stretches from the northern boundary to Yardie Creek in the south and is sealed. Other roads in the park are a mixture of sealed and unsealed. Some campsites have resident hosts in peak season.

Boat Harbour camping area

4WD access only. Reached off Yardie Creek Rd, 5 km south of Yardie Creek crossing. Bring drinking water. Gas/fuel stove only. Additional map ref.: STAWA 140 B3.

Lakeside camping area

Signposted off Yardie Creek Rd, about 10 km south of park entrance. Bring drinking water. Gas/fuel stove only. Additional map ref.: STAWA 140 B3.

Mesa Camp camping area

Signposted off Yardie Creek Rd, about 8 km south of park entrance. Bring drinking water. Gas/fuel stove only. Additional map ref.: STAWA 140 B3.

Neds Camp camping area

Signposted off Yardie Creek Rd, about 7 km south of park entrance. Bring drinking water. Gas/fuel stove only. Additional map ref.: STAWA 140 B3.

North Mandu camping area

Signposted off Yardie Creek Rd, about 23 km south of park entrance. Bring drinking water. Gas/fuel stove only. Additional map ref.: STAWA 140 B3.

North T Bone camping area

Signposted off Yardie Creek Rd, about 9 km south of park entrance. Bring drinking water. Gas/fuel stove only. Additional map ref.: STAWA 140 B3.

One K Camp camping area

4WD access only. Reached from Yardie Creek Rd, 1 km south of Yardie Creek crossing. Bring drinking water. Gas/fuel stove only. Additional map ref.: STAWA 140 B3.

Osprey Bay camping area

Signposted off Yardie Creek Rd, about 34 km south of park entrance. Bring drinking water. Gas/fuel stove only. Additional map ref.: STAWA 140 B3.

Pilgramunna camping area

Signposted off Yardie Creek Rd, about 29 km south of park entrance. Bring drinking water. Gas/fuel stove only. Additional map ref.: STAWA 140 B3.

Tulki Beach camping area

Signposted off Yardie Creek Rd, about 16 km south of park entrance. Bring drinking water. Gas/fuel stove only. Additional map ref.: STAWA 140 B3.

Yardie Creek camping area

Signposted off Yardie Creek Rd, about 44 km south of park entrance. Bring drinking water. Gas/fuel stove only. Additional map ref.: STAWA 140 B3.

Further information: CALM, Exmouth **Tel.:** (08) 9949 1676 **Email:** exmouth@calm.wa.gov.au **Park entrance fee:** $9.00 per vehicle **Camping fees:** From $5.00 per person/night; fees collected by ranger or campsite hosts **Note:** Camping areas may change from time to time due to regeneration and revegetation

Range to reef

Ningaloo Reef is the largest fringing coral reef in Australia, and is the only reef in the world found so close to a continental landmass – just 100 metres offshore at its nearest point. It is a major diving and snorkelling destination; those interested should contact operators based in the towns of Coral Bay or Exmouth.

Baywatch

Mangrove Bay offers superb conditions for wildlife-watching. A bird hide overlooks a shallow lagoon, from where visitors can sit in well-shaded comfort and identify the various seabirds and waders that wander past. A nearby fauna hide offers glimpses of kangaroos and emus among other species.

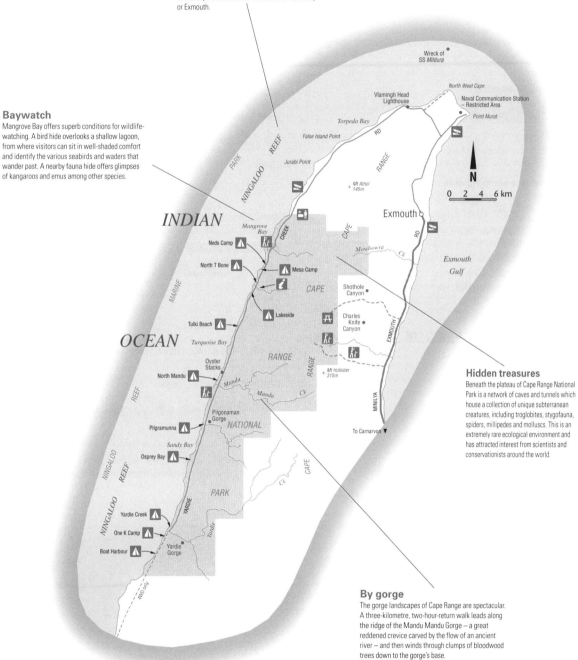

Hidden treasures

Beneath the plateau of Cape Range National Park is a network of caves and tunnels which house a collection of unique subterranean creatures, including troglobites, stygofauna, spiders, millipedes and molluscs. This is an extremely rare ecological environment and has attracted interest from scientists and conservationists around the world.

By gorge

The gorge landscapes of Cape Range are spectacular. A three-kilometre, two-hour-return walk leads along the ridge of the Mandu Mandu Gorge – a great reddened crevice carved by the flow of an ancient river – and then winds through clumps of bloodwood trees down to the gorge's base.

Eagle Bluff camping area

Permit required. Signposted from Eagle Bluff Rd off Shark Bay Rd, 18 km south-east of Denham. Good birdwatching, fishing and snorkelling spot. Bring drinking water. Gas/fuel stove only. Additional map ref.: STAWA 129 B4.

Fowlers Camp camping area

Permit required. Signposted on Fowlers Camp Rd off Shark Bay Rd, 22 km south-east of Denham. Good beach fishing. Bring drinking water. Gas/fuel stove only. Additional map ref.: STAWA 129 B4.

Goulet Bluff camping area

Permit required. Signposted from Goulet Bluff Rd off Shark Bay Rd, 36 km south-east of Denham. Bring drinking water. Gas/fuel stove only. Additional map ref.: STAWA 129 B4.

Whalebone Bay camping area

Permit required. On Whalebone Rd off Shark Bay Rd, 25 km south-east of Denham. Close to beach. Bring drinking water. Gas/fuel stove only. Additional map ref.: STAWA 129 B4.

Further information & bookings: Shire of Shark Bay **Tel.:** (08) 9948 1218 **Website:** www.sharkbay.asn.au **Permits:** Permits from Shire of Shark Bay by phone or in person (42 Hughes St, Denham, open Mon.–Fri. 8 am to 4 pm)

7. FRANCOIS PERON NATIONAL PARK

Francois Peron National Park is at the tip of the Peron Peninsula. Before it was gazetted as a national park, Peron Peninsula was a sheep-grazing station. The park protects various plants and shrublands, rugged coastlines and a variety of birds and wildlife. The waters surrounding the peninsula boast dugong, dolphins and loggerhead turtles. Access to the park is 4 km north of Denham off the Monkey Mia Rd. All roads within Francois Peron National Park are for high clearance 4WD vehicles only. As the roads are sandy, tyres should be deflated. In addition, the park has a number of claypans that should not be driven on.

Big Lagoon camping area

Signposted off main park road, 20 km north of Denham. Allow 45–60 minutes' travelling time from Denham. Beach boat launch. Bring drinking water. Gas/fuel stove only. Additional map ref.: STAWA 129 A3.

Herald Bight camping area

Signposted off main park road, 31 km north of Denham. Allow one hour's travelling time from Denham. Beach boat launch. Bring drinking water. Gas/fuel stove only. Additional map ref.: STAWA 129 A3.

South Gregories camping area

Signposted off main park road, 43 km north of Denham. Allow 1–1.5 hours' travelling time from Denham. Beach boat launch. Bring drinking water. Gas/fuel stove only. Additional map ref.: STAWA 129 A3.

Gregories camping area

Signposted off main park road, 43 km north of Denham. Allow 1–1.5 hours' travelling time from Denham. Beach boat launch. Bring drinking water. Gas/fuel stove only. Additional map ref.: STAWA 129 A3.

Bottle Bay camping area

Signposted off main park road, 43 km north of Denham. Allow 1–1.5 hours' travelling time from Denham. Beach boat

Big Lagoon, in Francois Peron National Park

launch. Bring drinking water. Gas/fuel stove only. Additional map ref.: STAWA 129 A3.

Further information: CALM, Denham **Tel.:** (08) 9948 1208 **Park entrance fee:** $9.00 per vehicle **Camping fees:** From $10.00 per site/night for 1–2 people; fees payable at self-registration station at park entrance near Peron Homestead

8. GASCOYNE JUNCTION

The township of Gascoyne Junction is where the Gascoyne and Lyons rivers meet, 175 km east of Carnarvon. Kennedy Range National Park lies to the north of the town.

Hackers Hectare camping area

At the Gascoyne River crossing in Gascoyne Junction. Bring drinking water and firewood. Suitable for an overnight stay only. Additional map ref.: STAWA 130 B1.

Further information & bookings: Shire of Upper Gascoyne **Tel.:** (08) 9943 0988

9. GERALDTON AREA

Geraldton is 424 km north of Perth and is a popular destination for fishing, sailing, surfing, diving and snorkelling. The surrounding shires have two delightful camping areas for travellers. To the north of Geraldton is Coronation Beach, a popular windsurfing and surfing beach, while to the east on the Greenough River is Ellendale Pool. This large freshwater pool is popular for swimming and canoeing.

Coronation Beach camping area

On Coronation Beach Rd off North West Coastal Hwy, 28 km north of Geraldton. Coronation Beach is 8 km west of the highway. Bring drinking water and firewood. Maximum 30-day stay. Additional map ref.: STAWA 113 Pt Map D1.

Further information: Shire of Chapman Valley **Tel.:** (08) 9920 5011 **Website:** www.chapmanvalley. wa.gov.au **Camping fees:** From $5.00 per vehicle/night; fees payable at honesty box or to ranger

Ellendale Pool camping area

Signposted along Ellendale Rd, 5 km north of Nangetty Walkaway Rd. Area is 47 km east of Geraldton. Bring drinking water. Gas/fuel stove only. Please take note of posted warning signs. Maximum three-night stay. Additional map ref.: STAWA 114 B3.

Further information: Shire of Greenough **Tel.:** (08) 9921 2533 **Website:** www.greenough.wa.gov.au

10. HAMELIN POOL

At Hamelin Pool is a historic Telegraph Station established in 1884 to service the Perth-to-Roebourne line. Not far from the station is a jetty where visitors can view interesting stromatolites. Hamelin Pool is reached off the Shark Bay Rd, 37 km west of the North West Coastal Hwy.

Hamelin Pool Caravan Park

On Hamelin Pool Rd off Shark Bay Rd. Camp kitchen. Additional map ref.: STAWA 129 C5.

Further information: CALM, Denham **Tel.:** (08) 9948 1208 **Bookings:** Hamelin Pool Caravan Park **Tel.:** (08) 9942 5905

Camping fees: Tent sites from $12.00 a site/night for 2 people, caravan sites from $16.00 per site/night for 2 people

11. KENNEDY RANGE NATIONAL PARK

The impressive Kennedy Range National Park is off the Ullawarra Rd, north of Gascoyne Junction. Within the park visitors can view ancient sea fossils, rock engravings, caves and waterfalls. During Aug.–Sept. a variety of wildflowers are on display. A walk to the top of the range offers the visitor expansive vistas in all directions.

Temple Gorge camping area

Signposted off Ullawarra Rd 60 km north of Gascoyne Junction. Bring drinking water and firewood. Gas/fuel stove preferred. Additional map ref.: STAWA 137 A5.

Further information & bookings: CALM, Carnarvon **Tel.:** (08) 9941 1801 **Road conditions:** Shire of Upper Gascoyne **Tel.:** (08) 9943 0988 **Camping fees:** There are no set camping fees – please make an appropriate donation in box at campsite

12. MULLEWA AREA

The Mullewa region is well known for its wildflower displays during July–Sept., in particular for the wreath flower, *Leschenaultia macrantha*. Other attractions around Mullewa include the Butterabby Gravesite and Tallering Peak and Gorge. Mullewa is 98 km north-east of Geraldton via the Geraldton–Mt Magnet Rd.

Noondamarra Pool camping area

Beside Greenough River. Signposted 29 km along Yuna–Tenindewa Rd, which runs off the Geraldton–Mt Magnet Rd 18 km south-west of Mullewa. Bring drinking water. Gas/fuel stove only. Additional map ref.: STAWA 114 C1.

Tenindewa Pioneer Well camping area

Signposted 4km along Yuna–Tenindewa Rd, which runs off the Geraldton–Mt Magnet Rd 18 km south-west of Mullewa. Bring drinking water. Gas/fuel stove only. Additional map ref.: STAWA 114 D1.

Further information:
Shire of Mullewa **Tel.:** (08) 9961 1007 *or* Mullewa Tourist Information Centre (open July–mid Oct.) **Tel.:** (08) 9961 1505

13. WILUNA

Wiluna is on the Goldfields Hwy 302 km north of Leonora. During its heyday of gold prospecting, Wiluna was a very prosperous town. As the start/finish point for both the Canning Stock Route and the Gunbarrel Hwy, Wiluna has all services required for intrepid travellers on these remote roads.

Club Hotel Caravan Park

On Wotton St in Wiluna behind Club Hotel. Firewood supplied. Additional map ref.: STAWA 133 A5.

Further information & bookings: Club Hotel **Tel.:** (08) 9981 7012 **Camping fees:** Tent sites from $8.80 per site/night for 2 people, caravan sites from $20.10 per site/night for 2 people

THE KIMBERLEY

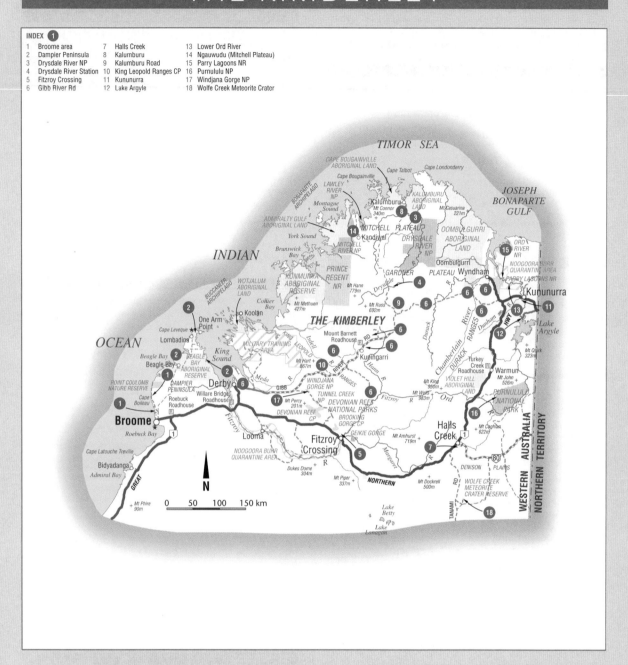

THE RUGGED AND REMOTE KIMBERLEY IS A REGION OF WILD COASTLINE, ANCIENT ROCK FORMATIONS, SPECTACULAR GORGES AND ABORIGINAL CULTURAL SITES. SOME OF THE MAJOR ATTRACTIONS INCLUDE THE ABORIGINAL COMMUNITIES ALONG THE COAST, THE SUPERB FISHING, THE ORD RIVER SCHEME, THE BUNGLE BUNGLES AND THE GIBB RIVER ROAD, A WORLD-RENOWNED TOURIST DRIVE FROM DERBY TO KUNUNURRA.

Extending for some 300 kilometres, the rugged King Leopold Ranges, protected within King Leopold Ranges Conservation Park, have strata of white and pink quartz sandstone, brown mudstone, grey–green basalt and grey dolerite. In the wet season large volumes of water cascade down the ranges on their way to King Sound. Also in the park are the rugged and spectacular Bell and Lennard gorges. In Bell Gorge a short walk leads from the carpark to the falls, where some excellent swimming can be enjoyed. Camping in the park is at Silent Grove and Bell Creek camping areas.

Fabulous fossils of extinct turtles and crocodiles, along with an ancient reef system, can be found in the limestone walls of Windjana Gorge and its caves. The Lennard River, which flows through Windjana Gorge National Park, supports a variety of birdlife, fish and freshwater crocodiles. The park offers great walking, birdwatching and photographic opportunities. Good facilities are provided at the park's two campgrounds.

Purnululu National Park is home to the spectacular Bungle Bungle Range. The magnificent orange-and-grey dome-shaped sandstone towers are intersected by beautiful palm-lined gorges. There are two vehicle-based camping areas in the park. Campers and visitors here can enjoy fantastic views and wonderful walking trails, including an easy circuit walk amongst the domes.

BEST CAMPSITES

Bell Creek camping area
King Leopold Ranges Conservation Park

Punamii-unpuu (Mitchell Falls) camping area
Ngauwudu (Mitchell Plateau)

Kurrajong camping area
Purnululu National Park

Quiet campground
Windjana Gorge National Park

Willie Creek camping area
Broome area

BEST TIME TO VISIT

From April to September, during the dry season.

1. BROOME AREA

Broome, a popular tourist destination, is the southern gateway to the Kimberley. During June and July the region's population swells with visitors, both Australian and international. Some come to absorb the town's rich history, from Aboriginal occupation through to its busy pearling years, and invariably all come to enjoy its beautiful beaches and great recreation. To the north of Broome via the Cape Leveque Rd are a number of council reserves where camping is permitted. Conventional-vehicle access to these sites is via unsealed roads. Road conditions do vary and should be checked before travelling. As these sites have no facilities, camping is for self-sufficient campers only. There is a maximum of three nights' stay at all sites. Fire danger periods are enforced – please check with local authorities for fire ratings before lighting any fire.

Barred Creek camping area

Signposted off Manari Rd, off Cape Leveque Rd, 39 km north of Broome. Bring drinking water and firewood. Gas/fuel stove preferred. Additional map ref.: STAWA 150 D3.

Prices Point camping area

Signposted off Manari Rd, off Cape Leveque Rd, 58 km north of Broome. Bring drinking water. Gas/fuel stove preferred. Additional map ref.: STAWA 150 C3.

Quondong Point camping area

On Quondong Beach Rd, off Manari Rd, off Cape Leveque Rd, 48 km north of Broome. Bring drinking water. Gas/fuel stove preferred. Additional map ref.: STAWA 150 C3.

Willie Creek camping area

Signposted off Manari Rd, off Cape Leveque Rd, 29 km north of Broome. Conventional vehicles should access with caution and check road conditions first. Natural boat launch. Bring drinking water. Gas/fuel stove preferred. Additional map ref.: STAWA 150 D3.

Further information:

Shire of Broome **Tel.:** (08) 9191 3456 **Email:** shire@broome.wa.gov.au **Website:** www.broome.wa.gov.au *or* Broome Visitors Centre **Tel.:** (08) 9192 2222 **Email:** tourism@broome.wt.com.au **Website:** www.ebroome.com/tourism

2. DAMPIER PENINSULA

The Dampier Peninsula is north of Broome. The major road along the peninsula is the Broome–Cape Leveque Rd. It is slow going, with travel time from Broome to Cape Leveque being about 3.5 hours. Travellers can visit some of the peninsula's Aboriginal communities and join in activities such as mudcrabbing, fishing and shell collecting as well as guided walks and bush tucker walks. At the Beagle Bay Community is the Sacred Heart Church, which was built in 1917 and has a beautiful pearl-shell altar (there is a fee of $5.00 per person to enter Beagle Bay Community; contact Beagle Bay office on tel. (08) 9192 4913). At Cape Leveque visitors will find beautiful white sandy beaches and a lighthouse. Please note that there are restricted-access areas along the peninsula including burial sites and traditional fishing grounds – please respect the owners' restrictions and keep to main roads. Do not drive on private roads and observe all 'no entry' signs.

Kooljaman camping area

This is 220 km north of Broome, reached via Broome–Cape Leveque Rd. Firewood supplied. Scenic flights and boat charters can be arranged. Other accommodation available. Bookings essential. Additional map ref.: STAWA 151 A1.

Further information & bookings: Kooljaman at Cape Leveque **Tel.:** (08) 9192 4970 **Email:** leveque@bigpond.com **Website:** www.kooljaman.com.au **Camping fees:** Unpowered site from $14.00 per adult/night, $7.00 per child (age 6–16) per night; for power add $4.00 per outlet/night

La Djardarr Bay Community camping area

Signposted on Broome–Cape Leveque Rd, 190 km north of Broome. Located 47 km east of Cape Leveque Rd. Firewood supplied. Bookings recommended. Additional map ref.: STAWA 151 A2.

Further information & bookings: La Djardarr Bay . Community **Tel.:** (08) 9192 4891 (phone number is seasonal and may be disconnected during the wet season) **Camping fees:** Unpowered site from $12.10 per person/night

Middle Lagoon Natures Hideaway camping area

Signposted on Broome–Cape Leveque Rd, 180 km north of Broome. It is 33 km west of Cape Leveque Rd. Solar hot showers. Other accommodation available. Bring firewood. Bookings recommended. Additional map ref.: STAWA 150 D2.

Further information & bookings: Middle Lagoon Natures Hideaway **Tel.:** (08) 9192 4002 **Camping fees:** Unpowered site from $13.00 per person/night, powered site from $16.00 per person/night

Mudnunn Community camping area

This is 190 km north of Broome. Signposted off Broome–Cape Leveque Rd at Lombadina airstrip. Bring drinking water. Firewood supplied. Bookings recommended. Additional map ref.: STAWA 151 A1.

Further information & bookings: Manager, Mudnunn Community **Tel.:** (08) 9192 4121 **Camping fees:** From $14.00 per person/night

3. DRYSDALE RIVER NATIONAL PARK

Drysdale River National Park covers over 448 000 ha. Within the park are rugged cliffs and gorges, creeks, rivers, and the Morgan and Solea waterfalls. Due to the park's remoteness there are excellent bushwalking and wildlife-watching opportunities. Access to the park's boundary, is by 4WD vehicle through Carson River Station off the Kalumburu Rd. From the boundary, entry into the park proper is for self-sufficient and experienced walkers only. There are no designated walking trails or facilities within the park. It is recommended that visitors to this region carry an EPIRB (emergency position indicating radio beacon). All visitors must register with the CALM office at Kununurra.

Carson River Station – Bulldust Yards camping area

On Carson River Station at the access point to Drysdale River National Park. Access permit and camping permit required. Self-sufficient campers only. Bring drinking water. Gas/fuel stove preferred. Additional map ref.: STAWA 154 B4.

Bush camping

Dispersed bush camping within park. Access permit and camping permit required. Self-sufficient and experienced walkers and campers only. No-trace camping applies. Bring drinking water. Gas/fuel stove only. Additional map ref.: STAWA 154 B4.

Further information: CALM, Kununurra **Tel.:** (08) 9168 4200 *or* Kalumburu Aboriginal Community **Tel.:** (08) 9161 4300 **Access fee:** $30.00 per vehicle, up to 5 people; collect permit and pay access fee to Kalumburu Aboriginal Community prior to entering **Camping fees:** *Carson River Station*: Contact Kalumburu Aboriginal Community for further details

4. DRYSDALE RIVER STATION

Drysdale River Station, covering over 400 000 ha, dates back to 1882; since then it has belonged to numerous owners and has a colourful history. The current owners have been on the station since 1985. Access is signposted off the Kalumburu Rd, 57 km north of the Gibb River Rd. Drivers of conventional vehicles should check road conditions before attempting – a 4WD vehicle is recommended. There is access for 4WD caravans.

Homestead Camp camping area

Signposted off Kalumburu Rd 57 km north of Gibb River Rd. Kalumburu Rd turn-off is 285 km west of Kununurra. Firewood supplied. Additional map ref.: STAWA 154 A5.

Miners Pool camping area

Signposted off Kalumburu Rd 2.5 km north of homestead turn-off, then 3 km east of Kalumburu Rd. Drinking water from river – boil before use. Firewood supplied. Additional map ref.: STAWA 154 A5.

Further information: Drysdale River Station **Tel.:** (08) 9161 4326 **Email:** drysdaleriver@bigpond.com **Website:** www.drysdaleriver.com.au **Camping fees:** *Homestead Camp*: From $9.00 per adult/night, $5.00 per child/night *Miners Pool*: From $5.00 per adult/night. Fees payable at Homestead reception or at shop, open 8 am–8 pm daily

5. FITZROY CROSSING

Fitzroy Crossing is on the sealed Great Northern Hwy, 391 km east of Broome, 256 km east of Derby and 289 km west of Halls Creek. The Fitzroy River flows for 1000 km to King Sound and the Indian Ocean.

Fitzroy River Lodge camping area

Signposted off Great Northern Hwy 2.3 km east of Fitzroy Crossing. Firewood supplied. Additional map ref.: STAWA 151 D4.

Tarunda Caravan Park

On Forrest Rd in Fitzroy Crossing. Camp kitchen. Dogs to be kept under strict control. Additional map ref.: STAWA 151 D4.

Further information & bookings:
Fitzroy River Lodge: **Tel.:** (08) 9191 5141
Tarunda Caravan Park: **Tel.:** (08) 9191 5330
Camping fees: Unpowered site from $9.90 per person/night, powered site from $23.00 per site/night for 2 people

6. GIBB RIVER ROAD

See also Kalumburu Road, *page 245*, King Leopold Ranges Conservation Park, *page 245, and* Windjana Gorge National Park, *page 247*

The Gibb River Rd is one of Australia's most famous roads. Originally built to transport cattle from the surrounding stations to Derby and Wyndham, it is now a major tourist route. The Gibb River Rd stretches for 650 km from Derby north-east to the junction of the Great Northern Hwy between Kununurra and Wyndham. Travellers along the Gibb River Rd will discover picturesque gorges, remote wilderness areas, Windjana Gorge National Park, Tunnel Creek, King Leopold Ranges and the Kalumburu Rd, which is accessed off the Gibb River Rd. Travellers should ensure their vehicle is well prepared and mechanically sound; a 4WD vehicle is recommended. Travel is best during the dry season, May–Nov. The surrounding stations are still working cattle properties and travellers should be aware of cattle on the road and also of the enormous road trains that transport cattle. The *Traveller's Guide to the Gibb River and Kalumburu Roads* is an excellent guide with up-to-date information and published yearly. It is available from visitor information centres for a small fee, or contact the Derby Visitor Centre on tel. (08) 9191 1426 for further details. Campsites may vary from year to year due to changed conditions after the wet season.

Birdwood Downs Station

A working station with tours and trail rides. Signposted along Gibb River Rd 20 km east of Derby. Bring gas/fuel stove. Bookings essential. Other accommodation available. Additional map ref.: STAWA 151 B3.

Further information & bookings: Birdwood Downs Station **Tel.:** (08) 9191 1275 **Email:** birdwood@wn.com.au
Camping fees: From $10.00 per person/night

Old Mornington Camp

Signposted off Gibb River Rd 247 km east of Derby. Located 100 km south-east of Gibb River Road. Scenic sites include Sir John Gorge, Dimond Gorge and Fitzroy River. Tours and canoe hire here. Other accommodation available. 4WD

vehicle and caravan access only. Flush toilets. Bring firewood. Additional map ref.: STAWA 152 A3.

Further information & bookings: Old Mornington Camp **Tel.:** (08) 9191 7406 **Camping fees:** From $10.00 per person/night

Beverley Springs Homestead camping area

Signposted off Gibb River Rd 251 km east of Derby. Located 43 km north of Gibb River Rd. Popular birdwatching area. Firewood supplied. Other accommodation is available. Additional map ref.: STAWA 151 D2.

Further information & bookings: Beverley Springs Homestead **Tel.:** (08) 9191 4646 **Email:** cpcamp1@ bigpond.com **Camping fees:** From $10.00 per person/night

Mount Barnett Roadhouse – Manning Gorge camping area

Mt Barnett Roadhouse is on Gibb River Rd 306 km east of Derby and 341 km west of Wyndham/Kununurra turn-off. 4WD vehicle and caravan access only. Camping area at Manning Gorge is 7 km north of roadhouse. Permit required to access camping area – it must be collected from roadhouse prior to proceeding to campsite. Flush toilets. Bring drinking water. Firewood supplied. Additional map ref.: STAWA 151 D2.

Further information & bookings: Mt Barnett Roadhouse **Tel.:** (08) 9191 7007 **Camping fees:** From $10.00 per person/night

Mount Elizabeth Station

Working cattle station signposted off Gibb River Rd, 338 km east of Derby and 309 km west of Wyndham/Kununurra turn-off. Located 30 km north of Gibb River Rd. 4WD vehicle and caravan access only. Day tours available. Swimming and fishing areas located a half-hour drive from campsite. Flush toilets. Firewood supplied. Bookings not necessary, but a phone call prior to arrival appreciated. Homestead accommodation also available. Additional map ref.: STAWA 152 A1.

Further information & bookings: Mt Elizabeth Station **Tel.:** (08) 9191 4644 **Email:** mt.elizabeth@bigpond.com
Camping fees: From $11.00 per person/night

Ellenbrae Station

Signposted off Gibb River Rd 476 km east of Derby and 171 km west of Wyndham/Kununurra turn-off. Located 5 km north of Gibb River Rd. 4WD vehicle and caravan access only. Showers have hot water donkey. Unmarked walking trails. Firewood supplied. Additional map ref.: STAWA 152 B1.

Further information & bookings: Ellenbrae Station **Tel.:** (08) 9161 4325 **Camping fees:** From $9.00 per person/night

Home Valley Station

This station is in a popular birdwatching area. It is signposted along Gibb River Rd 66 km west of Wyndham/Kununurra turn-off. Drivers of conventional vehicles and those towing caravans should check road conditions first. Flush toilets. Swimming pool. Firewood available for collection near campsite. Other accommodation available. Additional map ref.: STAWA 154 C5.

Further information & bookings: Home Valley Station **Tel.:** (08) 9161 4322 **Camping fees:** From $9.00 per person/night

El Questro Station

Signposted off Gibb River Rd 33 km west of Wyndham/Kununurra turn-off. Located 16 km south of Gibb River Rd. Wilderness Park Permit required ($12.50 per person valid for seven days; permits available on arrival). Drivers of conventional vehicles and those towing caravans should check road conditions before attempting. Dinghy hire, river cruises and helicopter flights on offer. Firewood for collection near campsite. Other accommodation available. Additional map ref.: STAWA 152 C1.

Further information & bookings: El Questro Station **Tel.:** (08) 9169 1777 **Website:** www.elquestro.com.au **Camping fees:** From $12.50 per person/night

Diggers Rest

On King River Rd, 45 km north of Gibb River Rd and 37 km south of Wyndham. Signposted from Wyndham. 4WD vehicle and caravan access only. Good birdwatching. Horseriding tours. Firewood supplied. Other accommodation available, including bush camping on the property – no facilities (fees from $7.00 per person/night). Additional map ref.: STAWA 154 C5.

Further information & bookings: Diggers Rest/Kimberley Pursuits Horse Treks **Tel.:** (08) 9161 1029 **Email:** kimberleypursuits@bigpond.com **Camping fees:** From $10.00 per person/night

Gibb River Road information:
Derby Visitor Centre **Tel.:** (08) 9191 1426 **Email:** derbytb@comswest.net.au **Website:** www.derbytourism.com.au or Kununurra Visitor Centre **Tel.:** (08) 9168 1177 **Email:** kununurratb@bigpond.com **Website:** www.eastkimberley.com or Wyndham Visitor Information Centre **Tel.:** (08) 9161 1281 **Road conditions:** Western Australia Road Condition Report Service **Tel.:** 1800 013 314

7. HALLS CREEK

Halls Creek was the site of Western Australia's first gold rush in 1887. The ruins of the old township site are located 17 km east. Local attractions include China Wall, Caroline Pool, Brockmans Hut, Palm Springs and Sawpit Gorge. Halls Creek is on the Great Northern Hwy, 359 km south of Kununurra and 289 km east of Fitzroy Crossing.

Halls Creek Caravan Park

On Roberta Rd in Halls Creek. Swimming pool. Additional map ref.: STAWA 152 C4.

Further information & bookings: Halls Creek Caravan Park **Tel.:** (08) 9168 6169 **Email:** lanus@bigpond.com.au **Camping fees:** Unpowered from $18.00 per site/night for 2 people, powered from $21.00 per site/night for 2 people

Old Halls Creek Lodge

On Duncan Rd 17 km east of Halls Creek. Signposted from Great Northern Hwy. Firewood supplied. Other accommodation available. Additional map ref.: STAWA 152 C4.

Further information & bookings: Old Halls Creek Lodge **Tel.:** (08) 9168 8999 **Camping fees**: Unpowered tent sites from $8.50 per person/night, unpowered van sites from $17.00 per site/night for 2 people, powered van sites from $20.00 per site/night for 2 people

8. KALUMBURU AREA

See also Kalumburu Road, next entry

The picturesque Aboriginal community of Kalumburu is 265 km north of the Gibb River Rd. Activities include visiting places of historic interest and enjoying a spot of fishing or mudcrabbing. An entry fee of $35.00 per vehicle (up to five people) is payable to visit Kalumburu and its surrounds (fee may go up in future). Contact the Kalumburu Aboriginal Corporation on tel. (08) 9161 4300 for further details.

Honeymoon Bay camping area

Located 27 km north of Kalumburu. Reached via McGowans Island Beach (see below). Fishing tours available. Firewood supplied. Additional map ref.: STAWA 154 B3.

Further information & bookings: French family **Tel.:** (08) 9161 4378 (phone number is seasonal and may be disconnected during the wet season) **Camping fees:** From $10.00 per person/night

Kalumburu Mission camping area

In Kalumburu community. Power available. Dogs by prior arrangement. Laundry facilities. Cafe on site. EFTPOS available (limited cash). Firewood supplied. Additional map ref.: STAWA 154 B3.

Further information & bookings: Kalumburu Mission **Tel.:** (08) 9161 4333 **Email:** kalumburumission@bigpond.com **Camping fees:** From $9.00 per person/night, school-aged children from $3.00 per night

McGowans Island Beach camping area

Located 15 km north of Kalumburu. Beach boat launch. Flush toilets. Firewood supplied. Additional map ref.: STAWA 154 B3.

Further information & bookings: Maraltadj family
Tel.: (08) 9161 4386 (phone number is seasonal and may be disconnected during the wet season) **Camping fees:** From $10.00 per person/night

Pago Mission camping area

This is 30–35 km north of Kalumburu. Access is via McGowans Island Beach. Historic area – ruins at mission. Bush camping for self-sufficient campers only. Bring drinking water. Firewood supplied. Additional map ref.: STAWA 154 B3.

Further information & bookings: Morgan family
Tel.: (08) 9161 4394 (phone number is seasonal and may be disconnected during the wet season) **Camping fees:** From $10.00 per vehicle/night up to 4–5 people

9. KALUMBURU ROAD

See also Kalumburu, *previous entry*

The Kalumburu Road is 267 km long. It stretches from the Gibb River Rd to the Kalumburu coast, leaving the Gibb River Rd 242 km west of the Wyndham/Kununurra turn-off and 413 km east of Derby. Travel is recommended only during the dry season and by 4WD vehicle. Numerous cattle stations are scattered along the road and travellers need to be aware of cattle and road trains. Vehicles must be well prepared and mechanically sound. The rest areas listed below are for 24-hour stops only – no extended stays.

Gibb River Crossing rest area

On Kalumburu Rd 3 km north of Gibb River Rd. Bring drinking water. Gas/fuel stove preferred. Additional map ref.: STAWA 152 A1.

Plain Creek rest area

On Kalumburu Rd 16 km north of Gibb River Rd. Bring drinking water. Gas/fuel stove preferred. Additional map ref.: STAWA 152 A1.

Further information:
Shire of Wyndham–East Kimberley **Tel.:** (08) 9168 1677 *or* Kununurra Visitors Centre **Tel.:** (08) 9168 1177
Email: kununurratb@bigpond.com
Website: www.eastkimberley.com
Road conditions: Western Australia Road Condition Report Service **Tel.:** 1800 013 314

10. KING LEOPOLD RANGES CONSERVATION PARK

The rugged 560-million-year-old King Leopold Ranges stretch for 300 km and are home to some of the Kimberley's most beautiful and picturesque gorges as well as numerous rare plants and animals. Visitors will enjoy spectacular scenery, bird- and animal-watching and bushwalking. The park is signposted off the Gibb River Rd 230 km east of Derby. A 4WD vehicle is necessary. Aside from camping, accommodation is available at the Mt Hart Wilderness Lodge; for details call tel. (08) 9191 4645 or visit www.mthart.com.au

Bell Creek camping area

On Silent Grove Rd 29.5 km north of Gibb River Rd. Water from creek – boil before use or bring own. Gas/fuel stove only. Additional map ref.: STAWA 151 D2.

Silent Grove camping area

On Silent Grove Rd 20 km north of Gibb River Rd. Flush toilets. Phone accepts phone cards only. Gas/fuel stove only. Additional map ref.: STAWA 151 D2.

Further information: CALM, Broome **Tel.:** (08) 9192 1036
Camping fees: From $9.00 per adult/night, $2.00 per child/night; fees collected by ranger

11. KUNUNURRA

Kununurra, on the Victoria Hwy, is the eastern gateway to the Kimberley. Visitors to Kununurra can explore Mirima National Park, take in the great views of the Ord Valley and Lake Kununurra from Kellys Knob lookout, try for a barra at Ivanhoe Crossing or visit Diversion Dam. There are numerous tour operators in town offering a variety of activities. Please note that the camping area listed below is for travellers with pets only, and all other travellers must use town caravan parks; contact visitor centre for details.

Kununurra Agricultural Society Showgrounds

On the corner of Ivanhoe Rd and Coolabah Drive, 600 m from town. Laundry facilities. Gas/fuel stove only. Proceed to caretaker's office before setting up camp. The site is closed 22–29 July annually for show. Additional map ref.: STAWA 154 D5.

Further information: Kununurra Visitors Centre
Tel.: (08) 9168 1177 **Email:** kununurratb@bigpond.com
Website: www.eastkimberley.com **Camping fees:** From $9.50 per person/night, extra $3.00 per night for power

12. LAKE ARGYLE

Lake Argyle covers an area 18 times the size of Sydney Harbour and is Australia's largest body of fresh water. The lake was created as part of the Ord River Irrigation Project, with the main Ord Dam being completed in 1972. Lake Argyle collects floodwaters during the wet season for use in drier months. Visitors can enjoy the scenery, take a boat cruise or do some birdwatching. Access to Lake Argyle is via Lake Argyle Rd, south of Kununurra.

Lake Argyle Caravan Park

On Lake Argyle Rd 70 km south of Kununurra. Laundry facilities. Firewood supplied. Bookings recommended June–Aug. Additional map ref.: STAWA 152 D1.

Further information & bookings: Lake Argyle Caravan Park
Tel.: (08) 9167 1050 **Email:** bigfish.in@bigpond.com
Camping fees: Unpowered tent sites from $7.00 per person/night, extra $4.50 per night for power **Dog bond:** Refundable bond of $20.00

13. LOWER ORD RIVER

See also Parry Lagoons Nature Reserve, *page 247*

The Lower Ord River is downstream (north) from Lake Argyle and Kununurra and flows into Cambridge Gulf. It is part of the Ord River Irrigation Project (see Lake Argyle, above). Access to the western riverbank is via Parry Creek Rd off Victoria Hwy, and to the eastern bank via Carlton Hill Rd off Weaber Plains Rd from the Victoria Hwy. Access is only possible by 4WD vehicle and roads may be closed during the wet

The dam wall of Lake Argyle

season. Please note that saltwater crocodiles frequent this area – do not swim in or camp near the river and if travelling with a dog keep it with you at all times.

Buttons Crossing camping area

On the west bank. Signposted on Parry Creek Rd off Victoria Hwy, 18.3 km north of highway. Permit required. Campfires only in existing fire sites. Bring drinking water and firewood. Additional map ref.: STAWA 154 D5.

Mambi Island camping area

On the west bank. Signposted on Parry Creek Rd off Victoria Hwy, 45.9 km north of highway. Permit required. Campfires only in existing fire sites. Bring drinking water and firewood. Additional map ref.: STAWA 154 D5.

Skull Rock camping area

On the east bank, 37 km north of Kununurra. Access off Carlton Hill Rd off Weaber Plains Rd, turn-off just east of Kununurra along Victoria Hwy. Permit required. Campfires only in existing fire sites. Bring drinking water and firewood. Additional map ref.: STAWA 154 D5.

Further information: Kununurra Visitors Centre **Tel.:** (08) 9168 1177 **Email:** kununurratb@bigpond.com **Website:** www.eastkimberley.com **Camping fees:** From $10.00 per vehicle/night; fees payable and permits from

visitor centre **Road conditions:** Shire of Wyndham–East Kimberley **Tel.:** (08) 9168 1677

14. NGAUWUDU (MITCHELL PLATEAU)

Ngauwudu is the name given to the Mitchell Plateau by the Wundambal Aboriginal people, who have lived in the region for thousands of years. The area is well known for the spectacular Mitchell Falls, King Edward River and Surveyors Pool. The palms native to the area grow up to 18 m, with some as old as 280 years. Aboriginal cave paintings can also be viewed. Please remember that Aboriginal sites are sacred. Do not touch paintings or engravings and do not remove artifacts. Access to Mitchell Plateau is along the Mitchell Plateau Rd off the Kalumburu Rd, turn-off 172 km north of the Gibb River Rd. A 4WD is essential. Self-sufficient campers only. Collect firewood only in designated collection zones.

Munurru (King Edward River Crossing) camping area

On Mitchell Plateau Rd 8 km west of Kalumburu Rd. 4WD camper-trailer access. Water from river – boil before use. Bring firewood. Gas/fuel stove preferred. Additional map ref.: STAWA 154 A4.

Punamii-unpuu (Mitchell Falls) camping area

On the Mitchell Plateau Rd 80 km west of Kalumburu Rd. Water from river – boil before use. Bring firewood. Gas/fuel stove preferred. Please note that there is no access to the area below the main falls from here. Additional map ref.: STAWA 153 D4.

Further information: CALM, Kununurra **Tel.:** (08) 9168 4200 **Camping fees:** Fees to be introduced in future, contact CALM for details

15. PARRY LAGOONS NATURE RESERVE

Parry Lagoons Nature Reserve is south-east of Wyndham, off the Great Northern Hwy. Popular with birdwatchers, the wetlands of Parry Lagoons are a feeding and breeding area for numerous birds as well as a stopover point for many migrating species. There is no camping in the reserve itself, however Parry Creek Farm is privately owned land within it. Dogs are permitted at Parry Creek Farm only and not within the reserve.

Parry Creek Farm camping area

On Parry Creek Rd. Signposted off Great Northern Hwy 20 km south of Wyndham. Limited drinking water, best to bring own. Some firewood supplied. For powered sites during June–Aug. a booking is recommended. Additional map ref.: STAWA 154 D5.

Further information & bookings:
CALM, Kununurra **Tel.:** (08) 9168 4200 *or*
Parry Creek Farm **Tel.:** (08) 9161 1139
Camping fees: Unpowered from $8.00 per person/night, powered from $20.00 per site/night for 1–2 people

16. PURNULULU NATIONAL PARK

The striking sandstone domes of the Bungle Bungle Range, within this park, were formed over 350 million years ago. Rivers and creeks have carved magnificent gorges, including Echidna Chasma, Frog Hole Gorge, Mini Palm Gorge and Cathedral Gorge. Access to the gorges is by foot only. The Piccaninny Gorge walk is for self-sufficient walkers only and requires overnight camping. Visit the visitor centre near the park entrance or contact CALM Kununurra for details on all walks including length and difficulty. Purnululu National Park is signposted from the Great Northern Hwy, 109 km north of Halls Creek and 250 km south of Kununurra. The park entrance is 53 km east of the highway, along Spring Creek Track, and is suitable for 4WD vehicles only. The park is closed to vehicles 1 Jan.–31 March.

Kurrajong camping area

Just north of the park entrance and visitor centre, along park's main road. Water from bore, boil before use or bring own. Firewood supplied. Additional map ref.: STAWA 152 D3.

Piccaninny Gorge Walking Trail camping area

The Piccaninny Gorge Walking Trail is a 30-km-return walk of moderate-to-difficult standard. Walkers must be self-sufficient and carry drinking water. Gas/fuel stove only. All walkers must register and deregister at the park visitor centre. Contact CALM for further details. Additional map ref.: STAWA 152 D3.

Walardi campsite

About 20 km south of the park entry and visitor centre, along park's main road. Water from bore, boil before use or bring own. Firewood supplied. Additional map ref.: STAWA 152 D3.

Further information: CALM, Kununurra **Tel.:** (08) 9168 4200
Park entrance fee: $9.00 per vehicle **Camping fees:** From $9.00 per person/night; fees payable at visitor centre

17. WINDJANA GORGE NATIONAL PARK

The narrow, 3.5-km-long Windjana Gorge was formed over millions of years, by the Lennard River winding its way through the limestone Napier Range. Fossils of extinct crocodiles, turtles and the giant marsupial *Diprotodon* have been found in the gorge and its caves. The area has an interesting history, from its early Aboriginal occupants to the arrival of explorers and pastoralists and a subsequent guerrilla war that lasted for three years. Ruins of the Lillimillura police outpost, 3 km east of Windjana, are still visible. Windjana Gorge National Park is 20 km east of the Gibb River Rd along the Fairfield–Leopold Downs Rd and is 145 km east of Derby. Access is via unsealed gravel roads that are suitable for conventional vehicles and caravans, however it is best to check road conditions before attempting.

Quiet campground

Signposted off Fairfield–Leopold Downs Rd 20 km east of Gibb River Rd. No generators. Gas/fuel stove preferred. Additional map ref.: STAWA 151 C3.

Generator campground

Signposted off Fairfield–Leopold Downs Rd 20 km east of Gibb River Rd. Generators allowed here but adhere to rules regarding hours of use. Gas/fuel stove preferred. Additional map ref.: STAWA 151 C3.

Further information: CALM, Broome **Tel.:** (08) 9192 1036
Camping fees: From $9.00 per adult/night, $2.00 per child/night; fees collected by ranger. Campground hosts on-site from April–Nov.

18. WOLFE CREEK METEORITE CRATER

The spectacular Wolfe Creek Meteorite Crater, on the edge of the Tanami Desert, was formed over 300 000 years ago when an iron meteorite weighing thousands of tons crashed to earth. The crater measures 850 m across. Aboriginal legend has it that the crater was formed by a rainbow snake when it came out of the ground on its way to form Sturt and Wolfe creeks. There is a steep rocky climb to the rim of the crater. Wolfe Creek Meteorite Crater is signposted off the Tanami Rd 112 km south of the Great Northern Hwy. The Tanami Rd leaves the Great Northern Hwy 18 km south of Halls Creek. Access is possible for conventional vehicles in the dry season but drivers should check road conditions before attempting.

Wolfe Creek Meteorite Crater camping area

Area is 23 km east of Tanami Rd. Bring drinking water. Gas/fuel stove only. Additional map ref.: STAWA 152 C5.

Further information: CALM, Kununurra **Tel.:** (08) 9168 4200

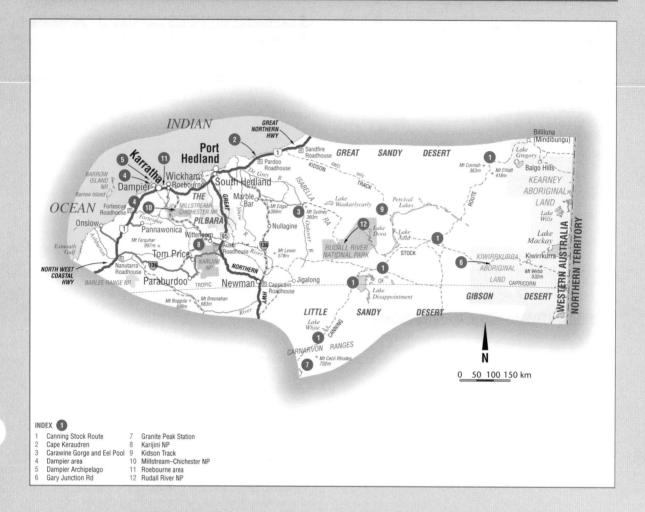

INDEX **1**

1	Canning Stock Route	7	Granite Peak Station
2	Cape Keraudren	8	Karijini NP
3	Carawine Gorge and Eel Pool	9	Kidson Track
4	Dampier area	10	Millstream–Chichester NP
5	Dampier Archipelago	11	Roebourne area
6	Gary Junction Rd	12	Rudall River NP

AMONG THE REGION'S IRON ORE AND NATURAL GAS OPERATIONS, THE PILBARA HAS SOME SPECTACULAR NATURAL SIGHTS, INCLUDING THE MAGNIFICENT GORGES AND WATERFALLS OF KARIJINI NATIONAL PARK, THE FANTASTIC DAMPIER ARCHIPELAGO, THE BEAUTIFUL JASPER BAR WEST OF MARBLE BAR, AND THE RED SAND-DUNE DESERTS THAT STRETCH TOWARDS THE NORTHERN TERRITORY BORDER. THE PILBARA ALSO HAS A NUMBER OF HISTORIC TOWNS – SUCH AS COSSACK, THE NORTH-WEST'S FIRST PORT, AND NULLAGINE, AN OLD GOLDMINING TOWN THAT IS STILL VISITED BY PEOPLE FOSSICKING FOR SEMI-PRECIOUS GEMS.

Stretching along the coast around Roebourne and Dampier are four council bush camping areas that provide basic facilities and excellent swimming, fishing and boating opportunities.

Millstream–Chichester National Park is a place of contrasts. In the Millstream section of the park are permanent pools and tropical vegetation including Millstream and date palms – this is like an oasis compared to the rugged, arid and sparsely vegetated Chichester section. The park is home to fruit bats, dollar birds and bustards, and a variety of mammals including native mice and rock rats. Wildflowers here include the striking Sturt's desert pea and mulla-mulla.

Set in the Hamersley Range, Karijini National Park has breathtaking scenery. Its beautiful gorges and tree-lined waterways dissect the mountains and escarpments, with the gorges in the north providing a refreshing refuge from the dry plains above. There are a number of walking trails of different grades and lengths in the park, taking in lookouts, waterfalls, clear pools and fern-lined chasms. The park's natural beauty provides excellent photographic opportunities and its two main camping areas are suitable for tents and caravans.

Campers travelling in a four-wheel drive who wish to experience remote bush camping in truly beautiful surroundings can stay in Rudall National Park, to the west of the Pilbara. Campers here must be fully self-sufficient.

BEST CAMPSITES

Deep Reach Pool camping area
Millstream–Chichester National Park

Cape Keraudren camping area
Cape Keraudren

Cleaverville camping area
Roebourne area

Dales camping area
Karijini National Park

Savannah Campground
Karijini National Park

BEST TIME TO VISIT

May to October.

1. CANNING STOCK ROUTE

See also Granite Peak Station, *page 251*

The Canning Stock Route stretches from Wiluna in the south to Billiluna in the north. Travelling for 1700 km through the Little Sandy Desert, the Gibson Desert, the Great Sandy Desert and the Tanami Desert, the Canning Stock Route is the longest stock route in the world. Along with the challenge to travel this remote road and see the beautiful desert scenery, the pioneering history of the Canning is one of the route's main attractions. Alfred Canning first surveyed the region in 1906–07. In March 1908 he and a party of 30 men set out from Wiluna to sink wells to water stock along the route. By July 1909, when they reached Flora Valley station, the party had sunk 31 wells. On their return journey they sunk 21 additional wells, arriving back at Wiluna in April 1910. Stock began using the route the following year. As then, travellers today need to be well prepared and fully self-sufficient. Vehicles need to be mechanically sound. Water is available from the wells along the track but should be boiled or treated before drinking. Please remember to always replace the well lids. It is suggested that travellers register and deregister their trip with the Wiluna and Halls Creek police.

Bush camping

Camping along the Canning Stock Route is generally wherever you find a spot to your liking. It is recommended that you camp away from wells and water supplies to help stop pollution. If you want a campfire you will have to carry your own firewood as wood is not available along the route. Be sure to carry a gas/fuel stove. Travelling with dogs in these remote areas is not recommended. Suggested bush campsites are listed in the order they are reached driving north from Wiluna.

North Pool
Well 3
Windick Springs
Well 6 – Pierre Spring
Calvert Range (requires detour of 100 km)
Durba Springs (toilets here)
Lake Disappointment – western edge
Well 24 – Curara Soaks
Well 26 – Tiwa Well
Well 30 – Dunda Jinnda
Well 33 – Gunowaggi
Bungabinni Native Well
Well 37 – Libral
Well 46 – Kuduarra
Breaden Valley
Well 50

Kunawarritji Aboriginal community camping area

On Kidson Track, 4 km west of Canning Stock Route, about 938 km north of Wiluna and 640 km south of Billiluna. Laundry facilities. Shop and fuel (see below). Other accommodation available. Bring firewood. Additional map ref.: STAWA 148 C4.

Further information & bookings: Kunawarritji Aboriginal Community **Tel.:** (08) 9176 9040 **Email:** kunawarritji@ bigpond.com **Camping fees:** From $8.00 per person/night; showers $5.00 per person

Canning Stock Route information:
Newman Tourist Information Centre **Tel.:** (08) 9175 2888
Police:
Wiluna **Tel.:** (08) 9981 7024
Halls Creek **Tel.:** (08) 9168 6000

Fuel:

Capricorn Roadhouse, Newman **Tel.:** (08) 9175 1535 **Details:** Can provide fuel dump at Well 23; needs to be prearranged 4–6 weeks in advance

Kunawarritji Aboriginal community **Tel.:** (08) 9176 9040 **Details:** Has diesel and unleaded; fuel does not need to be booked, but a phone call advising of estimated requirements is recommended prior to commencing trip; open Mon.–Fri. 10 am–11 am & 4 pm–5 pm, Sat. 9 am–noon, closed Sun. and public holidays

Billiluna Aboriginal community **Tel.:** (08) 9168 8988 **Details:** Has diesel and unleaded; open Mon.–Fri. 7 am–noon & 1 pm–3 pm, Sat. 9 am–11 am, closed Sun. and public holidays

Suggested maps and reading:

The Canning Stock Route, Westprint Heritage Maps
North West and *South West* sheets, HEMA Great Desert Tracks maps
Canning Stock Route: A Traveller's Guide, Ronele and Eric Gard, 2nd edition, Western Desert Guides, 1995
The Australian Geographic Book of the Canning Stock Route, editor David Hewitt et al, Australian Geographic, 1998

2. CAPE KERAUDREN

Cape Keraudren is protected in a small reserve north of Pardoo and 166 km north-east of Port Hedland. At the southern end of Eighty Mile Beach, Cape Keraudren is a perfect spot for beach lovers. Visitors here can enjoy the beautiful coastal scenery, take a stroll along the beach, swim in the clear blue waters and try their luck fishing. Cape Keraudren is reached via a signposted turn-off opposite the Pardoo Roadhouse on the Great Northern Hwy.

Cape Keraudren camping area

Cape Keraudren is located 14 km north of the highway turn-off. Bring drinking water and firewood. Additional map ref.: STAWA 147 A1.

Further information:

Shire of East Pilbara **Tel.:** (08) 9175 1924 *or*
Newman Tourist Bureau **Tel.:** (08) 9175 2888 *or*
Port Hedland Tourist Bureau **Tel.:** (08) 9173 1711
Reserve entrance fee: $10.00 per vehicle for up to 4 adults
Camping fees: From $5.00 per vehicle/night; fees payable to on-site ranger

3. CARAWINE GORGE AND EEL POOL

East of Marble Bar, Carawine Gorge and the nearby Eel Pool (Running Waters) are on the Oakover River. Both sites are on private property and the owners are happy for campers to enjoy these beautiful waterholes as long as they leave no trace of their visit. All campers must be self-sufficient. Access is via the Woodie Woodie Rd south of the Ripon Hills Rd. 4WD vehicle access only. As this is private property, it is a courtesy to phone ahead and let the owners know you will be visiting. Please respect their wishes by not bringing dogs or firearms onto the property. Take away all rubbish and wastes.

Carawine Gorge camping area

This is 13 km south-west of Woodie Woodie Rd. Signposted turn-off is 10 km south of Ripon Hills Rd, 166 km east of Marble Bar. Bring drinking water and firewood. Additional map ref.: STAWA 147 B3.

Eel Pool camping area

A short distance west of Woodie Woodie Rd. Access road is 34 km south of Ripon Hills Rd. Bring drinking water and firewood. Additional map ref.: STAWA 147 B3.

Further information: Mills family **Tel.:** (08) 9176 5900

4. DAMPIER AREA

The town of Dampier is on King Bay, 20 km north-west of Karratha. Visitors to Dampier can view Aboriginal rock engravings on Burrup Peninsula, take in the views of the harbour from William Dampier Lookout or enjoy a swim and picnic at Dampier Beach or Hearson's Cove.

Dampier Transit Caravan Park

Signposted on The Esplanade in Dampier. Laundry facilities. Gas/fuel stove only. Bookings recommended June–Oct. Additional map ref.: STAWA 145 A4.

Further information & bookings: Dampier Transit Caravan Park **Tel.:** (08) 9183 1109 **Email:** mich@starwon.com.au **Camping fees:** Unpowered tent sites from $11.00 per site/night for 2 people, powered from $13.20 per site/night for 2 people; unpowered van sites from $13.20 per site/night for 2 people, powered from $17.50 per site/night for 2 people

Fortescue River Mouth camping area

Signposted off North West Coastal Hwy around 80 km south-west of Dampier. Fortescue River Mouth is 27 km north-west of highway. Bring drinking water and firewood. Boaters should check tides before launching boats and watch for submerged rocks. Additional map ref.: STAWA 144 C5.

Forty Mile camping area

Signposted off North West Coastal Hwy around 60 km south-west of Dampier. Forty Mile is 13 km north of highway. Bring drinking water and firewood. Camping permitted 1 April–31 Oct. only; maximum of three months' stay. Additional map ref.: STAWA 144 D4.

Further information: Karratha Tourist Bureau **Tel.:** (08) 9182 1060 **Camping fees:** *Forty Mile:* From $5.00 per site/night or $30.00 per site/week; fees collected by on-site caretaker

5. DAMPIER ARCHIPELAGO

Comprising of 42 islands, the Dampier Archipelago lies in a 45 km radius around Dampier. The islands within the archipelago support a large range of native plants and animals. These include numerous snakes and reptiles, and in the waters themselves, various turtles, bottlenose dolphins, humpback whales and dugong. Visitors to the islands can view Aboriginal carvings, enjoy birdwatching and go boating, sea kayaking, diving, fishing, swimming and bushwalking. Camping is for self-sufficient campers only. Access to the Dampier Archipelago is by boat, with public boat ramps at Dampier and Karratha. If you don't have a boat, contact the Karratha Tourist Bureau for details on local charter boat companies. For further details on camping areas and restrictions, contact CALM Karratha. There is a maximum stay of five nights in the archipelago.

Beach camping

Camping available at beaches within the archipelago and on West Lewis and East Lewis islands. Contact CALM Karratha

for further details. Boat access only. Self-sufficient campers only. Bring drinking water. Gas/fuel stove only. Additional map ref.: Dampier STAWA 145 A4.

Further information:
CALM, Karratha **Tel.:** (08) 9143 1488 *or*
Karratha Tourist Bureau **Tel.:** (08) 9144 4600

6. GARY JUNCTION ROAD

Gary Junction Rd runs east from Gary Junction (where Gary Junction Rd and Gary Hwy meet) to the Tanami Track in the Northern Territory. It is remote and should be attempted only by well prepared and self-sufficient 4WD travellers. Permits are required in both Western Australia and the Northern Territory.

Jupiter Well camping area

On Gary Junction Rd 157 km east of Gary Junction. Gas/fuel stove preferred. Travelling with dogs in these remote areas is not recommended. Additional map ref.: STAWA 149 B5.

Further information: Ngaanyatjarraku Council
Tel.: (08) 8950 1711 **Permits:**
WA: Ngaanyatjarraku Council **Tel.:** (08) 8950 171
NT: Central Land Council **Tel.:** (08) 8951 6320

7. GRANITE PEAK STATION

Granite Peak Station is located 55 km east of the Canning Stock Route (Well 5). While travellers can access the route via a private track through the station and vice versa (a fee of $20.00 applies), the main access is via Granite Peak Rd from a turn-off 40 km east of Wiluna. The total distance from Wiluna to the station is 197 km.

Granite Peak Station camping area

Camp kitchen. Laundry facilities. Other accommodation available. Bring firewood. Contact homestead prior to proceeding through property. Additional map ref.: STAWA 133 C4.

Further information & bookings: Granite Peak Station
Tel.: (08) 9981 2983 **Email:** granitepeak@bigpond.com
Camping fees: Fees may have been implemented and

facilities upgraded since time of publication; check with station for details

Karijini National Park is within the Hamersley Range, to the east of Tom Price. The park protects some of the country's oldest rocks and is well known for its gorges, mountains and watercourses. Marvel at the spectacular views from one of the many lookouts. Some of the gorges within the park provide permanent pools of fresh water, in which a refreshing dip is a delight. Visitors also have a choice of walking trails that take in the park's natural features. From the east access is from Karijini Drive, off the Great Northern Hwy, and from the west access is along Karijini Drive from Tom Price.

Dales camping area

Signposted off Banjima Drive off Karijini Drive, 107 km north-east of Tom Price and 48 km north-west of Great Northern Hwy. Swim at nearby Fortescue Falls. Bring drinking water. Gas/fuel stove only. Additional map ref.: STAWA 143 B4.

Hamersley Gorge Truck Bay

On Nanutarra–Wittenoom Rd 63 km north of Tom Price. Suitable for an overnight stop only. Appropriate for caravans, motorhomes and campervans. Bring drinking water. Gas/fuel stove only. Additional map ref.: STAWA 142 D3.

Savannah Campground

Signposted access off Banjima Drive 31 km north of Karijini Drive. Bring drinking water. Gas/fuel stove only. Additional map ref.: STAWA 143 A3.

Further information: Karijini National Park Visitors Centre
Tel.: (08) 9189 8121 **Park entrance fee:** $9.00 per vehicle
Camping fees: From $10.00 per site/night for 1–2 people; fees payable at self-registration stations

Munjina Gorge, in Karijini National Park

9. KIDSON TRACK

See also Canning Stock Route, Kunawarritji Aboriginal community camping area, *page 249*

The Kidson Track, also known as the WAPET Rd, links the Kunawarritji Aboriginal community with the Great Northern Hwy, joining the highway 43.5 km south of Sandfire Roadhouse and covering 621 km in total. It is a remote and rugged 4WD-only road with no services and just emergency water between Kunawarritji and Sandfire every 50–100 km (Burrel Bore is the last water supply before the highway). These are to be used *only* in an emergency situation. Travellers should be self-sufficient and well prepared. At this stage permits do not apply to this road.

Razorblade Bore camping area

On the Kidson Track, 201 km west of Kunawarritji community. Bring firewood. Gas/fuel stove preferred. Travelling with dogs in these remote areas is not recommended. Additional map ref.: STAWA 148 A3.

Burrel Bore camping area

On the Kidson Track, 84 km west of Razorblade Bore. Bring firewood. Gas/fuel stove preferred. Travelling with dogs in these remote areas is not recommended. Additional map ref.: STAWA 148 A2.

Further information: Kunawarritji Aboriginal Community **Tel.:** (08) 9176 9040 **Email:** kunawarritji@bigpond.com

10. MILLSTREAM–CHICHESTER NATIONAL PARK

Millstream–Chichester National Park has a rich and diverse history of both Aboriginal occupation and pastoral lease. The park's visitor centre is in the homestead, which was built in 1920. The park offers two scenic drives, a range of walking trails, swimming in permanent waterholes and canoeing. Access to the southern section of the park is 15 km west of the Roebourne–Wittenoom Rd along the Millstream–Yarraloola Rd. Access to Snake Creek camping area in the north of the park is signposted off the Roebourne–Wittenoom Rd 87 km south of Roebourne. Alternative access to the park is via Hamersley Iron Access Rd; a permit is required to traverse this road.

Crossing Pool camping area

On Snappy Gum Drive off Crossing Pool Rd, off Millstream–Yarraloola Rd. Crossing Pool Rd is west of Roebourne–Wittenoom Rd. Drivers towing caravans should check road conditions before attempting. Bring drinking water. Gas/fuel stove only. Additional map ref.: STAWA 142 B1.

Deep Reach Pool camping area

Signposted off Millstream–Yarraloola Rd, which is off Roebourne–Wittenoom Rd, 98 km south of North West Coastal Hwy. Access road is 15 km west of Roebourne–Wittenoom Rd. Bring drinking water or boil water from river before use. Gas/fuel stove only. There may be a campground host here during busy periods. Additional map ref.: STAWA 142 B1.

Snake Creek camping area

Signposted off Roebourne–Wittenoom Rd approximately 90 km south of Roebourne. The camp area is 2 km south of Python Pool. Bring drinking water and firewood. Gas/fuel stove preferred. Additional map ref.: STAWA 145 B5.

Further information:
Millstream–Chichester National Park **Tel.:** (08) 9184 5144 *or* CALM, Karratha **Tel.:** (08) 9143 1488
Park entrance fee: $9.00 per vehicle **Camping fees:** From $10.00 per site/night for 1–2 people; fees collected by ranger

11. ROEBOURNE AREA

Roebourne, the oldest town in the Pilbara, has a history of mining and grazing. The town still boasts a number of historic buildings, these being the Union Bank built in 1888, a church built in 1894, and a gaol. Roebourne is on the North West Coastal Hwy 33 km east of Karratha. The Shire of Roebourne encourages the use of portable chemical toilets at all sites.

Balla Balla (Bulla Bulla) camping area

On Balla Balla Rd. Signposted off North West Coastal Hwy at Whim Creek, 85 km east of Roebourne. Balla Balla is 20 km north of the highway. Bring drinking water and firewood. Additional map ref.: STAWA 145 D4.

Cleaverville camping area

Signposted off North West Coastal Hwy 14 km west of Roebourne. Cleaverville is 13 km north of highway. Bring drinking water and firewood. Camping permitted 1 April–31 Oct. only; maximum of three months' stay. Additional map ref.: STAWA 145 B4.

Further information:
Shire of Roebourne **Tel.:** (08) 9186 8555 *or* Roebourne Tourist Bureau **Tel.:** (08) 9182 1060
Camping fees: *Cleaverville*: From $5.00 per site/night or $30.00 per site/week; fees collected by on-site caretaker

12. RUDALL RIVER NATIONAL PARK

Rudall River National Park features rugged wilderness and a wonderful history of Aboriginal occupation. Along with the headwaters of the Rudall River, the park boasts numerous waterholes, pools and soaks. Due to the remoteness of Rudall River National Park visitors should travel by 4WD vehicle, preferably in the company of another 4WD vehicle, and be well equipped and self-sufficient. Access to the park from Newman in the south is via the Talawana Track. Access from the north is via Telfer Goldmine; a permit is required for this route. Please note that access to the eastern section of the park is with a permit only, due to the Aboriginal communities living there. Contact CALM Karratha for access information and further details. It is advisable when travelling to this area to leave travel intentions with a family member and/or friend or with the Newman Police. Collecting firewood is prohibited in the park – bring your own.

Bush camping

Self-sufficient bush camping anywhere within park, but please stay on made roads and tracks. Permit required for eastern section. Bring drinking water and firewood. Additional map ref.: STAWA 147 D5.

Further information & bookings:
CALM, Karratha **Tel.:** (08) 9143 1488 *or* Telfer Goldmine **Tel.:** (08) 9158 6200

ROTTNEST ISLAND

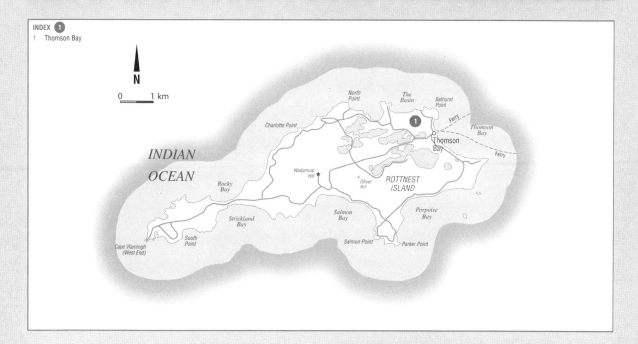

THE BEAUTIFUL ROTTNEST ISLAND LIES 18 KILOMETRES OFF THE COAST OF PERTH, AMID CRYSTAL-CLEAR WATERS. PRIVATE CARS ARE NOT PERMITTED ON THE ISLAND, SO EXPLORATION IS BY FOOT, BIKE, BUS OR THE HISTORIC LIGHT-RAILWAY.

Once on the island there is much to see and do, with walking trails leading to the island's best sites, both historic and natural. Places of interest include the Rottnest Museum, the Aboriginal cemetery, the historic buildings and the gun battery built in the 1930s.

Boasting beautiful beaches and bays, the island's coastline is popular for swimming, fishing, windsurfing and boating. The azure waters surrounding Rottnest are popular with divers and snorkellers who come to view the reefs, shipwrecks and marine life.

Quokkas, the small marsupials that inspired the island's name (Willem de Vlamingh mistook the animals for rats when he explored the island in 1696), can be seen across the island, while the woodlands, salt lakes, swamps, heath and coasts provide varied habitats for a huge number of bird species.

Rottnest Island's only camping area is at Thomson Bay, conveniently close to where the ferries dock from Perth, Hillarys Boat Harbour and Fremantle.

BEST TIME TO VISIT

All year. Summer is the most popular time for visitors, but in winter there is excellent fishing and surfing.

1. THOMSON BAY

Tall tuart trees shade the campsites in the Alison camping area, and facilities include hot showers, drinking water and free gas barbecues. Due to the island's popularity bookings are recommended and are essential during the summer periods.

Allison camping area

Gas/fuel stove only. All campers must proceed to the Accommodation Centre at Rottnest Island jetty prior to setting up camp. Bookings essential during all school and summer holidays. Additional map ref.: STAWA 65 C4.

Further information & bookings:
Rottnest Island Authority **Tel.:** (08) 9432 9111 or 1800 111 111
Website: www.rottnest.wa.gov.au or
Rottnest Island Visitor Information Centre **Tel.:** (08) 9372 9752
Camping fees: From $5.50 per adult/night, $2.75 per child (up to 12) per night

NORTHERN TERRITORY

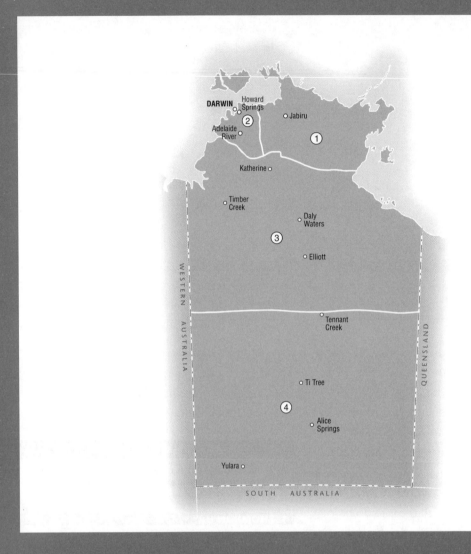

TOP 10 CAMPSITES

Twelve Mile Yards camping area
Elsey National Park, page 268

Smith Point camping area
Garig Gunak Barlu National Park, page 258

Gunlom camping area
Kakadu National Park, page 260

Shady Camp camping area
Mary River National Park (proposed), page 265

Nitmiluk Gorge Caravan and Camping Ground
Nitmiluk National Park, page 270

Bullita Homestead camping area
Gregory National Park, page 268

Jarrnarm camping area
Keep River National Park, page 269

Palm Valley camping area
Finke Gorge National Park, page 275

Ellery Creek Big Hole camping area
West MacDonnell National Park, page 281

Trephina Gorge campground
Trephina Gorge Nature Park, page 279

THE TERRITORY, VAST IN SIZE, EXTREME IN CLIMATE, REMOTE, AND FRONTIER-LIKE IN TERMS OF ACCESS AND FACILITIES, IS NOTHING IF NOT AN ADVENTURE, PARTICULARLY FOR THOSE WHO CHOOSE TO TRAVEL BEYOND THE USUAL ATTRACTIONS. IN POPULAR PLACES – ULURU, KAKADU – CAMPGROUNDS OFFER MOTEL-LIKE FACILITIES; IN OTHER REGIONS, SUCH AS THE VAST GRASSLANDS OF THE GULF AND THE DEEP DESERT HEART OF THE CENTRE, IT'S BACK TO BASICS.

World Heritage-listed Kakadu and adjoining Arnhem Land offer camping at either end of the scale. Kakadu, with its spectacular rock art and extraordinary range of landscapes, is a well-organised holiday centre with plenty of facilities. Arnhem Land is Aboriginal-owned land, and one of the country's most remote regions. You'll need a permit to visit, and a fair degree of self-sufficiency to travel comfortably.

Around Darwin things are more predictable. The magnificent Litchfield National Park, with its gorges, pools, waterfalls and rainforest, has several very popular sites. Tjuwaliyn (Douglas) Hot Springs Park offers crocodile-free swimming and camping, while on the more remote Daly River there are plenty of crocs, but the great barramundi fishing on offer is fair compensation.

Lying between the Top End and the Red Centre are places where you can experience the natural riches of the territory away from the crowds. Some places do get busy, such as Nitmiluk National Park, with its magnificent red gorges, and Elsey National Park, the official land of the Never Never. But at other sites, such as the far-flung Gregory and Keep River national parks, with their four-wheel drive tracks and walk-in campsites, privacy is virtually guaranteed.

The Red Centre is the territory's most recognised region, an arid reach of red sand dunes, ancient mountains and monoliths richly inscribed with art. Campers here have a great choice of parks and facilities, and also of landscapes. The options for that all-important early morning view might include the gum-lined watercourses of Trephina Gorge, the remote bush beauty of Ruby Gap Nature Park or the incomparable form of Uluru glowing beneath a rising sun.

Kata Tjuṯa, in Uluṟu–Kata Tjuṯa National Park

KAKADU AND ARNHEM LAND

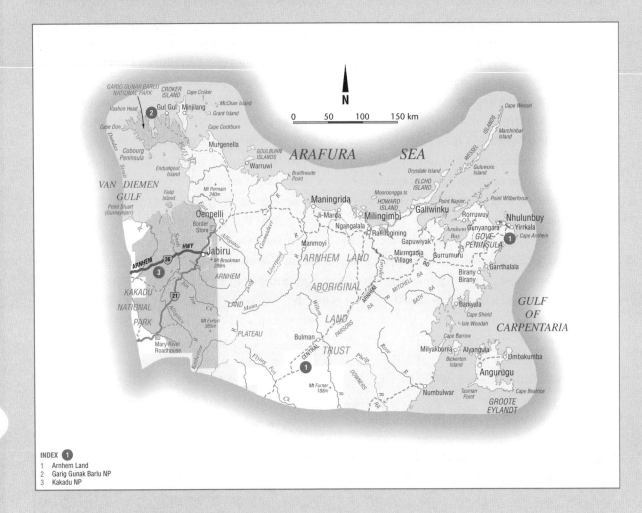

ARNHEM LAND ENCOMPASSES THE EASTERN HALF OF THE TOP END AND COVERS AN AREA OF 100 000 SQUARE KILOMETRES. IT TAKES IN THE COBOURG PENINSULA IN THE NORTH-WEST AND GOVE PENINSULA TO THE EAST, WHILE KAKADU NATIONAL PARK IS ON ITS WESTERN BORDER. ARNHEM LAND'S VAST UNTOUCHED AREAS ARE RICH IN CULTURE, WITH HUNDREDS OF INCREDIBLE ABORIGINAL ROCK-ART SITES. BOTH THE INLAND AND COASTAL SCENERY OF THIS REGION ARE SPECTACULAR.

Arnhem Land's coastline has stretches of white sandy beaches and clear blue waters. Local reefs and nearby islands offer excellent diving, snorkelling and superb fishing opportunities. Birdwatchers will delight in the number of rare seabirds that visit this remote shoreline.

Scattered throughout and along the coastline of east Arnhem Land are a number of camping areas that can be reached in four-wheel drive vehicles. The remote and idyllic setting of Smith Point camping area in Garig Gunak Barlu National Park on Cobourg Peninsula makes the long drive worthwhile for visitors. Leatherback and green turtles and dugongs can be found in the tropical waters of the surrounding Cobourg Marine Park but the waters are also home to saltwater crocodiles and marine stingers, so swimming here is not an option. However, visitors can enjoy the spectacular scenery and the walking trail from the campsite.

Kakadu National Park has a range of camping areas, including sites accessible by foot, four-wheel drive and conventional caravan. The world-renowned park is Australia's largest national park and has some wonderful natural sights and magnificent fauna. There is Aboriginal rock art, lookouts, waterfalls, waterways, gorges and plunge pools. Visitors can enjoy guided walks, or follow one of the many walking trails, go bird and wildlife watching and try their hand at photography.

BEST CAMPSITES

Smith Point camping area
Garig Gunak Barlu National Park

Gunlom camping area
Kakadu National Park

Mardugal camping area
Kakadu National Park

Barinura (Little Bondi Beach) camping area
Arnhem Land

Nanydjaka (Cape Arnhem) camping area
Arnhem Land

BEST TIME TO VISIT

The cooler months of the year, from April to October.

1. ARNHEM LAND

Arnhem Land is solely owned by the Aboriginal people who have lived there for some 60 000 years. Although Arnhem Land is one of earth's last wilderness regions, the town of Nhulunbuy on the Gove Peninsula has all services. The region's attractions include a strong Aboriginal spirit and culture, excellent fishing, spectacular scenery (including beautiful sunsets), bird- and wildlife-watching, scuba diving and snorkelling, boating and bushwalking. A travel permit must be obtained to enter Arnhem Land – contact the Northern Land Council. Travel in this area should only be attempted in a 4WD. Wood collection is allowed in some areas – please obey signs.

SOUTH OF ARNHEM LAND

Mainoru Outstation Store

Off Central Arnhem Rd just before Arnhem Land (this is the last fuel stop on the way to Nhulunbuy). Campsites beside Mainoru River. Store open 9 am–5 pm. Bring drinking water and firewood. Drivers of caravans should check road conditions first. Additional map ref.: ANNTM G4.

Further information & bookings: Mainoru Outstation Store **Tel.:** (08) 8975 4390 **Email:** mainoru@bigpond.com **Camping fees:** From $10.00 per vehicle/night

AROUND NHULUNBUY

Banambarrna (Rainbow Cliff) camping area

General Recreation Permit required. Area is about 11 km east of Nhulunbuy. Signposted off Main Rd (Melville Bay Rd). Bring drinking water and firewood. Additional map ref.: ANTTM J2.

Barinura (Little Bondi Beach) camping area

General Recreation Permit required. Area is about 39 km south-east of Nhulunbuy. Signposted off Dhupuma Rd. Bring drinking water and firewood. Additional map ref.: ANTTM J2.

Binydjarrna (Daliwoi Bay) camping area

General Recreation Permit required. This is about 33 km south of Nhulunbuy. Signposted off Dhupuma Rd. Bring drinking water and firewood. Additional map ref.: ANTTM J2.

Ganami (Wonga) camping area

General Recreation Permit and Special Permit required. This is about 57 km south-west of Nhulunbuy. Signposted off Central Arnhem Rd. Bring drinking water and firewood. Additional map ref.: ANTTM J2.

Ganinyara (The Granites) camping area

General Recreation Permit required. Boat access only. Access from Catalina Boat Ramp 15 km west of Nhulunbuy. Bring drinking water and firewood. Additional map ref.: ANTTM J2.

Gapuru (Memorial Park) camping area

General Recreation Permit and Special Permit required. This area is about 57 km south-west of Nhulunbuy. Signposted off Central Arnhem Rd. Bring drinking water and firewood. Additional map ref.: ANTTM J2.

Garanhan (Macassan Beach) camping area

General Recreation Permit required. Located about 35 km south-east of Nhulunbuy. Signposted off Dhupuma Rd. Bring drinking water and firewood. Additional map ref.: ANTTM J2.

Guwutjurumurru (Giddy River) camping area

General Recreation Permit required. This is about 41 km south-west of Nhulunbuy. Signposted off Central Arnhem Rd. Bring drinking water and firewood. Additional map ref.: ANTTM J2.

Lombuy (Crocodile Creek) camping area

General Recreation Permit required. Located west of Nhulunbuy. Signposted off Melville Bay Rd. Bring drinking water and firewood. Additional map ref.: ANTTM J2.

Lurrupukurru (Oyster Beach) camping area

General Recreation Permit required. This is about 37 km south of Nhulunbuy. Signposted off Dhupuma Rd. Bring drinking water and firewood. Additional map ref.: ANTTM J2.

Nanydjaka (Cape Arnhem) camping area

General Recreation Permit and Special Permit required. Area is about 49 km south of Nhulunbuy. Signposted off Dhupuma Rd. Bring drinking water and firewood. Additional map ref.: ANTTM J2.

Numuy (Turtle Beach) camping area

General Recreation Permit required. Located about 38 km south-east of Nhulunbuy. Signposted off Dhupuma Rd. Bring drinking water and firewood. Additional map ref.: ANTTM J2.

Ranura (Caves Beach) camping area

General Recreation Permit required. This is about 38 km south of Nhulunbuy. Signposted off Dhupuma Rd. Bring drinking water and firewood. Additional map ref.: ANTTM J2.

Wathaway (Goanna Lagoon) camping area

General Recreation Permit required. Located about 25 km south of Nhulunbuy. Signposted off Dhupuma Rd. Bring drinking water and firewood. Additional map ref.: ANTTM J2.

Wathaway (Latram River) camping area

General Recreation Permit required. This is about 23 km south of Nhulunbuy. Signposted off Dhupuma Rd. Bring drinking water and firewood. Additional map ref.: ANTTM J2.

Yarrapay (Rocky Point) camping area

General Recreation Permit required. Area is about 41 km south-east of Nhulunbuy. Signposted off Dhupuma Rd. Bring drinking water and firewood. Additional map ref.: ANTTM J2.

Further information & bookings:
Dhimurru Land Management Aboriginal Corporation **Tel.:** (08) 8987 3992 **Email:** dhimurru@octa4.net.au **Website:** www.octa4.net.au/dhimurru *or* East Arnhem Land Tourist Association **Tel.:** (08) 8987 2255 **Email:** arnhemland@ealta.org **Website:** www.ealta.org *or* Northern Land Council, Nhulunbuy **Tel.:** (08) 8987 2602 *or* Northern Land Council, Katherine **Tel.:** (08) 8972 2894 **Permits and fees:** Travel permit required from Northern Land Council to travel on Central Arnhem Rd; permit must be obtained before setting out and permits can take up to 2 weeks to process. General Recreation Permit required for all sites: $22.00 per adult, valid for 2 months. Special permit (additional to General Recreation Permit) required for Cape Arnhem, Wonga and Memorial Park: $11.00 per vehicle

2. GARIG GUNAK BARLU NATIONAL PARK

This park encompasses the entire Cobourg Peninsula, protecting natural grasslands, rainforests, swamps and lagoons. The surrounding Cobourg Marine Park protects dugong, turtles and other sea life. Garig is 300 km north of Jabiru and road access is by 4WD only through Arnhem Land. Check tide times at Cahills Crossing and possible road closures before setting out.

Smith Point camping area

On Coastal Drive off Garig Rd. 4WD access via Arnhem Land from Jabiru. Bring drinking water and firewood. Generators permitted at site no. 2. Bookings necessary and an application form must be completed. Due to a limit on vehicle numbers in the park, bookings are taken for June and July up to 12 months in advance, and for August 6 months in advance. Additional map ref.: ANTTM D1.

Further information & bookings: DIPE, Palmerston – Permit section **Tel.:** (08) 8999 4814 **Fees:** $232.10 covers camping fee for up to 5 adults (one vehicle) for 7 nights as well as road transit fee through Arnhem Land

3. KAKADU NATIONAL PARK see page 259

KAKADU NATIONAL PARK

Worthwhile stop
The Bowali Visitors Centre is an essential stop for all visitors. Displays tell the story of Kakadu from both indigenous and non-indigenous perspectives, and highlight the key things to see and do in the park.

Indigenous art
Kakadu has an estimated 5000 Aboriginal rock-art sites, including the works at Nourlangie on the Arnhem Land Escarpment. The Nourlangie Art Site Walk leads visitors past myriad works in a range of styles, including prime examples of x-ray art depicting the anatomy of humans and animals.

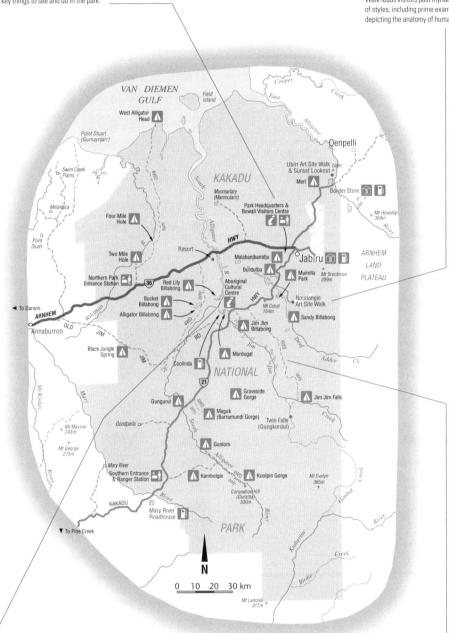

Croc tours
The spectacular wetland area called Yellow Water, or Ngurrungurrudjba, teems with birdlife, but the real stars are the resident crocodiles that surface regularly and frighten the tourists. Aim for a sunrise or sunset boat tour, when things are particularly active.

Natural heritage
Kakadu's staggering biodiversity was instrumental in earning the park a World Heritage listing. It contains the key habitats of northern Australia, including monsoonal rainforest, floodplains and woodlands, and boasts 1600 plant species, 280 bird species, 123 reptile species and 52 freshwater fish species. Enquire about the range of nature-based tours and walks on offer.

A declared World Heritage-area, Kakadu National Park is known worldwide. Its various features include escarpment lookouts and sandstone cliffs, wetlands and waterways, woodlands and monsoon forests, waterfalls, plunge pools and gorges, and extensive Aboriginal rock art. The park caters for visitors with activities such as birdwatching, boating, short strolls or longer bushwalks, and swimming and fishing in some areas. Ranger-guided walks, talks and slide shows are conducted throughout the dry season (April–Sept.). Visit the Bowali Visitors Centre for program details and other park information. Information and displays about Kakadu's Aboriginal heritage can be found at the Warradjan Aboriginal Cultural Centre. Kakadu National Park is 180 km east of Darwin and is reached via the sealed Arnhem Hwy from Darwin or the sealed Kakadu Hwy from Pine Creek north of Katherine. Along both roads is a park entrance station where park entry fees can be paid.

Alligator Billabong camping area

Signposted off Arnhem Hwy 37 km east of northern park entrance station. It is 26 km south of Arnhem Hwy. Bring drinking water and firewood. Gas/fuel stove preferred. Natural boat ramp. Additional map ref.: ANTTM E3.

Black Jungle Spring camping area

This is 52 km west of Kakadu Hwy on Old Jim Jim Rd, off Kakadu Hwy 56 km south of Jabiru. Self-sufficient camping, bring drinking water and firewood. 4WD access recommended. Additional map ref.: ANTTM D3.

Bucket Billabong camping area

Located 22 km south of Arnhem Hwy. Access via Red Lily Billabong. Bring drinking water and firewood. Gas/fuel stove preferred. Additional map ref.: ANTTM E3.

Burdulba camping area

Reached off Kakadu Hwy 15 km south of Jabiru. Access to carpark for conventional vehicles, then walk in to campsites. Bring drinking water and firewood. Additional map ref.: ANTTM E3.

Four Mile Hole camping area

Signposted off Arnhem Hwy 21 km east of northern park entrance station. Area is 34 km north of Arnhem Hwy. Bring drinking water and firewood. Gas/fuel stove preferred. Additional map ref.: ANTTM E3.

Graveside Gorge camping area

Accessed off Kakadu Hwy 72 km south of Jabiru. It is 44 km south-east of highway. Bring drinking water and firewood. Permits are needed to camp here and bookings are required. Experienced 4WD access only. Additional map ref.: ANTTM E3.

Gungurul camping area

Signposted off Kakadu Hwy 47 km north of Mary River Roadhouse and 100 km south of Jabiru. Small site. Bring drinking water and firewood. Additional map ref.: ANTTM E3.

Gunlom camping area

This is 35 km east of Kakadu Hwy on Gunlom Rd, which is signposted 11 km north of Mary River Roadhouse. Drivers of caravans should check road conditions. Bring firewood. Additional map ref.: ANTTM E4.

Kambolgie camping area

On Gunlom Rd 13 km east of Kakadu Hwy. Gunlom Rd turn-off is 11 km north of Mary River Roadhouse. Bring drinking water and firewood. Gas/fuel stove preferred. Additional map ref.: ANTTM E4.

Koolpin Gorge camping area

This is 44 km east of Kakadu Hwy, reached via Gunlom Rd. Permit required to camp here. Bring drinking water and firewood. Bookings essential. Locked gate at entry; key needed to access. Additional map ref.: ANTTM E4.

Jim Jim Falls after heavy rains

Jim Jim Billabong camping area

Signposted off Kakadu Hwy 61 km south of Jabiru. Area is 3 km east of highway. Bring drinking water and firewood. Additional map ref.: ANTTM E3.

Jim Jim Falls camping area

Reached via signposted Jim Jim Falls Rd off Kakadu Hwy 39 km south of Jabiru. Area is 58 km south-east of highway via 4WD track. Bring drinking water and firewood. Additional map ref.: ANTTM E3.

Maguk (Barramundi Gorge) camping area

Signposted off Kakadu Hwy 61 km north of Mary River Roadhouse. Area is 10 km east of highway. Bring drinking water and firewood. Additional map ref.: ANTTM E3.

Malabanjbanidju camping area

Signposted off Kakadu Hwy 15 km south of Jabiru. Bring drinking water and firewood. Additional map ref.: ANTTM E3.

Mardugal camping area

Signposted off Kakadu Hwy 52 km south of Jabiru. Boil drinking water before use. Bring firewood. Additional map ref.: ANTTM E3.

Merl camping area

This is 36 km north-east of Jabiru along Ubirr/Border Store Rd. Boat ramp and fishing areas nearby. Bring firewood. Additional map ref.: ANTTM E2.

Muirella Park camping area

Signposted off Kakadu Hwy 35 km south of Jabiru. Area is 6 km east of Kakadu Hwy. Limited drinking water, bring own supply and firewood. Additional map ref.: ANTTM E3.

Red Lily Billabong camping area

Signposted off Arnhem Hwy 37 km east of northern park entrance station. Area is 20 km south of Arnhem Hwy. Bring drinking water and firewood. Gas/fuel stove preferred. Boat fishing recommended. Additional map ref.: ANTTM E3.

Sandy Billabong camping area

Signposted via Muirella Park camping area. Located 6 km south of Muirella Park. 4WD vehicle recommended past Muirella Park. Popular birdwatching site. Bring drinking water and firewood. Additional map ref.: ANTTM E3.

Two Mile Hole camping area

Signposted off Arnhem Hwy 21 km east of northern park entrance station. Located 12 km north of Arnhem Hwy. Drivers of caravans should check road conditions. Bring drinking water and firewood. Gas/fuel stove preferred. Additional map ref.: ANTTM E3.

West Alligator Head camping area

Signposted off Arnhem Hwy 21 km east of northern park entrance station. Area is 81 km north of Arnhem Hwy. Bring drinking water and firewood. Gas/fuel stove preferred. Additional map ref.: ANTTM E2.

Further information & bookings: Bowali Visitors Centre, Kakadu National Park **Tel.:** (08) 8938 1120 **Email:** kakadunationalpark@ea.gov.au **Website:** www.ea.gov.au/parks/kakadu **Park entrance fee:** $16.25 per person (16 years and over) for 7 days (ticket can be revalidated for a further 7 days); fees payable at park entrance station on Arnhem Hwy or Kakadu Hwy **Camping fees:** From $5.40 per person/night (16 years and over); fees payable at information centre or to rangers **Permits:** Permits apply to Graveside Gorge and Koolpin Gorge; contact information centre for further details

The breathtaking escarpment country of Kakadu

INDEX ●1
1 Adelaide River
2 Copperfield Recreation Reserve
3 Douglas River Esplanade CP
4 Gunn Point
5 Leaning Tree Lagoon Nature Park
6 Litchfield NP
7 Mary River NP (proposed)
8 Tjuwaliyn (Douglas) Hot Springs Park
9 Umbrawarra Gorge Nature Park

SURROUNDING DARWIN ARE MANY NATURAL AND HISTORICAL ATTRACTIONS, AMONG THEM THE BEAUTIFUL AND SCENIC MARY RIVER AND LITCHFIELD NATIONAL PARKS, THE THERMAL POOLS AT TJUWALIYN (DOUGLAS) HOT SPRINGS PARK, THE DALY RIVER AND ITS SUPERB FISHING, THE HISTORIC GOLDMINING TOWN OF PINE CREEK, AND EVEN SOME AIRSTRIPS DATING BACK TO WORLD WAR II.

Mary River National Park (proposed) is east of Darwin, along the Arnhem Highway. The park's billabongs and paperbark forests offer excellent wildlife-watching, fishing and bushwalking. The viewing platform at Shady Camp provides views of Mary River and its crocodiles, while Couzens Lookout has a number of secluded campsites beside the river.

The spectacular Litchfield National Park is south of Darwin. Here magnificent waterfalls cascade from the escarpment of the Tabletop Range into deep pools. Walking tracks lead all through the park: to tropical rainforests, to the top of the escarpment, to swimming holes, to the large magnetic termite mounds and to the interesting weathered sandstone formations of the Lost City. Camping is possible at Florence, Wangi, Tjaynera (Sandy Creek) and Surprise Creek falls, with caravan access to Wangi Falls camping area. From the camping area here it is a short walk to the refreshing sandy pool below the falls.

The thermal pools of Tjuwaliyn (Douglas) Hot Springs Park not only attract people, who come to swim in the warm waters, but a huge variety of birdlife and quolls, bandicoots and flying foxes. The waters of the pools can be quite hot, so it's best to check the temperature before diving in. Camping is available beside the banks of the Douglas River.

A little further south are the beautiful steep red cliffs of Umbrawarra Gorge Nature Park. Meandering through the gorge is a creek where a large pool with a sandy beach can be reached via a walking track from the camping area.

BEST CAMPSITES

Wangi Falls camping area
Litchfield National Park

Buley Rockhole camping area
Litchfield National Park

Douglas Hot Springs camping area
Tjuwaliyn (Douglas) Hot Springs Park

Shady Camp camping area
Mary River National Park (proposed)

Umbrawarra Gorge camping area
Umbrawarra Gorge Nature Park

BEST TIME TO VISIT

Due to possible road closures during the wet season, the dry season (May–September) is the best time to visit.

1. ADELAIDE RIVER

On the Stuart Hwy, the town of Adelaide River was once an important supply depot during World War II. The Adelaide River War Cemetery is one of the largest war cemeteries in Australia.

Adelaide River Showgrounds

Signposted on Old Stuart Hwy (Dorat Rd) 2 km west of Adelaide River township. Firewood supplied. Bookings required for June–July. Additional map ref.: ANTTM C3.

Further information & bookings: Adelaide River Show Society **Tel.:** (08) 8976 7032 **Camping fees:** Unpowered from $11.00 per 2 people/night, powered from $13.50 per 2 people/night

2. COPPERFIELD RECREATION RESERVE

This reserve is 6 km south-west of Pine Creek. The Copperfield Dam is an ideal spot to relax and take a cool dip.

Copperfield Dam camping area

This is 6 km south-west of Pine Creek, signposted off the Stuart Hwy. There is a limit of three days' stay. Bring drinking water and firewood. Additional map ref.: ANTTM D4.

3. DOUGLAS RIVER ESPLANADE CONSERVATION PARK

Protecting part of the Douglas River, this conservation park provides many natural delights for the visitor. Enjoy the river's natural spas and thermal pools, take a walk along its banks and explore the riverine habitat, or try spotting some of the 100 different bird species in the region.

Douglas Daly Tourist Park

On Oolloo Rd 59 km south of Hayes Creek Wayside Inn. Signposted from the Stuart Hwy. Water from river, boil first or bring your own. Bring firewood. Register at shop for site allocation. Additional map ref.: ANTTM D4.

Further information & bookings:
DIPE, Batchelor **Tel.:** (08) 8976 0282 *or*
Douglas Daly Tourist Park **Tel.:** (08) 8978 2479
Email: douglasdalypark@bigpond.com
Camping fees: Unpowered from $7.00 per adult/night, $3.50 per child/night, family from $21.00 per night, powered from $15.20 per person/night, $22.20 for 2 people/night, $3.50 per child/night, family from $29.20 per night

4. GUNN POINT

To the north-east of Darwin, Gunn Point is on Shoal Bay. It is a popular fishing area. Conventional vehicles can only reach Gunn Point in dry weather. People towing caravans should check road conditions. The camping area is behind the beach.

Bush camping

On Gunn Point Rd, reached via Howard Springs Rd off Stuart Hwy. Area is 52 km from Stuart Hwy and 75 km north-east of Darwin. Bring drinking water and firewood. Additional map ref.: ANTTM C2.

Further information & bookings: Litchfield Shire Council **Tel.:** (08) 8983 1912

5. LEANING TREE LAGOON NATURE PARK

Leaning Tree Lagoon retains good water during the dry season, long after others have dried up, making it an ideal spot for birdwatchers. It is located 69 km south-east of Darwin and is signposted off the Arnhem Hwy.

Bush camping

Bring drinking water and firewood. Additional map ref.: ANTTM D3.

Further information & bookings: DIPE, Window on the Wetlands **Tel.:** (08) 8988 8188

6. LITCHFIELD NATIONAL PARK

Litchfield National Park, to the west of Batchelor, boasts the complete range of habitats found in the Top End. Visit magnetic termite mounds, take a refreshing dip at Buley Rockhole or at Wangi, Florence or Tjaynera (Sandy Creek) falls, view the waterfalls cascading from the Tabletop Range or enjoy a stroll along one of the signposted walking tracks. The park is reached via Litchfield Park Rd off the Rum Jungle Rd at Batchelor.

Buley Rockhole camping area

This is 44 km west of Batchelor. Signposted off Litchfield Park Rd. Bring drinking water and firewood. Generators not permitted. Additional map ref.: ANTTM C3.

Florence Falls 2WD camping area

Situated 46 km west of Batchelor. Signposted off Litchfield Park Rd. Bring firewood. Generators not permitted. Additional map ref.: ANTTM C3.

Florence Falls 4WD camping area

This is 46 km west of Batchelor. Signposted near 2WD camping area off Litchfield Park Rd. Bring drinking water and firewood. Generators not permitted. Additional map ref.: ANTTM C3.

Surprise Creek Falls camping area

4WD access only. Signposted off Litchfield Park Rd just past Greenant Creek or off Daly River Rd. Area is 30 km south of Litchfield Park Rd and 13 km north of Daly River Rd. Bring drinking water and firewood. Generators not permitted. Additional map ref.: ANTTM C4.

Tjaynera (Sandy Creek) Falls camping area

Signposted off Litchfield Park Rd just past Greenant Creek. Area is 7 km south of Litchfield Park Rd and is 4WD access only. Bring firewood. Generators not permitted. Additional map ref.: ANTTM C3.

Camping at Buley Rockhole, Litchfield National Park

Walker Creek camping area

Walk-in access only. Six sites along Walker Creek. Signposted off Litchfield Park Rd. Bring drinking water and firewood. Gas/fuel stove preferred. Additional map ref.: ANTTM C3.

Wangi Falls camping area

This is 66 km west of Batchelor. Signposted along Litchfield Park Rd. Bring firewood. Generators not permitted. Additional map ref.: ANTTM C3.

Further information & bookings: DIPE, Batchelor **Tel.:** (08) 8976 0282 **Camping fees:** From \$6.60 per adult/night, \$3.30 per child (age 5–15) per night; fees payable at self-registration stations

7. MARY RIVER NATIONAL PARK (PROPOSED)

Mary River National Park (proposed) is 150 km south-east of Darwin. The forests and freshwater billabongs within the park provide excellent fishing, bushwalking and wildlife-watching. Access to the camping areas is via the gravel Point Stuart Rd off the Arnhem Hwy. The collection of firewood in the park is prohibited.

Couzen's Lookout camping area

Signposted from Point Stuart Rd, 134 km south-east of Darwin off the Arnhem Hwy. Area is 34 km north-west of highway. Bring drinking water and firewood. Additional map ref.: ANTTM D3.

Shady Camp camping area

Signposted from Point Stuart Rd, 134 km south-east of Darwin off the Arnhem Hwy. Area is 45 km north of highway. Bring drinking water and firewood. Additional map ref.: ANTTM D3.

Further information & bookings: DIPE, Palmerston **Tel.:** (08) 8999 5511 **Camping fees:** From \$3.30 per adult/night, \$1.65 per child (age 5–15) per night; fees payable at self-registration stations

8. TJUWALIYN (DOUGLAS) HOT SPRINGS PARK

Protecting parts of the Douglas River, the park is well known for its thermal pools which attract a number of bird species as well as mammals. The park is 48 km south of Hayes Creek Wayside Inn and is signposted 30 km along Oolloo Rd off the Old Stuart Hwy.

Douglas Hot Springs camping area

Signposted off Oolloo/Douglas Daly Rd 48 km south of Hayes Creek Wayside Inn. Drinking water from artesian bore. Bring firewood. Additional map ref.: ANTTM D4.

Further information & bookings:
DIPE, Batchelor **Tel.:** (08) 8976 0282 *or*
Douglas Daly Tourist Park **Tel.:** (08) 8978 2479
Email: douglasdalypark@bigpond.com
Camping fees: From \$4.50 per adult/night, \$1.50 per child (age 5–15) per night; fees payable at self-registration station

9. UMBRAWARRA GORGE NATURE PARK

This park takes its name from the Umbrawarra Tin Mine that occupied this area until the early 1920s; at the time it was the Northern Territory's largest tin mine. As well as its mining history, the gorge has a rich Aboriginal heritage, being a Dreaming site. Visitors to Umbrawarra Gorge can see Aboriginal rock art and walk to rocky pools with sandy beaches that allow safe swimming. The gorge is also a popular rock climbing and abseiling area; permits are required for these activities, and you should get them before arrival. The park is signposted off the Stuart Hwy 3 km south of Pine Creek, then it is a further 22 km south-west along an unsealed road, accessible in dry weather only. This road can become very corrugated and is sometimes closed. The collection of firewood is prohibited in the park.

Umbrawarra Gorge camping area

The camping area is 25 km south-west of Pine Creek. Signposted off Stuart Hwy. Bring drinking water and firewood. Generators not permitted. Additional map ref.: ANTTM D4.

Further information & bookings: DIPE, Batchelor **Tel.:** (08) 8976 0282 **Camping fees:** From \$3.30 per adult/night, \$1.65 per child (age 5–15) per night; fees payable at self-registration station

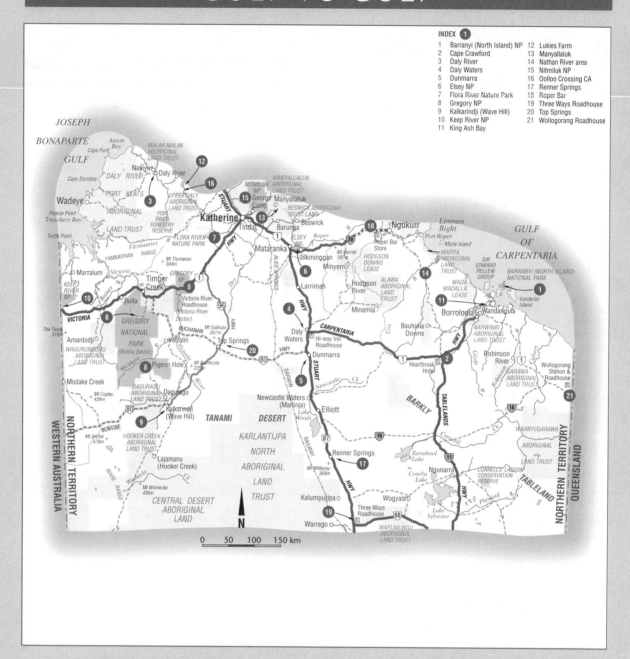

THIS STRETCH OF THE NORTHERN TERRITORY, FROM WESTERN AUSTRALIA TO QUEENSLAND, CONTAINS SOME OF THE TERRITORY'S MOST SPECTACULAR SCENERY, LIKE KATHERINE GORGE IN NITMILUK NATIONAL PARK AND ELSEY AND GREGORY NATIONAL PARKS.

The beautiful high sandstone cliffs of Katherine Gorge tower over the Katherine River. The best views of these magnificent coloured walls are from a boat cruise or canoe. Other scenic highlights of Nitmiluk National Park include the Aboriginal rock-art sites, lookouts and waterfalls. This park offers camping with excellent facilities at Nitmiluk Gorge and Leliyn (Edith Falls). Walking enthusiasts will enjoy the Jatbula Trail, a 66-kilometre walk from Katherine Gorge to Edith Falls.

Set amongst tall paperbark and palms, the thermal pool in Elsey National Park is a real oasis. Swimming in the warm waters of the pool is one of the major attractions of the park. Further east is the Twelve Mile Yards camping area, beside the Roper River; there is a boat ramp and canoe at the camping area for those who wish to venture down the river and do a spot of fishing. Walking tracks lead from the camping area along the river and to Mataranka Falls.

Gregory National Park houses significant evidence of Aboriginal culture and European occupation, including the old Bullita Homestead. There is spectacular gorge and range scenery, lookouts, walking trails, fishing and remote four-wheel drive touring opportunities. Access to the park is along the Victoria Highway and two of the park's campsites, which are suitable for caravans, are beside the highway. In the park proper, conventional vehicles can access two more camping areas, but the rest of the campsites are along remote old stock routes reachable by four-wheel drive vehicles only.

Alongside the Western Australia border is Keep River National Park, known for its beautiful and striking landforms. Visitors will see limestone cliffs, caves, gorges and rock archways. From the camping areas, walking trails lead to areas where visitors can view some of these rock formations. There are Aboriginal art sites at Nganalam and along the walking track from the Jarrnarm camping area.

BEST CAMPSITES

Twelve Mile Yards camping area
Elsey National Park

Nitmiluk Gorge Caravan and Camping Ground
Nitmiluk National Park

Bullita Homestead camping area
Gregory National Park

Limestone Gorge camping area
Gregory National Park

Jarrnarm camping area
Keep River National Park

BEST TIME TO VISIT

Dry season, May to August/September.

1. BARRANYI (NORTH ISLAND) NATIONAL PARK

The traditional home of the Yanyuwa Aboriginal people, this park is a remote haven within the Sir Edward Pellew group of islands, featuring long sandy beaches, a variety of birdlife and plenty of fish. Access is by boat only, involving a 35-km river trip from King Ash Bay then 15 nautical miles across the Gulf of Carpentaria. Visitors must be fully self-sufficient. Tours are also available to the island. Visitors should contact DIPE Borroloola before departure to confirm restricted areas on the island and check sea conditions.

Paradise Bay camping area

On north-west coast of island. Limited drinking water, best to bring your own. Firewood supplied. Gas/fuel stove preferred. Additional map ref.: ANTTM J6.

Further information & bookings: DIPE, Borroloola
Tel.: (08) 8975 8792

2. CAPE CRAWFORD

Cape Crawford, at the junction of the Carpentaria and Tablelands hwys, is 270 km east of Daly Waters and 117 km south-west of Borroloola. Scenic helicopter tours are available during the dry season.

Heartbreak Hotel camping area

At junction of Carpentaria and Tablelands hwys. Open 7 am–midnight. Firewood supplied. Additional map ref.: ANTTM H7.

Further information & bookings: Heartbreak Hotel
Tel.: (08) 8975 9928 **Camping fees:** Unpowered from $5.00 per person/night, $3.00 per child (age 7–14) per night, powered from $15.00 per 2 people/night

3. DALY RIVER

Daly River, 100 km west of the Stuart Hwy, is a popular fishing spot. Conventional vehicle access is possible along the gravel road. Note that some areas of Daly River are dry (no alcohol allowed).

Daly River Crossing bush camping area

Small area on Daly River Rd opposite police station. Bring drinking water and firewood. Additional map ref.: ANTTM C4.

Further information & bookings: Daly River Police Station
Tel.: (08) 8978 2466

4. DALY WATERS

This settlement, 4 km west of the Stuart Hwy, has a rich and varied history. The Overland Telegraph Line was laid through here in 1872 and in the 1890s, a pub was built for drovers camping in the area while on the stock route between the Kimberley and Queensland. It was also used as an airline refuelling stop. It is signposted from the Stuart Hwy 276 km south of Katherine.

Daly Waters Pub camping area

Located 4 km west of the Stuart Hwy. Open: 6 am–midnight. Fires are allowed; bring firewood or collect from around area. Additional map ref.: ANTTM F7.

Further information & bookings: Daly Waters Pub
Tel.: (08) 8975 9927 **Email:** dalywaterspub@bigpond.com
Camping fees: Unpowered from $5.00 per person/night,
powered from $7.00 per person/night

Hi-way Inn Roadhouse camping area

South of Daly Waters at junction of Stuart and Carpentaria
hwys. Open: 7 am–11 pm. Bring firewood. Additional map
ref.: ANTTM F7.

Further information & bookings: Hi-way Inn Roadhouse
Tel.: (08) 8975 9925 **Camping fees:** From $4.50 per
person/night

5. DUNMARRA

Dunmarra is on the Stuart Hwy. There is a historic marker
commemorating the joining of the Overland Telegraph Line
in 1872, about 35 km south of town.

Dunmarra Wayside Inn camping area

On the Stuart Hwy, between Tennant Creek and Katherine.
Open 6 am–midnight. Drinking water from bore. Firewood
supplied. Additional map ref.: ANTTM F7.

Further information & bookings: Dunmarra Wayside Inn
Tel.: (08) 8975 9922 **Camping fees:** Unpowered from $5.50
per person/night, powered from $16.50 per site (up to 4
people/night)

6. ELSEY NATIONAL PARK

This park is to the east of Mataranka, signposted off the
Stuart Hwy. It takes its name from the old Elsey Station,
home of Mrs Aeneas Gunn, author of the book *We of the
Never-Never*. The park's main attraction is the Rainbow
Spring and Thermal Pool section; fishing, swimming,
canoeing and walking are also popular. The collection of
firewood is prohibited in the park.

Twelve Mile Yards camping area

Signposted from John Hauser Drive off Homestead Rd, off
the Stuart Hwy. Area is 18 km east of Mataranka. Solar hot
water. Bring firewood. Generators not permitted. Additional
map ref.: ANTTM F5.

Further information & bookings: DIPE, Mataranka
Tel.: (08) 8975 4560 **Camping fees:** From $6.00 per
adult/night; fees payable to ranger/manager

7. FLORA RIVER NATURE PARK

This park is 122 km south-west of Katherine. It includes
25 km of the Flora River, with springs, waterfalls, cascades
and tufa formations. To help protect the local turtle population,
please use only lures when fishing. The collection of
firewood is prohibited in the park.

Djarrung Campground

Signposted from the Victoria Hwy 89 km south-west of
Katherine, then a further 46 km north to site. Solar hot water.

Bring drinking water and firewood. Additional map ref.:
ANTTM D5.

Further information & bookings: DIPE, Katherine
Tel.: (08) 8973 8888 **Camping fees:** From $3.30 per
person/night; fees payable at self-registration station

8. GREGORY NATIONAL PARK

Covering almost 13 000 sq. km, Gregory National Park
contains significant Aboriginal cultural sites along with
reminders of pastoral history. There is spectacular range
and gorge scenery, as well as excellent fishing, walking
trails and remote 4WD touring. During the peak season
(June–Aug.) there are slide shows and campfire talks.
Contact DIPE for further details. The park is in two sections:
the Eastern (Victoria River) Sector is 160 km west of
Katherine and the Western (Bullita) Sector is 275 km west of
Katherine. Access is from the Victoria Hwy. Due to the
remoteness and isolation of the 4WD tracks, intending
travellers should register with the Voluntary Registration
Scheme, tel. 1300 650 730. If you register with the scheme
you must deregister within 24 hours of trip completion.

Baines Campsite

On Bullita Stock Route, off Victoria Hwy, 32 km north-west
of Bullita Homestead. Bring drinking water and firewood.
Additional map ref.: ANTTM B6.

Big Horse Creek camping area

Signposted off Victoria Hwy 8 km west of Timber Creek.
Water from creek, boil before use. Bring firewood. Additional
map ref.: ANTTM B6.

Bullita Homestead camping area

On Bullita Access Rd 65 km south of Timber Creek. Bullita
Access Rd is signposted 10 km east of Timber Creek off the
Victoria Hwy. Drinking water from river, boil before use. Bring
firewood. Additional map ref.: ANTTM C6.

Dingo Yard camping area

On Wickham Track, 44.4 km south-east of Humbert/Wickham
track junction and 88 km south of trackhead information
shelter. Bring drinking water and firewood. Additional map
ref.: ANTTM C7.

Drovers Rest Campsite

On Bullita Stock Route 51 km north-west of Bullita
Homestead. Bring drinking water and firewood. Additional
map ref.: ANTTM B6.

Fig Tree Yard Campsite

On Humbert Track 15 km south of trackhead information
shelter. Bring drinking water and firewood. Additional map
ref.: ANTTM C7.

Limestone Gorge camping area

On Limestone Gorge Rd 52 km south of Timber Creek. Signposted from Bullita Access Rd 10 km east of Timber Creek off the Victoria Hwy. Bring drinking water and firewood. Swimming is at the nearby Limestone Billabong. Additional map ref.: ANTTM B6.

Paperbark Yard camping area

On Gibbie Creek Track, 22 km south-east of Dingo Yard and 66 km south of Humbert/Wickham track junction. Bring drinking water and firewood. Additional map ref.: ANTTM C7.

Spring Creek Yard camping area

On Bullita Stock Route 13 km west of Bullita Homestead. Bring drinking water and firewood. Additional map ref.: ANTTM B6.

Sullivan Creek camping area

Signposted off the Victoria Hwy 19 km east of Victoria River and 170 km west of Katherine. Bring drinking water and firewood. Additional map ref.: ANTTM C6.

Top Humbert Yard camping area

Located 800 m west of Humbert Track. Access track is 44 km south of trackhead information shelter. Bring drinking water and firewood. Additional map ref.: ANTTM C7.

Wickham Creek Waterhole Campground

On Broadarrow Track, 175 km south-west of Broadarrow/Wickham track junction and 93 km north of Buntine Hwy through areas of private property. Bring drinking water and firewood. Additional map ref.: ANTTM C7.

Further information & bookings: DIPE, Gregory National Park **Tel.:** (08) 8975 0888 **Camping fees:** From $3.30 per adult/night, $1.65 per child (age 5–15) per night; fees payable at self-registration stations

9. KALKARINDJI (WAVE HILL)

Kalkarindji (Wave Hill) is on the Buntine Hwy, 170 km south-west of Top Springs via a sealed road and 223 km east of the Western Australian border via an unsealed gravel road. It is beside the Victoria River. Public fossicking fields are nearby; enquire at the store for further details. Kalkarindji is a dry area and alcohol is not allowed.

Kalkarindji Caravan Park and Campground

On Buntine Hwy 170 km south-west of Top Springs. Kalkarindji Store is open 9 am–1 pm and 2 pm–5 pm. Bring drinking water. Gas/fuel stove only. Additional map ref.: ANTTM C8.

Further information & bookings: Kalkarindji Store **Tel.:** (08) 8975 0788 **Camping fees:** Unpowered from $11.00 per 2 people/night, powered from $16.50 per 2 people/night

10. KEEP RIVER NATIONAL PARK

Keep River National Park is beside the Western Australian border, 468 km west of Katherine along the Victoria Hwy. It is signposted 3 km east of the border. Known for its rugged sandstone formations, the park offers excellent bushwalking for visitors. Aboriginal art sites are also found here. The collection of firewood is prohibited in the park.

Gurrandalng camping area

This is 18 km north of Victoria Hwy entrance. Bring drinking water and firewood. Additional map ref.: ANTTM A6.

Jarrnarm camping area

Located 28 km north of Victoria Hwy entrance. Bring firewood. Additional map ref.: ANTTM A6.

Bush camping

Walk-in bush camping available for self-sufficient and experienced walkers. Contact ranger for further details. Bring drinking water. Gas/fuel stove preferred.

Further information & bookings: DIPE, Keep River National Park **Tel.:** (08) 9167 8827 **Camping fees:** From $3.30 per adult/night, $1.65 per child (age 5–15) per night; fees payable at self-registration stations

11. KING ASH BAY

King Ash Bay is 42 km north-west of Borroloola, on the McArthur River. The region is well known for its fishing; fishing tours are available.

Borroloola Boat and Fishing Club camping area

On King Ash Bay. Signposted off Bing Bong Rd 21 km north-east of Borroloola. Campsites beside McArthur River. Bring drinking water and firewood. Additional map ref.: ANTTM I6.

Further information & bookings: King Ash Bay Mini Mart **Tel.:** (08) 8975 9760 **Camping fees:** Unpowered from $10.00 per 2 people/night, powered from $15.00 per 2 people/night; fees payable at mini mart

12. LUKIES FARM

Lukies Farm is an ideal spot for fishing and seclusion – it has 15 km of river frontage to the Daly River. The farm is 29 km south-west of Douglas Daly Tourist Park.

Bush camping

Reached from Oolloo Rd. Bush campsites. Bring drinking water and firewood. Bookings required; key access to camping area with a refundable deposit for key. Additional map ref.: ANTTM C4.

Further information & bookings: Douglas Daly Tourist Park **Tel.:** (08) 8978 2479 **Email:** douglasdalypark@bigpond.com **Camping fees:** From $8.00 per adult/night

13. MANYALLALUK

Manyallaluk, 100 km east of Katherine, is owned by the Aboriginal people of the Mayali, Rembarrnga, Ngalkbon and Jawoyn language groups. The owners invite visitors to experience Aboriginal culture. There is plenty to do: enjoy one of the many guided tours, have a go at spear throwing or basket weaving or view old station buildings and ancient rock-art sites. Manyallaluk is a restricted area and alcohol is not allowed.

Manyallaluk Camping Ground

This is 35 km north of Central Arnhem Road and signposted from it. Bookings required. Additional map ref.: ANTTM E4.

Further information & bookings: Manyallaluk Community **Tel.:** (08) 8975 4727 **Camping fees:** From $5.50 per adult/night, $3.00 per child (age 7–16) per night

14. NATHAN RIVER AREA

There are dispersed bush campsites beside a number of river crossings along the Nathan River Rd (Roper Bar Store –Borroloola Rd) north of Nathan River Homestead. It is proposed that this area becomes a national park – if this happens dogs will no longer be allowed. 4WD vehicles are recommended; drivers of 2WD vehicles should check road conditions.

Cox River Crossing bush camping area

This area is 154 km south-east of Roper Bar Store and 34 km north of Nathan River Homestead. Bring drinking water and firewood. Additional map ref.: ANTTM H6.

Limmen Bight River Crossing bush camping area

This is 175 km south-east of Roper Bar Store and 13 km north of Nathan River Homestead. Bring drinking water and firewood. Additional map ref.: ANTTM H6.

Towns River Crossing bush camping area

Located 116 km east of Roper Bar Store and 72 km north of Nathan River Homestead. Bring drinking water and firewood. Additional map ref.: ANTTM H5.

Further information & bookings:
DIPE, Nathan River Homestead **Tel.:** (08) 8975 9940 or Roper Bar Store **Tel.:** (08) 8975 4636

15. NITMILUK NATIONAL PARK

The main feature at Nitmiluk National Park is the sandstone gorge carved by the Katherine River. Visitors can enjoy a short stroll along the riverbank or longer overnight bushwalks through the gorge – there are designated camping areas along the trails. Alternatively, paddle up the river through the gorge system in a canoe, view art and other evidence of the Jawoyn Aboriginal people's occupation of this area, or take a boat tour or scenic flight. The park's main entrance – and Nitmiluk Centre – is 30 km north-east of Katherine via sealed roads. Leliyn (Edith Falls) is signposted from the Stuart Hwy 40 km north of Katherine. The collection of firewood is prohibited in the park.

Leliyn (Edith Falls) Camping Ground

Located 61 km north-east of Katherine. Some firewood supplied. Generators not permitted. Additional map ref.: ANTTM E4.

Further information & bookings: Leliyn (Edith Falls) Camping Ground **Tel.:** (08) 8975 4869 **Camping fees:** From $6.60 per adult/night, $3.30 per child/night, $15.40 per family (2 adults and 4 children) per night

Nitmiluk Gorge Caravan and Camping Ground

On Giles Rd 30 km north-east of Katherine, signposted from the Stuart Hwy. Firewood supplied. Generators not permitted. Additional map ref.: ANTTM E4.

Further information & bookings: Nitmiluk Gorge Caravan and Camping Ground **Tel.:** (08) 8972 3150 **Camping fees:** From $8.00 per adult/night, $5.00 per child (age 5–15) per night, power an additional $4.00 per site/night

JATBULA TRAIL WALK-IN CAMPING AREAS

The Jatbula Trail is a 66-km, one-way walk from Nitmiluk Centre to Leliyn (Edith Falls). Permits are required for the walk and are available from Nitmiluk Centre (permit for the walk from Leliyn to Sweetwater Pool is available from Leliyn Camping Ground). Walkers must register and deregister.

Biddlecombe Cascades

This is 11.5 km along Jatbula Trail from Nitmiluk Centre. Water from natural source. Gas/fuel stove preferred. There is an ECD (Emergency Call Device) here. Additional map ref.: ANTTM E4.

Crystal Falls

Located 20.5 km along Jatbula Trail from Nitmiluk Centre. Water from natural source. Gas/fuel stove preferred. ECD here. Additional map ref.: ANTTM E4.

Seventeen Mile Falls

Situated 34.5 km along Jatbula Trail from Nitmiluk Centre. Water from natural source. Gas/fuel stove preferred. ECD here. Additional map ref.: ANTTM E4.

Edith River Crossing

This is 45.5 km along Jatbula Trail from Nitmiluk Centre. Water from natural source. Gas/fuel stove preferred. ECD here. Additional map ref.: ANTTM E4.

Sandy Camp Pool

Located 51 km along Jatbula Trail from Nitmiluk Centre. Water from natural source. Gas/fuel stove preferred. Additional map ref.: ANTTM E4.

Sweetwater Pool

This is 61.5 km along Jatbula Trail from Nitmiluk Centre; also accessible via the Sweetwater Pool Walking Trail 4 km north of Leliyn (Edith Falls) Camping Ground. Bring drinking water. Gas/fuel stove preferred. Additional map ref.: ANTTM E4.

SOUTHERN WALKS WALK-IN CAMPING AREAS

Canoe hire is available for those who prefer to paddle in. Permits are required, available from Nitmiluk Centre. Both walkers and canoeists must register and deregister.

Dunlop Swamp

Located 9 km east of Nitmiluk Centre via Smitt Rocks Walk. Bring drinking water. Gas/fuel stove preferred. Additional map ref.: ANTTM E4.

Smitt Rocks

This is 11 km east of Nitmiluk Centre via Smitt Rocks Walk or via canoe on Katherine River. Drinking water from river. Gas/fuel stove only. ECD here. Additional map ref.: ANTTM E4.

Eighth Gorge

Located 16 km east of Nitmiluk Centre via Eighth Gorge Walk or via canoe on Katherine River. Drinking water from river. Gas/fuel stove only. ECD here. Additional map ref.: ANTTM E4.

Further information & bookings: Nitmiluk Information Centre **Tel.:** (08) 8972 3150
Camping fees: *Jatbula Trail:* From $3.30 per person/night; $50.00 refundable deposit *Southern Walks:* Walkers from $3.30 per person/night, canoeists from $5.50 per person/night (own canoe); $20.00 refundable deposit

16. OOLLOO CROSSING CONSERVATION AREA

Oolloo Crossing on the Daly River is a popular spot for fishing. It is 77 km south of Hayes Creek. Access is in dry weather only via the signposted Oolloo Rd off the Stuart Hwy.

Bush camping

On Oolloo Rd. Dispersed bush camping along Daly River. Bring drinking water and firewood. Gas/fuel stove preferred. Additional map ref.: ANTTM C4.

Further information & bookings: DIPE, Batchelor **Tel.:** (08) 8976 0282

17. RENNER SPRINGS

Renner Springs is on the Stuart Hwy in the Ashburton Ranges. The Attack Creek Historical Reserve and a memorial to John McDouall Stuart are 85 km south of Renner Springs.

Renner Springs Desert Inn camping area

On the Stuart Hwy 160 km north of Tennant Creek. The attached roadhouse is open 6.30 am–11 pm. Additional map ref.: ANTTM F9.

Further information & bookings: Renner Springs Desert Inn **Tel.:** (08) 8964 4505 **Camping fees:** Unpowered from $5.50 per person/night, powered from $16.75 per 2 people/night

18. ROPER BAR

Roper Bar is 176 km east of Mataranka on the Roper Hwy. It is a popular fishing spot on the Roper River. Camping at the caravan park is beside the river.

Leichhardts Caravan Park

On Roper Hwy. Bring firewood. Additional map ref.: ANTTM G5.

Further information & bookings: Leichhardts Caravan Park **Tel.:** (08) 8975 4636 **Camping fees:** From $6.60 per adult/ night, $4.40 per child (age 4–14) per night

19. THREE WAYS ROADHOUSE

Located north of Tennant Creek at the junction of the Stuart and Barkly hwys. A walking trail from the roadhouse leads to the Flynn Memorial, which commemorates Rev. John Flynn, the founder of the Royal Flying Doctor Service.

Three Ways Roadhouse camping area

On Stuart Hwy 24 km north of Tennant Creek. Roadhouse open 6 am–11 pm. Bring firewood. Additional map ref.: ANTTM G10.

Further information & bookings: Three Ways Roadhouse **Tel.:** (08) 8962 2744 **Camping fees:** From $8.10 per adult/night

20. TOP SPRINGS

Top Springs is at the junction of the Buchanan and Buntine hwys. Services here include fuel, supplies, a bar, camping and motel rooms.

Top Springs Roadhouse camping area

Roadhouse open Sun.–Wed. 7 am–9 pm; Thurs.–Sat. 7 am–10 pm. Gas/fuel stove only. Drinking water from bore. Additional map ref.: ANTTM D7.

Further information & bookings: Top Springs Roadhouse **Tel.:** (08) 8975 0767 **Camping fees:** From $5.00 per person/night

21. WOLLOGORANG ROADHOUSE

Wollogorang Roadhouse (and station) is located on the unsealed Savannah Way, 270 km south of Borroloola and 6 km west of the Queensland border. The roadhouse operates organised fishing tours. Visitors with a 4WD can purchase a permit here for the 80-km Gulf Track. Travellers with 2WD vehicles should check road conditions before attempting the drive here.

Wollogorang Roadhouse camping area

Bring firewood. Roadhouse open 6 am to 9 pm. Additional map ref.: ANTTMK8.

Further information & bookings: Wollogorang Roadhouse **Tel.:** (08) 8975 9944 **Camping fees:** From $7.70 per person/night

THE RED CENTRE

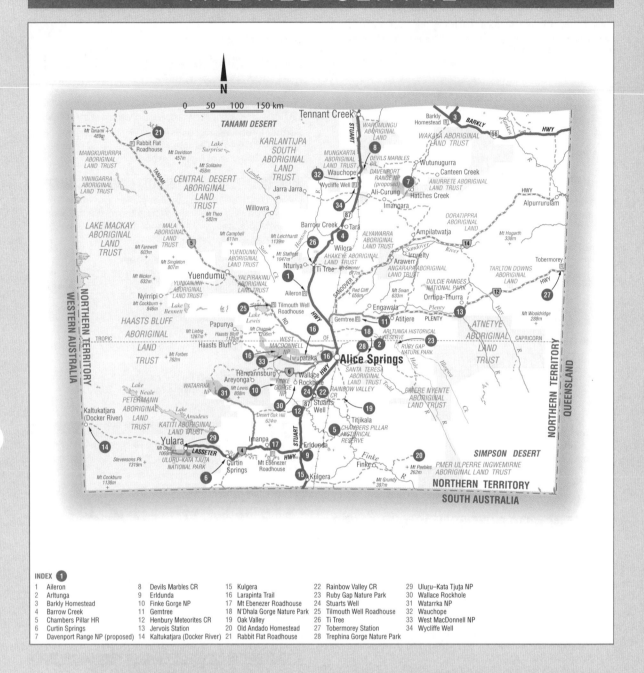

AUSTRALIA'S CENTRE OFFERS MAGNIFICENT ROCK FORMATIONS, PALM-FILLED GORGES, ANCIENT RIVERBEDS AND RED SAND-DUNE DESERTS, AS WELL AS ABORIGINAL CULTURAL SITES AND REMINDERS OF EUROPEAN EXPLORATION.

There is much to see in the Red Centre, from the majestic Uluru and Kata Tjuta to the impressive Chambers Pillar, the intriguing Devils Marbles, the spectacular Kings Canyon, the beautiful gorge system of the West MacDonnell Ranges, the ancient Finke River and its gorge, and the colourful sandstone bluffs and cliffs of Rainbow Valley. There are even craters that mark the spot where a huge meteorite crashed into the earth.

Many activities are on offer here, including walking and overnight hiking, cycling, bird-watching, gem fossicking and car touring. Visitors can explore old mine sites and World War II staging camps, take camel rides and join guided tours.

Campers in the Red Centre have a huge choice of parks and reserves with a range of facilities. There is everything from remote bush camping in the rugged Ruby Gap Nature Park and the scenic Finke Gorge National Park, walk-in sites along the Larapinta Trail throughout the spectacular West MacDonnell National Park, and the well-established campgrounds close to Kings Canyon and Uluru. Keen birdwatchers may wish to set up camp in Davenport Range National Park (proposed), where the permanent waterholes are an important refuge for waterbirds. If camping here be sure that you are well prepared and self-sufficient.

The sheer quartzite cliffs and gum-lined watercourses of Trephina Gorge Nature Park provide a beautiful setting for campers and are another one of the region's great features. A number of walks lead from Trephina Gorge campground, where caravan access is possible, to the gorge and a lookout; the more energetic may wish to attempt the seven-hour-return Ridgetop Trail.

BEST CAMPSITES

Ellery Creek Big Hole camping area
West MacDonnell National Park

Ormiston Gorge camping area
West MacDonnell National Park

Rainbow Valley camping area
Rainbow Valley Conservation Reserve

Trephina Gorge campground
Trephina Gorge Nature Park

Palm Valley camping area
Finke Gorge National Park

BEST TIME TO VISIT

During the cooler months, April to September.

1. AILERON

Aileron is between Alice Springs and Tennant Creek. The roadhouse is next to the historic Aileron Homestead. Services here include fuel, meals and supplies.

Aileron Roadhouse camping area

On the Stuart Hwy 132 km north of Alice Springs and 370 km south of Tennant Creek. Roadhouse open 7 am–10 pm. Firewood supplied. Additional map ref.: ANTTM F14.

Further information & bookings: Aileron Roadhouse **Tel.:** (08) 8956 9703 **Camping fees:** From $8.50 per person/night. Power only available up to 10 pm

2. ARLTUNGA

Arltunga is north-east of Alice Springs and was central Australia's first official town. When alluvial gold was found at Paddys Rockhole in 1887, hundreds of people flocked to the area to try their luck. At the Arltunga Historical Reserve visitors can explore old mine workings and cemeteries, and those with a current Northern Territory Fossickers Permit can fossick at the nearby fossicking reserve. Drop into the visitors centre for more details on the area's attractions. Ranger-guided tours are available May–Oct.; contact the visitors centre for further information. Arltunga is signposted from the Ross Hwy east of Alice Springs.

Arltunga Bush Hotel camping area

This is 110 km north-east of Alice Springs on the Arltunga Tourist Drive, via the Ross Hwy. Limited drinking water, bring your own. Firewood supplied. Additional map ref.: ANTTM G14.

Further information & bookings:
DIPE, Arltunga Historical Reserve **Tel.:** (08) 8956 9770 or Arltunga Bush Hotel **Tel.:** (08) 8956 9797
Camping fees: From $8.00 per adult/night, $4.00 per child (age 3–14) per night

3. BARKLY HOMESTEAD

Barkly Homestead is the last fuel stop before the Queensland border. It is 210 km east of Tennant Creek.

Barkly Homestead camping area

Signposted on the Barkly Hwy 187 km east of the Stuart Hwy. Open 6.30 am–midnight. Drinking water from bore. Bring firewood. Additional map ref.: ANTTM I10.

Further information & bookings: Barkly Homestead **Tel.:** (08) 8964 4549 **Camping fees:** From $6.00 per person/night

4. BARROW CREEK

Barrow Creek is between Tennant Creek and Alice Springs. Here you will find one of the few remaining Overland Telegraph stations, and can discover its interesting history. About 30 km to the north are the ruins of a WW II army staging camp.

Barrow Creek Hotel camping area

On the Stuart Hwy 220 km south of Tennant Creek and 285 km north of Alice Springs. Hotel open 7 am–11 pm.

Bring drinking water. Some firewood supplied. Additional map ref.: ANTTM F12.

Further information & bookings: Barrow Creek Hotel **Tel.:** (08) 8956 9753 **Camping fees:** Unpowered from $5.00 per person/night, powered from $6.00 per person/night

5. CHAMBERS PILLAR HISTORICAL RESERVE

A 50-m-high sandstone pillar is the major attraction of Chambers Pillar Historical Reserve. The pillar was named by John McDouall Stuart in April 1860 during his first attempt to cross Australia; the name is derived from one of Stuart's South Australian sponsors, James Chambers. Carved into the pillar are the names and dates of other early explorers. As well as this, Chambers Pillar has Aboriginal Dreamtime significance and is said to be the gecko ancestor Itirkawara. Chambers Pillar Historical Reserve is 164 km south of Alice Springs. It is south-west of Titjikala off the Old South Rd. Only 4WD vehicles can travel past the Titjikala turn-off. Dogs must be kept on leads and are only allowed in the carpark.

Chambers Pillar camping area

Signposted from Titjikala – 4WD only. Bring drinking water and firewood. Gas/fuel stove preferred. Generators not permitted. Additional map ref.: ANTTM F16.

Further information & bookings: DIPE, Alice Springs **Tel.:** (08) 8951 8211 **Camping fees:** From $3.30 per adult/night, $1.65 per child (age 5–15) per night, family (2 adults + 4 children) $7.70 per night; fees payable at self-registration station

6. CURTIN SPRINGS

Curtin Springs is located on the Lasseter Hwy to Uluru. It takes its name from the nearby springs which were named after John Curtin, the prime minister at the time that the first homestead was built here. Tours of Curtin Springs Station and of Mt Conner are available as well as camel rides. Enquire at the roadhouse for further information. Fuel, food and basic groceries are available. Dogs are welcome but must be kept on leads at all times in the campground.

Curtin Springs Roadhouse camping area

On the Lasseter Hwy 162 km west of Erldunda and 85 km east of Yulara. Roadhouse open 7 am–11 pm. Bring drinking water and firewood. Additional map ref.: ANTTM D16.

Further information & bookings: Curtin Springs Roadhouse **Tel.:** (08) 8956 2906 **Email:** curtinas@ozemail.com.au **Website:** www.curtinsprings.com **Camping fees:** Unpowered campsites free, with $1.00 per person for shower, powered sites $11.00 per site/night with free shower

7. DAVENPORT RANGE NATIONAL PARK (PROPOSED)

The Davenport Range has a diverse history with artifacts of Aboriginal occupancy and early European settlement. The region has many permanent waterholes, offering refuge for waterbirds and fish; it has been proposed as a national park to protect the fauna here. The park is east of the Stuart Hwy, off the Epenarra Rd which leaves the Stuart Hwy at Bonney Well 90 km south of Tennant Creek. The collection of firewood in the park is prohibited.

The startling formation of Chambers Pillar, in Chambers Pillar Historical Reserve

Policemans Waterhole camping area

Located 43 km south of Wutunugurra, which is 126 km east of the Stuart Hwy. Area is on Policemans Station Waterhole Rd and signposted off Loop Rd. Bring drinking water and firewood. Gas/fuel stove preferred. Additional map ref.: ANTTM H11.

Whistleduck Creek camping area

On Whistleduck Rd, 69 km east of the Stuart Hwy. Bring drinking water and firewood. Gas/fuel stove preferred. Additional map ref.: ANTTM G11.

Further information & bookings: DIPE, Tennant Creek **Tel.:** (08) 8962 4599 **Camping fees:** From $3.30 per person/ night; fees payable at self-registration stations

8. DEVILS MARBLES CONSERVATION RESERVE

These famous geological formations are a must-see, especially at sunrise or sunset when the reddish granite rocks are spectacular. The 'marbles' formed when large masses of granite broke and eroded into smaller slabs. Over the course of millions of years, erosion and flaking of the surface have formed rounded corners, shaping the granite into its present spherical or egg shapes. Take a stroll along the self-guide walk. Dogs must be kept on leads and confined to the carpark and camping area.

Devils Marbles camping area

Signposted from the Stuart Hwy 9 km north of Wauchope and 106 km south of Tennant Creek. Bring drinking water and firewood. Additional map ref.: ANTTM G11.

Further information & bookings: DIPE, Tennant Creek **Tel.:** (08) 8962 4599 **Camping fees:** From $3.30 per person/ night; fees payable at self-registration station

9. ERLDUNDA

Erldunda lies between Alice Springs and the South Australian border. Services here include fuel, supplies, meals, souvenirs and accommodation.

Erldunda Desert Oaks Roadhouse camping area

At junction of Stuart and Lasseter hwys, 201 km south of Alice Springs. Roadhouse open 7 am–9 pm. Firewood supplied. Additional map ref.: ANTTM F16.

Further information & bookings: Erldunda Desert Oaks Roadhouse **Tel.:** (08) 8956 0984 **Email:** erldunda@dove. com.au **Camping fees:** Unpowered from $8.00 per person/ night, powered from $13.00 per person/night

10. FINKE GORGE NATIONAL PARK

Finke Gorge National Park is signposted off Larapinta Drive 125 km west of Alice Springs. Palm Valley is the main attraction here, with its lush stands of red cabbage-palms which are unique to the area. Within the main gorge visitors will find high red cliffs, cool waterholes and river gums. The Finke River was part of an Aboriginal trade route and its permanent water – from soaks dug in the riverbed – supplied water to the Western Arrernte people in times of drought.

The Finke River 4WD Route is mostly sand driving and those planning to travel it must be well prepared. Contact DIPE for further details on this route. The collection of firewood in the park is prohibited.

Boggy Hole camping area

Along Finke River 4WD Route 30 km south of Larapinta Drive. 4WD necessary; self-sufficient campers only. Bring drinking water and firewood. Gas/fuel stove preferred. Generators not permitted. Additional map ref.: ANTTM E15.

Palm Valley camping area

This is 18 km south of Hermannsburg, signposted off Larapinta Drive. 4WD access only. Bring firewood. Generators not permitted. Additional map ref.: ANTTM E15.

Further information & bookings: DIPE, Alice Springs **Tel.:** (08) 8951 8211 **Camping fees:** *Boggy Hole:* From $3.30 per adult/night, $1.65 per child (age 5–15) per night *Palm Valley:* From $6.60 per adult/night, $3.30 per child (age 5–15) per night. Fees payable at self-registration stations

11. GEMTREE

Gemtree is 140 km north-east of Alice Springs. The surrounding area is popular with fossickers searching for semi-precious stones such as zircon and garnet. Novices can take a fossicking tour; enquire at the Gemtree Caravan Park for further details.

Gemtree Caravan Park

On Plenty Hwy 70 km east of junction of Stuart and Plenty hwys. Open 8 am–6 pm. Bring drinking water. Firewood supplied. Bookings recommended for June–July. Additional map ref.: ANTTM G14.

Further information & bookings: Gemtree Caravan Park **Tel.:** (08) 8956 9855 **Email:** gemtree@gemtree.com.au **Website:** www.gemtree.com.au **Camping fees:** Unpowered from $8.00 per person/night, powered from $20.00 per 2 people/night

12. HENBURY METEORITES CONSERVATION RESERVE

Henbury Meteorites Conservation Reserve is 145 km south-west of Alice Springs, close to the Stuart Hwy. The reserve contains twelve craters which were formed over 4700 years ago by fragments of the Henbury meteorite. The meteor, which weighed several tons, disintegrated before impact after travelling towards earth at over 40 000 km per hour. The largest crater in the reserve is 180 m wide and 15 m deep.

Henbury Meteorites camping area

This area is 131 km south-west of Alice Springs. Turn west at signpost on Stuart Hwy into Ernest Giles Rd, continue for 11 km and follow signs (area is 5 km north of Ernest Giles Rd). This section of Ernest Giles Rd is recommended for 4WD only; drivers of 2WD vehicles should check road conditions first. Bring drinking water and firewood. Generators not permitted. Additional map ref.: ANTTM F16.

Further information & bookings: DIPE, Alice Springs **Tel.:** (08) 8951 8211 **Camping fees:** From $3.30 per adult/

night, $1.65 per child (age 5–15) per night, family (2 adults + 4 children) $7.50 per night; fees payable at self-registration station

13. JERVOIS STATION

Jervois Station is on the Plenty Hwy. The station has a camping area 1 km off the highway, between the highway and homestead. Fuel is available for purchase.

Jervois Station camping area

This is 277 km east of the Stuart Hwy and 1 km north of the Plenty Hwy. Station open during daylight hours. Bring firewood. Additional map ref.: ANTTM I14.

Further information & bookings: Jervois Station **Tel.:** (08) 8956 6307 **Camping fees:** $5.00 per vehicle/night; toilet and hot shower facilities are available at the homestead, shower $2.00 each

14. KALTUKATJARA (DOCKER RIVER)

Kaltukatjara (Docker River) is 5 km east of the Western Australian border, on the unsealed Tjukaruru Rd (Outback Hwy) west of Yulara. (Over the border the road is known as the Great Central Road; see Great Central Road, The Goldfields region, Western Australia, for details of camping areas and permits.) En route to Kaltukatjara from the east you will pass Kata Tjuta and Lasseters Cave. The campground is within a scenic desert oak forest. Fuel is available in the township. To travel the Tjukaruru Rd a permit is required from the Central Land Council. People towing caravans should check road conditions.

Kaltukatjara Community camping area

Signposted off Tjukaruru Rd 1 km west of Kaltukatjara. Limited drinking water. Firewood supplied. Additional map ref.: ANTTM A16.

Further information & bookings: Docker River Council **Tel.:** (08) 8956 7337 **Permits:** Central Land Council **Tel.:** (08) 8951 6320 **Camping fees:** From $5.00 per person/night; fees payable at self-registration station

15. KULGERA

Kulgera is 18 km north of the South Australian border, and thus the first (or last) settlement in the Northern Territory on the Stuart Hwy. Services here include fuel, supplies, a bar and dining room, takeaway meals and accommodation.

Kulgera Roadhouse camping area

On Stuart Hwy 287 km south of Alice Springs. Roadhouse open 6 am–11.30 pm. Bring drinking water. Firewood supplied. Additional map ref.: ANTTM F17.

Further information & bookings: Kulgera Roadhouse **Tel.:** (08) 8956 0973 **Camping fees:** Unpowered from $6.00 per person/night, powered from $10.00 per person/night

16. LARAPINTA TRAIL

The Larapinta Trail is a 220-km walking track through West MacDonnell National Park. It runs west from Alice Springs along the backbone of the West MacDonnell and Chewings ranges to Mt Sonder, and is marked every kilometre. The trail crosses a variety of terrain, from ridgelines to sheltered gorges, and provides walkers with an opportunity to experience the magnificent landscapes and scenery of the

Centre. The trail has been designed in sections, allowing walkers to undertake parts of it as they choose. Contact DIPE for further details including water availability, guide books/pamphlets and maps. Walkers need to arrange their own pick-up and drop-off transport. It is recommended that all walkers register with the Voluntary Registration Scheme for safety purposes, tel. 1300 650 730. If you register with the scheme you must deregister within 24 hours of completing your trip.

SECTION 1 – TELEGRAPH STATION TO SIMPSONS GAP (23.7 KM)

Wallaby Gap camping area

This is 13 km west of the Telegraph Station and 300 m south of Wallaby Gap. Gas/fuel stove preferred. Additional map ref.: ANTTM F15.

Simpsons Gap camping area

Located 23.7 km west of the Telegraph Station. Vehicle access possible to Simpsons Gap carpark, which is 5 km north of Larapinta Drive. Gas/fuel stove preferred. Additional map ref.: ANTTM F15.

SECTION 2 – SIMPSONS GAP TO JAY CREEK (24 KM)

Bush camping

Suggested bush campsite 10 km west of Simpsons Gap. No facilities. Gas/fuel stove preferred. Additional map ref.: ANTTM F15.

Mulga Camp camping area

Located 13.4 km west of Simpsons Gap. Gas/fuel stove preferred. Additional map ref.: ANTTM F15.

Jay Creek camping area

Suggested camping areas beside Jay Creek, up- and downstream from Fish Hole (no camping allowed at Fish Hole as it is a sacred site and wildlife refuge). Gas/fuel stove preferred. Additional map ref.: ANTTM F15.

SECTION 3 – JAY CREEK TO STANDLEY CHASM (14 KM)

Millers Flat camping area

This is 8.9 km west of Jay Creek. Gas/fuel stove preferred. Additional map ref.: ANTTM F15.

SECTION 4 – STANDLEY CHASM TO BIRTHDAY WATERHOLE (18.3 KM)

Bush camping

There are three suggested bush campsites along this section, located 10.2 km, 16.7 km and 18 km west of

Standley Chasm. No facilities. Gas/fuel stove preferred. Additional map ref.: ANTTM F15.

Birthday Waterhole camping area

Located 18.3 km west of Standley Chasm. No facilities. Gas/fuel stove preferred. Only high-clearance 4WD vehicles can access Birthday Waterhole carpark. Additional map ref.: ANTTM F15.

SECTION 5 – BIRTHDAY WATERHOLE TO HUGH GORGE (15.2 KM)

Bush camping

There are two suggested bush campsites along this section, located 6.8 km and 11.5 km west of Birthday Waterhole. No facilities. Gas/fuel stove preferred. Additional map ref.: ANTTM F15.

Hugh Gorge camping area

This is 15.2 km west of Birthday Waterhole. No facilities. Gas/fuel stove preferred. Only high clearance 4WD vehicles can access Hugh Gorge carpark. Additional map ref.: ANTTM F15.

SECTION 6 – HUGH GORGE TO ELLERY CREEK (26.5 KM)

Ellery Creek Big Hole camping area

See West MacDonnell National Park, *page 281*

SECTION 7 – ELLERY CREEK TO SERPENTINE GORGE (26.5 KM)

No camping areas along this section.

SECTION 8 – SERPENTINE GORGE TO INARLANGA PASS (15.3 KM)

Serpentine Chalet Dam camping area

Bush campsite below Serpentine Chalet Dam 14.3 km west of Serpentine Gorge. No facilities. Gas/fuel stove preferred. Only 4WD vehicles can access Serpentine Chalet Ruins carpark. Additional map ref.: ANTTM F15.

SECTION 9 – INARLANGA PASS TO ORMISTON GORGE (27 KM)

Bush camping

Suggested bush campsites in gorge, about 11 km west of Inarlanga Pass, and at ridgetop lookout a further 2 km west. No facilities. Gas/fuel stove preferred. Additional map ref.: ANTTM E15.

Ormiston Gorge camping area

See West MacDonnell National Park, *page 281*

SECTION 10 – ORMISTON GORGE TO GLEN HELEN LODGE (12.5 KM)

There are no campsites between Ormiston Gorge and Glen Helen Lodge, however Glen Helen Lodge offers food and a range of accommodation. Walkers can also bush camp in sites along the Finke River between the trail and the lodge (lodge is 700 m south of the trail).

Bush camping

Campsites along Finke River between lodge and trail. No facilities. Gas/fuel stove preferred. Additional map ref.: ANTTM E15.

Glen Helen Gorge, near Glen Helen Lodge close to the Larapinta Trail

SECTION 11 – GLEN HELEN LODGE TO REDBANK GORGE (29 KM)

Rocky Bar Gap camping area

Bush campsite 15 km west of Glen Helen Lodge turn-off. No facilities. Gas/fuel stove preferred. Additional map ref.: ANTTM E15.

Redbank Gorge camping area

See West MacDonnell National Park, *page 281*

SECTION 12 – REDBANK GORGE TO MOUNT SONDER (16 KM RETURN)

No camping areas along this section.

Further information & bookings:
DIPE, Alice Springs **Tel.:** (08) 8951 8211

17. MOUNT EBENEZER ROADHOUSE

Mount Ebenezer is on the Lasseter Hwy. Mount Ebenezer Station is owned by the Imanpa Aboriginal community. Services here include fuel and accommodation as well as a dining room, bar and golf course. Local arts and crafts are sold at the roadhouse.

Mount Ebenezer Roadhouse camping area

Located on the Lasseter Hwy 57 km west of Erldunda. Roadhouse open 7 am–8 pm. Firewood supplied. Additional map ref.: ANTTM E16.

Further information & bookings: Mt Ebenezer Roadhouse **Tel.:** (08) 8956 2904 **Camping fees:** Unpowered from $5.00 per person/night, powered from $8.00 per person/night

18. N'DHALA GORGE NATURE PARK

N'Dhala Gorge Nature Park is 101 km east of Alice Springs. The park has significant Aboriginal cultural value – within it are over 5900 rock engravings along with spiritual sites and shelter areas. The marked walking trail has signs interpreting some of the engravings. Access to N'Dhala Gorge Nature Park is off the Ross River Homestead road, with the last 11 km being 4WD-access only.

N'Dhala Gorge camping area

Small campsite at park entrance, 11 km past Ross River Homestead (4WD only after this point) off Ross Hwy, 90 km east of Alice Springs. Bring drinking water and firewood. Generators not permitted. Additional map ref.: ANTTM G15.

Further information & bookings: DIPE, Alice Springs **Tel.:** (08) 8951 8211 **Camping fees:** From $3.30 per adult/night, $1.65 per child (age 5–15) per night; fees payable at self-registration station

19. OAK VALLEY

The Oak Valley community is 97 km south of Alice Springs. It is reached off the Old South Rd. Guided tours are available to Aboriginal art and engraving sites and to nearby alluvial fossil fields that date back 500 million years.

Oak Valley camping area

Drive 87 km south from Alice Springs down Old South Rd to signposted turn-off, then west for 10 km to gate. Firewood supplied. Additional map ref.: ANTTM F15.

Further information & bookings: Oak Valley Tours **Tel.:** (08) 8956 0959 **Email:** arnie@roonet.com.au **Website:** www.roonet.com.au **Camping fees:** From $8.00 per person/night

20. OLD ANDADO HOMESTEAD

Old Andado is a remote homestead on the western edge of the Simpson Desert. There is 2WD access from the west from Kulgera (on the Stuart Hwy) via Finke, although 4WD is recommended. Access from the north is 4WD only via the Old Andado Track from Santa Teresa. Drivers of conventional vehicles and caravans should check road conditions before travelling.

Old Andado Homestead camping area

Located on Old Andado Track, 270 km east of Kulgera and 321 km south of Alice Springs. Bring firewood. Additional map ref.: ANTTM H16.

Further information & bookings: Molly Clark, Old Andado Homestead **Tel.:** (08) 8956 0812 (phone March–Sept./Oct. only) **Camping fees:** From $7.00 per person/night; fees payable at homestead

21. RABBIT FLAT ROADHOUSE

Rabbit Flat Roadhouse is on Tanami Rd. Services here include fuel, supplies, a bar and camping. People towing caravans should check road conditions before travelling.

Rabbit Flat Roadhouse camping area

Roadhouse is 314 km north-west of Yuendumu and 125 km east of the Western Australian border, on Tanami Rd. Open 7 am–9 pm Fri.–Mon. only. Bring drinking water and firewood. Additional map ref.: ANTTM B11.

Further information & bookings: Rabbit Flat Roadhouse **Tel.:** (08) 8956 8744 **Camping fees:** From $3.00 per person/night

22. RAINBOW VALLEY CONSERVATION RESERVE

Rainbow Valley Conservation Reserve is 97 km south of Alice Springs. The coloured rock bands in the sandstone bluffs and cliffs are the main features of the reserve. A favourite spot for photographers, the cliffs and bluffs are at their best when highlighted with early morning or late afternoon light. Access to the reserve is via a soft sandy road and drivers of conventional vehicles are advised to check road conditions before travelling.

Rainbow Valley camping area

Signposted off the Stuart Hwy 75 km south of Alice Springs, then 22 km east. Bring drinking water and firewood. Gas/fuel stove preferred. Additional map ref.: ANTTM F15.

Further information & bookings: DIPE, Alice Springs **Tel.:** (08) 8951 8211 **Camping fees:** From $3.30 per adult/night, $1.65 per child (age 5–15) per night; fees payable at self-registration station

23. RUBY GAP NATURE PARK

Ruby Gap Nature Park is 150 km east of Alice Springs, 40 km past the Arltunga Historical Reserve with 4WD access only. After the discovery of some stones believed to be rubies in the bed of the Hale River during 1886, a 'ruby rush' began and over 200 people were reported to be prospecting here in May 1887. However, in the following year it was found that the stones were not rubies but high-grade garnets. With this the ruby rush died. Ruby Gap today offers beautiful gorge and river scenery. Visitors must register and deregister at the Arltunga Visitors Centre or on the Voluntary Registration Scheme, tel. 1300 650 730.

Bush camping

Dispersed camping along Hale River from park entrance to gorge (5 km). Suitable for self-sufficient campers. Bring drinking water and firewood. Additional map ref.: ANTTM H15.

Further information & bookings: PWCNT, Alice Springs **Tel.:** (08) 8951 8211 **Camping fees:** From $3.30 per adult/night, $1.65 per child (age 5–15) per night; fees payable at self-registration station

24. STUARTS WELL

Stuarts Well is on the Stuart Hwy south of Alice Springs. Services here include fuel, supplies and a restaurant and bar as well as guided tours and camel safaris.

Jims Place camping area

On the Stuart Hwy 90 km south of Alice Springs. Open 6 am–9 pm. Fire drums available but bring own firewood. Additional map ref.: ANTTM F15.

Further information & bookings: Jims Place **Tel.:** (08) 8956 0808 **Email:** cottours@topend.com.au **Camping fees:** Tent sites from $7.00 per person/night, van sites from $17.00 per 2 people/night; reduced rates apply to children

25. TILMOUTH WELL ROADHOUSE

Tilmouth is north-west of Alice Springs. Services at the roadhouse include supplies, fuel and a restaurant and bar.

Tilmouth Well Roadhouse camping area

On Tanami Rd 186 km north-west of Alice Springs. Roadhouse open 7 am–9 pm. Bring firewood. Bookings recommended June–Aug. Additional map ref.: ANTTM E14.

Further information & bookings: Tilmouth Well Roadhouse **Tel.:** (08) 8956 8777 **Camping fees:** From $6.00 per person/night, power additional $6.00 per site/night

26. TI TREE

Ti Tree is north of Alice Springs. The town has a gallery which sells local Aboriginal arts and crafts. The Ti Tree Roadhouse has fuel, a restaurant, a bar and accommodation.

Ti-Tree Roadhouse camping area

On the Stuart Hwy 193 km north of Alice Springs. Roadhouse open 6 am–10 pm. Gas/fuel stove only. Bookings recommended June–July. Additional map ref.: ANTTM F13.

Further information & bookings: Ti Tree Roadhouse **Tel.:** (08) 8956 9741 **Camping fees:** Unpowered from $6.00 per person/night or $11.00 per 2 people/night, powered from $17.00 per 2 people/night

27. TOBERMOREY STATION

Tobermorey Station is next to the Queensland border. Fuel and supplies are available here.

Tobermorey Station camping area

On the Plenty Hwy 494 km east of the Stuart Hwy. Open: 6 am–8 pm. Firewood supplied. Additional map ref.: ANTTM K13.

Further information & bookings: Tobermorey Station **Tel.:** (07) 4748 4996 **Camping fees:** From $20.00 per 2 people/night; extra $5.00 per additional person/night

28. TREPHINA GORGE NATURE PARK

In the East MacDonnell Ranges, Trephina Gorge is known for its river red gum-lined watercourses and sheer cliffs. The waterholes in the gorge attract a range of birds and other wildlife. There are three short walking trails within the park, while more experienced walkers can enjoy the Ridgetop Trail from Trephina Gorge to John Hayes Rockhole. Those planning on taking a cooling dip should be aware that the water in the swimming holes is extremely cold and prolonged exposure is not recommended. The entrance road is signposted off the Ross Hwy 66 km east of Alice Springs. The collection of firewood in the park is prohibited.

John Hayes Rockhole campground

This is 7 km north of the Ross Hwy, off the main park road. 4WD access only. Bring drinking water and firewood. Gas/fuel stove preferred. Additional map ref.: ANTTM G14.

Trephina Bluff campground

Located 9 km north of the Ross Hwy. Bring firewood. Gas/fuel stove preferred. Additional map ref.: ANTTM G14.

Trephina Gorge campground

This is 9 km north of the Ross Hwy. Bring firewood. Gas/fuel stove preferred. Additional map ref.: ANTTM G14.

Further information & bookings: DIPE, Alice Springs **Tel.:** (08) 8951 8211 **Camping fees:** From $3.30 per adult/night, $1.65 per child (age 5–15) per night; fees payable at self-registration stations

29. ULURU–KATA TJUTA NATIONAL PARK

Uluru is without doubt one of Australia's best known natural wonders. It was first sighted by Europeans in 1873 when explorer William Gosse led a party attempting to cross to the west. He sighted and named Mt Connor, then glanced to the west at a hill that upon closer inspection was found to be a rock. He named it Ayers Rock, after the then premier of South Australia Sir Henry Ayers. The Olgas, or Kata Tjuta, were sighted by Ernest Giles in 1872 and he named them after his financier, Baron von Mueller, who later changed the name to Mt Olga after Queen Olga. The entire region of Uluru and Kata Tjuta has a deep cultural significance for the local Aboriginal people, the Anangu. These two landmarks are now known by their traditional Anangu names. There are numerous walks at both sites. About 2 km before Uluru is the Uluru–Kata Tjuta National Park Cultural Centre, which is well worth spending some time in before proceeding to the rock. The park is south-west of Alice Springs and reached by the Lasseter Hwy, west off the Stuart Hwy. As camping is not permitted in the park, Ayers Rock Resort is the nearest campground.

Ayers Rock Resort campground

Signposted off Yulara Drive, off Lasseter Hwy, 247 km west of Stuart Hwy. Reception open 7 am–9 pm. Gas/fuel stove only. Additional map ref.: ANTTM C16.

Bookings: Ayers Rock Resort campground **Tel.:** (08) 8956 2055 **Website:** www.ayersrockresort.com.au **Camping fees:** Unpowered from $12.10 per person/night (for the first 2 people), powered from $28.60 per 2 people/night **Further information:** Uluru–Kata Tjuta National Park Cultural Centre **Tel.:** (08) 8956 3138 **Email:** uluru.informationdesk@ea.gov.au **Website:** www.ea.gov.au/parks/uluru **Park entry fee:** $16.25 per person (over 16 years), valid for 3 consecutive days

30. WALLACE ROCKHOLE

Wallace Rockhole is south-west of Alice Springs and is signposted off Larapinta Drive. The Aranda Aboriginal community has guided hiking and rock-art tours and sells traditional art and craft. Other services here include fuel and a general store. People towing caravans should check road conditions before travelling.

Wallace Rockhole Tourist Park camping area

From Alice Springs travel west along Larapinta Drive for 96 km then turn south at signposted turn-off. Rockhole is 17 km south of Larapinta Drive. Open 8 am–5.30 pm. Bring firewood. Bookings recommended for powered sites. Additional map ref.: ANTTM E15.

Further information & bookings: Wallace Rockhole Tourist Park **Tel.:** (08) 8956 7993 **Camping fees:** Unpowered from $8.00 per adult/night, $4.00 per child (age 5–15) per night, power an additional $1.00 per person/night

31. WATARRKA NATIONAL PARK

Watarrka National Park is south-west of Alice Springs. It is reached via Luritja Rd off Lasseter Hwy or from Alice Springs via Larapinta Drive (330 km, permit required for this route) or Luritja Rd off Ernest Giles Rd (333 km). Landscapes in the park range from moist gorges and rockholes to rugged crags. Visitors can picnic or enjoy one of the walking tracks. Some walking tracks are wheelchair accessible. Camping is not permitted within the park but Kings Creek Station and Kings Canyon Resort are both nearby. For information on activities within the park contact DIPE Alice Springs, tel. (08) 8951 8211.

Kings Canyon Resort camping area

Signposted off Luritja Rd, Kings Canyon Resort is 8 km north-west of the national park entrance road. Services include fuel and a tennis court, mini mart, bar and cafe. Bring firewood. Dogs must stay on leash and in the camping area. Additional map ref.: ANTTM D15.

Further information & bookings: Kings Canyon Resort **Tel.:** (08) 8956 7442 **Email:** reskcr@austarnet.com.au **Website:** www.voyages.com.au **Camping fees:** Unpowered from $14.00 per person/night (first 2 people), powered from $16.00 per person/night (first 2 people); rates drop for additional nights

Kings Creek Station camping area

Signposted off Luritja Rd, Kings Creek Station is located 35 km south-east of the national park entrance road. Other activities here include camel safaris, helicopter flights and quad-bike tours. Bring firewood. Additional map ref.: ANTTM D15.

Further information & bookings: Kings Creek Station **Tel.:** (08) 8956 7474 **Email:** info@kingscreekstation.com.au **Website:** www.kingscreekstation.com.au **Camping fees:** Unpowered from $11.20 per person/night, power an additional $3.00 per site/night; reduced rates apply for children

32. WAUCHOPE

Wauchope is 10 km south of Devils Marbles Conservation Reserve. The area was extensively mined for tungsten between WW I and WW II.

Wauchope Hotel camping area

Located on the Stuart Hwy 114 km south of Tennant Creek. Hotel open 6 am–11 pm. Bring firewood. Bookings essential. Additional map ref.: ANTTM G11.

Further information & bookings: Wauchope Hotel **Tel.:** (08) 8964 1963 **Camping fees:** Unpowered from $5.00 per person/night, powered from $14.50 per 2 people/night

33. WEST MACDONNELL NATIONAL PARK
see page 281

34. WYCLIFFE WELL

Wycliffe Well's history dates back to the construction of the Overland Telegraph Line. It is also well known for regular sightings of UFOs.

Wycliffe Well Holiday Park

Located on the Stuart Hwy 131 km south of Tennant Creek and 17 km south of Wauchope. Open 6.30 am–11 pm. Bookings preferred. Additional map ref.: ANTTM G12.

Further information & bookings: Wycliffe Well Holiday Park **Tel.:** (08) 8964 1966 **Email:** info@wycliffe.com.au **Website:** www.wycliffe.com.au **Camping fees:** Tent site from $20.00 per 2 people/night, powered site from $22.00 per 2 people/night

WEST MACDONNELL NATIONAL PARK

A gap and some gums

Simpsons Gap was carved through a rock face by the flow of water. It is framed by a set of towering cliffs, and offset by majestic river red gums and a picturesque creek bed and waterhole. This scenic site is just 25 kilometres from Alice Springs and can be reached by car, bike or foot.

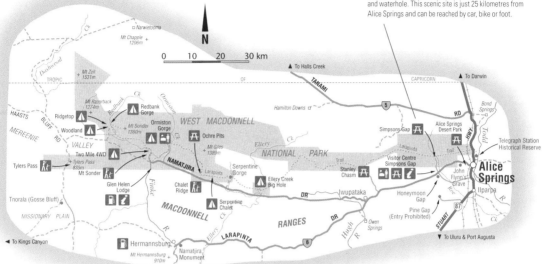

West MacDonnell National Park stretches from Alice Springs to Mt Zeil. Within the park are magnificent red gorges and deep waterholes. Visitors can enjoy picnicking, walking (including the epic Larapinta Trail), swimming and cycling on the track to Simpsons Gap. Please note that there are many more campsites in this park available to those walking the Larapinta Trail (see page 276 for details). The collection of firewood in the park is prohibited, gas/fuel stoves are preferred and generators are not permitted.

Ellery Creek Big Hole camping area

Signposted off Namatjira Drive. Also accessed via the Larapinta Trail, 26.5 km west of Hugh Gorge camping area. Bring drinking water. Additional map ref.: ANTTM E15.

Ormiston Gorge camping area

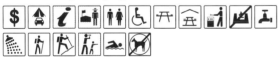

Signposted off Namatjira Drive. Also accessed via the Larapinta Trail, 27 km west of Inarlanga Pass. Additional map ref.: ANTTM E15.

Redbank Gorge camping area

Conventional vehicle access off Namatjira Drive. For those walking the Larapinta Trail, this site is 25.5 km west of the Glen Helen Lodge turn-off. Additional map ref.: ANTTM E15.

Ridgetop camping area

North of Woodland camping area. 4WD vehicles recommended. Bring drinking water. Additional map ref.: ANTTM E15.

Serpentine Chalet camping area

Signposted off Namatjira Drive. Bring drinking water. Additional map ref.: ANTTM E15.

Two Mile 4WD camping area

North of Namatjira Drive. Access is just west of the Glen Helen Lodge turn-off. 4WD vehicles necessary and self-sufficient campers only. Bring drinking water. Additional map ref.: ANTTM E15.

Woodland camping area

Access from Redbank Gorge Rd off Namatjira Drive. Conventional vehicles can reach camping area with care. Bring drinking water. Additional map ref.: ANTTM E15.

Further information & bookings: DIPE, Alice Springs **Tel.:** (08) 8951 8211 **Camping fees:** *Ellery Creek Big Hole, Redbank Gorge, Ridgetop and Woodland:* From $3.30 per adult/night, $1.65 per child (age 5–15) per night *Ormiston Gorge:* From $6.60 per adult/night, $3.30 per child (age 5–15) per night. Fees payable at self-registration stations

QUEENSLAND

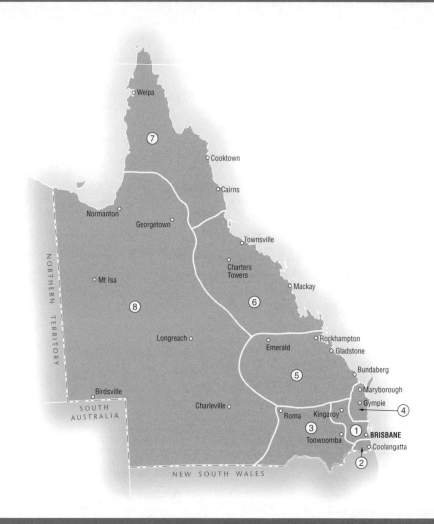

TOP 10 CAMPSITES

Dundubara camping area
Fraser Island (Great Sandy National Park), page 303

Charlie Moreland camping area
Kenilworth State Forest, page 305

Smalleys Beach camping area
Cape Hillsborough National Park, page 316

Joes Beach Camping area
Whitsunday Islands National Park, page 325

Kalpowar Crossing Campground
Lakefield National Park, page 334

Eliot Falls camping area
Jardine River National Park, page 331

Carnarvon Gorge camping area
Carnarvon National Park, page 309

Hunters Gorge Campground
Diamantina National Park, page 345

Burke and Wills Dig Tree camping area
Burke and Wills Dig Tree, page 343

Lawn Hill camping area
Boodjamulla (Lawn Hill) National Park, page 342

Q UEENSLAND IS KNOWN THE WORLD OVER FOR ITS DIVERSE AND BEAUTIFUL LANDSCAPES – TROPICAL ISLANDS, ANCIENT RAINFORESTS, RICH FARMING PLAINS, A VAST AND REDDENED OUTBACK AND ONE OF THE MOST SINGULARLY SPECTACULAR COASTLINES IN THE WORLD. THE HIGH NUMBERS OF TOURISTS TO THE STATE MEAN THAT GENERAL VISITOR FACILITIES ARE EXCELLENT, WITH CAMPING FACILITIES NO EXCEPTION. THE BIGGEST PROBLEM CAMPERS FACE HERE IS COMPETITION FOR AVAILABLE SITES, AND HIGH RAINFALL IN TROPICAL AREAS DURING THE WET SEASON, FROM OCTOBER TO APRIL.

In the immediate vicinity of the large and busy city of Brisbane are a number of well-preserved natural areas. Brisbane Forest Park, literally on the city's doorstep, has remote walk-in bush campsites in near-pristine surrounds. To the north-west lies the rugged bush and rainforest landscape of the Bunya Mountains, while in Moreton Bay peaceful offshore islands are just a quick ferry ride away.

The coastline to the immediate south and north of Brisbane – the Gold Coast and the Sunshine Coast – contains some of Australia's most famous beach scenery along with sophisticated holiday facilities. For something quieter, visit the World Heritage-listed Fraser Island, with its strong eco focus, or the national parks that protect the mountains and forests of the Gold Coast hinterland.

The tropical regions of Capricorn, the Mid Tropics and the Far North take in a vast stretch of Queensland's eastern coastline, all offering access to the exquisite scenery of the Great Barrier Reef. Exploring the colourful underwater world of the reef is a must, and those travelling by four-wheel drive can venture north of Cairns where the highlights include Aboriginal rock art around Laura as well as the near-trackless wilderness en route to the continent's most northern point, Cape York.

Agricultural Queensland is on display throughout the fertile Darling Downs region, where you will find a number of excellent conservation areas with good camping opportunities. The vast Outback and Gulf region is another mix of classic Australian farming scenery and untouched natural environments, including Boodjamulla (Lawn Hill) National Park, one of the country's top camping destinations.

South Molle Island, in the Great Barrier Reef

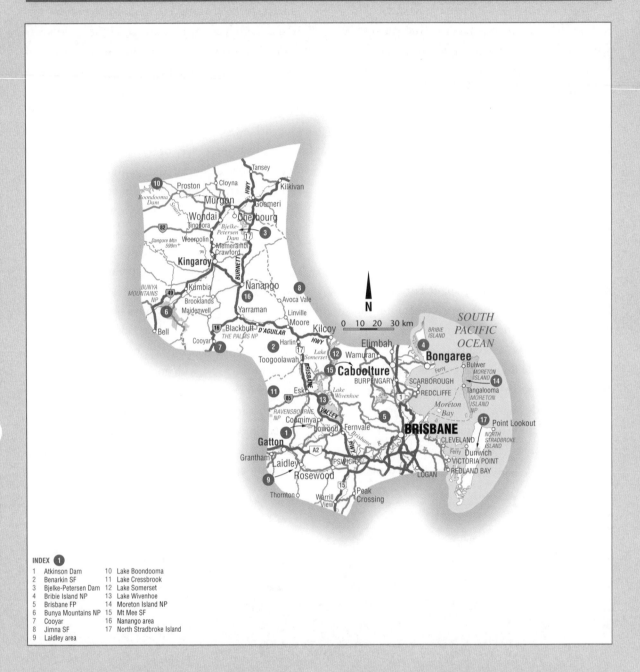

INDEX ❶

1	Atkinson Dam	10	Lake Boondooma
2	Benarkin SF	11	Lake Cressbrook
3	Bjelke-Petersen Dam	12	Lake Somerset
4	Bribie Island NP	13	Lake Wivenhoe
5	Brisbane FP	14	Moreton Island NP
6	Bunya Mountains NP	15	Mt Mee SF
7	Cooyar	16	Nanango area
8	Jimna SF	17	North Stradbroke Island
9	Laidley area		

THE HINTERLANDS OF BRISBANE
OFFER A RANGE OF NATURE-
BASED ACTIVITIES AND TOURING
DESTINATIONS. ONE HIGHLIGHT
IS THE HERITAGE CITY OF
IPSWICH, WHILE IN THE BLUE
WATERS OF MORETON BAY OFF THE COAST OF
BRISBANE ARE NORTH STRADBROKE, MORETON
AND BRIBIE ISLANDS.

A short drive from central Brisbane, in the
D'Aguilar Range, is the superb bushland of
Brisbane Forest Park. The park's forestry roads
double as great horse and mountain bike trails,
and there are a number of walk-in bush campsites.

Lake Wivenhoe, to the east of Esk, and
Lake Somerset, south of Kilcoy, have wonderful
foreshore camping spots. Campers will find
excellent facilities including hot showers and
drinking water, and the lakes are popular for
fishing, boating, canoeing, sailing and waterskiing.

The scenery in Bunya Mountains National
Park ranges from the tall dome-shaped crown of

the bunya pine to both moist and dry rainforests in the lower sections. There are three camping areas in the park and Dandabah, the main camping area, is accessible to caravans and has hot showers. Look out for the superbly coloured king parrots and crimson rosellas along with the red-necked wallabies and swamp wallabies.

The large sand island of North Stradbroke is a short ferry ride from Cleveland. It has wide golden beaches and the inland boasts spectacular bushland and magnificent freshwater lakes. Campers on 'Straddie' can opt for one of the many council-run caravan and camping areas, or foreshore bush camping along Main and Flinders beaches. A visit to the beautiful Blue Lake, and a swim, is a must.

Moreton Island is also known for its long, sandy beaches, high dunes and clear freshwater lagoons. It is reached by ferry, and once on Moreton a four-wheel drive is necessary as there are no sealed roads. Designated camping areas, with limited facilities, are on both the east and west coast, with beach camping also possible. North of Moreton Bay and connected to the mainland via a bridge is Bribie Island. Camping is also possible here, with two camping areas accessible by four-wheel drive and the other two by boat from Pumicestone Passage.

BEST CAMPSITES

Dandabah camping area
Bunya Mountains National Park

Main Beach camping area
North Stradbroke Island

Bush camping
Brisbane Forest Park

Amity Point camping area
North Stradbroke Island

Blue Lagoon camping area
Moreton Island National Park

BEST TIME TO VISIT

All year round. The islands are extremely popular and can become crowded during the summer periods.

1. ATKINSON DAM

Atkinson Dam is west of Brisbane and 10 km south-west of Coominya. The dam caters for watersports with swimming, fishing, waterskiing, canoeing and sailing being popular. Many people come to the dam to picnic.

Atkinson Dam Cabin Village

Signposted from Atkinson Dam Rd 8 km south-west of Coominya. Laundry facilities and shop. Bookings advisable for public holidays. Additional map ref.: STM Qld K8.

Further information & bookings: Atkinson Dam Cabin Village **Tel.:** (07) 5426 4211 **Email:** atkinson_dam.cab.vil@telstra.com **Camping fees:** From $7.00 per person/night; power additional $2.00 per site/night

Atkinson Dam Waterfront Caravan Park

Signposted from Atkinson Dam Rd 10 km south-west of Coominya. Laundry facilities and shop. Dogs allowed but enquire at office first. Bookings advisable. Additional map ref.: STM Qld K8.

Further information & bookings: Atkinson Dam Waterfront Caravan Park **Tel.:** (07) 5426 4151 **Camping fees:** From $6.60 per person (age 11 and over) per night, $3.30 per child (age 2–11) per night, power additional $2.75 per site/night

2. BENARKIN STATE FOREST

In the scenic Blackbutt Range, Benarkin State Forest has a diverse range of tree species: grey gums, white mahogany, blackbutts, tallowwood and hoop pine. The forest offers a range of activities, including bushwalking, horseriding and cycling. Those wishing to horseride or cycle must first obtain a permit. Benarkin State Forest is reached on Benarkin Forest Drive, which leaves D'Aguilar Hwy 5 km east of Blackbutt.

Clancys camping area

On Benarkin Forest Drive 13 km south of D'Aguilar Hwy and 18 km south-east of Blackbutt. On the National Bicentennial Trail. Camping permit required. Tank drinking water – boil before use or bring own. Firewood supplied. Additional map ref.: STM Qld K8.

Emu Creek camping area

On Benarkin Forest Drive 15 km south of D'Aguilar Hwy and 20 km south-east of Blackbutt. Camping permit required. Tank drinking water – boil before use or bring own. Firewood supplied. Additional map ref.: STM Qld K8.

Further information:
QPWS, Toowoomba **Tel.:** (07) 4639 4599 or Naturally Queensland Information Centre **Tel.:** (07) 3227 8197/8186 **Camping fees:** From $4.00 per person/night; permit from and fees payable at self-registration station

3. BJELKE-PETERSEN DAM

Bjelke-Petersen Dam, 13 km south-east of Murgon, is a popular place for watersports. The dam is surrounded by native bushland and the area has a variety of birds and other wildlife. The dam is signposted along Barambah Rd, which is off the Burnett and Bunya hwys. A Stocked Impoundment Permit is required to fish in the dam.

Yallakool Tourist Park

Signposted from Barambah Rd. Laundry facilities. Bookings recommended for powered sites. Additional map ref.: STM Qld K7.

Further information & bookings: Yallakool Tourist Park **Tel.:** (07) 4168 4746 **Email:** yallakooltp@burnett.net.au **Website:** www.yallakool.murgon.qld.gov.au **Camping fees:** Unpowered from $12.10 per site/night for 2 people, powered from $16.50 per site/night for 2 people

4. BRIBIE ISLAND NATIONAL PARK

Bribie Island is a sand island 34 km long and up to 8 km wide. It is east of Caboolture, at the northern end of Moreton Bay, and is separated from the mainland by Pumicestone Passage. The island is a popular destination for surfers, bushwalkers, birdwatchers, anglers and picnickers. Bribie Island is reached via the Caboolture–Bribie Island Rd or by boat.

Gallaghers Point camping area

This is 3.5 km north of the ranger headquarters at White Patch. Boat or 4WD access via White Patch Esplanade. Camping permit required. Bring drinking water and firewood. Can use existing fire sites but gas/fuel stove preferred. Additional map ref.: STM Qld K8.

Lime Pocket camping area

North of Mission Point on the western side of island. Boat access only. Camping permit required. Bring drinking water and firewood. Can use existing fire sites but gas/fuel stove preferred. Additional map ref.: STM Qld K8.

Mission Point camping area

North of Poverty Creek on the western side of island. Boat access only. Camping permit required. Bring drinking water and firewood. Gas/fuel stove preferred. Additional map ref.: STM Qld K8.

Ocean Beach camping area

Camping permit and 4WD Beach Access Permit required. 4WD beach access via North St, Woorim (check tide times). Camping area is 16 km north of beach access point and runs for 3 km. Bring drinking water and firewood. Can use existing fire sites but gas/fuel stove preferred. Additional map ref.: STM Qld K8.

Poverty Creek camping area

North of Gallaghers Point on the western side of island. Boat access only. Camping permit required. Bring drinking water

and firewood. Gas/fuel stove preferred. Additional map ref.: STM Qld K8.

Further information: QPWS, Bribie Island National Park **Tel.:** (07) 3408 8451 **Camping fees:** From $4.00 per person/night; permit from and fees payable at ranger headquarters, White Patch (vehicle access), or self-registration station at Mission Point (boat access) **4WD Beach Access Permit:** Caboolture Shire Council **Tel.:** (07) 5420 0100 **Permit fees:** Daily $21.50, weekly $31.00 or annual $72.00

5. BRISBANE FOREST PARK

Brisbane Forest Park is only a short drive from the centre of Brisbane. Visitors will find scenic lookouts, picnic and barbecue areas, a range of walking tracks, horse and cycle trails and a wildlife centre. Within the park are waterfalls, rainforests and eucalypt forests, native wildflowers and Aboriginal art sites. Park headquarters is at 60 Mount Nebo Rd, The Gap, and is the ideal place to start your exploration of the park. After you have applied for a camping permit and made a booking (1 week in advance) staff can recommend campsites and help plan your walking trip.

Bush camping

Bush campsites along various walking trails through the park. Suitable for self-sufficient campers only. Camping permit required. Bring drinking water. Gas/fuel stove only. Additional map ref.: STM Qld K8.

Further information & bookings: Brisbane Forest Park **Tel.:** (07) 3300 4855 **Email:** BrisbaneForestPark@epa.qld.gov.au **Website:** www.brisbaneforestpark.qld.gov.au **Permits:** Apply for camping permits at least 1 week in advance **Camping fees:** From $4.00 per person/night

6. BUNYA MOUNTAINS NATIONAL PARK
see page 288

7. COOYAR

The village of Cooyar is on the New England Hwy 90 km north of Toowoomba.

Cooyar Showgrounds

On Rangemore Rd, Cooyar, signposted off New England Hwy. Hot showers by arrangement. Water from tank – boil before use. Gas/fuel stove only. No camping during time of shows and campdrafts. Additional map ref.: STM Qld K7.

Further information & bookings: Cooyar Show Society Secretary **Tel.:** (07) 4692 6101 **Camping fees:** From $5.00 per site/night; fees collected by caretaker

Swing Bridge Park camping area

Beside Cooyar Creek. Reached via Munroe St, behind Cooyar Hotel. Bring firewood. There is a 48-hour limit to stays here. Additional map ref.: STM Qld K7.

Further information: Cooyar Fishing Club **Tel.:** (07) 4692 6150

8. JIMNA STATE FOREST

Clear mountain streams, swimming holes and scenic walking trails are some of the attractions in Jimna State Forest. Those with stamina may wish to climb the 241 steps to the top of the Jimna Fire Tower for magnificent views. Jimna is 40 km north of Kilcoy.

Peach Trees camping area

North-west of Jimna. Reached via Peach Trees Rd off Kilcoy–Murgon Rd. Camping permit required. Coin-operated shower. Water from tank – boil before use. Some firewood supplied. Additional map ref.: STM Qld K8.

Further information: QPWS, Kenilworth
Tel.: (07) 5446 0925 **Camping fees:** From $4.00 per person/night; permit from and fees payable at self-registration station

9. LAIDLEY AREA

Laidley has much to offer visitors: take in the views from Cunninghams Crest or Schultz lookouts, enjoy a picnic at Narda Lagoon Nature Reserve, walk or drive the self-guide Heritage Trail or throw in a line at Lake Dyer. Laidley is south of the Warrego Hwy and east of Toowoomba.

Centenary Park Camping Ground

Signposted from Mulgowie Rd in Thornton, 15 km south of Laidley. Bring firewood. Additional map ref.: STM Qld K8.

Further information & bookings:
Lockyer Valley Tourist Information Centre **Tel.:** (07) 5465 7642 or Laidley Shire Council **Tel.:** (07) 5465 1166 **Website:** www.laidley.qld.gov.au
Camping fees: First 3 nights free; for additional nights contact council for rates and details

Lake Dyer Camping and Caravan Ground

On Gatton–Laidley Rd 1.5 km west of Laidley. Refundable ($10.00) key deposit for amenities. Firewood supplied. Maximum stay of 1 week. Additional map ref.: STM Qld K8.

Further information & bookings:
Lake Dyer caretaker **Tel.:** (07) 5465 3698 or Laidley Shire Council **Tel.:** (07) 5465 1166
Website: www.laidley.qld.gov.au
Camping fees: First 2 nights free; additional nights unpowered from $9.50 per site/night, powered from $18.00 per site/night

10. LAKE BOONDOOMA

Lake Boondooma is an ideal spot for fishing, birdwatching, swimming, canoeing, sailing or just relaxing. It is 20 km north-west of Proston. The lake is reached via the Boondooma Dam Rd off the Wondai–Proston Rd. A Stocked Impoundment Permit is needed for fishing.

Lake Boondooma camping and recreation area

Camp fires allowed. Firewood supplied. Bookings recommended for powered sites. Additional map ref.: STM Qld K7.

Further information & bookings: Lake Boondooma camping and recreation area **Tel.:** (07) 4168 9694
Email: lakeboodooma@wondaishire.com **Website :** www.wondai.qld.gov.au **Camping fees:** Unpowered from

$10.00 per site/night for 2 adults, powered from $15.00 per site/night for 2 adults

11. LAKE CRESSBROOK

Lake Cressbrook, 50 km north of Toowoomba via Pechey on the New England Hwy, is an ideal place to relax and enjoy the surrounds. The lake is popular for fishing, windsurfing and boating and can be reached from Esk via the Esk–Hampton Rd. A Recreation Permit is required for water-based activities here. A weekly permit costs $5.75 per person and is available from on-site rangers and the council; contact the council for further details. A Stocked Impoundment Permit is also needed to fish in the lake.

Lake Cressbrook camping area

This is 13 km north-east of Pechey, signposted off New England Hwy from Crows Nest and Pechey. Only small caravans can access the site. Firewood supplied. Additional map ref.: STM Qld K8.

Further information: Toowoomba City Council
Tel.: (07) 4688 6540 **Camping fees:** From $5.80 per person/night; fees payable at self-registration station

12. LAKE SOMERSET

Lake Somerset is a popular watersports venue about 90 km north-west of Brisbane. Activities here include swimming, fishing, sailing, powerboating and waterskiing. The picturesque settings of Kirkleagh and Somerset Park on the lake's western shores are ideal camping areas. Access to Lake Somerset is along the Esk–Kilcoy Rd. A Stocked Impoundment Permit is needed to fish in the lake.

Kirkleagh camping area

About 10 km south of Kilcoy on Kirkleagh Rd, which is signposted off Kilcoy–Somerset Rd. Firewood supplied. Additional map ref.: STM Qld K8.

Further information:
Lake Somerset Ranger **Tel.:** (07) 5497 1093 or Lake Wivenhoe Information and Tourism Centre
Tel.: (07) 5427 8100
Camping fees: From $20.00 per vehicle (up to 6 people) per night; fees payable at entry office or to ranger **Boating permit:** Permit required for all registrable and/or trailer vessels; permit is $15.00 per week and is available from ranger

Somerset Park camping area

Signposted off Esk–Kilcoy Rd, 25 km north-east of Esk and 26 km south of Kilcoy. Firewood supplied. Additional map ref.: STM Qld K8.

Further information: Somerset Park caretaker
Tel.: (07) 5426 0108 **Camping fees:** From $15.00 per vehicle/night; fees payable to caretaker, who visits daily
Boating permit: Permit required for all registrable and/or trailer vessels; permit is $15.00 per week and is available from ranger

BUNYA MOUNTAINS NATIONAL PARK

Forests, pools and mountain scenery

There are a couple of popular walks leading from the Dandabah camping area. The Bunya Bunya walking track is an easy 500-metre stroll through a section of superb rainforest, while a more challenging four-kilometre circuit takes you past rock pools up towards a lookout, with a vista of dramatic mountain scenery.

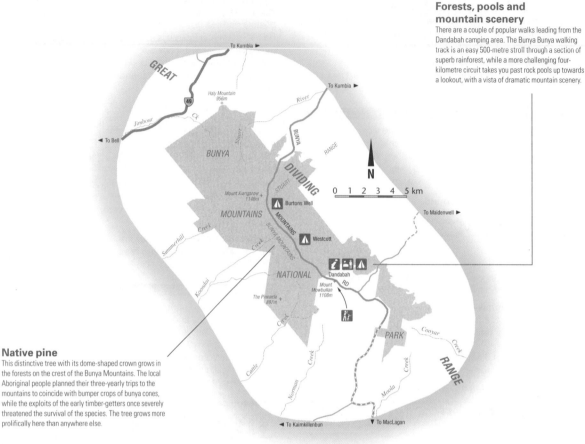

Native pine

This distinctive tree with its dome-shaped crown grows in the forests on the crest of the Bunya Mountains. The local Aboriginal people planned their three-yearly trips to the mountains to coincide with bumper crops of bunya cones, while the exploits of the early timber-getters once severely threatened the survival of the species. The tree grows more prolifically here than anywhere else.

The Bunya Mountains have a diverse history. Before European settlement Aboriginal tribes gathered here every three years for ceremonies, hunting and corroborees, while timber cutters were active here during the 1860s, the last sawmill closing in 1945. Throughout the park the bunya pine's distinctive dome-shaped crown rises above the surrounding rainforest. Bunya Mountains National Park is 55 km north-east of Dalby via Kaimkillenbun, 55 km south-west of Nanango via Maidenwell, and 56 km south-west of Kingaroy via Kumbia. Rangers request that visitors do not feed the birds or other wildlife in the park. Bookings are recommended for long weekends, school holidays, Easter and Christmas and can be made up to 6 months in advance.

Burtons Well camping area

On Bunya Mountains Rd 4 km north of Westcott camping area. Walk-in sites 5–20 m from parking area. Camping permit required. Donkey hot-water shower. Bring drinking water. Some firewood supplied. Gas/fuel stove preferred. Additional map ref.: STM Qld K7.

Dandabah camping area

On Bunya Ave off Bunya Mountains Rd, 60 km north of Dalby and 30 km west of Maidenwell. Camping permit required. Bring drinking water. Gas/fuel stove only. Additional map ref.: STM Qld K7.

Westcott camping area

On Bunya Mountains Rd 4 km north of Dandabah camping area. Walk-in sites 5–20 m from parking area. Camping permit required. Bring drinking water. Some firewood supplied. Gas/fuel stove preferred. Additional map ref.: STM Qld K7.

Further information: Naturally Queensland Information Centre **Tel.:** (07) 3227 8197/8186 **Further information & bookings:** Smart Service Queensland **Tel.:** 13 13 04 **Website:** www.qld.gov.au **Camping fees:** From $4.00 per person/night; permit from and fees payable at self-registration stations outside peak periods

13. LAKE WIVENHOE

Wivenhoe Dam was built in the 1950s to help reduce the damage caused by flooding to the Brisbane River system. Today the lake is a popular place for canoeing, sailing and fishing. Lake Wivenhoe is signposted off the Brisbane Valley Hwy north of Coominya. A Stocked Impoundment Permit is required to fish here and no outboard motors are allowed.

Captain Logan Camp

This is 11 km north of Coominya on Hay Rd, signposted off Brisbane Valley Hwy. Caravan access is limited to vans of single axle up to 4.9 m. Boat ramp nearby at Logan Inlet. No generators. Firewood supplied. Additional map ref.: STM Qld K8.

Lumley Hill camping area

Located 11 km north of Coominya on Hay Rd, signposted off Brisbane Valley Hwy. Boat ramp nearby at Logan Inlet. No generators. Firewood supplied. Bookings essential. Additional map ref.: STM Qld K8.

Further information & bookings: Lake Wivenhoe Camp manager **Tel.:** (07) 5426 4729 **Camping fees:** From $25.00 per site/night up to 4 people, power available at Lumley Hill for an additional $5.00 per site/night **Boating permit:** Permit required for all registrable and/or trailer vessels; permit is $15.00 per week

14. MORETON ISLAND NATIONAL PARK

Moreton Island provides peaceful surroundings in which to relax. Visitors can swim, fish and surf along the beautiful sandy beaches, dive or snorkel the Tangalooma Wrecks, swim in clear freshwater lagoons, view birds and wildlife and go walking or 4WD touring – a 4WD vehicle is the only form of motorised transport allowed on the island. Access to Moreton Island is by vehicle ferry.

Ben-Ewa camping area

This is 1 km north of the Wrecks on the island's west coast. Camping permit required. Bring firewood. Gas/fuel stove preferred. Additional map ref.: STM Qld K8.

Blue Lagoon camping area

On eastern side of island. Access road from Bulwer or Eastern Beach. Camping permit required. Bring firewood. Gas/fuel stove preferred. Additional map ref.: STM Qld K8.

Comboyuro Point camping area

On island's western shore, north of Bulwer. Camping permit required. Bring firewood. Gas/fuel stove preferred. Additional map ref.: STM Qld K8.

Eagers Creek camping area

On island's eastern beach. Access via Middle Rd from The Wrecks and Ben-Ewa. Camping permit required. Bring firewood. Gas/fuel stove preferred. Additional map ref.: STM Qld K8.

The Wrecks camping area

On island's western shore 3 km north of Tangalooma Resort. Vehicle ferry lands here. Camping permit required. Bring firewood. Gas/fuel stove preferred. Additional map ref.: STM Qld K8.

Beach camping

Camping permit required. Camp only in existing campsites and use only existing roads and tracks. Bring firewood. Gas/fuel stove preferred.

Further information: QPWS, Moreton Island National Park **Tel.:** (07) 3408 2710 **Camping fees:** From $4.00 per person/night; camping permit from and fees payable to ferry operators **Vehicle permits:** All vehicles must have a current vehicle permit; permits are $30.80 per vehicle, valid for 1 month; permit from and fees payable to ferry operators **Ferry operators:** Moreton Venture Ferry Service **Tel.:** (07) 3895 1000 or Combie Trader Ferry **Tel.:** (07) 3203 6399 or Tangalooma Passenger Launch **Tel.:** (07) 3268 6333

15. MOUNT MEE STATE FOREST

At the northern end of the D'Aguilar Range, Mount Mee State Forest includes a variety of forest types, from dry open forests to scribbly gum forests, rainforests and pine plantations. Visitors here can enjoy cool mountain streams and a number of lookouts and walking tracks. Conventional vehicle access is along Sellin Rd, 10 km west of the village of Mount Mee, which is on the Brisbane–Woodford Rd 22 km north of Dayboro and 13 km south of D'Aguilar on the D'Aguilar Hwy.

Archer camping area

On Lovedays Rd 17 km north of forest entry and 27 km north-west of Mount Mee. Camping permit and Permit to Traverse required (both must be obtained prior to arrival). Bring drinking water. Firewood supplied. Additional map ref.: STM Qld K8.

Neurum Creek camping area

On Neurum Creek Rd 7 km north of forest entry and 17 km north-west of Mount Mee. Camping permit required. Boil water before use. Firewood supplied. Additional map ref.: STM Qld K8.

Further information: Naturally Queensland Information Centre **Tel.:** (07) 3227 8197/8186 **Camping fees:** From $4.00 per person/night *Neurum Creek* Permit from and fees payable at self-registration station

16. NANANGO AREA

Nanango is on the Burnett Hwy 24 km south-east of Kingaroy. The town and its surrounds are steeped in history. Visitors to the region can fish, bushwalk, swim, visit historical sites, attend markets and enjoy local produce. Drop into the information centre for some friendly local advice.

Broadwater Recreational Reserve camping area

This reserve is 22 km north of Nanango. Signposted from Broadwater Access Rd off Burnett Hwy. Self-sufficient campers. Bring drinking water. Contact Nanango information centre if you wish to stay overnight; maximum 2 nights' stay. Additional map ref.: STM Qld K8.

First Settlers Park rest area

In Benarkin, which is signposted off D'Aguilar Hwy southeast of Nanango. 24-hour rest area. Suitable for caravans, vans and motorhomes only. Additional map ref.: STM Qld K8.

Maidenwell Rest Area

On Coomba Falls Rd in Maidenwell, 25 km south-west of Nanango. 24-hour rest area. Suitable for caravans, vans and motorhomes only. Hot showers in nearby town hall, key from general store. Bring drinking water and firewood. Additional map ref.: STM Qld K7.

Seven Mile Diggings camping area

This is 11 km south of Nanango. 4WD-only acccess via Old Coach Rd/Old Esk North Rd. Recreation permit required. Old fossicking area. No facilities. Self-sufficient campers. Bring drinking water and firewood. Maximum 2 nights' stay. Additional map ref.: STM Qld K8.

Further information: Nanango Visitor Information Centre **Tel.:** (07) 4171 6871 **Email:** tourism@nanango.qld.gov.au **Website:** www.nanango.qld.gov.au

17. NORTH STRADBROKE ISLAND

North Stradbroke Island is a popular holiday destination. It boasts white sandy beaches with crystal-clear water, magnificent freshwater lakes, Aboriginal and historical sites and fishing villages. Visitors can choose from a number of activities including picnicking, swimming, surfing, snorkelling, diving, fishing, sea kayaking and exploring – on foot, in a 4WD or on a bicycle – or just relax and take in the beautiful views. North Stradbroke Island is reached by vehicle ferry from Cleveland or Redland Bay. All campsites must be booked and paid for before arrival. Advance bookings are required for peak periods including school holidays, Christmas and New Year and Easter.

Adams Beach camping area

Just south of Dunwich. Bring own cooking equipment. Boat ramp nearby. Additional map ref.: STM Qld K8.

Adder Rock camping area

On East Coast Rd at Point Lookout, 20 km north-east of Dunwich. Laundry facilities. Firewood supplied. Additional map ref.: STM Qld K8.

Amity Point camping area

On Claytons Rd at Amity, 18 km north of Dunwich. Firewood supplied. Additional map ref.: STM Qld K8.

Bradburys Beach camping area

On Flinders Ave at One Mile, just north of Dunwich. Firewood supplied. Additional map ref.: STM Qld K8.

Cylinder Beach camping area

On East Coast Rd at Point Lookout, 21 km north-east of Dunwich. Laundry facilities. Additional map ref.: STM Qld K8.

Flinders Beach camping area

Beach camping at Flinders Beach. Access from Amity Point or Point Lookout. Located 19 km north of Dunwich. 4WD Beach Access Permit required. Drinking water and shower facilities available at Adder Rock. Small campfires permitted, bring firewood. Additional map ref.: STM Qld K8.

Main Beach camping area

Beach bush camping on Main Beach. Camping permitted 10 km south of beach-access causeway, which is 12.5 km east of Dunwich. Reached via Trans Island Rd from Dunwich. Alternative access from Point Lookout via George Nothling Drive. 4WD Beach Access Permit required. Bush camping, no facilities. Bring drinking water. Small campfires permitted, bring firewood. Additional map ref.: STM Qld K8.

Thankful Rest camping area

On East Coast Rd at Point Lookout, 20 km north-east of Dunwich. Additional map ref.: STM Qld K8.

Further information & bookings: North Stradbroke Island Visitor Information Centre **Tel.:** (07) 3409 9555 **Camping fees:** *Off-peak* Unpowered from $12.40 per site/night for 2 adults, powered from $19.60 per site/night for 2 adults *Peak* Unpowered from $17.40 per site/night, powered from $22.60 per site/night *Flinders Beach and Main Beach off-peak* From $7.80 per site/night for 2 adults *Peak* From $10.20 per site/night **4WD permits:** 48 hour $10.30, 1 week $15.40, 1 month $20.50, annual $82.20 **Ferry services:** Stradbroke Ferries (Cleveland) **Tel.:** (07) 3286 2666 *or* Islands Transport Pty Ltd (Redland Bay) **Tel.:** (07) 3829 0008

GOLD COAST AND HINTERLAND

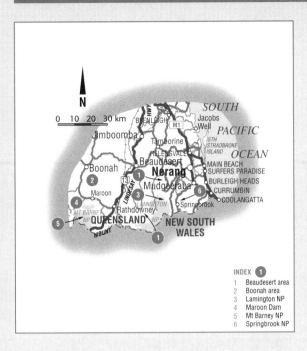

INDEX
1 Beaudesert area
2 Boonah area
3 Lamington NP
4 Maroon Dam
5 Mt Barney NP
6 Springbrook NP

THIS REGION IS AN INTERESTING MIX OF BEACHES, RESORTS AND RESTAURANTS ON THE GOLD COAST THAT CONTRAST WITH THE BEAUTIFUL MOUNTAINS, RAINFORESTS AND WATERFALLS OF THE HINTERLAND.

On the state border is the magnificent Springbrook National Park with natural beauties including rugged cliffs, fresh mountain streams, cool rainforests and eucalypt forests. In the western section of the park is the Natural Bridge, a rock archway across Cave Creek. Camping in the park is at the Gwongorella camping area, near lookouts over the spectacular Purlingbrook Falls. Walking trails leave from this camping area.

The spectacular wilderness of Lamington National Park is made up of beautiful rainforests, deep valleys, gorges, mountain ranges and waterfalls. The best way to view all the magnificent sights of the park is by foot along one of the many walking trails. Overnight bush camping is possible for those walkers who wish to venture a little further into the park and its forests. Vehicle-based camping is at Green Mountains Campground and at the Binna Burra Mountain campsite.

Further west is Beaudesert and its surrounding cattle-farming lands. Near Beaudesert are a number of council-owned camping areas that are well maintained and visited by supervisors. Each area is situated where campers can enjoy beautiful natural surroundings, take a refreshing dip in a creek or river and even try their hand at some fishing. Bookings do not apply to any of these sites – they are on a first-in, best-dressed basis.

The self-sufficient and experienced bushwalker can camp in the remote Mount Barney National Park. Walking tracks through the park are of moderate to extreme grade so walkers need to be fit. A shorter and less exhausting bushwalk leaves from the Yellow Pinch carpark through cool rainforest. To the west of the park is Mount May Reserve where vehicle-based camping is possible, but there are no facilities available.

BEST CAMPSITES

Gwongorella (Purlingbrook Falls) camping area
Springbrook National Park

Green Mountains Campground
Lamington National Park

Darlington Park camping area
Beaudesert area

Sharp Park camping area
Beaudesert area

Bigriggen Park camping area
Beaudesert area

BEST TIME TO VISIT

All year round.

1. BEAUDESERT AREA

Beaudesert is 70 km south of Brisbane on the Mount Lindesay Hwy and is an ideal base to take in the natural delights of the region. Visitors will find rivers to swim and fish in, abundant birds and other wildlife, bushwalking tracks and the beautiful Lamington National Park. As well, there are wineries and historical museums. The Beaudesert Shire Council runs many camping grounds within the shire.

Andrew Drynan Park camping area

On Running Creek Rd (The Lions Tourist Rd) 22 km south of Mount Lindesay Hwy and 46 km south of Beaudesert. Running Creek Rd is off the Mount Lindesay Hwy 5 km north of Rathdowney. Bring drinking water and firewood. Firewood available for purchase. Additional map ref.: STM Qld L8.

Further information & bookings: Andrew Drynan Park supervisor **Tel.:** (07) 5544 1281 **Camping fees:** From $3.50 per adult/night, $2.20 per child (age 5–15) per night; fees payable at self-registration station

Bigriggen Park camping area

On Bigriggen Rd off Upper Logan Rd, 9 km west of Rathdowney and 27 km south-west of Beaudesert. Upper Logan Rd is off Boonah–Rathdowney Rd 7 km west of Mount Lindesay Hwy. Bring firewood; also available to purchase. Additional map ref.: STM Qld L8.

Further information & bookings: Bigriggen Park manager **Tel.:** (07) 5463 6190 **Website:** www.erawan.com.au/bigriggen **Camping fees:** From $6.00 per adult/night, $3.00 per child (age 3–15 years) per night; fees payable at office

Burgess Park camping area

On Christmas Creek Rd 37 km south of Beaudesert. Christmas Creek Rd is signposted off Mount Lindesay Hwy. Bring drinking water and firewood. Additional map ref.: STM Qld L8.

Further information & bookings: Wildwood Park management **Tel.:** (07) 5544 8120 **Email:** info@wildwood. com.au **Website:** www.wildwood.com.au **Camping fees:** From $3.85 per adult/night and $2.20 per child (age 5–15 years) per night, plus insurance of $2.20 per campsite/night; fees payable at self-registration station

Darlington Park camping area

Signposted on Kerry Rd 24 km south of Beaudesert. Conventional vehicle access. Bring drinking water and firewood. Additional map ref.: STM Qld L8.

Further information & bookings: Wildwood Park management **Tel.:** (07) 5544 8120 **Email:** info@wildwood. com.au **Website:** www.wildwood.com.au **Camping fees:** From $3.85 per adult/night and $2.20 per child (age 5–15 years) per night, plus insurance of $2.20 per campsite/night; fees payable at self-registration station

Flanagan Reserve camping area

On Flanagan Reserve Rd off Upper Logan Rd, 13 km west of Rathdowney and 31 km south-west of Beaudesert. Upper Logan Rd is off the Boonah–Rathdowney Rd 7 km west of Mount Lindesay Hwy. Bring firewood; also available to purchase. Additional map ref.: STM Qld L8.

Further information & bookings: Flanagan Reserve supervisor **Tel.:** (07) 5544 3128 **Camping fees:** From $3.50 per adult/night, $1.75 per child (age 5–15 years) per night; fees payable at self-registration station

Sharp Park camping area

Beside Coomera River and on Beechmont Rd off Beaudesert–Nerang Rd, 4 km south-east of Canungra. Bring drinking water and firewood. Additional map ref.: STM Qld L8.

Further information & bookings: Sharp Park supervisors **Tel.:** 0409 550 745/740 **Email:** sharppark@qldnet.com.au **Camping fees:** From $7.00 per site/night; fees payable to on-site supervisors

Stinson Park camping area

On Christmas Creek Rd 42 km south of Beaudesert. Christmas Creek Rd is off Mount Lindesay Hwy at Laravale, 14 km south of Beaudesert. Bring drinking water and firewood. Additional map ref.: STM Qld L8.

Further information & bookings: Stinson Park supervisor **Tel.:** (07) 5544 8100 *or* Beaudesert Shire Council **Tel.:** (07) 5540 5339 **Camping fees:** From $3.50 per adult/night, $2.00 per child (age 5–15 years) per night; fees payable at self-registration station

2. BOONAH AREA

An hour's drive from Brisbane, Boonah and its surrounding countryside offer picturesque mountain scenery, national parks and lakes. Go bushwalking, waterskiing or fishing, climb a mountain, take in the views from a lookout or visit a historical museum. Boonah is 50 km west of Beaudesert and 56 km south of Ipswich via the Cunningham Hwy.

Boonah Showground

On Melbourne St, Boonah. Laundry facilities. Fires allowed in existing sites. Bring firewood. Additional map ref.: STM Qld L8.

Further information: Boonah Show Society **Tel.:** (07) 5463 1124 **Camping fees:** Unpowered tent site from $5.00 per person/night, powered caravan site from $15.00 per site/night for 2 people; fees collected by caretaker

Mount May Reserve

On Waterfall Creek Rd 35 km south of Boonah. Access via Newmans Rd or off Boonah–Rathdowney Rd, or via New Love Rd off Burnetts Creek Rd. Self-sufficient campers only. Bring drinking water and firewood. Additional map ref.: STM Qld L8.

Further information: Boonah Shire Visitor Information Centre **Tel.:** (07) 5463 2233

3. LAMINGTON NATIONAL PARK

Lamington National Park consists of 20 600 ha of forested valleys and ranges on the southern side of the Scenic Rim. The park is in two sections: Green Mountains and Binna Burra. The best way to appreciate the beauty of Lamington National Park is by taking one of the many walking tracks that range from short 1-km circuits to overnight hikes. Walkers will find rainforests, lookouts and waterfalls. Access to Green Mountains is via the 36-km narrow and windy Lamington National Park Rd from Canungra. Binna Burra is south of Beechmont via the Binna Burra Rd.

Binna Burra Mountain campsite

On Binna Burra Rd 10 km south of Beechmont. Laundry facilities. Bring firewood; also available to purchase. Bookings essential for weekends, holiday periods and van sites. Additional map ref.: STM Qld L8.

Further information & bookings: Binna Burra Lodge **Tel.:** (07) 5533 3622 **Email:** info@binnaburralodge.com.au **Website:** www.binnaburralodge.com.au **Camping fees:** From $10.00 per site/night, $5.00 per child (age 5–16) per night, power additional $3.50 per site/night

Green Mountains Campground

On Lamington National Park Rd 36 km south of Canungra. Staff on-site on weekdays and patrolling on weekends. Camping permit required. Coin-operated showers. Gas/fuel stove only. Bookings essential for weekends and holiday periods. Additional map ref.: STM Qld L8.

Further information: QPWS, Lamington National Park Green Mountains **Tel.:** (07) 5544 0634 **Further information & bookings:** Smart Service Queensland **Tel.:** 13 13 04 **Website:** www.qld.gov.au **Camping fees:** From $4.00 per site/night; fees payable 1 month in advance

Bush camping

Bush camping along various walking trails throughout park – campsites are recommended at time of booking and on completion of application for camping permit (both are essential, and bookings must be made at least 2 weeks in advance). Bring drinking water. Gas/fuel stove only.

Further information & bookings: QPWS, Lamington National Park Green Mountains **Tel.:** (07) 5544 0634 **Camping fees:** From $4.00 per site/night

4. MAROON DAM

Maroon Dam is 28 km south of Boonah at Maroon and is signposted from the Boonah–Rathdowney Rd. It is popular for fishing, canoeing and boating. A Stocked Impoundment Permit is necessary to fish here.

Pointro campsite

On Burnett Creek Rd at Maroon. Bring drinking water and firewood. Bookings recommended for long weekends, school holidays, Easter and Christmas. Additional map ref.: STM Qld L8.

Further information: Pointro campsite caretaker **Tel.:** (07) 5463 6209 **Email:** pip@outdoors.com **Camping fees:** From $6.00 per person/night; fees payable to caretaker

5. MOUNT BARNEY NATIONAL PARK

The rugged high peaks of Mount Barney have a rich history, from Aboriginal occupation to the first recorded European ascent in 1828. Visitors to the national park will be delighted by the undisturbed vegetation and the mountains' geology. Walking is suitable for experienced, fit and self-sufficient walkers. The park is south-west of Rathdowney and south of Boonah, signposted from the Barney View–Upper Logan Rd off the Boonah–Rathdowney Rd.

Bush camping

Walk-in bush campsites only. Walks are graded from moderate to extreme. Self-sufficient and experienced walkers only. Camping permit required (must arrange 3–6 weeks before visiting). Bring drinking water. Gas/fuel stove only. Additional map ref.: STM Qld L8.

Further information & bookings: QPWS, Coulson **Tel.:** (07) 5463 5041 **Camping fees:** From $4.00 per person/night

6. SPRINGBROOK NATIONAL PARK

The natural highlights of Springbrook National Park include sheer cliffs, deep gorges, plunging waterfalls, magnificent views, rainforests and the Natural Bridge. Visitors can also enjoy a stroll along a walking trail or go picnicking. Conventional-vehicle access to the camping area is off the Springbrook–Nerang Rd 30 km south of Mudgeeraba.

Gwongorella (Purlingbrook Falls) camping area

Signposted from Springbrook Rd, off the Springbrook–Nerang Rd. Walk-in sites (5–10 m). One caravan site only. Caravan access with care as road is steep and windy. Camping permit required. Boil water before use. Gas/fuel stove only. Bookings required; weekends and holiday periods are very popular. Additional map ref.: STM Qld L8.

Further information: QPWS, Springbrook National Park **Tel.:** (07) 5533 5147 **Further information & bookings:** Smart Service Queensland **Tel.:** 13 13 04 **Website:** www.qld.gov.au **Camping fees:** From $4.00 per person/night; permit from and fees payable at self-registration stations outside peak periods

DARLING DOWNS

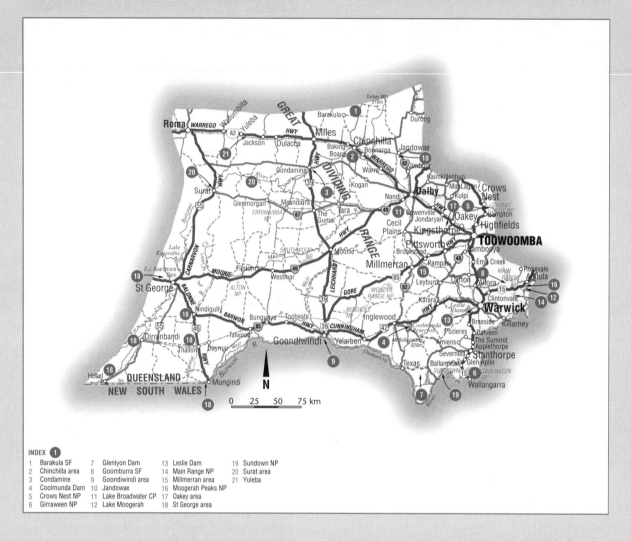

THE EXPANSIVE DARLING DOWNS STRETCH ACROSS UNDULATING PLAINS OF VINEYARDS AND GRAIN CROPS. DUE TO ITS FERTILE SOILS, MAGNIFICENT GARDENS CAN BE FOUND THROUGHOUT THE REGION AND IN THE LARGE TOWNS OF TOOWOOMBA AND WARWICK.

Separated into four different sections, Main Range National Park has a wonderful mix of rocky peaks and ridges where mountain heath grows, as well as beautiful rainforests, moist gullies and open eucalypt forests. Its mountain scenery is spectacular, with beautiful waterfalls, lookouts and walking trails. There are two campsites in the Cunninghams Gap section of the park: one along the highway west of

Cunninghams Gap and the other at Spicers Gap, where there is a small historic cemetery. In the Queen Mary Falls section of the park, a two-kilometre walking circuit leads to the base of the falls and circles back via the escarpment.

Girraween National Park features many granite outcrops, large boulders and precariously balanced rocks. The two camping areas in the park have excellent facilities including hot showers. Girraween National Park is a great spot for birdwatching – over 146 bird species have been recorded here, including the rare turquoise parrot. Other wildlife in the park includes wombats, spotted-tailed quolls, kangaroos, possums and gliders.

The 'traprock' country of Sundown National Park makes for some interesting exploration and fascinating views. Flowing through the park, the Severn River has carved sharp ridges and steep gorges. Swimming, fishing and canoeing are possible in the river and the larger waterholes. The park's main camping area, Broadwater, is beside the river and near a permanent waterhole. Other campsites accessible by four-wheel drive are in the north of the park.

South-west of Dalby, Lake Broadwater Conservation Park has lakeside camping. When the lake is full, campers can enjoy swimming, fishing, canoeing and boating. Birdwatching is also popular here as the surrounding forests are home to a variety of species.

BEST CAMPSITES

Spicers Gap camping area
Main Range National Park

Castle Rock camping area
Girraween National Park

The Lake camping area
Lake Broadwater Conservation Park

Wilga bush camping area
Lake Broadwater Conservation Park

Broadwater camping area
Sundown National Park

BEST TIME TO VISIT

All year round.

1. BARAKULA STATE FOREST

Barakula State Forest produces large quantities of cypress pine. It is 45 km north of Chinchilla, via the unsealed, dry-weather-only Barakula Town Rd. From Chinchilla travel west along the Warrego Hwy and take Auburn Rd north to Barakula.

Dogwood Creek camping area

This is 45 km north of Chinchilla via Barakula Town Rd off Auburn Rd. Camping permit required. Remote, self-sufficient camping. Bring drinking water and firewood. Additional map ref.: STM Qld K7.

Further information:
QPWS, Dalby **Tel.:** (07) 4669 9580 *or*
DPI Forestry, Barakula **Tel.:** (07) 4662 8366
Camping fees: From $4.00 per person/night; permit from and fees payable to QPWS Dalby or other QPWS offices

2. CHINCHILLA AREA

Chinchilla is on the Warrego Hwy 82 km north-west of Dalby and 185 km east of Roma. The town is a major centre for the surrounding industries, including timber, grain cattle and melons – 25 per cent of Australia's melons are produced in the Chinchilla region (rockmelons, watermelons and honeydews). The Chinchilla white gum and Hando's wattle are unique to the area. The helpful staff at the visitor information centre can tell you the region's sights.

Archers Crossing camping area

On Condamine River 24 km south-east of Chinchilla via Hopelands Rd. Detailed access information from visitor information centre. Boat ramp on southern side of river. Self-sufficient campers only. Bring drinking water. Additional map ref.: STM Qld K7.

Chinchilla Weir camping area

Located 9 km south of Chinchilla on Chinchilla–Tara Rd. Black soil area, dry-weather access only. Restrictions apply to fishing, contact visitor information centre for details. Bring drinking water and firewood. Maximum 2 nights' stay. Additional map ref.: STM Qld K7.

Grays Reserve camping area

This is 16 km south of Chinchilla. Access opposite 'Chinta' property on Chinchilla–Tara Rd. Dry weather access only. Self-sufficient campers only. Bring drinking water. Additional map ref.: STM Qld K7.

Further information: Chinchilla Visitor Information Centre **Tel.:** (07) 4668 9564

3. CONDAMINE

Condamine is on the Leichhardt Hwy 33 km south of Miles.

Caliguel Lagoon camping area

This is 7 km south of Condamine, reached via Condamine–Meandarra Rd. Bring drinking water and firewood. Additional map ref.: STM Qld K7.

Further information: Miles Historical Village **Tel.:** (07) 4627 1492

4. COOLMUNDA DAM

Coolmunda Dam, east of Inglewood, was built to provide irrigation water to the region's grain and cattle properties. The dam is stocked with silver perch, yellowbelly, cod and catfish and a Stocked Impoundment Permit is required to fish here.

Lake Coolmunda Caravan Park

On Coolmunda Dam access road 13 km east of Inglewood. Signposted off Cunningham Hwy. Firewood supplied. Bookings recommended for Easter and Christmas. Additional map ref.: STM Qld L7.

Further information & bookings: Lake Coolmunda Caravan Park **Tel.:** (07) 4652 4171 **Camping fees:** Unpowered tent sites from $13.50 per site/night for 2 people, powered sites from $15.50 per site/night for 2 people

5. CROWS NEST NATIONAL PARK

Crows Nest National Park is ablaze with colour during spring and summer, when the wildflowers bloom. The park is home to a wide range of wildlife, from sugar gliders and feathertail gliders to brush-tailed rock wallabies, eastern yellow robins, honeyeaters and rosellas. There are platypuses in the creeks. The park is 6 km east of Crows Nest and signposted from the New England Hwy.

Crows Nest camping area

Access via Three Mile Rd from Crows Nest. Camping permit required. Tank drinking water – boil before use or bring own. Donkey hot-water shower. Firewood supplied. Bookings recommended for long weekends, school holidays, Easter and Christmas. Additional map ref.: STM Qld K8.

Further information: QPWS, Crows Nest National Park **Tel.:** (07) 4698 1296 **Further information & bookings:** QPWS, Toowoomba **Tel.:** (07) 4639 4599 **Camping fees:** From $4.00 per person/night; permit from and fees payable at self-registration station outside peak periods

6. GIRRAWEEN NATIONAL PARK

Within Girraween National Park visitors will find massive granite outcrops and precariously balanced rocks. In spring colourful wildflowers bloom between the granite. The park is home to a large and diverse range of birds including the rare turquoise parrot; it is an excellent spot for birdwatchers. There are a number of walks to scenic sites. The park is reached from the New England Hwy 11 km north of Wallangarra and 26 km south of Stanthorpe.

Bald Rock Creek camping area

Signposted from Pyramids Rd off New England Hwy – camping area is 9 km from hwy. Pyramids Rd is 11 km north of Wallangarra and 7 km south of Ballandean. Camping permit required. Boil drinking water or bring own. Bring firewood. Bookings recommended at peak periods, long weekends, school holidays, Easter and Christmas. Additional map ref.: STM Qld L7.

Castle Rock camping area

Signposted from Pyramids Rd off New England Hwy – camping area is 9 km from hwy. Camping permit required. Boil drinking water or bring own. Bring firewood. Bookings recommended at peak periods, long weekends, school holidays, Easter and Christmas. Additional map ref.: STM Qld L7.

Bush camping

Remote walk-in bush campsites throughout park for self-sufficient and experienced walkers. Camping permit required. Bring drinking water. Gas/fuel stove only. Bookings and registration must be made 10 days in advance. Additional map ref.: STM Qld L7.

Further information: QPWS, Girraween National Park **Tel.:** (07) 4684 5157 **Further information & bookings:** Smart Service Queensland **Tel.:** 13 13 04 **Camping fees:** From $4.00 per person/night; permit from and fees payable at self-registration station outside peak periods

7. GLENLYON DAM

Glenlyon Dam, 97 km south-west of Stanthorpe and 52 km east of Texas, offers excellent boating and fishing. The dam is stocked with golden perch, silver perch, spangled perch, eel-tailed catfish and Murray cod. A Stocked Impoundment Permit is required to fish here. Access from the north is signposted off the Glenlyon Rd (Stanthorpe–Texas Rd), from the south off the Bruxner Hwy, and via Pinnancle Rd from Texas.

Glenlyon Dam Tourist Park

Signposted off Glenlyon–Texas Rd from Stanthorpe and from Bruxner Hwy 67 km north-west of Tenterfield. Laundry facilities. No generators. Firewood supplied. Stocked Impoundment Permits sold here. Bookings recommended and are essential for Easter and Christmas. Additional map ref.: STM Qld L7.

Further information & bookings: Glenlyon Dam Tourist Park **Tel.:** (02) 6737 5266 **Camping fees:** Unpowered from $15.00 per site/night for 2 people, powered from $20.00 per site/night for 2 people; key for amenities – refundable $5.00 deposit

8. GOOMBURRA STATE FOREST

Goomburra State Forest is within the Scenic Rim at the foothills of the Great Dividing Range. Spectacular views can be had from Sylvesters and Mt Castle lookouts. The forest is home to a diverse range of vegetation as well as platypuses, koalas, echidnas, feathertail gliders and mountain brushtail possums. From the camping area there are five walking trails of varying lengths. The forest is off the Cunningham and New England hwys.

Manna Gum and Poplar Flat camping areas

These camping areas are 35 km east of Allora. Signposted off New England Hwy via Inverramsay–Banshee Creek Rd or

reached via Goomburra Rd off Cunningham Hwy – 40 km from hwy. Camping permit required. Drinking water from tank, boil before use. Firewood supplied. Additional map ref.: STM Qld L8.

Further information: QPWS, Main Range National Park **Tel.:** (07) 4666 1133 **Email:** main.range@epa.qld.gov.au **Camping fees:** From $4.00 per person/night; permit from and fees payable at self-registration station

9. GOONDIWINDI AREA

Goondiwindi is on the New South Wales border, at the junction of the Cunningham, Barwon, Bruxner and Leichhardt hwys. There is a maximum stay of one night at all sites.

Bengalla Reserve rest area

Signposted along Old Warwick Rd 34 km east of Goondiwindi. Black soil area, dry weather access only. Bring drinking water and firewood. Additional map ref.: STM Qld L7.

Boonanga Reserve rest area

Camping beside Barwon River. Reached via Talwood–Boonanga Rd, 15 km south of Talwood. Talwood is 91 km west of Goondiwindi. Black soil area, dry weather access only. Bring drinking water and firewood. Additional map ref.: STM Qld L6.

Rainbow Reserve rest area

Accessed along Kildonan (Yelarbon) Rd, 17 km east of Goondiwindi. Camping beside the McIntyre River where road runs close to the river, prior to Eukabilla Rd. Black soil area, dry weather access only. Bring drinking water and firewood. Additional map ref.: STM Qld L7.

Further information: Goondiwindi–Waggamba Visitor Information Centre **Tel.:** (07) 4671 2653

10. JANDOWAE

Jandowae is 50 km north of Dalby. The nearby dam provides for picnicking, boating and fishing.

Jandowae Caravan Park

On High St in Jandowae. Bring firewood. Swimming pool. Dogs by arrangement only. Additional map ref.: STM Qld K7.

Further information: Jandowae Caravan Park **Tel.:** (07) 4668 5071 **Camping fees:** Tent sites from $6.00 per site/night up to 2 people, caravan sites from $9.00 per site/night up to 2 people

11. LAKE BROADWATER CONSERVATION PARK

When full, Lake Broadwater is a popular watersports venue. The forests and vegetation surrounding the lake is a haven for many bird species, making it a great birdwatching area. Lake Broadwater Conservation Park is 30 km south-west of Dalby and the lake is signposted off the Moonie Hwy. A permit is required for boating here.

The Lake camping area

Area is located 10 km along Lake Broadwater Rd, off Moonie Hwy. Camp outside log boundaries. Bring firewood. Additional map ref.: STM Qld K7.

Wilga bush camping area

Located 8 km along Lake Broadwater Rd, off Moonie Hwy. Bring drinking water and firewood. Additional map ref.: STM Qld K7.

Further information: Lake Broadwater Conservation Park **Tel.:** (07) 4663 3562 **Camping fees:** From $3.85 per person/night; fees collected daily or payable at honesty box

12. LAKE MOOGERAH

South of Aratula on the Cunningham Hwy, Lake Moogerah is an ideal venue for water activities such as swimming, fishing, sailing, canoeing and waterskiing. A Stocked Impoundment Permit is necessary to fish in this lake.

Lake Moogerah Caravan Park

On A. G. Muller Park Rd, signposted off Lake Moogerah Rd, 6 km south of Aratula. Campers kitchen and laundry facilities. Bring firewood. Bookings recommended for powered sites. Additional map ref.: STM Qld L8.

Further information & bookings: Lake Moogerah Caravan Park **Tel.:** (07) 5463 0141 **Camping fees:** Unpowered from $16.00 per site/night, powered from $19.00 per site/night

The Gorge Camping Reserve

On Gorge Rd off Charlwood Rd, 3 km south of Aratula. Bring drinking water and firewood. Bookings essential. Additional map ref.: STM Qld L8.

Further information & bookings: The Gorge Camping Reserve **Tel.:** (07) 5526 0683 **Camping fees:** From $3.00 per person/night

Yarramalong Outdoor Recreation Centre

At 688 Lake Moogerah Rd, 4 km south of Aratula. Canoe hire available. Bring firewood. Bookings recommended. Additional map ref.: STM Qld L8.

Further information & bookings: Yarramalong Outdoor Recreation Centre **Tel.:** (07) 5463 7369 **Email:** yarramalong@hypermax.net.au **Camping fees:** From $8.00 per adult/night, $6.00 per school-age child/night, $2.00 per 3–5-year-old child/night

13. LESLIE DAM

The scenic Leslie Dam, 14 km west of Warwick, is well known for its golden perch. As well as fishing, the dam is popular for picnicking, canoeing and sailing. It is signposted off the New England Hwy. A Stocked Impoundment Permit is necessary to fish in this dam.

Rocklands Camping Reserve

On Rocklands Rd, which is off Glen Rd off Washpool Rd from New England Hwy. Reserve is 18 km west of Washpool Camping Reserve. No built fireplaces, use existing fire sites. Bring drinking water and firewood. Additional map ref.: STM Qld L7.

Washpool Camping Reserve

This is 13 km west of Warwick. Reached on Washpool Rd, which is signposted off New England Hwy. Firewood supplied. Additional map ref.: STM Qld L7.

Further information: Washpool Camping Reserve caretaker **Tel.:** (07) 4661 7844 or 0418 870 354 **Camping fees:** From $4.50 per adult/night, $2.00 per child (12 years and under) per night; fees payable to caretaker

14. MAIN RANGE NATIONAL PARK

In the western section of the Scenic Rim, Main Range National Park stretches from Mt Mistake in the north to Wilsons Point on the New South Wales border and to Queen Mary Falls in the west. The park is a mixture of rainforest and open eucalypt forest sheltering diverse wildlife, and its rugged landscape and spectacular views make it popular with bushwalkers. Main Range National Park is 50 km east of Warwick and its main camping areas are reached from the Cunningham Hwy.

Cunninghams Gap camping area

On Cunningham Hwy 40 km east of Warwick and 3.5 km west of Cunninghams Gap. Camping permit required.

Drinking water from bore, boil before use or bring own. Firewood supplied. Additional map ref.: STM Qld L8.

Spicers Gap camping area

On East Spicers Gap Rd 18 km south-west of Aratula. Dry weather access only. Camping permit required. Limited drinking water – bring own. Gas/fuel stove only. Additional map ref.: STM Qld L8.

Bush camping

Bush campsites along walking trails (of various lengths and grades through the park. Self-sufficient campers only. Camping permit required – must be booked in advance. Bring drinking water. Gas/fuel stove only. Recommended campsites are advised at time of booking and on completion of application for camping permit.

Further information: QPWS, Main Range National Park **Tel.:** (07) 4666 1133 **Email:** main.range@epa.qld.gov.au **Camping fees:** From $4.00 per person/night *Cunninghams Gap and Spicers Gap* Fees payable at self-registration station

15. MILLMERRAN AREA

The Condamine River flows through Millmerran Shire, where a number of bush campsites are located near the river for fishing and boating. Millmerran is on the Gore Hwy 82 km south-west of Toowoomba. A rich and diverse agricultural area, Millmerran and its surrounds offer the visitor unique and interesting attractions.

Broadwater Reserve

On Millmerran–Leyburn Rd 30 km east of Millmerran. Dry weather access only. Bring drinking water and firewood. Additional map ref.: STM Qld K7.

Cecil Plains Recreation Area – Rest Area

Pull-up area in Cheetham St, Cecil Plains. Cecil Plains is 47 km north of Millmerran. There is a grey-water dump point

A walking trail in Main Range National Park

at Council Depot in Cheetham St. Additional map ref.: STM Qld K7.

Cecil Plains Weir – Apex Park

Park is 1 km from Cecil Plains via Cecil Plains–Toowoomba Rd. Bring drinking water and firewood. Additional map ref.: STM Qld K7.

Lemontree Weir

Weir is 20 km north of Millmerran via Lemon Tree Rd off Gore Hwy. Dry weather access only. Bring drinking water and firewood. Additional map ref.: STM Qld K7.

Walpole Park – Rest Area

Pull-up area suitable for fully self-contained units with own shower and toilet facilities. At Walpole Park on Charlotte St, Millmerran. A grey-water dump point lies opposite, in Charles St. Additional map ref.: STM Qld K7.

William Simmons Memorial Park – Rest Area

Pull-up area suitable for fully self-contained units with own shower and toilet facilities. At William Simmons Memorial Park on Commens St, Millmerran. Additional map ref.: STM Qld K7.

Yarramalong Weir

Situated 30 km east of Millmerran, on Shire Rd No. 96 off Millmerran–Leyburn Rd. Bring drinking water and firewood. Additional map ref.: STM Qld K7.

Further information:
Millmerran Shire Council **Tel.:** (07) 4695 1399
Email: millmerransc@growzone.com.au *or*
Millmerran Community Support Office **Tel.:** (07) 4695 1829
Camping fees: *Cecil Plains Recreation Area* $5.00 per unit/night for use of facilities and power, units not using facilities or power are free; payments to caretaker at 62 Cheetham St

16. MOOGERAH PEAKS NATIONAL PARK

Made up of four sections – Mt French, Mt Greville, Mt Edwards and Mt Moon – the rugged landscapes of Moogerah Peaks National Park offer a variety of walking trails. Attempt the steep cliffs and slopes in the Mt Moon section (for experienced walkers) or enjoy the short and easy lookout walks in the Mt French section.

Mount French camping area

This area is 11 km west of Boonah on Mount French Rd, which is 1 km south of Boonah off Boonah–Rathdowney Rd. Walk in (100 m) campsites from carpark. Camping permit required. Firewood supplied, gas/fuel stove preferred. Bookings recommended. Additional map ref.: STM Qld L8.

Further information: QPWS, Boonah **Tel.:** (07) 5463 5041
Further information & bookings: Smart Service Queensland **Tel.:** 13 13 04 **Website:** www.qld.gov.au **Camping fees:** From $4.00 per person/night; permit from and fees payable at self-registration stations outside peak periods

17. OAKEY AREA

The town of Oakey is on the Warrego Hwy 28 km north-west of Toowoomba.

Bowenville Reserve camping area

On the southern banks of Oakey Creek 33 km west of Oakey on Bowenville–Norwin Rd, 5 km south of Warrego Hwy. Turn-off from Warrego Hwy is at Bowenville 28 km west of Oakey. Bring drinking water and firewood. Additional map ref.: STM Qld K7.

Further information: Toowoomba Visitor Information Centre **Tel.:** (07) 4639 3797

18. ST GEORGE AREA

St George is at the junction of the Carnarvon, Balonne and Moonie hwys, 200 km west of Goondiwindi and 291 km east of Cunnamulla. A maximum stay of one night applies to all sites.

Balonne Minor Bridge camping area

This is 3 km west of Dirranbandi along Dirranbandi–Bollon Rd. Dirranbandi is 97 km south of St George. Bring drinking water. Additional map ref.: STM Qld L6.

Barneys Beach camping area

Beside the Moonie River, along Thallon–Dirranbandi Rd 3 km west of Thallon. Thallon is 76 km south-east of St George. Bring drinking water. Additional map ref.: STM Qld L6.

Barwon River camping area

Beside Barwon River in Mungindi. Mungindi is 118 km south-east of St George. Camping is on the northern bank. Bring drinking water. Additional map ref.: STM Qld L6.

Bokhara River camping area

Beside Bokhara River in Hebel. Hebel is 162 km south-west of St George and 65 km south-west of Dirranbandi. Bring drinking water. Additional map ref.: STM Qld L5.

Moonie River camping area

Beside Moonie River in Nindigully, 44 km south-east of St George. Bring drinking water. Additional map ref.: STM Qld L6.

Narran River camping area

Beside Narran River and reached via Dirranbandi–Hebel Rd, 37 km south of Dirranbandi. Bring drinking water. Additional map ref.: STM Qld L6.

Wallam Creek camping area

On the banks of Wallam Creek in Bollon, on Balonne Hwy 112 km west of St George. Bring drinking water. Additional map ref.: STM Qld L5.

Warroo Bridge camping area

This is 60 km north of St George. Take Wycombe School/ Warroo Bridge Rd off Carnarvon Hwy 51 km north of St George, then it is 9 km to the bridge. Camping is on north side of bridge only. Bring drinking water. Additional map ref.: STM Qld K6.

Further information: St George Shire Visitor Information Centre **Tel.:** (07) 4625 4996

Sundown National Park, along the New South Wales border, is 'traprock' country carved by the Severn River. Formed from ancient marine sediments, traprock is a very hard and dense rock. Visitors to Sundown can swim, fish and canoe in the Severn River. Access for conventional vehicles to Broadwater, in the south of the park, is signposted off the Glenlyon Dam Rd 76 km south-west of Stanthorpe. The park's eastern boundary is reached from Ballandean, with only 4WD or walk-in access from the boundary.

Broadwater camping area

On Permanents Rd, signposted off Glenlyon Dam Rd. Turn-off is 76 km south-west of Stanthorpe and campsite is 5 km in. Access for small caravans. Camping permit required. Firewood supplied. Additional map ref.: STM Qld L7.

Burrows Waterhole camping area

Reached from the park's eastern boundary 16 km west of Ballandean. Burrows Waterhole is 18 km from park entrance gate and is signposted along national park access road. Camping permit required. Water from river – boil before use. Camp fires allowed but only use existing fire sites. Bring firewood. Additional map ref.: STM Qld L7.

Red Rock camping area

Reached from the park's eastern boundary 16 km west of Ballandean. Red Rock is 7 km from park entrance gate and is signposted along national park access road. Camping permit required. Bring drinking water. Campfires allowed but use only existing fire sites. Bring firewood. Additional map ref.: STM Qld L7.

Bush camping

Walk-in bush camping sites throughout park. Recommended for experienced, self-sufficient campers. Camping permit required. Bring drinking water. Gas/fuel stove only. Contact Park Headquarters for up-to-date information on park conditions and water availability.

Further information: QPWS, Sundown National Park **Tel.:** (02) 6737 5235 **Further information & bookings:** Smart Service Queensland **Tel.:** 13 13 04 **Website:** www.qld.gov.au **Camping fees:** From $4.00 per person/night; permit from and fees payable at self-registration stations at Broadwater and at park entrance gate on eastern boundary

Surat is on the Carnarvon Hwy 78 km south of Roma and 116 km north of St George.

Balonne Bridge camping area

On the Carnarvon Hwy on the north side of Surat. Bring drinking water and firewood. Additional map ref.: STM Qld K6.

Bingi Crossing camping area

This is 45 km east of Surat off Surat–Tara Rd, which is off the Carnarvon Hwy. Bring drinking water. Additional map ref.: STM Qld K6.

Cow Paddocks camping area

This is 2 km east of Surat on Sawmill Rd. Call one of the numbers listed for access details. Bring drinking water. Additional map ref.: STM Qld K6.

Green Timbers Fishing Reserve camping area

Located 18 km south of Surat off the Carnarvon Hwy. Call one of the numbers for access details. Black soil road, dry weather access only. Bring drinking water. Additional map ref.: STM Qld K6.

Pialaway Reserve camping area

This is 85 km north-east of Surat. From Surat–Condamine Rd take Warkan Rd for 18 km to fishing reserve. Call one of the numbers for further access details. Bring drinking water. Additional map ref.: STM Qld K6.

Further information:
Cobb & Co. Changing Station, Surat **Tel.:** (07) 4626 5136 or Warroo Shire Council **Tel.:** (07) 4626 5299

Yuleba is on the Warrego Hwy 60 km east of Roma and 80 km west of Miles.

Judds Lagoon camping area

On Mongool Rd 3 km east of Yuleba. Bring drinking water and firewood. Additional map ref.: STM Qld K6.

Old Yuleba Town camping area

Located 13 km east of Yuleba. From Warrego Hwy turn south onto Forestry Rd 2 km east of Yuleba. Turn right onto Mongool Rd, then after the fourth grid turn right again. Bring drinking water. Additional map ref.: STM Qld K6.

Further information: Bendemere Shire Council **Tel.:** (07) 4623 5155 **Website:** www.bendemere.qld.gov.au

THE SUNSHINE COAST HAS A WONDERFUL MIX OF LONG SANDY BEACHES AND ROCKY HEADLANDS, FORESTED MOUNTAINS AND WATERFALLS.

Just north of the Sunshine Coast is World Heritage-listed Fraser Island, part of Great Sandy National Park. You can explore the island by foot or four-wheel drive: there are some spectacular beaches as well as clear creeks, pristine freshwater lakes and beautiful rainforests. A vast array of wildlife can be found here, including dingoes, wallabies, flying foxes, echidnas and possums. Tortoises inhabit the freshwater lakes and dolphins, dugongs, turtles and even whales are found in the surrounding waters of Hervey Bay and the South Pacific Ocean.

There are many places to camp on Fraser Island, from the well-facilitated areas of Central Station, Dundubara and Waddy Point to the campsites of Lake Boomanjin and Lake Allom, which have limited facilities. There is also bush camping along the island's beaches.

Back on the mainland, just west of Amamoor, is Amamoor State Forest. Two camping areas sit beside Amamoor Creek, which has deep holes suitable for swimming, and walking tracks lead from Cedar Grove camping area through the nearby forests. The popular Country Music Muster is held in August each year at the large Amamoor Creek camping area.

Further south, there is excellent camping in Kenilworth State Forest. Winding through the forest is the Kenilworth Forest Drive with scenic sights such as the cooling pools and picnic area of Peters Creek and Booloumba Falls.

Other features of the region include Wongi State Forest, boasting the Wongi Waterholes, and the Cooloola section of Great Sandy National Park – canoe down the Noosa River or explore the coloured sand cliffs of Rainbow Beach.

BEST CAMPSITES

Cedar Grove camping area
Amamoor State Forest

Charlie Moreland camping area
Kenilworth State Forest

Harrys Hut camping area
Great Sandy National Park – Woody Island

Central Station camping area
Fraser Island (Great Sandy National Park)

Lake Boomanjin camping area
Fraser Island (Great Sandy National Park)

BEST TIME TO VISIT

This region is suitable to visit all year round. However during and after wet weather some access roads and campsites may be closed.

1. AMAMOOR STATE FOREST

Amamoor State Forest is 20 km south-west of Gympie, reached from Amamoor Creek Rd west of Amamoor. The forest provides sightseeing, walking, picnicking and camping opportunities. The Amama Day Use Area is an excellent spot for picnicking and has three short walks. You might be lucky and spot a platypus here. Please note that if you wish to travel on any of the forest's restricted-access roads, a Permit to Traverse is required.

Amamoor Creek camping area

This is 4 km west of Amamoor Creek Rd. Camping permit required. Drinking water – boil before use. Some firewood supplied. Additional map ref.: STM Qld K8.

Cedar Grove camping area

Beside Amamoor Creek, 10 km west of Amamoor on unsealed Amamoor Creek Rd. Camping permit required. Drinking water – boil before use. Some firewood supplied. Additional map ref.: STM Qld K8.

Further information:
QPWS, Kenilworth **Tel.:** (07) 5446 0925 *or*
QPWS, Gympie **Tel.:** (07) 5480 6207
Camping fees: From $4.00 per person/night; permit from and fees payable at self-registration stations

2. BEERBURRUM STATE FOREST

Beerburrum State Forest is only an hour's drive north of Brisbane and is a mixture of native and pine forests. As well as being a sustainable timber source, the forest offers many recreation activities. Coochin Creek Camping and Day Use Area in the north-east of the forest is close to the site of Campbellville, a timber town which flourished 1881–90.

Coochin Creek Camping and Day Use Area

On Roys Rd 4 km east of Bruce Hwy and 9 km east of Beerwah. Camping permit required. Boat ramp nearby. Gas/fuel stove only. Additional map ref.: STM Qld K8.

Further information: Naturally Queensland Information Centre **Tel.:** (07) 3227 8197/8186
Camping fees: From $4.00 per person/night; permit from and fees payable at self-registration station

3. BORUMBA DAM

Borumba Dam is 11 km west of Imbil, which is 17 km north of Kenilworth, and was originally built in 1962. The Borumba Dam spillway was raised by 2.5 m in 1997 to allow the storage of an additional 12 000 megalitres. The dam is home to golden and silver perch, saratoga and bass. A Stocked Impoundment Permit is required to fish here. Conventional vehicle access is from Yabba Creek Rd.

Aerial view of Waddy Point, Fraser Island

Borumba Dam camping area

This is 11 km west of Imbil and reached along Yabba Creek Rd. Firewood supplied. Additional map ref.: STM Qld K8.

Further information: SunWater, Bundaberg
Tel.: (07) 4132 6200 **Camping fees:** From $7.50 per site/night up to 6 people; fees payable at self-registration station

4. BROOYAR STATE FOREST

Brooyar State Forest lies to the west of the Bruce Hwy. Visitors can enjoy the views from lookouts along Brooyar Forest Drive, paddle in the cooling shallow waters of Glastonbury Creek or stroll through rainforest along the old logging road from Glastonbury Creek Forest Recreation Area. Access from the north is via Petersen Rd, signposted off the Wide Bay Hwy 20 km west of Gympie, or from the south via a signposted road from Glastonbury on the Gympie–Woolooga Rd. Caravan access is from the north only and roads are unsealed.

Glastonbury Creek Forest Recreation Area

Beside Glastonbury Creek. Access via Petersen Rd from Wide Bay Hwy. Camping permit required. Water from creek – boil before use. Some firewood supplied. Additional map ref.: STM Qld K8.

Further information: QPWS, Kenilworth
Tel.: (07) 5446 0925 **Camping fees:** From $4.00 per person/night; permit from and fees payable at self-registration station

5. FRASER ISLAND (GREAT SANDY NATIONAL PARK)

See also Great Sandy National Park – Cooloola section *and* Great Sandy National Park – Woody Island, *page 304*

Stretching over 120 km, Fraser Island is the world's largest sand island. Its beauty and natural features are its main attractions: it has spectacular coloured sand cliffs and rocky headlands, beautiful white sandy beaches, pristine freshwater lakes, magnificent rainforests, mangroves and swamps. Visitors can reach all these by 4WD or on foot. Activities include fishing, wildlife spotting, birdwatching, 4WD touring, bushwalking, swimming and sightseeing. The island is reached by vehicle barge from Inskip Point, River Heads and Hervey Bay – contact QPWS Rainbow Beach for barge information. Camping and vehicle permits are to be obtained before arriving on Fraser Island. Collection of natural firewood is prohibited; firewood is available at Central Station, Dundubara and Waddy Point. If bringing your own firewood, only fresh-cut, milled timber is allowed. All visitors must be dingo-smart – ensure all food is securely stored and do not feed or encourage them. Obtain a copy of the QPWS's 'Be Dingo-Smart!' brochure for further details.

Central Station camping area

This is 10 km west of Eurong and 10 km east of Wanggoolba Creek. Campsites are over bollards/fence from carpark. Camping permit required. Coin-operated showers. Gas/fuel

stove only (at time of research QPWS were phasing out campfires here). Bookings required. Additional map ref.: STM Qld J8.

Dundubara camping area

Camping behind foredunes 76 km north of Hook Point and 20 km south of Indian Head. Suitable for off-road camper-trailers and trailers in limited numbers. Camping permit required. Coin-operated showers. Firewood supplied. Additional map ref.: STM Qld J8.

Garrys Anchorage camping area

On south-western coast. Access via 4WD or boat. Camping permit required. Bring drinking water. Gas/fuel stove preferred. Additional map ref.: STM Qld J8.

Lake Allom camping area

North-west of The Pinnacles on Northern Rd. Small site. Camping permit required. Bring firewood. Additional map ref.: STM Qld J8.

Lake Benaroon camping area

Hikers' campsite only, north of Lake Boomanjin and south of Central Station. Camping permit required. Recommended that hikers use storage lockers at site for storing food and packs. Self-sufficient campers only. Bring drinking water. Gas/fuel stove only. Additional map ref.: STM Qld J8.

Lake Boomanjin camping area

Located 6.5 km north-west of Dilli Village on Birrabeen Rd. Camping permit required. Wash-up area. Bring drinking water. Gas/fuel stove only. Additional map ref.: STM Qld J8.

Waddy Point camping area

There are two camping areas here: the top campground and the beachfront campground (limited facilities), 6–7 km north of Middle Rocks via Inland Track. Camping permit required. Wash-up area. Firewood supplied. Bookings required for top campground. Additional map ref.: STM Qld J8.

Wathumba camping area

This is 16 km west of Waddy Point. Access by 4WD or boat. Camping permit required. Use existing fire sites. Additional map ref.: STM Qld J8.

Beach camping

Beach camping on east and west coast of island, only in signposted areas. Camping permit required. Camp in existing campsites and use existing fire sites. Bring drinking water and firewood.

Further information:
QPWS, Rainbow Beach **Tel.:** (07) 5486 3160 *or*
QPWS, Eurong, Fraser Island **Tel.:** (07) 4127 9128
Further information & bookings: Smart Service Queensland
Tel.: 13 13 04 **Website:** www.qld.gov.au **Camping fees:**
From $4.00 per person/night; permit from and fees payable through Smart Service Queensland or at QPWS Rainbow Beach **Vehicle permit:** $30.80 per vehicle

6. GREAT SANDY NATIONAL PARK – COOLOOLA SECTION

See also Fraser Island (Great Sandy National Park), *previous entry*, and Great Sandy National Park – Woody Island, *next entry*

The Cooloola section of the Great Sandy National Park is on the coast north of Noosa Heads, east of Gympie and south of Rainbow Beach. Cooloola offers a large range of activities including bushwalking, camping, fishing, 4WD touring, canoeing, boating and sightseeing. It features coloured sand cliffs, rainforest, freshwater lakes and the Double Island Point Lighthouse. Visitors should check with QPWS before arrival regarding closures to roads, walking trails or campsites and fire restrictions.

Fig Tree Point camping area

Walk-in access 10.2 km north of Elanda Point. Boat access along Noosa River, 2 km north of Kinaba. Camping permit required. Water from river – boil before use. Firewood supplied. Gas/fuel stove preferred. Advance bookings necessary. Additional map ref.: STM Qld K8.

Freshwater Campground

Reached via Freshwater Rd from Bymien picnic area or via Teewah Beach. It is 19 km east of Rainbow Beach Rd and 1 km west of beach. Camping permit required. Communal fireplaces. Gas/fuel stove only at individual campsites. Bookings required for school holidays and long weekends. Additional map ref.: STM Qld J8.

Further information: QPWS, Rainbow Beach
Tel.: (07) 5486 3160 **Further information & bookings:**
QPWS, Freshwater **Tel.:** (07) 5449 7959 **Camping fees:**
From $4.00 per person/night; permit from and fees payable at self-registration station outside of booking periods

Harrys Hut camping area

Beside Noosa River, on Harrys Hut Rd 10 km east of Cooloola Way. Turn-off is 20 km north of Kin Kin. Access by foot, 4WD or boat. Camping permit required. Drinking water from tank or river – boil before use. Firewood supplied. Gas/fuel stove preferred. Advance bookings advisable for school holidays and long weekends. Additional map ref.: STM Qld K8.

Neebs Waterhole camping area

Walk-in access only from Cooloola Wilderness Trail. Area is 8.8 km south of Mullens carpark on Rainbow Beach Rd and

12.4 km north of Wandi Waterhole camping area. Camping permit required. For self-sufficient campers only. Bring drinking water. Gas/fuel stove only. Advance bookings necessary. Additional map ref.: STM Qld J8.

Noosa River campsites – 1, 2 and 3

Beside Noosa River. Boat/canoe access only. Camping permit required. Drinking water from river – boil before use. Gas/fuel stove only. Advance bookings necessary. Maximum camper numbers apply. Additional map ref.: STM Qld K8.

Noosa River campsites – 4, 5, 8, 9, 13 and 15

Beside Noosa River. Canoe access only; no motorised boats to these sites. Camping permit required. Drinking water from river – boil before use. Gas/fuel stove only. Advance bookings necessary. Additional map ref.: STM Qld K8, J8.

Poverty Point camping area

This is 6 km north of Rainbow Beach Rd. Access road is 12.6 km south of Rainbow Beach. 4WD access only. Camping permit required. For self-sufficient campers only. Bring drinking water and firewood. Fires only in existing fire sites. Additional map ref.: STM Qld J8.

Further information:
QPWS, Freshwater **Tel.:** (07) 5449 7959 *or*
QPWS, Rainbow Beach **Tel.:** (07) 5486 3160
Camping fees: From $4.00 per person/night; permit from and fees payable at self-registration station

Teewah Beach camping

Camping along Teewah Beach for 15 km between Little Freshwater Creek in the north and Noosa Shire boundary in the south. Camping permit required. Camp only in existing campsites. Bins along foreshore at intervals. For self-sufficient campers only. Bring drinking water and firewood. Fires only in existing fire sites. Self-registration stations at Little Freshwater Creek, on Kings Bore Rd and at southern boundary. Additional map ref.: STM Qld K8.

Wandi Waterhole camping area

Walk-in-only access on Cooloola Wilderness Trail. Area is 12.4 km south of Neebs Waterhole camping area and 9.5 km north of Harrys Hut camping area. Camping permit required. For self-sufficient campers only. Bring drinking water. Gas/fuel stove only. Advance bookings necessary. Additional map ref.: STM Qld K8.

Further information: QPWS, Rainbow Beach
Tel.: (07) 5486 3160 **Further information & bookings:** *All areas except Freshwater and Poverty Point* QPWS, Elanda Point **Tel.:** (07) 5485 3245 **Camping fees:** From $4.00 per person/night

7. GREAT SANDY NATIONAL PARK – WOODY ISLAND

See also Fraser Island (Great Sandy National Park), *page 303*, and Great Sandy National Park – Cooloola section, *previous entry*

Woody Island is between Fraser Island and Hervey Bay in the Great Sandy Strait. It is suitable for self-sufficient campers only, and access is by private boat. Permits are to be obtained before arriving on the island.

Bush camping

Bush camping on island. Camping permit required. Self-sufficient campers only. Bring drinking water. Gas/fuel stove only. Additional map ref.: STM Qld J8.

Further information: QPWS, Maryborough
Tel.: (07) 4121 1800 **Camping fees:** From $4.00 per person/night; permit from and fees payable at QPWS Maryborough

8. INSKIP PENINSULA RECREATION AREA

Inskip Peninsula Recreation Area is 11 km north of Rainbow Beach. This narrow peninsula has sandy beaches and it is a popular site for fishing and birdwatching. Two camping areas are accessible in conventional vehicles and caravans and two areas are 4WD only. Drivers of caravans should check road conditions first. No camping on foredunes.

Inskip Peninsula camping areas

Camping amongst casuarina trees in designated areas. Camping permit required. Bring drinking water and firewood. Gas/fuel stove preferred. Additional map ref.: STM Qld J8.

Further information: QPWS, Rainbow Beach
Tel.: (07) 5486 3160 **Camping fees:** From $4.00 per person/night; permit from and fees payable to QPWS, Rainbow Beach

9. KENILWORTH STATE FOREST

Kenilworth State Forest is reached from Sunday Creek Rd, which leaves the Maleny–Kenilworth Rd 6 km south of Kenilworth. The forest has scenic lookouts, rainforests, creeks, waterfalls and rugged landscapes. Over 120 bird species have been recorded here along with much other wildlife. Kenilworth State Forest is popular for car touring, camping, swimming, bushwalking, picnicking, mountain bike and horseriding (permits required for cycling and horseriding).

Booloumba Creek camping area – no. 1

Reached via Booloumba Creek Rd off Maleny–Kenilworth Rd. Camping permit required. Some firewood supplied. Advance bookings required. Additional map ref.: STM Qld K8.

Booloumba Creek camping area – no. 3

Accessed via Booloumba Creek Rd off Maleny–Kenilworth Rd. Camping permit required. Some firewood supplied. Advance bookings required. Additional map ref.: STM Qld K8.

Booloumba Creek camping area – no. 4

Reached via Booloumba Creek Rd off Maleny–Kenilworth Rd. Camping permit required. Some firewood supplied. Additional map ref.: STM Qld K8.

Charlie Moreland camping area

Accessed via Sunday Creek Rd, 4 km west of Maleny–Kenilworth Rd. Area is 10 km south-west of

Kenilworth. Camping permit required. Some firewood supplied. Additional map ref.: STM Qld K8.

Further information: QPWS, Kenilworth **Tel.:** (07) 5446 0925 **Bookings:** Smart Service Queensland **Tel.:** 13 13 04 **Website:** www.qld.gov.au **Camping fees:** *Booloumba Creek – nos 1 and 3* From $4.00 per person/night; permit from and fees payable through Smart Service Queensland *Booloumba Creek – no. 4 and Charlie Moreland* Permit from and fees payable at self-registration stations; contact QPWS Kenilworth for current fee schedule

10. MAPLETON STATE FOREST

The Mapleton Forest Drive takes in the major places of interest in Mapleton State Forest: the short, 400-m Pilularis Forest Walk, Pooles Dam, where a short walk leads to the top of a small waterfall, the Mapleton Day Use Area – a perfect place to picnic beside Cedar Creek – and Piccabeen Palm Groves Walk. The Mapleton Forest Drive is accessed from Mapleton, west of Nambour. In the forest's south-west is the Gheerulla Camping and Trail Bike Area, where up to 60 km of trails are available for touring by licensed trail-bike riders on registered vehicles – permits necessary.

Gheerulla Camping and Trail Bike Area

Beside Gheerulla Creek 8 km north-east of Kenilworth, reached from Eumundi–Kenilworth Rd. Camping permit required. Bring drinking water. Some firewood supplied. Additional map ref.: STM Qld K8.

Further information: QPWS, Kenilworth
Tel.: (07) 5446 0925 **Camping fees:** From $4.00 per person/night **Permits:** Permit to Traverse required to trail-bike ride in the area; contact QPWS Kenilworth for application

11. WONGI STATE FOREST

The Wongi Waterholes in the Wongi State Forest are a popular spot to cool off on a hot day. Wongi is Aboriginal for 'deep water'. Car touring, picnicking and camping are also enjoyed in the forest. Access is via Warrah Rd, off the Bruce Hwy 10 km north of Maryborough.

Wongi camping area

Signposted from Warrah Rd 10 km west of Bruce Hwy. Camping permit required. Bring drinking water. Some firewood supplied. Additional map ref.: STM Qld J8.

Further information:
QPWS, Maryborough **Tel.:** (07) 4121 1800 *or*
QPWS, Kenilworth **Tel.:** (07) 5446 0925
Camping fees: From $4.00 per person/night; permit from and fees payable at self-registration station

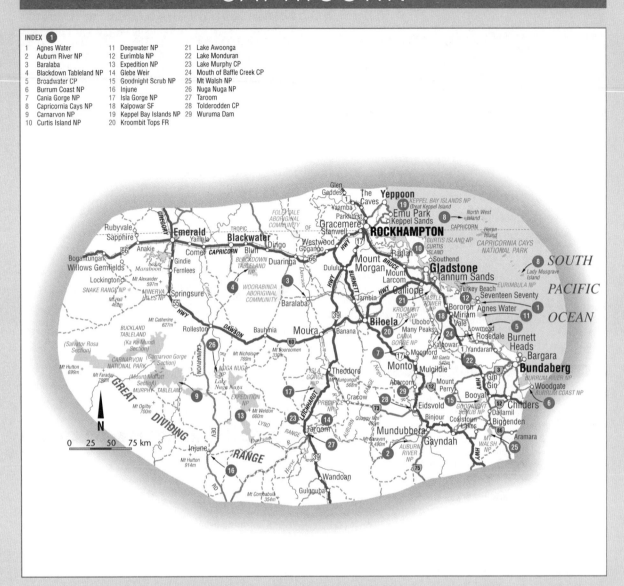

THE CAPRICORN REGION STRETCHES FROM THE MAJOR EASTERN TOWNS OF BUNDABERG, GLADSTONE AND ROCKHAMPTON ACROSS THE PLAINS TO THE RISING PLATEAUS OF THE GREAT DIVIDING RANGE. IN THE AREA THERE IS A MIX OF INDUSTRIES INCLUDING COAL MINING, ALUMINIUM REFINING, SUGARCANE-GROWING, CATTLE GRAZING AND TOURISM. OFF THE COAST ARE THE SOUTHERNMOST ISLANDS OF THE GREAT BARRIER REEF, A MECCA FOR CAMPERS, WITH TROPICAL BEACHES AND CORAL REEFS SUPERB FOR DIVING AND SNORKELLING.

North-east of Monto is Kalpowar State Forest, where camping is possible at the large, grassed Kalpowar camping and day use area beside Crane Creek. The scenic 20-kilometre Kalpowar Forest Drive leads through pine and native forests passing Bills Window Lookout, an old forestry workers hut and magnificent strangler figs.

Campers at Mimosa Creek camping area in Blackdown Tableland National Park can enjoy the park's natural beauty along one of the walking trails, or those with a four-wheel drive can tour the ten-kilometre Loop Road. Numerous lookouts, deep gorges, tall cliffs and the beautiful Rainbow Falls are found in the park.

To the far west of the region is the spectacular Carnarvon National Park. Here interesting sandstone features – arches, pillars and plateaus – have been formed by erosion over thousands of years. The park is separated into four sections, offering the visitor a range of facilities and experiences. Vehicle-based camping is possible in each section of the park, and there are a limited number of caravan sites at the Carnarvon Gorge camping area.

At the southern end of the Great Barrier Reef is Capricornia Cays National Park, where camping is possible on the coral cays of Masthead Island, North West Island and Lady Musgrave Island. These islands are north-east of Gladstone and the town of Seventeen Seventy. Off the coast of Rosslyn Bay Harbour camping is allowed on the islands of Keppel Bay Islands National Park – North Keppel Island has excellent facilities including toilets, tables and cold showers.

Lake Murphy Conservation Park, north-west of Taroom, is a great site for birdwatchers to set up camp and watch the visiting waterbirds. On the coast and to the south of Agnes Water are Broadwater Conservation Park and Deep Water National Park. Campsites in these two coastal parks, both popular for fishing, are accessible by four-wheel drive.

BEST CAMPSITES

Kalpowar camping and day use area
Kalpowar State Forest

Lady Musgrave Island
Capricornia Cays National Park

Glebe Weir camping area
Glebe Weir

Carnarvon Gorge camping area
Carnarvon National Park

Mimosa Creek camping area
Blackdown Tableland National Park

BEST TIME TO VISIT

This region can be visited all year round, but in the cooler months of the year – autumn to spring – the temperature is likely to be more comfortable.

1. AGNES WATER

The seaside town of Agnes Water is home to the most northern surf beach in Queensland. Agnes Water is 57 km east of Miriam Vale on the Bruce Hwy and 130 km north of Bundaberg.

Workmans Beach camping area

Signposted off Springs Rd just south of Agnes Water. Unpatrolled surf beach. Additional map ref.: STM Qld J7.

Further information: Miriam Vale Shire Council **Tel.:** (07) 4974 6222 **Camping fees:** From $4.00 per adult/ night, $3.00 per child (age 5–17) per night, family (2 adults + 2 children) $14.00 per night; fees collected by caretaker mornings and evenings

2. AUBURN RIVER NATIONAL PARK

The Auburn River flows through this park past forests of callistemons, stunted figs and rainforest. From the camping area a walking trail leads to a lookout above the river. Auburn River National Park is 42 km south-west of Mundubbera and is signposted along Hawkwood Rd off the Mundubbera–Durong Rd. The park is 7 km south of Hawkwood Rd.

Auburn River camping area

Signposted 20 km west of Mundubbera–Durong Rd along Hawkwood Rd. Camping permit required. Bring drinking water and firewood. Additional map ref.: STM Qld J7.

Further information: QPWS, Mundubbera **Tel.:** (07) 4165 5110 **Camping fees:** From $4.00 per person/ night; camping permit from and fees payable at self-registration station

3. BARALABA

The town of Baralaba is on the Dawson River, 96 km north-west of Biloela and 160 km south-west of Rockhampton. The river is a popular place for water activities.

Neville Hewitt Weir camping area

Camping at Neville Hewitt Weir in Baralaba. Bring drinking water. Some firewood available. Additional map ref.: STM Qld J6.

Further information:
Baralaba and Community Resource and Development Centre **Tel.:** (07) 4998 1142 *or*
Banana Shire Council **Tel.:** (07) 4992 9500

4. BLACKDOWN TABLELAND NATIONAL PARK

Blackdown Tableland National Park has beautiful wildflowers, magnificent waterfalls and tall eucalypt forests. Visitors can enjoy the various walks and lookouts. The park is signposted from the Capricorn Hwy 11 km west of Dingo and 35 km east of Blackwater; it is 34 km south of the highway. The access road is steep and unsealed, and not recommended for caravans.

Mimosa Creek camping area

Swimming nearby. Camping permit required. Bring drinking water and firewood. Gas/fuel stove preferred. Bookings required for school holidays and long weekends, and taken up to 12 months in advance. Additional map ref.: STM Qld H6.

Further information: QPWS, Blackdown Tableland National Park **Tel.:** (07) 4986 1964 (7.30 am–4 pm) **Further information & bookings:** Smart Service Queensland **Tel.:** 13 13 04 **Website:** www.qld.gov.au **Camping fees:** From $4.00 per person/night; permit from and fees payable through Smart Service Queensland or at self-registration station outside peak periods

5. BROADWATER CONSERVATION PARK

This park is on the coast between Rules Beach in the south and Agnes Water in the north. There is 4WD beach access only, and only at low tide. Drivers should check tides and entry point before proceeding onto beach.

Mitchell Creek camping area

Beach access off Rules Beach Rd north of Wartburg. Area is 7 km north of beach access point. Camping permit required. Bring drinking water. Gas/fuel stove only. Additional map ref.: STM Qld J7.

Further information & bookings:
QPWS, Agnes Water **Tel.:** (07) 4974 9350 or
QPWS, Bundaberg **Tel.:** (07) 4131 1600
Camping fees: From $4.00 per person/night; permit from and fees payable at self-registration station at beach access point

6. BURRUM COAST NATIONAL PARK

Burrum Coast National Park is in two sections: Woodgate and Kinkuna. Woodgate is a popular place to relax, birdwatch, walk, and fish and canoe in the Burrum River. It is reached via Walkers Point Rd from the town of Woodgate. The Kinkuna section is north of the Woodgate–Childers Rd and is reached by 4WD beach driving: check tides first as these can be dangerous for the inexperienced. Kinkuna is popular with wildlife-spotters, birdwatchers and bushwalkers. Swimmers should be aware that beaches in both sections are unpatrolled.

WOODGATE SECTION

Burrum Point camping area

Signposted from Walkers Point Rd from Woodgate. Area is 8 km south of Woodgate. 4WD access only. Camping permit required. Gas/fuel stove only. No generators. Bookings required for Christmas, Easter, school holidays and long weekends, and taken 6–12 months in advance. Additional map ref.: STM Qld J8.

KINKUNA SECTION

Beach camping

Beach camping on frontal dunes. Reached from the south via Woppis Rd off Woodgate–Childers Rd 3 km west of Woodgate,

and from the north via Palm Beach Rd off Coonarr Rd 8 km east of Bundaberg–Goodwood Rd. 4WD beach access, check tides first. Camping permit required. Self-sufficient campers only. Bring drinking water and firewood. Additional map ref.: STM Qld J8.

Further information and bookings:
QPWS, Woodgate **Tel.:** (07) 4126 8810 or
QPWS, Bundaberg **Tel.:** (07) 4131 1600
Camping fees: From $4.00 per person/night Burrum Point Permit from and fees payable at self-registration stations outside peak periods Kinkuna Self-registration stations at northern and southern entrances

7. CANIA GORGE NATIONAL PARK

Cania Gorge National Park preserves 3000 ha of sandstone cliffs and caves, rainforest and eucalypt forests. It is sign-posted off the Burnett Hwy 12 km north of Monto; its entrance is 14 km from the highway via a sealed road. Camping is not permitted within the national park, but two caravan parks are close by. At Lake Cania, 12 km further north, there is fishing and canoeing (Stocked Impoundment Permit required).

Cania Gorge Tourist Park

This park is 35 km north of Monto, 25 km north of the Burnett Hwy and 4 km from Lake Cania; it is reached through Cania Gorge National Park. Campers kitchen. Laundry facilities. Firewood for sale. Additional map ref.: STM Qld J7.

Further information & bookings: Cania Gorge Tourist Park **Tel.:** (07) 4167 8188 **Email:** info@caniagorge.com.au **Website:** www.caniagorge.com.au **Camping fees:** Off-peak: Campsite from $9.00 per adult/night, $4.00 per child (age 5–16) per night, powered from $20.50 per site/night for 2 people. Contact the park for peak fee schedule

Cania Gorge Tourist Retreat

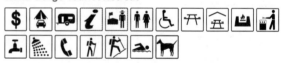

At park entrance. Campers kitchen. Laundry facilities. Firewood supplied. Bookings recommended during school holidays and Easter. Dogs allowed by prior application only. Additional map ref.: STM Qld J7.

Further information & bookings: Cania Gorge Tourist Retreat **Tel.:** (07) 4167 8110 **Email:** enquiries@ caniagorgeretreat.com.au **Website:** www.caniagorgeretreat. com.au **Camping fees:** Off-peak: Unpowered from $14.00 per site/night for 2 people, powered from $17.00 per site/night for 2 people; contact park for peak fee schedule

8. CAPRICORNIA CAYS NATIONAL PARK

This park is a group of coral cays, islands and reefs at the southern end of the Great Barrier Reef, to the east of Gladstone and Seventeen Seventy. The islands can only be reached by boat and are seasonally closed for camping; restrictions apply to recreational activities – detailed information is available from QPWS Gladstone. Maximum camper numbers apply and bookings are necessary.

Lady Musgrave Island

Lady Musgrave Island is 60 km north-east of Seventeen Seventy. Camping is on the western side of island. Boat access only. Camping permit required. Self-sufficient campers only. Bring drinking water. Gas/fuel stove only. Additional map ref.: STM Qld H8.

Masthead Island

Masthead Island is 60 km north-east of Gladstone. Camping is on the north-west corner of island. Boat access only. Camping permit required. Self-sufficient campers only. Bring drinking water. Gas/fuel stove only. Additional map ref.: STM Qld H7.

North West Island

North West Island is 75 km north-east of Gladstone. Camping is on the western shore of island. Boat access only. Camping permit required. Self-sufficient campers only. Bring drinking water. Gas/fuel stove only. Additional map ref.: STM Qld H7.

Further information: QPWS, Gladstone **Tel.:** (07) 4971 6500
Further information & bookings: Smart Service Queensland **Tel.:** 13 13 04 **Website:** www.qld.gov.au
Camping fees: From $4.00 per person/night; permit from and fees payable through Smart Service Queensland or at QPWS Gladstone

9. CARNARVON NATIONAL PARK

Carnarvon National Park covers 298 000 ha and contains spectacular sandstone cliffs, plateaus, gorges, pillars and arches as well as waterfalls, fern-filled gorges, Aboriginal rock-art sites, panoramic views, walking trails and varied wildlife. The park is separated into four main sections. The Carnarvon Gorge section is west of the Carnarvon Developmental Rd, 111 km north of Injune and 61 km south of Rolleston (access is possible in dry weather only). The ranger headquarters and the Mount Moffatt section are 165 km north-west of Injune and 220 km north of Mitchell (4WD vehicles recommended; drivers of conventional vehicles should check road conditions with Injune Visitor Information Centre, tel. (07) 4626 1053, or Roma Visitor Information Centre, tel. (07) 4622 4355. The Ka Ka Mundi section is 50 km south-west of Springsure and is signposted from the Springsure–Tambo Rd (Dawson Developmental Rd); from here it is a further 80 km south to the park entrance. The Salvator Rosa section is signposted 114 km south-west of Springsure and 144 km north-east of Tambo on the Springsure–Tambo Rd; it is a further 45 km south to the park entrance. Leave gates as found. The collection of firewood is prohibited – use only existing fire sites.

CARNARVON GORGE SECTION

Advance bookings and pre-payment are essential to camp in this section. Carnarvon Gorge camping area is open only during Easter and the state school holidays in April, June–July and Sept. – it is closed in summer. Carnarvon Gorge itself is open all year for day visitors.

Big Bend camping area

Walk-in access, 9.3 km up the gorge. Camping permit required. Bring drinking water or boil creek water. Gas/fuel stove only. Additional map ref.: STM Qld J5.

Carnarvon Gorge camping area

This is 45 km west of the Carnarvon Developmental Rd and signposted from there. Camping permit required. Limited caravan sites. Coin-operated showers. Gas/fuel stove only. Maximum 5 nights' stay. Additional map ref.: STM Qld J5.

Further information:
QPWS, Carnarvon National Park, Carnarvon Gorge **Tel.:** (07) 4984 4505 or
QPWS, Roma **Tel.:** (07) 4622 4266
Further information & bookings: Smart Service Queensland **Tel.:** 13 13 04 **Website:** www.qld.gov.au
Camping fees: From $4.00 per person/night; permit from and fees payable through Smart Service Queensland

MOUNT MOFFATT SECTION

The Mount Moffatt section is 158 km north-west of Injune, with the ranger headquarters 7 km further on. Advance bookings and pre-payment are essential to camp in this section during school holidays and Easter.

Dargonelly Rock Hole camping area

Along the park's main access road. Camping permit required. Access is possible for 4WD/off-road caravans – drivers should check road conditions first. Drinking water from bore – boil before use. Bring firewood (can collect from collection zone outside park). Gas/fuel stove preferred. Additional map ref.: STM Qld K6.

Rotary Shelter Shed camping area

About 25 km north of ranger headquarters. 4WD access only. Camping permit required. Limited water supply; bring drinking water. Bring firewood (can collect from collection zone outside park). Gas/fuel stove preferred. Additional map ref.: STM Qld J5.

Top Moffatt camping area

About 17 km east of ranger headquarters. 4WD access only. Camping permit required. Bring drinking water and firewood (can collect wood from collection zone outside park). Gas/fuel stove preferred. Additional map ref.: STM Qld J5.

West Branch camping area

This is 9 km north of ranger headquarters. Drivers of conventional vehicles should check road conditions before attempting; 4WD vehicles are recommended. Camping permit required. Drinking water from bore, boil before use. Bring firewood (can collect from collection zone outside park). Gas/fuel stove preferred. Additional map ref.: STM Qld J5.

Further information:
QPWS, Carnarvon National Park, Mount Moffatt **Tel.:** (07) 4626 3581 or
QPWS, Roma **Tel.:** (07) 4622 4266
Further information & bookings: Smart Service Queensland **Tel.:** 13 13 04 **Website:** www.qld.gov.au
Camping fees: From $4.00 per person/night; permit from and fees payable through Smart Service Queensland and at self-registration station at ranger headquarters outside peak periods

KA KA MUNDI SECTION

Conventional vehicles can reach here in dry weather only.

Bunbuncundoo Springs camping area

This is 130 km south-west of Springsure. Access is via Buckland Rd off Springsure–Tambo (Dawson Developmental)

Rd. Camping permit required. Bring drinking water and firewood. Gas/fuel stove preferred. Additional map ref.: STM Qld J5.

SALVATOR ROSA SECTION
Conventional vehicles can reach here in dry weather only.

Nogoa River campsite

This is 168 km south-west of Springsure and 198 km north-east of Tambo. Access off Springsure–Tambo (Dawson Developmental) Rd. Camping permit required. Water from river – boil before use or bring own. Bring firewood. Gas/fuel stove preferred. Additional map ref.: STM Qld J5.

Further information:
QPWS, Carnarvon National Park, Springsure
Tel.: (07) 4984 1716 *or*
QPWS, Roma **Tel.:** (07) 4622 4266
Camping fees: From $4.00 per person/night; permit from and fees payable at Springsure park headquarters or self-registration station at campsite

10. CURTIS ISLAND NATIONAL PARK
Curtis Island National Park lies at the north-eastern end of the large Curtis Island, which is off the coast north of Gladstone and south of Rockhampton. Access is by private boat from Gladstone or the Narrows. Contact QPWS for details.

Yellowpatch camping area

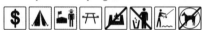

Bush camping in national park. Access via private boat. Camping permit required. Self-sufficient campers only. Bring drinking water. Gas/fuel stove only. Bookings essential. Additional map ref.: STM Qld H7.

Further information: QPWS, Gladstone **Tel.:** (07) 4971 6500
Further information & bookings: Smart Service Queensland **Tel.:** 13 13 04 **Website:** www.qld.gov.au
Camping fees: From $4.00 per person/night; permit from and fees payable through Smart Service Queensland or at QPWS Gladstone

11. DEEPWATER NATIONAL PARK
Deepwater National Park is south of Agnes Water. Access to the park is by Wreck Rock Rd from Agnes Water and 4WD vehicles are recommended; conventional vehicles (after checking road conditions) may be able to access Wreck Rock camping area from the south. The park's beach is popular with fisherfolk and those wishing to relax in a quiet, unspoiled area.

Middle Rock camping area

This is 14 km south of Agnes Water. 4WD access only via Wreck Rock Rd from Agnes Water. Camping permit required. Bring drinking water. Gas/fuel stove only. Additional map ref.: STM Qld J7.

Wreck Rock camping area

This is 16 km south of Agnes Water via Wreck Rock Rd. 4WD access from Agnes Water. Conventional vehicle access may be possible from the south via Wartburg, check road conditions; 4WD recommended. Camping permit required. Bring drinking water. Gas/fuel stove only. Bookings necessary during school and public holidays. Additional map ref.: STM Qld J7.

Further information: QPWS, Agnes Water
Tel.: (07) 4974 9350 **Further information & bookings:**
QPWS, Bundaberg **Tel.:** (07) 4131 1600 **Camping fees:** From $4.00 per person/night; permit from and fees payable at self-registration stations outside peak periods

12. EURIMBLA NATIONAL PARK
Eurimbula National Park is signposted from Agnes Water Rd 10 km west of Agnes Water. Captain Cook anchored in May 1770 at Bustard Bay, so named after a bustard (plains turkey) was shot in the area. For magnificent views over the bay and the rest of the park, take the short but steep walk to Ganoonga Noonga Lookout. Conventional vehicles can reach Bustard Beach. The collection of wood is prohibited in the park.

Bustard Beach camping area

Access via Bustard Beach Track, which is signposted off Eurimbula Access Rd 10 km west of Agnes Water. Bustard Beach is 15 km from Agnes Water Rd. Camping permit required. Limited rain water, best to bring drinking water. Gas/fuel stove only. Bookings are necessary during school and public holidays and are taken up to 3 months in advance. Additional map ref.: STM Qld J7.

Middle Creek camping area

About 35 km north-west of Agnes Water, reached (4WD vehicles only) off Eurimbula Access Rd. Camping permit required. Bring drinking water and firewood. Campfires allowed – use only current fire sites. Additional map ref.: STM Qld J7.

Further information: QPWS, Agnes Water
Tel.: (07) 4974 9350 **Further information & bookings:**
QPWS, Bundaberg **Tel.:** (07) 4131 1600 **Camping fees:** From $4.00 per person/night; permit from and fees payable at self-registration stations outside peak periods

13. EXPEDITION NATIONAL PARK
The 100-m-high Robinson Gorge is a highlight of the rugged sandstone country of Expedition National Park. Other features are Aboriginal stencils and artwork, views from Shepherds Peak, beautiful vegetation and birdlife. The park is 131 km west of Taroom and 103 km south of Bauhinia. It is signposted 18 km north of Taroom on the Leichhardt Hwy. Only 4WD vehicles can access the park and only in dry weather. This is a remote area; all campers must be well prepared and self-sufficient.

Spotted Gum campsite

This is 148 km west of Taroom. Signposted along Oil Bore Rd off Bauhinia Downs Rd. 4WD access only. Camping permit required. Bring drinking water and firewood. Additional map ref.: STM Qld J6.

Starkvale Creek campsite

Site is 147 km west of Taroom. Signposted along Oil Bore Rd off Bauhinia Downs Rd. 4WD access only. Camping permit required. Bring drinking water and firewood. Additional map ref.: STM Qld J6.

Further information: QPWS, Taroom **Tel.:** (07) 4627 3358
Camping fees: From $4.00 per person/night; permit from and fees payable at self-registration stations

14. GLEBE WEIR

Glebe Weir is a popular watersports venue. It is signposted off the Leichhardt Hwy 26 km north of Taroom. The weir is a further 26 km east.

Glebe Weir camping area

On Glebe Weir Rd off Leichhardt Hwy. Bring drinking water and firewood. Additional map ref.: STM Qld J6.

Further information & bookings: Taroom Shire Council **Tel.:** (07) 4627 3211 **Email:** mail@taroom.qld.gov.au **Camping fees:** From $5.00 per site/night; fees payable at self-registration station

15. GOODNIGHT SCRUB NATIONAL PARK

This densely forested park is home to abundant wildlife – birds, mammals, reptiles and butterflies. The forest of hoop pine towers above bottle trees, ironbark and spotted gum. A steep 4WD track leads to One Tree Hill Lookout, offering excellent views over the park and its surrounds. Goodnight Scrub National Park is 45 km south of Gin Gin and is signposted off the Bruce Hwy 10 km south of town. Access to the camping area is only possible in dry weather and the road is steep – drivers of caravans must exercise caution. The collection of firewood is prohibited in the park.

Burnett River bush camping

Access via Goodnight Scrub Rd. Camping permit required. Self-sufficient campers only. Bring drinking water and firewood. Gas/fuel stove preferred. Additional map ref.: STM Qld J8.

Further information: QPWS, Bundaberg **Tel.:** (07) 4131 1600 **Camping fees:** From $4.00 per person/night; permit from and fees payable at self-registration station at campsite turn-off

16. INJUNE

Injune is on the Carnarvon Developmental Rd 90 km north of Roma. The Injune district has many natural wonders including diverse flora and fauna, spectacular rock formations, beautiful lakes and Aboriginal paintings. Injune is an ideal base for exploring the surrounding region.

Injune Caravan Park

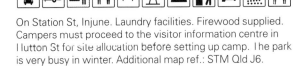

On Station St, Injune. Laundry facilities. Firewood supplied. Campers must proceed to the visitor information centre in Hutton St for site allocation before setting up camp. The park is very busy in winter. Additional map ref.: STM Qld J6.

Further information: Injune Visitor Information Centre **Tel.:** (07) 4626 1053 **Camping fees:** First 2 nights free, then $5.00 per site/night; fees payable at visitor information centre

17. ISLA GORGE NATIONAL PARK

The lookout at Isla Gorge National Park provides amazing views over the surrounding escarpments and eroded sandstone gorges. There are beautiful wildflower displays in spring. The park is signposted off the Leichhardt Hwy 55 km north of Taroom and 40 km south of Theodore.

Lookout camping area

Signposted off Leichhardt Hwy 55 km north of Taroom. Area is 1.5 km west of highway. Camping permit required. Undefined walking trails for experienced walkers only. Bring drinking water. Gas/fuel stove only. Additional map ref.: STM Qld J6.

Further information: QPWS, Taroom **Tel.:** (07) 4627 3358 **Camping fees:** From $4.00 per person/night; permit from and fees payable at self-registration station

18. KALPOWAR STATE FOREST

Kalpowar State Forest is 38 km north-east of Monto, and is reached by Fireclay Rd or Kalpowar–Gin Gin Rd, both off Monto–Gladstone Rd. The 20-km Kalpowar Forest Drive passes through pine and native forests and takes in all the main points of interest.

Kalpowar camping and day use area

On McNae Rd off Kalpowar–Gin Gin Rd, 46 km north-east of Kalpowar and 80 km north-west of Gin Gin. Camping permit required. Bring drinking water. Firewood supplied. Gas/fuel stove preferred. Additional map ref.: STM Qld J7.

Further information: QPWS, Bundaberg **Tel.:** (07) 4131 1600 **Camping fees:** From $4.00 per person/night; permit from and fees payable at self-registration station

19. KEPPEL BAY ISLANDS NATIONAL PARK

Keppel Bay Islands National Park includes 12 islands, all with a rich history – from Aboriginal occupation to exploration by Captain Cook to sheep grazing by early settlers. The islands are reached by private boat or water taxi from Rosslyn Bay Harbour, 15 km from Yeppoon. Maximum camper numbers apply to all islands and bookings are essential. The waters surrounding the islands are Marine Park; check with QPWS for zoning and allowed activities and with Queensland Fisheries for fishing regulations.

Conical Island

Bush camping on beach on eastern shore. Camping permit required. Self-sufficient campers only. Bring drinking water. Gas/fuel stove only. Additional map ref.: STM Qld H7.

Divided Island

Bush camping. Camping permit required. Self-sufficient campers only. Bring drinking water. Gas/fuel stove only. Additional map ref.: STM Qld H7.

Humpy Island

Camping along northern beach. Camping permit required. Self-sufficient campers only. Bring drinking water. Gas/fuel stove only. Additional map ref.: STM Qld H7.

Miall Island

Bush camping behind small beach and foredunes on the south-west shore. Camping permit required. Self-sufficient

campers only. Bring drinking water. Gas/fuel stove only. Additional map ref.: STM Qld H7.

Middle Island

Bush camping. Camping permit required. Self-sufficient campers only. Bring drinking water. Gas/fuel stove only. Additional map ref.: STM Qld H7.

North Keppel Island – Considine Beach Campground

Camping area on western shore of island. Camping permit required. Self-sufficient campers only. Bring drinking water (there is bore water for washing). Gas/fuel stove only. Additional map ref.: STM Qld H7.

Pelican Island

Bush camping. Camping permit required. Self-sufficient campers only. Bring drinking water. Gas/fuel stove only. Additional map ref.: STM Qld H7.

Further information:
QPWS, Rockhampton **Tel.:** (07) 4936 0511 or
QPWS, Rosslyn Bay **Tel.:** (07) 4933 6595
Further information & bookings: Smart Service Queensland **Tel.:** 13 13 04 **Website:** www.qld.gov.au
Camping fees: From $4.00 per person/night; permit from and fees payable through Smart Service Queensland

20. KROOMBIT TOPS FOREST RESERVE

Kroombit Tops Forest Reserve, adjoining Kroombit Tops National Park, is at the junction of the Dawes, Calliope and Milton ranges, 50 km south-west of Gladstone.
It is reached from the north via the Dawson Hwy then the Monto–Many Peaks Rd (turn-off 3–4 km west of Calliope), then Tablelands Rd. 4WD vehicles are recommended. Kroombit Tops Forest Reserve has spectacular views, lush rainforests and steep escarpments; for safety reasons visitors must take note of all signs. A Permit to Traverse is required here.

Griffiths Creek camping area

On Kroombit Tops Rd, off Tablelands Rd. Contact QPWS Gladstone for access details. 4WD vehicles recommended. Camping permit required. Bring drinking water and firewood. Additional map ref.: STM Qld J7.

The Wall camping area

Reached off Kroombit Tops Rd, off Tablelands Rd. Contact QPWS Gladstone for access details. 4WD vehicles recommended. Camping permit required. Bring drinking water and firewood. Additional map ref.: STM Qld J7.

Further information:
QPWS, Gladstone **Tel.:** (07) 4971 6500 or
QPWS, Rockhampton **Tel.:** (07) 4936 0511
Camping fees: From $4.00 per person/night
Permits: Camping permit and Permit to Traverse from QPWS

21. LAKE AWOONGA

Lake Awoonga is a popular spot for barramundi fishing, sailing, canoeing, waterskiing, swimming and birdwatching. Access to the lake is by Lake Awoonga Rd, which is

signposted off the Bruce Hwy at Benaraby, south of Gladstone. Regulations apply to fishing and waterskiing.

Lake Awoonga Caravan Park

On Lake Awoonga Rd 8 km west of Bruce Hwy. Laundry facilities. Campers kitchen. Firewood supplied. Key access to amenities block with a $5.00 refundable deposit. Bookings essential for public holidays and from June to Sept. Additional map ref.: STM Qld J7.

Further information & bookings: Lake Awoonga Caravan Park **Tel.:** (07) 4975 0155 **Email:** barraheaven@hotkey. com.au **Camping fees:** Unpowered from $8.00 per adult/ night, $4.00 per child/night, power additional $4.00 per site/night

22. LAKE MONDURAN

Lake Monduran is 21 km north of Gin Gin, signposted off the Bruce Hwy. The lake offers picnicking, fishing, boating, swimming and waterskiing.

Lake Monduran Recreation Area

Campers kitchen. Laundry facilities. Bring firewood. Dogs allowed but conditions apply; contact office for details. Bookings recommended during winter. Additional map ref.: STM Qld J7.

Further information & bookings: Lake Monduran Recreation Area **Tel.:** (07) 4157 3881 **Email:** monduran@kolan. qld.gov.au **Camping fees:** Unpowered from $5.50 per site/night up to 2 adults, powered from $11.00 per site/night up to 2 adults

23. LAKE MURPHY CONSERVATION PARK

The seasonal Lake Murphy is a wonderful spot for watching waterbirds. In 1844 Ludwig Leichhardt and his exploration party camped here on their journey to the Northern Territory. Lake Murphy is on the Bauhinia Downs–Expedition National Park Rd 31 km north-west of Taroom. Turn-off is 18 km north of Taroom on the Leichhardt Hwy.

Lake Murphy camping area

Area is 13 km along Bauhinia Downs–Expedition National Park Rd. Camping permit required. Bring drinking water and firewood. Additional map ref.: STM Qld J6.

Further information: QPWS, Taroom **Tel.:** (07) 4627 3358
Camping fees: From $4.00 per person/night; permit from and fees payable at self-registration station

24. MOUTH OF BAFFLE CREEK CONSERVATION PARK

The Mouth of Baffle Creek Conservation Park is north of Wartburg and is popular for beach fishing and surfing. Swimmers should be aware that the beach is unpatrolled and can be dangerous. Access is off Rules Beach Rd, off the Bundaberg–Agnes Water Rd, then by 4WD along the beach (at low tide only). Drivers should check tides and entry point before proceeding onto the beach.

Mouth of Baffle Creek camping area

On northern shore of Baffle Creek behind dune system, 2 km north of beach access point. Camping permit required. Camp only in current campsites. Self-sufficient campers only. Bring drinking water. Gas/fuel stove only. Additional map ref.: STM Qld J7.

Further information & bookings:
QPWS, Agnes Water **Tel.:** (07) 4974 9350 *or* QPWS, Bundaberg **Tel.:** (07) 4131 1600
Camping fees: From $4.00 per person/night; permit from and fees payable at self-registration station at beach access point

25. MOUNT WALSH NATIONAL PARK

The rugged landscape and diverse vegetation of Mount Walsh National Park provide excellent remote bushwalking and hiking for experienced walkers. Walkers need to be self-sufficient, well equipped and carry topographic maps and a compass. Access to the park is 2 km south of Biggenden on the Biggenden–Maryborough Rd. A carpark and picnic area is 5.4 km further south from here. Walkers should contact the ranger before visiting the park, as it is closed at times for safety reasons. A camping permit must be obtained before arrival.

Bush camping

Remote walk-in bush camping. Camping permit required. Self-sufficient, experienced bushwalkers only. Bring drinking water. Gas/fuel stove only. Additional map ref.: STM Qld J8.

Further information: QPWS, Maryborough **Tel.:** (07) 4121 1800 **Camping fees:** From $4.00 per person/night; permit from and fees payable at QPWS Maryborough

26. NUGA NUGA NATIONAL PARK

Nuga Nuga National Park is an important wetland area popular with birdwatchers. Lake Nuga Nuga is a beautiful sight in summer when it is covered with waterlilies. The park has Aboriginal cultural significance, with legends revolving around the lake and surrounding mountains. The park is 151 km north of Injune via Mulcahy Rd off the Carnarvon Developmental Rd. Access is possible in dry weather only and drivers should check road conditions first.

Bush camping

Camping permit required. Self-sufficient campers only. Bring drinking water. Gas/fuel stove preferred. Additional map ref.: STM Qld J6.

Further information: QPWS, Roma **Tel.:** (07) 4622 4266
Further information & bookings: Smart Service Queensland **Tel.:** 13 13 04 **Website:** www.qld.gov.au
Camping fees: From $4.00 per person/night; permit from and fees payable through Smart Service Queensland or QPWS Roma

27. TAROOM

The famous Leichhardt Tree which was blazed by Ludwig Leichhardt during his 1844 exploration is found in the main street of Taroom. Taroom is beside the Dawson River and on the Leichhardt Hwy 120 km north of Miles. Check with the shire council regarding dogs at Chain Lagoons, Sandy Creek Bridge and Widewater areas and to obtain detailed access information.

Taroom Caravan Park

On Short St, Taroom. Bring firewood. Additional map ref.: STM Qld J6.

Further information: Taroom Caravan Park caretaker **Tel.:** (07) 4627 3218 **Camping fees:** Unpowered tent site from $2.20 per person/night, powered van site from $11.00 per site/night up to 2 people

Chain Lagoons camping area

This is 15 km north-east of Taroom, via Old Theodore Rd off the Leichhardt Hwy. Bring drinking water. Gas/fuel stove preferred. Additional map ref.: STM Qld J6.

Sandy Creek Bridge camping area
Area is 8 km south-west of Taroom via Roma Rd. Bring drinking water. Gas/fuel stove preferred. Additional map ref.: STM Qld J6.

Widewater camping area

This is 3 km north of Taroom off the Leichhardt Hwy. Site is east of highway. Access in dry weather only. Bring drinking water. Gas/fuel stove preferred. Additional map ref.: STM Qld J6.

Further information:
Taroom District Development Association **Tel.:** (07) 4628 6113 *or* Taroom Shire Council **Tel.:** (07) 4627 3211

28. TOLDERODDEN CONSERVATION PARK

Tolderodden Conservation Park is reached from Cracow Rd, 6 km west of Eidsvold on the Burnett Hwy. The park's forest offers a peaceful retreat. Try your luck and throw a line in the Burnett River.

Bush camping

Beside the Burnett River. Drinking water from tank – boil before use. Bring firewood. Additional map ref.: STM Qld J7.

Further information: QPWS, Mundubbera **Tel.:** (07) 4165 5110

29. WURUMA DAM

Surrounded by natural bushland, Wuruma Dam is 48 km north of Eidsvold, which is on the Burnett Hwy. Stocked with silver and golden perch, bass and other fish species, the dam is a popular spot for fishing – a Stocked Impoundment Permit is required. At the dam is a picnic and camping area along with a playground. The dam is signposted off the Eidsvold–Monto Rd.

Wuruma Dam camping area

Along Cynthia Range Rd. Firewood supplied. Additional map ref.: STM Qld J7.

Further information: SunWater, Bundaberg **Tel.:** (07) 4132 6200

THE COASTAL AREAS OF THE MID
TROPICS BOAST SANDY BEACHES
AND EASY ACCESS TO THE
TROPICAL ISLANDS OF THE
GREAT BARRIER REEF. VISITORS
CAN DELIGHT IN THE REEF'S
BRIGHTLY COLOURED CORALS, MAGNIFICENT FISH,
TURTLES AND DUGONGS, SET SAIL IN A BOAT ON A
CALM DAY, OR SIMPLY SOAK UP THE SUNSHINE ON
ONE OF THE MANY SUPERB BEACHES. IN THE WEST
OF THE REGION VISITORS WILL FIND SOME

FASCINATING HISTORIC TOWNS LIKE CHARTERS
TOWERS, THE SITE OF ONE OF AUSTRALIA'S MOST
FAMOUS GOLD RUSHES.

The township of Eungella is 80 kilometres
west of Mackay, surrounded by the picturesque
and rugged Eungella National Park. The southern
section of the park is the most accessible part and
is popular with daytrippers and campers. Campers
can set up beside the Broken River then take their
time enjoying nature walks and scenic sights, or
try spotting a platypus in the river.

North-west of Eungella is the large Eungella Dam, a popular camping and watersports venue. Campers who throw in a line can try their luck at catching a barramundi or sooty grunter.

On the coast, 50 kilometres north of Mackay, are the rugged headlands and beaches of Cape Hillsborough National Park. The park has spectacular scenery, walking tracks to lookouts, picnic areas and the remains of Aboriginal fish traps. Smalleys Beach camping area, to the west of the park on Ball Bay, has limited facilities.

The Queensland Parks and Wildlife Service allows camping on some of the Great Barrier Reef islands. Many of these have no facilities, offering campers the chance to experience the peace and solitude of a tropical, and sometimes deserted, paradise. Campers here must be self-sufficient, carrying enough food and water supplies, and since campfires are prohibited on all Great Barrier Reef islands, they must bring stoves for cooking.

The Whitsunday Islands National Park, off Airlie Beach, includes four islands that allow camping: Hook, Henning, Whitsunday and Cid. Whitsunday Island has eight camping areas around its shores, situated amongst natural forests and a short walk from the beautiful sandy beaches. The popular Dunk Island is within Family Islands National Park. Campers at the Dunk Island Spit camping area can explore the island along one of the walking trails.

BEST CAMPSITES

Ball Bay Campground
Mackay area

Saddleback Island
Gloucester Islands National Park

Smalleys Beach camping area
Cape Hillsborough National Park

Eungella Dam camping area
Eungella Dam

Joes Beach camping area
Whitsunday Islands National Park

BEST TIME TO VISIT

In winter, when temperatures are comfortable and weather conditions are steady; from Nov.–April deadly marine stingers inhabit the waters surrounding the offshore islands.

1. ABERGOWRIE STATE FOREST

The diverse forests here provide habitats for a large number of bird species, and the waterholes in Broadwater Creek are an excellent spot to cool off after enjoying one of the forest's walking tracks. Those who prefer longer walks can take the 8-km one-way, medium-grade Dalrymple Gap Walking Track – walkers should contact QPWS to check track conditions before setting out. Abergowrie State Forest is 45 km north-west of Ingham via Abergowie Rd.

Broadwater camping area

Signposted off Abergowrie Rd, 45 km north-west of Ingham. Area is beside Broadwater Creek. Camping permit required. Bore water – boil before use. Firewood supplied. Additional map ref.: STM Qld F4.

Dalrymple Gap Walking Track camping area

Bush camping for walkers only, at southern and northern end of walking track. Dalrymple Gap Walking Track is 8 km, one way. The northern trackhead is 14 km south of Cardwell, signposted off the Bruce Hwy, and the southern trackhead is 37 km west of Ingham, signposted off Abergowrie Rd. Camping permit required. Self-sufficient campers only. Bring drinking water. Gas/fuel stove only. Additional map ref.: STM Qld F4.

Further information: QPWS, Ingham **Tel.:** (07) 4777 2822
Dalrymple Gap Walking Track Southern end: QPWS, Ingham, tel. (07) 4777 2822
Northern end: QPWS, Cardwell, tel. (07) 4066 8601
Camping fees: From $4.00 per person/night *Broadwater* Permit from and fees payable at self-registration station *Dalrymple Gap Walking Track* Permit from and fees payable to QPWS Ingham or Cardwell

2. BLACKWOOD NATIONAL PARK

Blackwood National Park is named after the tall acacia, or blackwood, which grow in the park. The varying ecosystems within the park provide refuge for a diverse range of wildlife and the park is popular with birdwatchers. It is only accessible by 4WD and is signposted from the Gregory Developmental Rd 180 km south-east of Charters Towers.

Blackwood camping area

4WD access. Camping area is at the gravel pit along the park's main access road. Camping permit required. Bring drinking water. Gas/fuel stove preferred. Additional map ref.: STM Qld G5.

Further information:
QPWS, Charters Towers **Tel.:** (07) 4787 3388 *or*
QPWS, Townsville **Tel.:** (07) 4721 2399
Camping fees: From $4.00 per person/night; permit from and fees payable to QPWS Charters Towers or Townsville

3. BOWLING GREEN BAY NATIONAL PARK

Bowling Green Bay National Park is off the Bruce Hwy south-east of Townsville. Alligator Creek tumbles down from Mt Elliot and the ranges, creating a scenic waterfall which can be reached by a walking trail from the camping area. The collection of firewood is prohibited in the park.

Bowling Green Bay camping area

Signposted off the Bruce Hwy 29 km south-east of Townsville, then 6 km to park boundary. Camping permit required. Solar hot showers. Firewood supplied. Bookings required from June–Sept. and for Easter and Christmas. Additional map ref.: STM Qld F5.

Further information: QPWS, Bowling Green Bay National Park **Tel.:** (07) 4778 8203 **Further information & bookings:** Smart Service Queensland **Tel.:** 13 13 04 **Website:** www.qld. gov.au **Camping fees:** From $4.00 per person/night; permit from and fees payable through Smart Service Queensland or at self-registration station outside peak periods

4. BURDEKIN FALLS DAM

Burdekin Falls Dam on Lake Dalrymple is 120 km south-east of Mingela, which is on the Flinders Hwy. The large lake is stocked with barramundi, making it a popular spot for fishing (a Stocked Impoundment Permit is required). Other water activities include sailing, canoeing and waterskiing. The dam is signposted off the Flinders Hwy at Mingela via Ravenswood Rd.

Burdekin Falls Dam Caravan Park

At Burdekin Falls Dam. Swimming pool. Gas/fuel stove only. No bookings – first in, best dressed. Christmas and Easter are extremely popular. Additional map ref.: STM Qld G5.

Further information: Burdekin Falls Dam Caravan Park **Tel.:** (07) 4770 3177 **Camping fees:** From $5.00 per person/night, power additional $5.00 per site/night

5. BYFIELD NATIONAL PARK

Byfield National Park is on the coast east of Byfield and north of Yeppoon. The park protects areas of coastal heath, eucalypt woodland and rainforest. It is reached from the Byfield Rd 43 km north of Yeppoon. The park entrance, where there is an information board, is 12 km from the Byfield Rd and the beach is a further 10 km via Nine Mile Beach Rd – beach access by 4WD only.

Nine Mile Beach camping area

Beach camping at northern end of Nine Mile Beach, 22 km from Byfield Rd. Access via Nine Mile Beach Rd from Byfield State Forest. Self-sufficient campers only. Bring drinking water and firewood. Additional map ref.: STM Qld H7.

Waterpark Point Headland camping area

Beach camping inside headland. Boat access only – boat landings at Corbetts Landing and Sandy Point. Camping permit required. Self-sufficient campers only. Bring drinking water. Gas/fuel stove only. Bookings necessary. Additional map ref.: STM Qld H7.

Further information: QPWS, Rockhampton **Tel.:** (07) 4936 0511 **Further information & bookings:** Smart Service Queensland **Tel.:** 13 13 04 **Website:** www.qld. gov.au **Camping fees:** *Waterpark Point Headland* From $4.00 per person/night; permit from and fees payable through Smart Service Queensland

6. BYFIELD STATE FOREST

Byfield State Forest is north of Yeppoon and south of Byfield via the Byfield Rd. Visitors can enjoy a stroll along one of the walking tracks, cool off in a creek or enjoy the sights and sounds of the forests. Dogs are allowed at Red Rock camping area only. Freshwater stonefish (bullrouts) are found at the Waterpark Creek and Upper Stony swimming areas; to avoid being stung, wear sturdy shoes when wading. Contact QPWS for further details regarding safety and recommended first aid for stings.

Red Rock camping area

This is 1 km east of Byfield Rd and signposted from it. Camping permit required. Undefined walking trails here. Bring drinking water. Firewood supplied. Additional map ref.: STM Qld H7.

Upper Stony camping area

Area is 10 km west of Byfield Rd and signposted from it. Camping permit required. Bring drinking water. Firewood supplied. Bookings necessary. Additional map ref.: STM Qld H7.

Waterpark Creek camping area

Located 2 km north of Byfield Rd and signposted from it. Camping permit required. Bring drinking water. Firewood supplied. Bookings necessary. Additional map ref.: STM Qld H7.

Further information: QPWS, Rockhampton **Tel.:** (07) 4936 0511 **Further information & bookings:** Smart Service Queensland **Tel.:** 13 13 04 **Website:** www.qld. gov.au **Camping fees:** From $4.00 per person/night *Red Rock* Permit from and fees payable at self-registration station *Upper Stony and Waterpark Creek* Permit from and fees payable through Smart Service Queensland

7. CAPE HILLSBOROUGH NATIONAL PARK

Cape Hillsborough National Park, 10 km east of Seaforth and about 55 km north of Mackay, has spectacular coastal scenery with rocky headlands and sandy beaches. The park is home to kangaroos and scrub turkeys along with a variety of land and sea birds. Visitors can take walking tracks to the various scenic areas within the park. The park is reached by Cape Hillsborough Rd off the Seaforth Rd, which leaves the Bruce Hwy 20 km north of Mackay. The waters around Cape Hillsborough National Park are within the Great Barrier Reef Marine Park – obtain a copy of the marine park's zoning map for permitted activities.

Smalleys Beach camping area

Area is north of Cape Hillsborough Rd and signposted from it. Camping permit required. Bring drinking water. Bring own fire container and firewood. Gas/fuel stove preferred. Additional map ref.: STM Qld G6.

Further information:
QPWS, Cape Hillsborough National Park **Tel.:** (07) 4959 0410 *or*
QPWS, Mackay **Tel.:** (07) 4944 7800
Camping fees: From $4.00 per person/night; permit from and fees payable at self-registration station

8. CAPE PALMERSTON NATIONAL PARK

Cape Palmerston National Park protects areas of Aboriginal cultural heritage as well as a range of plant and animal species. It is reached by Cape Palmerston Rd off the Greenhill Rd from Ilbilbie on the Bruce Hwy. The park's entrance is 14 km north-east of Ilbilbie. Driving within the park is by 4WD vehicle only and there are areas where beach driving is required – drivers need to check and be aware of tides. The waters around Cape Palmerston National Park are within the Great Barrier Reef Marine Park – obtain a copy of the marine park's zoning map for permitted activities.

Cape Creek campsite

South-west of Cape Palmerston. 4WD access only. Camping permit required. Self-sufficient campers only. Bring drinking water. Gas/fuel stove only. Additional map ref.: STM Qld G6.

Clarke Bay campsite

West of Cape Palmerston. 4WD access only. Camping permit required. Self-sufficient campers only. Bring drinking water. Gas/fuel stove only. Additional map ref.: STM Qld G6.

Windmill Bay campsite

On the eastern edge of park, south of Cape Palmerston. 4WD access only. Camping permit required. Self-sufficient campers only. Bring drinking water. Gas/fuel stove only. Additional map ref.: STM Qld G6.

Further information: QPWS, Mackay **Tel.:** (07) 4944 7800
Camping fees: From $4.00 per person/night; permit from and fees payable at self-registration stations at each campsite

9. CAPE UPSTART NATIONAL PARK

Cape Upstart National Park is a large headland north of Bowen and south of Ayr. It can only be reached by boat; nearby boat ramps are at Elliot River near Guthalungra or near Gumlu at Molongle Bay. The waters surrounding the park are in the Great Barrier Reef Marine Park – obtain a copy of the marine park's zoning map for permitted activities.

Coconut Bay camping area

This is 30 km north of Guthalungra. Boat access only. Camping permit required. Self-sufficient campers only. Bring drinking water. Gas/fuel stove only. Additional map ref.: STM Qld F5.

Further information: QPWS, Whitsunday Information Centre, Airlie Beach **Tel.:** (07) 4946 7022 **Camping fees:** From $4.00 per person/night; permit from and fees payable to QPWS Airlie Beach

10. CARDWELL AREA

Cardwell is on the Bruce Hwy 52 km north of Ingham and 96 km south of Innisfail. To the west of Cardwell are Blencoe Falls and Cashmere Crossing. Access to these is by an unsealed dry-weather-only road and 4WD is recommended. Contact the Shire of Hinchinbrook for detailed access information and road conditions.

Blencoe Creek bush camping

Camping beside Blencoe Creek 83 km west of Cardwell. 4WD recommended. Bush camping, no facilities. Bring drinking water and firewood. Gas/fuel stove preferred. Additional map ref.: STM Qld F4.

Cashmere Crossing bush camping

Camping at Cashmere Crossing on the Herbert River, 29 km west of Blencoe Creek. 4WD recommended. Bush camping, no facilities. Bring drinking water and firewood. Gas/fuel stove preferred. Additional map ref.: STM Qld F4.

Further information:
Hinchinbrook Shire Council **Tel.:** (07) 4776 4600 *or*
Hinchinbrook Visitor Information Centre **Tel.:** (07) 4776 5211

11. CATHU STATE FOREST

Clarke Range Lookout in Cathu State Forest provides stunning views east to the Whitsunday Islands. Visitors with a 4WD can enjoy the sights and activities along the Loop Rd, including the Muirs Rd walk and Kangaroo Creek. A Permit to Traverse is necessary. To reach Cathu State Forest take the Cathu–O'Connell River Rd from Calen on the Bruce Hwy.

Jaxut Camping and Day Use Area

This is 20 km west of Calen via Cathu–O'Connell River Rd. Access road is very steep and not suitable for large caravans. Camping permit required. Bring drinking water. Firewood supplied. Additional map ref.: STM Qld G6.

Further information: QPWS, Mackay **Tel.:** (07) 4944 7800
Camping fees: From $4.00 per person/night; permit from and fees payable at self-registration station

12. CHARTERS TOWERS AREA

See also Dalrymple National Park, page 318

The Fletcher Creek Camping Reserve is 45 km north of Charters Towers, beside Fletcher Creek near the entrance to Dalrymple National Park. Charters Towers is on the Flinders Hwy, 135 km south-west of Townsville and 243 km north-east of Hughenden.

Fletcher Creek Camping Reserve

Camping beside Fletcher Creek. Access via the Gregory Developmental Rd. Bring drinking water and firewood. Additional map ref.: STM Qld F5.

Further information:
Dalrymple Shire Council **Tel.:** (07) 4787 5600 *or*
Charters Towers and Dalrymple Visitor Information Centre **Tel.:** (07) 4752 0314

13. CONWAY NATIONAL PARK

Conway National Park features lush rainforests, coastal forests and grass trees. While enjoying one of the walks visitors may encounter brush turkeys and scrub fowl. The park is reached from Airlie Beach, which is 26 km east of the Bruce Hwy.

Swamp Bay camping area

Walk-in only site via Swamp Bay Track. Walk is 2.1 km one-way from carpark on Shute Harbour Rd. Camping permit required. Self-sufficient campers only. Bring drinking water. Gas/fuel stove only. Additional map ref.: STM Qld G6.

Further information: QPWS, Whitsunday Information Centre, Airlie Beach **Tel.:** (07) 4946 7022 **Camping fees:** From $4.00 per person/night; permit from and fees payable to QPWS Airlie Beach

14. CREDITON STATE FOREST

Crediton State Forest is in Mackay's hinterland, beside Eungella National Park and 8 km south of Eungella. This scenic open-eucalypt forest has 4WD opportunities. Detailed access information is available from the Mackay office of QPWS, where you can also apply for a camping permit and a Permit to Traverse.

Captains Crossing camping area

Accessible in dry weather only. Camping permit and Permit to Traverse required. Self-sufficient campers only. No facilities. Bring drinking water and firewood. Gas/fuel stove preferred. Additional map ref.: STM Qld G6.

Crediton Area camping area

Accessible in dry weather only. Camping permit and Permit to Traverse required. Self-sufficient campers only. No facilities. Bring drinking water and firewood. Additional map ref.: STM Qld G6.

The Diggings camping area

Accessible in dry weather only. Camping permit and Permit to Traverse required. Self-sufficient campers only. No facilities. Bring drinking water and firewood. Gas/fuel stove preferred. This area has many disused mine shafts – be careful and obey all safety signs. Additional map ref.: STM Qld G6.

Further information: QPWS, Mackay **Tel.:** (07) 4944 7800 **Camping fees:** From $4.00 per person/night **Permits:** Permit to Traverse and camping permit from and fees payable to QPWS Mackay

15. CUMBERLAND ISLANDS

This group of islands, comprising several national parks, lies off the coast north of Mackay. They have a range of vegetation and are home to a variety of birds and animals, while the surrounding waters are rich in marine species. The islands are in the Great Barrier Reef Marine Park – obtain a copy of the marine park's zoning map for permitted activities. They are reached by ferry or private boat from Mackay harbour. Bookings are essential for camping on all islands.

Carlisle Island

Boat access only. Camping on island's southern coast. Camping permit required. Bring drinking water. Gas/fuel stove only. Additional map ref.: STM Qld G6.

Cockermouth Island

This is north-east of Seaforth. Access via private boat or water taxi. Camping permit required. Self-sufficient campers only. Bring drinking water. Gas/fuel stove only. Additional map ref.: STM Qld G6.

Goldsmith Island

This is 30 km north-east of Seaforth. Access by private boat or water taxi. Camping permit required. Self-sufficient campers only. Bring drinking water. Gas/fuel stove only. Additional map ref.: STM Qld G6.

Keswick Island

East of Seaforth. Access via private boat or water taxi. Camping permit required. Self-sufficient campers only. Bring drinking water. Gas/fuel stove only. Additional map ref.: STM Qld G6.

St Bees Island

East of Cape Hillsborough. Access via private boat. Camping permit required. Self-sufficient campers only. Bring drinking water. Gas/fuel stove only. Additional map ref.: STM Qld G6.

Scawfell Island

This is 60 km north-east of Mackay. Access via private boat or water taxi. Camping permit required. Bring drinking water. Gas/fuel stove only. Additional map ref.: STM Qld G6.

Further information: QPWS, Mackay **Tel.:** (07) 4944 7800 **Further information & bookings:** Smart Service Queensland **Tel.:** 13 13 04 **Website:** www.qld.gov.au **Camping fees:** From $4.00 per person/night; permit from and fees payable through Smart Service Queensland or to QPWS Mackay

16. DALRYMPLE NATIONAL PARK

See also Charters Towers area, page 317

Dalrymple National Park features the Burdekin River, Mt Keelbottom and lava flows of the Toomba Basalt. The Burdekin River and its banks provide a habitat for waterbirds and attract birdwatchers. Dalrymple National Park is 46 km north-west of Charters Towers and reached by the Gregory Developmental Rd. Bushwalkers must complete a Remote Bushwalking Form and contact a QPWS office at least one week prior to arrival.

Burdekin River camping area

Camping beside Burdekin River. Camping permit required. Bring drinking water. Gas/fuel stove preferred. Bookings can be made but are not necessary. Additional map ref.: STM Qld F5.

Bush camping

Remote walk-in bush camping for self-sufficient, experienced walkers. Camping permit required. Bring drinking water. Gas/fuel stove only.

Further information:
QPWS, Charters Towers **Tel.:** (07) 4787 3388 *or* QPWS, Townsville **Tel.:** (07) 4721 2399
Camping fees: From $4.00 per person/night; permit from and fees payable to QPWS Charters Towers or Townsville

17. DRYANDER NATIONAL PARK

Dryander National Park is on the coast 3 km south-east of Dingo Beach and north-west of Airlie Beach. It is accessible by boat only from either Dingo Beach or Airlie Beach. The waters around the park are within the Great Barrier Reef Marine Park – obtain a copy of the marine park's zoning map for permitted activities.

Grimstone Point camping area

Camping permit required. Self-sufficient campers only. Bring drinking water. Gas/fuel stove only. Additional map ref.: STM Qld G6.

Further information: QPWS, Whitsunday Information Centre, Airlie Beach **Tel.:** (07) 4946 7022 **Camping fees:** From $4.00 per person/night; permit from and fees payable to QPWS Airlie Beach

18. EUNGELLA DAM

The dam, north-west of Eungella, was originally built for a thermal power station at Collinsville and to supply town water to Collinsville and Scottsville. Fishing on the dam is a popular pastime, with barramundi and sooty grunter stocked. A Stocked Impoundment Permit is required. Other recreational activities include waterskiing, swimming, canoeing and boating. The dam is signposted from Eungella.

Eungella Dam camping area

Bring drinking water and firewood. Additional map ref.: STM Qld G6.

Further information: SunWater, Mackay **Tel.:** (07) 4967 0941 **Camping fees:** From $3.85 per person/night; fees payable at self-registration station

19. EUNGELLA NATIONAL PARK

See also Finch Hatton Gorge, *page 319*

The rugged Eungella National Park preserves areas of central-Queensland rainforest. The park offers excellent visitor facilities including lookouts, picnic areas, a platypus viewing area, a camping area and a number of walks including the Rainforest Discovery Walks. Eungella National Park is 5 km south of Eungella and is signposted from there on the Eungella Dam Rd.

Fern Flat Campground

Camping permit required. Bring firewood or purchase from kiosk. Additional map ref.: STM Qld G6.

Further information:
QPWS, Eungella National Park **Tel.:** (07) 4958 4552 *or* QPWS, Mackay **Tel.:** (07) 4944 7800
Camping fees: From $4.00 per person/night; permit from and fees payable at self-registration station

20. FAMILY ISLANDS NATIONAL PARK

Family Islands National Park is a group of islands off the coast north of Cardwell and reached by boat from Mission Beach. The islands are within the Great Barrier Reef Marine Park – obtain a copy of the marine park's zoning map for permitted activities.

Coombe Island

Bush camping. Private boat access from Mission Beach. Camping permit required. Self-sufficient campers only. Bring drinking water. Gas/fuel stove only. Bookings necessary. Additional map ref.: STM Qld E5.

Dunk Island Spit camping area

On west coast of island – 9 sites only. Camping permit required. Gas/fuel stove only. Maximum of 5 nights' stay. Bookings essential; advance bookings, up to 6 months ahead, apply for Easter, June–July and Christmas. Additional map ref.: STM Qld E5.

Further information & bookings: Dunk Island Resort **Tel.:** (07) 4068 8199 **Camping fees:** From $4.00 per person/night; permit from and fees payable to Dunk Island Resort

Wheeler Island

Bush camping. Private boat access from Mission Beach. Camping permit required. Self-sufficient campers only. Bring drinking water. Gas/fuel stove only. Bookings necessary. Additional map ref.: STM Qld E5.

Further information: QPWS, Cardwell **Tel.:** (07) 4066 8601 **Further information & bookings:** Smart Service Queensland **Tel.:** 13 13 04 **Website:** www.qld.gov.au **Camping fees:** From $4.00 per person/night; permit from and fees payable through Smart Service Queensland

21. FINCH HATTON GORGE

The magnificent Finch Hatton Gorge is part of Eungella National Park. The gorge is 40 km east of Eungella and 37 km west of Mirani. A carpark and picnic area is 10 km north of the Eungella–Mackay Rd – the turn-off is 1 km east of the Finch Hatton township. From the picnic area there is a 2.1-km walk through tropical rainforest up the gorge and to Araluen Falls. There is no camping in Finch Hatton Gorge but the Platypus Bush Camp, just outside the national park, is nestled in beautiful rainforest.

Platypus Bush Camp

This is 8 km north of Eungella–Mackay Rd and signposted from it. Hot-water donkey shower system. Water from river. Firewood supplied. Additional map ref.: STM Qld G6.

Further information & bookings: Platypus Bush Camp **Tel.:** (07) 4958 3204 **Email:** wazza@bushcamp.net **Website:** www.bushcamp.net **Camping fees:** From $7.50 per person/night

22. FIVE ROCKS CONSERVATION PARK

Five Rocks Conservation Park is north of Byfield National Park. It is reached by 4WD vehicle only from Waterpark Creek camping area in Byfield State Forest north of Yeppoon. The conservation park is about 20 km from the camping area. Enjoy walking along the beach and fishing.

Five Rocks camping area

4WD access only. Camping permit required. Bore water. Gas/fuel stove only. Additional map ref.: STM Qld H7.

Further information: QPWS, Rockhampton **Tel.:** (07) 4936 0511 **Camping fees:** From $4.00 per person/night; permit from and fees payable at self-registration station

23. GLOUCESTER ISLANDS NATIONAL PARK

The islands of Gloucester Islands National Park lie in an arc off the mainland east of Bowen and north of Airlie Beach. They are reached by boat from Shute Harbour and Dingo Beach, and four islands in the group allow camping. Detailed access information is available from the QPWS Whitsunday Information Centre, Airlie Beach. Gloucester Islands National Park is within the Great Barrier Reef Marine Park – obtain a copy of the marine park's zoning map for permitted activities. Maximum camper numbers apply at all campsites and bookings are essential for all islands.

Armit Island

Armit Island is west of Olden Island. Camping is on the south-western side of the island. Camping permit required. Self-sufficient campers only. Gas/fuel stove only. Additional map ref.: STM Qld G6.

Olden Island

Olden Island is south of George Point. Camping permit required. Self-sufficient campers only. Gas/fuel stove only. Additional map ref.: STM Qld G6.

Saddleback Island

To the south-east of Gloucester Island and west of George Point. Camping on the island's western side. Camping permit required. Self-sufficient campers only. Bring drinking water. Gas/fuel stove only. Additional map ref.: STM Qld G6.

GLOUCESTER ISLAND

Bona Bay camping area

On the south-western side of Gloucester Island, 10 km east of Bowen. Access from Bowen or Dingo Beach. Camping permit required. Self-sufficient campers only. Gas/fuel stove only. Additional map ref.: STM Qld G6.

East Side Bay camping area

On the east side of Gloucester Island. Camping permit required. Self-sufficient campers only. Bring drinking water. Gas/fuel stove only. Additional map ref.: STM Qld G6.

Further information: QPWS, Whitsunday Information Centre, Airlie Beach **Tel.:** (07) 4946 7022 **Further information & bookings:** Smart Service Queensland **Tel.:** 13 13 04 **Website:** www.qld.gov.au **Camping fees:** From $4.00 per person/night; permit from and fees payable through Smart Service Queensland or at the QPWS Whitsunday Information Centre, Airlie Beach

24. GOOLD ISLAND NATIONAL PARK

Goold Island is known for its flocks of sulphur-crested cockatoos and for the turtles and dugongs that can be seen feeding in the shallow waters to the south and west. The island is 17 km north-east of Cardwell and is reached by private boat or ferry service from there. The island is in the Great Barrier Reef Marine Park – obtain a copy of the marine park's zoning map for permitted activities.

Western Beach camping area

On west coast of island. Camping permit required. Bring drinking water. Gas/fuel stove only. Additional map ref.: STM Qld F5.

Further information & bookings: QPWS, Cardwell **Tel.:** (07) 4066 8601 **Camping fees:** From $4.00 per person/night; permit from and fees payable to QPWS Cardwell

25. HINCHINBROOK ISLAND NATIONAL PARK

Hinchinbrook Island is 8 km east of Cardwell. It is Australia's largest island national park and is renowned for its rainforest, swamps and mangroves. The waters surrounding the island support a large range of marine life including dugong and green turtles. The Thorsborne Trail is a popular 32-km (3–5 day) walking trail on the east coast of the island. The island is in the Great Barrier Reef Marine Park – obtain a copy of the marine park's zoning map for permitted activities. Access to the island is by private boat or water taxi from Cardwell and Dungeness. Bookings are necessary for all camping on the island.

Banshee Bay camping area

On east of island, to north of Ramsay Bay. Access by private boat only. Camping permit required. Self-sufficient campers only. Bring drinking water. Gas/fuel stove only. Additional map ref.: STM Qld F5.

Macushla camping area

In north of island, on east coast of Missionary Bay. Access by private boat or commercial operator. Camping permit required. Bring drinking water. Gas/fuel stove only. Additional map ref.: STM Qld F5.

Sunset Beach camping area

On east of island. Access by private boat only. Camping permit required. Self-sufficient campers only. Bring drinking water. Gas/fuel stove only. Additional map ref.: STM Qld F5.

The Haven camping area

On west coast of island, in Hinchinbrook Channel. Private-boat access only. Camping permit required. Bring drinking water. Gas/fuel stove only. Additional map ref.: STM Qld F5.

Bush camping

Other areas of bush camping on the east coast. Private-boat access or walk-in only. Camping permit required. Self-sufficient campers only. Bring drinking water. Gas/fuel stove only.

THORSBORNE TRAIL CAMPING AREAS

Bookings are necessary to walk this trail. Bookings are through QPWS Cardwell and can be made up to 12 months in advance for holiday periods. Camping areas are listed in the order they are reached from the northern trackhead at Ramsay Bay.

Nina Bay camping area

This is 4 km south of Ramsay Bay trackhead. Camping permit required. Water from nearby creek – boil before use. Gas/fuel stove only. Additional map ref.: STM Qld F5.

Little Ramsay Bay camping area

Area is 2.5 km south of Nina Bay. Camping permit required. Water from nearby creek – boil before use. Gas/fuel stove only. Additional map ref.: STM Qld F5.

Zoe Bay camping area

This is 10.5 km south of Little Ramsay Bay. Camping permit required. Water from nearby creek – boil before use. Gas/fuel stove only. Additional map ref.: STM Qld F5.

Sunken Reef Bay camping area

Side trip east of Diamantina Creek. Diamantina Creek is 6.5 km south of Zoe Bay. Camping permit required. Water from nearby creek – boil before use. Gas/fuel stove only. Additional map ref.: STM Qld F5.

Mulligan Falls camping area

Area is 7.5 km south of Zoe Bay and 1 km south of Diamantina Creek. Camping permit required. Water from nearby creek – boil before use. Gas/fuel stove only. Additional map ref.: STM Qld F5.

George Point camping area

Southern trackhead of trail, 7.5 km south of Mulligan Falls. Camping permit required. Water from Mulligan Falls. Gas/fuel stove only. Additional map ref.: STM Qld F5.

Further information & bookings:
QPWS, Cardwell **Tel.:** (07) 4066 8601 *or*
Smart Service Queensland **Tel.:** 13 13 04
Website: www.qld.gov.au
Camping fees: From $4.00 per person/night; permit from and fees payable through Smart Service Queensland or QPWS Cardwell

26. KINCHANT DAM

Kinchant Dam is 40 km west of Mackay and is signposted off the Peak Downs Hwy at Eton. The dam is an excellent site for relaxing or indulging in activities such as waterskiing, jet-skiing, canoeing, swimming, fishing and boating (a Stocked Impoundment Permit is necessary to fish here). Birdwatching and walking are other popular pastimes.

Kinchant Waters

Laundry facilities. Firewood supplied. Additional map ref.: STM Qld G6.

Further information & bookings: Kinchant Waters
Tel.: (07) 4954 1453 **Camping fees:** Unpowered from $5.00 per person/night, powered from $6.50 per person/night (fees are under revision)

27. LAKE PROSERPINE

Stocked with barramundi and sooty grunter, Lake Proserpine is popular with fisherfolk (a Stocked Impoundment Permit is required). The lake is also suitable for boating, waterskiing, canoeing and swimming. Lake Proserpine is 28 km west of Proserpine, which lies on the Bruce Hwy. Just 1.5 km from the lake is Camp Kanga.

Camp Kanga

This is 24 km west of Proserpine and reached by Crystal Brook Rd. Laundry facilities. Bring firewood. Boat ramp at Lake Proserpine. Bookings recommended, and dogs allowed by application only. Additional map ref.: STM Qld G6.

Further information & bookings: Camp Kanga
Tel.: (07) 4947 2600 **Email:** campkanga@mrbean.net.au
Website: www.peterfaustdam.com **Camping fees:**
Unpowered from $11.00 per site/night for 2 people, powered from $13.00 per site/night for 2 people

28. LINDEMAN ISLANDS NATIONAL PARK

The scenic islands of this national park are east of the Whitsunday Passage. Access to the islands is via boat from Shute Harbour or Laguna Quays. Detailed access information is available from the QPWS Whitsunday Information Centre in Airlie Beach. Lindeman Islands National Park is within the Great Barrier Reef Marine Park – obtain a copy of the marine park's zoning map for permitted activities. Maximum camper numbers apply to all campsites and bookings are necessary.

Lindeman Island

Camping at Boat Port, on north-western side of island. Camping permit required. Self-sufficient campers only. Bring drinking water. Gas/fuel stove only. Additional map ref.: STM Qld G6.

Thomas Island

Camping at Naked Lady Beach on island's west coast. Thomas Island is south-east of Shaw Island. Camping permit required. Self-sufficient campers only. Bring drinking water. Gas/fuel stove only. Additional map ref.: STM Qld G6.

SHAW ISLAND

Burning Point camping area

Burning Point is on the south-western side of Shaw Island, which is east of Lindeman Island. Camping permit required. Self-sufficient campers only. Bring drinking water. Gas/fuel stove only. Additional map ref.: STM Qld G6.

Neck Bay camping area

Neck Bay is at the northern end of Shaw Island. Camping permit required. Self-sufficient campers only. Bring drinking water. Gas/fuel stove only. Additional map ref.: STM Qld G6.

Further information: QPWS, Whitsunday Information Centre, Airlie Beach **Tel.:** (07) 4946 7022 **Further information & bookings:** Smart Service Queensland **Tel.:** 13 13 04 **Website:** www.qld.gov.au **Camping fees:** From $4.00 per person/night; permit from and fees payable through Smart Service Queensland or at QPWS

29. LUMHOLTZ NATIONAL PARK

Visitors to the Wallaman Falls section of Lumholtz National Park will see spectacular waterfalls, beautiful rainforests and eucalypt forests, while in the Mount Fox section there is evidence of the region's volcanic past. The Wallaman Falls section is 51 km west of Ingham (conventional vehicles can reach it); the Mount Fox section is 75 km south-west of Ingham (4WD recommended).

Mount Fox section bush camping

4WD access via Abergowrie Rd. Contact QPWS Ingham for further access details. Camping permit required. Self-sufficient campers only. Bring drinking water. Gas/fuel stove only. Bookings necessary. Additional map ref.: STM Qld F4.

Wallaman Falls camping area

Signposted along Wallaman Falls Rd off Trebonne Rd from Ingham. Camping permit required. Bring drinking water. Gas/fuel stove only. Additional map ref.: STM Qld F4.

Yamanie camping area

Located 54 km west of Ingham, with 4WD access via Abergowrie Rd. Contact QPWS Ingham for further access details. Camping permit required. Self-sufficient campers only. Bring drinking water. Gas/fuel stove only. Bookings necessary. Additional map ref.: STM Qld F4.

Further information & bookings: QPWS, Ingham **Tel.:** (07) 4777 2822 **Camping fees:** From $4.00 per person/night; permit from and fees payable at self-registration station at Wallaman Falls or QPWS Ingham

30. MACKAY AREA

The busy coastal city of Mackay is on the Bruce Hwy and is surrounded by sugarcane farms. Mackay provides easy access to the islands off its coast and is close to many national parks. In Mackay visitors can take a walk around the city to view the historical buildings, take a tour of a sugar mill, enjoy the views from one of the city's lookouts or relax on a beach.

Ball Bay Campground

Foreshore location 35 km north of Mackay. Signposted off Cape Hillsborough Rd. Firewood supplied. Additional map ref.: STM Qld G6.

St Helens Beach camping area

In the township of St Helens, 54 km north of Mackay. Firewood supplied. Additional map ref.: STM Qld G6.

Seaforth Camping Reserve

This is 45 km north of Mackay and is signposted along Seaforth–Yakapari Rd. Firewood supplied. Additional map ref.: STM Qld G6.

Further information:
Mackay City Council **Tel.:** (07) 4968 4444 or
Mackay Visitor Information Centre **Tel.:** (07) 4952 2677
Camping fees: From $12.10 per site/night for up to 2 adults + 3 children; fees collected daily

31. MOLLE ISLANDS NATIONAL PARK

Molle Islands National Park is east of Shute Harbour and west of Whitsunday Island. It is reached by boat from Shute Harbour. Detailed access information is available from the QPWS Whitsunday Information Centre in Airlie Beach. Molle Islands National Park is within the Great Barrier Reef Marine Park – obtain a copy of the marine park's zoning map for permitted activities. Maximum camper numbers apply to all campsites and bookings are necessary; boat transfer tickets must be arranged before booking sites.

Denman Island camping area

Denman Island is east of South Molle Island. Camping permit required. Self-sufficient campers only. Bring drinking water. Gas/fuel stove only. Additional map ref.: STM Qld G6.

Long Island

Camping at Sandy Bay on western side of island. Long Island is south of South Molle Island. Camping permit required. Self-sufficient campers only. Bring drinking water. Gas/fuel stove only. Additional map ref.: STM Qld G6.

North Molle Island

Camping at Cockatoo Beach at southern end of island. Camping permit required. Self-sufficient campers only. Limited tank water at site – bring drinking water. Gas/fuel stove only. Additional map ref.: STM Qld G6.

Planton Island

Planton Island is east of South Molle Island. Camping permit required. Self-sufficient campers only. Bring drinking water. Gas/fuel stove only. Additional map ref.: STM Qld G6.

Tancred Island

Small island close to Shute Harbour. Camping permit required. Self-sufficient campers only. Bring drinking water. Gas/fuel stove only. Additional map ref.: STM Qld G6.

SOUTH MOLLE ISLAND

Paddle Bay camping area

At north-western tip of South Molle Island, 500 m from the western end of resort. Camping permit required. Self-sufficient campers only. Bring drinking water. Gas/fuel stove only. Additional map ref.: STM Qld G6.

Sandy Bay camping area

On south-western side of island, 4.1 km from the resort golf course. Camping permit required. Self-sufficient campers only. Bring drinking water. Gas/fuel stove only. Additional map ref.: STM Qld G6.

Further information: QPWS, Whitsunday Information Centre, Airlie Beach **Tel.:** (07) 4946 7022 **Further information & bookings:** Smart Service Queensland **Tel.:** 13 13 04 **Website:** www.qld.gov.au **Camping fees:** From $4.00 per person/night; permit from and fees payable through Smart Service Queensland or at QPWS Whitsunday Information Centre, Airlie Beach

32. MURRAY FALLS STATE FOREST PARK

Murray Falls State Forest Park is at the foothills of the Kirrama Range. The 10-m drop of Murray Falls can be viewed from several vantage points along the short river-boardwalk that leads from the camping area. Visitors should heed all safety signs here as rocks can be slippery and dangerous. Access to the park is signposted off the Bruce Hwy 22 km north of Cardwell and 14 km south of Tully. Murray Falls is about 20 km west of the highway. Swimming is possible at the day use area. No swimming above the boardwalk.

Murray Falls camping area

Signposted from Bruce Hwy. Camping permit required. Drinking water from tank – boil before use. Firewood supplied. Additional map ref.: STM Qld F4.

Further information: QPWS, Cardwell **Tel.:** (07) 4066 8779 **Camping fees:** From $4.00 per person/night; permit from and fees payable at self-registration station

33. NEWRY ISLANDS NATIONAL PARK

The Newry Islands group lies off the coast 50 km north-west of Mackay. The hilly islands were once part of the mainland. Wildlife on the islands includes koalas, possums and echidnas. The surrounding waters provide food for dugongs. Access to the islands is by boat from the boat launch at Victor Creek 4 km from Seaforth. The Newry Islands National Park is within the Great Barrier Reef Marine Park – obtain a copy of the marine park's zoning map for permitted activities. Bookings are essential.

Outer Newry Island

Camping on the island's west coast. Camping permit required. Maximum 7 nights' stay. Bring drinking water. Gas/fuel stove only. Additional map ref.: STM Qld G6.

Rabbit Island

Camping on the island's south-east coast. Camping permit required. Bring drinking water. Gas/fuel stove only. Additional map ref.: STM Qld G6.

Further information: QPWS, Mackay **Tel.:** (07) 4944 7800 **Further information & bookings:** Smart Service Queensland **Tel.:** 13 13 04 **Website:** www.qld.gov.au **Camping fees:** From $4.00 per person/night; permit from and fees payable through Smart Service Queensland or at QPWS Mackay

34. ORPHEUS ISLAND NATIONAL PARK

Orpheus Island National Park has some interesting geological features formed by molten rock millions of years ago. The island is in the Great Barrier Reef Marine Park – obtain a copy of the marine park's zoning map for permitted activities. Orpheus Island is off the coast from Halifax and is reached by private boat or special charter. Boat ramps are at Taylors Beach and Lucinda.

Little Pioneer Bay camping area

On island's north-western coast. Camping permit required. Self-sufficient campers only. Bring drinking water. Gas/fuel stove only. Additional map ref.: STM Qld F5.

South Beach camping area

On island's south-eastern coast. Camping permit required. Self-sufficient campers only. Bring drinking water. Gas/fuel stove only. Additional map ref.: STM Qld F5.

Yanks Jetty camping area

On island's south-western coast. Camping permit required. Self-sufficient campers only. Bring drinking water. Gas/fuel stove only. Additional map ref.: STM Qld F5.

Further information:
QPWS, Cardwell **Tel.:** (07) 4066 8779 *or*
QPWS, Ingham **Tel.:** (07) 4777 2822
Camping fees: From $4.00 per person/night; permit from and fees payable to QPWS Cardwell or Ingham

35. PALUMA RANGE NATIONAL PARK

The large Paluma Range National Park features creeks and valleys, waterfalls, rainforests and eucalypt woodlands. Visitors can go picnicking, walking, camping or take in the magnificent views from a lookout. The Mount Spec section of the park is signposted from the Bruce Hwy 61 km north-west of Townsville and 40 km south-east of Ingham; the Jourama Falls section is signposted from the Bruce Hwy 24 km south-east of Ingham and 91 km north-west of Townsville.

Big Crystal Creek camping area

Signposted off the Bruce Hwy 61 km north-west of Townsville. Access road is 2 km north of Paluma turn-off. Camping permit required. Drinking water from bore – boil before use. Gas/fuel stove only. Additional map ref.: STM Qld F5.

Jourama Falls camping area

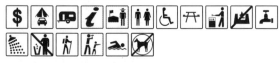

This is 6 km west of the Bruce Hwy and signposted from it 24 km south-east of Ingham. Camping permit required. Drinking water from bore – boil before use. Gas/fuel stove only. Advance bookings essential during holiday periods. Additional map ref.: STM Qld F5.

Further information: QPWS, Ingham **Tel.:** (07) 4777 2822 *Jourama Falls* QPWS, Paluma Range National Park, tel. (07) 4777 3112 **Further information & bookings:** Smart Service Queensland **Tel.:** 13 13 04 **Website:** www.qld.gov.au **Camping fees:** From $4.00 per person/night; permit from and fees payable through Smart Service Queensland or at self-registration station

36. PELORUS ISLAND

Pelorus Island is a small island to the east of Lucinda. The island's west coast has beautiful coral reefs which are ideal for snorkelling. It is reached by private boat or commercial operator from Taylors Beach.

Pelorus Island camping area

Small area on island's western coast. Self-sufficient campers only. Bring drinking water and firewood. Gas/fuel stove preferred. Additional map ref.: STM Qld F5.

Further information:
Hinchinbrook Shire Council **Tel.:** (07) 4776 5211 *or* Hinchinbrook Visitor Information Centre **Tel.:** (07) 4776 5211

37. REPULSE ISLANDS NATIONAL PARK

The Repulse Islands lie to the south of Cape Conway and are 15 km east of Laguna Quays. Access by boat from Laguna Quays. Detailed access information is available from the QPWS Whitsunday Information Centre in Airlie Beach. Repulse Islands National Park is within the Great Barrier Reef Marine Park – obtain a copy of the marine park's zoning map for permitted activities. Maximum camper numbers apply and bookings are essential.

South Repulse Island

South Repulse Island is 15 km east of Laguna Quays. Camping permit required. Self-sufficient campers only. Bring drinking water. Gas/fuel stove only. Additional map ref.: STM Qld G6.

Further information: QPWS, Whitsunday Information Centre, Airlie Beach **Tel.:** (07) 4946 7022 **Further information & bookings:** Smart Service Queensland **Tel.:** 13 13 04 **Website:** www.qld.gov.au **Camping fees:** From $4.00 per person/night; permit from and fees payable through Smart Service Queensland or at QPWS Whitsunday Information Centre, Airlie Beach

38. WHITE MOUNTAINS NATIONAL PARK

White Mountains National Park features rugged landscapes of white sandstone. The park is a blaze of colour during winter and early spring, and nature lovers will delight at the various reptiles, birds and wallabies found here. White Mountains National Park is 140 km south-west of Charters Towers and 80 km north-east of Hughenden. It is reached from the Flinders Hwy. Bushwalkers must complete a Remote Bushwalking Form in advance.

Canns Camp Creek campground

North of Flinders Hwy. Access road is 5 km south of lookout. Check with QPWS Charters Towers for access information to campground. Camping permit required. Bring drinking water. Gas/fuel stove only. Additional map ref.: STM Qld G4.

Bush camping

Remote walk-in bush camping in park for self-sufficient, experienced bushwalkers. Walkers must be well prepared. Remote Bushwalking Form to be completed. Bring drinking water. Gas/fuel stove only. Additional map ref.: STM Qld G4.

Further information: QPWS, Hughenden **Tel.:** (07) 4741 1113 **Further information & bookings:** QPWS, Charters Towers **Tel.:** (07) 4787 3388 **Camping fees:** From $4.00 per person/night; permit from and fees payable to QPWS Hughenden or Charters Towers

39. WHITSUNDAY ISLANDS NATIONAL PARK

The islands of this national park have beautiful beaches and many scenic highlights. They lie east and north-east of Shute Harbour and are reached by boat from Shute Harbour or Airlie Beach. Detailed access information is available from the QPWS Whitsunday Information Centre in Airlie Beach. Whitsunday Islands National Park is within the Great Barrier Reef Marine Park – obtain a copy of the marine park's zoning map for permitted activities. Maximum camper numbers apply to all campsites and bookings are essential. Boat transfer tickets must be arranged before booking campsites.

CID ISLAND
Cid Island is west of Whitsunday Island.

Cid Island camping area

Camping at Homestead Bay. Camping permit required. Self-sufficient campers only. Bring drinking water. Gas/fuel stove only. Additional map ref.: STM Qld G6.

HENNING ISLAND
Henning Island is south-west of Whitsunday Island.

Geographers Bay camping area

On south coast of Henning Island. Camping permit required. Self-sufficient campers only. Bring drinking water. Gas/fuel stove only. Additional map ref.: STM Qld G6.

Northern Spit camping area

On north coast of Henning Island. Camping permit required. Self-sufficient campers only. Bring drinking water. Gas/fuel stove only. Additional map ref.: STM Qld G6.

HOOK ISLAND

Hook Island is north of Whitsunday Island.

Bloodhorn Beach camping area

On west coast of island. Camping permit required. Self-sufficient campers only. Bring drinking water. Gas/fuel stove only. Additional map ref.: STM Qld G6.

Crayfish Beach camping area

On east coast of island. Camping permit required. Self-sufficient campers only. Bring drinking water. Gas/fuel stove only. Additional map ref.: STM Qld G6.

Curlew Beach camping area

On south coast of island. Camping permit required. Self-sufficient campers only. Bring drinking water. Gas/fuel stove only. Additional map ref.: STM Qld G6.

Maureens Cove camping area

On north coast of island. Camping permit required. Self-sufficient campers only. Bring drinking water. Gas/fuel stove only. Additional map ref.: STM Qld G6.

Steens Beach camping area

On north-west coast of island. Camping permit required. Self-sufficient campers only. Bring drinking water. Gas/fuel stove only. Additional map ref.: STM Qld G6.

WHITSUNDAY ISLAND

Whitsunday Island is east of Shute Harbour.

Chance Bay camping area

On south coast of island. Camping permit required. Self-sufficient campers only. Bring drinking water. Gas/fuel stove only. Additional map ref.: STM Qld G6.

Dugong Beach camping area

On west coast of island. Camping permit required. Self-sufficient campers only. Gas/fuel stove only. Additional map ref.: STM Qld G6.

Joes Beach camping area

On west coast of island. Camping permit required. Self-sufficient campers only. Bring drinking water. Gas/fuel stove only. Additional map ref.: STM Qld G6.

Naris Beach camping area

On west coast of island. Camping permit required. Self-sufficient campers only. Bring drinking water. Gas/fuel stove only. Additional map ref.: STM Qld G6.

Peter Bay camping area

On north-east coast of island. Camping permit required. Self-sufficient campers only. Bring drinking water. Gas/fuel stove only. Additional map ref.: STM Qld G6.

Sawmill Beach camping area

On west coast of island. Camping permit required. Self-sufficient campers only. Gas/fuel stove only. Additional map ref.: STM Qld G6.

Turtle Bay camping area

On south coast of island. Camping permit required. Self-sufficient campers only. Bring drinking water. Gas/fuel stove only. Additional map ref.: STM Qld G6.

Whitehaven Beach camping area

On east coast of island. Camping permit required. Self-sufficient campers only. Bring drinking water. Gas/fuel stove only. Additional map ref.: STM Qld G6.

Further information: QPWS, Whitsunday Information Centre, Airlie Beach **Tel.:** (07) 4946 7022 **Further information & bookings:** Smart Service Queensland **Tel.:** 13 13 04 **Website:** www.qld.gov.au **Camping fees:** From $4.00 per person/night; permit from and fees payable through Smart Service Queensland or at QPWS Whitsunday Information Centre, Airlie Beach

QUEENSLAND'S FAR NORTH IS A WONDERLAND OF UNSPOILED COASTLINES AND ISLANDS, REEFS, RAINFORESTS AND RIVERS, REMOTE TOWNS AND VILLAGES AND BEAUTIFUL NATIONAL PARKS. THE VERY TIP OF THE REGION, CAPE YORK, IS ONE OF AUSTRALIA'S MOST POPULAR FOUR-WHEEL DRIVE DESTINATIONS.

To the south-west of Cairns is the popular watersports venue of Lake Tinaroo. There are camping areas around the eastern shores of the lake in Danbulla State Forest. These areas are reached along a 28-kilometre forest drive that passes Lake Euramoo – a crater lake – the historic chimneys and School House, the Mobo Creek Crater and the Cathedral Fig, an impressive strangler fig. Each camping area has access to the lake for fishing, boating, canoeing and swimming.

North of Cairns to the tip of Cape York are many magnificent national parks. The beautiful Cedar Bay (Mangkal-Mangkalba) National Park, south of Cooktown, has bush camping near the coast that can only be reached by a 17-kilometre walking track. Remote beach camping is also possible in Cape Melville National Park, north of Cooktown, but a four-wheel drive is necessary.

The superb Lakefield National Park stretches south from Princess Charlotte Bay to near Laura. Its waterways are popular with fisherfolk and the local crocodiles! There is a huge choice of camping areas spread across the park's three sections but all campsites are accessible by four-wheel drive only. Along with great fishing, the park has incredible Aboriginal cultural sites and some remnants of European history.

Further up the cape are the remote and spectacular Iron Range and Jardine River national parks. Both offer excellent remote-camping opportunities for the well equipped and self-sufficient and have magnificent coastlines, waterfalls, lookouts, rainforests and open woodlands – all home to a huge variety of wildlife.

Offshore lie some of Australia's most memorable camping spots, in the islands of the Great Barrier Reef. Camping is available on Flinders Island, Lizard Island, Turtle Island and Nymph Island. Lizard Island National Park lies around 30 kilometres north-east of Cape Flattery, on the edge of the continental shelf. The tangle of wilderness that climbs across this cluster of islands makes a beautiful contrast to the clear, turquoise waters of the Great Barrier Reef. For self-sufficient campers, a spot like this is nothing short of paradise.

BEST CAMPSITES

Noah Beach camping area
Daintree National Park

Eliot Falls camping area
Jardine River National Park

Kalpowar Crossing Campground
Lakefield National Park

Downfall Creek camping area
Danbulla State Forest

Goldsborough Valley camping area
Goldsborough State Forest

BEST TIME TO VISIT

The dry season, April to October, offers the best weather and comfortable temperatures. Marine stingers inhabit the waters around the Great Barrier Reef from November to April.

A beach near Cape Tribulation, north of Cairns

1. BABINDA

The town of Babinda is on the Bruce Hwy 24 km north of Innisfail. A short drive west of Babinda are the Boulders. Here Babinda Creek cascades over large granite outcrops into some waterholes, providing an excellent place to cool off. A number of walking tracks lead from the Boulders. There is a maximum stopover of 48 hours for both campsites.

Babinda Creek Rest Area

East of Bruce Hwy. Turn-off is opposite information centre. Cross the railway line then turn right. Sealed access. Additional map ref.: STM Qld E4.

The Boulders Rest Area

Located 6 km west of Babinda on Boulders Rd. Signposted from the Bruce Hwy. Only 5 sites – if sites are full, move on. Additional map ref.: STM Qld E4.

Further information: Babinda Information Centre **Tel.:** (07) 4067 1008

2. BARNARD ISLAND GROUP NATIONAL PARK

The Barnard Island Group National Park, south-east of Innisfail, is a favourite place for birdwatchers. The islands can be reached by sea kayak or private boat from Mourilyan Harbour or Kurrimine Beach. The islands are within the Great Barrier Reef Marine Park – obtain a copy of the marine park's zoning map for permitted activities. Bookings are necessary to camp in the national park. The maximum stay is 7 nights and in peak periods, 4 nights.

Kent Island camping area

In the North Barnard Group. Camping on island's west coast. Camping permit required. Self-sufficient campers only. Bring drinking water. Gas/fuel stove only. Additional map ref.: STM Qld E5.

Stephens Island camping area

In the South Barnard Group. Camping on western spit. Camping permit required. Self-sufficient campers only. Bring drinking water. Gas/fuel stove only. Please note that access to rest of island is prohibited 1 Sept.–31 March. Additional map ref.: STM Qld E5.

Further information: QPWS, Cairns **Tel.:** (07) 4046 6600
Further information & bookings: Smart Service Queensland **Tel.:** 13 13 04 **Website:** www.qld.gov.au
Camping fees: From $4.00 per person/night; permit from and fees payable through Smart Service Queensland

3. BARRON GORGE NATIONAL PARK

Barron Gorge National Park is home to tropical rainforests, spectacular waterfalls, rugged mountains and gorges. A wide range of wildlife inhabits the park from butterflies, birds and reptiles to frogs. Visitors can view all of its natural beauty and the man-made sights on foot or via the skyrail or scenic train. Barron Gorge National Park is north-west of Cairns and is reached from Kuranda via the Kennedy Hwy.

Speewah camping area

This is 25 km south of Kuranda. Reached from the Kennedy Hwy 10 km west of Kuranda, then 15 km east to site via Speewah Rd and Stony Creek Rd. Trackhead for walks in park is nearby. Camping permit required. Bring drinking water. Gas/fuel stove preferred. Additional map ref.: STM Qld E4.

Further information:
QPWS, Cairns **Tel.:** (07) 4046 6600 *or*
QPWS, Atherton **Tel.:** (07) 4091 1844
Camping fees: From $4.00 per person/night; permit from and fees payable at self-registration station

4. CAPE MELVILLE NATIONAL PARK

The beautiful and remote Cape Melville National Park is on the coast north of Cooktown. The park's coastline is made up of sandy beaches and rugged headlands, while inland the landscape is dominated by large granite boulders. Due to its isolation a number of endemic plants and animals are found in the park. It is reached from the west from Lakefield National Park (280 km/6 hours) or from the south from Cooktown via Starcke Homestead along the Coast Rd (250 km/12 hours). Both routes are long and arduous, requiring 4WD vehicles and caution. The route from Cooktown can be extremely difficult.

Bush camping

Bush camping, mainly along the beach. Camping permit required. Self-sufficient campers only. Bring drinking water and firewood. Gas/fuel stove preferred. Additional map ref.: STM Qld D4.

Further information:
QPWS, Cooktown **Tel.:** (07) 4069 5777 *or*
QPWS, Cairns **Tel.:** (07) 4046 6600
Camping fees: From $4.00 per person/night; permit from and fees payable to QPWS Cooktown or Cairns, or to ranger headquarters in Lakefield National Park (preferred option if travelling that way)

5. CEDAR BAY (MANGKAL-MANGKALBA) NATIONAL PARK

Visitors to Cedar Bay National Park will find beautiful sandy beaches and tropical rainforests. Cedar Bay is about 45 km south of Cooktown and the area has special cultural value to the traditional Aboriginal owners. There is also a European history of tin mining here. Access to Cedar Bay is by foot or boat only. For boat launching and landings contact QPWS for further details. The walking track, 17 km one-way and a difficult grade, leaves from Home Rule Rainforest Lodge, which is 3 km east of Rossville on the Cooktown–Bloomfield Rd. Walkers can leave their vehicles here. Fishing and collecting of any kind is prohibited in the park.

Home Rule Rainforest Lodge camping area

On the Cooktown–Bloomfield Rd. Signposted 42 km south of Cooktown (conventional vehicle access) and 37 km north of Bloomfield River Crossing (4WD access only). Trackhead for Cedar Bay walking track nearby. Firewood supplied. Additional map ref.: STM Qld D4.

Further information & bookings: Home Rule Rainforest Lodge **Tel.:** (07) 4060 3925 **Camping fees:** From $8.00 per adult/night, $4.00 per child/night

Bush camping

Walk-in access, 17 km from trackhead of Cedar Bay walking track. Camping permit required. Use existing campsites only. Bring drinking water. Gas/fuel stove only. Additional map ref.: STM Qld D4.

Further information:
QPWS, Cairns **Tel.:** (07) 4046 6600 *or*
QPWS, Mossman **Tel.:** (07) 4098 2188
Camping fees: From $4.00 per person/night; permit from and fees payable to QPWS Cairns or Cooktown

6. DAINTREE NATIONAL PARK

The Cape Tribulation section of Daintree National Park (the Mossman Gorge section does not allow camping) is a long narrow strip of coastal land bordered by the Bloomfield River to the north, the Daintree River to the south and the McDowall Range to the west. Daintree National Park is well known for its lush rainforests, superb coastal scenery and rugged mountains. Throughout the Cape Tribulation section visitors will find facilities such as picnic areas, viewing platforms and boardwalks to various scenic sites, and there is a camping area at Noah Beach. Conventional vehicle access to this section is by the Cape Tribulation Rd after crossing the Daintree River 30 km north of Mossman.

Noah Beach camping area

On Cape Tribulation Rd 55 km north of Mossman and 8 km south of Cape Tribulation. Camping permit required. Bring drinking water. Gas/fuel stove only. Maximum stay of 7 nights. Additional map ref.: STM Qld E4.

Further information:
QPWS, Cairns **Tel.:** (07) 4046 6600 *or*
QPWS, Mossman **Tel.:** (07) 4098 2188
Camping fees: From $4.00 per person/night; permit from and fees payable at self-registration station

7. DANBULLA STATE FOREST

Danbulla State Forest is on the north-east side of Lake Tinaroo in the Atherton Tablelands. The forest has a wealth of plant and animal life, including numerous frog and bird species as well as possums. Visitors are well catered for with forest walks, picnic sites, swimming, camping and boating. Access is along the Danbulla Forest Drive north-east of Tinaroo Dam, which is 16 km north-east of Atherton.

Downfall Creek camping area

On Danbulla Forest Drive 7 km north-east of Tinaroo Dam. Camping permit required. Boil drinking water. Bring firewood. Additional map ref.: STM Qld E4.

Fong-On Bay camping area

Off Danbulla Forest Drive just over 18 km from Tinaroo Dam. It is 4.7 km to site from turn-off. Camping permit required. Boil drinking water. Bring firewood. Additional map ref.: STM Qld E4.

Kauri Creek camping area

On Danbulla Forest Drive 10 km north-east of Tinaroo Dam. Camping permit required. Boil drinking water. Bring firewood. Additional map ref.: STM Qld E4.

Platypus camping and day use area

On Danbulla Forest Drive 5 km north-east of Tinaroo Dam. Camping permit required. Boil drinking water. Bring firewood. Additional map ref.: STM Qld E4.

School Point camping and day use area

Off Danbulla Forest Drive 18 km east of Tinaroo Dam. It is 1 km to site from turn-off. Camping permit required. Boil drinking water. Bring firewood. Additional map ref.: STM Qld E4.

Further information: QPWS, Atherton **Tel.:** (07) 4091 1844
Camping fees: From $4.00 per person/night; permit from and fees payable at self-registration stations

8. DAVIES CREEK NATIONAL PARK

Camping in this national park is beside the boulder-lined Davies Creek amongst tall eucalypt forest. The road to Davies Creek is 14 km east of Mareeba off the Kennedy Hwy (Mareeba–Kuranda Rd). 4WD vehicles are recommended; drivers of conventional vehicles should check road conditions before attempting. A Permit to Traverse is required and must be obtained before arrival.

Davies Creek camping area

Site is 12 km south of Kennedy Hwy. 4WD access recommended. Camping permit and Permit to Traverse required. Bring drinking water or boil creek water. Bring firewood. Additional map ref.: STM Qld E4.

Further information:
QPWS, Cairns **Tel.:** (07) 4046 6600 *or*
QPWS, Atherton **Tel.:** (07) 4091 1844
Camping fees: From $4.00 per person/night; permit from and fees payable at self-registration stations **Permit:** For Permit to Traverse contact QPWS Atherton – Permit Officer, tel. (07) 4091 8103

9. DINDEN STATE FOREST

Dinden State Forest, which features tall eucalypt forests, is in the Atherton Tableland. It is signposted off the Kennedy Hwy 14 km east of Mareeba. 4WD vehicles are recommended and a Permit to Traverse must be obtained before setting out.

Bush camping

From the Kennedy Hwy it is 22 km south to this camping area. 6 sites only. 4WD access. Camping permit and Permit to Traverse required. Bring drinking water or boil creek water. Bring firewood. Bookings essential. Additional map ref.: STM Qld E4.

Further information & bookings: QPWS, Atherton **Tel.:** (07) 4091 1844 **Camping fees:** From $4.00 per person/night; permit from and fees payable to QPWS Atherton **Permit:** For Permit to Traverse contact QPWS Atherton – Permit Officer, tel. (07) 4091 8103

10. FLINDERS GROUP NATIONAL PARK

The seven islands of the Flinders Group National Park are part of the sea country of the Yiithuwarra Aboriginal people and have important Aboriginal sites. The group is east of the Cape York Peninsula between Cape Melville and Princess Charlotte Bay and is reached by charter or private boat. The group is remote – contact QPWS for detailed access information. The national park is surrounded by the Great Barrier Reef Marine Park – obtain a copy of the Great Barrier Reef Marine Park zoning map for details of permitted activities.

Flinders Island camping area

Located 14 km west of Cape Melville. Camping permit required. Bring drinking water. Gas/fuel stove only. Additional map ref.: STM Qld D4.

Further information:
QPWS, Cooktown **Tel.:** (07) 4069 5777 *or*
QPWS, Cairns **Tel.:** (07) 4046 6600
Camping fees: From $4.00 per person/night; permit from and fees payable to QPWS Cairns or Cooktown

11. FRANKLAND ISLANDS NATIONAL PARK

The Frankland Island group is about 20 km off the coast from Deeral, which is 43 km south of Cairns on the Bruce Hwy. There is boat access only to these islands. The national park is within the Great Barrier Reef Marine Park – obtain a copy of the marine park's zoning map for permitted activities. The maximum stay here is 7 nights and at peak periods, 4 nights.

High Island camping area

Access via private boat. Camping on north-west side of island. Camping permit required. Bring drinking water. Gas/fuel stove only. Bookings necessary. Additional map ref.: STM Qld E5.

Russell Island camping area

Access via private boat or charter. Camping on northern side of island. Camping permit required. Bring drinking water. Gas/fuel stove only. Bookings necessary. Additional map ref.: STM Qld E5.

Further information & bookings: QPWS, Cairns **Tel.:** (07) 4046 6600 **Camping fees:** From $4.00 per person/night; permit from and fees payable to QPWS Cairns

12. GOLDSBOROUGH STATE FOREST

The crystal-clear Mulgrave River flows through the Goldsborough Valley 25 km south of Cairns. The river and valley have a varied history, from Aboriginal occupation through to goldmining, timber-getting and agriculture. Nowadays the Mulgrave River is ideal for a cooling dip or for canoeing. Access to the Goldsborough State Forest is along Goldsborough Valley Rd off the Gillies Hwy (Gordonvale–Atherton Rd). The turn-off is 3 km south-west of Gordonvale.

Goldsborough Valley camping area

On banks of Mulgrave River 25 km south-west of Gordonvale. Camping permit required. Firewood supplied. Additional map ref.: STM Qld E4.

Further information: QPWS, Cairns **Tel.:** (07) 4046 6600
Camping fees: From $4.00 per person/night; permit from and fees payable at self-registration station

13. GRANITE GORGE NATURE PARK

Granite Gorge is a square mile of tumbled rock and stone created millions of years ago by volcanoes. Visitors to the park can walk beside the creek that winds through the gorge, sit back and enjoy the scenic natural surroundings or do some bird- and wildlife-spotting. Guided tours are available. Access to Granite Gorge Nature Park, which is 12 km west of Mareeba, is by Chewco Rd from Mareeba. There is an entry fee for day visitors.

Granite Gorge camping area

Signposted off Chewco Rd 7 km west of Mareeba. Gorge is a further 5 km from the turn-off. Firewood supplied. Additional map ref.: STM Qld E4.

Further information & bookings: Granite Gorge Nature Park **Tel.:** (07) 4093 2174 or (07) 4093 2259 **Camping fees:** Contact park for current fees. Powered sites available

14. HOPE ISLANDS NATIONAL PARK

East Hope Island is a sand cay 27 km south-east of Cooktown, surrounded by the Great Barrier Reef Marine Park (obtain a copy of the marine park's zoning map for details of permitted activities). The island is reached by private boat only and the maximum stay is 7 nights.

East Hope camping area

Bush camping, permit required. Bring drinking water. Gas/fuel stove only. Additional map ref.: STM Qld D4.

Further information:
QPWS, Cairns **Tel.:** (07) 4046 6600 *or*
QPWS, Mossman **Tel.:** (07) 4098 2188
Further information & bookings: Smart Service Queensland **Tel.:** 13 13 04 **Website:** www.qld.gov.au
Camping fees: From $4.00 per person/night; permit from and fees payable through Smart Service Queensland or at QPWS Cairns or Mossman

15. IRON RANGE NATIONAL PARK

Iron Range National Park is on the north-east coast of Cape York Peninsula. The park's varying vegetation, from rainforest to open woodland, is home to much wildlife including green pythons, spotted cuscus and a variety of bird species. The park has a varied history from Aboriginal occupation through to the landing of Europeans in the late 1700s and mid 1800s, goldmining during the 1930s, and use as a staging post for American troops during World War II. The park can be reached by 4WD vehicle only – from the Peninsula Developmental Rd take Lockhart River Rd 20 km north of the Archer River Roadhouse. The ranger headquarters is 114 km north-east of the Peninsula Developmental Rd and 9 km west of the Lockhart River. If lighting a fire use existing fire sites and do not collect firewood in the park.

Chili Beach camping area

This is 32 km north of ranger headquarters and 41 km north-west of the Lockhart River. Camping permit required. Self-sufficient campers only. Bring drinking water and firewood. Gas/fuel stove preferred. Additional map ref.: STM Qld C3.

Cooks Hut camping area

Located 7.5 km north of ranger headquarters and 16.5 km north-west of the Lockhart River. Camping permit required. Self-sufficient campers only. Bring drinking water and firewood. Gas/fuel stove preferred. Additional map ref.: STM Qld C3.

Gordon Creek Crossing camping area

This area is 8 km north of ranger headquarters and 17 km north-west of the Lockhart River. Camping permit required. Self-sufficient campers only. Bring drinking water and firewood. Gas/fuel stove preferred. Additional map ref.: STM Qld C3.

Rainforest camping area

This is 7 km north of ranger headquarters and 16 km north-west of the Lockhart River. Camping permit required. Self-sufficient campers only. Bring drinking water and firewood. Gas/fuel stove preferred. Additional map ref.: STM Qld C3.

Further information: QPWS, Iron Range National Park **Tel.:** (07) 4060 7170 **Further information & bookings:** Smart Service Queensland **Tel.:** 13 13 04 **Website:** www.qld.gov.au **Camping fees:** From $4.00 per person/night; permit from and fees payable through Smart Service Queensland or at self-registration station at ranger headquarters

16. JARDINE RIVER NATIONAL PARK

The remote Jardine River National Park contains 237 000 ha of wilderness at the top of Cape York Peninsula. The park lies between the Telegraph Rd and the east coast of the peninsula and includes Queensland's largest perennial stream, the Jardine River. There are a number of Aboriginal cultural sites within the park and it is home to many bird species such as the palm cockatoo and yellow-billed kingfisher. The vegetation of Jardine River National Park ranges from rainforest to open forest, scrubland and swamplands. The park is reached by 4WD vehicle only from Telegraph Rd, with access to various scenic sites off the Southern Bypass Rd and Northern Bypass Rd. Ranger headquarters is at Heathlands, 13 km east of the Telegraph Rd and 33 km north of the Southern Bypass Rd turn-off. This area is extremely remote and all travellers should be self-sufficient and well prepared. The park should only be visited in the dry season. If lighting a fire use existing fire sites and do not collect firewood in the park. Drivers must be aware of oncoming traffic on the local roads as many head-on accidents have occurred due to vehicles travelling in the opposite direction driving in the same wheel ruts.

Captain Billy Landing camping area

Signposted off Southern Bypass Rd. Area is 27 km east of bypass road and 55 km north-east of ranger headquarters. Camping permit required. Bring drinking water and firewood. Gas/fuel stove preferred. No beach access to Ussher Point. Additional map ref.: STM Qld B3.

Eliot Falls camping area

On Telegraph Rd 8.5 km north of Northern Bypass Rd turn-off. Camping permit required. Boil water. Bring drinking

water and firewood. Gas/fuel stove preferred. No swimming at Eliot Falls, but swimming at nearby Twin Falls. Additional map ref.: STM Qld B3.

Jardine River camping area

Reached from Telegraph Rd 29 km north of Eliot Falls. Alternative access via Northern Bypass Rd 49 km from Eliot Falls. Camping permit required. Water from river – boil before use. Bring firewood. Gas/fuel stove preferred. Additional map ref.: STM Qld B3.

Ussher Point camping area

Located 7 km north of Jardine River. Area is 62 km (about 4 hours' drive) east of Telegraph Rd. Camping permit required. Bring drinking water and firewood. Gas/fuel stove preferred. Additional map ref.: STM Qld B3.

Further information: QPWS, Jardine River National Park **Tel.:** (07) 4060 3241 **Camping fees:** From $4.00 per person/night; permit from and fees payable at self-registration stations at Captain Billy Landing, Eliot Falls and ranger headquarters

17. KOWANYAMA AREA

Kowanyama is an Aboriginal community in the west of Cape York Peninsula. It is 105 km north-west of Dunbar off the Burke Developmental Rd. The area is popular for barramundi fishing. Camping is only allowed 1 June–mid-Oct. (barramundi season). Bookings are necessary and are taken from Feb. onwards.

Bull Crossing, Shelso and Surprise Creek camping areas

East of Kowanyama, contact land office for access details. Boat launch suitable for small boats. Self-sufficient campers only. Bring drinking water and firewood. Additional map ref.: STM Qld D2.

Topsy Creek camping area

This is 45 km west of Kowanyama on the Gulf of Carpentaria. Boat launch suitable for small boats. Self-sufficient campers only. Bring drinking water and firewood. Additional map ref.: STM Qld D2.

Further information & bookings: Kowanyama Land Office **Tel.:** (07) 4060 5187 **Camping fees:** From $30.00 per vehicle/night

18. LAKEFIELD NATIONAL PARK see page 332

19. LAKE TINAROO

The large reservoir of Lake Tinaroo provides ample opportunities for water-based activities: fishing for barramundi, sooty grunter and red claw (a Stocked Impoundment Permit is necessary) as well as boating and canoeing, waterskiing, windsurfing and swimming. Other activities include bird-watching, sightseeing and car touring in the nearby Danbulla State Forest. Lake Tinaroo is 16 km north-east of Atherton.

LAKEFIELD NATIONAL PARK

Lakefield National Park is Queensland's second-largest national park, protecting important wetland and woodland areas, sites of Aboriginal cultural significance and reminders of European settlement and exploration. The park is west of Cooktown and east of the Peninsula Developmental Rd. The main access road to the park is off the Peninsula Developmental Rd just north of Laura; this road is often suitable for conventional vehicles but drivers should check road conditions first. Other access is by 4WD from Cooktown via Battle Camp Rd or from Musgrave Roadhouse on the Peninsula Developmental Rd 107 km south of Coen. Some camping areas can be reached by 4WD vehicles towing heavy-duty 4WD trailers; check with ranger headquarters first (headquarters are at New Laura, Lakefield and Bizant). Boating and fishing are popular, but canoeing and swimming are not recommended due to crocodiles in the rivers, creeks and waterholes of the park. The park and its camping areas are remote – visitors should be well prepared and self-sufficient. When lighting a fire use existing fire sites and do not collect firewood in the park.

NEW LAURA AREA
New Laura ranger headquarters is on Lakefield Rd 54 km north of Laura.

Twelve Mile Waterhole camping area

Located 12 km east of Lakefield Rd; turn-off is opposite New Laura ranger headquarters. Camping permit required. Bring drinking water and firewood. Gas/fuel stove preferred. Additional map ref.: STM Qld D4.

Catfish Waterhole camping area

This is 1 km west of Lakefield Rd; turn-off is 16 km north of New Laura ranger headquarters. Camping permit required. Bring drinking water and firewood. Gas/fuel stove preferred. Additional map ref.: STM Qld D4.

Dingo Waterhole camping area

Located 23 km east of Lakefield Rd; turn-off is 25 km north of New Laura ranger headquarters. Camping permit required. Bring drinking water and firewood. Gas/fuel stove preferred. Additional map ref.: STM Qld D4.

Horseshoe Lagoon camping area

Area is 1 km north of Battle Camp Rd; turn-off is 29 km east of Old Laura Homestead. Camping permit required. Bring drinking water and firewood. Gas/fuel stove preferred. Additional map ref.: STM Qld D4.

Kennedy Bend Waterhole camping area

On Lakefield Rd 8 km north of New Laura ranger headquarters. Camping permit required. Bring drinking water and firewood. Gas/fuel stove preferred. Additional map ref.: STM Qld D4.

Lake Emma camping area

On Battle Camp Rd, about 32 km east of Old Laura Homestead. Camping permit required. Bring drinking water and firewood. Gas/fuel stove preferred. Additional map ref.: STM Qld D4.

Leichhardt Waterhole camping area

This is 6 km north of Battle Camp Rd; turn-off is 29 km east of Old Laura Homestead. Camping permit required. Bring drinking water and firewood. Gas/fuel stove preferred. Additional map ref.: STM Qld D4.

Mick Fienn Waterhole camping area

This area is 23 km east of Lakefield Rd; turn-off is 25 km north of New Laura ranger headquarters. Camping permit required. Bring drinking water and firewood. Gas/fuel stove preferred. Additional map ref.: STM Qld D4.

Old Faithful Waterhole camping area

Located 17 km east of Lakefield Rd; turn-off is 23 km north of New Laura ranger headquarters. Camping permit required. Bring drinking water and firewood. Gas/fuel stove preferred. Additional map ref.: STM Qld D4.

Six Mile Waterhole camping area

Area is 3 km east of Lakefield Rd; turn-off is 15 km south of New Laura ranger headquarters. Camping permit required. Bring drinking water and firewood. Gas/fuel stove preferred. Additional map ref.: STM Qld D4.

Welcome Waterhole camping area

This is 2 km north of Leichhardt Waterhole. Camping permit required. Bring drinking water and firewood. Gas/fuel stove preferred. Additional map ref.: STM Qld D4.

Further information:
QPWS, New Laura **Tel.:** (07) 4060 3260 *or*
QPWS, Cairns **Tel.:** (07) 4046 6600
Camping fees: From $4.00 per person/night; permit from and fees payable at self-registration station at New Laura ranger headquarters; campers must fill in reservation board when obtaining permit

LAKEFIELD AREA
Lakefield ranger headquarters is on Lakefield Rd 35 km north of New Laura ranger headquarters.

Hanushs Waterhole camping area

Area is 16 km north of Lakefield ranger headquarters; turn-off is 13 km north of headquarters. Camping permit required. Bring drinking water and firewood. Gas/fuel stove preferred. Additional map ref.: STM Qld D4.

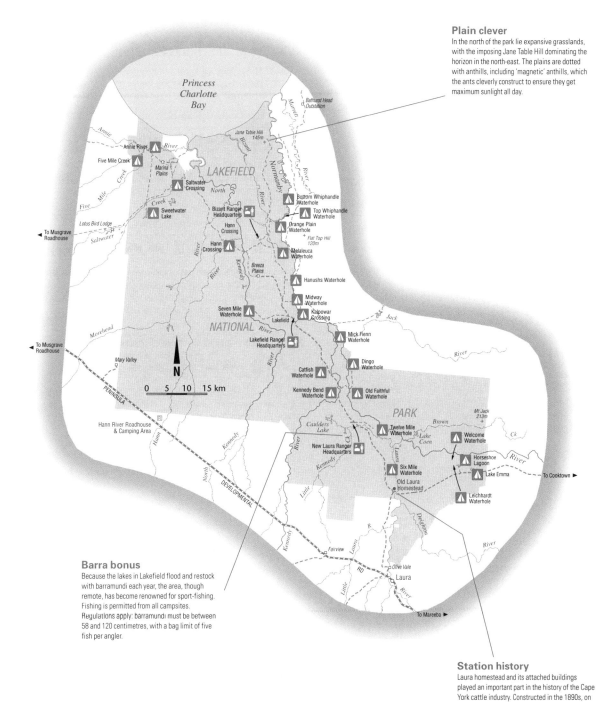

Plain clever

In the north of the park lie expansive grasslands, with the imposing Jane Table Hill dominating the horizon in the north-east. The plains are dotted with anthills, including 'magnetic' anthills, which the ants cleverly construct to ensure they get maximum sunlight all day.

Barra bonus

Because the lakes in Lakefield flood and restock with barramundi each year, the area, though remote, has become renowned for sport-fishing. Fishing is permitted from all campsites. Regulations apply: barramundi must be between 58 and 120 centimetres, with a bag limit of five fish per angler.

Station history

Laura homestead and its attached buildings played an important part in the history of the Cape York cattle industry. Constructed in the 1890s, on the track to the Palmer River goldfields, the homestead sheltered successive owners of the 12 800-hectare Laura Station. Abandoned in the 1960s, the buildings were restored once the park was gazetted in 1978.

Kalpowar Crossing Campground

Located 3 km east of Lakefield ranger headquarters. Camping permit required. Boat access at causeway. Bring drinking water and firewood. Gas/fuel stove preferred. Bookings recommended 6–12 weeks in advance for June–Aug. Additional map ref.: STM Qld D4.

Melaleuca Waterhole camping area

Area is 24 km north of Lakefield ranger headquarters; turn-off is 21 km north of headquarters. Camping permit required. Bring drinking water and firewood. Gas/fuel stove preferred. Additional map ref.: STM Qld D4.

Midway Waterhole camping area

This is 9 km north of Lakefield ranger headquarters; turn-off is 5 km north of headquarters. Camping permit required. Bring drinking water and firewood. Gas/fuel stove preferred. Additional map ref.: STM Qld D4.

Further information:
QPWS, Lakefield **Tel.:** (07) 4060 3271 *or*
QPWS, Cairns **Tel.:** (07) 4046 6600
Camping fees: From $4.00 per person/night; permit from and fees payable at self-registration station at Lakefield ranger headquarters; campers must fill in reservation board when obtaining permit

Seven Mile Waterhole camping area

This is 13 km north-west of Lakefield ranger headquarters. Camping permit required. Bring drinking water and firewood. Gas/fuel stove preferred. Additional map ref.: STM Qld D4.

BIZANT AREA

Bizant ranger headquarters is on Lakefield Rd 28 km north of Lakefield ranger headquarters.

Annie River camping area

Area is 60 km north-west of Bizant ranger headquarters; turn-off is 46 km north-west of headquarters, then site is a further 14 km north. Camping permit required. Bring drinking water and firewood. Gas/fuel stove preferred. Additional map ref.: STM Qld D3.

Bottom Whiphandle Waterhole camping area

Located 16 km north-east of Bizant ranger headquarters. Camping permit required. Bring drinking water and firewood. Gas/fuel stove preferred. Additional map ref.: STM Qld D4.

Five Mile Creek camping area

This is 65.5 km north-west of Bizant ranger headquarters; turn-off is 46 km north-west of headquarters, then site is a further 19.5 km north. Camping permit required. Bring drinking water and firewood. Gas/fuel stove preferred. Additional map ref.: STM Qld D3.

Hann Crossing camping area

On Lakefield Rd 29 km north-west of Lakefield ranger headquarters and 6 km south-west of Bizant ranger headquarters. Camping permit required. Bring drinking water and firewood. Gas/fuel stove preferred. Additional map ref.: STM Qld D4.

Orange Plain Waterhole camping area

This is 10 km east of Bizant ranger headquarters. Camping permit required. Bring drinking water and firewood. Gas/fuel stove preferred. Additional map ref.: STM Qld D4.

Saltwater Crossing camping area

On Lakefield Rd 41 km north-west of Bizant ranger headquarters. Camping permit required. Bring drinking water and firewood. Gas/fuel stove preferred. Additional map ref.: STM Qld D3.

Sweetwater Lake camping area

Area is 48 km north-west of Bizant ranger headquarters; turn-off is 46 km north-west of headquarters, then 2 km south to site. Camping permit required. Bring drinking water and firewood. Gas/fuel stove preferred. Additional map ref.: STM Qld D3.

Top Whiphandle Waterhole camping area

This is 12.5 km north-east of Bizant ranger headquarters. Camping permit required. Bring drinking water and firewood. Gas/fuel stove preferred. Additional map ref.: STM Qld D4.

Further information:
QPWS Bizant **Tel.:** (07) 4060 3258 *or*
QPWS, Cairns **Tel.:** (07) 4046 6600
Camping fees: From $4.00 per person/night; permit from and fees payable at self-registration station at Bizant ranger headquarters; campers must fill in reservation board when obtaining permit *Hann Crossing* Sites 3–10 have self-registration station; people camping at sites 1, 2, 11–17, 19 and 20 must obtain permit and complete reservation board at ranger headquarters

Lake Tinaroo Holiday Park

On Dam Rd at Tinaroo Falls. Laundry facilities. Firewood supplied. Bookings essential for Easter and Christmas holiday periods. Additional map ref.: STM Qld E4.

Further information & bookings: Lake Tinaroo Holiday Park **Tel.:** (07) 4095 8232 **Website:** www.ppawd.com/kairi-tinaroo **Camping fees:** Unpowered sites from $15.00 per site/night for 2 adults, powered from $20.00 per site/night for 2 adults

20. LIZARD ISLAND NATIONAL PARK

Lizard Island National Park is within the Great Barrier Reef World Heritage Area 93 km north-east of Cooktown. Obtain a copy of the Great Barrier Reef Marine Park's zoning map for details of permitted activities. The islands have a strong Aboriginal history and are reached by boat or air. Maximum camper numbers apply and there is a maximum stay of 10 nights.

Watsons Bay camping area

Camping at northern end of Watsons Bay. Self-sufficient campers only. Camping permit required. Boil water for drinking. Gas/fuel stove only. Bookings essential. Additional map ref.: STM Qld D4.

Further information: QPWS, Cairns **Tel.:** (07) 4046 6600 **Further information & bookings:** Smart Service Queensland **Tel.:** 13 13 04 **Website:** www.qld.gov.au **Camping fees:** From $4.00 per person/night; permit from and fees payable through Smart Service Queensland or at QPWS Cairns

21. MUNGKAN KANDJU NATIONAL PARK

The Coen and Archer rivers are the main features of this park. Its 457 000 ha offer excellent birdwatching and remote hiking for experienced bushwalkers. Remains of Aboriginal and pastoral history can be found within the park. Access to the park is by 4WD off the Peninsula Developmental Rd 24 km north of Coen. The ranger headquarters is 72 km west of the Peninsula Developmental Rd. It is a remote area and suitable for self-sufficient, well prepared campers only.

Bush camping

Bush camping throughout park. Camping permit required. Self-sufficient campers only. Bring drinking water and firewood. Gas/fuel stove preferred. When lighting a fire use existing firesites. Bookings are necessary for Archer Bend section; book 6–12 weeks in advance through QPWS Rokeby. Additional map ref.: STM Qld C3.

Further information:
QPWS, Mungkan Kandju National Park, Rokeby **Tel.:** (07) 4060 3256 *or* QPWS, Cairns **Tel.:** (07) 4046 6600 **Camping fees:** From $4.00 per person/night; permit from and fees payable to QPWS Rokeby; ranger will advise of camping sites at time of obtaining permit

22. NORTHERN CAPE YORK

Cape York has some of Australia's most spectacular scenery, with tropical wetlands and rainforests, magnificent coast-lines, plunging waterfalls and wild rivers. The drive to the top of the cape is considered one of Australia's most exciting 4WD trips. However, the roads can be challenging, with numerous river crossings and changing road conditions. When travelling in the area it is advisable to first check road conditions with local authorities. Travellers need to be well prepared and ensure vehicles are mechanically sound. Northern Cape York is reached via the Telegraph Rd off the Peninsula Developmental Rd. The dry season, June–Sept., is the peak period here and the preferred time to visit.

Jardine River ferry camping area

At Jardine River ferry crossing on Northern Bypass Rd, 290 km north of Archer River Roadhouse (ferry hours: 8 am–12 noon and 1 pm–5 pm). Water from river – boil before use. Firewood supplied. Additional map ref.: STM Qld B3.

Further information:
Jardine River ferry **Tel.:** (07) 4069 1369 *or* Injinoo Community Council **Tel.:** (07) 4069 3252 **Camping fees:** From $5.00 per person/night

Loyalty Beach Campground and Fishing Lodge

Signposted from Seisia and 3 km north of Seisia Wharf. Suitable for 4WD trailers. Beachfront location. Laundry facilities. Bring firewood. Dogs allowed but must be under strict control at all times. Additional map ref.: STM Qld B3.

Further information: Loyalty Beach Campground and Fishing Lodge **Tel.:** (07) 4069 3372 **Email:** fishcapeyork@bigpond.com **Camping fees:** From $8.80 per person/night, children half price

Punsand Bay Safari and Fishing Lodge

This is 30 km north of Bamaga. Laundry facilities. Swimming pool. Boat can be launched from beach. Ferry trips to Thursday Island and other tours. Firewood supplied. Dogs allowed but must be under strict control at all times. Bookings recommended June–Sept. Additional map ref.: STM Qld B3.

Further information and bookings: Punsand Bay Safari and Fishing Lodge **Tel.:** (07) 4069 1722 **Camping fees:** From $10.00 per person/night

Seisia Campground

In Seisia, with beachfront location. Suitable for 4WD trailers. Bring firewood. Ferry trips to Thursday Island. Boat hire. Additional map ref.: STM Qld B3.

Further information: Seisia Campground **Tel.:** (07) 4069 3242 **Email:** seisiaresort@bigpond.com **Camping fees:** Unpowered from $7.00 per adult/night, powered from $9.00 per adult/night, children half price

Umagico Camping Ground

On Umagico Beach at Umagico, 4 km south-west of Bamaga. Beachfront location. Firewood supplied. Dogs allowed at time of research but this may change – check before arrival. Additional map ref.: STM Qld B3.

Further information: Umagico Supermarket
Tel.: (07) 4069 3273 **Camping fees:** From $8.80 per person/night; register, pay fees and collect key from Supermarket

Bush camping

There are many bush campsites throughout the northern cape area, in particular at river crossings from the Dulhunty River north; at Somerset near Pajinka; at Muttee Head which is 19 km north-west of Telegraph Rd; and at Vrilya Point west of Northern Bypass Rd. A booklet with detailed information is supplied by Jardine River ferry operators (ferry hours: 8 am–12 noon and 1 pm–5 pm). Suitable for self-sufficient campers only. Bring drinking water and firewood. Additional map ref.: STM Qld B3.

Further information: Injinoo Community Council
Tel.: (07) 4069 3252 **Camping fees:** Covered in Jardine River ferry fee **Ferry fee:** $88.00 return per normal 4WD vehicle, additional $11.00 per trailer, $33.00 return per motorbike

Nymph Island is located between Turtle Group National Park and Lizard Island National Park. Access is by private boat or charter. Contact QPWS Cooktown for access details. The park is surrounded by the Great Barrier Reef Marine Park – obtain a copy of the marine park's zoning map for details of permitted activities. There are no facilities and campers must be self-sufficient.

Nymph Island camping area

Camping is on northern edge of island. Camping permit required. Self-sufficient campers only. Bring drinking water. Gas/fuel stove only. Additional map ref.: STM Qld D4.

Further information:
QPWS, Cooktown **Tel.:** (07) 4069 5777 *or*
QPWS, Cairns **Tel.:** (07) 4046 6600
Further information & bookings: Smart Service Queensland **Tel.:** 13 13 04 **Website:** www.qld.gov.au
Camping fees: From $4.00 per person/night; permit from and fees payable through Smart Service Queensland or at QPWS Cooktown or Cairns

Payable gold was found along the Palmer River on 29 June 1873. Soon thousands had flocked to the area, but the gold rush did not last long, ending in the 1880s. Today visitors will find old mine sites, relics and rusting machinery. The reserve is 280 km north-west of Cairns and is reached by 4WD vehicle

On the road in Cape York

only. From the Peninsula Developmental Rd take Whites Creek turn-off to Granite and Cannibal creeks, then continue north to Dog Leg Creek Junction south of Maytown. Prospecting and gold detectors are prohibited here.

Bush camping

Contact QPWS for detailed access information. Camping permit required. Self-sufficient campers only. Bring drinking water and firewood. Additional map ref.: STM Qld E4.

Further information:
QPWS, Chillagoe **Tel.:** (07) 4094 7163 *or*
QPWS, Cairns **Tel.:** (07) 4046 6600
Camping fees: From $4.00 per person/night; permit from and fees payable to QPWS Chillagoe or Cairns

25. PENINSULA DEVELOPMENTAL ROAD

The Peninsula Developmental Rd stretches from Mareeba to Weipa, over a distance of 750 km. This mostly unsealed road is the main Cape York road. Check with local authorities for current road conditions. Camping areas are listed in the order they are reached travelling north.

Mount Carbine Roadhouse camping area

On Peninsula Developmental Rd, 70 km north of Mareeba and 84 km south of the Palmer River. Roadhouse open 7 am–7 pm daily. Bring drinking water and firewood. Additional map ref.: STM Qld E4.

Further information: Mount Carbine Roadhouse **Tel.:** (07) 4094 3043 **Camping fees:** From $7.00 per site/night

Palmer River Roadhouse camping area

On Peninsula Developmental Rd, 84 km north-west of Mount Carbine and 31 km south of Lakeland. Roadhouse open 7 am–10 pm daily. Firewood supplied. Additional map ref.: STM Qld E4.

Further information: Palmer River Roadhouse **Tel.:** (07) 4060 2020 **Camping fees:** Tent site from $9.00 per site/night for 2 people, van sites from $12.00 per site/night for 2 people

Lakeland Caravan Park

On Peninsula Developmental Rd (Sesame St) in Lakeland, 54 km south-west of Helenvale and 64 km south-east of Laura. Bring firewood. Additional map ref.: STM Qld D4.

Further information: Lakeland Caravan Park **Tel.:** (07) 4060 2162 **Camping fees:** Check for current fees

Hann River Roadhouse camping area

On Hann River crossing of Peninsula Developmental Rd, 74 km north-west of Laura and 62 km south-east of Musgrave Roadhouse. Open 7 am–9 pm daily. Firewood supplied. Additional map ref.: STM Qld D3.

Further information: Hann River Roadhouse **Tel.:** (07) 4060 3242 **Camping fees:** From $7.00 per person/night

Musgrave Roadhouse camping area

On Peninsula Developmental Rd 62 km north-west of Hann River Roadhouse and 107 km south of Coen. Open 7.30 am–10 pm daily. Bring firewood. Additional map ref.: STM Qld D3.

Further information: Musgrave Roadhouse **Tel.:** (07) 4060 3229 **Camping fees:** From $6.00 per adult/night

Coen Camping Ground

On Regent St in Coen, 107 km north of Musgrave Roadhouse and 64 km south-east of Archer River Roadhouse. Bring firewood. Additional map ref.: STM Qld C3.

Further information: Armbrust & Co. **Tel.:** (07) 4060 1134 **Camping fees:** From $6.60 per adult/night, school-aged children half price, power additional $1.00 per site/night; fees payable at Coen general store

Archer River Roadhouse

Close to Archer River on Peninsula Developmental Rd, 64 km north-west of Coen. Open 7 am–10 pm daily. Bring firewood. Additional map ref.: STM Qld C3.

Further information: Archer River Roadhouse **Tel.:** (07) 4060 3266 **Camping fees:** From $6.00 per person/night

26. PORMPURAAW AREA

The Pormpuraaw Aboriginal community is on the western coast of Cape York 207 km west of Musgrave Roadhouse. The road to it is generally open from late May, depending on the wet season. 4WD vehicles are recommended; drivers of conventional vehicles should check road conditions at the roadhouse. It is a popular fishing area. All visitors are required to check in at the Pormpuraaw Community Council offices on arrival.

Chapman River Mouth camping area

This is 2.5 km south of Pormpuraaw. Camping permit required. 4WD recommended. Bring drinking water and firewood. Natural boat launch. Additional map ref.: STM Qld D2.

Moonkan River Mouth camping area

Area is 7.5 km north of Pormpuraaw. Camping permit required. 4WD recommended. Bring drinking water and firewood. Natural boat launch. Additional map ref.: STM Qld D2.

Further information: Pormpuraaw Community Council **Tel.:** (07) 4060 4175 **Website:** www.pormpuraaw.qld.gov.au **Camping fees:** From $25.00 per vehicle/night; permit from and fees payable at council offices

27. SNAPPER ISLAND NATIONAL PARK

Snapper Island National Park is 20 km north of Port Douglas and is surrounded by the Great Barrier Reef Marine Park – obtain a copy of the marine park's zoning map for details of permitted activities. Visitors to Snapper Island, which can only be reached by private boat, can enjoy fishing and snorkelling near the reef. Maximum camper numbers apply.

Snapper Island camping area

Camping in south-west of island near anchorage point. Camping permit required. Undefined walking trails. Self-sufficient campers only. Bring drinking water. Gas/fuel stove only. Bookings essential. Additional map ref.: STM Qld E4.

Further information: QPWS, Cairns **Tel.:** (07) 4046 6600
Further information & bookings: Smart Service Queensland **Tel.:** 13 13 04 **Website:** www.qld.gov.au
Camping fees: From $4.00 per person/night; permit from and fees payable through Smart Service Queensland or at QPWS Cairns or Port Douglas

28. TULLY GORGE STATE FOREST PARK

The Tully Gorge State Forest Park offers a range of activities including walking, picnicking, camping and swimming, as well as spectacular views of the Tully River from scenic lookouts. The Tully River is well known for its whitewater rafting – the river is graded and recommended for experienced paddlers. Tully Gorge State Forest Park is signposted from Tully.

Tully Gorge camping area

Small area suitable for cars and small vans only, 42 km north-west of Tully via Cardstone Rd off the Bruce Hwy. Camping permit required. Drinking water from bore – boil before use. Firewood supplied. Additional map ref.: STM Qld E4.

Further information: QPWS, Cardwell **Tel.:** (07) 4066 8779
Camping fees: From $4.00 per person/night; permit from and fees payable at self-registration station

29. TURTLE GROUP NATIONAL PARK

Turtle Group National Park is north of Cooktown between the mainland and Lizard Island National Park. It is surrounded by the Great Barrier Reef Marine Park – obtain a copy of the marine park's zoning map for details of permitted activities. The islands can only be reached by private boat or charter. Contact QPWS Cooktown for access details. There are no facilities and campers must be self-sufficient.

Turtle Group camping areas

Camping allowed on three islands in the group (contact QPWS Cooktown for details). Camping permit required. Self-sufficient campers only. Bring drinking water. Gas/fuel stove only. Additional map ref.: STM Qld D4.

Further information:
QPWS, Cooktown **Tel.:** (07) 4069 5777 or
QPWS, Cairns **Tel.:** (07) 4046 6600
Further information & bookings: Smart Service Queensland **Tel.:** 13 13 04 **Website:** www.qld.gov.au
Camping fees: From $4.00 per person/night; permit from and fees payable through Smart Service Queensland or at QPWS Cooktown or Cairns

30. TWO ISLANDS NATIONAL PARK

This park is 13 km south-east of Cape Flattery, which is about 50 km north of Cooktown. The park – two small wooded islands – is an important seabird nesting area. Obtain a copy of the Great Barrier Reef Marine Park zoning map for details of permitted activities. Access to the park is by private boat or charter. There are no facilities and campers must be self-sufficient. Camping is seasonal, check with QPWS for dates.

Bush camping

On western tip of island. Camping permit required. Self-sufficient campers only. Bring drinking water. Gas/fuel stove only. Bookings essential. Additional map ref.: STM Qld D4.

Further information: QPWS, Cairns **Tel.:** (07) 4046 6600
Further information & bookings: Smart Service Queensland **Tel.:** 13 13 04 **Website:** www.qld.gov.au
Camping fees: From $4.00 per person/night; permit from and fees payable through Smart Service Queensland or QPWS Cairns

31. UNDARA VOLCANIC NATIONAL PARK

The Undara lava tubes are the longest of their kind in the world, with one flow extending 160 km. These lava systems were formed hundreds of thousands of years ago. The lava tubes can only be seen on a guided tour and to avoid disappointment, a tour should be booked before arrival. Undara Volcanic National Park is reached from the Gulf Developmental Rd.

Undara Experience camping area

This is 16 km south of the Gulf Developmental Rd and is signposted from it 17 km west of the Kennedy Hwy. Facilities include a laundry, bars and restaurants, a swimming pool and an internet cafe. Firewood for sale. Bookings essential. Additional map ref.: STM Qld F4.

Further information & bookings: Undara Experience **Tel.:** (07) 4097 1411 or 1800 990 992 **Email:** res@undara.com.au **Website:** www.undara.com.au **Camping fees:** Unpowered sites from $6.00 per person/night, power additional $6.00 per site/night

32. WEIPA AREA

Weipa is at the northern end of the unsealed Peninsula Developmental Rd, 190 km north-west of the Archer River Roadhouse and on the eastern shores of the Gulf of Carpentaria. Weipa and its surrounds have an interesting history, from Aboriginal occupation through to the building of a Presbyterian mission, bauxite mining and tourism. Visitors can enjoy excellent fishing, sailing or boating, and even a tour of the mining operations. Conventional vehicles can reach Weipa via the Peninsula Developmental Rd but it is recommended that caravans are 4WD/off-road.

Cullen Point and Janie Creek camping area

Reached via Mapoon Rd. Janie Creek is 10 km north of Mapoon and 95 km north of Weipa; Cullen Point is 21 km north of Mapoon. Camping permit required. Self-sufficient campers only. Bring drinking water and firewood. Cullen Point has showers and drinking water. Additional map ref.: STM Qld B2.

Further information: Mapoon Council **Tel.:** (07) 4090 9124
Camping fees: From $5.00 per person/night *Cullen Point*

Camping permit from and fees payable at Weipa Camping Ground (Kerr Point Rd, tel. (07) 4069 7871) *Janie Creek* Camping permit from and fees payable at Weipa Camping Ground or ranger station 7 km north of Mapoon **Vehicle permit:** From $30.00 per vehicle/month

False Pera Head camping area

North of Aurukun. Reached by Aurukun Rd off Peninsula Developmental Rd. Camping permit required. Self-sufficient campers only. Some tank water supplied, best to bring drinking water. Bring firewood. Alcohol is prohibited at False Pera Head and large fines apply if found. Additional map ref.: STM Qld C2.

Further information: Aurukun Land and Sea Management **Tel.:** (07) 4060 6831 **Camping fees:** From $6.00 per person/night **Permit:** Application for camping permit must be completed at least 2 weeks in advance; contact Aurukun Land and Sea Management for form and details **Vehicle permit:** From $20.00 per vehicle

Pennefather River and Stoneys Crossing camping areas

Pennefather River is signposted off Mapoon Rd and is 71 km north of Weipa. Stoneys Crossing is 30 km east of Mapoon Road and 58 km north-east of Weipa. Camping permit required for both areas. Self-sufficient campers only. Bring firewood. Additional map ref.: STM Qld C2.

Further information: Napranum Land and Sea Centre, Napranum **Tel.:** (07) 4069 9477 **Camping fees:** From $5.00 per person/night; permit from and fees payable to Napranum Land and Sea Centre (open 8 am–4.30 pm Mon–Thurs., 8 am–3 pm Fri.), permit from and fees payable at Weipa Camping Ground outside these hours **Vehicle permit:** From $30.00 per vehicle/month

Weipa Camping Ground

On Kerr Point Rd in Weipa, beside the water. 4WD caravan access. Swimming pool. Firewood supplied. Fishing and mining tours can be arranged. Additional map ref.: STM Qld C2.

Further information: Weipa Camping Ground **Tel.:** (07) 4069 7871 **Email:** campweipa@bigpond.com **Camping fees:** From $9.00 per person/night, power additional $2.00 per vehicle/night

33. WOOROONOORAN NATIONAL PARK

Mt Bartle Frere is Queensland's highest peak at 1622 m – it dominates the rugged wilderness of Wooroonooran National Park. The park is 25 km south of Cairns, just south of Gordonvale and to the west of the Bruce Hwy. To reach the mountain and its summit walkers must first walk the difficult Mt Bartle Frere Trail, which is accessed from the west via Gourka Rd off Topaz Rd and from the east from Josephine Falls parking area 8 km west of the Bruce Hwy. The walk is recommended for fit, experienced, self-sufficient walkers and the climb to the summit is for experienced climbers only.

Henrietta Creek camping area

This is 30 km east of Millaa Millaa and 35 km west of Innisfail, signposted off the Palmerston Hwy and located right beside it. Camping permit required. Bring drinking water and firewood. Additional map ref.: STM Qld E4.

MOUNT BARTLE FRERE TRAIL

The following campsites are listed in the order they would be reached if walking the whole trail from west to east.

Gourka Gourka camp

Conventional vehicle access via Gourka Gourka Rd east of Malanda. Camping permit required. Self-sufficient campers only. Bring drinking water. Gas/fuel stove only. Additional map ref.: STM Qld E4.

The Junction camp

4WD or walk-in access only. This is 2 km east of Gourka Gourka. Camping permit required. Self-sufficient campers only. Bring drinking water. Gas/fuel stove only. Additional map ref.: STM Qld E4.

Top Western camp

Walk-in access along Mt Bartle Frere Trail. This is 6.5 km east of the Junction. Camping permit required. Self-sufficient campers only. Bring drinking water. Gas/fuel stove only. Additional map ref.: STM Qld E4.

Top Eastern camp

Walk-in access along Mt Bartle Frere Trail. This is 1.25 km south-east of Top Western via the summit of Mt Bartle Frere. Camping permit required. Self-sufficient campers only. Bring drinking water. Gas/fuel stove only. Additional map ref.: STM Qld E4.

Big Rock camp

Walk-in access along Mt Bartle Frere Trail. This is 4 km south-east of Top Eastern and 3 km north-west of the Josephine Falls parking area (no camping allowed here). Camping permit required. Self-sufficient campers only. Bring drinking water. Gas/fuel stove only. Additional map ref.: STM Qld E4.

Further information:
Henrietta Creek QPWS, Innisfail **Tel.:** (07) 4064 5115
Mt Bartle Frere Trail QPWS, Miriwinni **Tel.:** (07) 4067 6304
Camping fees: From $4.00 per person/night; permit from and fees payable at self-registration stations (self-registration stations along the Mt Bartle Frere Trail are located at the Josephine Falls parking area and at The Junction camp)

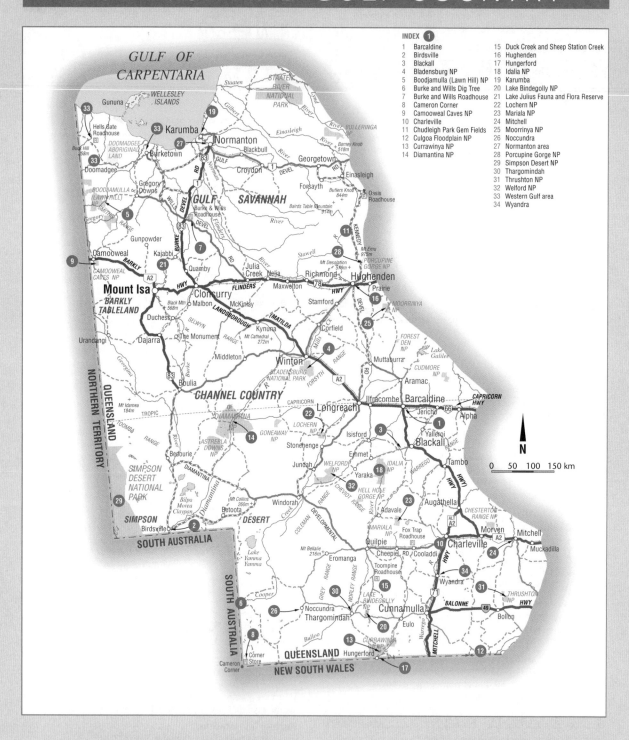

THIS VAST REGION STRETCHES FROM THE BLUE WATERS OF THE GULF OF CARPENTARIA SOUTH TO THE STATE'S BORDERS WITH SOUTH AUSTRALIA AND NEW SOUTH WALES. IT TAKES IN REMOTE OUTBACK PLAINS AND CHANNEL COUNTRY AS WELL AS THE WELL-KNOWN OUTBACK TOWNS OF BIRDSVILLE, LONGREACH, WINTON AND MOUNT ISA.

People who enjoy the solitude and history of the outback will be delighted with the wide choice of camping areas. There's camping at the site of the infamous Burke and Wills Dig Tree, at Cameron Corner – the junction of the Queensland, South Australian and Northern

Territory borders – beside the Barcoo River in Blackall, home to a monument to the legendary shearer Jackie Howe, and along the QAA Line crossing the Simpson Desert.

Boodjamulla (Lawn Hill) National Park is north of Mount Isa. The park has spectacular gorge country, beautiful riverine forests and the fascinating Riversleigh area, laden with ancient fossil deposits. The park's camping area has excellent facilities and a number of caravan sites.

Red sand dunes dominate the landscape of Diamantina National Park, and its purple gibber plains and flood plains together make the park a photographer's delight. Its fascinating heritage can be seen in historical sites along the Warracoota Drive. The park's two campgrounds are close to waterholes, allowing fishing and canoeing.

Just south of Winton are the sandstone ranges, plateaus and flat-topped mesas of Bladensburg National Park. Once a grazing property, the old homestead is now the park's information centre. Access to the park and its main camping area, Bough Shed Hole, is along the scenic Route of the River Gums, which is suitable for conventional vehicles and caravans during dry weather.

Another park that was once a grazing property is Lochern National Park, 150 kilometres south-west of Longreach. Lining the Thomson River and the park's waterholes are coolabahs and river tea trees that provide shelter for a variety of wildlife. Bush camping is possible beside the Thomson River and Broadwater Waterhole, both of which can be reached by conventional vehicles and caravans during dry weather.

BEST CAMPSITES

Burke and Wills Dig Tree camping area
Burke and Wills Dig Tree

Lawn Hill camping area
Boodjamulla (Lawn Hill) National Park

Hunters Gorge Campground
Diamantina National Park

Bough Shed Hole camping area
Bladensburg National Park

Wyandra Camping Reserve
Wyandra

BEST TIME TO VISIT

During the cooler months, from March to September.

1. BARCALDINE

Barcaldine is at the junction of the Capricorn and Landsborough hwys, 106 km east of Longreach and 105 km north of Blackall. Due to the town's good artesian water supply and abundant fruit orchards it is known as the 'garden city of the west'. Visit the Australian Workers Heritage Centre, the Tree of Knowledge and the Artesian Memorial.

Barcaldine Showgrounds

On Pine St, Barcaldine. Dogs allowed, but not in showground arena. Additional map ref.: STM Qld H4.

Further information: Barcaldine Shire Council
Tel.: (07) 4651 1211 **Camping fees:** From $15.00 per site/night for vans, second night free; fees collected by ranger

Lloyd Jones Weir camping area

Located 15 km south-west of Barcaldine. From Barcaldine travel 5 km south on the Blackall Rd then turn west onto the Barcaldine Downs Rd. Travel 9 km to the weir access road. Drinking water from bore. Bring firewood. Additional map ref.: STM Qld H4.

Further information: Barcaldine Visitor Information Centre
Tel.: (07) 4651 1724

2. BIRDSVILLE

Birdsville is Queensland's most remote town, located 375 km west of Windorah. It is home to the famous Birdsville Hotel and the Birdsville Races, which are held the first weekend in September. Access to Birdsville from the north is via Bedourie (193 km) and from the south via the Birdsville Track from Marree in South Australia (517 km).

Birdsville Caravan Park

On Florence St, Birdsville. Laundry facilities. Cafe and coffee shop. Bring firewood. Bookings recommended March–Nov.; bookings essential for race weekend, and no pets allowed at this time. Additional map ref.: STM Qld J1.

Further information & bookings: Birdsville Caravan Park
Tel.: (07) 4656 3214 **Email:** birdsvillecvanpk@growzone.com.au
Camping fees: From $6.00 per person/night, power additional $6.00 per vehicle/night

3. BLACKALL

Blackall is on the Landsborough (Matilda) Hwy 105 km south of Barcaldine. It was on a station near Blackall that Jackie Howe set his shearing world record of 321 sheep in under eight hours using hand shears. A statue to the legendary shearer is in the centre of town.

Barcoo River camping area

Camping on the banks of the Barcoo River. Access via Isisford Rd. Camping permit required. Free public toilets and hot showers available in Short St in front of information centre. Bring drinking water and firewood. Additional map ref.: STM Qld J4.

Further information: Blackall Visitor Information Centre
Tel.: (07) 4657 4637 **Email:** bhwa@b190.aone.net.au
Camping fees: From $5.00 per vehicle/night; permit from

and fees payable at visitor information centre, Short St, before setting up camp

4. BLADENSBURG NATIONAL PARK

This former grazing property now protects a number of waterholes and significant cultural sites. Within the park are diverse landscapes, vegetation – including huge plains of Mitchell and Flinders grass – and wildlife. Bladensburg National Park is reached via the Route of the River Gums 8 km south of Winton off the Winton–Jundah Rd. It is accessible for conventional vehicles in dry weather only. Collecting firewood is not permitted within the park.

Bough Shed Hole camping area

This is 22 km south of Winton via the Route of the River Gums. Camping permit required. Unmarked walks along the creek. Popular birdwatching spot. Bring drinking water and firewood. Gas/fuel stoves preferred. Additional map ref.: STM Qld H3.

Scrammy Gorge camping area

Area is 42 km south of Winton, via ranger station which is 17 km south of Winton. 4WD access only. Camping permit required. Swimming possible after rains. Bring drinking water and firewood. Gas/fuel stove preferred. Additional map ref.: STM Qld H3.

Further information: QPWS, Bladensburg National Park **Tel.:** (07) 4657 1192 **Camping fees:** From $4.00 per vehicle/ night *Bough Shed Hole* Camping permit from and fees payable at self-registration station *Scrammy Gorge* Camping permit from and fees payable at ranger station

5. BOODJAMULLA (LAWN HILL) NATIONAL PARK

The spectacularly scenic Boodjamulla National Park is beside the Northern Territory border, 220 km south-west of

Burketown via Gregory Downs and 340 km north-west of Mount Isa via Riversleigh. The park is well known for its magnificent gorge created by Lawn Hill Creek. It also has walking trails and canoeing opportunities, and is home to the Australian Fossil Mammal Site (Riversleigh) World Heritage Area. At Riversleigh visitors can view ancient fossil deposits, some dating back 25 million years. Conventional vehicles and caravans can reach the park via Gregory Downs along the Wills Developmental Rd. From Gregory Downs the road is unsealed. Collecting firewood is prohibited in the park.

Lawn Hill camping area

Just inside park near ranger headquarters. 4WD access to park from the south, from Mount Isa via Riversleigh; conventional vehicle access from Wills Developmental Rd at Gregory Downs. Camping permit required. Communal fireplaces. Bring firewood. Gas/fuel stove preferred. Bookings essential May–end-Sept. and taken up to 8 weeks in advance. Additional map ref.: STM Qld F1.

Adels Grove camping area

This area is 10 km east of the park. Access details same as Lawn Hill camping area, but Adels Grove can cater for customers who wish to fly in. Water from river – boil before use. Bring firewood. Dog-minding service available for those who wish to visit the national park. Bookings essential during peak period (June–Aug.). Additional map ref.: STM Qld F1.

Further information & bookings: Adels Grove **Tel.:** (07) 4748 5502 **Camping fees:** From $8.00 per person/night

Lawn Hill Gorge, Boodjamulla National Park

Further information: QPWS, Boodjamulla (Lawn Hill) National Park **Tel.:** (07) 4748 5572 **Further information & bookings:** Smart Service Queensland **Tel.:** 13 13 04 **Website:** www.qld.gov.au **Camping fees:** From $4.00 per person/night; permit from and fees payable through Smart Service Queensland

6. BURKE AND WILLS DIG TREE

The famous Dig Tree, on Cooper Creek, marks the site where Burke and Wills were expecting to meet the remainder of their expedition party, their final chance for survival. However all they found was the blazed tree and a limited amount of buried supplies. The calamitous story of the 'Victorian Exploration Expedition' is a fascinating part of Australia's history. The Dig Tree is signposted from the Adventure Way, about 57 km east of Innamincka (South Australia) and 320 km west of Thargomindah. Drivers of conventional vehicles and caravans should check road conditions before attempting.

Burke and Wills Dig Tree camping area

Camping beside Cooper Creek. Bring drinking water. Firewood supplied. Additional map ref.: STM Qld K2.

Further information: Thargomindah Information Centre **Tel.:** (07) 4655 3055 **Camping fees:** No set fee but a donation box is on site

7. BURKE AND WILLS ROADHOUSE

The Burke and Wills Roadhouse is located roughly halfway along the Wills Developmental Rd. This road leaves the Flinders Hwy at Julia Creek and continues in a north-west direction to Gregory Downs and the Gregory River.

Burke and Wills Roadhouse camping area

At junction of Wills Developmental Rd and Burke Developmental Rd, 232 km north-west of Julia Creek, 192 km north of Cloncurry and 195 km south of Normanton. Open 7 am–10 pm daily. Firewood supplied. Additional map ref.: STM Qld F2.

Further information: Burke and Wills Roadhouse **Tel.:** (07) 4742 5909 **Camping fees:** Unpowered from $4.50 per person/night, powered from $9.00 per person/night

8. CAMERON CORNER

Cameron Corner is the point where the Queensland, New South Wales and South Australian borders meet. It is named after John Brewer Cameron, a New South Wales Lands Department surveyor who led a survey here. Conventional vehicles can reach Cameron Corner but a 4WD is recommended; 4WD caravans and camper-trailers only.

Cameron Corner camping area

Camping behind Corner Store. Toilets and hot showers are available at store ($3.00 per shower). Bring drinking water. Some firewood available. Additional map ref.: STM Qld L2.

Further information: Corner Store **Tel.:** (08) 8091 3872 **Camping fees:** From $5.00 per vehicle/night; proceeds to RFDS

9. CAMOOWEAL CAVES NATIONAL PARK

There is not much on the surface of Camooweal Caves National Park, except for some sinkholes that give promise of the beautiful and complex cave system below. Camooweal

Caves are suitable for well-equipped and experienced cavers only; a caving permit is required, contact QPWS for details. The entrance to the park is signposted 8 km south of Camooweal along the Urandangi Rd. Access is possible in dry weather only and 4WD vehicles are recommended; drivers of conventional vehicles should check road conditions before attempting.

Caves Waterhole camping area

This is 22 km south of Camooweal. Camping permit required. Bring drinking water and firewood. Additional map ref.: STM Qld G1.

Further information: QPWS, Mount Isa **Tel.:** (07) 4743 2055 **Camping fees:** From $4.00 per person/night; permit from and fees payable at self-registration station

10. CHARLEVILLE

Charleville is on the Warrego River and is reached from both north and south by the Mitchell Hwy, from the east by the Warrego Hwy and from the west by the Diamantina Developmental Rd. Local attractions include the Historic House Museum, the Stiger Vortex rain-making guns from 1902 – which failed to break a drought – and the observatory.

Ward River bush camping area

Camping beside Ward River. Area is on Diamantina Developmental Rd 20 km west of Charleville. Bush camping, no facilities. Bring drinking water and firewood (some can be found). Additional map ref.: STM Qld K5.

Further information: Charleville Visitor Information Centre **Tel.:** (07) 4654 3057

11. CHUDLEIGH PARK GEM FIELDS

The road to the Chudleigh Park Gem Fields is signposted 155 km north of Hughenden along the Kennedy Developmental Rd. The fields and camping area are on private property 15 km west of the turn-off. Dogs are allowed in the campsite, but be aware that the owners bait the area for pests. Gems such as peridot and sapphires were first found here at the time of World War I. A current fossicking licence is required if you wish to fossick here.

Bush camping

Bush camping for self-sufficient campers only. Bring drinking water and firewood. Gas/fuel stove preferred. This is private property, so be very fire-aware. If you light a fire, do not leave it unattended and extinguish it with water. As a courtesy, phone ahead and let the owners know that you will be visiting; contact Hughenden Visitor Information Centre for owner's details. Additional map ref.: STM Qld F4.

Further information: Hughenden Visitor Information Centre **Tel.:** (07) 4741 1021

12. CULGOA FLOODPLAIN NATIONAL PARK

Formerly Byra Station, Culgoa Floodplain National Park protects floodplain and wetland habitats and is popular with birdwatchers (over 150 bird species have been noted). Aboriginal cultural sites and other heritage sites can be found within the park, located 130 km south-west of Dirranbandi on the New South Wales border. The park is reached by following signs for Byra from Goodooga in New South Wales (park is 30 km north-west of Goodooga; contact QPWS for

CURRAWINYA NATIONAL PARK

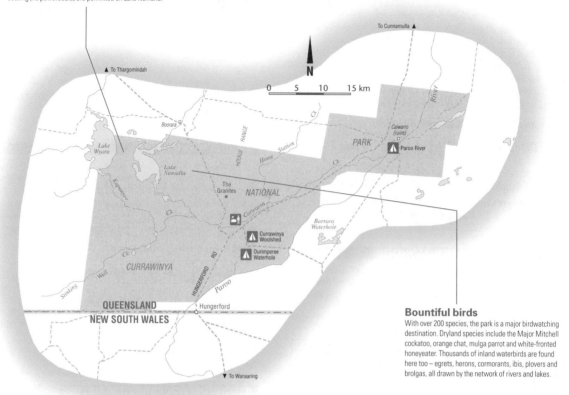

Lake landscapes
Two large lakes provide the park with a scenic centrepiece. Lake Numalla is freshwater, while nearby Lake Wyara is saline. In seasons of high rainfall, little lakes and claypans form amid the dunes that separate them. Swimming and boating (no powerboats) are permitted on Lake Numalla.

Bountiful birds
With over 200 species, the park is a major birdwatching destination. Dryland species include the Major Mitchell cockatoo, orange chat, mulga parrot and white-fronted honeyeater. Thousands of inland waterbirds are found here too – egrets, herons, cormorants, ibis, plovers and brolgas, all drawn by the network of rivers and lakes.

Currawinya National Park is a park of contrasts, with semi-arid rocky ranges and sandplains as well as rivers, lakes and wetlands. There are also Aboriginal sites and remains of early pastoral days. The lakes and wetlands are ideal sites for birdwatching. Explore and photograph the Granites. The park is reached from the south from Hungerford on the New South Wales border and from the north by a road 4 km west of Eulo off the Thargomindah–Cunnamulla Rd. All access roads are unsealed and may become unpassable after wet weather. Check road conditions before attempting. Collecting firewood is not permitted within the park.

Currawinya Woolshed

Group accommodation in woolshed complex, which is east of ranger base off Hungerford Rd, 20 km north of Hungerford. Bookings required. Self-contained accommodation. Full kitchen with fridge and freezer. Bookings required. Contact ranger for bookings and further details. Additional map ref.: STM Qld L4.

Ourimperee Waterhole

This is 25 km north of Hungerford. Access off Hungerford Rd 20 km north of Hungerford, then 5 km east to site. Conventional vehicle access possible in dry weather only. Camping permit required. Bring own firewood. Gas/fuel stove preferred. Additional map ref.: STM Qld L4.

Paroo River bush camping

Bush camping when river is not in flood. Area is 53 km north of Hungerford and 72 km south of Eulo. Access off Hungerford Rd 50 km north of Hungerford, then 3 km east to bush campsites. Camping permit required. Toilet facilities at nearby old Caiwarro homestead ruins. Bring drinking water and firewood. Fishing restrictions apply, contact QPWS for details. Additional map ref.: STM Qld L4.

Further information & bookings: QPWS, Currawinya National Park **Tel.:** (07) 4655 4001 **Camping fees:** From $4.00 per person/night; permit from and fees payable at self-registration station at ranger headquarters

detailed park map and access information). 4WD vehicles are recommended, and access is possible in dry weather only. This is a remote park and campers must be self-sufficient.

Bush camping

Bush camping, no facilities. Camping permit required. Bring drinking water. Gas/fuel stove only. Additional map ref.: STM Qld L5.

Further information: QPWS, Roma **Tel.:** (07) 4622 4266 **Further information & bookings:** Naturally Queensland Information Centre **Tel.:** (07) 3227 8197 **Camping fees:** From $4.00 per person/night; permit from and fees payable to Naturally Queensland Information Centre or QPWS

13. CURRAWINYA NATIONAL PARK see page 344

14. DIAMANTINA NATIONAL PARK

Diamantina National Park is south-east of Boulia and south-west of Winton. The area became a cattle property from 1875 and relics of this and of Aboriginal occupation can be found in the park. Warracoota Drive takes visitors to historic sites and areas to birdwatch and fish. The park is reached from the north via Kennedy Developmental Rd and from the south via Diamantina Developmental Rd. Access roads and all park roads are unsealed – 4WD vehicles and off-road 4WD caravans are recommended. Access is possible in dry weather only. Ranger headquarters is 186 km south-east of Boulia and 306 km south-west of Winton. Visitors must be self-sufficient in food, water and fuel. Collecting firewood is not permitted within the park.

Gumhole Campground

This is 21 km west of ranger headquarters off Boulia Rd. 4WD vehicles and vans recommended. Camping permit required. Bring drinking water and firewood. Gas/fuel stove preferred. Additional map ref.: STM Qld H2.

Hunters Gorge Campground

Camp is 4 km north of Boulia Rd; turn-off is 10 km west of ranger headquarters. 4WD vehicles and caravans recommended. Camping permit required. Bring drinking water and firewood. Gas/fuel stove preferred. Additional map ref.: STM Qld H2.

Further information:
QPWS, Diamantina National Park **Tel.:** (07) 4657 3024 *or* QPWS, Longreach **Tel.:** (07) 4652 7333
Camping fees: From $4.00 per person/night; permit from and fees payable at self-registration station, ranger headquarters

15. DUCK CREEK AND SHEEP STATION CREEK

Opal mines have been worked in this area since the 1890s. These two fossicking areas are within the Toompine opal fields – get detailed access information from the Quilpie Visitor Information Centre. If you intend to fossick for opals, a fossickers licence is required.

Bush camping

This is 62 km south-east of Toompine Roadhouse and 130 km south of Quilpie. Access in dry weather only. People towing caravans should check road conditions before

attempting. Self-sufficient campers only. Bring drinking water. Gas/fuel stove preferred. Additional map ref.: STM Qld K4.

Further information:
Quilpie Visitor Information Centre **Tel.:** (07) 4656 2166 *or* Quilpie Mining Registrar Office **Tel.:** (07) 4656 1266 **Camping fees:** From $2.50 per person/night; permit from and fees payable to Quilpie Visitor Information Centre or Quilpie Mining Registrar Office **Fossickers licence:** From $5.26 per person/month; available from Quilpie Visitor Information Centre or Quilpie Mining Registrar Office

16. HUGHENDEN

Hughenden is on the banks of the Flinders River, along the Flinders Hwy 243 km south-west of Charters Towers. The town's Flinders Discovery Centre houses fossils found in the area along with a replica skeleton of a dinosaur found south of Hungerford.

Allan Terry Caravan Park

On Resolution St, Hughenden. Close to all town facilities including swimming pool and shops. Laundry facilities. Campers kitchen. Firewood supplied. Additional map ref.: STM Qld G4.

Further information: Allan Terry Caravan Park **Tel.:** (07) 4741 1190 **Camping fees:** Unpowered sites from $10.00 per site/night for 2 people, powered sites from $14.00 per site/night for 2 people, additional fee for vans that wish to run air-conditioning units

17. HUNGERFORD

The small town of Hungerford is on the New South Wales border, 118 km south of Eulo and 102 km north of Wanaaring in New South Wales. Access from New South Wales is through the Dingo Fence. Roads to Hungerford pass through pastoral land – be aware of cattle. Roads can become impassable after rain. A friendly town, Hungerford was once a Cobb & Co. staging post and it is close to Currawinya National Park and the Paroo River.

Southern Cross Caravan Park

In Hungerford. Firewood supplied. Additional map ref.: STM Qld L4.

Further information:
Thargomindah Information Centre **Tel.:** (07) 4655 3055 *or* Bulloo Shire Council **Tel.:** (07) 4655 3133
Camping fees: From $5.50 per tent/night, powered van sites from $11.00 per site/night; fees collected daily by caretaker

18. IDALIA NATIONAL PARK

Idalia National Park has excellent opportunities for wildlife observation and birdwatching, along with historic sites, lookouts, bushwalks and scenic drives. As the park is isolated visitors need to be self-sufficient. The park is 126 km south-west of Blackall and signposted along the Benlidi–Idalia Rd, off the Yaraka Rd west of Blackall. 4WD vehicles are recommended.

Monks Tank camping area

Located 14 km north-west of ranger headquarters and 126 km south-west of Blackall. Camping permit required. Bush camping, no facilities. Self-sufficient campers only. Bring drinking water. Gas/fuel stove preferred. Additional map ref.: STM Qld J4.

Further information:
QPWS, Idalia National Park **Tel.:** (07) 4657 5033 or
QPWS, Longreach **Tel.:** (07) 4652 7333
Camping fees: From $4.00 per person/night; permit from
and fees payable at self-registration station, ranger
headquarters or to QPWS Longreach

19. KARUMBA

Karumba is situated where the Norman River enters the Gulf
of Carpentaria, 70 km north-west of Normanton. Karumba is
a popular destination for barramundi fishing.

Karumba Point Tourist Park

On Colonel Kitchen Rd (the road to Karumba Point), Karumba.
Saltwater swimming pool. Firewood supplied. Dogs allowed
but conditions apply, contact office for details. Bookings
apply May–Aug.; advance bookings taken from Christmas
onwards. Additional map ref.: STM Qld E2.

Further information & bookings: Karumba Point Tourist
Park **Tel.:** (07) 4745 9306 **Email:** craftynomads@bigpond.com
Camping fees: Unpowered from $16.00 per site/night for
2 people, powered from $19.00 per site/night for 2 people

20. LAKE BINDEGOLLY NATIONAL PARK

Lake Bindegolly National Park features the saline lakes
Bindegolly and Toomaroo and the freshwater Lake
Hutchinson. These are important breeding and feeding
habitats for waterbirds and many other animals. There is
a 9-km circuit walk around Lake Bindegolly. The park is on the
Bulloo Developmental Rd 34 km east of Thargomindah.
Camping is not permitted within the park, but a council
camping reserve is located just opposite. Firewood must be
collected outside park and camping reserve due to rare trees.

Bulloo Developmental Road camping reserve

Opposite Lake Bindegolly National Park on Bulloo
Developmental Rd. Camp at least 100 m from edge of lake.
Pets not allowed in national park. Bring drinking water and
firewood. Gas/fuel stoves preferred. If you light a fire please
ensure that it is watched at all times and extinguished
properly; the area surrounding the camping reserve has rare
trees. Additional map ref.: STM Qld L4.

Further information:
Lake Bindegolly National Park **Tel.:** (07) 4655 3173 or
Bulloo Shire Council **Tel.:** (07) 4655 3133

21. LAKE JULIUS FAUNA AND FLORA RESERVE

Visitors to Lake Julius Fauna and Flora Reserve can enjoy a
walk along the river, see old goldmines, throw in a line or do
some boating. The reserve is 110 km north of Mount Isa and
is signposted off the Barkly Hwy 19 km east of the town.
4WD vehicles and off-road caravans/trailers are
recommended.

Lake Julius Recreation Centre

On Lake Julius Rd 110 km north of Mount Isa (84 km of road
is unsealed – 4WD recommended). Boat ramp nearby.
Bookings not necessary, but phone call is advised before
arrival. Additional map ref.: STM Qld G1.

Further information & bookings: Lake Julius Recreation
Centre **Tel.:** (07) 4747 2186 **Camping fees:** From $2.85 per
person/night

22. LOCHERN NATIONAL PARK

Once a grazing property, Lochern National Park now protects
a range of plant habitats. The park has 20 km of frontage to
the Thomson River, which provides some excellent camping
and fishing opportunities. The park and its ranger headquarters are 150 km south-west of Longreach and 330 km
south of Winton via Lark Quarry. Access from Longreach is
signposted off the Longreach–Jundah Road 100 km south of
Longreach. Conventional vehicles can reach the park in dry
weather only and people towing caravans should check road
conditions before attempting.

Broadwater Waterhole camping area

Area is 2 km north of park's main road. Turn-off is 7 km west
of Thomson River and 7 km east of park headquarters access
road. Camping permit required. Bring drinking water and
firewood. Additional map ref.: STM Qld J3.

Lochern Shearers Quarters camping area

This is 1 km east of ranger headquarters. Turn-off to ranger
headquarters is 50 km west of Longreach–Jundah Rd. Permit
required. Bring drinking water and firewood. Bookings
recommended. Additional map ref.: STM Qld J3.

Thomson River camping area

This is 31 km west of Longreach–Jundah Rd, signposted
from the road 100 km south of Longreach. Camping permit
required. Bring drinking water and firewood. Additional map
ref.: STM Qld J3.

Further information:
QPWS, Lochern National Park **Tel.:** (07) 4658 5959 or
QPWS Longreach **Tel.:** (07) 4652 7333
Camping fees: Broadwater Waterhole and Thomson River
From $4.00 per person/night Lochern Shearers Quarters
From $10.00 per person/night. Permits from and fees
payable at self-registration station, ranger headquarters or
to QPWS Longreach

23. MARIALA NATIONAL PARK

Mariala National Park is ideal for nature-based activities
including wildlife-watching, birdwatching, bushwalking and
photography. The park is remote and all visitors must be self-
sufficient with food, water and fuel. As there are no marked
walking trails, bushwalking is only suited to experienced
walkers equipped with compass and maps. Mariala National
Park is 128 km north-west of Charleville and 55 km east of
Adavale, reached by the Charleville–Adavale Rd. Access
roads are unsealed and can become impassable after rain.
4WD vehicles are recommended.

Bush camping

Camping permit required. Self-sufficient campers only. Bring
drinking water. Gas/fuel stove only. Map ref.: STM Qld K4.

Further information: QPWS, Charleville **Tel.:** (07) 4654 1255
Camping fees: From $4.00 per person/night; permit from
and fees payable to QPWS Charleville

24. MITCHELL

Mitchell is on the Maranoa River, 89 km west of Roma and 178 km east of Charleville on the Warrego Hwy. Relax in the Great Artesian Spa, fish in the Maranoa River or enjoy the self-guide river walk. No bookings are taken here – it is first in, best dressed, with the peak period running April–Sept.

Fisherman Rest camping area

This is 4 km west of Mitchell. Signposted off Warrego Hwy. Bring drinking water and firewood. Additional map ref.: STM Qld K5.

Major Mitchell Caravan Park

On Warrego Hwy in Mitchell, close to all town amenities. Firewood supplied. Campers must proceed to the Great Artesian Spa for site allocation prior to setting up camp. Additional map ref.: STM Qld K5.

Neil Turner Weir camping area

On River St in Mitchell, beside Maranoa River. Firewood supplied. Additional map ref.: STM Qld K5.

Further information: The Great Artesian Spa, Cambridge St, Mitchell **Tel.:** (07) 4623 1073 **Camping fees:** *Major Mitchell Caravan Park* First 2 nights free, then unpowered sites from $5.00 per site/night, powered sites from $5.50 per site/night, ensuite sites from $13.75 per site/night; fees payable at the Great Artesian Spa

25. MOORRINYA NATIONAL PARK

Moorrinya National Park has a wonderful history of Aboriginal occupation and sheep farming. The park protects a variety of vegetation types and wildlife. Moorrinya National Park is along the Torrens Creek–Aramac Rd 85 km south of Torrens Creek, which lies on the Flinders Hwy. 4WD vehicles are recommended.

Bush camping

4WD vehicles only. Camping permit required and campsites advised by ranger at time of collecting permit. Self-sufficient campers only. Bring drinking water. Gas/fuel stove only. Additional map ref.: STM Qld G4.

Further information: QPWS, Moorrinya National Park **Tel.:** (07) 4741 7374 **Camping fees:** From $4.00 per person/night; permit from and fees payable at ranger headquarters, Old Shirley Homestead (in south of park, 5 km west of Torrens Creek–Aramac Rd)

26. NOCCUNDRA

Once a busy town, Noccundra is now just a hotel on the banks of the Wilson River. It is located off the Adventure Way 140 km west of Thargomindah.

Wilson River camping area

Beside Wilson River, just south of Noccundra Hotel. Toilet and shower facilities in hall opposite hotel. Bring drinking water. Some firewood supplied. Additional map ref.: STM Qld K3.

Further information:
Thargomindah Information Centre **Tel.:** (07) 4655 3055 *or* Noccundra Hotel **Tel.:** (07) 4655 4317

27. NORMANTON AREA

Normanton, the Gulf's major town, is on the Norman River and is a very popular spot for barramundi fishing. Normanton is at the northern end of the Burke Developmental Rd (Matilda Hwy) 372 km north of Cloncurry.

Leichhardt Lagoon camping area

On the Gulf Developmental Rd 26 km east of Normanton. On Norman River. Bring drinking water. Some firewood supplied. Additional map ref.: STM Qld E2.

Further information: Leichhardt Lagoon **Tel.:** (07) 4745 1330 **Camping fees:** From $6.00 per person/night

Normanton Caravan Park

On Brown St in Normanton. Camping permit required. Swimming pool. Laundry facilities. Gas/fuel stove only. Bookings recommended April–Aug. Additional map ref.: STM Qld E2.

Further information & bookings: Normanton Caravan Park **Tel.:** (07) 4745 1121 **Camping fees:** Unpowered from $14.00 per site/night for 2 people, powered from $19.50 per site/night for 2 people

Shady Lagoon camping area

Signposted from Normanton–Karumba Rd 10 km north of Normanton. Site is a further 25 km from turn-off and is beside the Norman River. Open Easter–Oct. Hot-water donkey shower system. Some firewood supplied. Additional map ref.: STM Qld E2.

Further information: Shady Lagoon **Tel.:** (07) 4745 1160 **Camping fees:** From $10.00 per vehicle/night

28. PORCUPINE GORGE NATIONAL PARK

The vibrantly coloured sandstone cliffs above Porcupine Creek are a striking sight for visitors to Porcupine Gorge National Park. The cliffs provide excellent photographic opportunities. The pools of Porcupine Creek are home to tortoises and the gorge to a variety of birds. Porcupine Gorge National Park is reached by the Kennedy Developmental Rd 70 km north of Hughenden. It is accessible in dry weather only – check road conditions first.

Pyramid Campground

Reached via Emu Plains Rd off Kennedy Developmental Rd. Check road conditions first. Camping permit required. Bring drinking water. Gas/fuel stove only. Additional map ref.: STM Qld G4.

Further information:
QPWS, Hughenden **Tel.:** (07) 4741 1113 *or*
QPWS, Charters Towers **Tel.:** (07) 4787 3388
Camping fees: From $4.00 per person/night; permit from and fees payable at self-registration station

29. SIMPSON DESERT NATIONAL PARK

The Simpson Desert is the world's largest parallel sand-dune desert. It straddles the corners of Queensland, South Australia and the Northern Territory. The park boundary is 75 km west of Birdsville. Travelling through the desert is for self-sufficient and well-equipped travellers in 4WD vehicles only. If travelling through South Australia a Desert Parks Pass is required (see page 170).

Bush camping

Bush camping throughout park. Camp within 500 m either side of the QAA Line. Camping permit required. Self-sufficient campers only. Bring drinking water and firewood. Additional map ref.: STM Qld J1.

Further information:
QPWS, Birdsville **Tel.:** (07) 4656 3272 *or*
QPWS, Longreach **Tel.:** (07) 4652 7333
Camping fees: From $4.00 per person/night; permit from and fees payable at QPWS Birdsville or Longreach

30. THARGOMINDAH

Thargomindah is on the banks of the Bulloo River 198 km west of Cunnamulla and 193 km south of Quilpie. Visitors can try their luck fishing in the Bulloo River, take a tour of the hydro plant – the town used the pressure of their artesian bore water to generate electricity for many years – or visit the museum in Leahy Historical House.

Explorers Caravan Park

On Dowling St, Thargomindah, beside Bulloo River. Campers kitchen with stove, fridge and microwave. Laundry facilities.

Limited tank water and bore water. Firewood supplied. Bookings recommended June–July. Additional map ref.: STM Qld K3.
Further information & bookings: Explorers Caravan Park **Tel.:** (07) 4655 3307 **Email:** bulloosc2@bigpond.com
Camping fees: Unpowered from $14.00 per site/night for 2 people, powered from $17.50 per site/night for 2 people

31. THRUSHTON NATIONAL PARK

Thrushton National Park protects areas of mulga, spinifex and heathland. There are also a variety of tree species in the park including brigalow, river red gum and forest gum, while koalas are known to frequent the Neabul Creek area. There are wildflowers during spring and the park is popular with birdwatchers and nature observers. Thrushton National Park is 27 km north-east of Bollon, 116 km north-west of St George and 160 km south of Mitchell. Contact QPWS Roma to obtain a map with access information. The park is remote and visitors must be self-sufficient and well prepared.

Bush camping

Off Balonne Hwy 11 km east of Bollon and 100 km west of St George. Park boundary is 16 km north of highway. Leave all gates as found. From Mitchell access is via Mitchell–Bollon Rd 147 km south of Mitchell, then park boundary is 13 km east. Camping permit required. Self-sufficient campers only. Bring drinking water. Gas/fuel stove preferred. Additional map ref.: STM Qld K5.

Further information: QPWS, Roma **Tel.:** (07) 4622 4266
Further information & bookings: Smart Service Queensland **Tel.:** 13 13 04 **Website:** www.qld.gov.au
Camping fees: From $4.00 per person/night; permit from and fees payable through Smart Service Queensland or QPWS Roma

Wildflowers in the Simpson Desert

32. WELFORD NATIONAL PARK

Welford National Park is north-east of Windorah and south-east of Jundah. It has contrasting landscapes, from red sand dunes to open grasslands, and visitors can enjoy one of the two tourist drives, birdwatching or fishing in the Barcoo River. The park is reached from the south by the Jundah–Quilpie Rd, which leaves the Diamantina Developmental Rd 50 km east of Windorah. The park is 57 km north of the Diamantina Developmental Rd. Ranger headquarters is 10 km east of the Jundah–Quilpie Rd. Some access roads and internal park roads are unsealed. 4WD vehicles are recommended; drivers of conventional vehicles should check road conditions first.

Jetty Campground

East of Little Boomerang Waterhole and One Tree campgrounds. Camping permit required. Self-sufficient campers only. Bring drinking water. Gas/fuel stove preferred. Additional map ref.: STM Qld J3.

Little Boomerang Waterhole Campground

Access off Jundah–Quilpie Rd 50 km south of Jundah, then 40 km west. Camping permit required. Self-sufficient campers only. Bring drinking water. Gas/fuel stove preferred. Additional map ref.: STM Qld J3.

One Tree Campground

East of Little Boomerang Waterhole. Camping permit required. Self-sufficient campers only. Bring drinking water. Gas/fuel stove preferred. Additional map ref.: STM Qld J3.

Rocks Campground

East of Jundah–Quilpie Rd. Access is just west of ranger headquarters. Camping permit required. Self-sufficient campers only. Bring drinking water. Gas/fuel stove preferred. Additional map ref.: STM Qld J3.

Trafalgar Campground

East of Jundah–Quilpie Rd. Access is east of ranger headquarters. Camping permit required. Self-sufficient campers only. Bring drinking water. Gas/fuel stove preferred. Additional map ref.: STM Qld J3.

Further information:
QPWS, Welford National Park **Tel.:** (07) 4658 5994 *or* QPWS, Longreach **Tel.:** (07) 4652 7333
Further information & bookings: Smart Service Queensland **Tel.:** 13 13 04 **Website:** www.qld.gov.au
Camping fees: From $4.00 per person/night; permit from and fees payable at self-registration station at Little Boomerang Waterhole or through Smart Service Queensland

33. WESTERN GULF AREA

The Western Gulf area covers the Gulf Track from Burketown to the Northern Territory border. Access to this part of the state is possible for conventional vehicles, with roads being a mixture of sealed and maintained unsealed roads, but drivers should enquire with local authorities about road conditions. The best time to travel these roads is during the dry season.

Burketown Caravan Park

On Sloman St in Burketown. Laundry facilities. Fishing tours can be arranged. Bring firewood. Additional map ref.: STM Qld E1.

Further information: Burketown Caravan Park **Tel.:** (07) 4745 5118 **Email:** stay@burketowncaravanpark.com.au **Website:** www.burketowncaravanpark.com.au **Camping fees:** Unpowered from $16.00 per site/night for 2 people, powered from $19.00 per site/night for 2 people

Escott Lodge

This is 17 km west of Burketown and signposted from there. Laundry facilities. Swimming pool. Natural boat ramps. Firewood supplied. Bookings recommended May–Aug. Additional map ref.: STM Qld E1.

Further information & bookings: Escott Lodge **Tel.:** (07) 4748 5577 **Camping fees:** Unpowered from $7.00 per person/night, powered from $8.50 per person/night

Hells Gate Roadhouse

On Savannah Way 173 km west of Burketown and 52 km east of the state border. Open 7 am–10 pm daily. Laundry facilities. Firewood supplied. Bookings advisable. Additional map ref.: STM Qld E1.

Further information & bookings: Hells Gate Roadhouse **Tel.:** (07) 4745 8258 **Camping fees:** From $6.00 per person/night

Kingfisher Camp

This is about 50 km south of Hells Gate Roadhouse and 30 km west of Doomadgee. 4WD vehicles, caravans and trailers are recommended. Laundry facilities. Good birdwatching. Boat hire. Guided tours available. Bring firewood. Additional map ref.: STM Qld E1.

Further information: Kingfisher Camp **Tel.:** (07) 4745 8212 or (07) 4745 8132 **Website:** www.ozemail.com.au/~bowthorn **Camping fees:** From $8.00 per person/night

34. WYANDRA

The quiet and friendly town of Wyandra is just off the Mitchell Hwy, 99 km north of Cunnamulla and 97 km south of Charleville. The Wyandra Museum displays the diesel motor used to power the town until 1970, and there are also a number of heritage houses.

Wyandra Camping Reserve

Off Moody St, Wyandra, behind school. Showers are unheated and with natural bore water, therefore water is cooler at times. Firewood supplied. Additional map ref.: STM Qld K4.

Further information & bookings: Cunnamulla Visitor Information Centre **Tel.:** (07) 4655 2481 **Camping fees:** First two nights free; a donation box is on site for additional nights

TASMANIA

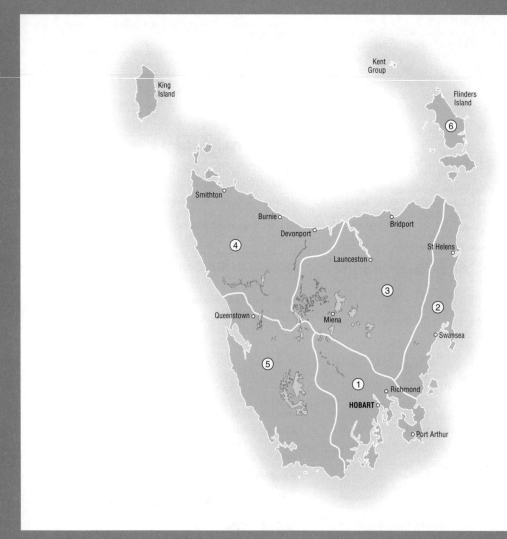

Tasmania accounts for just one per cent of the total land area of Australia, but it boasts a disproportionately large number of environments famous for their beauty, rarity and ecological significance. Tasmania is Australia's premier wilderness state, and one of the world's great outdoor destinations.

Fanning out around Hobart is an intricate coastal landscape of islands, channels, peninsulas and river estuaries, framed by forests and fretted mountains. The historic settlements of Port Arthur and Richmond and the remote wilds of Bruny Island are among the many attractions here.

With its mild weather, beautiful beaches and peaceful fishing villages, the east coast is Tasmania's premier seaside destination. Visit Freycinet National Park, where you'll find excellent camping grounds, as well as Wineglass Bay – one of the world's most beautiful beaches.

The Midlands and the north offer the experience of rural Tasmania, a place of vineyards, orchards, rolling fields, historic towns and grand colonial manors. Skiers and snow campers can get back to nature in Ben Lomond National Park, while anglers can head for the lakes of the Central Highlands.

Nature dominates throughout the north-west and the south-west wilderness areas. Located here are the World Heritage features that have put Tasmania on the map: the magnificent glaciated lakes and mountains of Cradle Mountain–Lake St Clair National Park, the wild rivers and ancient forests of the Franklin–Gordon region, and the remote coastline of the far south, where the only way in is on foot.

Remote in a different way is Flinders Island, a sparsely populated outcrop of civilization lying amid the turbulence and splendour of Bass Strait. Camp near the granite tors of Strzelecki National Park and visit the famous geese at Lady Barron.

Tasmania is a state where tourism and nature go hand-in-hand. Camping is enormously popular and well catered for. Facilities may be basic in remote areas, but there will always be something to recommend a spot, be it a great view or proximity to some outstanding natural feature.

PARKS PASS

A Parks Pass is generally required to visit Tasmania's national parks. There are a number of options available and you should be able to find something that suits your needs. At the time of writing, fees were as follows:

DAILY PASS
$10.00 per vehicle, carrying a maximum of eight people, or $3.50 per individual

HOLIDAY PASS (Valid for up to two months)
$33.00 per vehicle, carrying a maximum of eight people, or $13.50 per individual

ANNUAL PASS
To visit all parks – $46.00 per vehicle, carrying a maximum of eight people. To visit one park – $20.00 per vehicle, carrying a maximum of eight people

There is a 20% discount off the annual pass fee for those with a Seniors Card, Pensioner Concession Card or Health Care Card

Contact Parks and Wildlife for details of where to obtain a pass, tel. 1300 368 550

Dove Lake and Cradle Mountain at dawn

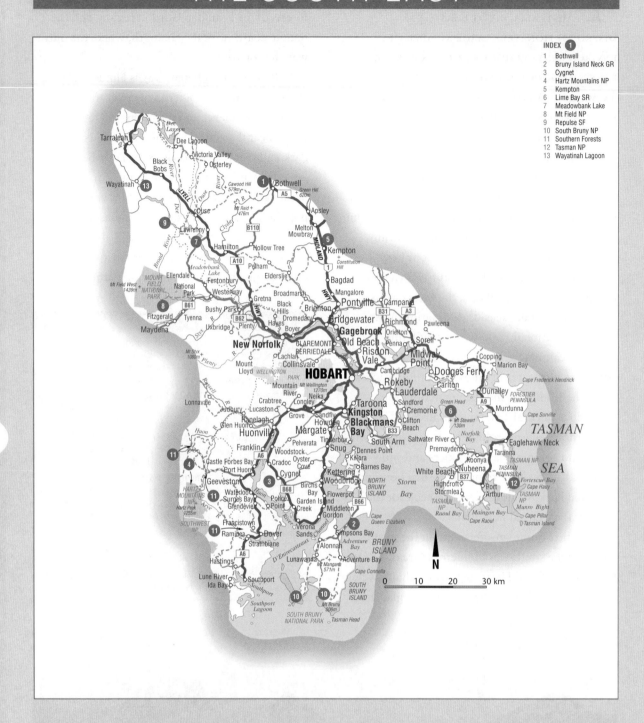

THIS REGION OF TASMANIA HAS WONDERFUL TOURING DESTINATIONS ALONG WITH SUPERB FORESTS, MOUNTAINS, COASTAL AREAS AND INTERESTING HISTORICAL SITES TO EXPLORE.

On the Tasman Peninsula are Tasman National Park and Lime Bay State Reserve; both offer excellent coastal campsites and access to the Coal Mines Historic Site and Port Arthur Historic Site nearby. Fortescue Bay campground within Tasman National Park is a great base to enjoy the excellent boating, canoeing and sea kayaking opportunities around the park's rugged coastline. If bushwalking is your passion, follow the Tasman Trail between Eaglehawk Neck and Fortescue Bay.

The beaches of Lime Bay State Reserve also offer excellent walking and the camping area is near a small beach that is safe for swimming. During summer the reserve has a colourful display of wildflowers.

Off the south-east coast of Tasmania is Bruny Island, which can be reached by car ferry from Kettering. The isthmus connecting North and South Bruny Island offers visitors the chance to swim, fish and see little (fairy) penguins and short-tailed shearwaters (muttonbirds). South Bruny National Park at the southern tip of the island has magnificent coastal scenery, including the rugged cliffs of Fluted Cape and Tasman Head.

South-west of Hobart, the picturesque southern forests spread across the valleys of the Huon, Arve, Weld, Picton, Esperance and Lune rivers, and adjacent mountainsides. The Arve Road is a popular touring destination with its excellent scenery, lookouts, walks and picnic areas. Beside the Huon River is the Tahune Forest Reserve, where campers can indulge in some fishing, canoeing, swimming, or strolling through the forests of huon pine. Take a walk along the Tahune Forest AirWalk, a 500-metre-long walkway through the treetops, with fantastic views over the Huon and Picton river junction.

BEST CAMPSITES

Lime Bay camping area
Lime Bay State Reserve

Jetty Beach camping area
South Bruny National Park

Tahune Forest Reserve camping area
Southern Forests

Land of the Giants campground
Mount Field National Park

Fortescue Bay campground
Tasman National Park

BEST TIME TO VISIT

All year round. The region is popular during the warmer months; it can be quite cool during winter.

1. BOTHWELL

Situated in the Clyde River valley, 74 km north-west of Hobart, Bothwell has over 50 buildings that have been classified or recognised by the National Trust. As well, the village is home to Australia's oldest golf course.

Bothwell Camping Ground

In Market Place, Bothwell. Gas/fuel stove only. Key access to showers. Additional map ref.: TVM L16.

Further information & bookings: Central Highlands Council **Tel.:** (03) 6259 5503 **Website:** www.tasmaniacentral.tas.gov.au **Camping fees:** Unpowered $5.00 per site/night, powered $10.00 per site/night; fees payable and keys available at council office, Alexander St, Bothwell. Contact caretaker outside office hours

2. BRUNY ISLAND NECK GAME RESERVE

Bruny Island can be reached by ferry from Kettering. The reserve is just to the south of the 'neck' that joins the north and south islands. The signposted route off the B66 road leads to the campsite, just behind the beach. There is limited access for caravans.

The Neck camping area

Located on Lutregala Rd and signposted from the B66 main road, 26 km south of the ferry terminal and 3 km north of Adventure Bay/Alonnah junction turn-off. Bring drinking water and firewood. Additional map ref.: TVM M21.

Further information:
Parks & Wildlife, Bruny Island **Tel.:** (03) 6293 1419 *or* Parks & Wildlife, Huonville **Tel.:** (03) 6264 8460

3. CYGNET

The centre of a fruit- and wine grape-growing area, Cygnet was originally named Port de Cygnet Noir (Black Swan Port) due to the number of swans in the bay. Explore the Pelverata Falls or take a stroll along one of the beaches in the area. Cygnet is on the B68 (Channel Hwy), 18 km south of Huonville.

Cygnet Caravan Park

In Mary St, Cygnet. Bring firewood. Bookings essential in early Jan. during the local Folk Festival. Additional map ref.: TVM L20.

Further information & bookings: Cygnet Caravan Park **Tel.:** (03) 6295 1869 **Camping fees:** Unpowered from $8.00 per 2 people/night, powered from $12.00 per 2 people/night

4. HARTZ MOUNTAINS NATIONAL PARK

This park is 24 km west of Geeveston and is signposted along the C632 from Geeveston. Encompassing a variety of landscapes and vegetation, it offers magnificent views and walking tracks. All walkers must register – and deregister at end of walk – at information booth within the park. Carry large-scale maps. Contact ranger for further details.

Bush camping

Walk-in bush camping allowed within park as per Parks & Wildlife bush camping regulations (must be 500 m from any road or day use area). Self-sufficient walkers only. Bring drinking water. Gas/fuel stove only. Additional map ref.: TVM K20.

Further information: Parks & Wildlife, Huonville **Tel.:** (03) 6264 8460 **Parks Pass:** Required

5. KEMPTON

This historic town on the A5 (Midland Hwy) is a 35-minute drive from Hobart. Visit the historic churches and graveyards or browse in the antique and craft shops.

Kempton overnight bay

On Main St off Midland Hwy, next to the blue church. Overnight stay only. Additional map ref.: TVM M16.

Further information: Southern Midlands Council **Tel.:** (03) 6254 5000

6. LIME BAY STATE RESERVE

Lime Bay State Reserve is on northern tip of Tasman Peninsula. The beaches at Lime Bay offer excellent walking and during summer there is a wonderful display of wildflowers in the reserve. Visit the ruins of the convict station at the nearby Coal Mines Historic Site. The reserve is reached from Premaydena, which is signposted off the A9 (Arthur Hwy) at Taranna.

Lime Bay camping area

At end of Coal Mines Rd, off Saltwater River Rd from Premaydena. Area is 16 km north of Premaydena. Bring drinking water and firewood. Gas/fuel stove preferred. Additional map ref.: TVM P19.

Further information & bookings: Parks & Wildlife, Taranna **Tel.:** (03) 6250 3497 **Camping fees:** $3.30 per adult/night, $1.65 per child/night, family (2 adults + 2 children) $8.25 per night; fees payable at self-registration station

7. MEADOWBANK LAKE

Meadowbank Lake is 10 km from Hamilton, which is on the A10 (Lyell Hwy) about 75 km north-west of Hobart. The lake is part of the Derwent River system, and is popular for waterskiing and fishing.

Bethune Park camping area

Grassed area on western foreshore of lake, at the end of Dunrobbin Bridge. Access signposted, through gate on western foreshore along Ellendale Rd, 2 km west of its junction with A10. Bring drinking water and firewood. Boat ramp on eastern foreshore. Map ref.: Additional map ref.: TVM K17.

Further information: Central Highlands Council **Tel.:** (03) 6286 3202 **Website:** www.tasmaniacentral.tas.gov.au

8. MOUNT FIELD NATIONAL PARK

A little over an hour's drive from Hobart, Mt Field National Park is one of Tasmania's oldest national parks. It protects a diverse range of wildlife and flora, from alpine vegetation to rainforest and tall gum forests. Visit Russell Falls and the visitor centre. The park is signposted from the C609 (Lake Dobson Rd), which is off the B61 (Gordon River Rd) north-west of New Norfolk.

Land of the Giants campground

The campground is beside the Tyenna River and is signposted along C609 off B61, 41 km north-west of New Norfolk. Gas/fuel stove only. Additional map ref.: TVM K17.

Further information & bookings:
Parks & Wildlife, Mt Field **Tel.:** (03) 6288 1149 *or* Land of the Giants campground **Tel.:** (03) 6288 1526 **Parks Pass:** Required
Camping fees: Unpowered $6.00 per adult/night, $4.00 per child (age 6–17) per night; powered $8.50 per adult/night, $4.00 per child/night; fees payable at self-registration station

9. REPULSE STATE FOREST

This forested area on the western foreshore of Lake Repulse is accessed via the road to Dunrobbin Bridge off the A10 (Lyell Hwy). Once over the bridge, take the first turn-off right (at 2.7 km) into Dawsons Rd. Continue for 11 km to the entrance of Repulse State Forest, then follow the signs to Lake Repulse.

Bush camping

Many tracks lead to bush campsites on lake foreshore. Some sites have natural boat launches. Bring drinking water and firewood. Additional map ref.: TVM J16.

Further information: Forestry Tasmania, Derwent **Tel.:** (03) 6233 7449

10. SOUTH BRUNY NATIONAL PARK

The park, at the southern end of South Bruny Island, offers coastline areas with magnificent scenery, abundant wildlife and some rare vegetation. Bruny Island can be reached by car ferry from Kettering.

Cloudy Corner camping area

Signposted from Cloudy Beaches, 3 km from the beach entrance off C644 (Cloudy Bay Rd) and 10 km south of Lunawanna. Beach can be accessed by 4WD; check tide times beforehand. Boat can be launched from beach. Bring drinking water and firewood. Gas/fuel stove preferred. Additional map ref.: TVM M22.

Jetty Beach camping area

Signposted from C629 (Cape Bruny Rd), 19 km south of Lunawanna. Bring drinking water and firewood. Gas/fuel stove preferred. Boat can be launched from beach. Additional map ref.: TVM M22.

The Pines camping area

This area close to Cloudy Bay Beach is signposted from C644 (Cloudy Bay Rd) and is 9 km south of Lunawanna. Bring drinking water and firewood. Gas/fuel stove preferred. Additional map ref.: TVM M21.

Further information:
Parks & Wildlife, Bruny Island **Tel.:** (03) 6293 1419 *or*
Parks & Wildlife, Huonville **Tel.:** (03) 6264 8460
Parks Pass: Required

11. SOUTHERN FORESTS

This area encompasses much of the state's southern mountains and valleys within the catchment areas of the Weld, Picton, Arve, Huon, Lune and Esperance rivers. Due to high rainfall, the forests here are mostly wet eucalypt. Activities include walking, rafting, fishing and camping.

Arve River picnic and camping area

Signposted along Arve Rd, 15 km west of Geeveston. Firewood supplied. Additional map ref.: TVM K20.

Hastings Forest Tour picnic and camping area

This camping area, on either side of the Esperance River, can be reached via the Esperance River Rd. Take the turn-off from the A6 (Huon Hwy) at Strathblane (4 km south of Dover) and continue for 8 km to reach the campsite. There is limited vehicle- and caravan-based camping in clearings and limited walk-in sites near facilities. Water from river – boil before use. Firewood supplied. Additional map ref.: TVM L21.

Tahune Forest Reserve camping area

Located beside the Huon River, on Arve Road Forest Drive 30 km north-west of Geeveston. A 400-m walk to tent sites; limited van sites. Facilities are a short distance from campsites. Firewood supplied. Additional map ref.: TVM K20.

Further information:
Forestry Tasmania, Geeveston **Tel.:** (03) 6297 0012 *or*
Tahune Forest AirWalk office, Tahune Forest Reserve camping area **Tel.:** (03) 6297 0068

12. TASMAN NATIONAL PARK

Along with beautiful coastal scenery, Tasman National Park also offers bushwalking, swimming and fishing opportunities. The campground at Fortescue Bay is signposted from the A9 (Arthur Hwy) while access to the north of the park is via C338 (Blowhole Rd).

Bivouac Bay campsite

Walk-in bush camping along Tasman Trail, north of Fortescue Bay. Trail can be accessed from Fortescue Bay campground or from Waterfall Bay Rd to the north. Gas/fuel stove only. Bring drinking water and maps. Additional map ref.: TVM Q20.

Camp Falls campsite

Walk-in bush camping along Tasman Trail, south of Waterfall Bay carpark. Northern section of trail can be accessed from Waterfall Bay Rd; Fortescue Bay campground provides access from the south. Gas/fuel stove only. Bring drinking water and maps. Additional map ref.: TVM Q19.

Fortescue Bay campground

Signposted off A9 (Arthur Hwy) at Fortescue Rd, the turn-off is midway between Taranna and Port Arthur. The campground is 12 km east of this A9 junction. Bring firewood. Bookings recommended for peak periods. Additional map ref.: TVM Q20.

Further information & bookings:
Parks & Wildlife, Taranna **Tel.:** (03) 6250 3497 *or*
Fortescue Bay campground **Tel.:** (03) 6250 2433
Parks Pass: Required
Camping fees: $5.50 per person/night or $11.00 per 2–6 people/night; fees payable to caretaker at Fortescue Bay

13. WAYATINAH LAGOON

This lagoon is north-west of New Norfolk and is signposted from A10 (Lyell Hwy). Wayatinah is home to the six-station Lower Derwent hydro-electric scheme. The lagoon offers excellent trout fishing.

Wayatinah Camping and Caravan Park

On Wayatinah Rd in Wayatinah village, 75 km north-west of New Norfolk. Bring firewood. Bookings essential for school holidays and long weekends. Additional map ref.: TVM J16.

Further information & bookings: Wayatinah Camping and Caravan Park **Tel.:** (03) 6289 3317 **Email:** peterwayatinah@bigpond.com **Website:** www.wayatinahcamping.com
Camping fees: Unpowered from $9.00 per 2 adults/night, powered from $12.00 per 2 adults/night, children under 16 $2.00/night

THE PICTURESQUE EAST COAST OF TASMANIA FEATURES SANDY BEACHES, EXCELLENT FISHING AND STRIKING COASTAL SCENERY.

Maria Island, which can be reached by ferry from Triabunna, draws many walkers and cyclists.

Visitors can absorb Maria Island's rich and varied history, including its days as a penal settlement, and view the magnificent scenery and flora and fauna. The Marine Reserve surrounding most of the island protects a huge variety of marine life, and diving and snorkelling offer a chance to view this marine wonderland.

The beautiful white beaches and rugged granite cliffs and peaks of Freycinet National Park are home to abundant wildlife and colourful wildflowers. Freycinet is a bushwalkers' paradise with walking trails that range from short strolls to remote overnight hikes. Other activities include scenic drives, swimming, snorkelling and diving. The main campground is near the park's entrance.

Heading north from Bicheno to St Helens are the Lagoons Beach and Little Beach coastal reserves and the St Helens Point and Scamander conservation areas. Their camping areas have a range of facilities and swimming and fishing are popular. North of St Helens, the blue waters and sandy beaches of the Bay of Fires Conservation Area attract divers, snorkellers, anglers and swimmers. Campers here have a large choice of sites, all with fantastic views.

North of the Bay of Fires, campers can set up amongst the casuarinas in Mount William National Park. The park is ablaze with colour during spring and summer when the wildflowers are in bloom. Here visitors can enjoy the Forester Kangaroo Drive, which can be completed by car or mountain bike – hundreds of forester kangaroos can be spotted along this route.

BEST CAMPSITES

Mayfield Bay camping area
Mayfield Bay Conservation Area

Freycinet Main campground
Freycinet National Park

Cosy Corner camping area
Bay of Fires Conservation Area

Moulting Bay camping area
Humbug Point Nature Recreation Area

Stumpys Bay campsites
Mount William National Park

BEST TIME TO VISIT

Spring to autumn.

1. BAY OF FIRES CONSERVATION AREA

The Bay of Fires is on the north-east coast of Tasmania, north of St Helens, and is reached by the A3 (Tasman Hwy) from Launceston. Beautiful white sandy beaches and blue water lure divers, swimmers and fisherfolk to this area. The numerous campsites in the south are signposted from The Gardens Rd, which is off the C850 (Binalong Bay Rd) from St Helens. Policemans Point in the north is reached from Ansons Bay Rd. Check road conditions before travelling. At time of writing, dogs were prohibited in Bay of Fires Conservation Area, however this ruling may have changed. Call Parks & Wildlife at St Helens to confirm current regulations.

SOUTHERN CAMPING AREAS

Big Lagoon camping area

Access off The Gardens Rd, 2 km north of bridge over Sloop Lagoon. Travel for 1 km to turn-off into Bay of Fires Conservation Area. Many tracks to bush campsites on lagoon's shore. Bring drinking water and firewood. Additional map ref.: TVM R9.

Cosy Corner camping area

Signposted off The Gardens Rd, 5.4 km from Binalong Bay Rd. Bring drinking water and firewood. Additional map ref.: TVM R9.

Grants Lagoon camping area

Signposted off The Gardens Rd, 1.3 km from Binalong Bay Rd. Bring drinking water and firewood. Additional map ref.: TVM R9.

Jeanneret Beach camping area

Signposted off The Gardens Rd, 3.2 km from Binalong Bay Rd. Bring drinking water and firewood. Additional map ref.: TVM R9.

Seaton Cove camping area

Access off The Gardens Rd, 6.3 km from Binalong Bay Rd. The road to this small camping area is opposite Old Gardens Rd turn-off. Bring drinking water and firewood. Additional map ref.: TVM R9.

Sloop Lagoon camping area

Access via Old Gardens Rd, signposted from The Gardens Rd, 6.3 km from Binalong Bay Rd. Many tracks off Old Gardens Rd lead to bush campsites on lagoon's shore. Bring drinking water and firewood. Additional map ref.: TVM R9.

Sloop Reef camping area

Reached from The Gardens Rd, 6.8 km from Binalong Bay Rd. Bring drinking water and firewood. Additional map ref.: TVM R9.

Swimcart Beach camping area

Signposted off The Gardens Rd, 4 km from Binalong Bay Rd. Bring drinking water and firewood. Additional map ref.: TVM R9.

NORTHERN CAMPING AREA

Policemans Point camping area

Signposted off C843 (Ansons Bay Rd). Camping area is 5.2 km from turn-off. Bring drinking water and firewood. Additional map ref.: TVM R8.

Further information: Parks & Wildlife, St Helens
Tel.: (03) 6376 1550

2. DOUGLAS–APSLEY NATIONAL PARK

This park is north-west of Bicheno and is reached from the A3 (Tasman Hwy). Access to southern section is via Rosedale Rd (off A3), 4 km north of Bicheno, while access to northern part of park is via the gravel E Rd off Tasman Hwy. Take the short walk to Apsley Waterhole or the three-hour Apsley Gorge circuit. Those who prefer longer walks can attempt the three-day Leeaberra Track – its trackhead is reached from E Rd. Note that it is important to walk the track north to south to prevent the spread of root rot. Walkers should also ensure they clean boots and tent pegs before and after visiting. The collection of firewood is prohibited in the park.

Apsley Waterhole camping area

This is 11 km north-west of Bicheno; signposted off Rosedale Rd. Park at carpark and walk 200 m into campsite. Water from river – boil before use. Gas/fuel stove preferred. Additional map ref.: TVM R13.

Heritage Falls and Tevelein camping areas

Walk-in sites along the Leeaberra Track, a walk that begins in north of park. Self-sufficient bushwalkers only. Bring drinking water. Gas/fuel stove only. Obtain large-scale maps and contact ranger for further details.

Further information: Parks & Wildlife, Freycinet
Tel.: (03) 6256 7080 **Parks Pass:** Required **Fire restrictions:** Solid-fuel fire ban 1 Oct.–30 April; gas/fuel stove only during this period, unless days of total fire ban

3. FREYCINET NATIONAL PARK see page 359

4. HUMBUG POINT NATURE RECREATION AREA

Humbug Point is on Georges Bay, south of Binalong Bay. It is reached by Binalong Bay Rd from St Helens. The area is abundant with birdlife and is popular with birdwatchers and bushwalkers. At time of writing dogs were prohibited in Humbug Point Nature Recreation Area, however this ruling may change. Call Parks & Wildlife at St Helens to confirm current ruling.

A lookout in Douglas–Apsley National Park

FREYCINET NATIONAL PARK

Scenic drives

Spectacular coastal views are the main feature along the 6.4-kilometre unsealed road from the Freycinet Lodge to Cape Tourville. The Friendly Beaches are reached via a signposted turn-off on the Coles Bay Road. Carpark lookouts along the way reveal miles of deserted beaches in a near pristine state.

Sweeping coast

This crescent of azure sea and white sand, bordered by forested mountains and pink granite tors, is claimed as one of the world's most beautiful beaches. To see it in all its glory, take the two-hour Wineglass Bay Lookout Walk to the saddle of land between Mount Amos and Mount Mayson.

Freycinet National Park features forests, quiet beaches, rocky headlands and an excellent range of walking tracks. Coles Bay, nestling in a sheltered nook of Great Oyster Bay is a good base from which to explore the area. Access to the park is via the C302 (Coles Bay Rd) off the A3 (Tasman Hwy), 11 km south of Bicheno.

Bluestone Bay camping area

4WD access. Turnoff is 4.9 km along Cape Tourville lighthouse road. Gas/fuel stove only. Additional map ref.: TVM S14.

Freycinet Main campground

Signposted from Freycinet Drive. Powered sites. Gas/fuel stove only. Additional map ref.: TVM R14.

Friendly Beaches camping area

Signposted from C302 (Coles Bay Rd), 9 km south of A3 (Tasman Hwy) junction. Bring drinking water. Gas/fuel stove only. Additional map ref.: TVM R14.

Honeymoon Bay camping area

Signposted along Freycinet Drive. Gas/fuel stove only. Open 18 Dec.–March long weekend and Easter only. Additional map ref.: TVM R14.

The Sand Dunes camping area

Signposted along Freycinet Drive just past main campground. Gas/fuel stove only. Open 18 Dec.–March long weekend and Easter only. Additional map ref.: TVM R14.

Bush camping – Bryans Beach, Cooks Beach, Hazards Beach and Wineglass Bay

Walk-in bush campsites for self-sufficient walkers. Carry large-scale maps. Gas/fuel stove only. Contact ranger for details of water availability. Walkers must register and de-register at the information/self-registration station in the main carpark.

Further information & bookings: Parks & Wildlife, Freycinet Visitors Centre **Tel.:** (03) 6256 7000
Parks Pass: Required **Camping fees:** Unpowered $5.50 per adult/night, $2.75 per child (age 6–17) per night; powered $6.60 per adult/night, $3.30 per child/night. Fees payable at office or self-registration station outside ballot season. Ballot system applies for Christmas holidays (applications by 1 Oct.) for Freycinet Main, The Sand Dunes and Honeymoon Bay camping areas

Dora Point camping area

Signposted from Binalong Bay Rd, 8 km north of St Helens, then 4.5 km into camping area. Bring drinking water and firewood. Gas/fuel stove preferred. Additional map ref.: TVM R10.

Moulting Bay camping area

Signposted from Binalong Bay Rd, 7 km north of St Helens. Boat can be launched from beach. Bring drinking water and firewood. Gas/fuel stove preferred. Additional map ref.: TVM R10.

Further information: Parks & Wildlife, St Helens **Tel.:** (03) 6376 1550

5. LAGOONS BEACH COASTAL RESERVE

This coastal reserve, south-east of St Marys, is good for fishing and swimming. Note that the collection of firewood is prohibited in this area.

Lagoons Beach camping area

North of Chain of Lagoons. Entrance is signposted 2 km north of A3/A4 junction. Bring drinking water and firewood. Additional map ref.: TVM R12.

Further information: Parks & Wildlife, Freycinet **Tel.:** (03) 6256 7080

6. LITTLE BEACH COASTAL RESERVE

The coastal location of this reserve, east of St Marys, makes it ideal for fishing and swimming. Note that the collection of firewood is prohibited in this area.

Little Beach camping area

Signposted, 3 km north of Lagoons Beach Coastal Reserve. Limited access for caravans. Bring drinking water and firewood. Additional map ref.: TVM R11.

Further information: Parks & Wildlife, Freycinet **Tel.:** (03) 6256 7080

7. LITTLE SWANPORT RIVER RESERVE

The reserve is beside the Little Swanport River where it meets the A3 (Tasman Hwy), 20 km north of Triabunna. Note that the collection of firewood is prohibited in this area.

Little Swanport River camping area

Small site at northern end of bridge over Little Swanport River along A3 (Tasman Hwy). Bring drinking water and firewood. Gas/fuel stove preferred. Additional map ref.: TVM Q15.

Further information: Parks & Wildlife, Freycinet **Tel.:** (03) 6256 7080

8. MARIA ISLAND NATIONAL PARK

Access to Maria Island is by a half-hour ferry trip. The ferry leaves from Louisville, 6 km north of Orford and goes thrice daily to Darlington. Maria Island has a rich and varied history, including periods as a penal settlement in 1825–32 and 1842–50. There are numerous walks on the island which take in its history and flora and fauna. As there is no access for cars, Maria Island is a popular bike-riding spot.

Darlington camping area

In Darlington, a 10-minute walk south of ferry terminal. Additional map ref.: TVM Q17.

Encampment Cove camping area

Located 13 km south of Darlington. Access is signposted. Firewood supplied. Gas/fuel stove preferred. Additional map ref.: TVM Q17.

Frenchs Farm camping area

This camping area is 11 km south of Darlington. Access is signposted. Gas/fuel stove only. Additional map ref.: TVM Q17.

Further information & bookings: Parks & Wildlife, Maria Island **Tel.:** (03) 6257 1420 **Parks Pass:** Required **Camping fees:** $4.40 per adult/night, $2.20 per child (age 6–17) or pensioner/night; fees payable at self-registration station **Ferry service:** Tel. 0427 100 104

9. MAYFIELD BAY CONSERVATION AREA

This conservation area is off the A3 (Tasman Hwy), 15 km south of Swansea. The beaches at Mayfield Bay offer diving, swimming and fishing. Visit Three Arch Bridge, built by convicts in 1845 . Note that the collection of wood is not permitted in this area.

Mayfield Bay camping area

Signposted off A3 (Tasman Hwy), 15 km south of Swansea. Boat launching facilities available. Bring drinking water and firewood. Additional map ref.: TVM Q15.

Further information & bookings: Parks & Wildlife, Freycinet **Tel.:** (03) 6256 7080 **Camping fees:** $2.00 per site/night; fees payable by donation in donation box at campsite

10. MOULTING LAGOON GAME RESERVE

Moulting Lagoon is an internationally listed wetland habitat for birds. It is the largest known swan breeding area in Tasmania and is home to many other waterbird species. The reserve is on the shores of the lagoon and is reached via the Coles Bay Rd from the A3 (Tasman Hwy).

Moulting Lagoon camping area

Signposted from Coles Bay Rd, 12 km north of Coles Bay and 3.6 km south of turn-off to Friendly Beaches. Bring drinking water and firewood. No pets allowed at this site. Additional map ref.: TVM R14.

MOUNT WILLIAM NATIONAL PARK

TASMAN

SEA

N

0 2 4 6 km

Unusual lighthouse
This unusual granite lighthouse was built in the 1890s and is still operational, although not manned. The lighthouse is closed to the public, but there is a picnic area nearby, with views of the azure waters, fine white sands and red granite outcrops so typical of the region.

Saltwater fishing
Tasmania's east coast is the preferred spot for the state's saltwater anglers, and Mount William attracts its fair share of enthusiasts. Within the park there are boat launches at Musselroe Bay, Eddystone Point and Stumpys Bay (campsite three). There is good inshore fishing for Australian salmon, flathead and whiting, particularly just outside the estuary of Anson Bay.

Mount William National Park offers great coastal scenery, fishing, diving and wildlife-watching. In the south of the park is the Eddystone Point Lighthouse. The park is in the far north-east of Tasmania and is reached from the north via the C843 and C845 roads from Gladstone and from St Helens in the south via the C843 road to Ansons Bay and then the C846.

NORTHERN CAMPING AREAS

Stumpys Bay – campsite no. 1

Signposted from Forester Kangaroo Drive off C845, 10 km north of ranger base. Bring drinking water and firewood. Additional map ref.: TVM R7.

Stumpys Bay – campsite no. 2

Signposted from Forester Kangaroo Drive off C845, 10.4 km north of ranger base. Bring drinking water and firewood. Additional map ref.: TVM R7.

Stumpys Bay – campsite no. 3

Signposted from Forester Kangaroo Drive off C845, 11 km north of ranger base. Boat ramp requires 4WD. Bring drinking water and firewood. Generators can be used here, following park regulations. Additional map ref.: TVM R7.

Stumpys Bay – campsite no. 4

Signposted from Forester Kangaroo Drive off C845, 13 km north of ranger base. Bring drinking water and firewood. Additional map ref.: TVM R7.

Top Camp campground

This area is 28 km north-east of Gladstone and 8 km north of ranger base. It is signposted from the C845 in Poole. Bring drinking water and firewood. Additional map ref.: TVM R7.

SOUTHERN CAMPING AREA

Deep Creek camping area

Follow the C843 from Gladstone and take the C846 (Eddystone Point Rd) turn-off. The campsite is 3 km north of Eddystone Point Rd junction. Bring drinking water and firewood. Additional map ref.: TVM R8.

Further information: Parks & Wildlife, Mt William
Tel.: (03) 6356 1173 **Parks Pass:** Required

River and Rocks camping area

The area is off River and Rocks Rd, which is signposted from Coles Bay Rd, 12 km south of its junction with the A3. Bring drinking water and firewood. Additional map ref.: TVM R14.

Further information: Parks & Wildlife, Freycinet
Tel.: (03) 6256 7080

11. MOUNT WILLIAM NATIONAL PARK
see page 361

12. MUSSELROE BAY CONSERVATION AREA

This conservation area north of Mt William National Park is a popular birdwatching spot. Access to it from the north is via the C844 (Cape Portland Rd) from Gladstone and to the south via Poole along the C843 and C845 roads from Gladstone.

Little Musselroe Bay camping area

This area is 25 km north of Gladstone, reached from signposted Little Musselroe Rd off Cape Portland Rd. Bring drinking water and firewood. Vehicle access only possible Christmas–Easter; at other times site is walk-in only (300 m from parking area). Additional map ref.: TVM Q7.

Musselroe Bay camping area

Signposted along C845 road from Poole. Many camping areas along road. Bring drinking water and firewood. Additional map ref.: TVM R7.

Further information: Parks & Wildlife, Bridport
Tel.: (03) 6356 1173 **Parks Pass:** Not required

13. NINE MILE BEACH COASTAL RESERVE

This reserve is on the northern shores of Great Oyster Bay. Activities include swimming and fishing in the Swan River or in Great Oyster Bay.

Bagot Point camping area

Signposted from Dolphin Sands Rd, off A3 (Tasman Hwy) 2 km north of Swansea. Camping area is behind the beach at the end of Nine Mile Beach Rd, 18–20 km north-east of Swansea. Bring drinking water. Gas/fuel stove only. Additional map ref.: TVM R14.

Further information: Parks & Wildlife, Freycinet
Tel.: (03) 6256 7080

14. ORFORD

Orford, located beside the Prosser River, is on the A3 (Tasman Hwy), 81 km north-east of Hobart. Enjoy one of the numerous walks to places of interest in the area.

Raspins Beach Camping Park

Signposted from Tasman Hwy in Orford, 9 km south of Triabunna. Fire pots supplied, bring firewood. Gas/fuel stove preferred. Boat ramp nearby. Additional map ref.: TVM Q17.

Further information & bookings: Raspins Beach Camping Park **Tel.:** (03) 6257 1771 **Camping fees:** Tent sites from

$12.00 for up to 2 people/night; powered from $14.00 for up to 2 people/night

15. ST HELENS POINT CONSERVATION AREA

This conservation area is east of St Helens, on the shores of Georges Bay. There are many campsites on the eastern foreshore, between Dianas Basin and the beach. Fishing, swimming, surfing and canoeing are some of the activities to be enjoyed here. Note that camping is not permitted at St Helens Point, only at the designated camping area. At the time of writing, dogs were prohibited in St Helens Point Conservation Area, but this ruling may have changed. Call Parks & Wildlife at St Helens to confirm current regulations.

Dianas Basin camping area

Signposted off A3 (Tasman Hwy), 8.5 km south of St Helens. Bring drinking water and firewood. Additional map ref.: TVM R10.

Further information: Parks & Wildlife, St Helens
Tel.: (03) 6376 1550

16. SCAMANDER CONSERVATION AREA

Located to the north of Scamander, this conservation area is midway between St Helens and St Marys. The discovery of middens and tools has produced evidence of a rich Aboriginal history. At time of writing, dogs were prohibited in Scamander Conservation Area, but this ruling may have changed. Call Parks & Wildlife at St Helens to confirm current regulations.

Paddys Island camping area

Signposted off A3 (Tasman Hwy), 10 km south of St Helens. Bring drinking water and firewood. Additional map ref.: TVM R10.

Shelly Point camping area

Signposted off A3 (Tasman Hwy), 15 km south of St Helens. Bring drinking water and firewood. Additional map ref.: TVM R10.

Further information: Parks & Wildlife, St Helens
Tel.: (03) 6376 1550

17. SCAMANDER FOREST RESERVE

North of Scamander, this reserve is reached from the C421 road; alternatively it is signposted from Beaumaris via Eastern Creek Rd for 11 km and then Trout Rd. Try your luck fishing for bream in the Scamander River.

Trout Creek camping area

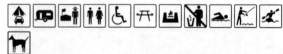

Located 13.5 km west of Beaumaris on Trout Rd, 2.5 km from the junction with Eastern Creek Rd. Bring drinking water and firewood. Additional map ref.: TVM R10.

Further information: Forestry Tasmania, Fingal
Tel.: (03) 6374 2102

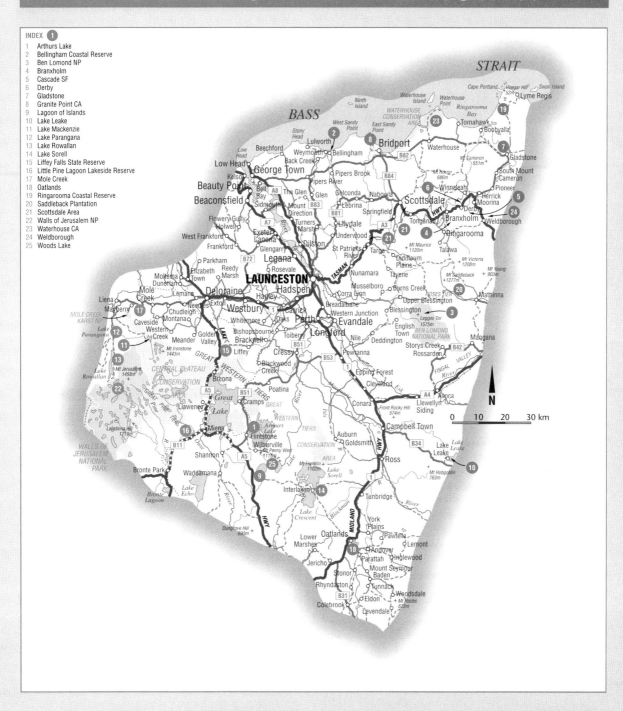

THIS LARGE REGION STRETCHES FROM THE BASS STRAIT COAST DOWN TO THE MIDLAND LAKES, EAST TO GLADSTONE AND WEST TO MOLE CREEK. EXCELLENT BOATING AND FISHING ARE POSSIBLE ALONG THE COAST AND IN THE MANY LAKES OF THE CENTRAL PLATEAU, WHILE THE BEN LOMOND AND WALLS OF JERUSALEM NATIONAL PARKS HAVE STRIKING MOUNTAIN SCENERY.

Campers have a huge choice of reserves and parks, from the beachside campgrounds of Bellingham Coastal Reserve, Granite Point Conservation Area and Ringarooma Coastal Reserve to the pretty inland areas around Derby and Scottsdale. The lakes are a magnet for anglers, as trout are plentiful, while for the hardy there is a high campsite below a summit in Ben Lomond National Park and remote walk-in sites in the Walls of Jerusalem National Park.

The large Waterhouse Conservation Area is on the coast facing Bass Strait, east of Bridport. There are many campsites here amongst the coastal vegetation and around the lakes and lagoons. This conservation area is popular for fishing and beachcombing. Further south, the picturesque Liffey Falls are on the slopes of the Great Western Tiers and framed by temperate rainforests of myrtle and sassafras. Access to the falls is via a walking track from the camping area in Liffey Falls State Reserve.

The lakes of the central plateau – Arthurs Lake, Lake Sorell, Woods Lake and Lagoon of Islands – have a range of camping options. At Arthurs Lake there is a choice between Pumphouse Bay or Jonah Bay camping grounds – both have facilities and boat ramps. Bush campsites are located around the shores of the Lagoon of Islands and Woods Lake (access to Woods Lake is by four-wheel drive only) while there are two campsites with good facilities at Lake Sorell.

BEST CAMPSITES

Mole Creek Caravan Park
Mole Creek

Jonah Bay Camping Ground
Arthurs Lake

Bush camping
Lagoon of Islands

Ben Lomond campground
Ben Lomond National Park

Lower Liffey Reserve campsite
Liffey Falls State Reserve

BEST TIME TO VISIT

Spring through to autumn.

1. ARTHURS LAKE

Arthurs Lake is located about 50 km north of Bothwell, within the Central Plateau Conservation Area. It is a mecca for keen fisherfolk and is reached from the west by the Poatina Rd from the A5 (Lake Hwy).

Jonah Bay Camping Ground

Signposted along B51 (Poatina Rd), 9 km north of its junction with the A5 and 32 km south of Poatina. Bring drinking water and firewood. Additional map ref.: TVM L13.

Pumphouse Bay Camping Ground

Signposted along B51 (Poatina Rd), 5 km north of its junction with the A5 and 36 km south of Poatina. Hot showers Oct.–April only. Firewood supplied. Additional map ref.: TVM L13.

Further information & bookings: Parks & Wildlife, Liawenee **Tel.:** (03) 6259 8148 **Camping fees:** *Jonah Bay:* $2.20 per adult/night, $1.10 per child/night, family (2 adults + 2 children) $5.50 per site/night *Pumphouse Bay:* $3.30 per adult/night, $1.65 per child/night. Fees payable at self-registration stations

2. BELLINGHAM COASTAL RESERVE

This reserve is beside the seaside village of Bellingham which is 40 km north-east of George Town and 27 km west of Bridport. It is reached via the C852 road off the B82 road.

Bellingham camping area

This small camping area is signposted from Clifford St off Howard St in Bellingham, 6 km north of B82. Boat ramp nearby. Bring drinking water and firewood. Additional map ref.: TVM M8.

Further information: Parks & Wildlife, Prospect **Tel.:** (03) 6336 5312

3. BEN LOMOND NATIONAL PARK

This well-known park, 50 km south-east of Launceston, can be reached via the Ben Lomond Rd off the C401 from Blessington. Within the park, the Ben Lomond Range, a plateau rising to over 1575 m, attracts downhill and cross-country skiers in winter. In summer, bushwalkers, birdwatchers and nature enthusiasts flock to the alpine heathlands.

Ben Lomond campground

Access via Ben Lomond Rd, 13 km south of Upper Blessington. Bring firewood. Additional map ref.: TVM P11.

Bush camping

Remote bush camping is permitted throughout the park for self-sufficient bushwalkers. Bring drinking water. Gas/fuel

stove only. Obtain large-scale maps and contact ranger for further details.

Further information: Parks & Wildlife, Prospect
Tel.: (03) 6336 5312 **Parks Pass:** Required

4. BRANXHOLM

Branxholm is east of Scottsdale on the A3 (Tasman Hwy). The Branxholm district was once an important tin-mining area. Visit a hop farm or take a gemstone tour.

Branxholm camping area

Beside the Ringarooma River and close to the A3 (Tasman Hwy) in Branxholm village, this area is 25 km east of Scottsdale and 8 km west of Derby. Bring drinking water. Additional map ref.: TVM P9.

Further information & bookings: Branxholm Supermarket
Tel.: (03) 6354 6168 **Camping fees:** Unpowered from $6.00 per 2 people/night, powered from $10.00 per 2 people/night; fees payable at Branxholm Supermarket, Scott St (Tasman Hwy)

5. CASCADE STATE FOREST

This forest is just south of Derby and borders the Cascade Dam. The dam was originally built for the Briesis Tin Mine in Derby but is now used for irrigation purposes. From Derby Town Hall, follow the signposted route along the Cascade Rd to the campsite.

Cascade Dam camping area

This small site beside the dam is reached via Cascade Rd, 4.5 km south of Derby. Bring drinking water and firewood. Additional map ref.: TVM P9.

Further information: Forestry Tasmania, Scottsdale
Tel.: (03) 6352 6466

6. DERBY

This former tin-mining town, 104 km north-east of Launceston, is now classified as a Historic Town. The Tin Mine Museum in town has history displays, gemstones and tin-panning.

Derby Park camping area

On A3 (Tasman Hwy) in Derby, 33 km east of Scottsdale. Camping area is beside the Ringarooma River. Bring drinking water. Gas/fuel stove only. Additional map ref.: TVM P9.

7. GLADSTONE

Gladstone is in the far north-east of the state, 132 km from Launceston on the B82 road. The area has many interesting geological formations and gem fossicking is popular here.

Gladstone Hall camping area

On Carr St (Waterhouse–Boobyalla Rd) in Gladstone, 35 km north-east of Derby. Camping area is behind the town hall. Additional map ref.: TVM Q8.

Further information: Gladstone General Store
Tel.: (03) 6357 2182 **Camping fees:** $2.00 per site/night for power; fees collected by caretaker

8. GRANITE POINT CONSERVATION AREA

This conservation area in the north-east corner of the state can be reached via the B82 Rd from Bridport.

Bridport Caravan Park

Signposted from Bentley St in Bridport. Beachside location. Campsites set amongst natural coastal vegetation. Campfires allowed, bring own fire pot and firewood. Laundry facilities available. Bookings recommended for peak periods. Additional map ref.: TVM N8.

Further information & bookings: Bridport Caravan Park
Tel.: (03) 6356 1227 **Camping fees:** Unpowered from $10.00 per 2 adults and children (under 16) per night; powered from $14.50 per 2 adults and children (under 16) per night

9. LAGOON OF ISLANDS

The Lagoon of Islands is a popular fishing spot in the central plateau region. It is reached by the Interlaken Rd off the A5 (Lake Hwy).

Bush camping

Signposted along C527 (Interlaken Rd), 4 km east of the A5. Gas/fuel stove preferred. Bring drinking water. Additional map ref.: TVM L14.

Further information: Hydro Tasmania **Tel.:** (03) 6230 5660

10. LAKE LEAKE

Lake Leake is 4 km north of the B34 road between Campbell Town and Swansea. It is a popular spot with anglers seeking trout.

Lake Leake camping area

Camping area is 34 km east of Campbell Town and 41 km north-west of Swansea, reached via Lake Leake Rd off B34. Bring drinking water. Firewood supplied. Bookings preferred. Additional map ref.: TVM P14.

Further information & bookings: Lake Leake caretaker
Tel.: (03) 6381 1319 **Camping fees:** From $6.00 per site/night

11. LAKE MACKENZIE

Lake Mackenzie is a trout-fishing spot in the highlands of Tasmania. It is reached via Lake Mackenzie Rd off the C171 (Mersey Forest Rd), 20 km west of Mole Creek, then 21 km south-east to this open campsite and fishing area.

Bush camping

At the end of Lake Mackenzie Rd, off C171. Access road may be closed during bad weather. Small exposed site best suited to anglers. Gas/fuel stove preferred. Bring drinking water and firewood. Additional map ref.: TVM H12.

Further information: Hydro Tasmania, Gowrie Park
Tel.: (03) 6491 2800

12. LAKE PARANGANA

Lake Parangana is south-west of Mole Creek, 7.5 km along the C171 road (Mersey Forest Rd). The turn-off for the C171 is 20 km west of Mole Creek.

Bush camping

Scattered bush camping areas on western foreshore of lake. Access road is just south of Parangana Dam wall through picnic area. Gas/fuel stove preferred. Bring drinking water, or boil water from lake. Bring firewood. Additional map ref.: TVM H12.

Further information: Hydro Tasmania, Gowrie Park
Tel.: (03) 6491 2800

13. LAKE ROWALLAN

Lake Rowallan is south-west of Mole Creek and just south of Lake Parangana. It is reached via the C171 (Mersey Forest Rd).

Bush camping

Signposted from Mersey Forest Rd (C171). Turn-off for C171 is 20 km west of Mole Creek. Many roads lead off Mersey Forest Rd to bush camping areas on eastern foreshore of lake. Gas/fuel stove preferred. Bring drinking water, or boil water from lake. Bring firewood. Additional map ref.: TVM H12.

Further information: Hydro Tasmania, Gowrie Park
Tel.: (03) 6491 2800

14. LAKE SORELL

Lake Sorell is within the Great Western Tiers Conservation Area. It is reached via the Interlaken Rd, between the A5 (Lake Hwy) to the west and National Highway 1 (Midland Hwy) to the east.

Dago Point camping area

This area is at Interlaken, which is 26 km east of A5 and 26 km west of National Hwy 1. Bring firewood. Additional map ref.: TVM M14.

Silver Plains Camp Ground

Signposted off Interlaken Rd, 22 km east of A5 and 30 km west of National Hwy 1. Bring firewood. Restrictions have been placed on camping at Silver Plains due to introduced European carp being found in Lake Sorell. Please contact Parks & Wildlife Liawenee for further information. Additional map ref.: TVM L14.

Further information: Parks & Wildlife, Liawenee
Tel.: (03) 6259 8148 **Camping fees:** Currently under revision; fees collected by ranger

15. LIFFEY FALLS STATE RESERVE

This reserve is nestled on the slopes of the Great Western Tiers amongst rainforest, 15 km west of Bracknell. As well as the Liffey Falls, there are a number of smaller waterfalls within the reserve. Enjoy the nature walk through tree ferns and tall eucalypts. The reserve is reached by the C513 (Gulf Rd/Liffey Rd).

Lower Liffey Reserve campsite

Signposted from Bracknell along the C513 (Gulf Rd/Liffey Rd). Bring drinking water and firewood. Additional map ref.: TVM K12.

Further information: Parks & Wildlife, Trevallyn
Tel.: (03) 6336 2678

16. LITTLE PINE LAGOON LAKESIDE RESERVE

Little Pine Lagoon Lakeside Reserve is west of Miena, and is reached by the B11 road, 7 km from its junction with the A5 (Lake Hwy).

Little Pine Lagoon Lakeside Reserve camping area

Signposted from the B11. Bring drinking water. Gas/fuel stove only. Additional map ref.: TVM J14.

Further information: Parks & Wildlife, Liawenee
Tel.: (03) 6259 8148 **Camping fees:** $3.30 per adult/night, $1.65 per child/night; fees payable at self-registration station

17. MOLE CREEK

Mole Creek is an ideal base from which to explore the nearby lakes and King Solomons and Marakoopa caves. Mole Creek is on the B12 road, 23 km west of Deloraine.

Mole Creek Caravan Park

Signposted from B12, 3 km west of Mole Creek village, beside Sassafras Creek. Firewood supplied. Fires only allowed on creek side of camping area. Additional map ref.: TVM H11.

Further information & bookings: Mole Creek Caravan Park
Tel.: (03) 6363 1150 **Camping fees:** Unpowered $12.00 per family/site per night, powered $15.00 per family/site per night; fees payable to caretaker

18. OATLANDS

This heritage town on the Midland Hwy, 35 km south of Ross, has a number of unique sandstone buildings constructed in the 1830s. Take a walking tour of the town to see its 19th-century stone mill and convict-built gaol. For those interested in a spot of fishing, head for Lake Dulverton to cast a line.

Oatlands overnight bay

Signposted on The Esplanade in Oatlands. Oatlands is 42 km south of Campbell Town. Overnight stay only. Additional map ref.: TVM M15.

Further information: Southern Midlands Council
Tel.: (03) 6254 5000

19. RINGAROOMA COASTAL RESERVE

This reserve is in the north-east corner of the state, on Ringarooma Bay. It is reached by the C844 (Cape Portland Rd) from Gladstone. The campsite is at the northern end of Boobyalla Beach.

Petal Point camping area

This area is 20 km north-west of Gladstone and is reached by the C844 (Cape Portland Rd). Bring drinking water and firewood. Additional map ref.: TVM Q7.

Further information: Parks & Wildlife, Bridport
Tel.: (03) 6356 1173

20. SADDLEBACK PLANTATION

West of Mathinna, Saddleback Plantation encompasses the popular Griffin camping area which has grassy sites beside the South Esk River. The area is well known for trout fishing.

Griffin camping area

This camping area is 8–10 km west of Mathinna, beside Griffin Park Rd which is reached off C401 (west end) or C423 (east end). Water from river, boil first. Bring firewood. Additional map ref.: TVM P11.

Further information: Forestry Tasmania, Fingal
Tel.: (03) 6374 2102

21. SCOTTSDALE AREA

Scottsdale, 63 km north-east of Launceston, is regarded as the hub of the north-east. The town is surrounded by some of Tasmania's richest agricultural and forest land.

Myrtle Park Recreation Ground

On A3 (Tasman Hwy) in Targa, 30 km south-west of Scottsdale. Campground is beside St Patricks River. Bring drinking water and firewood. Bookings recommended Dec.–Jan. Additional map ref.: TVM N10.

Further information & bookings: Caretaker
Tel.: (03) 6399 3368 **Camping fees:** From $3.00 per couple/family per night

North East Park Camp Ground

Along Ringarooma Rd east of Scottsdale. Bring firewood. Additional map ref.: TVM N9.

Further information & bookings: Caretaker
Tel.: (03) 6352 2017 (6–8 pm only) **Camping fees:** Unpowered from $7.50 per site/night, powered from $10.00 per site/night; fees collected by caretaker

22. WALLS OF JERUSALEM NATIONAL PARK

Located 23 km from the junction of the Walls of Jerusalem Track and the C171 (Mersey Forest Rd) to Lake Rowallan, this park features majestic mountain scenery and alpine lakes. The park is open for day or overnight walkers only. Walkers must carry large-scale maps and be aware of and ready for dramatic weather change while visiting this park;

Solomons Throne, in Walls of Jerusalem National Park

they must also register and deregister at the registration station along the track (near the carpark). The entrance to the park is 30 minutes' walk from the carpark; no vehicles are allowed within the park. Contact ranger for further information.

Bush camping

Walk-in bush campsites for self-sufficient walkers. Bring drinking water. Gas/fuel stove only. Additional map ref.: TVM H12

Further information: Parks & Wildlife, Mole Creek
Tel.: (03) 6363 5182 **Parks Pass:** Required

23. WATERHOUSE CONSERVATION AREA

This large conservation area on the northern coast of Tasmania is reached by Homestead Rd from Waterhouse on the B82 road, 25 km north-east of Bridport. There are many camping areas on the coast and around its inland lakes and lagoons. Some access roads can be rough, so check road conditions before travelling. There are 4WD beach boat launches throughout the conservation area.

Big Waterhouse Lake camping area

Signposted off Homestead Rd, 4 km from B82 junction. Drive in 3 km from turn-off. Bush campsites along access road. Bring drinking water and firewood. Additional map ref.: TVM P7.

Blackmans Lagoon camping area

Signposted off Waterhouse Rd, 22 km north-east of Bridport. Camping in general vicinity of boat ramp and adjacent pine trees. Bring drinking water and firewood. Additional map ref.: TVM P7.

Herbies Landing camping area

The small site is signposted from Homestead Rd, 11 km from B82 junction. Boat launching facilities available. Bring drinking water and firewood. Additional map ref.: TVM P7.

Ransons Beach camping area

Located along Homestead Rd 14.5 km from B82 junction. Boat launching facilities available. Bring drinking water and firewood. Additional map ref.: TVM P7.

South Croppies Point camping area

Signposted off Homestead Rd, 6 km from B82 junction. Drive in 5 km from turn-off. Bush campsites along road. Bring drinking water and firewood. Additional map ref.: TVM P7.

Waterhouse Beach camping area

Signposted off Homestead Rd, 6 km from B82 junction. Drive in 5 km from turn-off. Bush campsites along road. Bring drinking water and firewood. Additional map ref.: TVM P7.

Waterhouse Point camping area

Signposted from Homestead Rd, 12 km from B82 junction. Many roads to sites; some sites may be suitable for small vans. Bring drinking water and firewood. Additional map ref.: TVM P7.

Waterhouse Point camping area no. 2

Reached from Homestead Rd, 14 km from B82 junction. Many roads to sites but access road is sandy, 4WD recommended. Bring drinking water and firewood. Additional map ref.: TVM P7.

Further information: Parks & Wildlife, Bridport
Tel.: (03) 6356 1173

24. WELDBOROUGH

Located on the A3 (Tasman Hwy), Weldborough is 38 km north-west of St Helens. Visit the Weldborough Pass Scenic Reserve enroute to Weldborough where you can see some of the oldest myrtles and ferns in the country.

Weldborough Hotel camping ground

Beside A3 in Weldborough, 21 km south-east of Derby and 42 km north-west of St Helens. Bring firewood. Additional map ref.: TVM Q9.

Further information & bookings: Weldborough Hotel
Tel.: (03) 6354 2223 **Camping fees:** Unpowered from $6.00 per person/night, powered from $8.00 per person/night

25. WOODS LAKE

The lake is reached by the A5 (Lake Hwy), then the B51, 47 km north of Bothwell. The signposted turn-off to the lake is the C525 (Arthurs Lake Rd). Woods Lake's foreshore is 12 km from the turn-off. Access is only possible with a 4WD vehicle.

Bush camping

Many tracks lead to bush campsites around northern foreshore of lake. Natural boat launches. Bring drinking water, or boil water from lake. Bring firewood. Additional map ref.: TVM L14.

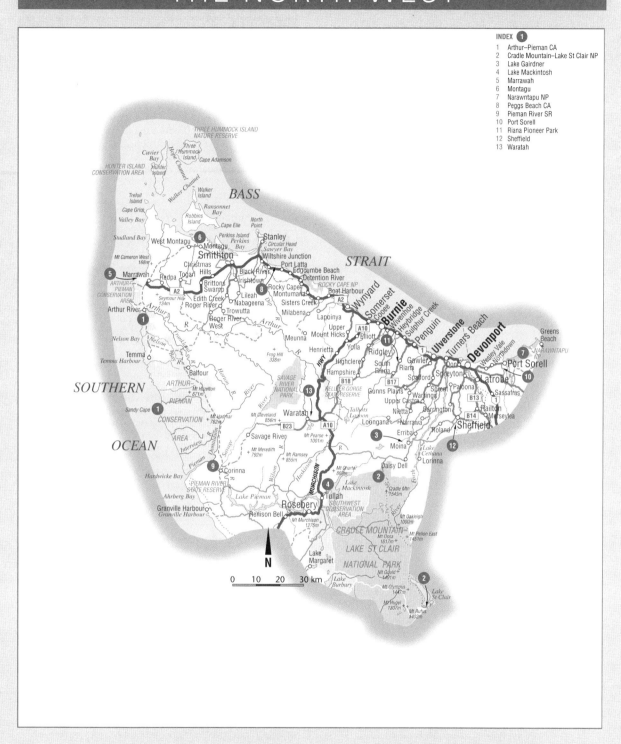

THE NORTH-WEST OF TASMANIA OFFERS VISITORS THE CHANCE TO EXPLORE THE SPECTACULAR CRADLE MOUNTAIN–LAKE ST CLAIR NATIONAL PARK, THE RUGGED WEST COAST SOUTH TO THE PIEMAN RIVER AND THE SCENIC COAST ALONG BASS STRAIT.

East of Devonport is Narawntapu National Park, where campers can enjoy the coastal scenery and do some beachcombing. There is a boat ramp here and it is possible to waterski off Bakers Point. Other activities in the park include bushwalking, swimming and horseriding.

Arthur–Pieman Conservation Area stretches about 70 kilometres from the town of Arthur

River south to the Pieman River. In this large conservation area are magnificent beaches and coastal scenery, waterfalls on the Nelson Bay River, and the old mining town of Balfour. Visitors can enjoy fishing, sea kayaking, diving and surfing. The Peppermint Campground is next to the Parks and Wildlife office in Arthur River while the large Manuka Campground is just north of town. There are other sites with beach access further south of Arthur River.

The Corinna Campground lies beside the mighty Pieman River in the Pieman River State Reserve. This is an ideal camping area for those who wish to explore the river by boat or canoe. Along its banks are forests of huon pine, laurel, sassafras and giant tree ferns. For those without their own boat, commercial cruises operate along the Pieman River.

The precious Cradle Mountain–Lake St Clair National Park is World Heritage-listed. This stunning park protects spectacular mountains, steep gorges, glacial lakes and mountain streams. The jagged Cradle Mountain in the north dominates the area. Excellent views can be had across Dove Lake to the mountain. In the south of the park, Lake St Clair, which was carved out by glacial ice millions of years ago, is the main feature. The Overland Track, a five-to-eight-day walk from Cradle Valley to Lake St Clair, is world renowned; camping along the track is in the vicinity of shelter huts. Those who prefer shorter walks can camp at the established campgrounds in the north and south of the park and take one of the many day walks.

BEST CAMPSITES

Campsite no. 3 – Bakers Point
Narawntapu National Park

Black River camping area
Peggs Beach Conservation Area

Manuka Campground
Arthur–Pieman Conservation Area

Cradle Mountain Camp Ground
Cradle Mountain–Lake St Clair National Park

Cynthia Bay Camp Ground
Cradle Mountain–Lake St Clair National Park

BEST TIME TO VISIT

Spring to autumn. It is best to visit Cradle Mountain–Lake St Clair National Park during the warmer months from November to April.

1. ARTHUR–PIEMAN CONSERVATION AREA
see page 371

2. CRADLE MOUNTAIN–LAKE ST CLAIR NATIONAL PARK

Cradle Mountain–Lake St Clair National Park is one of Tasmania's most popular parks, with many visitors walking the world-renowned 85-km Overland Track between Cradle Valley in the north of the park and Lake St Clair in the south. There are also many day walks of varying lengths – contact rangers for further details and information. The park features the rugged contours of Cradle Mountain and its surrounding alpine and rainforest vegetation and Lake St Clair, the deepest lake in Australia. This glaciated landscape is part of the Tasmanian Wilderness World Heritage Area.

CRADLE MOUNTAIN

Cradle Mountain Camp Ground

Signposted from Cradle Mountain Rd, 54 km south-west of Sheffield and 2 km before park's entry station. Open fires in camp cookhouses only. Firewood supplied. Bookings for powered sites recommended during peak period, Nov.–May. Other accommodation also available. Additional map ref.: TVM G11.

Further information & bookings: Cradle Mountain Camp Ground and Cosy Cabins **Tel.:** (03) 6492 1395 **Email:** cradle@cosycabins.com **Website:** www.cosycabins.com/cradle **Parks Pass:** Not required **Camping fees:** Unpowered from $9.00 to $11.00 per person/night, powered from $11.00 to $13.00 per person/night

LAKE ST CLAIR

Cynthia Bay Camp Ground

Signposted along Lake St Clair Rd, 5 km in from A10 (Lyell Hwy) at Derwent Bridge. Firewood supplied. Bookings for powered sites recommended during Jan. Other accommodation also available. Additional map ref.: TVM H14.

Further information & bookings: Lake St Clair Wilderness Holidays **Tel.:** (03) 6289 1137 **Email:** lakestclair@trump.net.au **Parks Pass:** Required **Camping fees:** Unpowered from $12.00 per 2 people/night, powered from $15.00 per 2 people/night

THE OVERLAND TRACK

The Overland Track winds its way through Cradle Mountain–Lake St Clair National Park and is a great way to see this amazing wilderness area. One of Australia's best-known treks, it takes five-to-eight days to complete and is for self-sufficient and experienced walkers only. The Overland Track Kit, which includes a map, notebook, trip planner and general information, is available from the Parks & Wildlife visitor centres. Gas/fuel stove only. Water available from drinking tanks at huts. Pit toilets at hut sites. All walkers must register and deregister at trackheads. Carry large-scale maps.

ARTHUR–PIEMAN CONSERVATION AREA

River trips
The Arthur River runs through a tiny fishing village of the same name. Much of the river is inaccessible except by boat; boat cruises leave from town, and there is a local canoe/boat hire outlet. The fishing is good – expect trout or blackfish for dinner.

Wildlife paradise
This remote and all but trackless wilderness protects a large number of animals, including Bennetts wallabies, Tasmanian pademelons, wombats, Tasmanian devils and spotted-tailed quolls. There is also abundant birdlife including three rare species: ground parrots, hooded plovers and orange-bellied parrots.

This remote conservation area is on the north-west coast and is reached from Smithton via the A2 (Bass Hwy) to Marrawah then south along the C214. It covers the region between the Arthur River in the north and the Pieman River in the south, and is over 100 000 hectares in area. There is a range of activities for the visitor, including fishing, diving, sea kayaking and surfing.

Manuka Campground

Signposted along Arthur River Rd, 200 m north of Arthur River township. Bring drinking water and firewood. Additional map ref.: TVM A8.

Nelson Bay Campground

Signposted along C214 road, 11 km south of Arthur River. Continue 2 km from road junction. Campsites to the right on grassed area. Bring drinking water and firewood. Additional map ref.: TVM A9.

Peppermint Campground

Signposted along Arthur River Rd in Arthur River village, next to Parks Office. Bring drinking water and firewood. Additional map ref.: TVM A8.

Prickly Wattles Campground

Signposted along Arthur River Rd, 2 km south of Arthur River Bridge. Bring drinking water and firewood. Additional map ref.: TVM A8.

Sandy Cape camping area

This area is 50 km south of Arthur River. Access by 4WD only, via Temma or Balfour Track off Corinna Rd. Should only be attempted by experienced drivers with well-equipped 4WD vehicles. Check track conditions with ranger first and obtain an Off Road Authority. Beach near camping area offers good swimming. Bring drinking water and firewood. Additional map ref.: TVM B10.

Bush camping

Walk-in bush camping allowed throughout park. Carry large-scale maps and contact Parks Office for further details. Gas/fuel stove preferred. Bring drinking water.

Further information & bookings: Parks & Wildlife, Arthur River **Tel.:** (03) 6457 1225 **Parks Pass:** Not required **Camping fees:** $5.00 per site/night (up to 5 people); fees payable at Parks Office during work hours. Use self-registration box at Parks Office after hours

Waterfall Valley Hut
10 km from Ronny Creek carpark.
Additional map ref.: TVM G12.

Windermere Hut
7.7 km from Waterfall Valley Hut.

New Pelion Hut
16.75 km from Windermere Hut.

Kia Ora Hut
9 km from New Pelion Hut.

Windy Ridge Hut
10 km from Kia Ora Hut.

Narcissus Hut
9 km from Windy Ridge Hut.

Echo Point Hut
6.5 km from Narcissus Hut (end point at Lake St Clair Visitor Centre is 11 km from Echo Point Hut).

Further information:
Parks & Wildlife Visitor Centre, Cradle Mountain
Tel.: (03) 6492 1133 *or*
Parks & Wildlife Visitor Centre, Lake St Clair
Tel.: (03) 6289 1172
Parks Pass: Required

3. LAKE GAIRDNER

This beautiful lake is to the west of Moina. It is reached from the C132 (Cradle Mountain road).

Lake Gairdner camping area

Access road is 1 km west of Moina off C132. From this junction travel west for 4 km to small grassed campsites near bridge over Iris River. Bring drinking water and firewood. Additional map ref.: TVM G11.

4. LAKE MACKINTOSH

Lake Mackintosh is a hydro dam adjacent to the town of Tullah, which is on the A10 (Murchison Hwy). It offers anglers excellent trout fishing.

Lake Mackintosh camping area

North of dam wall via Mackintosh Dam Rd, 5 km north-east of Tullah. Bring drinking water and firewood. Additional map ref.: TVM E12.

Further information & bookings: West Coast Council
Tel.: (03) 6471 4700 **Email:** wcc@westcoast.tas.gov.au

5. MARRAWAH

Marrawah, a popular surfing area, is 51 km south-west of Smithton. It is reached from the A2 (Bass Hwy).

Green Point camping area

This area is 2 km west of Marrawah. Access via Beach Rd off Green Point Rd. Bring drinking water and firewood. Additional map ref.: TVM A8.

Further information: Circular Head Council
Tel.: (03) 6452 4800 **Email:** council@circularhead.tas.gov.au

6. MONTAGU

Montagu is 15 km north-west of Smithton along the C215 road. The area has good swimming and fishing.

Montagu Camping Ground

This area is 4 km north-east of Montagu and is signposted from Old Port Rd off the C215. Bring drinking water. Firewood supplied. Open 1 Nov.–30 April (dates may vary – check before travel). Bookings required. Additional map ref.: TVM B7.

Further information & bookings: Circular Head Council
Tel.: (03) 6452 4800 **Email:** council@circularhead.tas.gov.au *or* caretaker **Tel.:** (03) 6452 1076 **Camping fees:** $7.00 per site/night for up to 2 adults + 2 children or $35 weekly

7. NARAWNTAPU NATIONAL PARK

This park, 40 km east of Devonport, can be reached via the B71 road and then the C740. Formerly known as Asbestos Range National Park, the park offers many activities including numerous walks, safe beaches for swimming and fishing as well as nature study and horseriding (permits required).

Campsite no. 1 – Springlawn

Signposted from C740 road, just within the park boundary. Bring drinking water. Firewood supplied. Additional map ref.: TVM J9.

Campsite no. 2 – Bakers Point

Signposted along main park road, 5 km from Ranger Station. Gas/fuel stove only. Bring drinking water. Additional map ref.: TVM J9.

Campsite no. 3 – Bakers Point

Signposted along main park road, 5 km from Ranger Station. Drinking water available – boil before use. Firewood supplied. Additional map ref.: TVM J9.

Campsite no. 4 – Horse Yards

Signposted from C740 road at park entrance. Limited drinking water. Firewood supplied. People with horses must give notice 48 hours prior to arrival. Permit required. Additional map ref.: TVM J9.

Further information & bookings: Parks & Wildlife, Narawntapu **Tel.:** (03) 6428 6277 **Parks Pass:** Required
Camping fees: $4.40 per adult/night, $2.20 per child (age 6–17) per night; fees payable at self-registration station at Springlawn

8. PEGGS BEACH CONSERVATION AREA

This is located on the north coast of Tasmania between Stanley and Wynyard. Activities include fishing, swimming and beachcombing.

Black River camping area

Signposted along A2 (Bass Hwy), 16 km south-east of Stanley and 44 km west of Wynyard. Bring drinking water and firewood. Additional map ref.: TVM D7.

Peggs Beach camping area

Signposted along A2 (Bass Hwy), 18 km east of Stanley and 42 km west of Wynyard. Bring drinking water and firewood. Additional map ref.: TVM D7.

Further information & bookings: Parks & Wildlife, Smithton **Tel.:** (03) 6452 4998 **Camping fees:** $2.20 per person/night; fees payable at self-registration station

9. PIEMAN RIVER STATE RESERVE

The Pieman River State Reserve covers the banks of the Pieman River at the southern end of the Arthur–Pieman Conservation Area. Corinna, which lies in the reserve, was once a booming goldmining town. As well as its rich history, the Corinna area is known for its magnificent wilderness, bushwalks and good trout fishing. Take time out to enjoy a river cruise along the Pieman River. Corinna is reached from the north via the C247 road from Savage River (26 km) or from the south via the C249 road from Zeehan (48 km).

Corinna Campground

Located in Corinna. Firewood supplied. No power. Bookings recommended. Cabin accommodation also available. Additional map ref.: TVM C12.

Further information & bookings: Corinna Camp Ground **Tel.:** (03) 6446 1170 **Camping fees:** $3.50 per adult/night, $1.70 per child (age 5–16) per night

10. PORT SORELL

East of Devonport, Port Sorell is on the Rubicon River estuary. Close to the beaches of Bass Strait, it is a popular area for water activities.

Port Sorell Lions Club Caravan Park

On Port Sorell Rd in Port Sorell, 15 km east of Devonport. Fire pots and firewood available. Laundry facilities, shop and playground. Bookings recommended. Additional map ref.: TVM J9.

Further information & bookings: Port Sorell Lions Club Caravan Park **Tel.:** (03) 6428 7267 **Camping fees:** Unpowered from $11.00 per site/night, powered from $15.00 per site/night

11. RIANA PIONEER PARK

Riana is a small village in a dairy and agricultural region south of Penguin. It is reached via the B17 road from Penguin. Once here, visit the nearby deer farm.

Riana Pioneer Park camping ground

Signposted from B17 (Pine Rd) in Riana, 17 km south of Penguin. Boil drinking water before use. Limited firewood supplied. Additional map ref.: TVM G9.

Further information & bookings: Secretary/caretaker **Tel.:** (03) 6437 6137 **Camping fees:** Unpowered from $6.00 per 2 people/night, powered from $9.00 per 2 people/night

12. SHEFFIELD

Nestled in the foothills of Mt Roland, Sheffield is known as the 'Town of Murals', thanks to the 46 murals depicting the region's history on buildings throughout the town and district. Sheffield is 30 km south of Devonport via the B14 road.

Sheffield Caravan Park

On Albert St in Sheffield. Dogs at management's discretion – check before travel. Laundry facilities. Bookings recommended during Christmas holiday period. Additional map ref.: TVM H10.

Further information & bookings: Manager at Sheffield Backpackers **Tel.:** (03) 6491 2611 **Camping fees:** Unpowered from $11.00 per 2 people/night, powered from $16.00 per 2 people/night

13. WARATAH

Waratah, once home to the world's richest tin mine, is only five minutes drive along the B23, west of its junction with the A10 (Murchison Hwy). Activities in the area include panning for gold, trout fishing and river cruises.

Waratah camping ground

On Smith St in Waratah. Key access to toilet and shower facilities. Additional map ref.: TVM E10.

Further information & bookings: Wynyard–Waratah Shire Council, Waratah **Tel.:** (03) 6439 7100 (9 am–5 pm) *or* Bischoff Hotel **Tel.:** (03) 6439 1188 **Camping fees:** Tent site $8.80 per site/night, unpowered van site from $8.80 per site/night, powered van site from $11.00 per site/night

TASMANIA'S SOUTH-WEST IS A REGION OF GREAT BEAUTY, ALMOST WHOLLY MADE UP OF NATIONAL PARK. THERE ARE MAJESTIC RIVERS LINED WITH THICK FORESTS, MIDDENS AND CAVES, SOARING MOUNTAINS, AND A SPECTACULAR COASTLINE WITH EXCELLENT FISHING OPPORTUNITIES.

Campers interested in catching their own seafood can set up at Macquarie Heads just south of the picturesque town of Strahan. The campground here offers wonderful fishing, and there is even a boat ramp for those who wish to venture further out.

Lake Burbury, east of Queenstown, is popular for water activities such as boating, waterskiing and fishing. The camping area here is a large grassed area on the shoreline with excellent views across the lake.

Franklin–Gordon Wild Rivers National Park protects the Franklin, Gordon, Jane and Denison rivers. Their waters are popular with experienced whitewater rafters and canoeists, while nature lovers can enjoy the short walks through the park's magnificent rainforests. Experienced hikers can camp along the challenging Frenchmans Cap Track.

Southwest National Park covers a large area encompassing the beautiful lakes Pedder and Gordon in its north and the spectacular coastline along the Southern Ocean in the south and west. Two spectacular long-distance walking tracks traverse the park, and the lakes offer wonderful trout fishing, boating and canoeing. Campers at the open grassed area of Edgar campground, on the southern edge of Lake Pedder, may be lucky enough to view one of the resident platypus, while people at the smaller, secluded Huon River campground can enjoy its tall forest surroundings. In the south of the park is an open camping area adjacent to Cockle Creek, where safe swimming and fishing is possible.

BEST CAMPSITES

Edgar campground
Southwest National Park

Boltons Green campground
Southwest National Park

Lake Burbury camping area
Lake Burbury

Cockle Creek campground
Recherche Bay Nature Recreation Area

Gilhams Beach campground
Recherche Bay Nature Recreation Area

BEST TIME TO VISIT

Spring through to early autumn.

1. FRANKLIN–GORDON WILD RIVERS NATIONAL PARK

Protecting the Franklin, Gordon, Jane and Denison rivers, Franklin–Gordon Wild Rivers National Park is part of the Tasmanian Wilderness World Heritage Area. Take one of the short walks and explore the magnificent rainforests along the Lyell Hwy; for more experienced walkers there is the Frenchmans Cap Track that takes four-to-five days to complete.

Collingwood River campsite

Small site on both sides of the Collingwood River. Sign-posted along A10 (Lyell Hwy), 48 km east of Queenstown and 40 km west of Derwent Bridge. Bring drinking water or boil river water before use. Some firewood supplied. There are Grade 6 rapids on the Collingwood River, suitable for experienced canoeists and rafters only. Additional map ref.: TVM G14.

FRENCHMANS CAP TRACK

This three-to-four-day walk to the summit of the park's most prominent peak takes in the Loddon Plains, Lake Vera, Barron Pass and Lake Tahune before ascending Frenchmans Cap. Those intending to walk this track must register and deregister at trackhead. Trackhead and walker registration is signposted along Lyell Hwy, 3 km west of the Franklin River Bridge, 30 km west of Derwent Bridge and 40 km east of Queenstown. Track is suitable for experienced, self-sufficient walkers with high level of fitness only. Carry large-scale maps. Contact Parks & Wildlife for further details. Gas/fuel stove only.

Franklin River
Campsites located off A10 (Lyell Hwy), before Franklin River crossing. Additional map ref.: TVM G15.

Lake Vera
16 km from A10 (Lyell Hwy); campsites located a short distance over bridge from Vera Hut. Walkers can also stay in hut. (There are campsites located between the Franklin River and Lake Vera for those walking at a slower pace.)

Lake Tahune
9 km from Lake Vera; campsites near Tahune Hut. Walkers can also stay in hut. Frenchmans Cap is a further 1 km from here.

Further information: Parks & Wildlife, Queenstown
Tel.: (03) 6471 2511 **Parks Pass:** Required

2. LAKE BURBURY

This large lake east of Queenstown is a popular watersports venue with fishing, canoeing, and waterskiing opportunities.

Lake Burbury camping area

Signposted from A10 (Lyell Hwy), 21 km east of Queenstown and 67 km west of Derwent Bridge. Gas/fuel stove only. Additional map ref.: TVM E14.

Thureau Hills camping area

Signposted access to boat ramp and camping area along A10 (Lyell Hwy), 15 km east of Queenstown. Bring drinking water and firewood. Additional map ref.: TVM E14.

Further information & bookings:
West Coast Council, Queenstown **Tel.:** (03) 6471 5880 *or* Lake Burbury Camping Area caretaker **Tel.:** (03) 6471 1311 (after 5.30 pm)
Camping fees: $5.00 per site/night; fees payable to caretaker

3. LAKE KING WILLIAM

Lake King William is to the south-west of Derwent Bridge and is a popular spot for trout fishing.

Bush camping

Scattered bush camping areas near boat ramp, off A10 (Lyell Hwy), 4 km west of Derwent Bridge (access road not signposted). Gas/fuel stove preferred. Bring drinking water. Additional map ref.: TVM H14.

Further information: Hydro Tasmania **Tel.:** (03) 6230 5660

4. RECHERCHE BAY NATURE RECREATION AREA

Recherche Bay is in the southern corner of the state and offers excellent swimming, fishing and beach walks. It is reached via the C636 (Cockle Creek Rd) off the A6 (Huon Hwy) just north of Southport.

Catamaran campground

Signposted from Cockle Creek Rd, 23 km from its junction with the A6. Bring drinking water and firewood. Additional map ref.: TVM L22.

Cockle Creek campground

Signposted from Cockle Creek Rd, 26 km from its junction with the A6. Campground is north of bridge at Cockle Creek. Bring drinking water and firewood. Area on far side of bridge is national park – no pets allowed. Additional map ref.: TVM L22.

Finns Beach campground

Signposted from Cockle Creek Rd, 22 km from its junction with the A6. Bring drinking water and firewood. Additional map ref.: TVM L22.

Gilhams Beach campground

Signposted from Cockle Creek Rd, 21 km from its junction with the A6. Bring drinking water and firewood. Additional map ref.: TVM L22.

Further information: Parks & Wildlife, Huonville **Tel.:** (03) 6264 8460

5. SOUTHWEST NATIONAL PARK

Covering over 600 000 ha of remote and wild country, Southwest National Park is Tasmania's largest park. In the south of the park is the South Coast Track, an awe-inspiring five-to-ten-day walk along the wild south coast between Cockle Creek and Melaleuca. The Port Davey Track, another wilderness walk, follows the historic route to Port Davey and Bathurst Harbour. There are shorter tracks for less experienced walkers – ask ranger for details. In the north of the park are lakes Gordon and Pedder, both excellent for trout fishing. A visit to the Gordon Dam and Hydro Visitors Centre is also worthwhile.

COCKLE CREEK

Boltons Green campground

South of Dover on Cockle Creek Rd, 28 km from its junction with the A6 (Huon Hwy). Camping area is just over bridge at Cockle Creek. Ranger on site during summer. Bring drinking water and firewood. Additional map ref.: TVM L22.

Further information: Parks & Wildlife, Huonville **Tel.:** (03) 6264 8460 **Parks Pass:** Required

LAKE PEDDER

Edgar campground

Signposted along the C607 (Scotts Peak Dam Rd), 30 km south of its junction with the B61. This junction is 43 km east of Strathgordon and 50 km west of Westerway. Firewood supplied. Additional map ref.: TVM H19.

Huon River campground

This small site is 7 km past Edgar campground. Bring drinking water. Firewood supplied. Boat ramp nearby at Scotts Peak Dam. This is also the trackhead for Port Davey Track. Additional map ref.: TVM H19.

Teds Beach campground

Signposted from the B61 (Strathgordon Rd), 38 km west of Scotts Peak Dam Rd and 3 km east of Strathgordon. Gas/fuel stove only. Additional map ref.: TVM G18.

Further information: Parks & Wildlife, Mt Field **Tel.:** (03) 6288 1149 **Parks Pass:** Required

PORT DAVEY TRACK

This walking track from Scotts Peak to Melaleuca is for self-sufficient and experienced walkers only. It takes three-to-four days to complete and involves one river crossing. Walkers must register and carry large-scale maps. Trackhead and walker registration is at Huon River campground. Gas/fuel stove only. Contact Park & Wildlife for details.

Huon River campground
See listing above.

The historic town of Strahan, on Macquarie Harbour

Junction Creek
7 km from Huon River campground.

Crossing River
10 km from Junction Creek.

Spring River
24 km from Crossing River (some campsites exist between Crossing River and Spring River for those walking at a slower pace).

Bathurst Narrows
10 km from Crossing River.

Melaleuca
12 km from Bathurst Narrows. Basic hut accommodation available here in addition to camping. Can continue on along South Coast Track (see next entry) or arrange flight out of nearby airstrip.

Further information & bookings: Parks & Wildlife, Mt Field
Tel.: (03) 6288 1149 **Parks Pass:** Required

SOUTH COAST TRACK

This walking track from Cockle Creek to Melaleuca is for self-sufficient and experienced walkers only. It takes five-to-ten days to complete and involves boat crossing. Walkers must register and carry large-scale maps. Trackhead and walker registration is at Cockle Creek. Gas/fuel stove only. Contact Park & Wildlife for details.

Boltons Green campground
See listing on page 376.

South Cape Rivulet
11 km from Boltons Green campground.

Granite Beach (east)
8 km from South Cape Rivulet.

Surprise Bay
3 km from Granite Beach.

New River Lagoon
9 km from Surprise Bay.

Deadmans Bay
9 km from New River Lagoon.

Louisa River
13 km from Deadmans Bay.

Point Eric
16 km from Louisa River.

Melaleuca
12 km from Point Eric. Basic hut accommodation available here in addition to camping. Can continue on along Port Davey Track (see previous entry) or arrange flight out of nearby airstrip.

Further information: Parks & Wildlife, Huonville
Tel.: (03) 6264 8460 **Parks Pass:** Required

6. STRAHAN

This holiday town on the northern shores of Macquarie Harbour offers the visitor a range of outdoor activities. Take a cruise down the Gordon River, ride the rapids on the Franklin River, paddle a sea kayak in Macquarie Harbour or take a 4WD tour to explore the Henty Dunes on Ocean Beach.

Macquarie Heads camping area

This camping area is at the end of C251 (Macquarie Heads Rd), 15 km south of Strahan. Access is signposted. Bring firewood. Additional map ref.: TVM D15.

Further information & bookings:
West Coast Council, Queenstown **Tel.:** (03) 6471 5880 *or* Strahan Visitors Centre **Tel.:** (03) 6471 7622
Camping fees: $5.00 per site/night

FLINDERS ISLAND

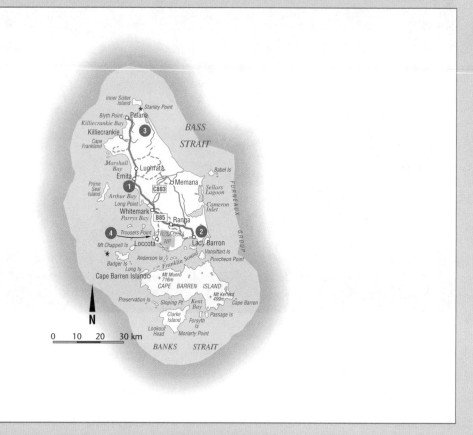

TASMANIA

FLINDERS ISLAND, THE LARGEST OF THE 53 ISLANDS THAT MAKE UP THE FURNEAUX GROUP, HAS MUCH TO OFFER THE WILDLIFE ENTHUSIAST, NATURE LOVER AND AVID BUSHWALKER.

Flinders Island can be reached by air or sea, but once on the island there is no public transport. Vehicles can be hired on the island, but those with a little more energy might prefer to hire a bicycle or bring their own. There is much to see and do here: visit the Wybalenna Historic Site and beautiful beaches, fossick for Killiecrankie 'diamonds', scuba dive near the shipwrecks around the island, fish, take in the magnificent views from the lookouts and enjoy some bushwalking. The island is home to abundant wildlife and birds, such as short-tailed shearwaters (muttonbirds) and Cape Barren geese.

In the north of the island camping is beside the North East River, a popular fishing site. On the west coast there is a cleared camping area opposite the beach north of Whitemark, and to the south of the island camping is at Yellow Beach, east of Lady Barron.

In the south-west corner of Flinders Island is Strzelecki National Park. Strzelecki Peak offers a great bushwalking challenge and magnificent views. Campers at Trousers Point, opposite the park, can enjoy swimming, fishing and diving as well as exploring the beach and the colourful rocky coastline.

BEST CAMPSITES

North East River camping area
North East River

Allports Beach camping area
Emita

BEST TIME TO VISIT

Spring to autumn.

1. EMITA

Situated in the north-west of the island, Emita is the location of the Wybalenna Historic Site, one of the most important historic sites in Tasmania. As the Aboriginal population of Tasmania dwindled in the 1830s, this settlement was created in an attempt to save the race from extinction. It became the home of 133 Aboriginal people who were relocated here. The site has since been restored by the National Trust. Emita also has a museum exhibiting relics from the Bass Strait shipwrecks.

Allports Beach camping area

Cleared area opposite beach, signposted off Palana Rd. Bring drinking water and firewood. Additional map ref.: TVM Q2.

2. LADY BARRON

Home to the protected Cape Barren goose, Lady Barron is a small settlement on the south-east corner of Flinders Island. Take a boat tour from here to explore some of the other islands in the Furneaux Group.

Yellow Beach camping area

Accessed from Lady Barron, this area is located 10 km east of Lady Barron in the south of the island. Bring drinking water and firewood. Additional map ref.: TVM R4.

Further information: Flinders Council Area Marketing & Development Office **Tel.:** (03) 6359 2380 **Email:** amdo@trump.net.au **Website:** www.flinders.tco.asn.au

3. NORTH EAST RIVER

This popular fishing and camping area is on the far northern tip of Flinders Island.

North East River camping area

This is 15 km north-east of Killiecrankie. Many tracks lead off North East River Rd to sites beside river. Bring drinking water and firewood. Be wary of undertows when swimming here. Additional map ref.: TVM Q1.

4. TROUSERS POINT

Trousers Point is located to the west of Strzelecki National Park, a magnificent park in the island's south-west featuring tall granite peaks, beautiful wildflowers and wonderful views of the surrounding islands. There is excellent swimming, fishing, diving and snorkelling at Trousers Point.

Trousers Point camping area

Signposted from the C806, 10 km south of Whitemark. Bring firewood. Gas/fuel stove preferred. Additional map ref.: TVM Q4.

Further information: Parks & Wildlife, Strzelecki National Park **Tel.:** (03) 6359 2217 **Parks Pass:** Required

Strzelecki Peak, in Strzelecki National Park

Map Symbols

Roads

FREEWAY / HIGHWAY	HIGHWAY
sealed	unsealed
MAIN ROAD	MAIN ROAD
sealed	unsealed
MINOR ROAD	MINOR ROAD
sealed	unsealed

VEHICULAR TRACK

RAILWAY

152
distance in kilometres

Route markers

1 A2   National highway route markers

1 A8   National route markers

16 B500   State route markers

Town and feature symbols

State capital city	○ **ADELAIDE**
Town, over 50 000 inhabitants	○ **Wollongong**
Town, 10 000–50 000 inhabitants	○ **Cessnock**
Town, 5000–10 000 inhabitants	○ Broome
Town, 1000–5000 inhabitants	○ Coober Pedy
Town, 200–1000 inhabitants	○ Northampton
Town, under 200 inhabitants	○ Lake King
Aboriginal community	○ Doomadgee
Roadhouse	⊞ Hells Gate Roadhouse
Place of interest	● Bungle Bungles
Landmark feature	● Poeppel Corner

Area features

ABORIGINAL LAND

NATIONAL PARK

OTHER RESERVE

PROHIBITED AREA

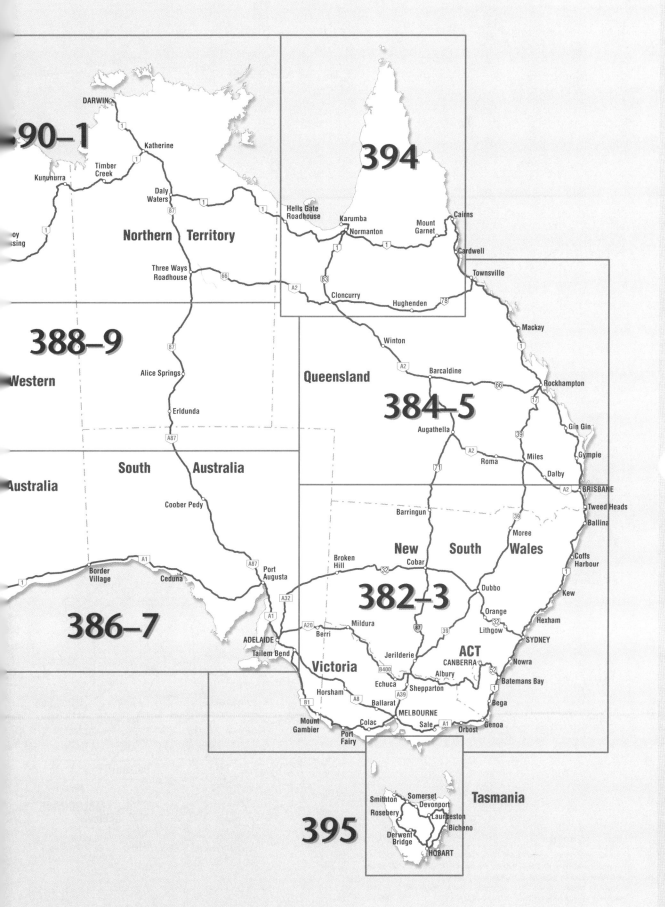

90–1

394

388–9

384–5

386–7

382–3

395

Northern Territory

Western

Australia

South   Australia

Queensland

New   South   Wales

ACT

Victoria

Tasmania

DARWIN

Katherine

Timber
Creek

Kununurra

Daly
Waters

Three Ways
Roadhouse

Alice Springs

Erldunda

Coober Pedy

Border
Village

Ceduna

Port
Augusta

ADELAIDE

Tailem Bend

Mount
Gambier

Port
Fairy

Colac

Horsham

Ballarat

MELBOURNE

Sale

Echuca

Shepparton

Mildura

Berri

Broken
Hill

Cobar

Dubbo

Orange

Lithgow

SYDNEY

Kew

Hexham

Jerilderie

Albury

Barringun

Moree

Bega

Genoa

Orbost

Batemans Bay

Nowra

CANBERRA

Hells Gate
Roadhouse

Karumba

Normanton

Cloncurry

Hughenden

Winton

Barcaldine

Augathella

Roma

Miles

Dalby

BRISBANE

Tweed Heads

Ballina

Coffs
Harbour

Gympie

Gin Gin

Rockhampton

Mackay

Townsville

Cardwell

Cairns

Mount
Garnet

Smithton

Rosebery

Derwent
Bridge

HOBART

Somerset

Devonport

Launceston

Bicheno

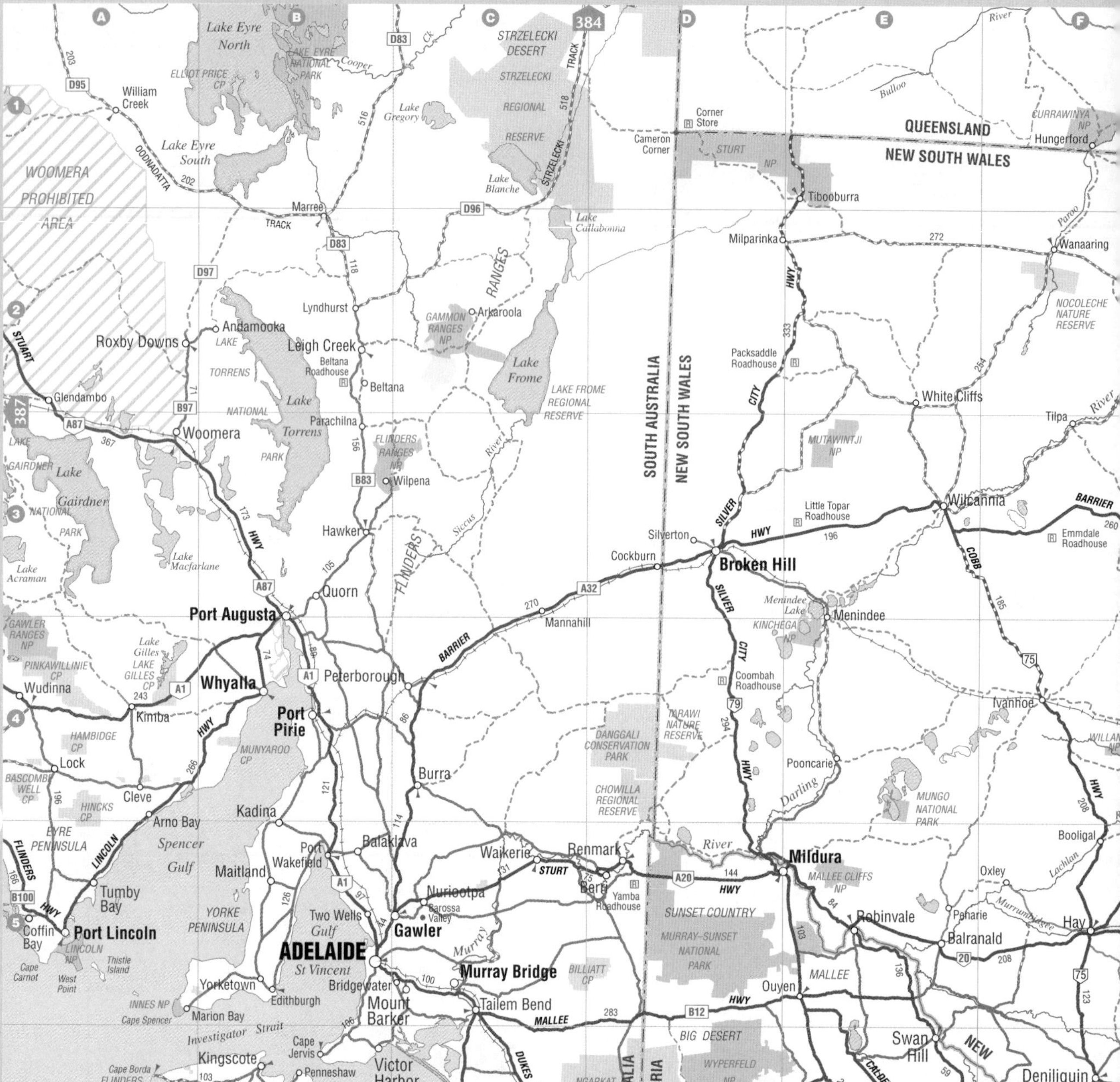

INTER-CITY ROUTES

	DISTANCE
Adelaide–Darwin via Stuart Hwy [A1] [A87] [87] [1]	3037 km
Adelaide–Perth via Eyre & Great Eastern hwys [A1] [1] [94]	2716 km
Adelaide–Sydney via Sturt & Hume hwys [A20] [20] [31]	1415 km
Adelaide–Melbourne via Dukes & Western hwys [M1] [A8] [M8]	732 km
Adelaide–Melbourne via Princes Hwy [M1] [A1] [M1]	906 km

QUEENSLAND
NEW SOUTH WALES

SOUTH AUSTRALIA | NEW SOUTH WALES

SOUTH AUSTRALIA | VICTORIA

SOUTHERN

OCEAN

BASS

ADELAIDE
MELBOURNE
Broken Hill
Mildura
Port Augusta
Whyalla
Port Lincoln
Mount Gambier
Ballarat
Bendigo
Geelong
Horsham
Warrnambool
Portland

WOOMERA PROHIBITED AREA

KANGAROO ISLAND

Spirit of Tasmania Ferries
Melbourne to Devonport

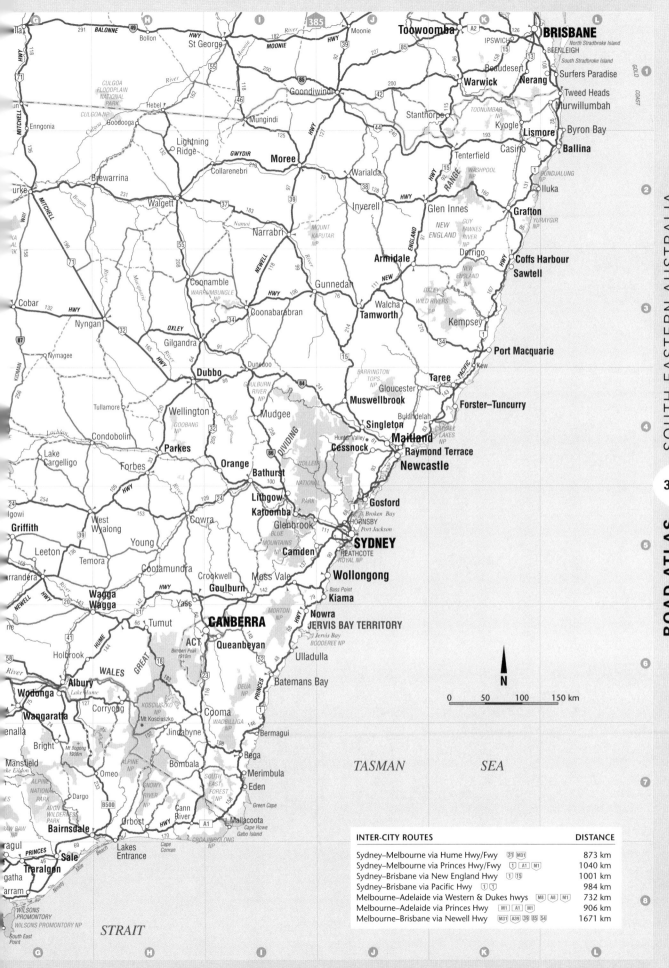

INTER-CITY ROUTES		DISTANCE
Sydney–Melbourne via Hume Hwy/Fwy	31 M31	873 km
Sydney–Melbourne via Princes Hwy/Fwy	1 A1 M1	1040 km
Sydney–Brisbane via New England Hwy	1 15	1001 km
Sydney–Brisbane via Pacific Hwy	1 1	984 km
Melbourne–Adelaide via Western & Dukes hwys	M8 A8 M1	732 km
Melbourne–Adelaide via Princes Hwy	M1 A1 M1	906 km
Melbourne–Brisbane via Newell Hwy	M31 A39 39 85 54	1671 km

TASMAN SEA

STRAIT

N

0   50   100   150 km

Ngunarra

TABLELANDS

Lake Sylvester

RANKEN

391

Murun Murula

BOODJAMULLA (LAWN HILL) NP

Gregory Downs

394

GULF

SAVANNAH

Forsayth

Elmas

377

HWY

Gregory River

WILLS

141

Norman River

BARKLY

11

Barkly Homestead

RANKEN RD

Camooweal

263

66

A2

CAMOOWEAL CAVES NP

HWY

168

Gunpowder

Kajabbi

DEVEL

83

182

DEVEL

RD

Burke & Wills Roadhouse

BURKE

Flinders River

Clara River

250

Stawell River

BLACKBR NP

WAKAYA ABORIGINAL LAND TRUST

Canteen Creek

2

389

Alpururulam

Quamby

Mount Isa

118

Cloncurry

137

FLINDERS

Julia Creek

78

259

Richmond

Hughend

SANDOVER

14

579

HWY

162 RD

Urandangi

URANDANGI RD

Duchess

A2

McKinlay

343

LANDSBOROUGH (MATILDA

Stamford

DEVEL

212

Corfield

Sandover R

3

Arthur Creek

486

Orrtipa-Thurra

12

HWY

Dajarra

295

83

Burke River

Kynuna

Middleton

360

KENNEDY

(OUTBACK

DEVEL

HWY

RD

Winton

BLADENSBURG NATIONAL PARK

KENNEDY

HWY

174

Mut

PLENTY (OUTBACK

Plenty River

Tobermorey

NORTHERN TERRITORY

QUEENSLAND

Georgina River

Boulia

KENNEDY

A2

Longreach

Ilfr

ATNETYE ABORIGINAL LAND TRUST

TROPIC

OF

CAPRICORN

191

Mayne River

DIAMANTINA NATIONAL PARK

GONEAWAY NP

4

Hale R

Todd R

Bedourie

242

ASTREBLA DOWNS NP

CHANNEL COUNTRY

Stonehenge

Isisford

SIMPSON

SIMPSON

DESERT

DIAMANTINA

266

Thomson River

Barcoo River

5

PMER ULPERRE INGWEMIRNE ABORIGINAL LAND TRUST

DESERT

NATIONAL

191 EYRE DEVEL RD

Diamantina River

DEVEL

Jundah

WELFORD NP

Poeppel Corner

PARK

Birdsville

BIRDSVILLE

Betoota

266

DEVEL RD

Windorah

336

6

WITJIRA

NATIONAL PARK

SOUTH

SIMPSON DESERT CONSERVATION PARK

AUSTRALIA

Lake Etamunbanie

Haddon Corner

Adava

SIMPSON DESERT REGIONAL RESERVE

Goyder Lagoon

Lake Yamma Yamma

Eromanga

Quilpie

387

Macumba

Ephemeral Lakes

SIMPSON DESERT REGIONAL RESERVE

516

STURT STONY DESERT

INNAMINCKA REGIONAL RESERVE

Too Ro

Oodnadatta

OODNADATTA

Neales River

BIRDSVILLE

Mungerannie Hotel

Cooper Creek

Innamincka

Noccundra

Thargomindah

7

203

Lake Eyre North

LAKE EYRE NATIONAL PARK

Warburton Ck

Cooper Creek

STRZELECKI DESERT

D96

518

Bullo River

CURRAWINYA NP

Hungerf

William Creek

ELLIOT PRICE CP

Lake Gregory

STRZELECKI REGIONAL RESERVE

STRZELECKI

Cameron Corner

Corner Store

QUEENSLAND

NEW

8

WOOMERA PROHIBITED AREA

TRACK

Lake Eyre South

Lake Blanche

STURT NP

Tibooburra

Milparinka

272

Wanaaring

202

D83

Marree

D95

D97

382

Lake Callabonna

INTER-CITY ROUTES   **DISTANCE**

Brisbane–Sydney via New England Hwy [15] [1]	1001 km
Brisbane–Sydney via Pacific Hwy [1] [1]	984 km
Brisbane–Melbourne via Newell Hwy [54] [85] [39] [A39] [M31]	1671 km
Brisbane–Darwin via Warrego Hwy [1] [87] [66] [A2]	3406 km
Brisbane–Cairns via Bruce Hwy [1]	1699 km

SOUTH

PACIFIC

OCEAN

GREAT

BARRIER

REEF

0   50   100   150 km

N

LITTLE SANDY DESERT

GIBSON DESERT
NATURE
RESERVE

388 HWY

MUNGILLI
ABORIGINAL
LAND

NGAANYATJARRA

Warakurna
Warakurna
Roadhouse

GUNBARREL

231

RD

Lake
Naberu

CARNARVON RANGES

CANNING STOCK ROUTE

Lake
Carnegie

Carnegie
Homestead

Boyd
Lagoon

Lake
Breaden

ABORIGINAL

Surveyor Generals
Corner

Pipalyatjara

HWY)

Warburton
Roadhouse

LAND

Warburton

CENTRAL

AUSTRALIA

ABORIGINAL

LAND TRUST

WESTERN AUSTRALIA

SOUTH AUSTRALIA

Wiluna

Lake
Way

GOLDFIELDS

Mount
Keith

174

WANJARRI
NATURE
RESERVE

DE LA POER RANGE
NATURE RESERVE

Lake
Wells

Tjukayirla
Roadhouse

CENTRAL
(OUTBACK

250

HWY

Lake
Throssel

315

GREAT

YEO LAKE
NATURE
RESERVE

CONNIE

SUE

Neale Junction

NEALE
JUNCTION
NATURE
RESERVE

Leinster

141

131

HWY

Cosmo Newbery

COSMO NEWBERY
ABORIGINAL LAND

GREAT   VICTORIA   DESERT

GREAT

VICTORIA

DESERT

NATURE

RESERVE

124

Laverton

Rason Lake

Jubilee
Lake

Leonora

Lake
Carey

Lake
Minigwai

PLUMRIDGE
LAKES
NATURE
RESERVE

HWY

Kookynie

Lake
Ballard

Lake
Barlee

Lake Raeside

275

Menzies

91

GOONGARRIE
NP

Lake
Rebecca

CONNIE

SUE

4WD only

NULLARBOR

392

MOUNT
MANNING
NATURE
RESERVE

Broad Arrow

QUEEN VICTORIA SPRINGS
NATURE RESERVE

Deakin

Loongana

Reid

RAILWAY

Kalgoorlie–Boulder

Lake
Yindarlgooda

Cundeelee

TRANS

AUSTRALIA

Coolgardie

36

94

Kambalda

Lake Lefroy

Zanthus

Rawlinna

Mundrabilla
Roadhouse

Eucla

GOLDFIELDS
WOODLANDS
NP

186

94

EASTERN

HWY

BURRA ROCK
NR

BOORABBIN
NP

Widgiemooltha

166

Lake
Cowan

Cocklebiddy

HWY

195

Madura

1

Marvel
Loch

JILBADJI
NATURE
RESERVE

94

191

EYRE

HWY

Balladonia

182

Caiguna

158

EYRE

Red Rocks Point

Norseman

DUNDAS
NATURE
RESERVE

1

Point Dover

1

Lake Dundas

NUYTSLAND
NATURE
RESERVE

Point Culver

GREA

Varley

313

FRANK HANN
NP

PEAK
CHARLES
NP

Salmon Gums

Lake Tay

Young R.

203

Grass Patch

CAPE
ARID
NP

Israelite Bay

Point Dempster

Lake King

LAKE
MAGENTA
NR

Condingup

65

Cape Pasley

Ravensthorpe

COAST

187

HWY

Esperance

CAPE LE GRAND
NP

SOUTH

1

113

Hopetoun

N

Jerramungup

FITZGERALD
RIVER
NP

Bremer Bay

Cheyne Bay

0   50   100   150 km

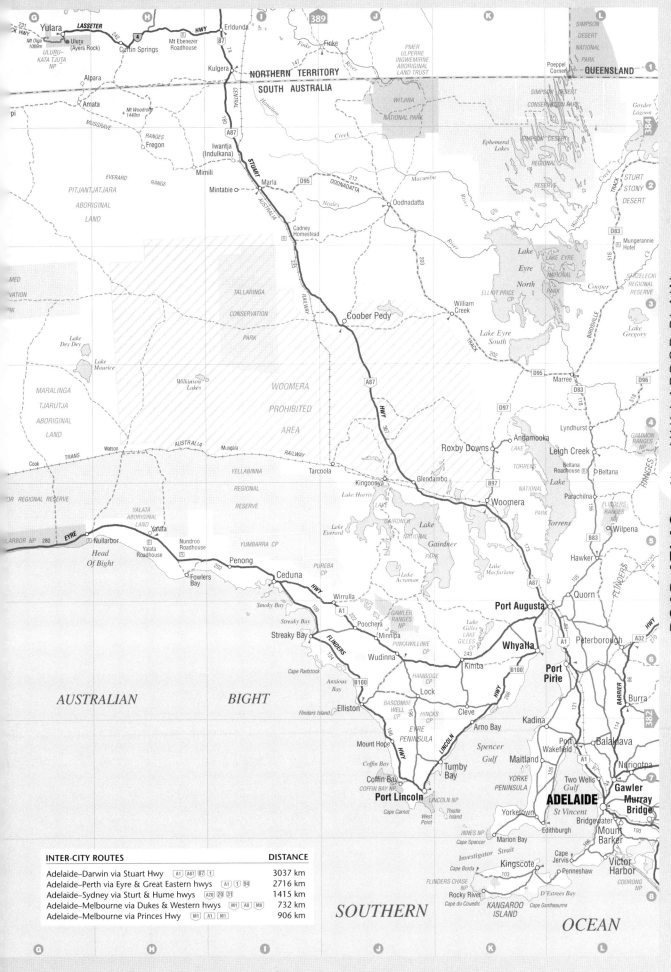

INTER-CITY ROUTES		DISTANCE
Adelaide–Darwin via Stuart Hwy A1 A87 87 1		3037 km
Adelaide–Perth via Eyre & Great Eastern hwys A1 1 94		2716 km
Adelaide–Sydney via Sturt & Hume hwys A20 20 31		1415 km
Adelaide–Melbourne via Dukes & Western hwys M1 A8 M8		732 km
Adelaide–Melbourne via Princes Hwy M1 A1 M1		906 km

SOUTHERN

OCEAN

AUSTRALIAN   BIGHT

A B C D E F

1

390

KEEP NP

Kununurra

VICTORIA

Amanbidji

WAG AB LAN

Hall Point

PRINCE REGENT NATURE

KUNMUNYA ABORIGINAL RESERVE

GARDNER PLATEAU

284

Drysdale R

River

PARRY LAGOONS NR

85

46

36

34

151

191

Koolan

Collier Bay

Charnley River

River

Gibb River

DOON DOON ABORIGINAL LAND

Lake Argyle

Cape Leveque

One Arm Point

Lombadina

Isdell

MILITARY TRAINING AREA

KIMBERLEY

Mount Barnett Roadhouse

Kupingarri

Turkey Creek Roadhouse

Turkey Creek (Warmun)

HWY

161

Mistake Creek

MAL ABO LAN TRU

2

Pender Bay

Beagle Bay

Beagle Bay

Cape Baskerville

Coulomb Point

POINT COULOMB NR

Cape Boileau

Broome

Roebuck Bay

Cape Villaret

Gourdon Bay

BEAGLE BAY ABORIGINAL RESERVE

Derby

Willare Bridge Roadhouse

Roebuck Roadhouse

145

King Sound

Meda

River

43

Fitzroy

KING

RIVER

KING LEOPOLD RANGES CP

DEVONIAN REEF

NATIONAL PARKS

LEOPOLD

RANGES

River

Ord

River

Fitzroy

365

219

GREAT

1

Looma

MOOGOORA BURR QUARANTINE AREA

River

1

Fitzroy Crossing

NORTHERN

388

Halls Creek

1

DUNCAN

DENISON PLAINS

PURNULULU NP

Bungle Bungles

80

RD

40 Cre

WESTERN AUSTRALIA

NORTHERN TERRITORY

34

HWY

286

1

NORTHERN

GREAT

286

Cape Jaubert

Eighty Mile Beach

De Grey

3

False Cape Bossut

Bidyadanga

4

Sandfire Roadhouse

WARNINGS: In outback Australia, long distances separate some towns. Travellers should familiarise themselves with prevailing conditions before departure and take care to ensure their vehicle is roadworthy. Adequate supplies of petrol, water and food should be carried at all times.

In northern Australia, rainfall during the wet season (October to March) can make some roads impassable. Full information on road conditions should be obtained from local authorities before departure.

If visitors intend diverting off public roads within Aboriginal Land areas, a permit is required from the relevant Aboriginal authority.

Beware of crocodiles in rivers, estuaries and coastal areas.

Sturt

Billiluna (Mindibungu)

404

TANAMI

Balgo Hills

Lake Gregory

KEARNEY ABORIGINAL LAND

ROUTE

Lake Wills

RD

GREAT SANDY DESERT

De Grey River

Lake Waukarlycarly

Tobin Lake

Percival Lakes

Lake Mackay

5

393

River

Oakover

Lake Dora

RUDALL RIVER NATIONAL PARK

Lake Auld

Lake George

STOCK

Kiwirrkurra

Lake Macdonald

Kint

6

WALAGUNYA ABORIGINAL LAND

Jigalong

JIGALONG ABORIGINAL LAND

TROPIC

OF

CAPRICORN

GIBSON DESERT

CENTRAL

Lake Hopkins

Lake Disappointment

Lake Earnham

AUSTRALIA

Kaltukatjara (Docker River)

7

LITTLE SANDY DESERT

GIBSON DESERT NATURE RESERVE

MUNGILLI ABORIGINAL LAND

HWY

NGAANYATJARRA

ABORIGINAL

Warakurna

Warakurna Roadhouse

231

HWY)

RD

105

ABORIGINAL

Surveyor Generals Corner

Pipalyatjara

8

CANNING

CARNARVON

RANGES

Lake Naberu

Carnegie Homestead

Lake Carnegie

GUNBARREL

Lake Breaden

Boyd Lagoon

Lake Breaden

Warburton Roadhouse

Warburton

GREAT 250 (OUTBACK

CENTRAL

LAND TRUST

N

0 50 100 150 km

A B C 386 D E F

250

Borroloola

GARAWA ABORIGINAL LAND TRUST

Daly Waters
CARPENTARIA
Hi-way Inn Roadhouse
Dunmarra
Robinson River
Heartbreak Hotel
Wollogorang Station & Roadhouse
Hells Gate Roadhouse
CHINA WALL

Yarralin
BUCHANAN
Top Springs
STUART
Newcastle Waters (Marlinja)
Elliott
BARKLY
STOCK ROUTE
BARKLY
TABLELANDS
WAANYI/GARAWA ABORIGINAL LAND TRUST
BOODJAMULLA (LAWN HILL) NP

Dagaragu
Kalkarindji (Wave Hill)
KARLANTIJPA ABORIGINAL LAND TRUST
Renner Springs
Tarrabool Lake
Creswell
Ngunarra
Fish Hole Creek
Murun Murula
TABLELAND

Lajamanu (Hooker Creek)
Three Ways Roadhouse
Likkaparta
Corella Lake
Lake Sylvester
Wogyala
RANKEN
BARKLY

CENTRAL DESERT ABORIGINAL LAND TRUST
TANAMI DESERT
Tennant Creek
Barkly Homestead
WAKAYA ABORIGINAL LAND TRUST
Camooweal
CAMOOWEAL CAVES NP

Rabbit Flat Roadhouse
Mungkarta
Devils Marbles
Wauchope
Wycliffe Well
Ali-Curung
DAVENPORT RANGE NP (proposed)
Wutunugurra
Canteen Creek
Hatches Creek
Alpururulam
Urandangi

Jarra Jarra
Imangara
Barrow Creek
Tara
Ti Tree
Tobermorey

Yuendumu
Yuelamu
Laramba
Aileron
Tilmouth Well Roadhouse
SANDOVER
Bundey
Arthur Creek
Orrtipa-Thurra
DONOHUE

Nyirripi
Lake Bennett
Papunya
Mt Liebig
Mt Zeil +1510m
PLENTY (OUTBACK)
Gemtree
RANGES
TROPIC OF CAPRICORN
ATNETYE ABORIGINAL LAND TRUST

Lake Lewis
Mt Zeil
WEST
MACDONNELL NP
Alice Springs
SANTA TERESA ABORIGINAL LAND TRUST
SIMPSON DESERT

Lake Neale
Areyonga
Haasts Bluff
Glen Helen Homestead
Iwupataka
Hermannsburg
FINKE GORGE NP
Ltyentye Purte (Santa Teresa)
HAASTS BLUFF ABORIGINAL LAND TRUST
MACDONNELL

Lake Amadeus
Kings Canyon
WATARRKA NP
Stuarts Well
SIMPSON DESERT NATIONAL PARK

Yulara
LASSETER
Mt Olga 1069m
Uluru (Ayers Rock)
Curtin Springs
Mt Ebenezer Roadhouse
Erldunda
Finke
PMER ULPERRE INGWEMIRNE ABORIGINAL LAND TRUST
Poeppel Corner
ULURU-KATA TJUTA NP

Alpara
Kulgera
NORTHERN TERRITORY
SOUTH AUSTRALIA
WITJIRA NATIONAL PARK
SIMPSON DESERT CONSERVATION PARK

Kanypi
Amata
Mt Woodroffe +1440m
MUSGRAVE RANGES
CENTRAL
Goyder Lagoon

PITJANTJATJARA ABORIGINAL LAND
Fregon
Iwantja (Indulkana)
Ephemeral Lakes
SIMPSON DESERT REGIONAL RESERVE

EVEREST RANGE
Mimili
Marla

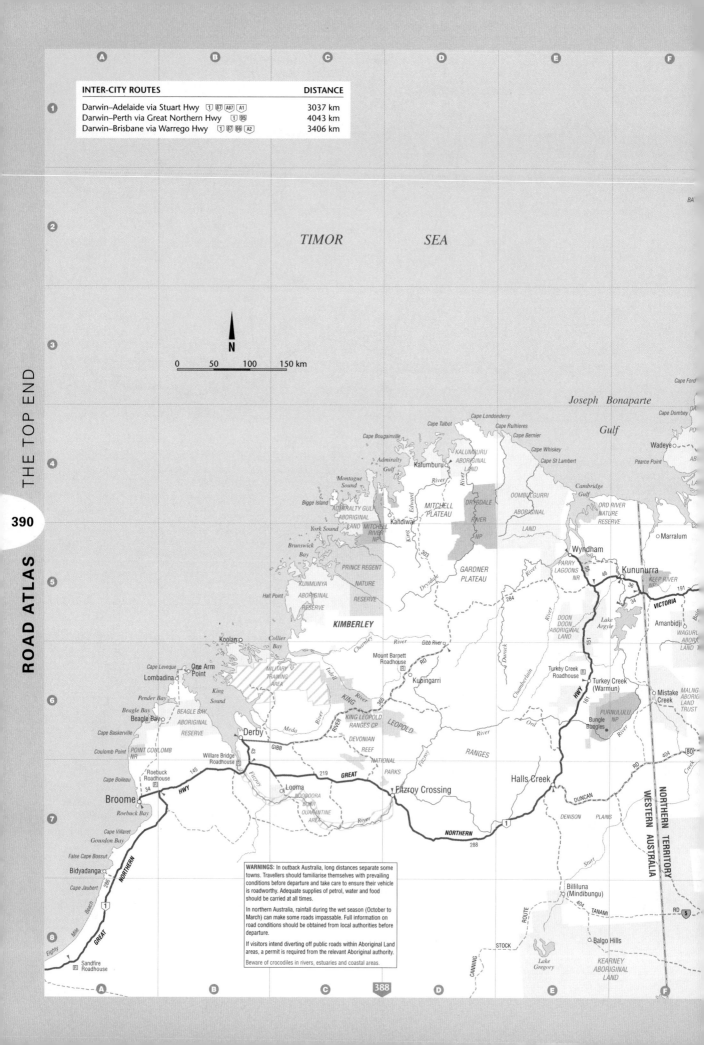

INTER-CITY ROUTES	DISTANCE
Darwin–Adelaide via Stuart Hwy ① 87 A87 A1	3037 km
Darwin–Perth via Great Northern Hwy ① 95	4043 km
Darwin–Brisbane via Warrego Hwy ① 87 66 A2	3406 km

TIMOR   SEA

0   50   100   150 km

N

Joseph Bonaparte

Cape Ford

Cape Londonderry
Cape Talbot   Cape Ruthieres
Cape Bougainville   Cape Bernier   Gulf   Cape Dombey

Cape Whiskey
Cape St Lambert   Wadeye

KALUMBURU
ABORIGINAL
LAND   Pearce Point

Admiralty   Kalumburu
Gulf
Montague   River
Sound   Cambridge
Bigge Island   MITCHELL   Gulf   Marralum
PLATEAU   DRYSDALE
ADMIRALTY GULF   River   NP
ABORIGINAL   Kandiwal   OOMBULGURRI   ORD RIVER
York Sound   LAND MITCHELL   ABORIGINAL   NATURE
RIVER   LAND   RESERVE
NP   King   Wyndham
Brunswick   303
Bay   River   PARRY
Edward   LAGOONS   Kununurra
PRINCE REGENT   GARDNER   NR
KEEP RIVER   191
RUNMUNYA   NATURE   PLATEAU   46   NP
ABORIGINAL   RESERVE   Drysdale   284   36   34
Hall Point   RESERVE   River   VICTORIA
River   Amanbidji
KIMBERLEY   151   Lake
Chumley   River   Gibb River   Argyle   WAGURL
Koolan   Collier   DOON   ABORIG
Bay   Mount Barnett   DOON   LAND
Cape Leveque   Roadhouse   RD   ABORIGINAL
One Arm   365   Duncan   LAND   Mistake
Lombadina   Point   Kubingarri   River   Turkey Creek   Creek   MALNG
KING   Roadhouse   ABORIG
Pender Bay   King   Turkey Creek   LAND
Beagle Bay   RIVER   KING LEOPOLD   151   (Warmun)   TRUST
Beagle Bay   Sound   RANGES CP   HWY   PURNULULU
Cape Baskerville   BEAGLE BAY   River   Bungle   NP   404
ABORIGINAL   DEVONIAN   Bungles   80
Coulomb Point   RESERVE   Derby   Meda   REEF   River
POINT COULOMB   GIBB   LEOPOLD   Ord
NR   Willare Bridge   43   NATIONAL   RANGES   RD
Roadhouse   Fitzroy   219   PARKS   Fitzroy   DUNCAN
Roebuck   145   GREAT   Halls Creek
Cape Boileau   Roadhouse   Looma   DENISON   PLAINS   NORTHERN
34   NOOGOORA   River   TERRITORY
Broome   HWY   BURR   Fitzroy Crossing   WESTERN
QUARANTINE   288   Sturt   AUSTRALIA
Roebuck Bay   AREA   NORTHERN
Cape Villaret
Gourdon Bay
False Cape Bossut   Bililuna
Bidyadanga   (Mindibungu)
NORTHERN   404   RD   5
Cape Jaubert   286   TANAMI
Beach   ①
Mile   Balgo Hills
GREAT   STOCK   KEARNEY
Eighty   Lake   ABORIGINAL
Sandfire   Gregory   LAND
Roadhouse   CANNING
ROUTE

WARNINGS: In outback Australia, long distances separate some
towns. Travellers should familiarise themselves with prevailing
conditions before departure and take care to ensure their vehicle
is roadworthy. Adequate supplies of petrol, water and food
should be carried at all times.

In northern Australia, rainfall during the wet season (October to
March) can make some roads impassable. Full information on
road conditions should be obtained from local authorities before
departure.

If visitors intend diverting off public roads within Aboriginal Land
areas, a permit is required from the relevant Aboriginal authority.

Beware of crocodiles in rivers, estuaries and coastal areas.

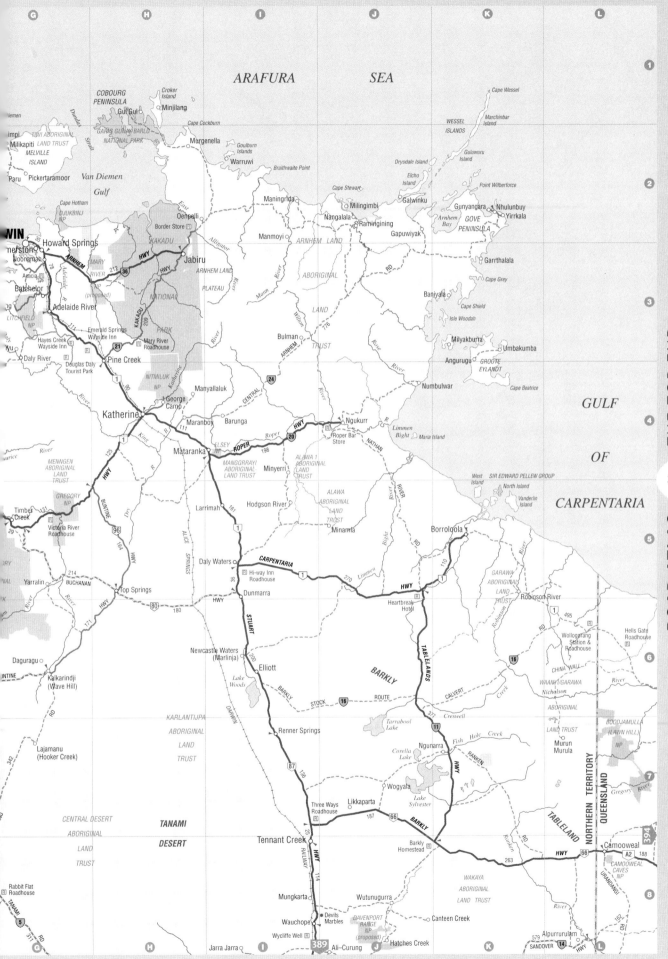

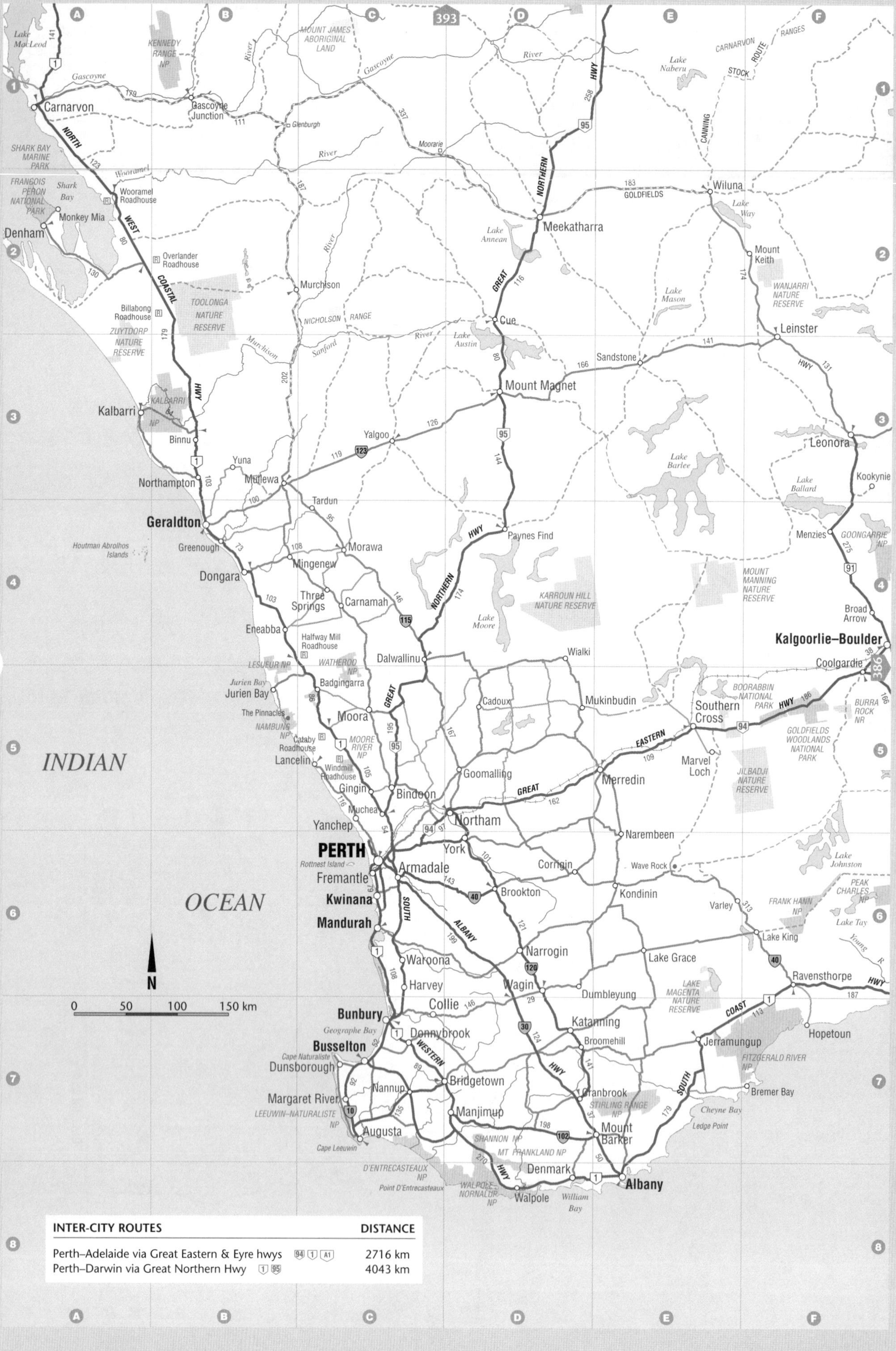

INDIAN

OCEAN

N

0   50   100   150 km

PERTH
Fremantle
Kwinana
Mandurah

Geraldton
Carnarvon
Denham
Monkey Mia
Kalbarri
Northampton
Bunbury
Busselton
Dunsborough
Margaret River
Augusta
Albany
Denmark
Walpole

Meekatharra
Cue
Mount Magnet
Yalgoo
Mullewa
Greenough
Dongara
Morawa
Mingenew
Carnamah
Three Springs
Eneabba
Dalwallinu
Jurien Bay
Moora
Lancelin
Gingin
Bindoon
Yanchep
Muchea
Armadale
York
Northam
Goomalling
Merredin
Southern Cross
Coolgardie
Kalgoorlie–Boulder
Leonora
Wiluna
Leinster
Menzies
Broad Arrow
Kookynie
Sandstone
Paynes Find
Wialki
Mukinbudin
Cadoux
Marvel Loch
Narembeen
Corrigin
Brookton
Kondinin
Varley
Lake King
Ravensthorpe
Hopetoun
Bremer Bay
Mount Barker
Cranbrook
Jerramungup
Broomehill
Katanning
Wagin
Dumbleyung
Lake Grace
Narrogin
Collie
Harvey
Waroona
Donnybrook
Bridgetown
Manjimup
Nannup

INTER-CITY ROUTES	DISTANCE
Perth–Adelaide via Great Eastern & Eyre hwys 94 1 A1	2716 km
Perth–Darwin via Great Northern Hwy 1 95	4043 km

INDIAN

OCEAN

N

0   50   100   150 km

WITTENOOM: The blue asbestos dust present in and around Wittenoom may cause cancer if inhaled. While the risk from such fibres to short-term visitors is significantly less than to residents, the Ashburton Shire Council advocates avoidance of the Wittenoom area.

Roebuck Roadhouse
Cape Boileau
Broome
34
Roebuck Bay
Cape Villaret
Gourdon Bay
False Cape Bossut
Bidyadanga
Cape Jaubert
Eighty Mile Beach
NORTHERN HWY
286
GREAT SANDY DESERT
139
GREAT
Sandfire Roadhouse
Pardoo Roadhouse
142
Port Hedland
Cape Thouin
190
GREAT
De Grey River
193
Shaw
Bamboo Creek
Lake Wankarlycarly
388
Dampier   Wickham
Karratha Roadhouse
Regnard Bay
Cape Preston
Barrow Island
Roebourne
32
Whim Creek
Karratha
95
PIPPINGARRA ABORIGINAL LAND
Marble Bar
138
251
NORTHERN
YANDEYARRA ABORIGINAL LAND
THE PILBARA
Nullagine
HWY
1
Fortescue Roadhouse
104
Vale River
MILLSTREAM-CHICHESTER NP
287
297
Oakover
RUDALL RIVER NP
COASTAL
117
Fortescue
Robe
MUNGAROONA RANGE NR
Onslow
80
Pannawonica
HAMERSLEY
160
Wittenoom
42
Auski Roadhouse
35
River
WALAGUNYA ABORIGINAL LAND
North West Cape
CANE RIVER CONSERVATION PARK
136
River
110
RANGE
162   HWY
Exmouth
CAPE RANGE NP
Exmouth Gulf
88
Nanutarra Roadhouse
136
Tom Price
68
KARIJINI NATIONAL PARK
Mt Meharry 1251m
Newman
Capricorn Roadhouse
Jigalong
JIGALONG ABORIGINAL LAND
WEST
Wyloo
219
Paraburdoo
CAPRICORN
50
9
79
111
BARLEE RANGE NATURE RESERVE
Ashburton
160
Coral Bay
129
NORTH
104
TROPIC
OF
River
LITTLE SANDY DESERT
Lyons
River
MT AUGUSTUS NP
COLLIER RANGE NATIONAL PARK
Kumarina Roadhouse
Lake Nabern
ROUTE
Minilya Roadhouse
141
MOUNT JAMES ABORIGINAL LAND
Gascoyne
River
258
NORTHERN
CANNING
CARNARVON   STOCK   RANGES
Lake MacLeod
KENNEDY RANGE NP
Gascoyne Junction
Gascoyne
River
Bernier Island
1
179
111
Glenburgh
337
Moorarie
95
Carnarvon
Dorre Island
SHARK BAY MARINE PARK
123
Wooramel
River
183
GOLDFIELDS
Wiluna
Lake Way
FRANCOIS PERON NATIONAL PARK
Shark Bay
Monkey Mia
Wooramel Roadhouse
WEST
80
187
Murchison
River
Lake Annean
Meekatharra
116
Mount Keith
174
WANJARRI NR
386
Denham
Dirk Hartog Island
130
Overlander Roadhouse
GREAT
Lake Mason
Leinster
COASTAL
179
Billabong Roadhouse
TOOLONGA NATURE RESERVE
Murchison
NICHOLSON RANGE
Sanford
River
Cue
Lake Austin
80
Sandstone
166
141
131
HWY
ZUYTDORP NATURE RESERVE
202
Mount Magnet
Leonora
Kalbarri
KALBARRI NP
Murchison
123
Binnu
Yalgoo
126
392

A B C D E F

1

2

3

4

5

6

7

8

TORRES STRAIT

Badu Island

Moa Island

Thursday Island

Prince of Wales Island

Cape York

Endeavour Strait

Injinoo

Bamaga

CORAL

Jardine

GREAT

Vrilya Point

JARDINE RIVER NP

Orford Bay

GREAT

SEA

HEATHLANDS RESOURCES RESERVE

Shelburne Bay

Cape Grenville

BARRIER

Mapoon

Red Beach

Temple Bay

Duyfken Point

Weymouth Bay

BARRIER

GREAT

Weipa

Portland Roads

Lockhart River

Cape Direction

REEF

Pera Head

GULF

DIVIDING

Aurukun

MUNGKAN KANDJU NATIONAL PARK

Archer River Roadhouse

Cape Sidmouth

REEF

CAPE PENINSULA

MARINE

OF

Coen

Kendall River

CAPE

Princess Charlotte Bay

Flinders Is

Cape Melville

CARPENTARIA

Holroyd River

YORK

107

Musgrave Roadhouse

LAKEFIELD

CAPE MELVILLE NATIONAL PARK

Normanby

PARK

Edward River

DIVIDING

Lizard Island

Pormpuraaw

PENINSULA

DEVEL

NATIONAL

Cape Flattery

Wallaby Island

Coleman River

MITCHELL-ALICE RIVERS NP

Hann River Roadhouse

203

PARK

Hope Vale

Kowanyama

Mitchell

Alice

River

Laura

RANGE

Helenvale

Cooktown

RD

Palmer

River

Lakeland

Wujal Wujal

Ayton

Staaten

Palmer River Roadhouse

Cape Tribulation

WELLESLEY ISLANDS

Mornington Island

River

STAATEN RIVER NATIONAL PARK

DEVEL

Walsh

Lynd

Maryfarms

178

DAINTREE NP

Daintree

Mossman

Port Douglas

Bentinck Island

Point Burrowes

Gilbert

River

81

Green Island

Mareeba

Cairns

Hells Gate Roadhouse

Chillagoe

Gordonvale

495

BURKE

Tate

River

Atherton

Mt Bartle Frere 1611m

BRUCE

98

Karumba

51

Tirranna Roadhouse

Burketown

GULF

Mount Garnet

Babinda

Nicholson

Doomadgee

River

229

153

Blackbull

Einasleigh

BULLERINGA NP

128

Innisfail

Normanton

River

HWY

Silkwood

Tully

Dunk Island

391

Croydon

148

DEVEL

Mount Surprise

82

RD

Cardwell

BOODJAMULLA (LAWN HILL) NP

Gregory Downs

195

Clara

Georgetown

148

UNDARA VOLCANIC NP

KENNEDY

LUMHOLTZ NP

Gregory

141

WILLS

River

Einasleigh

Forsayth

Abergowrie

Ingham

7

Burke & Wills Roadhouse

SAVANNAH

82

Oasis Roadhouse

Greenvale

1

HWY

Gunpowder

GULF

Flinders

River

GREGORY

Blue Water Springs Roadhouse

383

Rollingstone

Camooweal

182

250

BLACKBRAES NP

260

GREAT BASALT WALL NP

CAMOOWEAL CAVES NP

Kajabbi

DEVEL

River

Stawell

PORCUPINE GORGE NP

WHITE MOUNTAINS NP

Charters Towers

BARKLY

188

Quamby

Clarke

River

Clarke

243

HWY

A2

URANDANGI RD

162

Mount Isa

83

118

Cloncurry

FLINDERS

137

Julia Creek

78

259

Richmond

Hughenden

384

Pentland

55

HWY

A2

Prairie

Torrens Creek

78

FLINDERS RD

0 50 100 150 km N

Cape Patton
Apollo Bay

Phillip Island

383 Leongatha
Wonthaggi   Inverloch   Foster   Yarram
Port Welshpool
Cape Liptrap   Waratah Bay
Tidal River
WILSONS PROMONTORY
WILSONS PROMONTORY NP
South East Point
Ninety Mile Beach

BASS   STRAIT

VICTORIA
TASMANIA

Cape Wickham
Egg Lagoon
LAVINIA NATURE RESERVE
KING ISLAND
Currie   Naracoopa
Grassy
Stokes Point

Palana
WINGAROO CONSERVATION AREA
Memana
FLINDERS ISLAND
Whitemark
STRZELECKI NP
Lady Barron
FURNEAUX GROUP
Cape Barren Island
Clarke Island
BANKS   STRAIT

Hunter Island   Three Hummock Island

INTER-CITY ROUTES   **DISTANCE**
Hobart–Launceston via Midland Hwy ①   200 km
Hobart–Devonport via Midland & Bass hwys ① B52   286 km

Cape Grim   Robbins Island

Cape Naturaliste

Smithton
Marrawah   51   A2   BASS
ROCKY CAPE NP
Wynyard   Somerset
Burnie
HWY   Ulverstone   Port Sorell   George Town   Bridport   Gladstone
Arthur   81   HWY   57   1   MOUNT WILLIAM NP   Eddystone Point
River   Devonport   Beauty Point
ARTHUR PIEMAN CONSERVATION AREA
Scottsdale
SAVAGE RIVER NATIONAL PARK   119   TASMAN   99   A3   HWY
Sandy Cape   Waratah   54   49   St Helens
CONSERVATION AREA   Hadspen   70   28
Hardwick Bay   Corinna   A10   Mersey   Deloraine   Launceston   St Marys
Rosebery   River   Westbury   Evandale   BEN LOMOND NP   74   16   23
Cradle Mountain   MURCHSON   CRADLE MTN   56   MIDLAND   DOUGLAS APSLEY NP   Long Point
Granville Harbour   Zeehan   LAKE ST CLAIR NP   Great Lake   A4   Avoca   MacLean Bay
53   CENTRAL PLATEAU   Arthurs Lake   78   43   Bicheno
Strahan   Queenstown   WALLS OF JERUSALEM NP   GREAT WESTERN TIERS CA   Campbell Town
Cape Sorell   582   LYELL   Lake St Clair   Miena   Ross   HWY
Strahan   River   Derwent Bridge   33   Swansea
Macquarie Harbour   26   Bronte Park   A5   87   A3
A10   LAKE   82   Great Oyster Bay
Birthday Bay   HWY   Bothwell   Oatlands   FREYCINET NP
FRANKLIN-GORDON WILD RIVERS NP   89   57   Schouten Island
SOUTHWEST   Gordon River   36   MILITARY TRAINING AREA
Point Hibbs   Franklin & Gordon rivers   Melton Mowbray   Triabunna   MARIA ISLAND NP
Endeavour Bay   CONSERVATION   62   Maria Island
Elliott Bay   AREA   Lake Gordon   113   TASMAN   Richmond
Strathgordon   MOUNT FIELD NP   Bridgewater   Sorell   73
New Norfolk   32   21   TASMAN PENINSULA
Lake Pedder   HWY   35   Storm Bay
Huonville   HUON   HOBART   A9
SOUTHWEST NATIONAL PARK   Huon R.   HWY   26   Tasman Peninsula
Port Davey   63   A6   Gordon   Port Arthur   TASMAN NP
Dover
South West Cape   Southport   Bruny Island
South East Cape   SOUTH BRUNY NP

SOUTHERN

OCEAN

TASMAN

SEA

N
0   25   50   75 km

INDEX

This index lists camping areas, individual campsites, and place names found in the road atlas. Camping areas could be the name of a park or forest, town or area. Campsites appear in italics.

398

401

404

410

411

Explore Australia Publishing Pty Ltd
12 Claremont Street
South Yarra, Victoria 3141, Australia

First edition published by Explore Australia Publishing Pty Ltd, 2003

10 9 8 7 6 5 4 3 2

Printed and bound in China by Midas Printing (Asia) Limited

Disclaimers: The authors and publisher cannot accept responsibility for any errors or omissions in this book. While information was correct at the time of research, please be aware that conditions constantly change. Campsites are subject to closure without notice and fees may rise. Also, the representation on the maps of any road or track is not necessarily evidence of public right of way or of safe travelling conditions. It is the responsibility of the user to obtain permits/ permission, check road conditions and amenities, and check the status of campsites prior to setting out.

Publisher's note: The publisher welcomes information and suggestions for correction or improvement to the text and maps within this book. Write to the Publications Manager, Explore Australia Publishing, 12 Claremont Street, South Yarra, Victoria 3141, Australia, or email explore@hardiegrant.com.au

Cover and opening photographs
Front cover: Camping in Southwest National Park, Tasmania (Grant Dixon)
Back cover: Sea kayaks, Schouten Island, Tasmania (Grant Dixon)
Title page: West MacDonnell National Park, Northern Territory (Cathy Savage and Craig Lewis)
Contents: Wooroonooran National Park, Queensland (Tourism Queensland/Peter Lik); Finke Gorge National Park, Northern Territory (Cathy Savage and Craig Lewis); Leeuwin–Naturaliste National Park, Western Australia (Cathy Savage and Craig Lewis); Burrum Coast National Park, Queensland (Tourism Queensland/Lincoln Fowler); Coffin Bay, South Australia (South Australian Tourism Commission); Walls of Jerusalem National Park, Tasmania (Geoff Murray)

Explore Australia Special Editions
Explore Australia books can be purchased in bulk for use in promotions or as premiums. We are also able to offer special editions and personalised jackets, corporate imprints, and excerpts from all of our books, tailored specifically to meet your own needs.

To find out more, please contact:

Special Sales
Explore Australia Publishing Pty Ltd
12 Claremont Street
South Yarra
Victoria 3141
Australia
Tel.: (61 3) 9827 8377
Email: anthonygribble@hardiegrant.com.au

Acknowledgements

Project Manager
Astrid Browne

Cartographers
Paul de Leur, Claire Johnston, Bruce McGurty, Colin Critchell

Editors
Rachel Pitts, Clare Coney, Astrid Browne

Editorial Assistant
Emma Schwarcz

Additional writing
Ingrid Ohlsson, Rachel Pitts

Cover design
KPD

Internal design
Adrian Saunders

Picture research
Rachel Pitts

Typesetting
Mike Kuszla, J&M Typesetting

Indexing
Fay Donlevy

Pre Press
Splitting Image Colour Studio Pty Ltd

Internal photo credits

Abbreviations
B: J. P & E. S. Baker; CS & CL: Cathy Savage & Craig Lewis; DS: Don Skirrow; EAP: Explore Australia Publishing; JD: Jeff Drewitz; KS: Ken Stepnell; NR: Nick Rains; SATC: South Australian Tourism Commission; TQ: Tourism Queensland; TT: Tourism Tasmania

Page vi: Australian Picture Library/John & Lorraine Carnemolla; viii: CS & CL; ix: EAP/NR; x: CS & CL; xi: EAP/NR; xii: CS & CL; xiii: TQ; xiv, xvi & xviii: CS & CL; 1: JD; 5: JD; 14: EAP/B; 40: EAP/B; 43: EAP/B; 48: EAP/B; 55: EAP/B; 58: B; 60: EAP/B; 71: EAP/Mike Archer; 79: JD; 87: Rachel Pitts; 89: John Meier; 111: EAP/KS; 115: Rachel Pitts; 129: EAP/NR; 138: EAP/KS; 141: John Meier; 146: Tourism Victoria; 149: Rachel Pitts; 153: SATC; 157: EAP/B; 161: EAP/NR; 165: SATC; 175: EAP/KS; 191: SATC; 195: EAP/B; 199: EAP/DS; 203: CS & CL; 211: EAP/KS; 228: EAP/B; 238: EAP/DS; 246: EAP/DS; 251: EAP/DS; 255: EAP/NR; 260, 261 & 264: Northern Territory Tourist Commission; 274: EAP/NR; 277: EAP/NR; 283: TQ; 298: TQ; 302: TQ; 327: TQ; 336: TQ; 342: TQ; 348: TQ; 351: JD; 358: TT; 367: JD; 377: TT; 379: TT

Aboriginal lands and parks and reserves
The maps in this book were produced with data from the following organisations:

New South Wales National Parks and Wildlife Service
Australian Capital Territory Land Information Centre
National Parks and Wildlife South Australia
Primary Industries and Resources South Australia
Department of Conservation and Land Management Western Australia
Department of Indigenous Affairs Western Australia
Parks and Wildlife Commission Northern Territory, Strategic Planning and Development Unit
Northern Territory Department of Infrastructure, Planning and Environment
Environmental Protection Agency (Queensland)
Queensland Department of Natural Resources
Forestry Tasmania

Explore Australia Publishing indemnifies the above government authorities, which remain custodians and retain copyright of their data used in this publication. Data on Aboriginal lands and parks and reserves is current to 2000.